BUSINESS and SOCIETY

Corporate Strategy, Public Policy, Ethics

McGraw-Hill Series in Management
Fred Luthans and Keith Davis, Consulting Editors

BUSINESS and SOCIETY
Corporate Strategy, Public Policy, Ethics

Sixth Edition

William C. Frederick
University of Pittsburgh

Keith Davis
Arizona State University

James E. Post
Boston University

McGraw-Hill Book Company

New York   St. Louis   San Francisco   Auckland   Bogotá   Caracas   Colorado Springs   Hamburg
Lisbon   London   Madrid   Mexico   Milan   Montreal   New Delhi   Oklahoma City   Panama
Paris   San Juan   São Paulo   Singapore   Sydney   Tokyo   Toronto

3 4 5 6 7 8 9 0   DOCDOC   8 9 3 2 1 0 9 8

ISBN 0-07-015561-5

This book was set in Palatino by the College Composition Unit
   in cooperation with Waldman Graphics, Inc.
The editor was Kathleen L. Loy;
the designer was Charles A. Carson;
the production supervisor was Friederich W. Schulte.
The cover Illustrator was Roy Wiemann.
New drawings were done by Fine Line Illustrations, Inc.
Project supervision was done by The Total Book.
R. R. Donnelley & Sons Company was printer and binder.

Library of Congress Cataloging-in-Publication Data

Frederick, William Crittenden (date).
   Business and society.

   (McGraw-Hill series in management)
   Davis's name appears first on the earlier editions.
   Includes index.
   1. Industry—Social aspects.   I. Davis, Keith,
(date).   II. Post, James E.   III. Title.
IV. Series.
HD60.F72   1988   658.4'08   87-21436
ISBN 0-07-015561-5

ABOUT THE AUTHORS

William C. Frederick is Professor of Business Administration at the University of Pittsburgh. He teaches and conducts research on corporate social responsibility, public affairs management, and business ethics and values. He is a former chairperson of the Social Issues in Management division of The Academy of Management, and in 1984 was the recipient of that division's Sumner Marcus Award for contributions to the division and to the field of business and society studies. He is coauthor of *Social Auditing: Evaluating the Impact of Corporate Programs* and editor of *Research in Corporate Social Performance and Policy: Empirical Studies of Business Ethics and Values*. He has been a management education consultant to private foundations, corporations, and governments in the United States and abroad. He holds a doctorate in economics from the University of Texas.

Keith Davis is Professor Emeritus of Management at Arizona State University. He has a Ph.D. from Ohio State University and formerly taught at Indiana University and the University of Texas. He is a former president of The Academy of Management and is a Fellow in both The Academy of Management and the International Academy of Management. He is author of numerous books and articles, including *Human Behavior at Work*; was named a Beta Gamma Sigma Distinguished Scholar; and has lectured at several universities in the United States and abroad. The first edition of *Business and Society*, coauthored with Robert L. Blomstrom, won a national book award in 1966; and several of his books have been translated into other languages. He has been an active contributor to the business and society field for over thirty years.

James E. Post is Professor of Management and Public Policy at Boston University. He has degrees in law and management; teaches business-government relations, corporate social responsibility, and public affairs management; and has lectured extensively throughout the United States and abroad. His many books include *Private Management and Public Policy* (with Lee E. Preston), *Risk and Response: Management and Social Change in the American Insurance Industry*, and *Corporate Behavior and Social Change*. He has been a consultant and advisor to the World

Health Organization, The Population Council, and the Rockefeller Foundation, and an expert witness before various committees of the U.S. Senate and House of Representatives on the impact of multinational business operations on public health in developing countries. He is a past chairperson of the Social Issues in Management division of The Academy of Management and has been a member of the editorial board of the *Academy of Management Review.*

CONTENTS

PREFACE

We welcome readers—whether students, teachers, executives, or other interested persons—to use this book as a way of broadening and deepening their understanding of the ways business and society interact with each other. Our purpose is to clarify these relationships by describing their most prominent features, analyzing the issues that are typical of the business-and-society interface, and suggesting policy guidelines that may carry both business and society toward workable, livable, and mutually beneficial solutions.

Instructors, including those who have used previous editions and others who are looking for a fresh approach to the field, will be interested in knowing what changes have been made in this edition.

Two new chapters have been added. A new Chapter 4, **Corporate Stakeholders and Public Issues**, presents the concept of corporate stakeholders and shows how stakeholder management can be used to improve a company's overall performance. The new Chapter 15, **Business and Media Relations**, contains a thorough discussion of media relationships and responsibilities, including the media's impact on business and other groups in society.

All chapters have been thoroughly updated and revised. Chapters dealing with ideology, ecology and the environment, and international business have been reorganized, with a more effective presentation of these topics.

Six new case studies have been included, each one offering comprehensive coverage of current issues. All of these new cases have multiple themes but are focused on public policy dilemmas that business faces overseas, corporate takeovers, hazardous waste management and cleanup, marketing dilemmas of multinational corporations, doing business in South Africa, and environmental disasters. **Four revised cases** deal with the definition of corporate social responsibility, product recalls, public policy reforms affecting business, and plant closings. The case studies have been deliberately selected to illustrate examples of both effective and ineffective environmental management.

A new feature of this edition is a series of **Critical Incidents** that deal with topical issues. These Critical Incidents illustrate real-world events, pose decision-making situations for students, and provide practice in grappling with actual business problems.

The text contains **discussion of many current topics**, including insider trading, corporate mergers, drug testing, biotechnology, AIDS in the workplace, passive smoking, media images of business and social groups, free market developments in China, political action committees, chemical spills, Big Power politics, developments in South Africa, and many other similar issues of lasting importance.

With the addition of a **new coauthor—Professor James E. Post of Boston University**—this new edition places a heavy emphasis on **corporate strategic management**, and it continues the fifth edition's focus on **public policy** and **ethics**. In light of the growing international complexities of business, a **broad, geopolitical perspective** is employed, with examples of both United States-based and foreign-based corporations. **An analytic framework** that involves the use of new models and helpful diagrams continues the book's conceptual approach to business and society relationships.

For instructors who adopt the book for classroom use, **a completely revised instructor's manual** is available. It is now a practical guide that can be used before class to prepare teaching materials, class lecture notes, and in-class assignments. It contains teaching guides for each chapter and each case study, sample examinations, suggestions for in-class and out-of-class projects, a list of term paper topics, an audiovisual bibliography of films and cassettes, transparency masters of all figures in the book for use on an over-head projector, and other such teaching aids.

Acknowledgments

Writing a comprehensive textbook is a collaborative effort. The authors wish to express their gratitude for the assistance and support of many colleagues and friends who contributed ideas, reviewed the manuscript, conducted ancillary research, or helped otherwise to produce this book.

Underlying the entire structure of the book is a very comprehensive body of theory and research produced by many scholars during the past four decades. This body of literature now defines the major outlines and contains the central questions of the business-and-society field of inquiry. We are indebted to all of those scholars, past and present, who have helped build this structure of theory and research. Many of their ideas and insights may be found throughout this book.

A number of people made specific contributions to the book's content. John F. Mahon provided much of the information for the Superfund case study. James Weber prepared the case study on Bhopal and assisted in gathering information for other case studies and a number of text chapters. Michelle Poirier also conducted research and prepared materials for several chapters and case studies. Brenda Manning helped design the new format for the Instructor's Manual, and she wrote major portions of the manual and coordinated the authors' work on it.

We were helped by several faculty colleagues who reviewed portions of the manuscript and offered suggestions. They included James A. Craft, University of Pittsburgh; Robert B. Dickie, John F. Mahon, and Edwin A. Murray, Jr., all of Boston University; Paul Shrivastava, New York University; and Sandra A. Waddock, Boston College. A very special and valuable form of assistance was rendered by the following persons who reviewed and made suggestions for improvement in the book's overall plan: William Anthony, Florida State University; Oya Culpan, Pennsylvania State University (Capital Campus); David Flynn, State University of New York at Albany; Edwin C.

Leonard, Indiana University–Purdue University at Fort Wayne; Thomas Martin, Southern Illinois University; and Janet Stern Soloman, Towson State University–Purdue, University at Fort Wayne; and Janet Stern Soloman, Towson State University.

Fully as valuable and indispensable as any of the collaborative efforts involved in writing the book were the professional and administrative support activities of Diane Robinson, Robin Carter, and Ann Stawowczyk.

We deeply appreciate the willing support and encouragement of all these friends and colleagues whose skills and insights have enhanced the quality of the book.

We are pleased also to remind readers about the earlier contributions of Robert L. Blomstrom who was coauthor of the first four editions of the book.

William C. Frederick
Keith Davis
James E. Post

INTRODUCTION AND OVERVIEW

*I*n this introduction, we wish to explain the overall design of the book, which is divided into four major parts. We have written the book so that it tells its story in a logical sequence. The book's "plot" is simple but profound: **Business executives who wish to direct their companies in the successful pursuit of profits must take into consideration the broad social environment. Their decisions, policies, and actions—their plans for the present and the future—their strategies and tactics for achieving the company's goals—all of these must be undertaken in ways that include and integrate major elements of the social and political world surrounding company operations.**

The *penalties* for failing to observe this simple precaution can be severe: A company's financial future can be jeopardized, its employees can lose their jobs, and much harm can be done to individuals and groups in society. On the other hand, the *rewards* of factoring environmental concerns into business decisions and policies can be great: Customer loyalty can be gained, thereby securing or expanding a company's share of the market; investors may be attracted to a company with a good record of social concern, thereby increasing invested capital; employee morale can be boosted, thus enhancing the firm's productivity by making people proud to work for the firm; company managers can enjoy larger amounts of influence in shaping public policies that affect business; and all employees from top to bottom can gain satisfaction from knowing that their company's social responsibilities and ethical obligations are a realistic part of daily work.

The book's central characters—the "heroes" and "heroines"—are the people who devote their professional lives to business careers. We make no distinctions based on social class, organizational rank, gender, race, national origin, color of skin, ethnic affiliation, religion, age, or physical and mental condition. The distinctive mark of the business professional is none of these. Rather, the essential trait is a knowledge of business combined with a high degree of skill in applying that knowledge to practical problems. Whether the business professional is an accountant, a personnel expert, a computer analyst, a manager, a financial specialist, a marketing research analyst, an industrial engineer, a lawyer specializing in business affairs, an executive secretary or an administrative assistant—all share a common heritage and an indispensable trait, namely, the ability to confront a problem and to search for a practical solution.

Combining the "plot" with the "central characters" produces the book's "narrative," which deals mainly with a complex range of business-and-society relationships and issues. Some of these interactions are bumpy and controversial. Business and society do not always get along well with one another. Many social issues are highly charged with emotion. A few of them seem to pit business and society against one another in bitter struggles. The reasons for these difficulties are explained as the book's narrative proceeds.

Even though the business-and-society interface is sometimes scarred by the brickbats hurled by people on both sides, a strong "subplot" running through the entire book deals with the ability of business and society to cooperate smoothly. More often than not—and certainly more often than the general public realizes—business and society collaborate in solving problems that neither one acting alone could solve. These "social partnerships," as we call them, are the key to a more effective social role for business and are one way to increase socially responsible business actions.

A Road Map for Reading This Book

Figure 1 is a diagram showing the overall plan of the book and illustrating how each chapter fits into that plan.

The book's major focus is **The Socially Responsive Corporation**, which is shown at the top of the diagram. A socially responsive corporation has the ability to interact positively and humanely with people and groups in its social environment.

Chapters 1 through 9 in Part I, The Corporation in Society, and Part II, The Corporation and Government, describe various **Tools for Environmental Analysis and Corporate Strategic Planning.** These chapters identify for business leaders, corporate managers, public officials, and various groups in society the most effective ways to analyze and understand business-and-society problems. These approaches also enable corporations to plan strategically to attain their goals and to carry out their economic mission in society, while acting in socially responsible ways. The chapters in Parts I and II contain *the conceptual core* of the book. These concepts can be, and actually are, used by business corporations as tools to resolve business-and-society problems. The primary goal of Parts I and II is to identify these tools and to demonstrate how they can be used to analyze environmental problems facing business.

In Part III, Corporate Stakeholders, and Part IV, Managing in a Turbulent World, we apply the tools from Parts I and II to a broad range of business-and-society issues and problems. Specific **Corporate Stakeholders** are discussed in Chapters 7 through 15. Each of these stakeholders makes demands on business, thus requiring managers to develop strategies for coping with their demands and pressures.

Broad **Environmental Management Challenges** that are typical of today's turbulent world are analyzed in Chapters 15 through 18. A high degree of social sophistication and management skill is needed by business managers if their companies are to find acceptable ways to deal with such problems. It is here that one sees the difficulties, as well as the opportunities, of knowing and applying the tools of environmental analysis (from Parts I and II) to complex situations. We should mention that the overlap that includes Chap-

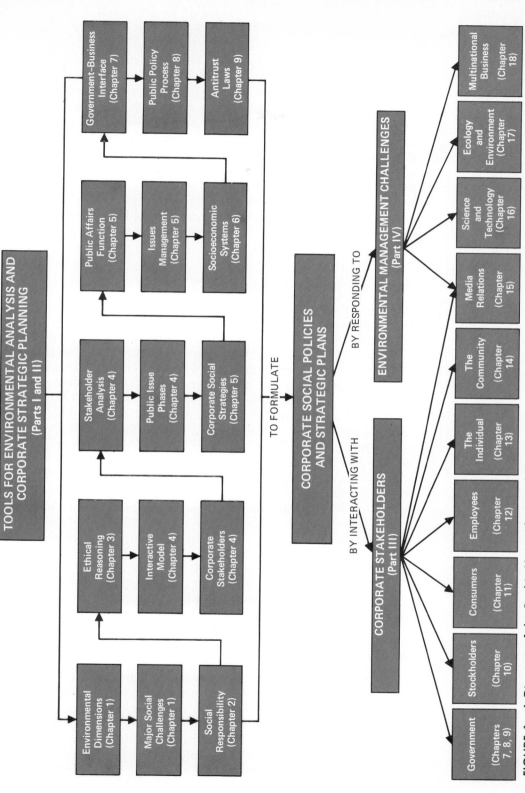

FIGURE 1   A Diagram of the Book's Major Ideas and Themes.

ter 15's topic, the media, as both a corporate stakeholder and as a management challenge is deliberate.

Figure 1, by itself, can only suggest the bare outlines of socially responsive corporate behavior and what is required to produce it. The outline can be filled in and a greater understanding can be achieved after reading and mastering the entire book. However, this chart can be used as an orienting guide and road map while reading the book. It will enable the reader to see where she or he is at as one reads the separate chapters. It can be especially helpful in grasping the relation of any one chapter to the book's overall themes. We hope readers will use it for these purposes. Looking at the diagram each time a new chapter is started would be a wise step for anyone. Figure 1 is reproduced again in Chapter 19, where a summary and overview of the entire book are presented.

A Special Note to Instructors

Although the book is designed to unfold its story chapter by chapter, we realize that many instructors prefer to cover specific topics in other sequences or to omit some topics altogether. For that reason, the chapters are written to stand alone as independent units that can be assigned in any preferred order. Cross references to related subject matter appear in some of the chapters, although such guides are written to serve as helpful linkages rather than to impose an arbitrary order of presentation. We do believe that the book's first five chapters will have a maximum effect if read relatively early. The final chapter can be used either as a summary of the book's major themes, which can be read at the conclusion of the course, or as an introductory overview at the beginning.

The ten case studies that appear at the end of the book are not included in Figure 1 because each case study has been written deliberately so that it includes more than one theme or issue. Therefore, the cases are not anchored to one particular location within the book's narrative but can be assigned at several different points depending on the instructor's preference.

The Critical Incident that appears at the end of each chapter is intended to pose a problem requiring a decision or the formulation of a policy related to the topic of that chapter. These Critical Incidents can be used instead of the longer case studies, or they can be assigned as a practice vehicle before assigning the case studies.

A Note for All Readers

Readers of this book have our assurance that we have tried to present a balanced, even-handed picture of business and society relationships. While no one can be perfectly neutral on controversial issues, it is possible and desirable to present both sides, to show the consequences of each argument, and to provide references to other materials that develop the arguments in greater detail. This approach and philosophy have guided the design and writing of each chapter of the book.

The authors make no secret of their commitment to the major theme of the text, namely, that socially responsive corporations are good for society and good for business. But our experience as teachers has taught us that there are many valid ways to define and approach business-and-society problems. Each student's viewpoints and beliefs deserve to be heard, examined, and put to the test of argumentation. We like to think that we have learned as much or more from our students as they have learned from us. We hope all readers will find something here that can enrich their personal and professional lives.

BUSINESS and SOCIETY
Corporate Strategy, Public Policy, Ethics

PART 1

THE CORPORATION IN SOCIETY

Chapter One

CORPORATE SOCIAL POLICY: THE ISSUES AND CHALLENGES

All business firms conduct their operations within a very complex social environment. In order to succeed, a company must have a well-conceived social policy that effectively meets a variety of social demands and expectations. This chapter outlines the issues and challenges facing corporate managers as they make decisions and formulate policies for their companies.

CHAPTER OBJECTIVES

After reading this chapter, you should be able to

- Explain the complexity of business's social environment
- Show how corporate managers can use environmental knowledge in decision making
- Describe six fundamental social challenges facing business
- Demonstrate that a corporation's social policies are a critical element in achieving effective business performance

*I*n order to get an idea of just how complex a job it is to manage a modern business firm, put yourself in the position of top management of Union Carbide Corporation on a morning in early December 1984.

While still at home preparing to go to your office at the company's headquarters in Danbury, Connecticut, you receive a message that a fatal accident has occurred at one of the company's foreign plants. By the time you get to your office, another report has come in. It is feared that between 50 and 100 persons have died as a result of chemical fumes that leaked from a Union Carbide plant in Bhopal, a city in north-central India. This plant produces pesticides and herbicides used to treat crops and croplands. Without such chemical products, Indian farmers would not be able to provide enough food to feed millions of Indian citizens.

Now thoroughly alarmed by the magnitude of this accident, you seek additional information through company channels. As the day goes along, however, it is difficult to get any clear messages from the Bhopal plant managers, and you are forced to rely on an awkward system of relaying communications through Union Carbide's office in Hong Kong. In the meantime, news organizations begin to report what happened in Bhopal. Some of these reports say that the death toll is in the hundreds with more casualties being reported each hour. Some speak of a night of horror and confusion among Bhopal inhabitants living close to the pesticide plant; others report a large cloud of poisonous vapor that spread across sections of the city, killing those asleep in their homes as well as others who tried to flee.

Before this first day is over, you already know that your company has an immense crisis on its hands. Before the week is over, you realize that it is the biggest and most tragic industrial accident in the history of the world. The death toll is thought to be well over 2,000. In addition, perhaps as many as 200,000 Bhopal citizens have been seriously injured by inhaling the poisonous fumes; some of these, including many children and older folks, face a lifetime of poor eyesight, breathing difficulties, fatigue, and inability to work.

As if the human tragedy were not enough, you find that your company is facing lawsuits of unparalleled complexity. The survivors claim damages for deaths of family members and for illnesses among those not killed. A question arises whether these trials should be held in India where the accident occurred and where the victims lived, or whether they should be heard by courts in the United States where the parent corporation has its world headquarters. Government officials in Bhopal and in India's capital at New Delhi intervene to protect the rights of Indian citizens. Lawyers from the United States rush to India to file legal claims for the Bhopal survivors. Union Carbide's chief executive officer, who flies to the site of the tragedy to offer help, is arrested by Indian authorities and advised to leave the country for his own safety. The Indian plant is closed by order of Indian authorities. The prime minister of India becomes involved in behind-the-scenes negotiations about how to handle the claims of its citizens.

As a top manager of this troubled company, you wonder just how all of these legal, human, governmental, and political complexities are to be straightened out. Will investors sell off their Union Carbide stock, thus depressing its price? Will lenders be reluctant to extend more credit? Will governments everywhere impose stricter standards and controls on all chemical companies? You wonder if the liability costs of the accident will be enough to drive the company into bankruptcy. You understand that, whatever the final outcome, it may be years before your company is back to normal in its operations. You fear that the public may not ever forget this tragic episode and that the shadow of Bhopal may haunt the company throughout your own career. You would like to know if the company has the necessary resolve, the imagination, the international political sophistication, the legal expertise, and a sufficient humane concern for the grief this accident has caused to get through the crisis. Will it be able to meet its legal and social responsibilities while preserving its financial integrity and its ability to produce needed items for consumers throughout the world?

Union Carbide's tragic involvement in the lives of Bhopal's citizens, although an extreme example because of its magnitude and complexity, provides a useful object lesson for anyone who manages or who plans to manage a business firm of any size. *Business "success" is judged, not simply by a company's technological or financial performance, but by how well that company interacts with and serves social, legal, political, governmental, and broad human interests.* If this lesson is overlooked or perhaps forgotten by busy managers, their firms most likely will suffer the consequences, which may be severe and long-lasting.

Fortunately, it is possible to learn this basic lesson and put it to work in all business firms. That is the purpose of this book. As you read this chapter, keep Bhopal in mind. Try to imagine what went wrong at Union Carbide. What could that company's managers have done to avoid the human tragedy and the almost overwhelming legal and financial difficulties faced by the company? Take a positive view of the possibilities, rather than an easier negative one provided by hindsight. The task of managers is to anticipate and solve problems, not just to react to them. Start now by learning the lesson of Bhopal.

BUSINESS'S COMPLEX SOCIAL ENVIRONMENT

Today's business firms do not operate in a social vacuum. Instead, they constantly find themselves in a virtual whirlwind of social problems and controversies. Business managers are buffeted by many complicated and threatening components of the social environments in which their firms do business. The environmental dimensions that have the greatest effect on business operations are depicted in Figure 1-1 and are discussed next.

The International Dimension

Conducting business on an international scale is very complex. Business interests are vitally affected by geopolitical maneuvering among the great nation-states; for example, the United States, Britain, and France all have oil companies operating in the Middle East, and companies from many different countries are helping to build the Soviet gas pipeline into Western Europe. Some industries, such as arms manufacturers and military contractors, profit from geopolitical tensions when some nations want to defend themselves from other nations with modern weapons. Global competitive pressures may

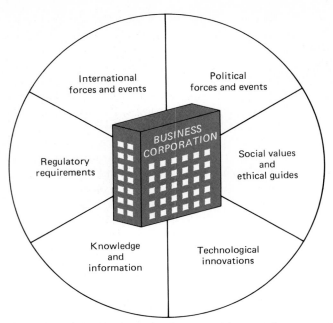

FIGURE 1-1.   Dimensions of business's social environment.

make or break an industry; for example, imported shoes, steel, and auto-mobiles pose vital threats to United States firms. Varying and sometimes contradictory cultural standards and practices pose serious questions of mo-rality for businesses; this is true for foreign companies operating in South Africa. Revolutionary changes of government may lead to loss of a company's facilities; such events occurred in Cuba and Chile. Terrorism may be directed against companies as a way of promoting a particular political view; this happens when air flights are highjacked. Warfare may destroy installations, interfere with supply lines, or wipe out markets; conflicts in Vietnam and Nicaragua produced such results. Indigenous religions, such as fundamen-talist Islam in Iran, may be opposed to the modernism introduced by business products and new technology. The great tensions between the rich countries of the Northern hemisphere and the poorer ones of the Southern hemisphere often lead some public action groups and international organizations to con-demn United States business firms for exploiting the poor and enriching themselves; protest movements in Chile, the Philippines, and other nations in Asia and Africa have made these charges.

Business managers must be alert to international forces and the under-lying tensions they represent. Union Carbide's experiences in Bhopal are a classic example of how important this kind of knowledge can be to a com-pany's future.

The Regulatory Dimension

Governments around the world and at all levels—federal, state, local, and international—regulate business in many ways. Large companies typically must deal with hundreds of regulatory agencies, thousands of regulations, and a continuing flood of new rules each year. Government regulations always affect business decision making, frequently interfere with what managers would like to do, and usually add to the costs of doing business. Many corporate managers dislike these curbs but must deal with them anyway since they are a fact of life in all societies. The most effective companies learn to cope with government regulations; they understand that the regulations frequently represent social goals and priorities considered to be important by a society.

Union Carbide found itself having to deal with many levels of government laws, government regulations, and court jurisdictions in the aftermath of the Bhopal tragedy. The company's future depended to a very large degree on its ability to cope successfully with this network of government regulations.

The Political Dimension

Government regulation is closely related to the political dimension. Political leaders, elected officials, and those appointed to important political posts can be powerful allies or determined opponents of business interests. Because politicians wield great power and because they often express the views and interests of those who put them in office, they are important participants in debates about business and economic policies. Sometimes these political viewpoints are at odds with business needs and business thinking; however, on other occasions politicians can produce results—for example, tax laws or import protections—that are very favorable to business. Learning how to cope with these political currents is an absolute necessity for all business firms.

Clearly, Union Carbide needed a thorough familiarity with political currents and key politicians in Bhopal, in India, and in the United States if it was to weather the crisis created by the chemical leak.

The Technological Dimension

Technology permeates the business scene. It brings benefits as well as headaches. Innovations (for example, a lap-top personal computer) that give competitive advantage to a firm are welcome. Technological surprises sprung by competitors (for example, a superior software package) are not so welcome, nor are technological crises, such as the one in Bhopal or the nuclear accidents at Three Mile Island in Pennsylvania and Chernobyl in the Soviet Union. Technology may improve productivity but at the expense of employees' jobs and security. One industry's technological improvement (for example, plastics for building automobile bodies) may be another's bad news (for example, steel makers may be out of jobs). Managers must learn to ride these technological ups and downs, anticipating new developments and making them a part of the company's strategic plans.[1]

[1]Michael Tushman and David Nadler, "Organizing for Innovation," *California Management Review*, Spring 1986, pp. 74–92.

The Value Dimension

Ethics and values are deeply embedded in the social environment. They can have a significant impact on business activities. The rising interest in health, nutrition, and wellness has created new markets (from health foods to spas) and threatened others (tobacco products, alcoholic beverages, and fatty foods). Minorities and women have brought new values and attitudes into the workplace; they have sought more opportunities and insisted on a larger measure of social justice in the workplace. The demands of religious activists and social protest groups often reflect or anticipate society's shifting value priorities and ethical orientations. For example, Nestlé and other makers of infant formula were forced to modify their marketing practices in Third World nations when groups protested against the overselling of the formula under conditions likely to damage the health of babies. The protesting groups in several nations obviously placed a higher social value on infant health than on the marketing practices of the manufacturers. In general, the companies most likely to be socially approved have managers who are aware, not only of broad social value changes, but also of how their own company's values compare with public attitudes.

In the wake of the Bhopal disaster, many complex ethical questions appeared, and it was important for Union Carbide's managers to display a concern for the human costs imposed on Indian citizens by a foreign company. Finding a solution that would be consistent with the value systems and public attitudes of both India and the United States was the crux of Union Carbide's dilemma.

The Knowledge Dimension

The amount and availability of information have grown to immense proportions with the advent of the computer. In advanced industrial societies, mountains of data can be available in an instant merely by touching a few keys on a computer terminal. Converting this information into useful knowledge is a big task for today's business firms. It requires knowing what to do with the information, knowing how to organize it, deciding who should get it, and determining how a company can take advantage of it in the marketplace. The universal availability of instant knowledge has virtually eliminated the communication "float" or lag which formerly acted to cushion the company, its employees, and the public from the shock of awareness and change. With easier access to information about business, corporations are now more vulnerable to being attacked and criticized by outside groups—including market competitors, government regulators, social critics, whistleblowers, and the general public—who know more about the corporation and know it quicker.

Lack of reliable information greatly hampered Union Carbide's management in trying to deal effectively with the Bhopal situation. Vital information about how the chemical leak was triggered was missing or withheld. In the early hours of the accident, communication links between company headquarters and the plant were weak and uncertain. In this thin information atmosphere—unlike that found in the industrially advanced United States—the company encountered great difficulty in managing the crisis. And with vital information about the accident's cause missing or withheld, the company found itself vulnerable to vigorous public criticism.

Business has no choice; it cannot escape a very complicated social environment. Business leaders have to learn how to operate within it. Their day-to-day decisions, as well as their efforts to plan strategically for the future, are totally dependent upon having knowledge about the social environment. Union Carbide found it out the hard way. *But there is an easier way. We begin here with a basic question that needs to be on the minds of all business managers and professionals: How can knowledge of the broad and complicated business environment be made an integral part of management thinking, planning, decision making, policy formulation, and action?*

MANAGEMENT'S NEED FOR ENVIRONMENTAL KNOWLEDGE

One way to persuade managers to learn more about the social environment is to show them the practicality of such knowledge. This approach appeals to the pragmatic traits of most business professionals. Environmental information can be used by business firms for three major purposes; these are shown in Figure 1-2.

Corporate Strategic Planning

Strategic planning occurs when the top managers of a business firm make deliberate decisions about the purposes of the company, decide what kind of company they want it to be and what line of business it should be in, set some specific goals (for example, growth, increased market share, diversification, or profit targets), and set in motion the activities and programs that will carry the company in the desired directions. This kind of planning looks far into the future and so is usually called "long-term" planning. A strategy is devised for getting from the here-and-now to a desirable future. To succeed, such a strategy must be rooted in reality but also have some imagination and creativity. Some theorists believe that imagination and creativity are the key to all workable strategic plans.[2]

For example, *consider the recent experience of the United States Steel Corporation. Faced by aging steel mills, costly pollution controls, high labor costs, competing products such as plastics, declining demand for its basic products, increased foreign competition, and difficulty in raising needed capital, the company's management embarked on a program to diversify and strengthen its business. Beginning in the early 1980s, it closed obsolete plants; concentrated its new capital investments in low-cost regions; forced its unions into giving concessions on work rules, wages, and benefits; put pressure on the federal government*

[2]See Linda Smircich and Charles Stubbart, "Strategic Management in an Enacted World," *Academy of Management Review*, vol. 10, no. 4, 1985, pp. 724–736.

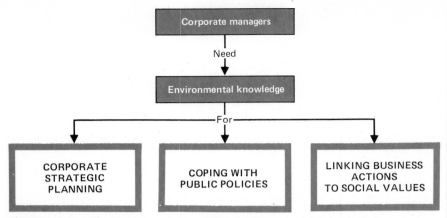

FIGURE 1-2. Management's need for environmental knowledge.

to provide protection against foreign steel producers; entered into joint production with a large South Korean steel producer; and, in moves that shocked many observers, bought Marathon Oil for $5.8 billion and later merged with Texas Oil & Gas in a multibillion-dollar transaction. By the mid-1980s, the bulk of United States Steel's revenues came from its nonsteel businesses. It was no longer primarily a steel company. As a way of symbolizing the company's more diversified character, officials changed its name to USX Corporation.

The company's managers and board of directors, when faced with tough market conditions, had to ask themselves what kind of company they wanted to run. Their long-term strategic plan involved diversification, limited modernization of domestic steel facilities, drastic cutbacks in basic steel production, and linkages with foreign producers.

In putting this plan into effect, the company was in constant and often contentious contact with the social environment. Steelworkers' unions howled when forced to give concessions and when jobs were lost because of plant closings or labor-saving technology. Local communities were devastated when their tax base was narrowed and unemployment rolls increased. Local, state, and federal politicians brought pressure on the company to rescind its decisions. Social protest groups picketed the offices, homes, and even churches of top executives. Attempts were made by employees to take over abandoned steel plants by using the power of eminent domain to establish employee ownership. Congress was outraged when the company tried to import basic steel slabs from a British steel company at the very moment when it was asking Congress for protection from foreign steel competition.

It is obvious that the success of U.S. Steel's strategic plan did not rest solely on financial, production, and marketing analysis. Devising and implementing the plan also required intense and continuous interaction with a very active social environment. All of the dimensions of that environment—international, regulatory, political, technological, ethical, and informational—were directly involved. The company's leaders did well in some of these planning dimensions but not so well in others. The point is that the strategic plan's success was highly *dependent on the social environment. A knowledge of that environment was a basic requirement in devising and implementing the strategic plan.*

Many other well-known companies have drawn up new strategic plans to meet changed business conditions. Major oil companies, large banks, high-technology firms, and many older smokestack companies have followed suit. In all of these cases, inputs from the social environment were an essential component of the company's strategic plan.[3]

Chapter 5 explains in greater detail how companies establish their long-run policies and plan strategically to reach their long-run goals. Such strategic planning is as important for small and midsized companies as for large ones, because all business firms continuously interact with a broad and complex social environment. And the effects of these goal-setting and planning activities reach far down into the ranks of employees, providing signals to them about the company's plans for the future and how those plans affect the jobs of individual employees. For these reasons, a knowledge of corporate strategic planning, particularly its goals and long-run purposes, is important for everyone in business, not just the planners and managers at the higher levels.

Public Policy toward Business

A second very practical reason why business managers need to know as much as possible about the social environment is related to public policy. *Public policy refers to governmental actions taken to promote the general public interest.* Many public policies, ranging from taxes to national defense to protecting the environment, affect business directly. These public policies and programs often make the difference between profits and failure.

> For example, *United States auto makers gained relief from Japanese competition when the two governments agreed on a plan, a public policy, to limit imports of Japanese cars into the United States. Earlier, Chrysler was saved from bankruptcy by a bailout plan enacted by Congress. In another case, Digital Equipment and other computer manufacturers were blocked by government directives from selling computers to the Soviet Union. When relations between Libya and the United States became tense, United States oil companies in Libya were forced by pressure from the White House to close down their operations. In the mid-1980s, the emerging biotechnology industry faced uncertainty due to a lack of public policy guidelines regarding new developments such as genetic engineering.*[4]

In all such cases, a knowledge of public policy and how it is established was vital to business. The affected companies had to wade into the "roiling waters" of politics, Big Power tensions, ideological conflicts, and big financial

[3]For a discussion of strategic planning that places great emphasis on the social environment, see R. Edward Freeman, *Strategic Management: A Stakeholder Approach,* Boston: Pitman, 1984. See also Archie B. Carroll and Frank Hoy, "Integrating Corporate Social Policy into Strategic Management," *Journal of Business Strategy,* Winter 1984, pp. 48–57.

[4]"Why Biotech Can't Wait to Be Regulated," *Business Week,* May 5, 1986, p. 29.

stakes. Politics, government regulation, and public policy often are at the very heart of the social environment. Today, a company has to operate as effectively in Washington (and other world capitals) as on Wall Street. That means it needs to know the ins and outs of congressional committees, how regulatory agencies make their decisions, how to communicate the company's needs to the proper authorities at the right time and in appropriate language, and how and when to take legal action in its own interest. Sophisticated business leaders understand the importance of public policies toward business. They know their firms must master the subtleties, and suffer some of the shocks, that are a part of the public policy realm.

This kind of public policy know-how can be as important to smaller business firms as to the largest ones. They too must learn how to cope effectively with city, county, state, and federal laws and regulations that affect their operations.

Ethical Standards and Social Values

A thorough knowledge of ethics and values is another requirement of effective corporate leadership. *Ethics and values are standards of right and wrong behavior.* Every individual person, every organization and human group, and all societies are guided by ethics and values. They keep human behavior going in desirable directions. They are an "early warning system" for behavior that does not meet basic human needs and desires for a good life for all. They enable everyone in society—both individuals and organizations—to have a general idea of what is acceptable, as well as what cannot be tolerated.

These ethical standards and social values apply to business behavior as well as to all other aspects of life. Business is expected to adhere to these notions of right and wrong conduct as it makes decisions and pursues its goals. If it does not do so, the company and its managers will be in trouble sooner or later. The larger the gap between what business does and what society expects, the bigger the risk a company runs. On the other hand, any company that matches its own actions to society's ethical standards is richly rewarded by public acceptance and approval.

> For example, *Johnson & Johnson twice was the target of terrorist attacks by someone who put poison in Tylenol capsules, killing innocent customers. Both times, the company's managers acted swiftly to remove the affected product from stores. They also abandoned the capsule form of Tylenol, which is especially vulnerable to tampering. In taking these steps, Johnson & Johnson was recognizing one of society's most fundamental ethical standards—the right to life. They matched the company's actions to society's ethical expectations. Although losing great amounts of money in each recall, the company restored the confidence of its customers, thereby retaining their loyalty for the new forms of Tylenol and for the company's many other health care products.*[5]

[5]"The Tylenol Rescue," *Newsweek*, March 3, 1986, pp. 52–53. For more details, see "Johnson & Johnson and the Tylenol Crises," in the case study section of this book.

Corporations do not always act with this kind of ethical integrity. When they do not, they lose a great deal, as shown in the following episode:

> *E. F. Hutton, a leading stock brokerage firm, was found to be handling its banking transactions in ways that inflated its own profits and defrauded banks. At first it denied the charges, but later the company admitted these fraudulent practices. Internal company documents revealed that some high-level officers knew that lower-level managers were engaged in illegal and unethical activities and had actually encouraged them informally. The firm pleaded guilty to 2,000 counts of mail and wire fraud, paid a $2-million criminal fine, lost many customers and some of its most productive employees, and suffered extremely negative publicity in a business where, as one observer said, "Their only product is their name, their reputation."* [6]

The lesson is clear. All business firms need to be aware of ethical standards and social values, design their policies and plans to match those standards, and be sure that all employees adhere to them. When this is done, the rewards are great. Not doing so exposes a company to strong public disapproval and severe social sanctions.

A FRAMEWORK FOR IDENTIFYING ENVIRONMENTAL PROBLEMS

One good way to understand business's environmental problems—and then do something practical about them—is to take an analytical approach to them. The first few chapters in this book present various concepts and ideas that can be used to identify and analyze these problems. We begin now with the first of these analytic concepts—the fundamental social challenges to business.

Fundamental Social Challenges to Business

We said earlier that business's social environment is very complex. A very large variety of problems and issues occur. At times, these environmental pressures are so numerous and so complicated that they seem overwhelming. They are never simple. However, most of these problems fall into broad general categories. Certain basic themes tend to occur over and over again. The specifics of any given problem may differ from one business firm to another or from one time period to another, but it is possible to discern certain patterns that remain stable over extended periods. Knowing what those basic patterns are can be a powerful aid in analyzing business and society issues, because knowing the fundamental nature of the problem is the logical starting point of trying to work out a solution.

---

[6]"Why the E. F. Hutton Scandal May Be Far from Over," *Business Week*, February 24, 1986, pp. 98–101.

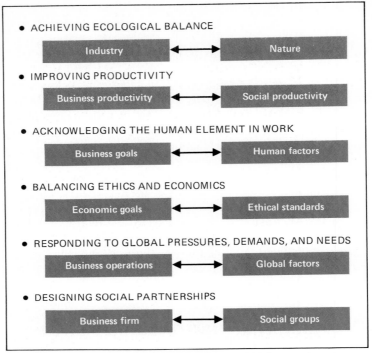

- ACHIEVING ECOLOGICAL BALANCE

  Industry ⟷ Nature

- IMPROVING PRODUCTIVITY

  Business productivity ⟷ Social productivity

- ACKNOWLEDGING THE HUMAN ELEMENT IN WORK

  Business goals ⟷ Human factors

- BALANCING ETHICS AND ECONOMICS

  Economic goals ⟷ Ethical standards

- RESPONDING TO GLOBAL PRESSURES, DEMANDS, AND NEEDS

  Business operations ⟷ Global factors

- DESIGNING SOCIAL PARTNERSHIPS

  Business firm ⟷ Social groups

FIGURE 1-3.   Six fundamental social challenges to business.

We refer to these underlying patterns as *the six fundamental social chal-lenges to business,* as listed in Figure 1-3. These challenges—which also are business opportunities—run like constant threads through all business and society relations. Rarely is one found without one or more of the others also being present.

One of the first analytical steps to be taken in trying to understand any business and society problem is to decide which one or more of these social challenges is involved. Is it a problem of ecological damage, as in Bhopal? Is an ethical issue involved, as in E. F. Hutton? Are scarce resources being wasted? Is there a human factor—perhaps an employee's privacy—at issue? Are plant closings that are made to improve a company's productivity cre-ating community distress and hardship? Frequently, a company may be faced with a situation that includes several of these challenges. As revealed in Figure 1-4, questions like these should be asked at the beginning of any discussion about business's social problems. Knowing the basic nature of the problem is a good first analytical step. Taking this step helps simplify what otherwise might seem to be an impossibly complicated situation. It puts order into the analysis. Corporate policymakers can then plan their actions with greater certainty and with the hope of achieving better results for their firms and for society.

Each of these major social challenges will be discussed briefly now, with additional attention given to all of them in later chapters.

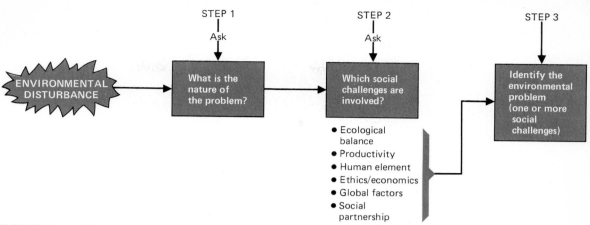

FIGURE 1-4. Three steps in analyzing a company's environmental problems.

Achieving Ecological Balance

One of the most important social challenges to business is to find a happy medium between industrial production and nature's limits. Industrial production is bound to produce waste and pollution, along with needed goods and services. The ground must be dug up or the oceans explored to find minerals. The waters must be dirtied to wash and process raw materials and to clean and cool machinery. The air will be clouded with combustion by-products from factories, cars, trucks, buses, and airplanes. Tons of solid waste are created when ores are recovered. The sounds of engines roaring, explosives going off, pulleys squealing, jackhammers rat-a-tat-tatting, drilling machinery revolving, gears clashing, machinery pounding, and space rockets taking off are those of a technological society in full swing. The various forms of pollution and waste are the price society pays for abandoning a quieter and more peaceful rural life—the kind depicted in Old Master paintings hanging in art museums. All industrial societies—whether the United States, Japan, the Soviet Union, or France—create a portion of the world's pollution and waste simply because these are the unavoidable by-products of a high level of industrial activity.[7]

The social challenge to business in an industrial society, therefore, is not to stop all pollution and waste but to reduce its volume, lessen its burden on society, and help to clean it up once it occurs.

> For example, *all power plants pollute the air. It is a necessary price society pays for having electric power. But smokestack scrubbers can reduce the amount of pollutants going into the environment. In the same way, all automobiles puff harmful exhausts into the air; they cannot operate in any other way. But catalytic converters can convert some of these exhausts into less harmful by-products.*

---

[7]The laws of nature that make pollution and waste inevitable are explained imaginatively in Jeremy Rifkin, *Entropy: A New World View*, New York: Viking, 1980.

Copper mining, coal mining, and bauxite mining devastate surface land and produce enormous and unsightly heaps of waste materials that may drain dangerous chemicals into nearby lakes and streams. But it is possible to reclaim some of this land, restoring its former beauty and making it into productive cropland. Oil tanker accidents and disastrous oil spills are almost bound to occur, given the great volume of such traffic; but better design, greater care in navigation, improved maintenance, and innovative cleanup techniques can reduce the negative results.

The challenge of achieving a sound ecological balance between nature and industrial production first appeared on a large scale during the 1960s in the advanced industrial societies. Since then, this social concern has spread around the world, following the contours of the world's industrial system. Public interest is heightened when a dramatic episode occurs, such as the Three Mile Island nuclear accident in 1979 or the Bhopal tragedy in 1984 or the Chernobyl nuclear disaster in the Soviet Union in 1986. In such cases, as well as in numerous, less-publicized others, the problem is to achieve a livable balance between human needs and nature's limits.

As long as people seek the life-supporting benefits of industrialism, they will face the challenge of ecological balance. An unchecked growth of industry—without considering threats to the environment—is no longer possible or desirable, either in the United States or elsewhere. The reason is that the resultant burden of pollution and waste produced worldwide would not be tolerated by most peoples and might seriously threaten life itself. This social challenge, like the others discussed below, will be with business for a long time.

Improving Business and Social Productivity

A society's productivity depends on how efficiently it uses resources. Customarily, we tend to think of resources as minerals and other raw materials used in production. However, human resources—managers and employees—and financial capital also contribute to society's productive output. If these natural, human, and capital resources are combined and managed effectively by business firms, then the productivity of both business *and* society can be high. *Productivity is an input-output relationship, where the goal is to increase the productive outputs faster than the resource inputs.* A society's well-being depends largely on having a high and rising level of productivity.

Productivity can be increased by anything that improves the efficiency with which industrial inputs are converted into outputs. New or improved technology, better-educated employees, less red tape, and higher morale among workers are some key factors that improve productivity.

Who is responsible for productivity? In the United States, business is primarily responsible, because society has entrusted the production of goods and services to private business firms. The public depends on business to be efficient in converting productive inputs into ever greater outputs of higher quality.

Productivity can refer to a single business firm, an industry, or an entire society. Highly productive *companies* are efficient and profitable. Highly productive *societies* are healthy and growing, and they have many opportunities for improving the quality of life for their citizens. Most of the time, when a business firm improves its productivity, the benefits are felt throughout society. For example, when IBM brings out a new, lower-cost computer model, many individuals and companies welcome it as a more efficient and cheaper way to get work done.

Sometimes, however, steps taken by a company to improve its own productivity can work against the interests and the productivity of a group or an entire community. While *economic* costs may be lowered for the company, *social* costs may be simultaneously increased for the community.

For example, *when United States Steel Corporation decided in the 1980s to close down obsolete and noncompetitive steel mills in Pennsylvania and Indiana, its own productivity was improved. But the health and welfare of jobless steelworkers and their local communities were damaged. U.S. Steel's improved productivity did not improve the productivity of Pennsylvania and Indiana milltowns. On the other hand, the company strengthened its ability to compete and to remain an important cog in the industrial machinery of the United States, so the nation's overall productivity may have been improved.*

The productivity needs of business and society have to be considered together. Business decisions—made for the purpose of improving a company's productivity—sometimes can cause serious problems in society and can actually lower productivity and increase social costs for others.

In the same way, a business's productivity can be threatened by the actions of groups in society. If employees demand (and get) more in pay and other benefits than they produce, productivity will be impaired. Or if labor costs of one firm are driven up above the competitive levels paid by other firms, other industries, or other nations, the productivity of that business firm, industry, or nation will be lower in relation to its competitors. Government, too, bears responsibility for society's productivity, especially when it imposes rules and regulations on businesses which increase costs without stimulating production or when these added costs outweigh the social benefits.

Improving society's overall productivity requires a joint effort by all major institutions. What once might have been the sole responsibility of business has now become a matter of public concern. Business is now challenged to help find the best ways to improve a society's well-being through increasing its own productivity. In doing so, however, business cannot ignore the needs of others in society. *Linking business's needs and society's needs by improving the productivity of both is the essence of this social challenge.*

Acknowledging the Human Element in Work

A third social challenge for business is harnessing human skills and talents for productive work while, at the same time, protecting human dignity and health. Because work is done by people (as well as machines), an enormous number of complex human problems occur in the workplace. A partial listing includes the following:

- Most business employees, including managers, want to be recognized as the unique individuals they are, and they want to be treated with personal dignity. This desire requires businesses to reach a compromise between *the individualized needs and talents* of their employees and *the company's requirements* for a common effort from all employees to achieve the company's goals.
- Safeguarding an *employee's privacy* has become more important in recent years. Computerized data banks filled with medical information, credit ratings, job performance evaluations, marital status, and other sensitive material about the employee pose a threat to privacy if the information is misused. Often, though, business has collected this kind of information in order to make sound hiring and promotion decisions.
- Allowing a greater degree of *employee participation* in business decision making has steadily become more important. In addition to the wage and benefit demands made by labor unions, employees now want more say in the pace of work, how it is organized, and which employees will do it.
- Beginning in the 1960s, many groups demanded an end to *workplace discrimination.* Racial and ethnic groups, women, older workers, religious groups, foreign-born employees, and handicapped persons have insisted upon equal job opportunities. Equal opportunity became a social demand that business could not ignore. This demand added to the complexities of hiring, training, and developing an effective work force.
- Still another social demand—for *a safer and healthier job environment*—continues to be a major issue. The risks of on-the-job injury or illness in factories and on farms have risen with more complex machinery and an increased use of exotic chemicals. While a "risk free" job environment is impossible to achieve, business now is expected by its employees to lower the risks to acceptable levels.
- *Security*—in one's present job and in one's retirement years—has high priority for today's employees. Some employers cannot meet these social demands and still remain profitable. Others may satisfy the social demands but suffer low economic returns. Balancing job and retirement security against rising labor costs is a constant challenge to business ingenuity.
- Looming perhaps larger than any of these new employee demands is the change in *attitudes toward work* itself. In a relatively prosperous society, people begin to value nonwork activities, such as leisure, more highly. They are less willing to consider work as their central life interest. When this happens, the work ethic declines. The new challenge for business is to adjust its policies and practices to this changed attitude toward work.

All of these new employee trends, taken together, make up one of business's greatest and most constant social challenges: learning how to deal effectively and sympathetically with the human element in work, while meeting the public's demands for goods and services at reasonable prices.[8]

Balancing Ethics and Economics

As noted earlier in this chapter, business is increasingly expected to consider ethics when it makes decisions. *The social challenge is to find ways to integrate economics and ethics.* Society wants business to produce needed goods and services, but it also expects business to conduct its economic operations in ethical ways. Harmonizing these two social expectations is the essence of this challenge.

All human societies have ethical systems that define what is meant by right and wrong, fairness, justice, truthfulness, and similar ideas dealing with morality and rightness. Individuals who live in those societies learn from childhood what is considered ethical and unethical. Religious institutions, parents, teachers, and others instill a sense of fairness, justice, and general ethical behavior. As a result, most persons develop a strong sense of ethics which then acts as one's conscience when faced with questions of right and wrong. In addition to individual conscience as an ethical guide, societies spell out their ethics in laws, customs, and religious beliefs. When questions arise, these community standards are then used to sort out right from wrong and to define what is ethical or unethical.

A society's ethics—its sense of right and wrong—tends to permeate all business operations in some way. Sometimes this ethical component may be strong. At other times it may be weakly expressed or perhaps nonexistent. Ethical problems in business occur when business practices deviate from society's notions of what is right and moral. Most of the time, ethics and business go hand in hand, because many companies have discovered that good ethics is good business.

The question, therefore, is not, should business be ethical? Nor is it, should business be economically efficient? Society wants business to be both—at the same time. The challenge to business is to find a balance between these two social demands—high economic performance and high ethical standards.[9]

Responding to Global Pressures, Demands, and Needs

Business is a worldwide institution, touching even the most remote village in some way. Japanese cars, United States computer systems, Italian wines, British insurance, Swiss banking services, Brazilian coffee, and Taiwanese transistor radios—all the result of business activities—are common through-

[8]For further discussion see Keith Davis and John W. Newstrom, *Human Behavior at Work: Organizational Behavior*, 7th ed., New York: McGraw-Hill, 1985.

[9]For a detailed analysis see Thomas Donaldson, *Corporations and Morality*, Englewood Cliffs, N.J.: Prentice-Hall, 1982.

out much of the world. Big multinational corporations headquartered in Western Europe, North and South America, Australia, Japan, and other nations do business around the globe. The world's peoples have become accustomed to business and are dependent on it for many of their needs. They want what business can produce.

A growing world population that is estimated to be around 6 billion in 2,000 A.D. needs to be fed, clothed, housed, educated, and otherwise supported. Even in those nations where private business plays a small role— China and the Soviet Union, for example—international trade with business firms and farmers in other nations can help feed and clothe people and equip factories with machinery. Another type of help is business's investments in the world's poorer nations, thus boosting economic growth there. Business also can work cooperatively with international organizations, such as the Food and Agricultural Organization or the World Bank, to find ways to improve food production and build a sounder economic system.

Beginning in the 1980s, many United States business firms realized that foreign competition is getting tougher. Several Third World nations began to produce steel more cheaply and efficiently than United States firms. Japanese autos and electronic products took increasing shares of the United States market. Textiles, glass products, shoes, and other consumer items were imported in greater amounts, which put economic pressures on domestic firms. A strong dollar—that is, one that makes United States products more expensive for foreigners and the price of their goods less expensive for United States buyers—made things even tougher for many United States exporters. This new challenge of foreign competition brought new joint ventures between American and foreign businesses—for example, in auto making (ventures with Japanese and European producers) and steel production (joint arrangements with Japanese and Korean steel companies). In some cases, United States corporations shifted production to lower-cost labor markets overseas, thus depriving American citizens of jobs but creating more jobs for workers in poorer nations.

Doing business on a global scale is far more complex than doing business domestically, because companies must operate in societies with differing cultural traditions, laws, values, and public attitudes. Multinational corporations need to be aware of these cultural differences while trying to be as economically efficient as possible. World opinion is more likely to support private business, rather than another type of production system, if business not only helps the world's people economically but also shows a sensitivity to their cultural traditions and social needs.[10]

The social challenge to business in a global economy is to conduct operations in ways that acknowledge the world's economic needs, the changing competitive scene, and varying cultural patterns.

---

[10]A good overview of the cultural and political differences faced by multinational corporations is given in Vern Terpstra, *The Cultural Environment of International Business*, Cincinnati: South-Western, 1978.

Designing Social Partnerships

The 1980s marked an important turning point in business's relations with society. The American public seemed to prefer less government intrusion into business affairs, far less than during the 1960s and 1970s when many new regulations and government agencies were created. Both the President and Congress advocated more reliance on private business, more free market solutions to social problems, and more voluntary social responsibilities for business.

Society during the 1980s seemed to be saying, "If today's social problems are to be solved, neither government nor business can be expected to do the job alone. The problems are too big, too complex, and too costly. Why should government and business not work together cooperatively to find solutions?" This kind of thinking has produced the concept of social partnership. *Social partnerships bring together groups that normally compete with and criticize one another, such as government and business, or management and labor, or environmentalists and power plant operators, who then work together to find solutions to common problems.*

For example, *National Steel Corporation decided either to close or to sell its plant in Weirton, West Virginia, because of high labor costs and foreign competition. Employees proposed to buy the facility and run it themselves. Since the entire Weirton community was so dependent on the steel mill, many local citizens and the municipal authorities supported the idea of an employee buyout. National Steel agreed to sell to the employees on favorable terms; a newly formed union agreed to take major pay cuts to lower labor costs to competitive levels; an employee stock ownership plan (ESOP) was set up to transfer ownership to the employees; local government officials cooperated; new managers were hired to run the plant; and the renamed Weirton Steel became the nation's largest employee-owned company. In its first years of operation, the mill made money, saved many local jobs, kept the local economy strong, and proved that broad cooperation could help solve a difficult problem.*

Social partnerships are usually the result of hard work and compromise on all sides. After all, management and labor are traditional adversaries on such matters as wages, fringe benefits, and working conditions, so it is not always easy to work together in a cooperative spirit. The most successful social partnerships are usually based on certain principles and attitudes that help reduce tensions and increase the likelihood of a positive outcome.

The core principles that allow social partnerships to operate successfully are shown in Figure 1-5 and listed below.

- *All interested groups participate* in formulating plans.
- *Decentralized decision making* replaces concentrated power in business and government.
- *Cooperation among potential adversaries* is used to find a way out of present difficulties.

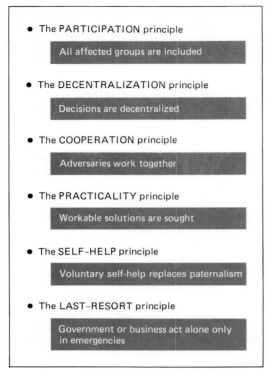

FIGURE 1-5. Working principles of social partnerships.

- *A practical-minded "whatever it takes" attitude* is adopted by the social partners.
- *Voluntary self-help* is the rule, rather than reliance on a paternalistic government program.
- *Government or business acting alone is used only as a last resort* in a critical emergency situation.

These social partnership principles can be used—and in an increasing number of cases are actually used—by businesses to help solve social problems.[11] Business has much to contribute to society, in addition to its direct production of goods and services. But it cannot carry the entire load. It needs to pool its management talents, its planning skills, and its resources with government and other community groups. It needs to find ways to get the cooperation of its employees and unions. It needs to invite all groups and communities affected by its actions to participate in its decisions and policies.

Social partnerships are useful to business because they are a practical way to link social needs with business purposes and business talents. They permit business to participate fully as one member of a problem-solving co-

[11]See Harvey Brooks, Lance Liebman, and Corinne S. Schelling (eds.), *Public-Private Partnership: New Opportunities for Meeting Social Needs,* Cambridge, MA.: Ballinger, 1984.

alition, without giving up business's traditional profit orientation. They provide a vehicle through which business and social groups can cooperate in finding solutions to complex social problems.

SUMMARY

Business and society are thoroughly intertwined with each other. An action taken by one inevitably affects the other. For this reason, it is vitally important for business managers to be aware of the social environment and interact with it skillfully and carefully. Overall business success is measured, not just by a company's financial performance but also by how well it serves broad social and public interests. Corporate managers can use a knowledge of the social environment for strategic planning, for coping with public policies aimed at business, and for aligning business behavior with society's ethical standards and values.

DISCUSSION AND REVIEW QUESTIONS

1. Review Figure 1-1, which depicts the various dimensions of business's social environment. Then identify how many of those dimensions were present in the Bhopal episode described in the opening paragraphs of this chapter. In your opinion, which one of those environmental dimensions was probably the most important to top-level managers of Union Carbide?

2. Review the three major uses of environmental knowledge shown in Figure 1-2. Describe how Union Carbide's officials might use their knowledge of the social environments of India and the United States to carry out the three purposes outlined in Figure 1-2.

3. Of the six major social challenges summarized in Figure 1-3, some would have been more important to Union Carbide in the Bhopal accident than others. First, tell which social challenges were involved. Then, rank them in order of importance *to the company*. Would the survivors in Bhopal rank the social challenges in the same order as the company? Explain your answer.

4. Review the principles of social partnerships shown in Figure 1-5. In your opinion, could any of these principles have been used *prior to* the Bhopal accident to reduce the chances of this tragedy? How many of those principles could be applied *after* the accident to help resolve the problem?

5. Examine recent copies of the *Wall Street Journal, Business Week, Fortune,* or some similar business publication for an example of a company that has been affected in some way by the social environment. Use Figures 1-1, 1-2, 1-3, or 1-4 to help you identify environmental relationships. In your opinion, did the company choose an appropriate strategy for responding? Explain why or why not.

CRITICAL INCIDENT

Not in My Backyard

PPG Industries, Inc., is a leading manufacturer of glass, chemicals, fiberglass, and industrial coatings and resins, with headquarters in Pittsburgh. During the company's April 1982 stockholders' meeting, seven persons who owned one share each of PPG stock objected angrily to a company plan to store its toxic wastes in an abandoned limestone mine owned by the company and located partially under their homes. The seven were residents of Norton, Ohio, near Akron, and they carried a petition signed by over 8,000 Norton residents opposing the waste disposal idea. A local group called Citizens Opposed to the Destruction of our Environment (CODE) had been formed to represent the views of Norton homeowners.

PPG's top management expressed sympathy with the concerns of Norton residents but maintained that the storage area would pose no significant risk to public health. All wastes would be put into sealed containers, stored in the 2,200-foot-deep mine, and kept under constant surveillance by the company. The company also planned to rent storage space to other companies within a 500-mile radius who would store their toxic wastes in the mine, too. This method would be preferable to previous arrangements made by PPG to dispose of its hazardous wastes through contractors who sometimes were careless in handling or safeguarding them. Besides, said the company's chief executive officer, wastes like these are an unavoidable by-product of manufacturing, and over 50 million tons of them are produced each year in the United States. Some place has to be found for them, and the Norton site was a logical and economical place.

CODE members, however, charged that the property value of their homes had been lowered. No one wanted to buy homes located over a chemical dump. Some also feared that the drums would eventually leak and possibly contaminate local water supplies. Some Norton residents who lived along the area's highways mentioned the possibility of accidents involving trucks bringing the wastes to the Norton area.

In spite of these concerns expressed by CODE representatives, PPG's chief executive said that the company would continue to seek permits from state and federal environmental agencies for the plan.

During the same stockholders' meeting, PPG announced that its earnings for the first three months of 1982 had declined by 56 percent when compared with the same period in 1981. The generally poor economic conditions in the housing and automobile industries had reduced demand for some of PPG's major product lines. Nevertheless, first-quarter earnings for 1982 were over $24 million on sales of $752.2 million.[12]

1. Identify the major social challenges presented to PPG by this episode. In your opinion, did the company meet those challenges well? Defend your answer.

[12]Michael Schroeder, "Ohio Residents Fight PPG Dump Plan," *Pittsburgh Post-Gazette*, April 16, 1982, p. 12.

2. One of the six social challenges mentioned in Figure 1-3 might have been the key to solving PPG's social dilemma in Norton. Which one of the six was it?

3. If you had been a corporate strategic planner for PPG, what plan of action could you have recommended to top management for handling the Norton situation? Assume that you want to achieve the company's economic objectives while simultaneously satisfying community opinion in Norton.

Chapter Two

CORPORATE SOCIAL RESPONSIBILITY

Whether corporations should deliberately try to act in socially responsible ways is a matter of intense debate. This chapter examines both sides of the issue, but first it examines the meaning of corporate social responsibility. Learning how to make carefully balanced judgments about business's social activities is an important requirement of modern corporate management.

CHAPTER OBJECTIVES

After reading this chapter, you should be able to

- Discuss the basic principles of corporate social responsibility
- Learn what corporate social responsibility requires corporations to do
- Analyze the arguments for and against corporate social responsibility
- Learn how to make balanced judgments about a corporation's social activities
- Understand how corporate social responsibility and corporate strategic planning are related to each other

The modern business corporation is one of the most powerful and influential institutions in the world. Its productive output constitutes much of the material wealth of the world. Its jobs provide a livelihood for millions of employees around the globe. For many people, it provides psychological shelter and comfort as well as material support and security. It embodies many central values of society. From its laboratories and technicians comes a constant stream of new products. The corporation's managerial expertise is admired and copied by other institutions. Corporate executives serve as trustees of universities, board members of many public and civic organizations, and governing officers of churches, and they are appointed or elected to important government positions. Corporate philanthropy sustains many community enterprises, charitable groups, artistic activities, and educational institutions. No one can doubt the key role played by corporations in improving the quality of life for many people. It has become, in the words of one observer, "the central institution of our age."[1]

On the other hand, a corporation at times can have a negative impact on the lives of people, as revealed in the following episode.

> *General Motors, one of the world's largest corporations, decided in 1980 that it needed to build a new automobile assembly plant if it was to remain competitive. The demand for lighter, fuel-efficient cars plus the use of robots and new assembly-line techniques required that the traditional factories be redesigned and new plants be built. The new plants required much more land than the older ones, so finding a site would not be easy. GM decided it would have to move its Cadillac and Fisher Body operations out of Detroit unless city officials could find the needed 500 acres.*
>
> *The only suitable location for a new plant included a residential area of Detroit known as Poletown. At stake were the homes of over 3,000 mostly elderly residents and the ethnic identity of an old neighborhood. The new auto plant would destroy Poletown.*
>
> *Wanting to save the jobs made possible by the new plant, Detroit city officials used legal powers to acquire the Poletown site, which they then sold to GM. Poletown buildings were demolished, homeowners were evicted and relocated after being paid for their property, and the new GM plant was built.[2]*

Events like the one in Poletown raise questions about the responsible use of corporate power. Some people criticize General Motors for not being more socially responsible to Poletown's residents. Others say that the company exhibited a great deal of social responsibility by agreeing to build a plant in Detroit, thereby saving local jobs and stimulating the city's economy.

Just what constitutes socially responsible business action is complex. Learning how to make balanced judgments about corporate power and about a corporation's social responsibilities is the purpose of this chapter.

CORPORATE SOCIAL RESPONSIBILITY

The concept of corporate social responsibility has always been very controversial. Some people are very much in favor of it, while others are strongly opposed. Fundamentally, the controversy has been about the proper role

[1]Kenneth Mason, "The Multinational Corporation: Central Institution of Our Age," in Robert B. Dickie and Leroy S. Rouner (eds.), *Corporations and the Common Good*, South Bend, IN: University of Notre Dame Press, 1986, p. 78.

[2]For additional details, see Joseph Auerbach, "The Poletown Dilemma," *Harvard Business Review*, May–June 1985, pp. 93–99, and readers' reactions, *Harvard Business Review*, January–February 1986, pp. 185–186.

and function of the business corporation in modern society. People have debated about the behavior, performance, and power of the corporation: Should it stick strictly to business and put all of its efforts into profit making? Or should it, while still trying to make profits, also take steps to improve society in other ways, even at the risk of lowering its overall profits? These are big questions. They concern the very nature of the function of business. No wonder people get agitated or disturbed about the questions! While there are no easy answers, we can shed additional light on the issues by tracing the origin and development of the concept of corporate social responsibility.

The Origin of Corporate Social Responsibility

The idea of corporate social responsibility in the United States began in the early part of the twentieth century. Corporations at that time were being criticized for being too big, too powerful, and antisocial, and they were accused of engaging in anticompetitive practices. Efforts were made to curb corporate power through antitrust laws and other regulations.

A few farsighted business executives advised the business community to use its power and influence for broad social purposes, rather than solely for making the highest possible profits. This approach appealed to increasing numbers of people in business, and the idea eventually became the concept of corporate social responsibility.

Some of the wealthier business leaders such as steelmaker Andrew Carnegie became great philanthropists who gave much of their wealth to educational and charitable institutions. Others, such as automaker Henry Ford, developed paternalistic programs to support the recreational and health needs of their employees. All these business leaders believed that business had a responsibility to society that went beyond or worked in parallel with its efforts to make profits.[3]

As a result of these early ideas about business's expanded role in society, two broad principles emerged. These principles have shaped business thinking about social responsibility for most of the twentieth century. They are the foundation for the modern idea of corporate social responsibility.

The Charity Principle

The notion that the wealthier members of society should be charitable toward those less fortunate is very ancient. Members of royalty through the ages have been expected to provide for the poor, as have those people who, from feudal times to the present, have vast holdings of property. Biblical passages invoke this most ancient principle, as do the sacred writings of other world religions. When Andrew Carnegie and other wealthy business leaders endowed public libraries, supported settlement houses for the poor, gave money to educational institutions, and contributed funds to many other community organizations, they were continuing this long tradition of being "my brother's keeper."

[3]Morrell Heald, *The Social Responsibilities of Business: Company and Community, 1900–1960,* Cleveland: Case-Western Reserve Press, 1970.

This kind of private aid to the needy members of society was especially important in the early decades of this century. At that time, there was no Social Security system, no Medicare for the elderly, no unemployment pay for the jobless, no United Fund to support a broad range of community needs, no Veterans Administration hospital system for war veterans, and no organized disaster relief system to handle the victims of storms and floods. There were few organizations capable of helping immigrants adjust to life in a new country, counselling troubled families, sheltering women and children victims of physical abuse, aiding alcoholics, treating the mentally ill or the physically handicapped, or taking care of the destitute. When wealthy industrialists reached out to help others in these ways, they were accepting some responsibility for improving the conditions of life in their communities.

Before long, community needs outpaced the riches of even the wealthiest people and families. When that happened, beginning in the 1920s, much of the charitable load was taken on by business firms themselves rather than by the owners alone. The symbol of this shift from *individual* philanthropy to *corporate* philanthropy was the Community Chest movement in the 1920s, the forerunner of today's United Fund drives that are widespread throughout the United States. Business leaders gave vigorous support to this form of corporate charity and urged all business firms and their employees to unite their efforts to extend aid to the poor and the needy. In other words, what once had been a responsibility of wealthy individuals and families now became more of a shared responsibility of business firms, their employees, and their top-level managers.[4]

For many of today's business firms, corporate social responsibility means this kind of participation in community affairs—making charitable contributions. In a later chapter, we discuss corporate philanthropy in more detail since it is such an important part of the social responsibility picture. But charitable giving is not the only form of corporate social responsibility. The founders of the doctrine also had another principle in mind.

The Stewardship Principle

Many of today's corporate executives see themselves as stewards or trustees who act in the public's interest. Although the companies for which they work are privately owned and although they try to make profits for the stockholders, the company's resources are managed and directed by professional managers who believe that they have an obligation to see that the general public benefits from the company's actions. According to this viewpoint, corporate managers are placed in a position of public trust. They control vast resources whose use can affect the public in fundamental ways. Because they exercise this kind of crucial influence, corporate managers incur a responsibility to use those resources in ways that are good not just for the stockholders but for society generally. In this way, they become stewards, or trustees, for society. As such, they are expected to act with a special degree of responsibility in making business decisions.

[4]Heald, op. cit.

An early statement of this viewpoint was made by Frank W. Abrams, who was then board chairman of Standard Oil Company of New Jersey, later known as Exxon:

> Businessmen are learning that they have responsibilities not just to one group but to many. . . . The job of professional management . . . is to maintain . . . a harmonious balance among the claims of the various interested groups: the stockholders, employees, customers, and the public at large. . . . [No] corporation can prosper for any length of time today if its sole purpose is to make as much money as possible, as quickly as possible, and without concern for other values.[5]

Two decades later, the Committee for Economic Development, a highly influential group of business executives, echoed the same philosophy:

> The modern professional manager also regards himself . . . as a trustee balancing the interests of many diverse participants and constituents in the enterprise. . . . Thus, recent generations of professional managers have been opening up more and more channels of communication and participation for various corporate constituencies. Whereas the traditional management structure was almost exclusively concerned with raw materials, manufacturing, sales, and finance, the modern management group includes executives who give specialized attention to all the constituencies: employees, stockholders, suppliers, customers, communities, government, the press, and various interest groups.[6]

This kind of thinking eventually produced the modern theory of stakeholder management, which is described more fully in Chapter 4. According to this theory, corporate managers need to interact skillfully with all groups who have a "stake" in what the corporation does. If they do not do so, their firms will not be fully effective economically or fully accepted by the public as being socially responsible.[7]

These two principles, the charity principle and the stewardship principle, became the foundation of corporate social responsibility. The *charity principle* urged business firms to give voluntary aid to society's unfortunate or needy groups. The *stewardship principle* urged them to be trustees of the public interest, which meant that they should act in the interest of all members of society who are affected by the corporation's operations. A business firm guided by these two principles would be considered a socially responsible one, and it would be acting in its own long-term self-interest.

The Modern Meaning of Corporate Social Responsibility

Figure 2-1 shows how the principles of charity and stewardship form the modern idea of corporate social responsibility. Corporate philanthropy or gift giving—freely and voluntarily extended to those in society who are in need—

---

[5]Frank W. Abrams, "Management's Responsibilities in a Complex World," *Harvard Business Review*, May 1951, pp. 29–30, 31.

[6]Research and Policy Committee of the Committee for Economic Development, *Social Responsibilities of Business Corporations*, New York: Committee for Economic Development, June 1971, pp. 22–23.

[7]R. Edward Freeman, *Strategic Management: A Stakeholder Approach*, Boston: Pitman, 1984.

	CHARITY PRINCIPLE	STEWARDSHIP PRINCIPLE
DEFINITION	Business should give voluntary aid to society's needy persons and groups.	Business, acting as a public trustee, should consider the interests of all who are affected by business decisions and policies.
MODERN EXPRESSION	• Corporate philanthropy • Voluntary actions to promote the social good	• Acknowledging business and society interdependence • Balancing the interests and needs of many diverse groups in society
EXAMPLES	• Corporate philanthropic foundations • Private initiatives to solve social problems • Social partnerships with stakeholder groups	• Stakeholder approach to corporate strategic planning • Optimum longrun profits, rather than maximum shortrun profits • Enlightened self-interest attitude

FIGURE 2-1. Foundation principles of corporate social responsibility.

is the modern expression of the charity principle. The stewardship principle is given meaning today when corporate managers recognize that their decisions affect the lives of many people in society and that they have a responsibility to balance the interests of many groups rather than focus on any one group alone. Business and society are interdependent. Decisions that affect one also affect the other. This mutuality of interests places a responsibility on business to exercise care and social concern in formulating policies and conducting business operations.

Companies vary considerably in their approach to social actions. Some companies do only what is absolutely necessary or required by laws and regulations; they act according to *social obligation*. Others may recognize a somewhat wider circle of social relationships and are willing to make charitable contributions as well as interact with stakeholder groups who have an interest in what the company does; they act according to the principles of *social responsibility*. Other companies are far more open to social influence and communication with external groups. They try to anticipate social issues that may affect themselves, and they work in direct partnership with stakeholders. They also may give more attention to broad ethical principles of right and wrong behavior (which are fully explained in Chapter 3). Companies of the latter type act according to the principles of *social responsiveness* (which are fully explained in Chapter 5). Thus, corporations, when interacting with society, exhibit varying degrees of social commitment.[8]

[8]This classification is explained more fully in S. Prakash Sethi, "Dimensions of Corporate Social Responsibility," *California Management Review,* Spring 1975, p. 63.

Since about 1950, some companies have tended to move from attitudes of social obligation to attitudes of social responsibility and to attitudes of social responsiveness. This trend means that some corporate managers realize that the social environment is becoming increasingly important in conducting business in today's world. However, many companies remain in the social obligation phase, while increasing numbers have adopted social responsibility attitudes. Chapters 4 and 5 tell what companies must do to reach the most advanced stage of social responsiveness.

Types of Socially Responsible Actions by Business

General ideas about social responsibility need to be translated into specific actions. Socially responsible companies can adopt social programs, set social goals, honor stakeholder interests, and seek optimum profits, rather than maximum profits. Each of these four specific actions is discussed next.

Social Programs

Figure 2-2 shows ten major fields of action identified by the Committee for Economic Development, and six top priorities named by the life and health insurance industry, as being suitable areas for socially responsible initiatives by business.

Just how these general preferences are translated into action programs by life and health insurance companies is illustrated by the following examples:

> The State Mutual Life Assurance Company of America in Worcester, Massachusetts, supports a local affiliate of Habitat for Humanity. This organization secures decayed inner-city property at little or no cost, and with a combination of contributions and hard work ("sweat equity") by tenants and owners, restores the property for occupancy. Pacific Mutual Life in Newport Beach, California, spearheaded a drive to open a YWCA Hotel for Homeless Women that houses women who have lost their homes through desertion of a spouse, loss of a job, crime, fire, emotional trauma, or similar loss of support. Metropolitan Life of New York aids Dwelling Place in Manhattan, which provides food and temporary housing for the homeless; City Harvest, an organization that runs soup kitchens and food pantries for the hungry; and Impact on Hunger, which works to combat worldwide hunger. The philosophy guiding these efforts is summed up in a comment by the chairman of Northwestern Life: "The essence of corporate public involvement is that the problems of the community, short- and long-run, become the problems of the company." [9]

Social Goals as Business Policy

Some companies have decided to pursue social goals as a way of doing good and making money at the same time. Control Data Corporation, headquartered in Minneapolis, provides a good example of this approach:

[9]"What the Companies Are Doing," *Response,* November 1985, p. 6.

BUSINESS ACTIVITIES TO IMPROVE SOCIETY (Committee for Economic Development, 1971)	PRIORITIES FOR CORPORATE PUBLIC INVOLVEMENT (American Council of Life Insurance and Health Insurance Association of America, 1985)
• **Economic growth and efficiency** Improving productivity Cooperating with government • **Education** Giving aid to schools and colleges Assisting in managing schools and colleges • **Employment and training** Training disadvantaged workers Retraining displaced workers • **Civil rights and equal opportunity** Ensuring equal job opportunities Building inner-city plants • **Urban renewal and development** Building low-income housing Improving transportation systems • **Pollution abatement** Installing pollution controls Developing recycling programs • **Conservation and recreation** Protecting plant and animal ecology Restoring depleted lands to use • **Culture and the arts** Giving aid to arts institutions • **Medical care** Helping community health planning Designing low-cost medical care programs • **Government** Improving management in government Modernizing and reorganizing government	• **Education** • **The elderly** • **The hard-to-employ** • **Health and wellness** • **Housing** • **Hunger and the homeless**

FIGURE 2-2.   Types of socially responsible actions by business. (*Source: Research and Policy Committee of the Committee for Economic Development*, Social Responsibilities of Business Corporations, *New York: Committee for Economic Development, 1971; and Stanley G. Karson, "Corporate Public Involvement: Priorities for Insurance Companies,"* Response, *May 1986, p. 2.*)

Up through the early 1980s, Control Data had built three inner-city plants in St. Paul, Minneapolis, and Washington, D.C. All three plants were profitable, and they provided jobs for inner-city residents and helped urban poverty areas to build an improved economic base. Control Data's sophisticated computer-based learning program, called PLATO, uses television, audiovisual aids, telephone, and satellite transmission to spur training in vocational education and among the handicapped in over 100 company learning centers. In addition, City Venture Corporation plans and manages revitalization projects in some cities, and Rural Ventures Corporation works at improving the productivity of small farms and encouraging small businesses in rural areas by giving them access to data banks on agricultural and business information.

Control Data's chief executive officer, William Norris, stated that the solution to the nation's growing unmet social needs depended upon whether ". . . Cor-

porate America will assume a new role. Simply stated, corporations must use their vast resources more efficiently by taking the initiative, in cooperation with other sectors of society, to address major unmet needs as profitable business opportunities.''[10]

While not all of Control Data's social projects have turned a profit, the hope is that most of them will in the long run. In the meantime, many communities and people have been assisted in resolving some serious problems of education and development.

Honoring Stakeholder Interests

Acting on the stewardship principle described earlier, some companies make special efforts to acknowledge that many groups have an important stake in corporate actions. One such company is Cummins Engine, headquartered in Columbus, Indiana. As one Cummins official said, "we will be responsible to all of our stakeholders for all that we do."

Cummins put this principle into practice in the following ways: members of the board of directors were deliberately chosen to represent a broad spectrum of public interests; racial equality was promoted throughout the company, with special emphasis being placed on opportunities for black managers; the company spent large sums of money to reduce emissions in the diesel engines it manufactured and it led the industry in working with government officials to find workable pollution control standards. Cummins's guidelines to insure the privacy of its employees became part of state and federal privacy policy; and the company offered to upgrade the architectural face of the town in which it was headquartered by paying internationally known architects to design new public buildings, including churches, libraries, schools, and banks. By these actions, Cummins was attempting to serve the interests of its major stakeholders in responsible ways. At the same time, it remained a profitable enterprise, even though economic pressures were occasionally severe. When plants were closed, generous severance payments were provided to employees who were laid off and special efforts were made to help them find new jobs.[11]

Substituting Optimum Profits for Maximum Profits

Maximum profits are the "official" goal of all business activities. Sometimes, however, business judgments are deliberately made that result in less than a maximum return. In these cases, companies seem willing to settle for op-

---

[10]See "Control Data Corporation: Programs for Disadvantaged People and Areas" in Rogene A. Buchholz, William D. Evans, and Robert A. Wagley, *Management Response to Public Issues: Concepts and Cases in Strategy Formulation,* Englewood Cliffs, NJ: Prentice-Hall, 1985, pp. 226–238.

[11]For more details, see "Cummins Engine: Community Relations" in Buchholz, Evans, and Wagley, op. cit., pp. 239–249.

timum profits rather than maximum profits. *An optimum profit is a return considered to be satisfactory by the managers or owners of a business.* It may be lower than what is actually possible, and it is higher than the minimum return necessary to keep the company in business. An optimum profit may be the best a company can earn when operating under economic and social constraints. When this happens, the company is said to be "satisficing" rather than "maximizing" its profits.

Optimum profits are sometimes accepted for reasons of social responsibility. In the Poletown episode mentioned at the beginning of this chapter, General Motors might have been better off in a profit sense to build its new assembly plant somewhere in the Sunbelt. The costs would have been lower and the plant might have been completed sooner. It also could have avoided the charges that it disregarded the needs of Poletown residents. In other words, GM could have maximized its profits by moving this operation out of Detroit entirely. Instead, it decided to remain because it felt a sense of obligation to the city of Detroit and to its employees there. It knew that moving would deliver a severe economic blow to Detroit's economy. By accepting somewhat less than a maximum return on its new plant, GM was settling for an optimum profit—that is, one that GM executives believed was satisfactory, given all the circumstances.

Another example of settling for optimum profits is seen among companies that ceased or reduced operations in South Africa. According to the Investor Responsibility Research Center in Washington, D.C., by 1985 one-half of the largest United States banks voluntarily refused to lend money to the South African government, and one-fourth of them banned loans to private South African borrowers as well. Many other American companies reduced or stopped operations there entirely. Some of the immediate pressure for these decisions was economic and financial, since South Africa's economy suffered from the effects of social turmoil and racial unrest. But a number of corporations also felt the pressure of public protest from groups opposed to the South African system of racial separation. To these firms, optimum profits seemed better and more desirable than the maximum profits that could have been made by continuing operations in such an unstable social environment.

Corporations frequently aim for optimum profits rather than maximum returns. When the reasons for doing so are social, it is an example of social responsibility in action.

THE DEBATE ABOUT CORPORATE SOCIAL RESPONSIBILITY

There are strong arguments on both sides of the debate about business's social responsibilities. A person should learn what the arguments are for both points of view. Then he or she can be in a better position to judge business actions in the social environment and to make more balanced business judgments.

- Balances power with responsibility
- Discourages government regulation
- Promotes long-run profit
- Improves a company's image
- Responds to changing public needs and expectations
- Corrects social problems caused by business
- Applies useful resources to difficult problems
- Recognizes business's moral obligations

FIGURE 2-3. Arguments for corporate social responsibility.

Arguments for Corporate Social Responsibility

Who favors corporate social responsibility? Many business executives believe it is a good idea. So do social activist groups who want to preserve the environment, protect consumers, preserve the safety and health of employees, prevent job discrimination, conserve energy supplies, protect the elderly, oppose television shows featuring violence and crime, and preserve jobs threatened by plant closures. Government officials also look for corporate compliance with laws and regulations that protect the general public from abusive business practices. In other words, both the supporters and critics of business have reasons for wanting corporations to act in socially responsible ways. The major arguments they use are listed in Figure 2-3.

Balances Power with Responsibility

The modern business corporation possesses much power and influence. Most people believe that responsibility must accompany power, whoever holds it. This relationship between power and responsibility produces what has been called the Iron Law of Responsibility. *The Iron Law of Responsibility says that in the long run, those who do not use power in ways that society considers responsible will tend to lose it.*[12] For example, companies that are callous in closing plants or careless in disposing of toxic wastes may face an angry public that will then impose restrictions or penalties on them. Toy makers who produce hazardous toys may lose out to more responsible competitors, or they may face expensive recalls ordered by government. As one group of executives said, "increasingly the public reacts very strongly against those in positions of great power who are arrogant or insensitive to either their legal or social responsibilities."[13]

Discourages Government Regulation

One of the most appealing arguments for business supporters is that voluntary social acts may head off an increased amount of government regulation. Some regulation may reduce freedom for both business and society,

[12]For an early expression of this idea, see Keith Davis and Robert Blomstrom, *Business and Its Environment*, New York: McGraw-Hill, 1966, pp. 174–175.

[13]Research and Policy Committee of the Committee for Economic Development, op. cit., p. 21.

and freedom is a desirable public good. In the case of business, regulations tend to add economic costs and restrict flexibility in decision making. From business's point of view, freedom in decision making allows business to maintain initiative in meeting market and social forces. This view also is consistent with political philosophy that wishes to keep power as decentralized as possible in a democratic system. It is said that government is already a massive institution whose centralized power and bureaucracy threaten the balance of power in society. Therefore, if business by its own socially responsible behavior can discourage new government restrictions, it is accomplishing a public good as well as its own private good.[14]

Promotes Long-Run Profits

At times, social initiatives by business produce long-run business profits. A corporate gift to an engineering school, though costly in the present, might in time provide a flow of talented graduates to work for the company. Or voluntarily recalling an unsafe product might cost a company millions of dollars now and even risk loss of that company's share of that market (this happened when Johnson & Johnson recalled poisoned Tylenol capsules), but it may gain great public favor and goodwill, as well as convince its customers that it is reliable and trustworthy. By sacrificing short-run profits in order to save lives, the company probably increased overall profits in the long run.

Improves a Company's Public Image

The general public tends to have a low opinion of business, as revealed in many public opinion polls.[15] Whether deserved or not, this view is widespread and persistent. When a company gets into trouble, many of business's critics cite the incident as being typical of business's poor conduct. In order to offset this unfavorable image, many business leaders work hard to convince the public that business creates much good for society. In addition to producing things people want and need, creating jobs, increasing incomes, and generally enhancing society's standard of living, a socially responsible firm can improve the general quality of life for a community. Control Data and Cummins Engine, whose activities were described previously, create very positive images for themselves as well as for business in general. Such socially responsible companies become symbols of what is possible and achievable, thus demonstrating that business is not always the villain it is perceived to be by the public.

Responds to Changing Public Needs and Expectations

Social expectations of business have increased dramatically since the 1960s: demands for a cleaner environment, equal opportunity for minorities and women, safer products, fuel-efficient cars, less reliance on nuclear power,

[14]For a discussion that supports this idea, see Tad Tuleja, *Beyond the Bottom Line*, Washington, DC: Facts on File, 1985.

[15]Ann Crittenden, "The Age of 'Me-First' Management," *New York Times*, August 19, 1984, p. F-1.

and similar social conditions have put business on the spot. The public now, more than ever before, expects higher levels of social performance from business.

It is likely that concern about social response is a sign of deep, far-reaching social change. Certain basic forces are at work that will, in the long run, change society's expectations of social outputs from business; more will be expected. The old idea of expecting only economic outputs from business—an outcome that business achieved well—is no longer enough. Corporate leaders who grasp the nature of these basic social changes will be able to guide their companies more effectively in directions preferred by the public.[16]

Corrects Social Problems Caused by Business

Many people believe business has a responsibility to society for the harm it has sometimes caused. Industrial pollution affects everybody, causing health problems and damaging the environment. Since business creates environmental damage, should it not be responsible for cleaning up the problem? Others have said that business's personnel practices and policies sometimes invade employees' privacy or create inequities between men and women workers or discriminate against handicapped persons or older employees. In such cases, it is thought that business firms have a responsibility to help correct these social problems.

Applies Useful Business Resources to Difficult Problems

Some people point out that business has valuable resources that can be applied to social problems. Other institutions in society are not always successful in tackling social problems, partly because they lack sufficient funds, management know-how, and sophisticated planning tools that are a normal part of business operations. So why not put the resources of business to work on social problems? Such a challenge often presents a problem of priorities, for if business applies its resources to society, it may have fewer resources to devote to its economic goals. Also, some people who favor this argument have an exaggerated notion of a corporation's total wealth as well as the ability of its managers to redirect company resources away from established functions. In spite of these qualifications, the viewpoint is appealing when one considers the obvious skills and talents that reside in the business system.

Recognizes Business's Moral Obligations

Many business critics assert that business has a moral obligation to help society. This viewpoint considers a society's moral and ethical rules to have higher priority for corporate managers than other considerations, including business profits and other economic goals. If social justice demands that equal

---

[16]James O'Toole, *Vanguard Management*, New York: Doubleday, 1985.

pay be given for equal work performed by both men and women, then a company is morally obligated to have equal pay scales. Or if the moral principle of the right to life is threatened by shoddy construction methods that risk the lives of workers, business should immediately correct these methods. According to this viewpoint, moral obligations outstrip all other kinds of obligations corporate managers may have to others, including economic returns to stockholders.[17]

All of these arguments in favor of corporate social responsibility—some made by business people and some made by business critics—add up to a very powerful new conception of business's role in society. Taken together, they claim that both business and society are better off with strong business involvement in socially responsible actions because business gains public acceptance and secures its economic position in the long run, and because society is helped with some of its most difficult problems.

Two more points deserve mention before considering the counterarguments on the other side. First, the advocates of social responsibility usually say that *socially responsible companies should act voluntarily* rather than be coerced by government regulations or general public opinion. In fact, some people maintain that *only* voluntary actions can be considered to be socially responsible, because if a firm has to be forced to do something that it should do anyway, then it is not being very responsible. Second, *socially responsible business firms actually are promoting their own enlightened self-interest.* One authoritative source declared that "the corporate interest broadly defined by management can support involvement in helping to solve virtually any social problem, because people who have a good environment, education, and opportunity make better employees, customers, and neighbors for business than those who are poor, ignorant, and oppressed. The doctrine of enlightened self-interest is also based on the proposition that if business does not accept a fair measure of responsibility for social improvement, the interests of the corporation may actually be jeopardized."[18]

Arguments against Corporate Social Responsibility

Who opposes corporate social responsibility? Many people in the business world do. They believe that business should stick strictly to profit making and leave social matters to other groups in society. They are joined by some professional economists who fear that the pursuit of social goals by business will lower the economic efficiency of firms, thereby depriving society of important goods and services. Some groups are skeptical about trusting business with social improvements; they prefer governmental initiatives and programs. According to some of the more radical critics of the private business system, social responsibility is nothing but a clever public relations smokescreen to hide business's true intentions to make as much profit as possible. Figure 2-4 summarizes these arguments that are discussed next.

[17]Thomas Donaldson, *Corporations and Morality,* Englewood Cliffs, NJ: Prentice-Hall, 1982.

[18]Research and Policy Committee of the Committee for Economic Development, op. cit., p. 28.

- Lowers economic efficiency and profits
- Imposes unequal costs among competitors
- Imposes hidden costs on society
- Creates internal confusion and unjustified public expectation
- Gives business too much power
- Requires special social skills which business lacks
- Lack of social accountability
- Places responsibility on the corporation instead of individuals

FIGURE 2-4.   Arguments against corporate social responsibility.

Lowers Economic Efficiency and Profits

According to one argument, any time a business firm uses some of its resources for social purposes, it risks lowering its efficiency. For example, if a company decides to keep an obsolete factory open because it wants to avoid the negative social impact that a closing would have on the local community, its overall economic and financial performance may suffer because of that factory. As a result, the company's costs may be higher than necessary and its profits lower. Stockholders may receive less return on their investment than desirable, and that might make it more difficult for the company to get additional capital for future growth. In the long run, the company's attempt to be socially responsible might backfire: its costs would be inflated, its competitive strength reduced, and its profits lowered to an undesirable level.

This viewpoint says to all businesses, "Concentrate on producing goods and services and selling them at the lowest competitive prices." When that economic task is done well, the most efficient firms survive, consumers' economic needs are well served, and profits are both a reward for past performance and an incentive to future economic activity. Above all, a company's resources should not be devoted to noneconomic or nonprofit purposes. Even though well intended, such social activities lower business's efficiency, thereby depriving society of the high levels of economic production needed to maintain everyone's standard of living.[19]

Imposes Unequal Costs among Competitors

Suppose a coal mine operator who wishes to be socially responsible decides to install more safety equipment than the law requires, spends extra money to find and train women miners, and goes to the expense of removing all waste materials and restoring the land around the mine to its original condition. Suppose now that competing coal mine owners do not take these socially responsible steps. As a result their costs are lower and their profits are higher. In cases like this, the socially responsible firm penalizes itself and even runs the risk of going out of business, especially in a highly competitive market.

[19]Milton Friedman and Rose Friedman, *Free to Choose*, New York: Avon, 1981.

This kind of problem becomes apparent also when companies compete with foreign corporations. If one nation requires higher and more costly pollution control standards, or greater job safety criteria, or more stringent pre-market testing of consumer drugs than other nations, it imposes higher costs on business. This cost disadvantage means that competition cannot be equal. Foreign competitors who are the least socially responsible will actually be rewarded because they will be able to capture most of the market.

Imposes Hidden Costs on Society

Many social proposals undertaken by business do not pay their own way in an economic sense; therefore, someone must pay for them. Ultimately, society pays all costs, although it may seem that a corporation is paying the bill. Some people believe that social benefits are costless, but socially responsible businesses will try to recover all of their costs in some way. For example, stockholders may receive lower dividends; employees may be paid less; or consumers may pay higher prices. If the public knew that it must eventually pay these costs, and if it knew how high the true costs were, it might not be so insistent that companies act in socially responsible ways. The same might be true of government regulations intended to produce socially desirable business behavior. By driving up business costs, these regulations probably increase prices and lower productivity, in addition to making the nation's tax bill higher.[20]

Creates Internal Confusion and Unjustified Public Expectations

A great deal of social involvement by business may divide the interests of its managers and create confusion about the firm's major goals. Conflicting signals coming from the chief executive may hamper strong leadership from other executives in the organization. "Are we here to improve the architectural esthetics of our headquarters town, or to produce diesel engines?" may be asked by some Cummins Engine personnel. Although socially aware managers have the best of intentions, they actually may make their companies less effective rather than more so. Debating about business goals and purposes—whether they should be economic or social—diverts organizational energies from the main job of producing goods and services. It is a luxury that neither business nor society can afford.

At the same time, an emphasis on social response may cause the public to develop expectations of business that are impossible to accomplish. This problem frequently occurs when business's charitable gifts give life to a community organization which then returns again and again for additional support. When these expectations are not satisfied, a company's public image can be tarnished, and it may lose important public support it needs.

[20]Murray L. Weidenbaum, *Business, Government, and the Public,* 2d ed., Englewood Cliffs, NJ: Prentice-Hall, 1980.

Gives Too Much Power to Business

Some critics say that business corporations already are too powerful economically and that it would be a mistake for them to gain even more social influence. Taking responsibility for solving social problems would only concentrate an undesirable amount of power in the hands of business leaders, while weakening the public institutions that are supposed to handle such problems. The best safeguard for a diverse, pluralistic society and its many free institutions is to make business responsible for economic problems while leaving social problems to other institutions.

Requires Special Social Skills That Business Lacks

Business people are not trained primarily to solve social problems. They may know all about production, marketing, accounting, finance, computer analysis, and personnel work, but what do they know about urban problems, or racial tensions, or world hunger, or how to cope with teenage drug abuse? Putting them in charge of such social matters might lead to blunders and poorly conceived approaches. Or business analysts might be tempted to believe that methods which succeed in normal business operations will also be applicable to complex social issues, although social analysts have discovered that different approaches are required when working in the social arena. Control Data, for example, experienced great difficulty with its urban renewal programs because of the many social and political tensions created by such activities.[21]

Lack of Social Accountability

If business is to be responsible for social improvements, then it should be held accountable for how well it performs. But there are no *direct* lines of accountability between a business corporation and the general public. If community organizations believe that corporate contributions are inadequate, they can do little but complain. If a company moves one of its facilities to a foreign nation because labor costs are lower there, those left behind cannot do much about it. The lack of direct accountability for social activities is one of the shortcomings of allowing a business firm to be responsible for social matters. The social arena is not the same as the market for economic goods; in the latter case, any business firm that does not perform satisfactorily is held accountable to the buying public, which may decide to take its business to another company. There is a direct penalty for not performing well. In government programs aimed at solving social problems, politicians sooner or later have to face the electorate and answer to them for what they have or have not done. But corporate executives are not elected to office by the public, nor are they punished if a social initiative does not succeed. Therefore, one should not entrust important social questions to them.

[21]Buchholz, Evans, and Wagley, op. cit., pp. 226–238.

Places Responsibility on the Corporation Instead of on Individuals

The entire idea of *corporate* responsibility is misguided, according to some critics. Only *individual persons* can be responsible for their actions. People make decisions; organizations do not. An entire company cannot be held liable for its actions; only those individuals who are involved in promoting and carrying out a policy qualify for responsibility. Therefore, it is wrong to talk about the social responsibility of *business* when it is the social responsibility of *individual business persons* that is involved. If individual business managers want to contribute their own personal money to a social cause, let them do so; but it is wrong for them to contribute their company's funds in the name of corporate social responsibility. This would be just a smokescreen or disguise used by people with special interests or biases to promote their own points of view. As one critic has said, "Corporations are not morally responsible for anything they do," meaning that the responsibility is on the individual, not the company.[22]

Together, these arguments claim that corporate social responsibility places added burdens on both business and society without producing the intended effect of social improvement or does so at excessive cost.

MAKING JUDGMENTS ABOUT CORPORATE SOCIAL RESPONSIBILITY

With opinion so evenly divided and with so many solid arguments both for and against social initiatives by corporations, how can thoughtful and concerned people make up their minds on this important issue? As noted earlier, the answers will probably help decide the basic role of business in society, and that involves the welfare of most people. The following guidelines can help in making judgments about corporate social responsibility.

- The very existence of such effective pros and cons suggests that neither side has all the right answers. Anyone who is blindly committed to just one point of view may be overlooking some legitimate points that need to be considered. Even those who believe that all business firms should actively promote social responsibility must acknowledge the difficulties and drawbacks that sometimes accompany such policies. As an example, consider General Motors' Poletown dilemma. In trying to be socially responsible by keeping jobs in the Detroit region, GM took actions that resulted in the destruction of Poletown. But if the company had been socially responsible by saving Poletown and moving its plant to the Sun Belt, many Detroit auto workers would have lost their jobs and Detroit's economy

[22]Manuel G. Velasquez, "Why Corporations Are Not Morally Responsible for Anything They Do," *Business and Professional Ethics Journal,* Spring 1983, pp. 1–18.

Statements for Corporate Social Responsibility	Percentage of CEOs Agreeing
• Responsible corporate behavior can be in the best economic interest of the stockholders.	92.2 %
• Efficient production of goods and services is no longer the only thing society expects from business.	88.8 %
• Involvement by business in improving its community's quality of life will also improve long run profitability.	78.4 %
• A business that wishes to capture a favorable public image will have to show that it is socially responsible.	77.6 %
• If business is more socially responsible, it will discourage additional regulation of the economic system by government.	70.7 %
• The idea of social responsibility is needed to balance corporate power and discourage irresponsible behavior.	36.5 %

Statements against Corporate Social Responsibility	Percentage of CEOs Disagreeing
• Business already has too much social power and should not engage in social activities that might give it more.	77.0 %
• A firm that ignores social responsibility can obtain a competitive advantage over a firm that does not.	69.3 %
• Involvement in socially responsible activities threatens business by diverting time and money away from its primary business purpose.	68.1 %
• It is unwise to allow business to participate in social activities where there is no direct way to hold it accountable for its actions.	67.6 %
• Business leaders are trained to manage economic institutions and not to work effectively on social issues.	60.5 %
• Consumers and the general public will bear the costs of business social involvement because businesses will pass these costs along through their pricing structure.	15.8 %

FIGURE 2-5. **Executive attitudes toward corporate social responsibility** (*Source: Robert Ford and Frank McLaughlin, "Perceptions of Socially Responsible Activities and Attitudes: A Comparison of Business School Deans and Corporate Chief Executives," Academy of Management Journal, September 1984, pp. 670–671.*)

would have suffered. Social responsibility decisions are never easy. It is best to consider all sides of the issue.

- Most social issues are complex, so what works in one case might not work in all. Some companies might be notably successful (or lucky) in tackling a social problem, while others might not do so well. Taking a flexible approach that allows several alternatives is probably the wisest course of action.
- Both sides need to be open-minded about the benefits and costs of corporate social initiatives. Most attempts by business to be socially responsible provide benefits for some segments of society as well as for business. However, these benefits are gained only at a cost. Therefore, one must ascertain how large these costs are, who will pay them, and whether the benefits are worth the costs. Sometimes they are; other times, they are not.

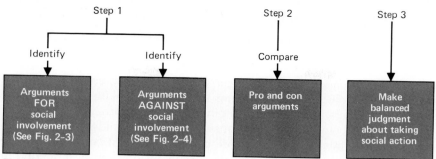

FIGURE 2-6. Analyzing the pros and cons of corporate social responsibility.

Although the social responsibility debate continues, the general trend since the 1960s has been toward more social involvement by corporations. Figure 2-5 reveals the views of a cross section of chief executive officers of corporations who accept this new kind of responsibility. In addition, the actual pressures on business firms to respond to social demands have steadily increased, leaving them less discretion to carry on the debate. These external pressures leave business with little choice but to respond in humane ways while still protecting its ability to remain economically productive. Being socially responsible does not change the basic economic mission of business, because society still expects business to provide goods and services efficiently and at a profit. Rather, social responsibility introduces new social performance criteria for business so that companies respond to *both* the economic needs and the social goals of a changing society. This double-edged "social contract" between business and society reflects the core idea of corporate social responsibility.

Taking an Analytical Approach to Corporate Social Responsibility

Although the debate about social responsibility is a philosophical one involving the basic purpose and meaning of business in society, it is possible to take an analytical approach to the questions raised by the debate. Doing so is desirable for business managers because it can help them to make better decisions. Many individuals and groups in society want and expect business to act in socially responsible ways. It has become a fact of life for most business firms. When faced with such public attitudes, managers who are fully aware of the arguments for and against social involvement—and who have carefully examined the situation facing their company—will be in better position to chart a sensible course of action.

Figure 2-6 shows how business managers can apply the pros and cons of social responsibility to any situation in which social involvement might be an issue. The three essential steps in the analysis are to *identify* the pros and cons that are applicable, to *compare* the relative strength of the pros and cons, and to *make a balanced judgment* about the company's social involvement based on this information.

Strategic Planning and Corporate Social Responsibility

The concept of social responsibility can be related to a company's strategic planning in two basic ways.

First, it can help a business firm decide *what kind of company it wants to be*. Control Data's chief executive officer decided that the company should become deeply involved in social actions as a way of making a profit while aiding various groups in society. Cummins Engine is another company that was committed to being socially responsive to its stakeholders. These decisions to be socially involved were guided by the top executives' vision of the kind of company they preferred to manage. This vision then became one of the goals of strategic planning in each company. Managers and employees at all levels understood that social goals were an important target of planning. This commitment shaped their thinking, their planning, and their actions.

Second, the idea of corporate social responsibility—regardless of whether a company accepts or rejects it—helps management decide *how the firm will try to reach its goals*. Having set a long-term goal of being socially involved, Control Data and Cummins Engine then adopted certain social programs and allocated funds to support those activities. These two companies were strongly committed to social responsibility and were willing to "put their money where their mouth is" in order to make it work. Their strategic plans therefore included a social responsibility budget.

What do companies that favor less social involvement than these two corporations do? Do they make any use of the concept of social responsibility in their strategic plans? Yes. By preferring more of the arguments against social involvement, such companies basically decide to put more long-term emphasis on economic goals. To reach those goals, their strategic plans allocate fewer resources to social purposes.

Both types of corporations will have to live with their strategic choices. Both will continue to be affected by the many diverse dimensions of the social environment. The acceptance of corporate social responsibility does not guarantee a safe road to the future for any firm, as Control Data discovered in the mid-1980s when it encountered financial difficulties (which, however, were not caused by its social programs). Neither does the failure to be socially responsible absolutely block a company from attaining its strategic planning goals, although it may pay a very high price in bad publicity and new government regulations. But neither type of corporation can avoid the issues raised by the social responsibility debate. Sooner or later, those issues will have to be faced.

Unfortunately, a large number of companies are perhaps indifferent to social responsibility and make little or no effort to integrate it into their plans for the future. They are stuck in the social obligation phase of development, doing only the minimum required by the law. However, no company is entirely able to escape the influence of public attitudes and social expectations. The Iron Law of Responsibility has a way of catching up with companies that forget this basic relationship of business and society. Companies that plan their futures by acknowledging social factors as well as economic ones are more likely to *have* a secure future.

SUMMARY

Two principles of social action help define the meaning of corporate social responsibility. The charity principle commits business to extending aid to society's needy. The stewardship principle expresses the idea that business firms and their managers should act as stewards or trustees of the public interest, using business resources to promote the interests of all stakeholders affected by a company's operations.

In the debate about social responsibility, good points can be made both for and against social involvement by business. But with the general trend toward greater social actions by business, the major issue has become how much social involvement is desirable. An open-minded, balanced attitude toward the issues is the best position to assume.

DISCUSSION AND REVIEW QUESTIONS

1. Without looking back at this chapter, define the two major principles of corporate social responsibility and identify four types of socially responsible actions that can be taken by business firms. Give an example of each type of social action. If you have difficulty remembering these ideas, review the materials again.

2. Consider the social activities of two companies mentioned in this chapter—Cummins Engine and Control Data. In your judgment, what are the two strongest arguments listed in Figure 2-3 that support these social actions? What are the two best arguments from Figure 2-4 that you can use to criticize the companies' social strategies?

3. With others in the class, role-play the following situation. One student takes the role of chief executive officer of General Motors. Another student plays the role of Detroit's mayor. A third student represents the citizens of Poletown. A fourth one is the mayor of Sun Belt City who wants GM to build its new plant in her city. Refer to the Poletown situation described at the beginning of this chapter. In evaluating General Motors' actions, determine what arguments *for and against* the corporation's social responsibility each role player will be likely to make. Could there have been a better outcome than the one that actually occurred? Discuss the possibilities.

4. Assume that you are the owner of a genetic engineering firm that employs 50 people. The company's main activity is to produce genetic materials that are "engineered" to help control pests and weeds on farmland. Critics claim that these artificially produced genetic materials, if released into the environment, may have harmful consequences of unknown proportions. In this situation what social responsibility do you think your company has? Refer to the pro and con arguments in Figures 2-3 and 2-4 before developing your answer.

5. Draw up a short questionnaire using some of the statements that appear in Figure 2-5. Ask other students or a group of business persons to indicate whether they agree or disagree with the statements. Then compare their responses with the business executives' viewpoints listed in Figure 2-5. How do you explain the differences between the groups?

CRITICAL INCIDENT

Continental State Bank

Continental State Bank is located in a large Eastern city of over 1 million people. Fifteen years ago the neighborhood where the bank is located was one of the city's more affluent sections, and the bank prospered. Since that time the neighborhood has deteriorated rapidly and fallen into disrepair. Now it is populated by low-skilled wage earners and the urban poor. The majority of residents are members of minority groups. During the period, deposits have declined from $68 million to $58 million in spite of inflation, and bank profits have declined accordingly.

The state in which the bank is located does not allow branch banking; thus, bank management thinks that in order to restore the bank's former level of operations, it must move to another location in a more affluent neighborhood where many of its former customers have moved. Major stockholders strongly support this view, because they have seen their investment decline in value. The bank's management has secured an option on a location 3 miles distant, and the bank is considering a move.

The bank was forced to release its plans for a move when it routinely applied to the state banking commission for approval of a bank at the new location. When neighborhood people learned of the move, they rose in protest. A store owner stated that the bank was the last source of stability in the neighborhood and that if the bank left, the neighborhood would deteriorate further. Others claimed that the neighborhood would be without necessary banking facilities, because the closest other bank was over 2½ miles away. A local activist demanded: "Reach out to the little people who need you." An owner of a cafe claimed that the bank deliberately discouraged customers so that it would have an excuse to move. He claimed that half the businesses in the neighborhood banked elsewhere because the bank had been unresponsive to their needs.

Bank representatives replied that the bank had spent large sums of money for market development without results. They claimed that other banks were close enough to serve the neighborhood. One representative explained the bank's position as follows: "We have a right to grow like any other business, and we are not a public agency established to solve community problems at the expense of stockholders." He added that Continental Bank would be glad to lease or sell its bank property to another bank if the residents could secure or organize one.

An outside observer familiar with the situation said that it could be summarized in one fundamental question: Is the bank's major responsibility to its shareholders or to the neighborhood it serves?

1. After reviewing Figure 1-4 in Chapter 1 and Figure 2-6 in this chapter, write out your responses to each of the analytical steps regarding Continental State Bank's situation. Compare your answers with those given by other students.

2. After you have taken the six analytical steps above, determine what policy you think is appropriate for the bank to adopt. Would such a policy be socially responsible? Defend your preferred policy in terms of the arguments summarized in Figures 2-3 and 2-4.

3. How good a job do you think the bank did in planning strategically for its future—both before its neighborhood changed, and at the time described above? In your opinion, did the bank include a thorough knowledge of the social environment in its long-term planning? Explain your viewpoints.

Chapter Three

ETHICS AND VALUES IN BUSINESS

Ethics is everybody's business, from top management to employees at all levels. One of business's most important social challenges is to conduct its affairs ethically while simultaneously achieving high levels of economic performance. Just why ethical problems arise in business, and what can be done about them, are explained in this chapter.

CHAPTER OBJECTIVES

After reading this chapter, you should be able to

- Explain the meaning of ethics in business
- Describe why ethical problems occur in business
- Understand how to analyze business's ethical problems
- Identify various types of corporate crime
- See how business can improve its ethical performance

T G&Y Stores, a national retailing corporation with headquarters in Oklahoma City, sued seven of its buyers, charging them with accepting $735,000 in cash and other gifts from the company's vendors. One of the buyers who purchased shoes for the retailing chain allegedly built a nest egg of $525,000 from these kickbacks. TG&Y also sued twelve of the stores that allegedly had paid these bribes to TG&Y's buyers.[1]

[1]Hank Gilman, "Bribery of Retail Buyers Is Called Pervasive," *Wall Street Journal*, April 1, 1985, p. 6.

"Money laundering" provides another example. The Bank of Boston Corporation shipped over $1 billion in cash to banks in Switzerland and other European nations without reporting these transactions to United States bank regulators. Twenty-one other banks also failed to file the required forms for big cash transactions. Drug-enforcement officials fear that such large cash flows may possibly cloak secret drug sales, gambling earnings, or other illicit gains that are hidden in banks and "cleaned up" or "laundered" so as to appear they were made honestly.[2]

Ethical problems in business can arise also in a very personal, human way. When orders dropped in one small manufacturing company, the supervisor knew she would have to lay off a loyal, hard-working employee in two months. Company rules did not allow her to tell the employee in advance, for fear he would quit while still needed or not work as hard as he usually did after being told. The supervisor believed that it was unfair to the employee, but she had to enforce all company rules and policies. For her, the ethical dilemma had both personal and professional dimensions.[3]

Episodes like these raise ethical questions for a number of reasons. Sometimes, society is harmed. At other times, an individual profits unfairly at the expense of others. Frequently, a business firm suffers higher costs when money is embezzled or when the firm has to pay hidden costs for its supplies. Money laundering cloaks illegal activities and protects lawbreakers.

However, business frequently demonstrates a high level of ethical performance. Twice within a five-year period, Johnson & Johnson protected its customers by recalling stocks of Tylenol capsules when poison was found in some Tylenol bottles on store shelves. In a similar case, Parker Brothers voluntarily withdrew its all-time best-selling toy when two children choked to death after swallowing some of its parts. Both companies spent millions of dollars on the recalls.

This chapter provides perspective on the ethical problems found in business. It also explains how ethical issues can be analyzed and how all companies can improve their ethical performance. Remember that one of the major social challenges faced by business, as discussed in Chapter 1, is to *balance* ethics and economics. Society wants business to be ethical *and* economically profitable at the same time.

THE MEANING OF ETHICS

When one is dealing with ethics clear thinking is extremely important, because most ethical issues and problems are controversial, involving emotional questions of right and wrong behavior. A good first step is to have a clear definition of ethics.

[2]"Money Laundering," *Business Week,* March 18, 1985, pp. 74–82.

[3]A number of similar ethical puzzles are presented in Barbara Ley Toffler, *Tough Choices: Managers Talk Ethics,* New York: Wiley, 1986.

What Is Ethics?

Ethics is a set of rules that define right and wrong conduct. These ethical rules tell us when our behavior is acceptable and when it is disapproved and considered to be wrong. Ethics deals with fundamental human relationships. Ethical rules are guides to moral behavior. For example, all societies have ethical rules forbidding lying, stealing, deceiving, and harming others, just as they also have ethical rules that approve of honesty, keeping promises, helping others, and respecting the rights of others. Such basic rules of behavior are thought to be essential for the preservation and continuation of organized life.

For many people, religious beliefs and organizations are a major source of ethical guidance and moral meaning. The family institution also imparts a sense of right and wrong to children as they grow up, as do schools and other similar influences such as television. The totality of these learning experiences creates in each person a concept of ethics, morality, and socially desirable behavior.

Ethical rules are present in all societies, all organizations, and all individual persons, although they may vary greatly from one to another. Your ethics may not be the same as your neighbor's; or one particular religion's notion of morality may not be identical to another's; or what is considered ethical in one society may be forbidden in another society. In spite of this diversity, ethics is a universal human trait. All people everywhere need rules to govern their conduct, rules that tell them whether their actions are right or wrong, moral or immoral, approved or disapproved.

What Is Business Ethics?

Business ethics is *not* a special set of ethical rules different from ethics in general and applicable only to business. *Business ethics is the application of general ethical rules to business behavior.* If a society's ethical rules say that dishonesty is unethical and immoral, then anyone in business who is dishonest with employees, customers, creditors, stockholders, or competitors is acting unethically and immorally. If protecting others from harm is considered to be ethical, then a business firm that recalls a defective and dangerous product is acting in an ethical way.

In the TG&Y episode, both the buyers who took the bribes and the bribers acted unethically because they deceived others, took unfair advantage of them, and then concealed their own selfish actions. They broke the rules of fair play. Likewise, the banks that allowed laundered money to flow through their accounts not only broke the law but protected criminals who harmed society and who brought tragedy into the lives of drug users and addicts. The supervisor who failed to give an employee advance notice of being fired was not breaking the law, but she felt unethical in not telling the whole truth. When business firms or people in business violate the rules that define right and wrong behavior, they are acting unethically, and they also may be acting illegally. The link as well as the difference between ethics and law are discussed later in this chapter.

Why Is Business Ethics Important?

Why should business pay attention at all to ethics? What prevents a business firm from piling up as many profits as it can, in any way it can, regardless of ethical rules? We gave one reason in Chapters 1 and 2. In most cases, the general public *expects* business to exhibit high levels of ethical performance and social responsibility. Parker Brothers spent $10 million in recalling the toy that was involved in the death of two children because company executives knew that its customers and the general public would approve its attempts to protect childrens' lives, even though the likelihood of further accidents was remote.

A second factor encouraging business firms and their employees to act ethically is to prevent harm to society. One of the strongest ethical principles is stated very simply: "Do no harm." A company that is careless in disposing of toxic chemical by-products that may cause disease and death is breaking this ethical injunction. Many ethical rules operate to protect society against various types of harm, and business is expected to observe these common-sense ethical principles.

A third reason for promoting ethical behavior is to protect business firms from abuse by unethical employees or unethical competitors. Bribery and kickback schemes penalize honest business firms: "One New York apparel vendor says he lost a $4 million account with one of the nation's largest retailers because he, unlike one competitor, didn't bribe the buyer with $20,000 cars and pricey stereo systems."[4]

High ethical performance also protects the individuals who work in business. Employees resent invasions of privacy (such as unjustified polygraph tests) or being ordered to do something against their personal convictions (such as "midnight dumping" of toxic wastes) or working under hazardous conditions (such as entering unventilated coal mines). Businesses that treat their employees with dignity and integrity reap many rewards in the form of high morale and improved productivity. People feel good about working for an ethical company because they know they are protected along with the general public.

WHY ETHICAL PROBLEMS OCCUR IN BUSINESS

In spite of the positive benefits of good ethical practices, ethical problems do occur in business. Some of the main reasons are listed in Figure 3-1.

Personal Gain

Personal gain, or even greed, causes some ethical problems. Business sometimes employs people whose personal values are less than desirable. They will put their own welfare ahead of all others, regardless of the harm done to fellow employees, the company, or society. In the process of selecting

[4]Gilman, op. cit.

- Personal gain/dubious character
- Individual values in conflict with organizational goals
- Managers' values and attitudes
- Competitive pressures
- Cross-cultural contradictions

FIGURE 3-1 The sources of ethical problems in business.

employees there is an effort to weed out ethically undesirable applicants, but ethical qualities are difficult to anticipate and measure. The embezzler, the expense account padder, the chronic sick leaver, and the bribe taker slip through. Lacking a perfect screening system, business is not likely to eliminate this kind of unethical behavior entirely. Moreover, business has to proceed carefully in screening applicants, taking care not to trample on individuals' rights in the search for potentially unethical employees. Contrary to popular opinion, personal gain is not the most important reason why unethical practices occur in business, which is a point discussed later in this chapter.

Individual Values in Conflict with Organizational Goals

Ethical conflicts in business frequently occur when a company pursues goals or uses methods that are unacceptable to some of its employees. "Whistle-blowing" may be the outcome, if an employee "goes public" with a complaint after failing to convince the company to correct the alleged abuse.

> In one case, *a pilot for Eastern Airlines charged in court that he had been given undesirable flight assignments and was suspended from work for insisting that certain safety improvements should be made on cockpit equipment that later was implicated in a fatal airplane crash.* In another case, *a senior design engineer for Ford Motor Company brought suit after the company demoted him and later brought about his termination because he objected to hazardous design features of the Ford Pinto's windshield and gas tank.* He said, "Our main purpose as Ford employees was to increase corporate profits. . . . In short we were forced to indulge in poor engineering practices, and had to assume responsibility for components we knew were marginal in design—or worse."[5]

The protesting employees in these companies were not troublemakers; they tried to work through internal company procedures to get the problems corrected. The ethical dilemma arose because the company's goals and methods required the employees to follow orders that they believed would harm themselves, other employees, customers, or the general public. As far as they were concerned, they were being asked to do something unethical. When

[5]These episodes are described in greater detail in Alan F. Westin, *Whistle-Blowing! Loyalty and Dissent in the Corporation*, New York: McGraw-Hill, 1981. The quotation is from pp. 120–121.

	U.S.A.	Japan	Korea	Australia	India	International Sample
Will it work? (pragmatic approach)	57.3%	67.4%	53.1%	40.2%	34.0%	52.9%
Is it right? (ethical approach)	30.3	9.9	9.0	40.2	44.1	24.4
Is it pleasant? (affective approach)	1.2	7.0	8.5	5.4	2.2	5.1
Mixed (Combination of the three approaches)	11.2	15.8	29.4	14.2	19.6	17.6
Number of managers	997	374	211	351	623	750*

*150 managers from each of the five nations.

FIGURE 3-2   Major decision-making orientations of managers from five nations. (*Source: George W. England,* The Manager and His Values, *Cambridge, Mass.: Ballinger, 1975, p. 20. Used with permission.*)

company officials would not change the company's practices, the employees "blew the whistle" by revealing the situation to the general public.[6]

Managers' Values and Attitudes

Managers are the key to whether a company will act ethically or unethically. As major decision makers and policymakers, they have more opportunities than others to set an ethical tone for their company. Employees look to the top levels of authority for ethical guidance. The values held by these top managers are all-important in promoting ethical activities.

One pioneering study of managerial values classified managers according to three key questions they might ask themselves when making a decision: Will it work? Is it right? Is it pleasant? The results for managers in five different nations are shown in Figure 3-2. Only three out of ten United States managers put ethics first when considering a business decision, although they (as well as Japanese and Korean managers) may believe that those decisions that "work" are also ethical ones.

The same research revealed that the values most likely to influence a manager at work are service to customers, company loyalty, organizational efficiency, ability, achievement, and high productivity.[7]

[6]For a discussion of the tendency of organizations to put their employees in situations like these, see H. R. Smith and Archie B. Carroll, "Organizational Ethics: A Stacked Deck," *Journal of Business Ethics,* vol. 3, 1984, pp. 95–100.

[7]George W. England, *The Manager and His Values,* Cambridge, MA: Ballinger, 1975. Another comprehensive study of the values of managers in different nations is reported in Geert Hofstede, *Culture's Consequences: International Differences in Work-Related Values,* Beverly Hills, CA: Sage, 1980.

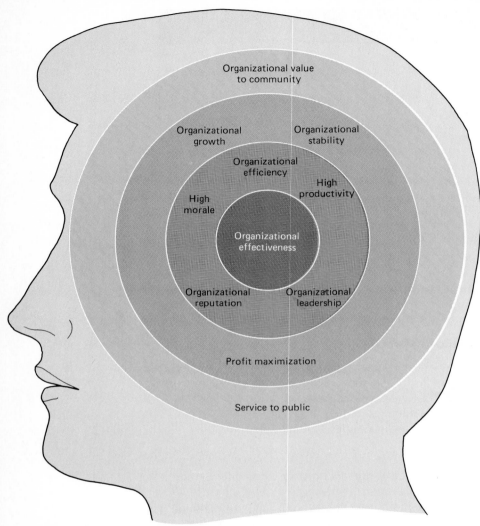

Organizational value
to community

Organizational
growth

Organizational
stability

Organizational
efficiency

High
productivity

High
morale

Organizational
effectiveness

Organizational
reputation

Organizational
leadership

Profit maximization

Service to public

(Goals listed on the inner circles were ranked higher than those on the outer circles.)

FIGURE 3-3   Important organizational goals of managers. (*Source: Warren H. Schmidt and Barry Z. Posner,* Managerial Values and Expectations: The Silent Power in Personal and Organizational Life, *New York: American Management Associations, 1982, p. 39. Copyright 1982. Reprinted by permission of the publisher. All rights reserved.*)

Additional light was shed on managers' values by a 1982 report on a group of over 1,400 corporation executives.[8] When asked to choose values that they consider important, 88 percent of the managers ranked responsi-

[8]Warren H. Schmidt and Barry Z. Posner, *Managerial Values and Expectations: The Silent Power in Personal and Organizational Life,* New York: American Management Associations, 1982. See also Barry Z. Posner and Warren H. Schmidt, "Values and the American Manager: An Update," *California Management Review,* Spring 1984, pp. 202–216.

REASON FOR BEING UNETHICAL	1982 Survey (1,443 Managers) RANK	1977 Survey (1,227 Managers) RANK
Behavior of superiors in company	1	1
Behavior of one's equals in company	2	4
Industry's ethical climate	3	3
Society's moral climate	4	5
Formal company policy or lack thereof	5	2
Personal financial need	6	6

FIGURE 3-4 Factors that contribute to unethical behavior in business. (*Source: Steven N. Brenner and Earl A. Molander, "Is the Ethics of Business Changing?" Harvard Business Review, January–February 1977, p. 66, copyright 1977 by the President and Fellows of Harvard College, all rights reserved; and Barry Z. Posner and Warren H. Schmidt, "Values and the American Manager: An Update," California Management Review, Spring 1984, p. 212.*)

bility and honesty at the top, with capable (67%), imaginative (55%), logical (49%), and ambitious (37%) coming next in order.

One reason for these value preferences is the influence their companies have on managers. Another reason is the professional responsibility that managers feel concerning their jobs. As far as they are concerned, they owe strong allegiance to their companies. Figure 3-3 demonstrates that organizational effectiveness is their central goal while at work. If the organization can be made effective through good management, they tend to believe that other goals (such as service to the public) will follow.

When asked to rank the factors that might cause them to make unethical decisions, readers of the *Harvard Business Review*, most of them managers, identified the behavior of their superiors as most influential, followed by the other factors listed in Figure 3-4. Another group of managers in 1982 agreed that their superiors' behavior was most important and personal financial need was least important in contributing to unethical decisions. Peer behavior was ranked second by this group, while the 1977 managers believed that a formal ethics policy (or its total absence) could be the second most important factor.

These research findings show that the values and attitudes of managers are a critical element in a company's ethical performance. Giving strong ethical leadership and setting a high ethical tone through the example of their own behavior are essential steps for a corporation's managers, especially top-level executives whose visibility and influence are the greatest.

Competitive Pressures

When companies are squeezed by severe competition, they sometimes engage in unethical activities in order to beat out a competitor. Rivalry between employees for advancement can motivate some kinds of unethical behavior, as apparently happened among branch bank managers in Florida who "looked the other way" when suspiciously large cash deposits were made for purposes of laundering illicit drug profits.

Perhaps the best example of how economic pressures can push a company to take an unethical position is the case of Firestone Tire & Rubber Company.

> In the late 1970s, Firestone produced and sold its Radial 500 tire, which had a higher-than-average failure rate, thus causing crashes, injuries, and deaths. Although under great pressure from government officials to recall the tire, the company resisted for several years but eventually agreed reluctantly to withdraw it from sale. During this time, the tire industry worldwide was undergoing a competitive "shakeout" due to overcapacity and slackening sales. Withdrawing the Radial 500 would have meant severe economic penalties for Firestone, perhaps even bankruptcy, since a substitute product was not immediately available.[9] Question: Under the circumstances, would you have recalled the tire, thereby risking your company's failure and the jobs of Firestone employees, or would you have put the safety of Firestone's customers first?

Cross-Cultural Contradictions

Some of the knottiest ethical problems occur as corporations do business in other societies where ethical standards differ from those at home. For example, United States sleepwear manufacturers discovered that the chemical they used to flameproof childrens' pajamas might cause cancer if absorbed through the skin. When these pajamas were banned from sale in the United States, some manufacturers sold the pajamas to distributors in other nations that had no such restrictions. Some say that "dumping unsafe products" is unethical; others counterargue that acceptable safety standards differ among nations and that honest differences of opinion exist among scientists and safety experts.

Parallel problems can be found when companies operate in nations with repressive governments, such as South Africa, or when another country's customs permit (or may even legalize) questionable payments that others would call bribes. Some companies have built factories in nations whose pollution control laws are less stringent than United States regulations; they are charged with "exporting pollution."

In all such cases, what is thought to be ethically acceptable by one nation is considered unethical in another. The resultant ethical dilemmas can be difficult ones for business firms and their managers to solve.

HOW TO USE ETHICAL REASONING

What business needs is a set of guidelines for thinking about ethics. The guidelines should help corporate managers and employees (1) identify the nature of the ethical problem, and (2) decide which course of action is likely

---

[9]See Rogene A. Buchholz, William D. Evans, and Robert A. Wagley, "Firestone Tire and Rubber: Radial '500' Recall," *Management Response to Public Issues*, Englewood Cliffs, NJ: Prentice-Hall, 1985, pp. 310–321.

METHOD	CRITICAL DETERMINING FACTOR	AN ACTION IS ETHICAL WHEN . . .	LIMITATIONS
Utilitarian	Comparing benefits and costs	Net benefits exceed net costs	Difficult to measure some human and social costs Majority may disregard rights of minority
Rights	Respecting rights	Basic human rights are respected	Difficult to balance conflicting rights
Justice	Distributing fair shares	Benefits and costs are fairly distributed	Difficult to measure benefits and costs Lack of agreement on fair shares

FIGURE 3-5   Three methods of ethical reasoning.

to produce the most ethical result. The following three methods of ethical reasoning can be used for these analytical purposes, as summarized in Figure 3-5.

Utility: Comparing Benefits and Costs

One approach to ethics emphasizes the overall amount of good that can be produced by an action or a decision. Should a company close one of its older plants and move production to its modern facility in another part of the country (or world)? The answer would depend on how much good is produced by the move, compared to the harm that could result. If the company is better off after the move than before, then it would claim that the move was ethical because more good than harm resulted. On the other hand, the workers left jobless by the plant closing would probably say that the company was unethical to move away because the harm done to them and their community was great. Both sides are looking at the _results and consequences_ of shifting production elsewhere. This kind of results-oriented ethical reasoning tries to determine whether the overall outcome produces more good than harm—more "utility" or usefulness than negative results.

This kind of ethical approach is called _utilitarian reasoning_. It is often referred to as _cost-benefit analysis_ because _it compares the costs and benefits of a decision, a policy, or an action._ These costs and benefits can be economic (expressed in dollar amounts) or social (the effect on society at large) or human (usually a psychological or emotional impact). After adding up all the costs and all the benefits and comparing them with one another, the net cost or the net benefit should be apparent. If the benefits outweigh the costs, then the action is ethical because it produces "the greatest good for the greatest number" of people in society. If the net costs are larger than the net benefits, then it is probably unethical because more harm than good is produced.

The main drawback to utilitarian reasoning is the difficulty of accurately measuring both costs and benefits. Some things can be measured in monetary terms—goods produced, sales, payrolls, and profits. But other items are trickier—employee morale, psychological satisfactions, and the worth of a human life. Human and social costs are particularly difficult to measure with precision. But unless they can be measured, the cost-benefit calculations will be incomplete, and it will be difficult to know whether the overall result is good or bad, ethical or unethical.

Another limitation of utilitarian reasoning is that the rights of those in the minority may be overridden by the majority. Closing an outmoded plant may produce "the greatest good for the greatest number," but this good outcome will not change the fact that some workers left behind may be unable to find decent jobs. The problem is especially difficult for older workers or those not well educated or members of minority groups. A utilitarian solution may leave them in the lurch. They will not agree that this method of reasoning produces an ethical outcome.

In spite of these drawbacks, cost-benefit analysis is widely used in business. Businesses judge their own success or failure on this basis. If benefits (that is, earnings) exceed costs (for materials, labor, capital, and equipment), the firm makes a profit and is considered to be an economic success. If its costs are continuously higher than its revenues, financial failure is just around the corner. Because this method, when used to measure economic and financial outcomes, works well, business managers sometimes are tempted to rely on it to decide important ethical questions without being fully aware of its limitations or the availability of still other methods that may improve the ethical quality of their decisions. One of these other methods is to consider the impact of business decisions on human rights.

Rights: Determining and Protecting Entitlements

Human rights are another basis for making ethical judgments. *A right means that a person or group is entitled to something or is entitled to be treated in a certain way.* The most basic human rights are those claims or entitlements that enable a person to survive, to make free choices, and to realize one's potential as a human being. Denying those rights or failing to protect them for other persons and groups is normally considered to be unethical. Respecting others, even those with whom we disagree or whom we dislike, is the essence of human rights, provided that others do the same for us. This approach to ethical reasoning holds that individuals are to be treated as valuable ends in themselves just because they are human beings. Using others for your own purposes is unethical if, at the same time, you deny them their goals and purposes. For example, a union that denies a group of women employees an opportunity to bid for all jobs for which they are qualified is depriving them of some of their rights. Or a company that carelessly disposes of hazardous wastes may be guilty of ignoring the rights of others and simply using the environment for its own selfish purposes.

The main limitation of using rights as a basis of ethical reasoning is the difficulty of balancing conflicting rights. For example, an employee's right to privacy may be at odds with an employer's right to protect the firm's cash by testing the employee's honesty with a polygraph. Some of the most difficult balancing acts have occurred when minorities and women have competed with white males for the right to hold jobs in business and government. Rights also clash when United States multinational corporations move production to a foreign nation, causing job losses at home but creating new jobs abroad. In such cases, whose job rights should be respected?[10]

In spite of this kind of problem, the protection and promotion of human rights is an important ethical benchmark for judging the behavior of individuals and organizations. Surely most people would agree that the denial of a person's fundamental rights to life, freedom, privacy, growth, and human dignity is generally unethical. By defining the human condition and pointing the way to a realization of human potentialities, such rights become a kind of common denominator of ethical reasoning, setting forth the essential conditions for ethical actions and decisions.

Justice: Is It Fair?

A third method of ethical reasoning concerns justice. "Is it fair or just?" is a common question in human affairs. Employees want to know if pay scales are fair. Consumers are interested in fair prices when they shop. When new tax laws are proposed, there is much debate about their fairness—where will the burden fall, and who will escape paying their fair share?

Justice (or fairness) exists when benefits and burdens are distributed equitably and according to some accepted rule. For society as a whole, social justice means that a society's income and wealth are distributed among the people in fair proportions. A *fair* distribution does not necessarily mean an *equal* distribution. The shares received by the population depend on the society's approved rules for getting and keeping income and wealth. These rules will vary from society to society. Most societies try to consider peoples' needs, abilities, efforts, and the contributions they make to society's welfare. Since these factors are seldom equal, fair shares will vary from person to person and from group to group.

Determining what is just and unjust is often a very explosive issue because the stakes are so high. Since distributive rules usually grant privileges to some groups based on tradition and custom, sharp inequalities between groups can generate social tensions and sharp demands for a change to a fairer system. An "equal opportunity" rule—that is, a rule that gives everyone the same starting advantages in life (to health, to education, and to career choices)—can lead to a fairer distribution of society's benefits and burdens.

Justice reasoning is not the same as utilitarian reasoning. A person using utilitarian reasoning adds up costs and benefits to see if one is greater than the other; if benefits exceed costs, then the action would probably be considered ethical. A person using justice reasoning considers who pays the costs and who gets the benefits; if the shares seem fair (according to society's rules), then the action is probably just. Is it ethical to move a factory from Boston to Houston? The utilitarian would say "yes" if the net benefits to all

[10]For a discussion, see Patricia H. Werhane, *Persons, Rights, and Corporations,* Englewood Cliffs, NJ: Prentice-Hall, 1985.

parties are greater than the costs incurred by everyone. A person using justice reasoning would say "yes" if the benefits and costs caused by the move were fairly borne by all parties affected by the move. The utilitarian reasoner is interested in the *net sum*. The justice reasoner is interested in *fair shares*.

A major limitation of justice reasoning is the difficulty of measuring benefits and costs precisely. The utilitarian has the same problem. Another limitation is that many of society's benefits and burdens are intangible, emotional, and psychological, as well as tangible material things. People deprived unfairly of life's opportunities do not willingly accept their condition. Few people, even those who are relatively well off, are ever entirely satisfied with their shares of society's wealth. For these reasons, the use of justice reasoning is tricky: although everyone is intensely interested in being treated fairly, many are skeptical that justice is ever fully realized. In spite of these drawbacks, though, justice reasoning is a method of ethical analysis that can be applied to many business situations.

Applying Ethical Reasoning to Business Activities

Anyone in the business world can use these three methods of ethical reasoning to gain a better understanding of ethical issues that arise at work. More often than not, all three can be applied at the same time. Using only one of the three methods is risky and may lead to an incomplete understanding of all the ethical complexities that may be present. It also may produce a lopsided ethical result that will be unacceptable to others.

Figure 3-6 diagrams the kind of analytical procedure that is useful to employ when one is confronted with an ethical problem or issue. Two general rules can be used in making such an analysis.

The Unanimity Rule

If you want to know whether a decision, a policy, or an activity is ethical or unethical, you first ask the three questions listed in Figure 3-6. If the answers to all three questions are "yes," then the decision or policy or activity is probably ethical. If answers to all three are "no," then you probably are looking at an unethical decision, policy, or activity. The reason why you cannot be absolutely certain is that different people and groups may (1) honestly and genuinely use different sources of information, (2) may measure costs and benefits differently, (3) may not share the same meaning of justice, or (4) may rank various rights in different ways. Nevertheless, anytime an analyst obtains unanimous answers to these three questions—all "yes's" or all "no's"—it is an indication that a strong case can be made for either an ethical or an unethical conclusion.

The Priority Rule

What happens when the Unanimity Rule does not apply? What if there are two "yes's" and one "no," or another combination of the various possibilities? In that case, a choice is necessary. The analyst (who may be a business

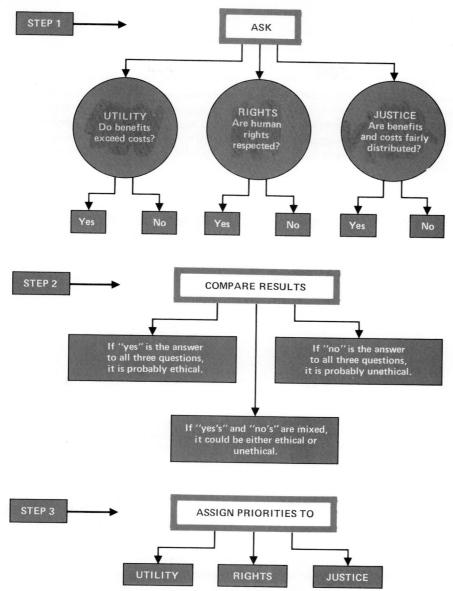

FIGURE 3-6   An analytical approach to ethical problems.

manager or other employee) then has to assign priorities to the three methods of ethical reasoning. What is most important to the analyst, employee, or organization—utility? rights? or justice? What ranking should they be given? A judgment must be made, and priorities must be determined.

Unfortunately, there are no easy ways to do this. As we pointed out in Chapter 1, every business firm has to be aware of its social environment and public opinion. The ethical spotlight often shines directly on business decision makers, so they are not entirely free to establish ethical priorities without considering how others will react. There is a natural tendency for managers and employees to assign a high priority to those things that benefit their company and preserve their jobs. As a result, they may prefer to decide ethical issues on a narrow cost-benefit basis, even if others' rights are threatened or an injustice occurs. When this happens, the affected groups are quick to challenge the company's ethical priorities. The final outcome is difficult to predict, and it usually depends on the effectiveness of the various ethical arguments and the relative amount of influence exercised by the groups involved.

Individuals in the business world, as well as companies, have to set their own personal ethical priorities while at work. Should you pad your expense account? Should you accept an expensive stereo system from a sales representative who wants to do business with your company? Should you agree to hire a waste hauler who is known to dump toxic wastes illegally? Should you sign your name to a financial report you know to be false? Employees often encounter these ethical challenges at work and must apply the Priority Rule to their own actions. In doing so, they find out what kind of person they are and what their true values are. A high degree of personal integrity can go a long way toward insuring that business firms act in ethically proper ways.[11]

ETHICS, LAW, AND CORPORATE CRIME

Law and ethics are not quite the same. Laws are similar to ethics because both are rules defining proper and improper behavior. In general, *laws* have an ethical basis because they *are a society's attempt to formalize its rules regarding right and wrong behavior*. But sometimes there is not a perfect match between the law and important ethical principles.

> *In 1986 some of the nation's large convenience chains decided to quit selling* Playboy *and* Penthouse *because some of their customers and various organized groups objected to sexually explicit photographs and articles in the magazines. Sale of these magazines was not illegal, but the protesters argued that selling them was immoral because the material degraded women and encouraged sexual promiscuity among readers. For these groups, pornography laws were inadequate for coping with an ethical crisis.*
>
> *About the same time, many groups in the United States objected to United States corporations doing business in South Africa on grounds that racial laws there deprived the majority black population of fundamental human rights. They claimed that racial laws and basic ethical principles were in direct conflict. On*

---

[11]For several examples, see Toffler, op. cit.; James A. Waters, Frederick Bird, and Peter D. Chant, "Everyday Moral Issues Experienced by Managers," *Journal of Business Ethics,* **5** (1986), pp. 373–384; and Robbin Derry, "Moral Reasoning in Work-Related Conflicts," in William C. Frederick (ed.), *Research on Corporate Social Performance and Policy,* vol. 9, Greenwich, CT: JAI Press, 1987 (in press).

the other hand, those opposed to corporate withdrawal from South Africa pointed out that their companies were not breaking any law by conducting business there. Their attitude was, "As long as it is legal, it is not unethical."

These episodes demonstrate that legality cannot always define when something is ethical or unethical. Although laws attempt to codify a society's notions of right and wrong, they are not always able to do so completely. Obeying the law is usually one way of acting ethically, and the public generally expects business to be law-abiding. But at times, the public expects business to recognize that ethics is broader than the law and to act accordingly.

Illegal Corporate Behavior

Although estimates vary, lawbreaking in business is not unusual, as shown by the following studies.

One survey undertaken by Fortune _revealed that 11 percent of major United States corporations had been found guilty of breaking federal laws from 1970 to 1980. The crimes included conspiracies to fix prices and rig bids; kickbacks, bribery, and illegal rebates; illegal political contributions by corporations; criminal fraud; and tax evasion. The list of crimes and corporate lawbreakers would have been even longer but the survey did not include overseas cases, monopolistic practices, price signaling among competitors, illegal practices among medium-sized and small businesses, or failure to comply with local and state laws._[12]

Another study of 582 leading corporations found that 60 percent were discovered to be in violation of the law by various federal agencies during 1975 and 1976. Over half had broken the law an average of 4.8 times. The bigger the company, the greater were the number of violations, although the study concluded that "The world of giant corporations does not necessarily require illegal behavior in order to compete successfully. The fact that 40 percent of the corporations in this study did not have a legal action instituted against them . . . attests to this conclusion."[13]

Business crimes cause serious financial losses. Securities frauds cost over $1 billion annually; worthless or misrepresented pharmaceutical drugs amount to nearly $500 million each year; and almost $1 billion is spent each year on fraudulent home repairs. The U.S. Chamber of Commerce has estimated that white-collar crime costs the nation $40 billion annually.[14]

[12]Irwin Ross, "How Lawless Are Big Companies?" _Fortune,_ December 1, 1980, pp. 56–64.

[13]Reported in S. Prakash Sethi, "Corporate Law Violations and Executive Liability," in Lee E. Preston (ed.), _Corporate Social Performance and Policy,_ vol. 3, Greenwich, CT: JAI Press, 1981, pp. 72–73. For additional information, see Marshall B. Clinard and Peter C. Yeager, _Corporate Crime,_ New York: Free Press, 1980; and Peter C. Yeager, "Analyzing Corporate Offenses: Progress and Prospects," in James E. Post (ed.), _Research on Corporate Social Performance and Policy,_ vol. 8, Greenwich, CT: JAI Press, 1986.

[14]Larry Watts, "Organizational Strategy and Criminal Behavior," presented to Academy of Management annual meeting, August 1985, pp. 3–5. See also "The Limited War on White-Collar Crime," _Fortune,_ June 22, 1985, pp. 91–100.

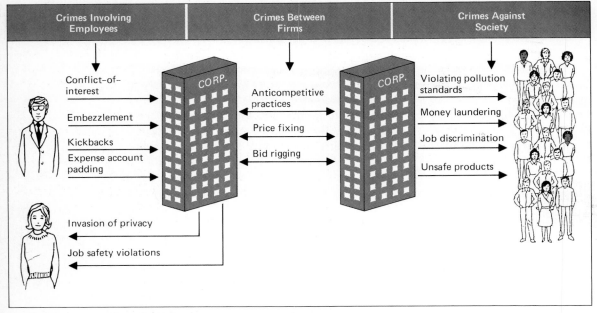

FIGURE 3-7 Major types of corporate crime.

Illegal activities in business put great scars on business's image. A 1985 public opinion poll that asked, "Do you think most American corporate executives are honest, or not?," found 55 percent saying "no" and only 32 percent saying "yes."[15] As long as this view is held by the public, business will have a difficult time being accepted as an ethical institution, even if the majority of business decisions and actions are entirely ethical.

Types of Corporate Crime

Not all crimes committed in business are alike. As shown in Figure 3-7, some are committed by employees against their own company, some are directed against other companies, and others harm corporate stakeholders and the public interest.

Crimes against One's Own Company

Employees can harm their own company when they take bribes, embezzle company funds, pad expense accounts, or engage in conflict-of-interest activities such as hiring unqualified family members or channeling company business to outside firms in which they have a financial interest. In these cases, employees have violated their duty of loyalty and fidelity to their employer. They have enriched themselves unjustly at the employer's expense. Companies try to combat this kind of crime by carefully screening

---

[15]Adam Clymer, "Low Marks for Executive Honesty," *New York Times*, June 9, 1985, pp. F-1, F-6, reporting a New York Times/CBS poll.

prospective employees, installing surveillance techniques, establishing tight accounting controls, and issuing detailed guidelines in the form of codes of ethics.

Crimes against Other Companies or Business Entities

Some criminal actions are taken by one company against another for the purpose of financial or competitive gain. If a group of electrical contractors agrees secretly to fix the prices of its services and to divide the available business among its members, their industrial customers will have to pay unfairly high prices. Such actions are forbidden by law. "Inside trading" is another violation; it occurs when someone gets advance information about a potential change in the price of a company's stock and then proceeds to buy or sell the stock before others know about it. As a result, other stockholders who could not take advantage of the "inside" information lose money or lose an opportunity to profit from such an investment. In one sensational 1986 case, a New York investment banker was accused of making over $50 million in illegal profits from inside trading. Inside trading allows some individuals or investment banking firms to gain unjust and unfair advantages over others.

Crimes against Corporate Stakeholders and the Public Interest

When corporations carelessly dump dangerous wastes where they may harm people or the environment, or when they fail to comply with safety regulations intended to protect their employees, they are committing crimes against the general public or specific stakeholder groups. The same is true when they produce consumer goods (such as childrens' toys) that are defective and dangerous. Society has acted through its legal system to forbid such harmful behavior, so business has an obligation and an ethical duty to comply with the law. If it does not do so, the rights of many corporate stakeholders and the general public are violated.

Who Is Morally Responsible—the Individual or the Corporation?

When crimes in business are committed, who should be held responsible? Consider the following situations.

> *McDonnell Douglas, a leading aircraft manufacturer, and four of its leading executives, were indicted for fraud, bribery, conspiracy, and lying to conceal improper overseas payments to promote sales of its DC-10 airplane. The com-*pany *admitted guilt to most of these charges and paid fines of more than $1.2 million. The four high-ranking* individual executives *were not fined or jailed.*
>
> *The same thing happened when E. F. Hutton & Company was charged with defrauding banks of millions of dollars in interest. Although the* firm *paid a criminal fine of $2 million and reimbursed government prosecutors $750,000 for the costs of the investigation, not a* single *officer, executive, or employee was charged, fined, or jailed.*

When trying to locate moral and ethical responsibility within a corporate system, one may find that if those individuals who actually make illegal and unethical decisions are not held legally accountable for their actions, others may believe that they, too, can break the law without being penalized. Some people say that a corporation is nothing but a structural shell and a legal fiction that has no meaning apart from the individuals who work there. Due to its impersonal and artificial character, the *company* cannot be held responsible for anything it does. According to this viewpoint, moral and ethical responsibility rests entirely on the *individuals* who make the decisions, set the policies, and take the actions.[16]

HOW TO IMPROVE ETHICAL PERFORMANCE IN BUSINESS

Any business firm that wishes to do so can improve the quality of its ethical performance. It requires supportive top-management attitudes, an open corporate culture, and organizational changes that help employees at all levels deal with ethical dilemmas that arise in their work.

Top Management Attitudes

The attitudes of high-ranking executives are crucial in determining whether a company and its employees will perform ethically or unethically. A chief executive officer who projects a strong ethical concern, who lets employees know what is expected as they do their work, and who personally puts these ethical attitudes into practice establishes a positive ethical tone throughout the entire company. Sanford McDonnell, chairman of McDonnell Douglas Corporation, speaking of this kind of influence, said, "You have to keep reminding people [in the company] what you stand for. Unless you stress that—especially with the emphasis in a corporation on making profits—it's not always clear to people which way management wants them to go."[17]

Opening Up Corporate Culture to Broad Ethical Standards

Every corporation has a distinctive culture, just as every society has cultural traditions and ways of behaving that set it off from other societies. Life inside one company will not be exactly as it is in other companies. One expert put it this way: "The corporation is a community with a culture and value commitments. As a community it is an organizational context of persons and groups; a system of customs, expectations, values, and purposes; and a system of action and interactions."[18] This kind of internal corporate culture ex-

---

[16]Manuel Velasquez, "Why Corporations Are Not Morally Responsible for Anything They Do," *Business and Professional Ethics Journal*, Spring 1983, pp. 1–18.

[17]Quoted in Winston Williams, "White-Collar Crime: Booming Again," *New York Times*, June 9, 1985, p. F-6.

[18]Charles S. McCoy, *Management of Values: The Ethical Difference in Corporate Policy and Performance*, Boston: Pitman, 1985, p. 63. See also Lynn A. Isabella, "Culture, Key Events, and Corporate Social Responsibility," in Post, op. cit.; Thomas J. Peters and Robert H. Waterman, *In Search of Excellence: Lessons from America's Best-Run Companies*, New York: Harper & Row, 1982; and Edgar H. Schein, *Organizational Culture and Leadership*, San Francisco: Jossey-Bass, 1985.

erts a powerful influence on the behavior of everyone in the company. It sends signals to employees on what and how they are expected to perform while on the job.

Corporate managers need to remember that people expect a high standard of ethical behavior from business. They can reach that standard and improve ethical performance if their company's culture is (1) based on sound ethical principles and (2) open to dialogue about controversial ethical issues that disturb the public. In the final analysis, the strongest and most successful corporate culture is one capable of harmonizing a company's economic values with the social and ethical values of other groups in the environment.

Building Ethical Safeguards into the Company

Positive top-management attitudes and an ethically open corporate culture are important, but they are not enough. Companies also need to create ethical safeguards to be used as part of their normal operations. Employees need guidance on how to handle day-to-day ethical situations; their own personal ethical compass may be working well, but they need to receive directional signals from the company. Several organizational steps can be taken to provide this kind of ethical awareness and direction.

Codes of Ethics

According to Gary Edwards, director of the Ethics Resource Center, over 90 percent of large United States corporations had ethics codes in 1985.[19] *An ethics code describes the general value system, the ethical principles, and specific ethical rules that a company tries to apply.* These codes help employees know what is expected in ethical terms when they face an uncertain situation. Codes vary considerably among companies, but Figure 3-8 shows some of the most commonly included provisions. Interestingly, this study pointed out that "the codes' authors seem more concerned about conflict of interest [where the company is harmed] than with actions that directly affect the public at large."[20]

A code's impact on employee behavior is weakened if its purpose is primarily to make the company look good or if it is intended to give the company's top executives a legal defense when illegal or unethical acts are committed by lower-ranking employees. The most effective codes are those drawn up with the cooperation and participation of employees and those having specific rewards and penalties that are spelled out and enforced. Surveys report that the majority of managers think that a self-developed code will help improve ethical behavior in their industries.[21] Some companies have

---

[19]"Using Ethics to Keep Business Straight," *Security World,* September 1985, p. 13.

[20]Donald R. Cressey and Charles A. Moore, "Managerial Values and Corporate Codes of Ethics," *California Management Review,* Summer 1983, p. 58.

[21]Steven N. Brenner and Earl A. Molander, "Is the Ethics of Business Changing?" *Harvard Business Review,* January–February 1977, pp. 66–67. For additional discussion of ethics codes, see Robert Chatov, "What Corporate Ethics Statements Say," *California Management Review,* Summer 1980, pp. 20–29; and M. Cash Mathews, "Codes of Ethics: Organizational Behavior and Misbehavior," in Frederick, op. cit.

POLICY AREA	PERCENTAGE OF CODES DISCUSSING ITEM
Conduct on behalf of the firm	
Relations with U.S. governments	76.7
Relations with customers/suppliers*	75.0
Employee relations*	52.6
Relations with competitors*	50.0
Relations with foreign governments	42.2
Relations with investing public*	41.4
Civic and community affairs	34.5
Transactions with agents, consultants, and distributors	26.7
Environmental affairs	19.8
Host-country commercial relations	12.1
Other	2.6
Conduct against the firm	
Conflict of interest*	69.0
Other white-collar crimes (e.g., embezzlement)	16.4
Personal character matters	9.5
Other	1.7
*Items receiving relatively greater emphasis by more detailed discussion	

FIGURE 3-8 Policy areas included in corporate codes of ethics. (116 leading corporations) (*Source: Donald R. Cressey and Charles A. Moore, "Managerial Values and Corporate Codes of Ethics," California Management Review, Summer 1983, p. 56. Used with permission.*)

found that supplementing codes with an employee advisory committee to provide confidential advice to company personnel faced with an ethical dilemma is helpful.

Ethics Committees

In some corporations a standing committee of the board of directors is appointed to consider the ethical dimensions of company policies and practices. These committees are important for two reasons: first, they can inject ethics into the very highest levels of policy-making in the company; second, they serve a symbolic function that communicates to employees and external stakeholders the company's formal commitment to giving ethics an important hearing.[22]

Ethics Training Programs

Since business firms frequently train their employees in accounting methods, marketing techniques, safety procedures, and technical systems, why not give them training in ethics also? In fact, more corporations are doing so.

[22]S. Prakash Sethi, Bernard J. Cunningham, and Patricia M. Miller, *Corporate Governance: Public Policy–Social Responsibility Committee of Corporate Board: Growth and Accomplishment,* Richardson, TX: Center for Research in Business and Social Policy, University of Texas, 1979, pp. 7–8 and 40–41.

Allied Corporation, Chemical Bank, McDonnell Douglas, and General Dynamics are among the prominent companies with training programs for managers, supervisors, and anyone else likely to encounter an ethical question at work. The programs acquaint employees with official company policy on ethical issues and show how those policies can be translated into the specifics of everyday decision making. Sometimes, simulated case studies based on actual events in the company are used to illustrate how to apply ethical principles to on-the-job problems.[23]

Ethics Audits

Another step that tends to build ethical practices into a company's regular routines is to institute periodic ethics audits. These audits attempt to uncover opportunities for unethical behavior that might exist or that have occurred in the company. Executives can then judge how far these practices vary from the company's code and can determine the economic and public relations cost of allowing them to continue. Strategies can be adopted for closing the ethical gaps.

SUMMARY

Ethical business performance means adhering to society's basic rules that define right and wrong behavior. In doing so, business meets public expectations, prevents social harm, protects itself from abuses by employees and other firms, and preserves the dignity and integrity of individuals who work in business.

Law and ethics are not identical. Ethical rules tend to be broader and more basic than laws, and the general public wants business to act ethically as well as lawfully.

Any company can improve its ethical performance if its top managers project a strong ethical tone, if the company's culture is open to broad ethical standards, and if organizational safeguards are installed to encourage ethical behavior by all who work there.

DISCUSSION AND REVIEW QUESTIONS

1. Refer to the three examples given at the beginning of this chapter—conflict of interest at TG&Y, money laundering through banks, and not giving advance notice before firing an employee. In each case explain what harm was done, and to whom, by these unethical actions. What major ethical principles were violated in these episodes?

[23]Alan F. Otten, "Ethics on the Job: Companies Alert Employees to Potential Dilemmas," *Wall Street Journal*, July 14, 1986, p. 19.

2. By referring to *Fortune, Business Week, Wall Street Journal,* or local newspapers, identify one or more companies that have encountered ethical problems. Based on the news accounts and the discussion in this chapter, identify the apparent reasons why the ethical problem arose. Was it due to personal gain, a whistle-blowing conflict, managers' values, competitive pressures, cross-cultural contradictions, or some combination of these factors?

3. Review the three methods of ethical reasoning discussed in this chapter—utilitarian reasoning, rights reasoning, and justice reasoning. If the Priority Rule forced you to make a choice among them, which one seems to be the most important ethical idea to you? Which one do you believe is most often applied in business decision making?

4. Explain the difference between law and ethics. In your opinion, which one of these two contains the most fundamental principles of desired human behavior? If you were confronted with a choice of obeying a law that you believed to be unethical or acting on the basis of your own personal ethics, what would your choice be? Do you believe people in business should make the same choice you favor? Explain your position.

5. Suppose you were the judge in a trial of three executives who were found guilty of rigging bids and fixing prices on electrical contracts. As a result, their corporation gained several million dollars in business over a ten-year period in an industry that was fiercely competitive. In passing sentence, would you as judge penalize the three executives, or would you put the blame on the corporation? Or would you be lenient on both in view of the strong competitive pressures that encouraged them to act illegally? Defend your position.

6. Review several of this chapter's examples of unethical or illegal behavior by corporations or their employees. In each case, indicate which one of the methods of improving ethical performance—top management attitudes, an open corporate culture, and organizational safeguards—would have been most effective in preventing the undesirable behavior.

CRITICAL INCIDENT

Manville Corporation

Asbestos fibers, when inhaled, cause serious lung diseases, including cancer. The health dangers from working with asbestos have been known to medical and industry officials since the late 1920s, but asbestos workers were poorly informed about the risks they were undergoing. Since asbestos has been used for over a century as a flame retardant, an insulating material, and in many consumer products and buildings, millions of people have been exposed to possible health risks. Workers who mine it and those who shape it into finished products are especially at risk, since the tiny fibers permeate the working environment, cling to clothing, and are taken into the lungs. Even family members at home have been known to contract lung disorders from handling an asbestos worker's clothing. Medical experts estimate that 8,000 to 10,000 people will die from asbestos diseases each year until the turn of the century.

Johns-Manville Corporation, formed in 1901 and renamed Manville Corporation in 1981, became the leading manufacturer of asbestos. Many of its workers were exposed to asbestos fibers, and several thousand contracted various lung diseases, some of which do not show up until 20 to 40 years after initial exposure to the fibers. Many of these workers or their survivors sued Manville Corporation for damages; by 1982, 16,500 suits were pending and another 35,500 to 100,000 were expected to be filed. These suits claimed that Manville Corporation should have notified employees of the health risks but did not do so. Manville's lawyers claimed that the company took protective steps in the 1930s when it learned of the link between the raw fibers and lung cancer, but the company denied knowing until the mid-1960s that finished products containing asbestos also could be responsible for health problems. Evidence on this point is disputed, but juries in some cases thought Manville should have done more, as shown by their awards to victims which sometimes averaged $600,000 per case. Even at an expected average of $40,000 per case, the company was facing a total award bill of around $2 billion; others thought the costs might be as high as $40 billion.

Faced with possible financial ruin, Manville declared itself legally bankrupt in 1982, although at the time it was worth $1.1 billion and continued to make a profit on its other lines of business. The bankruptcy laws are usually reserved to protect an *insolvent* company from the demands of its creditors until a fair settlement plan can be approved by the bankruptcy court. Manville's legal bankrupt status halted settlement of all asbestos-related health claims against the company, and froze the claims of all other creditors, which amounted to $600 million. The company's unorthodox strategy involved separating its asbestos business from the rest of its business activities, setting up a separate fund to compensate victims, and continuing to operate as a profitable concern. Victims' lawyers objected vigorously to a plan that would let the company escape with much smaller awards than juries had been approving. A plan finally was worked out to establish a trust fund of up to $2.5 billion to pay compensation to victims over a 25-year period, and a second trust fund of $125 million to handle the costs of removing asbestos materials from buildings, including many schools. This plan could not go into effect until approved by the bankruptcy court.[24]

1. In filing for bankruptcy even though it was still a profitable business, Manville acted legally. Do you believe in taking this legal step, it also was acting ethically? Give reasons for your answer.

2. Using the analytical steps outlined in Figure 3-6, indicate the ethical and moral responsibilities Manville managers had to the company's employees

[24]For details, see Paul Brodeur, *Outrageous Misconduct: The Asbestos Industry on Trial*, New York: Pantheon, 1985; "Manville Concludes Plan to Settle Claims of Property Damage Linked to Asbestos," *Wall Street Journal*, August 25, 1986, p. 3; and "The Case for Asbestos," *Business Week*, September 29, 1986, pp. 40–41.

who were exposed to asbestos and Manville's ethical obligations to persons who used products containing asbestos. Does the Unanimity Rule apply to this case? If the Priority Rule is used, how would you personally rank the three methods of ethical reasoning that ought to be applied in this case?

3. By using hindsight, what steps do you believe Manville could have taken beginning in the 1930s and 1940s to minimize the amount of harm caused by asbestos? In answering, draw upon this chapter's discussion of ways to improve a company's ethical performance.

change corporate culture

develop co code of ethics.

Chapter Four

CORPORATE STAKEHOLDERS AND PUBLIC ISSUES

This chapter discusses the interdependence between business, government, and society, and the relationships between organizations and their public and private stakeholders. It defines stakeholders and explains the manner in which a thorough stakeholder analysis can be conducted. It closes with a discussion of how stakeholder concerns evolve into public issues.

CHAPTER OBJECTIVES

After reading this chapter, you should be able to

- Understand the interdependence between business, government, and society
- Describe an interactive model of business and society
- Describe corporate stakeholders
- Demonstrate key steps in conducting a stakeholder analysis
- Understand the critical interests and powers of key stakeholders
- Discuss the evolution of public issues affecting business

*E*very corporation has complex involvements with other people, groups, and organizations in society. Some of these are intended and desired, others are unintentional and not desired. The people and organizations with which corporations are involved have an interest or "stake" in the decisions, actions, and outputs of the corporations. They are "stakeholders," and they are a critical factor in determining the success or failure of a modern business corporation. This became painfully evident in late August of 1986, when People Express airlines attempted to sell an ailing subsidiary, Frontier Airlines.

People Express had purchased Frontier Airlines, a forty-year-old operation, in November 1985. Since that time, Frontier had cost People $10 million a month, a sum that even a flourishing company could not long afford. Because People itself was struggling, the company's management decided to cut its losses and sell Frontier.

In July 1986, United Airlines made an offer of $146 million for the Denver-based carrier; however, because of conflict in negotiations with the pilots and unions, the offer was retracted on August 27. During the six or seven weeks after the offer was made, Frontier continued to lose money and became an increasingly unattractive candidate for acquisition. Frontier shut down operations completely on August 24. People Express announced that a bankruptcy filing was imminent.

Many groups of stakeholders were adversely affected by this turn of events. Frontier's passengers were the most immediately inconvenienced; thousands of travelers were left stranded when the announcement was made, and very few of them were able to make other arrangements to reach their destinations on time.

Another group immediately affected was Frontier's 4,700 employees. Though many of them hoped to find work with Continental or United, Denver's two major carriers, many would remain unemployed for some time.

Residents of the mountain states and the people who traveled there also were concerned. The loss of Frontier might mean less competition, higher fares, and reduced service. Access to Denver's Stapleton International Airport, an important regional hub, would be limited. Oil, cattle, mining, freight, and tourism companies in the area claim that direct and easy access to Denver is critical to their prosperity.

The federal government, although not directly affected by Frontier's shutdown, was a stakeholder in that it represents the public and formerly regulated the airline industry. Deregulation was intended to increase competition and thereby increase operator efficiency and produce lower prices for travelers. In 1986, however, weak, unprotected carriers were folding. Not only were travelers inconvenienced, occasionally being given only hours' notice of flight cancellation, but larger carriers were buying up the smaller ones, which might reduce competition. Government officials and agencies had to decide how best to protect travelers from frequent service delays, employees from massive layoffs, and the market from potential monopoly players.

In the case of Frontier, government and the legal system played a very large role. Though the inability of the United pilots and management to come to terms was considered the major reason why Frontier was expected to file for bankruptcy, the situation was not entirely in their control. "Neither the executives of People Express nor the union leaders at Frontier had much influence over Frontier's sale to United. 'We see ourselves as a tennis ball, and we are battered from one court to another and we're not even in the game,' said Robert C. Kardell, chairman of the Frontier merger committee."[1]

BUSINESS-GOVERNMENT-SOCIETY: AN INTERDEPENDENT SYSTEM

As the Frontier Airlines episode demonstrates, business, government, and other elements of society are all highly interdependent. Very few business actions are without an impact on others in society, just as few actions by government are without direct or indirect impact on business. And, of course, business and government decisions continuously affect all segments of the general public. To manage these interdependencies, corporate managers need both a _conceptual understanding_ of the relationships and _practical skills_ for responding.

A Systems View

Management thinking has increasingly been based on general systems theory. According to this theory, all living organisms (systems) interact with and are affected by their host environments. The key to survival is the capacity to adapt—that is, to be appropriately responsive—to the changing conditions posed by the environment. For an organism such as the modern business corporation, systems theory provides a powerful way for managers to think about the relationships between their system (i.e., their company) and the rest of the world.

The traditional concept of business interacting with society only through transactions in the marketplace is certainly not true today, if it ever was. Market exchanges are only one of the ways in which business and society interact. Many social influences on business come from outside of the marketplace, as do many business influences on society. The impact of IBM's development of computer technology, for example, has certainly not been confined just to those parties with whom it does business. To the contrary, the computer has become a pervasive influence, due in no small measure to IBM's success in developing the technology, marketing it widely to many types of customers, and finding many ways to encourage the public to solve problems, play games, and develop new modes of analysis with computers.

One result of this close, inseparable relationship between business and society is that all business decisions have a social impact, much as a pebble thrown into a pond creates ever-widening ripples. Another result is that the vitality of business and even its survival depend on society's actions and attitudes. Business can be smothered under a heavy "blanket" of social demands. For example, a labor union may demand wages that exceed a company's ability to pay. Local taxes may be set at a punitive level, thereby

[1]Agis Salpukas, "Frontier Deal Is Dead, United Says," _New York Times_, August 28, 1986, p. D-4.

driving businesses to other regions. Environmental regulations may prove to be too costly, leading to plant closures and job losses. So, while business decisions can have both positive and negative impacts on society, the actions of a society often can determine whether a business firm will prosper or die.

That is why business and society, taken together, are *an interactive system.* Each needs the other. Each can influence the other. They are intertwined so completely that an action taken by one will inevitably affect the other. The boundary line between the two is blurred and indistinct. Business is a part of society, and society penetrates far and often into business.

An Interactive Model of Business and Society

In spite of the close relationship of business and society, not all business ties to society are the same. Some are closer than others and more directly related to a company's main economic functions in society. Figures 4-1 and 4-2 illustrate the different types of relationships between business and society.[2]

Figure 4-1 shows business interacting with other groups necessary to carry out its primary purpose of effectively providing society with goods and services. Stockholders and creditors provide capital funds; employees contribute their work skills; suppliers sell raw materials, energy, and other needed supplies; and wholesalers, dealers, and retailers help move the product from the plant to sales outlets and on to consumers. All business firms need customers willing to buy what is produced, and most companies compete with other companies that are selling identical or similar products and services. These are the fundamental interactions that a company has with society. They tell us why that company is in business, and what its economic mission is.

A business's "primary involvement" with society includes all the direct relationships necessary for it to perform its major mission of producing goods and services for society. These primary interactions are usually conducted through the free market, which is a buying and selling process. In other words, business buys employees' time and skills, buys supplies, borrows capital (for a price, called "interest"), sells stock, contracts with dealers and suppliers, and, of course, sells products to its customers in competition with other firms. The market system, discussed in Chapter 6, is the primary way in which business interacts with society.

However, Figure 4-2 reveals that business's relationships with society go beyond the marketplace. Another level of interactions occurs when other groups express an interest in what the company is doing. *A business's "secondary involvement" with society is the result of the impacts caused by the company's primary business mission or function.*

For example, *suppose that some Toyota cars and trucks contribute to air pollution in urban areas. In such a case, public health is affected. Toyota did not*

___

[2]This discussion is based largely on the concept of "interpenetrating systems" developed in Lee E. Preston and James E. Post, *Private Management and Public Policy,* Englewood Cliffs, NJ: Prentice-Hall, 1975, pp. 24–27 and chap. 7.

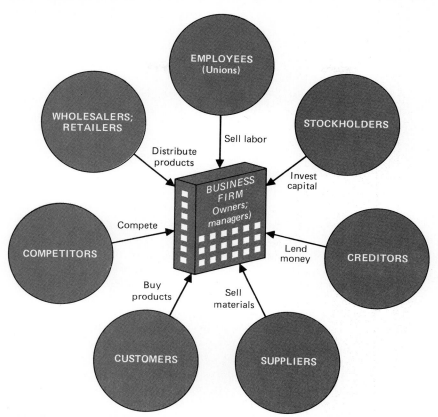

FIGURE 4-1. Business's primary interactions with society.

intend to create this effect when it sold cars; pollution was only an unintended result of its fundamental drive to make cars and sell them at a profit. Or consider what happens to a Japanese community that may be heavily dependent upon an automobile assembly plant when Toyota moves that plant to a United States location where transportation costs may be lower or energy supplies more abundant. The abandoned community may lose much of its tax base, joblessness may contribute to an increased crime rate, and the local housing market may become depressed, while the opposite effects might be felt at the new location. Toyota cannot escape these secondary impacts of its primary operations.

Calling these impacts "secondary" does not mean that they are less important than business's primary relationships with society. It means that they occur as a consequence of the normal activities of conducting business. Primary and secondary areas of involvement are not always sharply distinguished; often, one area "shades into" the other. For example, although two companies may have very different primary activities (e.g., one produces automobiles, the other hair spray), the secondary involvements (e.g., safety issues) may be similar.

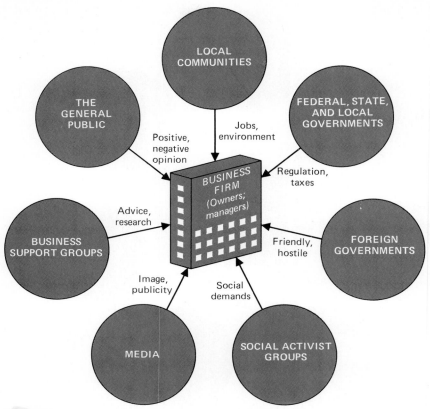

FIGURE 4-2. Business's secondary interactions with society.

These secondary interactions with other groups normally do not occur through the free market. As Figure 4-2 illustrates, a very extensive network of social groups may interact with business. All it takes to bring them into the picture is for the people they represent to be affected one way or another by a business firm's operations. The problems with which these groups are concerned are not easily approached or resolved by market action alone.

Consumers, for example, may not trust the market to establish fair prices. Plant closures may create semipermanent pockets of unemployment when workers either cannot or will not leave their home communities for jobs or higher wages elsewhere. Or coal miners may feel safer if government officials, rather than the owners, inspect mines for safety hazards. In these and similar cases, people form self-help groups or turn to the government for aid, often believing that their goals are better achieved by nonmarket means.

Combining business's primary and secondary interactions gives an interactive model of business and society relations, as shown in Figure 4-3. Primary interactions conducted through the free market are shown on the left. The sec-

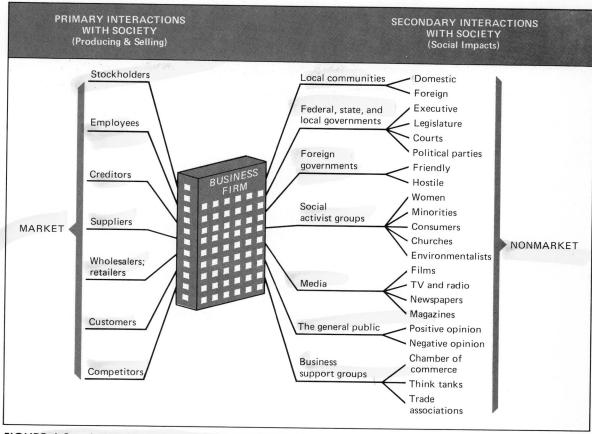

| PRIMARY INTERACTIONS WITH SOCIETY (Producing & Selling) | SECONDARY INTERACTIONS WITH SOCIETY (Social Impacts) |

FIGURE 4-3. An interactive model of business and society relations.

ondary interactions, which are carried out through nonmarket institutions, are depicted on the right. The main lessons that emerge from this interactive model are the following ones:

- In making decisions, business shares power with all primary and secondary groups. Shared decision making has become more and more typical of all businesses, large and small.
- The managers of business firms need to become skilled in the social and political factors involved in their secondary relations, as well as in the economic and financial aspects of their primary relations. Neither skill alone will suffice.
- A business firm's acceptance by society—its legitimacy as an approved institution—depends upon its performance in both the primary *and* secondary spheres. An automaker may be a successful manufacturer of reasonably priced cars that make a profit for the company but will encounter public disapproval if those cars are unsafe, polluting gas guzzlers.

The interactive model of business and society defines clearly the fundamental role of the business corporation in society. It recognizes that corporate decision makers need to take actions that protect and improve the welfare of society as a whole along with their own interests. The net effect is to enhance the quality of life in the broadest possible way, however the quality of life is defined by society. An effective relationship between business's actions and society's wants is thus achieved. Business acts in a manner that will accomplish social benefits along with the traditional economic gains that it seeks. It becomes concerned with its social as well as economic outputs, and with the total effect of its economic and institutional actions on society. In essence, business develops a sense of social community and human values to accompany its economic values.

THE STAKEHOLDER CONCEPT

When business interacts so often and so closely with society, a shared community of interest develops between a company and its surrounding social groups. When this occurs, corporate stakeholders are created. *Corporate stakeholders are all the groups affected by a corporation's decisions and policies* as shown in the following example:

> *Fifty to seventy children in the United States die annually from DPT vaccinations, which are given to prevent diphtheria, whooping cough, and tetanus. Because the vaccine industry has been in a crisis situation with skyrocketing liability insurance costs, Wyeth Laboratories, a division of American Home Products, is one of the few DPT producers left. Wyeth distributes only through Lederle Laboratories. The cost of the vaccine distributed by Lederle rose between 1983 and 1985 from 68 cents to $2.80 per dose, largely because of the increased cost of liability insurance and legal fees.*
>
> *Many groups—that is, stakeholders—are affected by this crisis. Consumers of the vaccine face higher purchasing costs and are threatened with a severe shortage of the vaccine if the few remaining producers withdraw from the market. Thousands of children would be endangered if Lederle withdrew from the business. In 1934, before the vaccine was widely used, more than 9,000 American children died of whooping cough alone.*
>
> *Lederle president Robert Johnson said: "We'd like to stay in this business as long as it is economically feasible." However, Johnson estimates that the dollars demanded in DPT lawsuits against the company are more than 100 times Lederle's annual DPT vaccine sales. "The breaking-off point would be not getting insurance."*
>
> *Government officials agree that some kind of legislation will be required to keep manufacturers producing and distributing DPT vaccine. The government has a special stake in keeping the supply of vaccine flowing because most states require that children be vaccinated with DPT before entering school. Bills have*

been introduced in Congress which would put a cap on amounts to be awarded for pain and suffering, and for death caused by DPT.[3]

Although the government—a stakeholder—can create conditions that would influence a company to stay or withdraw from a given market, the company itself—in this case, Lederle—will make the final decision. However, a company cannot act without regard to stakeholder interests. In addition to profit and business considerations, Lederle must consider the possibilities of a lawsuit by an injured consumer, plus the fact that production of the vaccine is necessary. Weighing conflicting considerations such as these is a part of any manager's job.

The interests of all corporate stakeholders need to be given serious consideration by the company. If their wishes are disregarded, they may combine to block or delay company operations. This happened in the nuclear power industry, where nuclear opponents and government regulations have stretched out the completion time of nuclear plants from six years to over twelve years.[4] In another famous case that continued for eighteen years, community and political action groups in New York State blocked Consolidated Edison Company from building a much-needed stored-water power plant on a scenic stretch of the Hudson River.

On the positive side, corporate stakeholders can be marshalled to aid and support a company that is in trouble financially.

Faced with possible bankruptcy, Chrysler Corporation in the late 1970s appealed to the United States Congress for an aid package to help it survive financial problems. The company successfully rallied many of its stakeholders to pressure Congress to grant the aid. Included were its many dealers, its unionized workers, banks that had lent money to the company, state and local governments that would be affected if the company failed, and the Canadian government, which did not want to see Chrysler plants in that country close down. Other stakeholders were elected politicians who feared the wrath of Chrysler employees if they permitted the company to fold, stockholders who had to forego regular dividends, and even some of Chrysler's biggest competitors who were reluctant to face possible charges of monopoly power if competition were narrowed to just two or three large United States automakers. Each group wanted to protect its stake in Chrysler.

The key point about corporate stakeholders is that they may, and frequently do, share decision-making power with a company's managers. Their justification for doing so is that they are affected by the company's operations. The community of interest created between a company and its stake-

[3]Adapted from Peter W. Berstein, "A Vaccine Crisis Lands in Congress," *Fortune,* April 29, 1985, p. 238.

[4]Office of Nuclear Reactor Programs, U.S. Department of Energy, "Update: Nuclear Power Program Information and Data," Washington, DC, July–September 1981.

holders can be a powerful aid to business, or it can be turned against a company. When stakeholders demand a voice in decision making and policy making, corporation managers need to respond with great skill if their primary business mission—producing goods and services—is to be achieved.[5]

Stakeholders and stakeholder relationships have changed over the years. Previously, managers only had to focus their attention on the product-market framework; they could focus on bringing products and services to market as efficiently and effectively as possible. Therefore, the number of stakeholders was limited. Thomas J. Watson, Sr., chairman of IBM in the 1950s, is said to have described management's role as one of balancing a "three-legged stool" consisting of employees, customers, and shareholders. He insisted on systematically changing the order in which he mentioned them in his talks and speeches to emphasize their equality.[6] In those days, theories of management emphasized the static or stable nature of both the organization and its environment.

This view of stakeholder relationships and management theory is inappropriate today, amidst increasingly uncertain and unstable environments. Where business firms previously had to consider only the needs of a few stakeholder groups, modern managers regularly have to consider the needs of owners, unions and employees, suppliers, customers, and many other constituencies.

Today, more comprehensive approaches are needed for the successful management of the entire enterprise—approaches that take into consideration the needs of a larger and more diverse group of stakeholders. John de Butts, who served as chairman of AT&T during the late 1970s, commented about the outdated three-legged stool: "The only image which recurs with uncomfortable persistence is not a piece of furniture at all. It's a porcupine—with the quills reversed."[7]

This complex situation creates a dilemma for the manager; each environmental shift must be understood individually and handled individually in order for the organization to adapt to it. At the same time, many changes may be occurring simultaneously, affecting many areas of the organization at once. Therefore, nothing can be done in a vacuum, and business planning must take into consideration this web of impacts. Stakeholder analysis is one modern approach to this management challenge.

STAKEHOLDER ANALYSIS

Stakeholder analysis helps the manager identify each stakeholder, each stakeholder's interest, and the changes in stakeholder perceptions of issues and

[5]James R. Emshoff and R. Edward Freeman, "Who's Butting into Your Business?" *The Wharton Magazine*, Fall 1979, pp. 44–59.

[6]Quoted in John de Butts, "A Strategy of Accountability," in William Dill (ed.), *Running The American Corporation*, Englewood Cliffs, NJ: Prentice-Hall, 1978, pp. 139–152.

[7]Ibid., p. 141.

- MAPPING STAKEHOLDER RELATIONSHIPS
- MAPPING STAKEHOLDER COALITIONS
- ASSESSING THE NATURE OF EACH STAKEHOLDER'S INTEREST
- ASSESSING THE NATURE OF EACH STAKEHOLDER'S POWER
- CONSTRUCTING A MATRIX OF STAKEHOLDER PRIORITIES
- MONITORING SHIFTING COALITIONS

FIGURE 4-4. Major steps in stakeholder analysis.

in the balance of influence over time. Stakeholder analysis involves several steps, as shown in Figure 4-4: mapping stakeholder relationships; mapping stakeholder coalitions; assessing the nature of each stakeholder's interest; assessing the nature of each stakeholder's power; constructing a matrix of stakeholder priorities; and monitoring shifting coalitions of stakeholders. Each of these analytic steps will be briefly described.

Managers utilize stakeholder maps in two ways. *First*, the stakeholder relationship map, like a snapshot, identifies the web of common actors whose interests must always be taken into account as the corporation's business strategy is pursued. In the case of a 7-Eleven convenience store, for example, this map would include suppliers of paper products, packaged goods, ready-to-eat fast foods, beverages, and periodicals. It also would include the kinds of customers typical of the convenience store industry, as well as employees. *Second*, the stakeholder map is used by managers to better understand the relationships among various actors on specific problems or issues. Use of the map assists managers in responding to the actors' concerns. Many 7-Eleven stores faced such a need for stakeholder maps in 1986 when their sale of *Playboy* and *Penthouse* magazines was challenged by consumer groups.

Mapping Stakeholder Relationships

The stakeholder diagrams shown in Figures 4-1 and 4-2 apply to most business organizations. To use stakeholder analysis in decision making, one should construct a more specific map of each firm's stakeholders. Such a diagram provides more detail; it illustrates the specific actors and groups with which a company interacts. For example, where the general map lists creditors, the specific map lists specific banks and lenders, and perhaps the percentage or amount of indebtedness for each. Similarly, the category "suppliers" can be refined by listing the suppliers by name, the materials supplied, and the amount of business done with them.

Mapping Stakeholder Coalitions

Managers need to "see" how particular stakeholders are aligned on specific issues to formulate effective responses to them. By mapping the coalitions of stakeholders on a particular issue, managers can better appreciate how much concern exists, and what actors need to be considered as actions are taken.

For example, 7-Eleven Stores found themselves the target of a consumer boycott to protest the sale of Playboy *and* Penthouse *magazines. Older and more conservative customers protested the sale of the magazines. When the chain decided to stop selling these magazines, other stakeholders became more actively involved. Those who regularly purchased the magazines strongly protested their withdrawal. Some of these people boycotted the stores to protest the company's decision to drop the magazines. The publishers of the magazines also became more involved than they had been when their magazines had been ordered regularly. The decision of a national buyer such as 7-Eleven to cancel its orders cost these suppliers a great deal in revenues. In addition to customers and suppliers, a variety of legal and public interest groups, which had not been stakeholders previously, also were drawn into the controversy.*

Assessing the Nature of Each Stakeholder's Interest

The next task in conducting a comprehensive stakeholder analysis is assessing the nature of each stakeholder's interest. Each stakeholder has a unique involvement, and managers must understand the differing interests and respond accordingly. For example, stockholders have an ownership interest in the organization. The economic health and success of the organization affect these people financially; their personal wealth is at stake. Customers, suppliers, and retailers have a market interest. All of these stakeholders are involved in market exchanges with the organization; they have a stake in "getting what they pay for." Customers want to receive quality goods for their purchasing dollar. Suppliers want to receive a fair price on a predictable basis for the materials or goods they sell to the firm. Retailers want to receive quality merchandise for resale in their stores. Thus, the nature of the stake is different for owners than it is for customers and suppliers. Owners are most interested in realizing a return on their investment, while customers and suppliers are most interested in gaining fair value in the exchange of goods and money. Neither has a great interest in the other's stake.

Governments, public interest groups, and local communities have another sort of relationship with the company. Theirs is one of nonmarket influence. They exert political, legal, social, and governmental pressures. They often are interested in influencing business to act in socially responsible ways. In general, their stake is broader than the financial stake of owners or persons who buy products and sell services to the company. They may wish to protect the environment, assure human rights, or advance other broad social interests. Managers need to track these stakeholder distinctions with great care.

Assessing the Nature of Each Stakeholder's Power

Different stakeholders have different types and degrees of power. Power, in this instance, means the ability to use resources to make an event happen or to secure a desired outcome. One authority describes three types of stake-holder power: voting power, economic power, and political power.[8]

Voting power (not referring to political, electoral voting) means that the stakeholder has a legitimate right to cast a vote. For example, each stock-holder has a voting power proportionate to the percentage of the company's stock that he or she owns. Stockholders typically have an opportunity to vote on such major decisions as mergers, acquisitions, and other extraordinary issues. Through the exercise of informed, intelligent voting, they may influence company policy so that their investment is protected and will produce a healthy return.

Customers, suppliers, and retailers have a direct economic influence on a company. Their power is *economic*. Suppliers can withhold supplies or refuse to fill orders if a firm does not meet its contractual responsibilities. Customers can choose to boycott products or entire organizations for any number of reasons; they may consider the goods to be too expensive, poorly made, unsafe, or inappropriate for consumption. They may refuse to buy any of the products a company sells if they consider one of the products especially unfit for sale, as did some of the customers who objected when 7-Eleven sold *Playboy* and *Penthouse*. Other customers may refuse to buy a company's products if the company enacts an improper policy. This was the case for those customers who regularly bought these magazines from 7-Eleven; they boycotted the store because they considered its new policy to be a form of censorship.

Government exercises *political power* by creating legislation, making regulations, or bringing lawsuits against corporations. In an open political system, other stakeholders may exercise political power too, using their resources to pressure government to adopt new laws or regulations or to take legal action against a company.

> In a landmark case, a group of citizens in Woburn, Massachusetts, sued W. R. Grace Company and Beatrice Foods for allegedly dumping toxic chemicals that leaked into underground wells used for drinking water. The deaths and illnesses of family members led the survivors to mobilize political power against Grace and Beatrice. Investigations were conducted by private groups and public agencies, and the toxic waste issue became politically important.

Of course, a single stakeholder is capable of exercising more than one type of power. The Woburn families sued the two corporations (political power), but they had other powers too. They could have led a boycott (economic power) against the companies, or purchased shares of stock in the companies and attempted to oust the directors and management through a proxy fight (voting power). Thus, stakeholders who are intent on forcing a corporation to change its behavior have a variety of options for doing so.

---

[8]R. Edward Freeman, *Strategic Management: A Stakeholder Approach*, Marshfield, MA: Pitman, 1984.

STAKEHOLDER	NATURE OF INTEREST— STAKEHOLDER WISHES TO:	NATURE OF POWER— STAKEHOLDER INFLUENCES COMPANY BY:
PRIMARY STAKEHOLDERS		
EMPLOYEES	• Maintain stable employment in firm • Receive fair pay for work • Work in safe, comfortable environment	• Union bargaining power • Work actions or strikes • Publicity
OWNERS/ STOCKHOLDERS	• Receive a satisfactory return on investments (dividends) • Realize appreciation in stock value over time	• Exercising voting rights based on share ownership • Exercising rights to inspect company books and records
CUSTOMERS	• Receive fair exchange: value and quality for dollar spent • Receive safe, reliable products	• Purchasing goods from competitors • Boycotting companies whose products are unsatisfactory or whose policies are unacceptable
SUPPLIERS	• Receive regular orders for goods • Be paid promptly for supplies delivered	• Refusing to meet orders if conditions of contract are breached • Supplying to competitors
COMPETITORS	• Be profitable • Gain a larger share of the market • See the entire industry grow	• Technological innovation, forcing competitors to "Keep up" • Charge lower prices
RETAILERS/ WHOLESALERS	• Receive quality goods in a timely fashion at reasonable cost • Reliable products that consumers trust and value	• Buying from other suppliers if terms of contract are unsatisfactory • Boycotting companies whose goods or policies are unsatisfactory
CREDITORS	• Receive repayment of loans • Collect debts and interest	• Calling in loans if payments are not made • Utilizing legal authorities to repossess or take over property if loan payments are severely delinquent • Refusing to extend additional credit
SECONDARY STAKEHOLDERS		
LOCAL COMMUNITIES	• Employ local residents in the company • Ensure that the local environment is protected • Ensure that the local area is developed	• Issuing or restricting operating licenses and permits • Lobbying government for regulation of the company's policies or methods of land use and waste disposal
SOCIAL ACTIVISTS	• Monitor company actions and policies to ensure that they conform to legal and ethical standards, and that they protect the public's safety	• Gaining broad public support through publicizing the issue • Lobbying government for regulation of the company
MEDIA	• Keep the public informed on all issues relevant to their health, well-being, and economic status • Monitor company actions	• Publicizing events that affect the public, especially those which have negative effects
BUSINESS SUPPORT (e.g., trade associations)	• Provide research and information which will help the company or industry perform in a changing environment	• Using its staff and resources to assist company in business endeavors and development efforts • Provide legal or "group" political support beyond that which an individual company can provide for itself
FOREIGN GOVERNMENT	• Economic development • Social improvements	• Permits to do business • Regulations
FEDERAL STATE AND LOCAL GOVERNMENTS	• Raise revenues through taxes • Economic development	• Regulations, licenses, and permits • Power to allow or disallow industrial activity
THE GENERAL PUBLIC	• Social values protected • Risks minimized • Prosperity for society	• Support activists • Press government to act • Condemn or praise individual companies

FIGURE 4-5. Primary and secondary stakeholders: Nature of interest and power.

Issues \ Stakeholders	7-Eleven Stores, Owners and Stockholders	Suppliers of sexually explicit magazines	Buyers of sexually explicit magazines	Customers opposed to sale of sexually explicit magazines	American Civil Liberties Union (ACLU)
Financial returns	1	1	NA	NA	NA
Ethics of sale of sexually explicit magazines	5	NA	NA	1	5
Free speech and censorship issues	5	1	3	5	1

1 = Critically important to stakeholder   5 = Not very important to stakeholder
3 = Somewhat important to stakeholder   NA = Stakeholder not concerned with this issue

FIGURE 4-6. Stakeholder-issues matrix for 7-Eleven stores. (*Source: Adapted from R. Edward Freeman,* Strategic Management: A Stakeholder Approach, *Marshfield, MA: Pitman, 1984, p. 114.*)

A company's managers must therefore understand the type of power each stakeholder group has or can readily acquire. This, too, is essential for effectively managing stakeholder relationships. Figure 4-5 illustrates the nature of the interest and power for the key stakeholders identified in Figures 4-1 and 4-2.

Constructing a Matrix of Stakeholder Priorities

Once stakeholders have been identified and an analysis has been made of the nature of each one's stake and power, a matrix can be constructed that combines all of this information. Not all stakeholders will be equally interested or involved in all issues. Different stakeholders will assign a different value to each issue and will set different priorities.

> For example, *local communities and public interest groups had very little interest in 7-Eleven stores until the sale of allegedly "pornographic" magazines became an issue. With that issue, however, they developed a very strong interest. And while customers in general were moderately interested in what was sold in the store, some of them—those strongly opposed to the sale of pornographic magazines and those who regularly purchased them—became highly interested.*

Figure 4-6 presents one possible stakeholder-issues matrix for 7-Eleven stores. By developing such a matrix, managers can illustrate the coalitions that might form around a specific issue and the types of interests they might have.

Monitoring Shifting Coalitions

Stakeholder coalitions are not static. The stakeholders that are highly involved with a company today may be less involved tomorrow. Issues that are most salient at one time may be replaced by other issues at another time; stakeholders who are most dependent on an organization at one time may be less dependent at another. To make matters even more complex, the process of shifting coalitions may not occur uniformly in all parts of a large corporation. Stakeholders involved with one part of a large corporation often will have little or no involvement with another part of the company. These shifts require periodic review of a company's stakeholders, redrawing stakeholder maps, and revising a company's stakeholder-issues matrix.

EVOLUTION OF PUBLIC ISSUES

As we demonstrated previously, any large company will have multiple stakeholder groups, each of which will have a different type and degree of influence on company operations and policy. The complexity of this situation can be intimidating; certainly more than a few managers have been tempted to simply ignore the stakeholders and get on with business. However, ignoring stakeholders will most likely make it impossible for the firm to do "business as usual." Managers need to be aware of and responsive to stakeholder interests and keep informed as interests and influences shift. To ignore the changing environment can lead to the birth of a "public issue."

A public issue or social issue is a problem which, because of its salience or the degree of its impact, attracts the attention of stakeholder coalitions. When a company dumps standard garbage in a garbage dump, that action is unimportant to everyone except the company's maintenance crew and the dump personnel. If, however, the company dumps toxic wastes in that same dump, the issue becomes extremely salient to local residents, environmental groups, and government agencies, as well as to the dump operator.

Often, the first sign of a rising public issue is a conflict or confrontation with a stakeholder group. Workers go on strike; protest groups picket in front of a company's offices; angry suppliers or customers sue the corporation for breach of contract. Such actions are sometimes a visible sign of a larger, more dangerous problem for the corporation. Naturally, calling strikes, picketing, and engaging in lawsuits do not occur without a reason or without prior history leading to the action. But at times, managers do not see the early warning signals of an emerging issue or controversy. By the time they recognize the existence of a problem, it may already be a crisis.

Public issues generally occur in a series of phases which, because of their natural evolution, can be thought of as a "life cycle." By recognizing the pattern through which issues evolve, and spotting the early warning signs, a corporation's management can anticipate problems and act to resolve them before they reach crisis proportions. The pattern of public-issue development includes four basic phases: changing stakeholder expectations; political ac-

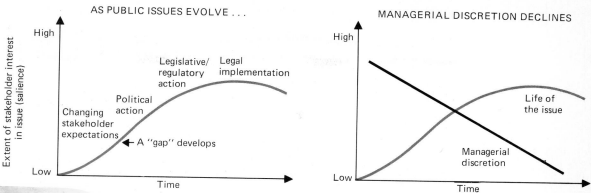

FIGURE 4-7. Phases of the public-issue life cycle. (*Source: Adapted from James E. Post,* Corporate Behavior and Social Change, *Reston, VA: Reston, 1978.*)

tion; legislative and regulatory action; and legal implementation, as shown in Figure 4-7.

Phase 1: Changing Stakeholder Expectations

Public issues begin to develop when a stakeholder group's expectations of how a company should behave is not met by the company's actual performance. This failure to meet expectations can take many forms, ranging from small groups of residents objecting to a local manufacturer's fouling of the air to the concern of animal lovers for the welfare of monkeys being used in scientific research in a laboratory. Once a gap develops between stakeholder expectations and the corporation's actual performance, the seeds of another public issue have been sown.

> *The tobacco industry has had to battle against an increasingly pervasive anti-smoking climate. In the 1920s, 1930s, and 1940s smoking was considered to be glamorous and sophisticated. Advertisements during the 1940s featured movie stars dressed in military garb, which gave the impression that smoking is not only glamorous but patriotic. The perception of smokers and smoking is very different today. "The public is increasingly defining smoking as unacceptable," said Dr. David Harris, the Suffolk County (NY) Health Commissioner. "It is demanding the right to live free from smoke, the right to life, liberty and the pursuit of happiness without smoke." And although tobacco industry representatives dispute the validity of studies linking health hazards to smoking, they agree "that in a society enamored with youth, beauty and fitness, smokers are increasingly seen as misfits." Said William Aylward, assistant president of the Tobacco Institute, "They've turned smokers into social pariahs."[9]*

[9]Lindsey Gruson, "Employers Get Tough on Smoking at Work," *New York Times,* March 14, 1985, p. B-8.

Phase 2: Political Action

It may take months or even years for an unhappy or concerned group of stakeholders to build a base of support sufficient to challenge a corporation. If an issue persists, however, the group may organize formally and campaign for its point of view through pamphlets, newsletters, brochures, and other forms of communication. They may attract the attention of the media, which will result in newspaper, television, or radio coverage. Such attention helps move the issue from one of citizen concern to one of political importance.

> *The political drive against smoking began in the 1960s with a flurry of unsuccessful lawsuits against tobacco companies. The landmark "turning of the tide," however, came in 1973, when the Civil Aeronautics Board relegated smokers to the back of the airplanes.*
>
> *Later political efforts included the formation of various antismoking groups, most notably the Group Against Smoking Pollution (GASP). Originally the group received calls from people complaining of illness caused by "passive smoke"—smoke from other people's cigarettes. Later, they responded to calls from companies wishing to establish smoking restrictions. Antismoking activists attribute corporate eagerness to set up such policies to dozens of legal cases in which nonsmokers have successfully sued companies for failing to protect them from passive smoke. (EPA statistics conclude that passive smoke kills up to 5,000 people each year.[10]) The courts have, in fact, sided with nonsmokers in every major suit of this nature since 1975.*

Politicians are interested in citizen concerns and often are anxious to advocate action on their behalf. Thus, the neighborhood group that complains about pollution from a local manufacturer may find a willing audience in the city council, a local zoning board, or a municipal official. Perhaps a local congressional representative will send a letter to a plant manager, send a staff investigator to study the situation, or even consider holding a public hearing to allow citizens to air their grievances. Such actions let a company's management know that an issue is now politically important. The government officials thus become new stakeholders with different types of power to use in closing the gap between expectations and performance. For the company that runs a local plant, resolution of an issue will require action that is satisfactory to government officials as well as to local citizens. The issue thus becomes much more complex for the company and its managers to resolve. Managerial discretion and freedom to act begin to decline.

Phase 3: Legislative and Regulatory Action

The political phase of an issue's life can be quite long. As more people are drawn into a conflict, there may emerge some ideas—or even a consensus—about a new law or regulation that can help to solve the problem. When

---

[10]Ibid.

legislative proposals or draft regulations begin to emerge, the underlying issue unquestionably moves to a new level of action and managerial importance.

> *Much legislative and legal action has been taken in favor of antismoking activists during the past decade. In September 1984, United States District Court Judge H. Lee Sarokin ruled that the health warning in cigarette advertisements and on labels does not shield a company from liability. His ruling also supported the argument that the cigarette industry is negating the health warning in cigarette ads by skillful publicity implying that they should not be taken seriously. One reason why courts may rule in favor of smokers in future claims is that, according to the National Institute of Drug Abuse, cigarettes are addictive—more addictive than heroin and alcohol.[11]*
>
> *Legislation has been enacted nationally and in several states. In mid-1984 the federal government required that health warnings on cigarette labels and advertisements be 50 percent larger and that messages be rotated quarterly to warn of more dangers associated with smoking. Suffolk County New York's smoking restrictions, in effect since August 1984, limit the areas in restaurants that can be used by smokers, and it allows nonsmokers in the workplace to declare their "immediate work area" a no-smoking zone. Also in 1984, the city commissioner in Gainesville, Florida, approved smoking restrictions that require smokers to ask for and receive permission from every employee in their work area before smoking. In March 1985, the New Jersey legislature approved four bills that prohibit smoking on buses and trains and in supermarkets and require restaurants to post their smoking policies on the door.*

Most managers have little direct influence or control over legislative and regulatory action. Instead, their company is represented by lawyers, lobbyists, and professional political consultants. Only top management is directly involved at this point, sometimes by testifying before government committees or regulatory agencies. For the most part, corporate lawyers and lobbyists are deciding what proposals are best and worst for the company.

Phase 4: Legal Implementation

Once a new law is passed or a regulation developed, government agencies take action to ensure that corporations comply with the new rules. A corporation may still challenge the validity of the law by testing it in a lawsuit. Thus, implementation of new laws and regulations is often accompanied by litigation and court activity. As in Phase 3, managers have relatively little discretion or freedom to act on the underlying conflict or problem. The company's lawyers are primarily responsible until the litigation is ended. At that point, the corporation is expected to implement the new rules and involve other appropriate levels of management in meeting the new requirements.

[11]Shirley Hobbs Scheibla, "Where There's Smoke . . . There's Certain to Be a Lawsuit," *Barron's*, January 7, 1985, p. 13.

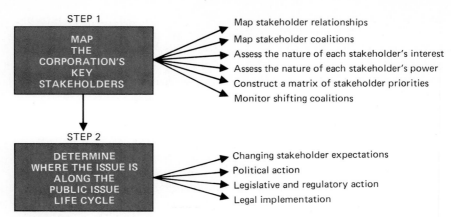

FIGURE 4-8. Analytic steps in responding to stakeholders.

In the case of smoking restrictions, most businesses are more than willing to comply. Though some restaurants bend the seating rules during slack hours, so as not to inconvenience customers, most companies have financial incentives for meeting or even exceeding smoking restrictions. Several studies show that smokers cost their employers millions of dollars every year. The owner of a New Jersey plumbing and heating supply business gave his employees a $2 per week bonus for not smoking. "Nonsmokers are worth more than people who smoke," he said. "They're out sick less. And smoking takes time from the job. Smokers are always stopping for a pack and running out of matches." An in-house survey at Good-year estimated that the almost 3,000 employees at the Akron headquarters cost the company about $2 million each year in smoking-related problems. And an insurance company with 2,000 employees in Washington state received a $500-a-month rebate from its janitorial service after implementing a smoking ban. "We now don't have to dump and clean ashtrays," said the service's president. "The dusting of the desktops is easier. . . . Upholstered furniture is easier to keep clean. Windows don't get dirty as fast."[12]

Stakeholder interest in an underlying issue tends to decline as a new law or regulation is implemented. If the law is violated or ignored, however, the issue will reemerge, as a gap once again develops between stakeholder expectations and the corporation's actual performance.

When public issues are left unresolved, the discretion of managers in finding acceptable ways of narrowing the gap is restricted. As more stakeholders become involved, it becomes harder to settle the underlying issue. In the end, the corporation may face a "solution" that is very costly, difficult to implement, and hard to manage. That is one of the best reasons to identify issues early and act to close the gaps between the corporate actions and the stakeholders' expectations. That is the essence of socially responsive management. Figure 4-8 outlines the analytic steps corporate managers can take in responding to stakeholders.

[12]Gruson, op. cit., pp. B-1, B-8.

SUMMARY

The relationship between business, government, and society is highly inter-dependent and complex. General systems theory states that all organisms or systems are affected by their host environments; thus, an organization must be appropriately responsive to changes and conditions in its environment in order to survive or succeed.

The web of interactions between business, government, and society naturally generates a corresponding system of stakeholders—groups affected by and influential in corporate decisions and actions. Stakeholder analysis helps managers define specifically who the company's stakeholders are, what their interests and sources of power are, and how these change over time.

Public issues normally develop through a sequence of four phases: first, a change in stakeholder expectations occurs, then political action, then legislative and regulatory action, and finally legal implementation. Managerial actions taken early in a public issue's life cycle give a company greater discretion and control over the eventual outcome.

DISCUSSION AND REVIEW QUESTIONS

1. What is the systemic relationship between business, government, and society? From current events discussed in the *Wall Street Journal* or *Business Week*, describe a company that is currently facing changes in this relationship. Who is being affected and how?

2. In 1986, Delta Airlines entered into an agreement to purchase Western Airlines. The agreement was "subject to the approval of both companies' stockholders." The Federal Aviation Agency and the Justice Department's Antitrust Division also had to review the proposed merger before it could be implemented. Read news items from the time of the merger and describe the merger in terms of the interactive model discussed in this chapter. Who are the primary and secondary stakeholders? Explain the interests of each of the stakeholders mentioned. What do they want from the merger? What powers do they have to affect the merger?

3. Select and visit, if possible, a local business or hospital in your community. Prepare a stakeholder map, showing the key parties with which the business or hospital interacts.

4. How do stakeholders vary in terms of the nature of their stake and the nature of their influence on an organization? For the company you described in the previous question, put yourself in the position of chief executive officer: How would you balance your actions and set priorities in response to the needs or demands of your various stakeholders?

5. In the early 1980s, General Motors revised much of its print advertising to include a qualifier stating that all Oldsmobile components came from the Oldsmobile division or another GM division. This was in response to consumer protests about Oldsmobiles advertised as including Oldsmobile engines, but which, in fact, held Chevrolet engines. Research the issue of the "Chevymobile" and describe it in terms of the public-issue life cycle.

CRITICAL INCIDENT

Food Mart Stores

Joe Smith, midwestern area manager of Food Mart Stores, was faced with a problem. Two stores in a suburban area of a medium-sized city in Missouri were scheduled to be closed. Just as this announcement was made, and with only one week left until closing, the townspeople sent hundreds of letters of protest to the president of the company, asking her to reconsider. She turned the problem over to Smith.

When Smith visited the town, he found that one of the stores located in the Stone Hill area seemed to be highly desired, while local citizens were indifferent to the other. At the former store, he was met by picketers and newspeople, all of whom seemed to have an unfavorable opinion of the company for closing the store. Smith found the residents of the Stone Hill area to be highly organized and community oriented; they had joined to form a strong, united front, complete with petitions, form letters, and protest banners, in less than twenty-four hours.

After investigating, Smith discovered the major reasons for the protest. The senior citizens, numbering one in ten in the community, were the most ardent opponents. Because they could not carry heavy loads long distances, these people shopped frequently. If the store closed, they would be forced to take a bus in and out of the central city several times a week, and few of them could afford to do that. Another group opposed to the closing were local families in low-income brackets. Family incomes averaged $9,000 in the neighborhood, compared to the city average of $11,000. Jane Katz, the protest organizer, also mentioned that when the Food Mart Store had first come to the area, it had forced all other local stores out of business; they would not be there now to service the residents if the only store left were to close.

The problem was not a simple one. Food Mart had been overhauling its operations for some time. Most of the small stores had been replaced with stores that were not only two or three times bigger, but which carried a much more diverse line of products than the basic food lines carried at the Stone Hill store. Renovations were rarely done, because they were very costly yet produced no increases in selling space. The company, through this expansion program, had increased its efficiency, which allowed it to offer price breaks without absorbing any of the costs. Therefore, all the patrons (stakeholders) of the new stores were receiving benefits from the program.

On the other hand, the patrons of the Stone Hill store would suffer if it closed, or even if a new larger location were opened which was not within walking distance. Katz felt that Food Mart, as a large corporation, could easily absorb the costs of running one store that produces somewhat lower revenues than the rest. She demanded only minimal service, and asserted that, for humanitarian reasons, the store should stay open.

Smith had to take several factors into consideration. The profits of the company would probably increase if the two stores were closed and moved to a large, mall location. This was important to the company, since it currently earned less than 2 percent on sales (before taxes and after operating costs). It also would be important to Smith, whose performance was evaluated on the profitability of his area. In addition, the patrons of the other new stores were benefiting from lower prices produced by the expansion program.

On the other hand, Smith could not ignore the protesters and the needs of the people in the community. The Food Mart Store had forced out all its local competition. The local citizens of Stone Hill would have no convenient alternative. Since Food Mart had been the cause of the public's dependence on it, did not the corporation owe something to this public? Perhaps if the store had to be closed for economic reasons, the closing could be held off until a new store had moved to the area to service the customers. On returning to his office, Smith had to determine what to recommend to Food Mart's president.

1. Who are the stakeholders in this case? Which are primary, and which are secondary? What is the nature of each stakeholder's influence, and how much influence does each seem to have? Use illustrations from throughout the chapter to shape your answers.

2. If Smith decides to close the store immediately, how will the business-government-society relationship come into play? How might the public issue life cycle unfold?

3. How should Smith handle the situation? Defend your recommendations and compare them with the viewpoints of others in the class.

Chapter Five

STRATEGIC MANAGEMENT AND SOCIAL RESPONSIVENESS

A corporation's core activities—its primary involvements—have the greatest impact on society. Business plans and commitments for the future will define tomorrow's primary involvements. By considering and carefully planning for the long-term effects of these decisions and policies, a company's management can be socially responsive. This chapter discusses how businesses integrate social responsiveness into the strategic decision process and infuse social responsibility into the core activities of the firm.

CHAPTER OBJECTIVES

After reading this chapter, you should be able to

- Describe four basic strategies of corporate response to the environment
- Discuss how strategic decisions are formulated with an awareness of environmental issues
- Define the factors essential for implementing corporate social policies
- Explain a model of managerial responsiveness to environmental issues and social demands
- Highlight the development of the public affairs function and issues management

*E*ffective strategic management involves the guidance and direction of the whole business enterprise. Therefore, it requires an understanding of two important concerns:

- Where and how the organization is going to change, develop, and operate in the present and in the future. These issues comprise the corporation's *strategy*, or basic plan, for relating current decisions to future goals and objectives.
- What general managers (as opposed to managers with narrow or technical responsibilities) do in integrating all of the interests and considerations into current decision making. The way managers perceive their environment, organize and order their thinking about those factors, and weigh the various interests of stakeholders in making decisions are all relevant factors.[1]

Managers must balance two sets of concerns simultaneously: current, short-term business needs and long-term survival and growth needs. This need is well illustrated by the situation facing the genetic-engineering industry:

> In May of 1984, environmental activist Jeremy Rifkin won a preliminary injunction (issued by United States District Court Judge John J. Sirica) to halt the testing of a genetically altered organism in the open environment. The decision prevented Steven E. Ludlow, a University of California scientist, from spraying a 200-foot row of potato vines with "ice-minus," a synthetic bacterium created to prevent frost from damaging plants.
>
> This was just the first of several court actions initiated by Rifkin which halted or slowed the development and testing of genetically altered organisms. Delays present a serious problem for firms in the genetic-engineering industry. Although they continue to conduct research, usually at great expense, the firms receive no guarantee that they will have a return on their investment. To make matters more complex, a company receives no guarantee that it will have an exclusive patent on any product it develops. In one case, Hoffman-La Roche, a Swiss pharmaceutical multinational, was awarded a United States patent for alpha interferon (a potential cancer fighter) in early 1985; Biogen, a Swiss biotechnology firm, had been awarded a European patent for the same product six months earlier. In such an unstable, unpredictable environment, strategic planning becomes both increasingly difficult and increasingly important.
>
> The dilemma hinges on an ongoing argument: biotechnology firms and scientists insist that the products they are developing will be far too valuable to humanity to be stopped by environmentalists and industry critics. According to these scientists, genetic developments will be able to improve everything from agriculture to medicine to bridge construction. Products currently in early stages of development include bacteria that eat toxic wastes, strains of grain that are inherently pest-resistant, organisms that would fight cancers and other currently fatal diseases, and a "diamond fiber" that could be used to make beams and support structures fifty times stronger than steel.

[1]Charles W. Hofer, Edwin A. Murray, Jr., Ram Charam, and Robert A. Pitts, *Strategic Management: A Casebook in Policy and Planning*, 2d ed., St. Paul, MN: West, 1984, Chap. 1.

> *Environmentalists agree that the potential rewards from genetic testing and development may be great, but they fear that too much unregulated progress may be dangerous. If testing is allowed to progress unwatched, the environment may be permanently and adversely altered. According to Rifkin, genetically altered organisms, if released in the environment, might be impossible to control. He pointed out, for example, that "ice-minus" could significantly alter the climate of an area, and while preventing frost damage, it could allow whole new strains of pests to enter and damage the crops.[2]*

No solution to this conflict presently exists. Most government regulatory officials think that the existing laws and regulations can be adapted to address the problem. Officials of the Food and Drug Administration (FDA), Environmental Protection Agency (EPA), and U.S. Department of Agriculture (USDA) have stated that existing methods of regulation, monitoring, and standard setting will probably be applied to the biotechnology field.[3]

Meanwhile, biotechnology firms must operate in an insecure, unpredictable environment. Most of their products require long-term commitments and, therefore, long-term strategies. Few companies have any guaranteed sources of short-term revenue or successful products already in the market. Strategy making is therefore almost impossible: long-term investment and research strategies are needed most, yet no future conditions are guaranteed; companies must be socially responsible in their activities, and yet limited experience in the field leaves almost no precedent by which action can be guided.

STRATEGIES OF RESPONSE

As managers in the biotechnology field attempt to plan and implement business strategies, they frequently encounter pressures and problems from the external environment. Usually, those problems and pressures can be identified with one or more other organizations, groups, or stakeholders. In societies where power is diffused and where individuals can freely make decisions in their own self-interest, managers are likely to find that their actions are challenged by others outside the organization. Some managers believe that such outside interferences are illegitimate, and they respond with an attitude that R. Edward Freeman calls "blame the stakeholder."[4] Government, environmentalists, and consumer activists are among the most popular villains.

[2]Michael Bowker, "The Hawkers of Heredity," *Sierra Club Bulletin,* January–February 1985, p. 28.

[3]David Hansen, "Regulation of Biotechnology Progress," *Chemical Engineering News,* January 7, 1985, p. 27.

[4]R. Edward Freeman, *Strategic Management: A Stakeholder Approach,* Marshfield, MA: Pitman, 1984, p. 23.

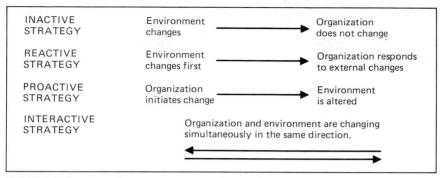

FIGURE 5-1.   Four basic strategies of social response.

Winston J. Brill, vice president of research and development for Agracetus, a Wisconsin biotechnology firm, illustrates such a position. In response to Rifkin's claims of impending disaster, he says "It's very easy to gain the media's attention by crying 'the sky is falling.' But the fact is, I couldn't make an organism that could cause a significant problem even if I wanted to. And to create one by accident is virtually impossible."[5]

There are, however, other approaches for coping with a changing environment. Some firms steadfastly adhere to their plans, no matter how strong the opposition or pressure from other actors in society. Some firms change only when forced to do so by strong outside pressures. Others actively attempt to move society in directions that will be to the company's advantage. A fourth approach is to try to find ways to harmonize a company's own goals with the changing needs, goals, and expectations of the public. These approaches are referred to, respectively, as an inactive strategy, a reactive strategy, a proactive strategy, and an interactive strategy of response to the environment. They are shown in Figure 5-1.

An Inactive Strategy

Many managers are apt to respond initially by resisting, altering their policies only as pressure and criticism mount. Occasionally, however, a company will absolutely refuse to change its behavior in response to the concerns of others.

For example, Quarex Industries, a publicly traded company that the President's Commission on Organized Crime reported had ties to organized crime, repeatedly failed health inspections by authorities in New York, paid small fines, and continued to "short weight" customers, sell unfit food, and operate some of the most unsanitary supermarkets in New York State.[6]

[5]Bowker, op. cit, p. 28.

[6]Walt Bogdavich, "A Food Firm Prospers Despite Often Failing Sanitary Inspections," *Wall Street Journal,* July 25, 1986, pp. 1, 12.

For such companies, nothing less than a government edict, court order, or imprisonment of managers will force a modification of behavior.

A Reactive Strategy

Utilizing a reactive strategy, a firm tries to cope with an unanticipated change in its environment *after* the significant change has occurred. Often, company practices will be modified only as strong pressures are applied.

> *Consider the actions of the makers of aerosol spray products. Scientists discovered in 1974 that the fluorocarbon compounds released into the air posed a threat to the protective ozone layer in the earth's atmosphere. Without its protection, the earth would be exposed to harmful solar radiation that can cause skin cancer and mutations in plants and animals. The manufacturers initially attempted to defend their products, but after mounting pressure, they acceded to a 1978 government regulation banning the use of damaging aerosols.*
>
> *In the mid-1980s, the controversy again heated up, as a large hole in the ozone layer was discovered over Antarctica. Pressure was exerted to have chlorofluorocarbons (widely used as refrigerants) and industrial solvents banned. In addition, health and environmental groups pushed for a multinational governmental ban of the damaging substances. Because of the costs involved, some companies can be expected to react only after legal pressure is applied.*

A Proactive Strategy

Companies utilizing proactive strategies are a step ahead of those that merely react, because they understand the need to get "on top" or ahead of changes that are occurring in their environments. Such companies may even try to manipulate the environment in ways that will be to their own advantage.

> *Although an ongoing conflict between environmentalists and biotechnology firms exists, the issue is less over the question of whether the developments and tests should continue than over how best to control them. Many in the industry, in fact, take a very proactive approach and actively promote regulation for a number of reasons. First, it would create some stability where none now exists—many companies literally have no idea whether the products they are spending millions of dollars to develop will ever be sold. Second, if regulations are developed and published, and if a biotechnology firm follows them, the company may be protected from future prosecution for environmental harm.*

An Interactive Strategy

When a company is able to anticipate environmental change and blend its own goals with those of the public, it has adopted an interactive strategy. An interactive strategy promotes harmonious relations between a firm and the public by reducing the gap between public expectations and business performance.

For example, *Rely tampons were promptly and effectively recalled by Procter & Gamble (P&G) when the product was statistically associated with toxic shock syndrome. Rather than resist external pressures (through an inactive or reactive strategy) or attempt to shape public opinion or change the minds of government officials (through a proactive strategy), P&G adopted an interactive position that protected public health and instilled consumer confidence in the company. The public expected socially responsible action and got it, which thereby preserved the company's credibility.*

Research has demonstrated that, under various conditions, the inactive, reactive, and proactive response strategies may produce temporary, short-run successes for companies. However, evaluations of longer-term successes strongly suggest that an interactive approach brings greater, more lasting benefits for both business and society.[7]

A strategy of response to the external environment is developed depending upon what has happened, and is now happening, in that environment and how it is understood. Managers have to understand that the environment is changing and that a strategic approach is needed to respond to it. Only then can any of these specific responses be employed. As one author says: "Major strategic shifts in the business environment require conceptual shifts in the minds of managers."[8] Thus, managers need to reexamine their assumptions and think about the present and future environment in a way that is accurate, practical, and up-to-date.

FORMULATING SOCIALLY RESPONSIVE STRATEGIES

Social responsiveness considerations permeate both the formulation and implementation of an organization's strategy. The strategy of a business involves basic decisions about its mission, purpose, and reason for being. These are value-laden decisions, affected by the values and ethics of management, the interests of various stakeholders, and the web of social issues and problems that are a vital dimension of the environment. In other words, a business strategy that will effectively guide an enterprise over time *cannot* possibly be formulated without taking management, stakeholder, and societal interests into account. These relationships are shown in Figure 5-2.

The Relevant Environment

In order to begin formulating a socially responsive strategy, one needs a framework of environmental information. Managers must understand what is occurring in many sectors of the external world. According to two authorities,[9] the environment that is relevant for businesses and their managers

[7]James E. Post, *Corporate Behavior and Social Change*, Reston, VA: Reston, 1978.

[8]Freeman, op. cit, p. 24.

[9]Liam Fahey and V. K. Narayanan, *Macroenvironmental Analysis for Strategic Management*, St. Paul, MN: West, 1986, pp. 28–29.

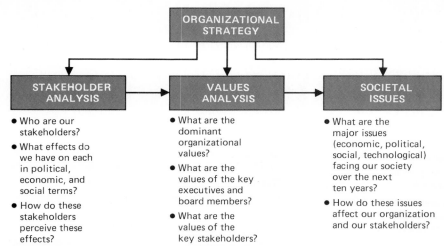

FIGURE 5-2.   **Strategy and social responsiveness.** (*Source: Adapted from R. Edward Freeman,* Strategic Management: A Stakeholder Approach, *Boston: Pitman, 1984, p. 92.*)

consists of four distinct segments: social, economic, political, and technological. The environment consists of an almost unlimited amount of information, including facts, trends, issues, and ideas. Each of these segments represents a focused area of information, a portion of which is important and relevant to the business.

- The *social segment* focuses on information about (1) demographics, (2) lifestyles, and (3) social values of a society. Managers have a need to understand changes in population patterns, characteristics of the population, emergence of new life-styles, and social values that seem to be in or out of phase with the majority of the population.
- The *economic segment* focuses on the general set of economic factors and conditions confronting industries in a society. For example, information about interest rates, unemployment, foreign imports, and many other such factors is relevant to virtually all businesses. The economic segment obviously has a large impact on all business organizations.
- The *political segment* deals with specific political relationships in society, changes in them, and the processes by which society makes political decisions. Changes in a tax code, for example, redistribute income and tax burdens. This involves political relationships between various segments of society. The creation or dissolution of regulatory institutions that set standards for business behavior are examples of change in the political process.
- The *technological* segment is concerned with the technological progress or advancements that are taking place in a society. New products, processes, or materials; the general level of scientific activity; and advances in fundamental science (e.g., biology) are the key concerns in this area.

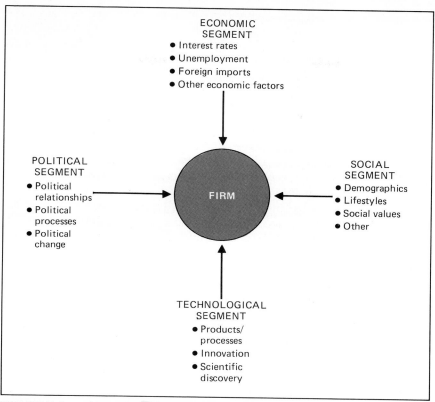

FIGURE 5-3.   The macroenvironment of business.

The macroenvironment, as presented in Figure 5-3, is a system of inter-related segments, each one connected to and influencing the others. The developments in genetic science, for example, occur in the technological segment. Their impact is evident in the economic segment, where new businesses are formed. They also affect the political segment, where regulation is discussed, and the social segment, where the ethical dimensions of genetic engineering are debated. By understanding each of these segments, their interrelationships, and those facts which are of direct and indirect importance to the organization, a manager will improve his or her understanding of the relevant environment in which strategies must be formulated.

Environmental Analysis

It is generally accepted that a business cannot be successful, or even survive, without adapting to a changing environment. Adaptation requires efforts to identify and assess emerging issues and trends that might prove to be critical to the organization's future. By anticipating future changes and their implications, a business can avoid the worst problems, prepare for those that are unavoidable, and take advantage of possible opportunities.

The process of environmental analysis occurs in four stages: *scanning* the environment to identify warning signals of potential environmental change or to detect environmental changes already taking place; *monitoring* specific environmental trends and patterns; *forecasting* the future direction of environmental changes; and *assessing* current and future environmental changes.[10]

Scanning

Scanning involves a general surveillance of all segments of the relevant environment to detect changes already under way and to identify hints of coming changes. Thus, scanning is both present-oriented and prospective, looking toward the "unknown future."

Scanning is perhaps the most unstructured environmental analysis activity, in that potentially relevant data are unlimited, inherently scattered, vague, and imprecise, and that they come from a multitude of sources.

> *Environmental scanners study newspapers, magazines, research reports, government publications, futurist publications, and obscure periodicals. They always look for basic trends and changes in the social, political, economic, and technological environments of business. Artistic trends expressed in contemporary painting, drama, or literature may contain hints of underlying changes in public moods or values. What may appear to be trivial style or fashion movements— for example, shorter hairstyles for men or space-age toys for children—may signify to an environmental scanner that cultural shifts are occurring that could affect business indirectly. Environmental scanning also involves contacting professional, scientific, governmental, and special interest groups.*

Monitoring

After potential changes and trends have been identified, sequences of events and streams of activities must be tracked and monitored. The monitoring activity allows the firm's management to keep track of important developments and respond to them more quickly and effectively. It also allows managers to separate true signals from false signals. Signals picked up during the original scanning may hint at a trend or development; they need to be verified before organizational decisions are made.

Monitoring is a very complex task. Patterns almost always are made up of many individual trends or events. A change in the "life-style" pattern may involve changes in entertainment, education, consumption, work habits, and residential location preferences. Patterns are difficult to define clearly in their early stages. One recent trend shows this point well:

> *As reported in the* New York Times, *"a politically conservative research center (in San Francisco) foresees an eventual alliance of conservatives, leftists of the 1960s and Americans with interests ranging from Eastern mysticism and the*

[10]Ibid., pp. 36–45.

occult to holistic medicine." These "strands in a thread of alternative thought" are working their way increasingly "into the nation's cultural, religious, social, economic and political life." In July 1986, representatives of some of the nation's largest corporations met in New Mexico to discuss how these alternative ideas and "human potential" or "self-help" programs might be used to help executives compete in the world marketplace. One scholar described the trend as "the most powerful force in the country today. I think it's as much a political movement as a religious movement and it's spreading into business management theory and a lot of other areas. If you look at it carefully you see it represents a complete rejection of Judeo-Christian and bedrock American values." [11]

Years may pass before this purported trend can be verified and understood, so the monitoring phase will be lengthy and complex. In general, effective monitoring for all organizations should produce a specific description of environmental trends and patterns that are occurring, identification of specific trends that need further monitoring, and identification of areas that need further scanning.

Forecasting

Scanning and monitoring describe current, unfolding events and developments. Since strategic planning and decision making require an orientation toward the future, managers must also project, or forecast, what will happen in the future.

Forecasting can be conducted on two fronts. Some trends are more predictable than others; thus, some forecasting is done in the realm of "the expected." For example, much demographic information can be projected, with a small margin of error, for five or ten years into the future. School enrollments, the number of entry-level jobs, and school dropout or graduation rates can be forecast with a reasonable degree of accuracy because of experience and the ability to double-check past forecasts.

This situation is not true for all developments, however. Many future situations and circumstances are sudden and unexpected. They cannot be projected based on available data and figures. The sudden popularity of metaphysical ideas and the occult, for example, was entirely unexpected by many people. Public skepticism of nuclear power also was not predicted by those who built the first nuclear power plants. Signals did exist, however, which should or could have been read and used to construct pictures of a "possible future."

Despite the problems and ambiguities involved in forecasting, most organizations recognize its importance and value. Today, many corporations have discovered that new techniques enable managers to integrate forecasts into their strategic planning process. [12]

---

[11]Robert Lindsey, "Spiritual Concepts Drawing a Different Breed of Adherent," *New York Times,* September 29, 1986, pp. A-1, B-12.

[12]Fahey and Narayanan, op. cit., Chap. 13.

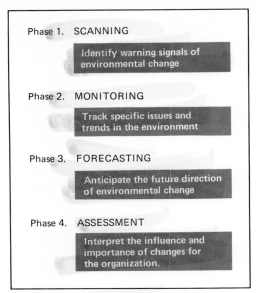

Phase 1. SCANNING

     Identify warning signals of environmental change

Phase 2. MONITORING

     Track specific issues and trends in the environment

Phase 3. FORECASTING

     Anticipate the future direction of environmental change

Phase 4. ASSESSMENT

     Interpret the influence and importance of changes for the organization.

FIGURE 5-4. Four phases of environmental analysis. (*Source: Adapted from Liam Fahey and V. K. Narayanan, Macroenvironmental Analysis for Strategic Management, St. Paul, MN: West, 1986.*)

Assessment

Scanning, monitoring, and forecasting produce information which is then assessed and interpreted to determine how the trends and developments might affect the company. The assessment phase, therefore, involves a great amount of interpretation and judgment on the part of the manager. Assessment requires identifying how, why, in what time frame, and to what degree certain predicted trends will affect the strategic plans of the organization.

Figure 5-4 illustrates the relationships between the four phases of the environmental analysis process. Figure 5-5 is an example of an environmental analysis summary prepared by a major United States manufacturing company.

IMPLEMENTING SOCIAL RESPONSIVENESS

Companies do not become socially responsive overnight. The process takes time. New attitudes have to be developed, new routines learned, and new policies and action programs designed. Many obstacles must be overcome in implementing socially responsive strategies. Some are structural, such as the reporting relationships between groups of managers; others are cultural, such as a historical pattern of only men or women in a particular job category.

International Issues
- Business is moving offshore for more components, manufacturing and engineering.
- South Africa will continue to be the focus of a wave of protest in the United States.

Economic and Employment Issues
- The budget deficit will be a top federal issue, because it causes the high dollar, high interest rates, and weak capital spending. The response will be spending cuts and/or tax increases.
- Industry pressures to improve productivity through automation and reduce costs through offshore procurement will result in fewer jobs for the U.S.

Government Regulation and Service Issues
- The public will be more supportive of traditional business opposition to government intervention.
- Public concern will increase over hazardous waste created by the manufacturers of high technology products. There will be more regulation of materials used in the manufacturing process.

Education Issues
- Greater business support for changes in elementary/secondary education will lead to more corporate involvement with legislative and policy groups.
- The need to create school climates for innovation and excellence will cause conflicts, particularly between decision makers and teacher unions.

Community Issues
- Neighborhood groups will take strong leadership roles in developing solutions on employment, economic development, and human service policies. These groups will continue to impact local decisions.
- The size of the underclass is growing, creating a generation of people with little hope or involvement in society. This group consists mainly of non-whites, single mothers, the aged, and children.

Defense Issues
- Concern over U.S. defense policies and the level of defense spending will continue to increase tensions among government, citizens, and defense contractors.
- The public is less willing to leave defense decisions to the experts, seeking ways to make their voices heard.

Work Force Issues
- Older workers will face more pressure to postpone retirement due to concerns about financial security.
- Constant changes in technological, business, and social areas will require continuous learning and retraining by employees.

Health Care Issues
- Employees will be asked to pay more for health benefits at the same time as the IRS seeks to tax these benefits.
- Ethical dilemmas will appear as advances in medical technology and limited resources require decisions on who receives care.

FIGURE 5-5. A corporate public affairs environmental outlook: 1985–1988.
(*Source: Adapted from a report by Honeywell, Inc. Used with permission.*)

A Model of Corporate Social Responsiveness

One model of how large organizations effectively implement socially responsive policies is illustrated in Figure 5-6.[13] There are three stages to the responsiveness process depicted in this model.

The Policy Stage

The first stage of social responsiveness involves being aware of which part of the surrounding environment needs to be responded to and acted upon

[13]Robert W. Ackerman, *The Social Challenge to Business*, Cambridge, MA: Harvard University Press, 1975; and Robert W. Ackerman and Raymond A. Bauer, *Corporate Social Responsiveness: The Modern Dilemma*, Reston, VA: Reston, 1976.

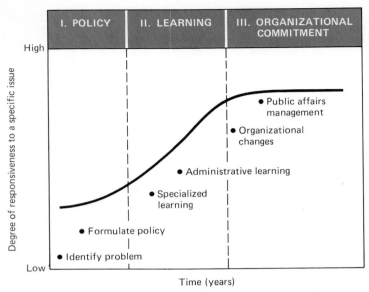

FIGURE 5-6. **A three-stage model of corporate social responsiveness.** (*Source: Adapted from Robert W. Ackerman,* The Social Challenge to Business, *Cambridge, MA: Harvard University Press, 1975; and Robert W. Ackerman and Raymond A. Bauer,* Corporate Social Responsiveness: The Modern Dilemma, *Reston, VA: Reston, 1976.*)

by the company. The response may occur after stakeholder expectations change, or it may result from a systematic environmental analysis. Whether or not stakeholder pressures exist, a company's management may think, based on the company's own environmental analysis, that a response is needed to emerging issues, concerns, or social trends. For example,

> *In September 1986, leading Boston businesses announced a $6-million program designed to guarantee financial aid to all graduates of the city's public high schools who get into college and to provide jobs for those who complete their education. This action reflected a continuing policy commitment by the chief executives of these companies. The businesses, mostly banks and insurance companies, were responding to statistics indicating that roughly 50 percent of the students in an entering high school class dropped out over the four-year attendance period.[14] Since the Boston school population was declining, the number of graduating students had been decreasing drastically. This trend meant a drastic shortage of applicants for entry-level jobs at many of the local insurance companies and banks. The businesses formulated a plan to support local schools and education. In addition to the funds provided, 350 Boston-area companies pledged to help provide jobs to high school graduates, and many offered to help pay for guidance counselors in the schools. This commitment served two purposes: the students and schools were helped, and the companies ensured themselves a future pool of applicants for entry-level jobs.*

[14]Fox Butterfield, "Funds and Jobs Pledged to Boston Graduates," *New York Times*, September 10, 1986, p. D-25.

Social responses need to be guided by policies that are carefully and deliberately developed by top management and the board of directors. Those policies provide a framework for shaping other aspects of the organization's response. New production policies, for example, may result in better quality control for consumer products, may remove job hazards, and may reduce water pollution all at the same time.

The Learning Stage

Once a social problem—for example, excessive numbers of high school dropouts—has been identified, and once a general policy—for example, an educational opportunity policy—has been adopted, the company must learn how to tackle the problem and make the new policy work. Two kinds of learning are needed: *specialized learning* and *administrative learning.*

Specialized learning occurs when a "sociotechnical" expert—for example, an inner-city educator who is thoroughly familiar with the culture, life-styles, motivations, and special problems of high school youth—*is employed to advise company officers and managers.* The kind of specialized knowledge that the sociotechnical expert brings to the company is particularly helpful in the early stages of social responsiveness when the company is dealing with an unfamiliar social problem, whether it be high school dropouts, prejudice against minorities in hiring practices, excessive pollution, or toxic chemical hazards.

Administrative learning occurs when a company's supervisors and managers—those who administer the organization's daily affairs—*become familiar with new routines that are necessary to cope with a social problem.* A technical expert can assist the company in taking its first steps to solve a problem but cannot do the whole job alone. Social responsiveness requires the full cooperation and knowledge of line managers as well as staff experts.

> *Managers of businesses involved in supporting the education systems in their cities have had to learn many new skills. For example, Dianne Sullivan, the president of Miraflores Designs in New York, pledged to help sixty East Harlem students. The day before school started in September 1986, she learned that they did not know which junior high school they were supposed to attend. Sullivan immediately telephoned the local school superintendent and solved the problem. Had she not done so, many of the students might have simply stayed home.* [15]

The Organizational Commitment Stage

One final step is needed to achieve full social responsiveness: an organization must "institutionalize" its new social policy. [16] The new policies and routines learned in the first two stages should become so well accepted throughout the entire company that they are considered to be a normal part of doing

[15]Jane Perlez, "Public Schools and the Private Sector," *New York Times,* September 14, 1986, p. 14.

[16]Robert Ackerman, "How Companies Respond to Social Demands," *Harvard Business Review,* July–August 1973, pp. 88–98.

business. In other words, they should be a part of the company and its standard operating procedures. For example, when managers respond to the needs of the local education system or the students without special directives from top management, the socially responsive policy can be considered to be institutionalized.

The normal organizational pressures to resist change mean that both effort and time are needed to improve a corporation's responsiveness. In the past, it took large corporations an average of six to eight years to progress from stage one to stage three on any given social issue or problem such as equal-employment opportunity or pollution control. Yet, some firms are more flexible than others, and some social problems are easier to handle than others, so the time involved may vary considerably. It is clear, however, that a combination of internal factors, especially management willpower, and external factors, especially continued stakeholder action on the problem, is necessary for effective change to occur.[17]

Making Social Responsiveness Operational

What does it take to move a company to a point of true organizational commitment to social responsiveness? What kinds of strategies and policies are required, and how should they be implemented? What roles do different levels of management play in transforming policy commitments into reality? How do staff professionals and operating managers work together to accomplish results? In other words, what has to happen inside a company before social responsiveness becomes a living reality?

Organizational Changes

Countless obstacles impede effective implementation of management policy in the modern corporation. To overcome them, top management often changes the factors that most affect resistance to change: administrative systems, organizational structures, corporate culture, and evaluation and reward systems. Companies that have demonstrated significant success in being socially responsive to their stakeholders and the environment have recognized that new machinery, as well as new attitudes and new incentives, are needed.

> *As Peter Jones, former senior vice president and corporate counsel of Levi Strauss, a company that has often appeared among lists of the most socially responsive companies in America, has written, "The key to getting the desired type of behavior in the modern corporation is providing enough countervailing pressures—either incentives or sanctions—to overcome the incentives to behave in the undesired way."*[18]

---

[17]See Robert H. Miles, *Managing the Corporate Social Environment: A Grounded Theory*, Englewood Cliffs, NJ: Prentice-Hall, 1986.

[18]Peter R. Jones, "Sanctions, Incentives and Corporate Behavior," in R. B. Dickie and L. Rouner (eds.), *Corporations and the Common Good*, South Bend, IN: University of Notre Dame Press, 1986, pp. 118–137.

Organizational Group	Required Action
Board of directors and top management	Improve interface with the environment and social inputs from it Develop social philosophy, commitment, and strategy Develop and communicate policies for social action Establish necessary staff organization, such as a public affairs department Commit resources to social action Revise incentive system so that social performance is rewarded Review corporate social performance
Staff organization	Scan the environment for better social inputs Advise management in areas of social policy Monitor social performance in the organization Act as a change agent in areas of social policy and performance Develop and maintain suitable appraisal systems for managerial and corporate social performance
Operating departments	Maintain operating interface with the environment Revise operating procedures to conform to social philosophy and policy Communicate social policy to employees and supervise their performance Apply resources to social performance Evaluate and report results to management

FIGURE 5-7. Actions required by different management groups for corporate social responsiveness.

Those countervailing pressures require a combination of organizational innovations in structures, decision processes, and incentives, such as the following ones.

The Board of Directors

As shown in Figure 5-7, a suitable corporate response often begins with the board of directors. The board determines the basic policy and strategy of the firm. Many corporate social actions are major ones that require board approval. The board needs to improve its interaction with the environment in order to gain more social understanding. The directors need to learn what is happening in the social world in the same way that they historically have sought to know what is happening in the economic world.

One way to increase social inputs to the board is to increase the number of "outside" members, as compared with insiders who also are top managers of the company. Outside directors generally have a broader perspective and sometimes may possess specialized social knowledge. Another suggestion is to appoint nontraditional people as board members: minorities, women, consumers, labor-union representatives, and others who might contribute distinctive social viewpoints to corporate policies.

Another development among some of the largest corporations is a public responsibility or public policy committee of the board of directors. The job of such a committee is to monitor the social environment, identify social and political issues most likely to affect the firm, and make recommendations to the full board for appropriate actions.[19]

The Chief Executive Officer

The chief executive officer (CEO) is the link between the board's policies and the top-management group that must put policies into action. Since the 1970s, CEOs have been spending substantial amounts of time on external affairs that affect their companies. A study undertaken by the Conference Board revealed that the majority of top executives surveyed spend one-quarter of their time managing external affairs, and that a sizable percentage of them devote up to 50 percent of their workweek to such duties.[20] An active and socially alert CEO can keep both the board and top management well-informed, thereby increasing the firm's chances of responding meaningfully to external pressures.

Top Management

While the board of directors and the CEO can work together to establish general social policies for a company, the top management group should translate these broad guidelines into operational plans and programs. For example, the board of directors of a large food manufacturer wanted to demonstrate the company's concern for members of the city's poorer neighborhoods. Top officers of the company, after consulting with production and marketing departments, decided to donate excess inventories of canned goods to selected community agencies. The costs of the program were absorbed by the public affairs department. In this way, a policy favored by the public affairs managers became a practical reality through top-management planning. The participation of many business firms in such major activities as Live-Aid, Hands Across America, and the Statue of Liberty restoration effort were implemented in similar ways.[21]

The Staff Role

Companies large enough to have staff units will depend on them for a number of support functions related to social policy. The staff is the firm's specialized organ for reaching out into the world and learning directions of social change so the firm may respond appropriately. Staff experts may advise top

[19]John Kohls, "Corporate Board Structures, Social Reporting, and Social Performance," in L. Preston (ed.), *Research in Corporate Social Performance and Policy*, vol. 7, Greenwich, CT: JAI Press, 1985, pp. 165–189. See also Michael L. Lovdal, Raymond A. Bauer, and Nancy H. Treverton, "Public Responsibility Committees of the Board," *Harvard Business Review*, May–June 1977.

[20]Phyllis S. McGrath, *Managing Corporate External Relations: Changing Perspectives and Responses*, New York: The Conference Board, 1976, p. 49. This information is updated in Seymour Lusterman, *The Organization and Staffing of Corporate Public Affairs*, New York: The Conference Board, 1987.

[21]"Lending a Helping Hand," *Time*, June 2, 1986, p. 25; and "People," *Time*, June 9, 1986, pp. 66–67.

management on social developments, monitor the company's social performance from inside, and help evaluate how well the firm is meeting its social program objectives.

Operating Units

Change eventually affects operating departments, and usually its impact is greatest there. Since traditional ways of work must be revised to conform with new programs, change always brings some operating costs, regardless of the benefits that eventually may occur. In the case of social involvement, there often are high beginning costs, while the benefits are long-range, often indirect, and sometimes not very evident to an individual department. As a result, from a department's point of view a cost-benefit analysis may be negative; therefore, management faces an additional task of helping departments to develop a long-term perspective. Nevertheless, it is in the plant, the office, the mine, and the field location—where a company actually conducts its business—that top-level social policies and goals either succeed or fail.

Incentive Systems

Success or failure in social programming generally depends on the same kinds of factors that operate in normal business situations. Is there enough money allocated for the program? Is a qualified person in charge? Is there proper follow-up and review? And, most important, are managers and employees motivated to be socially responsive?

As Peter Jones of Levi Strauss noted, implementation of corporate policies requires combinations of "carrots and sticks."[22]

> *One large electrical manufacturer audits the performance of its managers each year to determine how much progress has been made in equal opportunity hiring and promotions in the divisions. Annual bonuses are trimmed for those managers who cannot show progress. Such incentives and sanctions reinforce the message to all managers that the company is seriously committed to an equal employment policy.*

This approach is a vital way of convincing operating managers that the policy is not mere "window dressing."

Social Performance Evaluation

In order to evaluate its social performance, a firm needs some form of specialized social accounting or evaluation process. The *social audit* is a useful tool for this purpose.[23] *A social audit is a systematic study and evaluation of an or-*

---

[22]Jones, op. cit., pp. 118–137.

[23]A discussion of the social audit may be found in Raymond A. Bauer and Dan H. Fenn, Jr., *The Corporate Social Audit*, New York: Russell Sage, 1972; David H. Blake, William C. Frederick, and Mildred S. Myers, *Social Auditing: Evaluating the Impact of Corporate Programs*, New York: Praeger, 1976; and John J. Corson and George A. Steiner, *Measuring Business's Social Performance: The Corporate Social Audit*, New York: Committee for Economic Development, 1974.

ganization's social performance, as distinguished from its economic performance. The social audit provides management with information about the firm's social impact; it may be presented as a *social performance report* for managers and outsiders.

Public disclosure of the data collected in a social evaluation is an important issue. At one time, only financial-performance data were presented in annual reports. By the 1980s, however, the pressure for greater disclosure of social performance information had led 90 percent of the top 500 corporations to include information about their social activities in the company's annual report to shareholders. A few companies, such as General Motors, Bank of America, and Atlantic Richfield, published special yearly reports detailing the company's efforts to be a socially responsible member of the community. In the insurance industry, the Clearing House for Corporate Social Involvement has collected and published aggregates for member companies in such socially important areas of performance as equal employment opportunity, inner-city investments, and charitable contributions.

Perhaps the most visible example of social reporting by United States companies in the 1980s involved reports filed by more than 100 companies that agreed to abide by the Sullivan Principles in South Africa.[24] The principles specified standards of conduct toward black workers in hiring, wage rates, and working conditions. Companies that signed an agreement to abide by the principles publicly reported on their performance annually.

Social performance reporting in general is done on a mostly voluntary basis in the United States, but it is required in nations such as Germany, France, and Spain.[25] Social performance reporting is more highly advanced in Europe because of the commitment of both government and companies (e.g., the Swiss company Migros) to its implementation, and because of pressure from activist trade unions and socialist political parties.

Social performance evaluation produces several benefits for managers and their companies. It supplies data for comparison of social performance with policies and standards so that management can determine how well the organization is living up to its social objectives. In this context, reporting on affirmative action programs, environmental protection programs, and similar activities is like reporting on sales revenues and profits—it is a basis for evaluating the progress made with these programs.

Social audits also demonstrate top-management concern for social performance, and they encourage this concern throughout the company. They have symbolic value. The requirement to report on an activity provides an incentive for managers throughout the organization to actually "do something" to implement a social policy. The knowledge that senior management will carefully read and assess those reports further strengthens the corporate commitment to be socially responsive. In the process of preparing social

[24]See Investor Responsibility Research Center, *South Africa Review Service*, Washington, DC: IRRC, 1986.

[25]Meinolf Dierkes and Ariane Berthoin Antal, "Whither Corporate Social Reporting: Is It Time to Legislate?" *California Management Review*, Spring 1986, pp. 106–121.

reports and responding to the evaluations, employees become more aware of the social data and the implications of their actions. Corporate social objectives are thereby reinforced throughout the organization.

THE PUBLIC AFFAIRS FUNCTION

A major innovation in American management since the 1970s has been the emergence of the corporate public affairs function, which began when specialized departments and units were created to interact with specialized stakeholder interests, e.g., consumer affairs, government relations, urban affairs, media relations, and public relations. In many companies, these specialized staff departments have existed for years and have needed an overall coherence and direction. The public affairs function has emerged as the overall approach to coordinate these diverse stakeholder-management efforts.

According to one group of experts:

> [T]he essential role of public affairs units appears to be that of a _window out_ of the corporation through which management can perceive, monitor, and understand external change, and simultaneously, a _window in_ through which society can influence corporate policy and practice. This boundary-spanning role primarily involves the flow of information to and from the organization. In many firms it also involves the flow of financial resources in the form of political contributions to elected and would-be officials, and charitable contributions to various stakeholder groups in society.[26]

Between 1970 and 1980 more than half (58 percent) of 400 corporations had established a public affairs unit; a 1986 update of that study showed that the trend toward establishing public affairs continued during the 1980s.[27] Today, medium-sized and small businesses are joining larger companies in using the public affairs function as a means of coordinating political, social, and economic initiatives. Figure 5-8 summarizes a broad range of activities that are normally associated with public affairs management. Community relations and government relations (at both federal and state levels) account for much of the activity, but many companies also recognize the need to include corporate contributions and media relations as important components of the function.

Most companies have a high-ranking executive to head the public affairs function, so the public affairs unit usually has a direct input or voice in the company's major business policy decisions. According to a former senior vice president and director of public affairs at First Interstate Bank in California, this arrangement is an important key to infusing social responsiveness into the organization.

[26]Boston University Public Affairs Research Group, _Public Affairs Offices and Their Functions: A Summary of Survey Results,_ Boston: Boston University School of Management, 1981, p. 1.

[27]Boston University Public Affairs Research Group, _Public Affairs Offices and Their Functions: A Five-Year Update,_ Boston: Boston University School of Management, 1986.

Does your company consider the activity or function to be a part of public affairs?

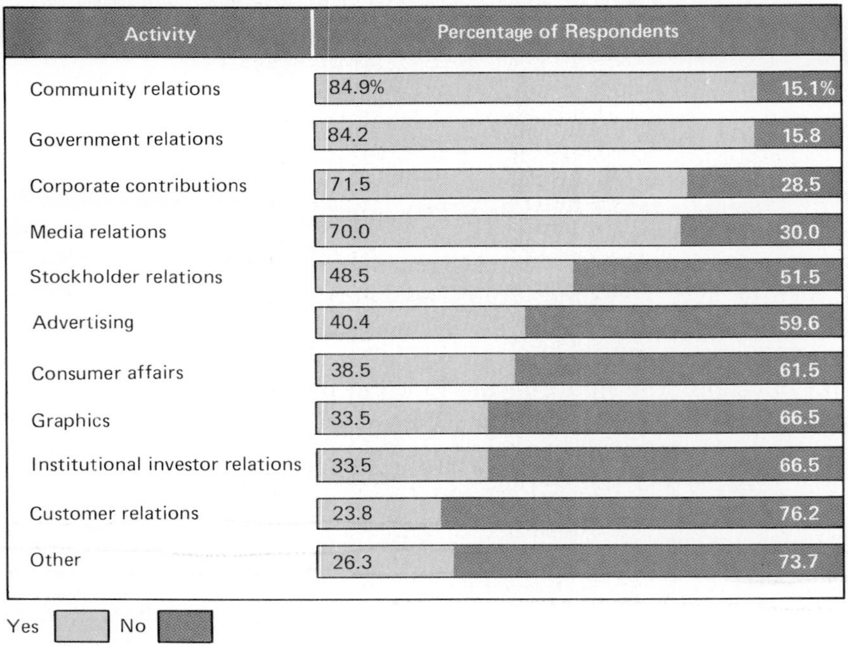

Activity	Percentage of Respondents	
Community relations	84.9%	15.1%
Government relations	84.2	15.8
Corporate contributions	71.5	28.5
Media relations	70.0	30.0
Stockholder relations	48.5	51.5
Advertising	40.4	59.6
Consumer affairs	38.5	61.5
Graphics	33.5	66.5
Institutional investor relations	33.5	66.5
Customer relations	23.8	76.2
Other	26.3	73.7

Yes ▢   No ▣

("Other" includes grass–roots lobbying and political action committees.)

FIGURE 5-8. Public affairs activities and functions of 400 corporations.

"The job of the public affairs professional should be to analyze the environment in order to strategically place the company in an offensive posture rather than a reactive one." This responsibility goes beyond a staff function for public affairs. This executive concludes: "public affairs people must redefine their role from being 'staff' people to being active participants in the decision making process. They must get top management involved in thinking about the external environment and in assessing the likely scenarios that will be coming down the road."[28]

This policy role involves asking many difficult questions.

The task of public affairs should be to ask: What are the public policy ramifications of a new product or service? What will this do to the community? Who will be offended or hurt, and who is helped? What are the social forces out there that will try to stop this action, and why? Are there outsiders we should be consulting with, such as "think tanks," foundations, or people in academia? How do we bring the "outside" key players "in" and make them feel part of the process? What will the press say? How will the political community react? And, if we can't do it this way, how about rethinking and redesigning it so we can get to the same result? In other words, the question should always be: Are we

---

[28]Lloyd B. Dennis, "Redefining the Role of Public Affairs," *New Management*, June 1986, pp. 50–53.

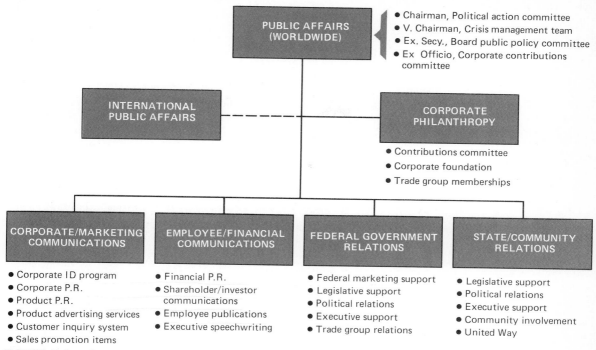

PUBLIC AFFAIRS (WORLDWIDE)
- Chairman, Political action committee
- V. Chairman, Crisis management team
- Ex. Secy., Board public policy committee
- Ex Officio, Corporate contributions committee

INTERNATIONAL PUBLIC AFFAIRS

CORPORATE PHILANTHROPY
- Contributions committee
- Corporate foundation
- Trade group memberships

CORPORATE/MARKETING COMMUNICATIONS
- Corporate ID program
- Corporate P.R.
- Product P.R.
- Product advertising services
- Customer inquiry system
- Sales promotion items

EMPLOYEE/FINANCIAL COMMUNICATIONS
- Financial P.R.
- Shareholder/investor communications
- Employee publications
- Executive speechwriting

FEDERAL GOVERNMENT RELATIONS
- Federal marketing support
- Legislative support
- Political relations
- Executive support
- Trade group relations

STATE/COMMUNITY RELATIONS
- Legislative support
- Political relations
- Executive support
- Community involvement
- United Way

FIGURE 5-9. Corporate public affairs organization.

anticipating as many facets of the issues as we can, and how much can we learn *before* we make a decision?[29]

Many companies have developed a public affairs function that meshes with the business decision-making system in three key ways. First, public affairs often is responsible for collecting, analyzing, and preparing *political and social intelligence* for management. Issues are identified, trends forecast, and the environment analyzed. Second, public affairs is responsible for *communicating* important information to a variety of management groups within the company. Special reports may be prepared for the board of directors, the chief executive officer, the planning department, and operating managers in different product divisions. Third, public affairs is responsible for developing and executing *action programs* that are targeted at key external stakeholders. Thus, a public affairs department may have a media contacts program, community affairs operations, and federal government lobbying activities. The public affairs organization chart of a manufacturing company, depicted in Figure 5-9, shows how these programs and functions are arranged.

Issues Management

Issues management helps a company cope with social change. *The issues and trends spotted by environmental scanners and social forecasters which are especially important to the company are singled out for special attention by management.*

> For example, *one major oil company identified 148 different government-related issues that could affect the company's many divisions. From that list, issues managers targeted thirty-eight that were considered significant and worth further study and tracking. While doing this, they also alerted top management to several key environmental events and trends that could affect the way government might react during the year; these included inflation and recession, Middle East developments, presidential and congressional elections, stabilizing the dollar, and Cold War trends.*

An issues-management program makes a valuable contribution to strategic planning by spotting particular issues of importance, analyzing their consequences to the firm, and putting that information into the hands of the company's strategic planners and policymakers.[30]

> *In the Mead Corporation the Human and Environmental Protection Department was transformed from a routine environmental research staff to an important player in the company's planning activities. Staff members made special efforts to focus on assuring company compliance with government regulations in all planned programs. Issues or problems of particular significance to the company were analyzed carefully for their social as well as their economic content and meaning. For example, when deciding the location of a new facility, company planners considered the attitudes and sentiments of the affected community before making any decision. Social factors, such as the decision's impact on local schools and on traffic patterns in the community, were made a part of the overall assessment. In earlier years, Mead—much like other companies—tended to ignore these social elements and concentrate solely on economic, financial, and technological matters.[31]*

Issues management has developed an identity as a specialized staff function in some companies (e.g., Clorox), and "issues managers" are increasingly found on corporate staffs. Even before the massive industrial accident in Bhopal, India, Union Carbide had issues managers to coordinate the company's activities in areas such as toxic substances and environmental and job safety. Corporate issues managers nationwide now have a professional organization devoted to the advancement of issues-management knowledge and skills and its complete integration into the strategic activities of corporations.

[30]See Robert L. Heath and Richard Alan Nelson, *Issues Management: Corporate Public Policymaking in an Information Society*, Beverly Hills, CA: Sage, 1986; and Francis W. Steckmest, *Corporate Performance: The Key to Public Trust*, New York: McGraw-Hill, 1982.

[31]"Capitalizing on Social Change," *Business Week*, October 29, 1979, p. 106.

SUMMARY

This chapter has described the relationship between the strategic business decisions made by managers and the social responsiveness concerns of corporate stakeholders. The challenge for modern management is to effectively make near-term and longer-term decisions that attempt to integrate stakeholder interests with the actions and values of management and emerging societal trends.

Environmental analysis is crucial to integrating social responsiveness and long-term strategic decisions. Through scanning, monitoring, forecasting, and assessment, managers can anticipate the future business environment.

The implementation of socially responsive strategies and policies is also a major challenge to business. By understanding the stages in the responsiveness process and the devices that have been utilized to make social responsiveness operational in organizations, the integration of business and social concerns can be achieved. The development of a public affairs function and the use of systematic issues-management approaches help to infuse an organization with social concerns.

DISCUSSION AND REVIEW QUESTIONS

1. A zinc-smelting company located near a small town has complied with all legal ordinances restricting the amount and kinds of pollutants discharged into the air. However, the plant's pollution control engineers told the manager of the smelter that it could make the air in the plant's vicinity even cleaner than the law required by installing some new pollution control machinery. This machinery would have only a slight negative effect on the smelter's profits. What strategy should the plant manager recommend to higher management in order to be socially responsive? Discuss.

2. Through library research, identify four or five large corporations that use environmental analysis to change their business strategy. Explain how scanning, monitoring, forecasting, and assessment have been helpful to the firm in analyzing segments of the macroenvironment.

3. Examine recent issues of the *Wall Street Journal, Business Week, Fortune,* or other business periodicals for examples of companies that have exhibited socially responsive behavior. Identify organizational changes that have helped each company to become more socially responsive.

4. Review the stages of corporate social responsiveness discussed in this chapter. In your opinion, which one of these stages would be the most difficult and time-consuming for a typical company? Give reasons for your position.

ORGANIZATIONAL

5. Review the biotechnology example at the beginning of the chapter. Explain what strategic policy issues are involved. How might the public affairs officers of those companies represent a "window out" and a "window in" to the organization?

CRITICAL INCIDENT

Star Wars Research and Corporate Social Responsibility

In recent years, much debate has occurred on issues of national defense. One such issue is whether or not companies should engage in research and development of technologies to be used in the Strategic Defense Initiative (SDI). This program, generally referred to as "Star Wars," is highly controversial. Its proponents claim that it will strengthen the United States' position in the balance of power, and therefore provide leverage during arms negotiations. Many others, however, think that development and implementation of a space weapons system would destabilize international relations.

The issue is complex, and it requires the consideration of many factors. As stated in an Investor Responsibility Research Center (IRRC) report,

> A thoughtful assessment of the program must take several things into account: estimates of the technical capabilities of possible space weapons systems; the tasks or goals that the weapons might be expected to accomplish; the political effects that SDI research or manufactured weapons could have on international and United States–Soviet relations, including arms negotiations; and the moral implications, if any, of such a weapons system.[32]

A church shareholder group first introduced the issue of space weapons into the arena of shareholder resolutions in 1984; it asked two companies to provide information about their involvement in military space programs. In 1986, five space weapons resolutions came to votes: Eastman Kodak was asked to create a committee to examine the ethical aspects of the company's space weapons work. Ford and United Technologies were asked to disclose their involvement in the development of space weapons. McDonnell Douglas was asked to hold a symposium on the issue, and Raytheon was asked to report on the amount of its current work that involves space weapons.

Proponents of the space weapons resolutions say they want companies to think of space weapons as "not just another business opportunity." Companies, on the other hand, have tended to argue that the kind of assessment outlined above properly belongs in the political arena. According to their representatives, if and when government policymakers determine that the need for a certain item exists and offer a contract for the production of the item, accepting that contract is, in fact, an ordinary business matter. For them, space weapons are just another business opportunity.

Several colleges and church organizations supported space weapons resolutions. Radcliff College supported the resolutions because they merely asked for an

---

[32]Helen E. Booth, *How Institutions Voted on Social Responsibility Shareholder Resolutions in the 1986 Proxy Season*, Washington, DC: Investor Responsibility Research Center, 1986, p. 36.

evaluation of a company's SDI programs rather than a particular judgment against them. Its explanation did not claim that space weapons production merited special attention but rather that making policy evaluations was good general practice: "Our committee agrees that private corporations do not make defense policy," said a committee spokesperson. But "in general, we feel that it is sound business practice for a corporation to review its rationale for taking action in developing policies in the areas of operations and products selection."[33]

SPACE WEAPONS RESOLUTIONS, 1986

	Requested Action	Institutions			
		Number Voting	For	Against	Abstain
Eastman Kodak	Ethical committee	46	15	27	4
Ford	Report	35	5	23	7
McDonnell Douglas	Symposium	22	2	16	4
Raytheon	Current sales	24	3	17	4
United Technologies	Report	30	2	23	5

More than twice as many institutions opposed the resolutions as supported them. The great majority of these institutions explained that they believed that space weapons were a matter of national policy and did not belong in the shareholder forum at all. As one bank commented: "The committee agreed with management's arguments that the U.S. government sets the national defense policy, not the companies." And a spokesperson for Yale University stated, "Yale believes that companies should consider the end use of their products, but that policy with respect to the development and deployment of space weapons should be determined by government rather than business."[34]

1. How should SDI defense contractors assess the information presented in this critical incident? What strategic implications exist for the companies?

2. If you were advising the top management of one of the defense-contractor companies mentioned, would you recommend further investment in SDI-related projects? Why? Why not? What criteria would you recommend be used to make this decision?

3. If you were a manager of pension funds for a group of church employees, what approach would you take to this issue? How could you demonstrate both social responsiveness and business skill in managing the fund?

4. How could managers of the defense contractors, pension funds, or universities engage in "issues management" in ways that would help them in establishing policies for their organizations?

[33]Ibid., p. 38.
[34]Ibid., p. 39.

PART 2

THE CORPORATION AND GOVERNMENT

Chapter Six

FREE ENTERPRISE AND COMPETING SOCIOECONOMIC SYSTEMS

Societies throughout the world organize their economic life according to one of three basic types of systems: free enterprise, central state control, or mixed state-and-private enterprise. The role of government is different in these three systems, and social problems are handled in a variety of ways. Business thinking about the role of government in the United States has undergone big changes as competing socioeconomic systems have risen to challenge free enterprise.

CHAPTER OBJECTIVES

After reading this chapter, you should be able to

- Describe the main features of free enterprise, central state control, and mixed state-and-private enterprise
- Be aware of trends in these socioeconomic systems
- Explain changes in business attitudes toward government
- Realize the importance of today's global ideological competition

Hilda Kreuger is a worker in a West German chemical plant making materials that eventually become plastic components used in a variety of consumer products. Recently she read that some of the chemicals she works with on a daily basis can cause cancer if the fumes are inhaled long enough, although scientists are not certain just how much exposure is necessary to endanger a person's health seriously. She also knows that disposing of the chemical's poisonous residue is a problem for the plant, especially after filling a big order for an industrial customer. Moreover, she wonders if the consumers who finally buy the finished plastic products might somehow be exposed to an unnecessary degree of risk.

Unknown to Hilda Kreuger, another worker in a similar plant in the Soviet Union has been pondering the same questions. Olga Ivanova, a first-line supervisor in a Leningrad chemical plant, is aware that some of her workers became ill in recent months when handling this same chemical compound. Fearful that the resultant absences will cause the factory to miss its production quota for the year, she wonders if something ought to be done about this particular chemical.

While Kreuger and Ivanova are struggling with the problem, Jane Armstrong is equally upset. The Houston chemical plant that employs her is the market leader in production of the suspect chemical, and she has been working in that department for almost five years. To discover now that she may have risked her health through contact with the fumes from production has her considerably worried. She knows too that the company has dumped much of the residue offshore and on land in ways that might eventually endanger others. Until now, she has always taken pride in the knowledge that her own children play with toys made from the plastic that originated in her plant, but now she worries about them and especially about the baby she expects to deliver in two months.

These three industrial workers face a common problem, but they will not try to solve it in the same way. In West Germany, where labor unions are strong and very much concerned about the welfare of their members, Hilda Kreuger will undoubtedly turn first to her plant's labor union representative for aid and advice. If the matter cannot be handled through normal discussions with management, it may eventually wind up on the agenda of the company's board of directors, which, in many German corporations, has labor union members.

Leningrad worker Olga Ivanova will take her problem to a representative of the plant's workers, too, but she knows that the union there has little independent power. The most she can hope for is that a mid-level director of labor affairs will bring the matter to the attention of the plant manager and perhaps to the plant's chief Communist party official. Even these two have limited power to take action to protect their workers, because the plant takes its orders from regional and national party officials who, in turn, are bound to the goals laid down in the country's five-year plan. If the plan has not made provision for the safe disposal of chemical residues or for the protection of workers and consumers, not much can be done by those who object to or worry about such problems.

Jane Armstrong may have more opportunities than her foreign counterparts to take corrective action. Her labor union is known for its concern for the safety of chemical workers, so she can count on help from that quarter. Her company has been a chemical industry leader in reducing health risks to workers, and it prides itself in being known as a socially responsive corporation. Local, county, state, and federal regulations provide guidelines for the safe disposal of chemical wastes. Environmental and consumer activist groups are available to hear Armstrong's story if she chooses to tell it to them, and she can ask her congressional representative in Washington to investigate the problem.

The point is that different countries have different ways of approaching social problems. Chemical workers in Japan, Brazil, and Nigeria have their own distinctive ways of coping with on-the-job risks, and these may be unlike those in West Germany, the Soviet Union, and the United States. A great deal depends on a country's history, traditions, political institutions, and social values. Some will rely almost exclusively on governmental approaches, others on organized interest groups, while others will try to accomplish the same goals through free market procedures.

Question: Which one of these three workers would you rather be, and which system appeals to you the most? Of course, everyone would probably prefer the system most like their own and the one that could provide the most protection on the job. But there is more to it than just self-protection. Some socioeconomic systems permit and encourage greater degrees of freedom than others. Some systems favor more participation in decision making than others. In some nations, government regulators get deeply involved, while in others the lead role is taken by private business. So your answer to the question concerns much more than just being safe on the job. The stakes are much bigger. Your answer—along with the answers of other citizens—helps determine what kind of society we shall have, how much freedom there will be, and what business will be expected to do in carrying out its economic and social responsibilities.

BASIC TYPES OF SOCIOECONOMIC SYSTEMS

The world's peoples, faced with solving their economic and social problems, generally organize themselves according to one of three basic systems: (1) *free enterprise,* (2) *central state control,* or (3) *mixed state-and-private enterprise.* In each system there is some combination of private efforts and government controls. *In all systems attention is given to social problems as well as economic ones; thus, they are called socioeconomic systems.* As shown in Figure 6-1, varying amounts of freedom and coercion are present in each system. Some systems are politically democratic and socially open, while others are dominated by a single political party that controls the government and centralizes economic and social decisions.

The kind of socioeconomic system any nation has depends greatly on that nation's history. For example, the strong ties between government and business in Japan result from a long tradition of close cooperation between public authorities and private merchants. The Soviet Union's centralized system is a direct result of the Marxist-inspired 1917 revolution, which favored control of all social, political, economic, and governmental institutions in the name of the working classes.

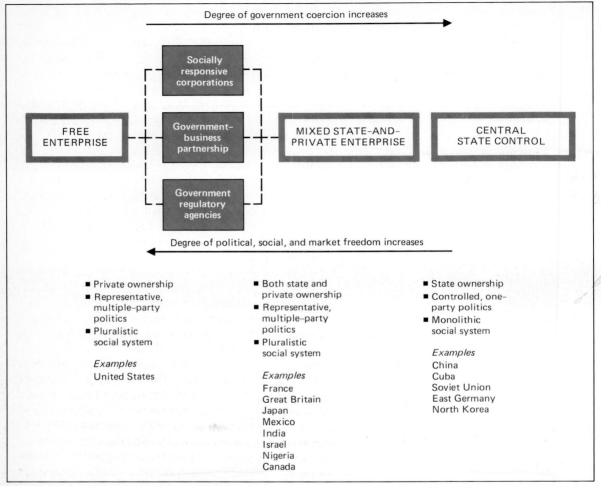

Degree of government coercion increases →

Socially responsive corporations

Government-business partnership

Government regulatory agencies

FREE ENTERPRISE

MIXED STATE-AND-PRIVATE ENTERPRISE

CENTRAL STATE CONTROL

← Degree of political, social, and market freedom increases

- Private ownership
- Representative, multiple–party politics
- Pluralistic social system

Examples
United States

- Both state and private ownership
- Representative, multiple–party politics
- Pluralistic social system

Examples
France
Great Britain
Japan
Mexico
India
Israel
Nigeria
Canada

- State ownership
- Controlled, one-party politics
- Monolithic social system

Examples
China
Cuba
Soviet Union
East Germany
North Korea

FIGURE 6-1. Major types of socioeconomic systems.

But history is not the whole story. Socioeconomic systems can change, sometimes drastically. After Fidel Castro and his supporters overthrew the Cuban government in 1959, a radical change took place. Foreign firms were taken over or expelled, farmland was nationalized, centralized economic planning was begun, new ties were forged with the Soviet Union, trade relationships with many nations were disrupted or terminated, many church officials were expelled, and new educational and health care institutions were adopted. Cuba's socioeconomic system moved toward centralized state control and away from its former close relationship with Western free enterprise economies. Other nations have moved in the opposite direction—Communist China in the 1980s encouraged more free markets and allowed greater freedom of expression than had been true earlier. These shifts show that socioeconomic systems are not "set in concrete"; they can and do change.

FREE ENTERPRISE

A free enterprise economy is based on the principle of voluntary association and exchange. People with goods and services to sell take them voluntarily to market, seeking to obtain a profit from the sale. Other people with wants to satisfy go to market voluntarily, hoping to find the things they want to buy. No one forces anybody to buy or to sell. Producers are drawn voluntarily to the market by their desire to make a profit. Consumers likewise go willingly to the marketplace in order to satisfy their many wants. The producer and consumer then make an economic exchange in which normally both of them receive an economic benefit. The producer earns a profit, and the consumer has a new good or service personally valued more highly than its cost.

A modern supermarket is a good example of the market system. The owners of the supermarket stock the shelves with hundreds of food items, knowing from past experience that their customers will pay enough money for the supermarket to earn a profit. No one has to force the supermarket to try to sell groceries. The owners voluntarily sell in order to make a profit.

The customers are willing to shop in the supermarket because in the past they have found the items they need. No one forces them to go to any particular store. They may shop around among several supermarkets for the best buys in order to stretch the family grocery budget as far as possible. They also may try to avoid the supermarket entirely by raising their own food, but most people now prefer the convenience of supermarket shopping and the wide variety of choices there.

As Figure 6-2 demonstrates, in such a market economy, production is for profit and consumption is for the satisfaction of wants. People try to promote their own interests in the marketplace. To make the system work

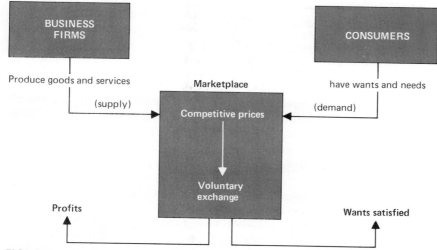

FIGURE 6-2.   Basic components of a free market system.

fairly, competition must be present. In other words a producer—the supermarket operator—has to set prices at about the same level as competing supermarkets or run the risk of losing customers and profits to lower-priced stores. All prices are the result, not of actions by monopolists or government officials, but of completely impersonal forces of supply (by producers) and demand (by consumers). When these conditions occur, producers voluntarily produce what consumers want, for that is the way to make a fair profit. At the same time, consumers achieve an optimum satisfaction of their wants at the lowest cost. In free competitive markets, the consumer is "king" or "queen" because producers must obey the wishes and demands of consumers if they want to make a profit.

In this kind of market system, the members of society satisfy most of their economic wants through these voluntary market transactions. Business firms (like the supermarket) that sell goods and services to consumers for a profit are at the same time fulfilling a social or public need. Consider society's need for cars, housing, energy, and entertainment—all produced mostly by private enterprise. Usually there is a very large overlap between society's needs and business's efforts to provide those needs through profit-making activities.

Free Enterprise in the United States

Very few economic systems conform strictly to the ideal conception of a free enterprise system. The United States comes the closest of any of the major industrial powers, partly because its historical traditions have favored free markets and partly because the American public prefers the economic and social freedom as well as the less-centralized government typical of free enterprise.

In order to cope with some of the economic and social problems that occur in a free enterprise system, the United States relies on three subsystems that supplement the activities of private business firms. These subsystems also may be found in nations with a mixed state-and-private enterprise system.

Government Regulatory Agencies

These agencies try to curb undesirable social and economic practices by encouraging compliance with government-mandated performance standards. The Environmental Protection Agency (EPA), created in 1970 to clean up pollution and police the environment, and the Occupational Safety and Health Administration (OSHA), which was given power by Congress to establish safety and health rules for the workplace, are two examples of such agencies. Regulatory agencies are used to supplement free enterprise in cases where social and economic problems cannot be resolved by the use of market incentives alone. Pollution, racial and religious discrimination, various consumer abuses, and anticompetitive tendencies fall into this category.

Government and Business Partnerships

A close working relationship—often called a *partnership*—between government and business is sometimes used to deal with social and economic problems that cannot be solved by either party acting alone.[1]

In such a partnership, *government* usually sets the goals, ranks them in order of importance, develops strategies for achieving them, and then creates conditions that permit private companies to carry out the work at a profit. The emphasis is on positive incentives rather than the negative penalties that often prevail in regulation. Once the government has created a framework for action, *business* uses its managerial, financial, and technical skills to tackle the problems. These public-private partnerships have been used to build low-income housing and mass transit systems in urban areas, and to retrain industrial workers displaced by technological changes in the workplace or by foreign competition.[2]

Socially Responsive Corporations

Free enterprise societies, as well as mixed state-and-private enterprise systems, rely on socially responsive corporations to help solve difficult social problems. If these private companies act in socially responsible ways—for example, to control pollution, combat job discrimination, protect the privacy and health of their employees, and curb unethical practices—the need for government regulation and intervention is lessened. Decisions are decentralized, and there is more room for private initiative and freedom of action.

These three subsystems demonstrate that the United States does not conform strictly to an abstract model of free enterprise or perfectly free markets. While private business initiatives tend to be favored, other institutions, including government, are frequently used to supplement free enterprise activities.

Free Enterprise Ideology

All socioeconomic systems have an ideology or guiding philosophy that explains and justifies the way economic activities are organized. This philosophy affects the attitudes and general outlook of managers and government officials concerning matters of economic policy and business decision making. In free enterprise societies, special attention is given to the role that should be played by government in economic and business affairs. The tendency is

---

[1]An early proposal along these lines was made by the prestigious Committee for Economic Development. See *Social Responsibilities of Business Corporations*, New York: Committee for Economic Development, 1971.

[2]A good discussion of these partnerships is in Harvey Brooks, Lance Liebman, and Corinne S. Schelling (eds.), *Public-Private Partnership: New Opportunities for Meeting Social Needs*, Cambridge, MA: Ballinger, 1984. See also R. Scott Fosler and Renee A. Berger, *Public-Private Partnership in American Cities: Seven Case Studies*, Lexington, MA: Lexington, 1982.

to assign the major economic role to private business, while leaving to government the tasks that cannot be undertaken by the private sectors of society, as well as maintaining order and protecting national security.

The advocates of a free enterprise socioeconomic system build their case on several basic principles. These principles have become deeply embedded in the business mind, guiding the thinking of many business people today. The core ideas of this powerful business ideology are the following:

- *Individualism.* The individual person is considered to be more important than society or its institutions. Society's institutions exist to protect and promote the interests of individual persons. The opposite is true in a collectivist state, where individuals are subordinated to the power of government, the military, or organized religion.
- *Freedom.* All individuals must be free to promote and protect their own personal interests. This means they must have freedom to own property, to choose a job and career, to move freely within the society and to other societies, and to make all of life's basic decisions without being coerced by others. In business affairs, it means companies should be left free to pursue profits, and markets should be free of government intervention.
- *Private property.* The bedrock institution on which free enterprise is founded is private property. Unlike socialist states where the government owns the productive system, property is held by private individuals or companies. The ownership of property allows one to control one's own destiny, rather than to have important decisions made by someone else.
- *Profit.* Profit is a gain made by owners who use their property for productive purposes. Although profits are sometimes made from using property unproductively—or, as in the case of some government-supported farmlands, from not using the property at all—a free enterprise economy tends to draw all property into productive uses because that is the way to make profits. Profits are a reward for making a productive contribution to society. They act as a powerful incentive to needed production.
- *Equal opportunity.* Equality of *opportunity* has long been an ideal of free enterprise thinking. This notion does not guarantee that everyone is, or should be, equal in life. It says only that each person should have an opportunity to begin life's race on about the same footing as all others. No special advantages—in education, access to jobs, or treatment at work—should be allowed to tip the scales in favor of one person over another.
- *Competition.* Competition is an indispensable part of free enterprise thinking. Once equality of opportunity is achieved for everyone, the way is open for competition to encourage the most skilled, the most ambitious, and the most efficient to rise to the top. Competition is society's way of encouraging high levels of economic performance from all of its citizens. Adam Smith's "invisible hand" of competition regulates and curbs economic power, rather than the "visible hand" of government regulators. It keeps business on the alert to do its best, or else a competitor will win customers away with a better product or service.
- *The work ethic.* Most Americans believe that work is desirable, good for one's health and self-esteem, necessary if society is to achieve high levels of

productivity, and even a fundamental right that should not be denied. This "work ethic" has fluctuated from period to period but remains an important part of free enterprise ideology. In the older Calvinist version of the work ethic, work was considered to be a way of using God-given talents to improve oneself. Eventually, this quasi-religious notion of work helped justify the pursuit of worldly wealth by merchants, financiers, and others in business.

- *Limited government.* The founders of free enterprise thinking advocated a government of very limited economic functions. "That government is best which governs least" was the ideal. Beyond protecting private property, enforcing contracts, and providing for general security, the government was expected to do little. A "hands off" policy toward business—often called *laissez faire*—is a preferred ideal of free enterprise theory, although obviously many changes have occurred since this ideal theory was first advanced.

Challenges to Free Enterprise in the United States

Over the years the original free enterprise ideology has been severely challenged by several major changes that have occurred in the business system and in society. Questions have been raised about the continued usefulness and relevance of free market philosophy as a useful guide to business thinking because the basic principles have been either ignored or rendered impractical in many instances. The most important of these challenges are depicted in Figure 6-3.

The growth of big business convinced many people that competition was not working properly to insure fair prices and fair dealing. *The Great Depression* of the 1930s brought on a greatly expanded role for government as regulator of economic affairs. Government also grew far beyond its originally intended scope as a result of *large-scale wars*, especially World Wars I and II. Individualism was challenged by the appearance of *mammoth organizations*—corporations, labor unions, government, agribusiness, the military establishment, massive educational systems, and even giant religious organizations. In each of these institutions, individuals found a more difficult time in expressing their views and having an influence on an organization's policies. *Social concerns* weakened some of free enterprise's cherished principles, as government regulatory programs substituted for market competition, some disillusioned employees became less committed to the traditional work ethic, and many consumers lost faith in business's ability to deal fairly with them and to produce reliable, effective, and safe products. Women and ethnic minority groups claimed that equality of opportunity was not working for them. *Interest group demands* continued to erode the notion of a government with limited functions: farmers wanted guaranteed prices, workers wanted a minimum wage, small business sought protection from large corporations, domestic producers appealed for protection from foreign competitors, the elderly pressed for retirement security, and many others asked for government aid of one kind or another. In responding to these demands, government grew beyond the limited functions spelled out in free enterprise ideology. *Government-sponsored global competition* also played a part in widening the gap between ideological principles and economic reality, particularly when state-owned or state-subsidized enterprises were able to penetrate the unprotected markets of free market nations and take business away from corporations operating by the competitive rules of free enterprise. Under these conditions, each nation tended to adopt protectionist laws that restricted the free play of market forces.

The resultant weakening of traditional business ideology was not simply an intentional abandonment of treasured ideals. It was instead a gradual, piecemeal trend based upon immediate needs and pressures being felt by different groups. Most of the adjustments and demands, when considered by themselves, seemed reasonable enough and were usually approved by the general public. But when considered together, they seemed to erode away much of the foundation of free enterprise ideology.

Changes in Business Attitudes toward Government

It is easy to understand the basic dilemma faced by United States business leaders. On the one hand, they strongly prefer a free enterprise system which

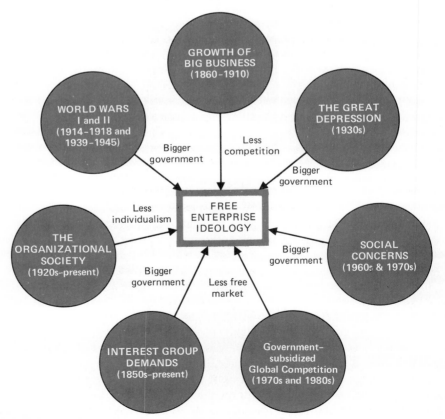

FIGURE 6-3. Major challenges to free enterprise ideology.

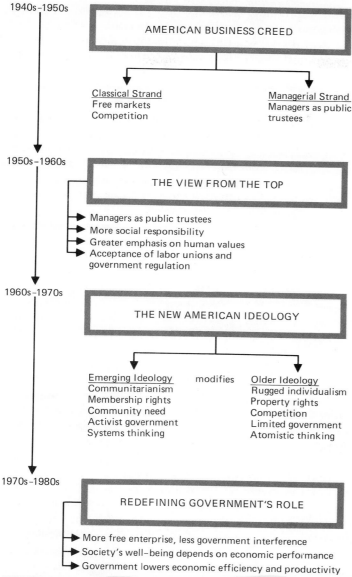

1940s–1950s

AMERICAN BUSINESS CREED

<u>Classical Strand</u>
Free markets
Competition

<u>Managerial Strand</u>
Managers as public
trustees

1950s–1960s

THE VIEW FROM THE TOP

▶ Managers as public trustees
▶ More social responsibility
▶ Greater emphasis on human values
▶ Acceptance of labor unions and
   government regulation

1960s–1970s

THE NEW AMERICAN IDEOLOGY

<u>Emerging Ideology</u>   modifies   <u>Older Ideology</u>
Communitarianism   Rugged individualism
Membership rights   Property rights
Community need   Competition
Activist government   Limited government
Systems thinking   Atomistic thinking

1970s–1980s

REDEFINING GOVERNMENT'S ROLE

▶ More free enterprise, less government interference
▶ Society's well–being depends on economic performance
▶ Government lowers economic efficiency and productivity

FIGURE 6-4. **Four stages in the development of United States business ideology.**

is as free from all types of control as possible. But they are fully aware of the legal, regulatory, social, and economic limits that have accumulated over the years, as shown in Figure 6-3. They may not like these limitations, but people in business tend to be practical-minded and able to adjust to new conditions. This realistic, pragmatic, "whatever-it-takes" attitude can be seen very clearly in the four distinct phases of ideological adjustment shown in Figure 6-4.

This ability to be flexible and to adjust to constantly changing conditions is a decided strength and admirable quality of business people. As revealed in the following sections, they do not want to be so flexible that they "give the store away," but their practical realism has permitted them to live with fluctuating amounts of social control.

"The American business creed" mentioned in Figure 6-4 refers to a study of business attitudes in the early 1950s that showed a gradual shift of business thinking away from the classical free enterprise philosophy. The new managerial point of view recognized that corporations have to interact responsibly with a large number of stakeholders, including employees (and sometimes labor unions), customers, local communities, and the general public. No longer could business concentrate solely on the stockholders as it attempted to make profits for them. Managers began to see themselves as public trustees rather than as merely private citizens.[3]

About ten years later, "the view from the top" confirmed this general trend in business thinking. This was a study of speeches made by several top-level corporate executives during the 1950s and early 1960s. Particularly strong in their thoughts was the importance of protecting and preserving human values as business decisions are made.[4]

The next step in the evolution of business philosophy occurred during the tumultuous 1960s when civil strife, urban decline, social protest, and political turmoil challenged business to play a leading role in helping society to solve its fundamental problems. "The new American ideology," proposed by George Cabot Lodge of the Harvard Business School, argued that United States society is moving away from the older free enterprise principles toward a philosophy more suitable to today's world and today's problems. The new philosophy emphasizes community needs (for jobs and environmental controls); cooperative planning by business, government, and labor; and less emphasis on individualism and property rights. He challenged business leaders to recognize this trend and to support it as one way of meeting public expectations of improved social performance by business.[5] Another manifestation of this general point of view was the issuance in the early 1970s of a famous statement on corporate social responsibilities by the Committee for Economic Development, mentioned earlier in this chapter and in Chapter 2.

The fourth phase of business thinking depicted in Figure 6-4 shows attitudes toward government in the 1980s. Business leaders began to feel that government had gone too far and had taken on too many tasks during society's attempts to deal with the social problems of the 1960s and 1970s. It was time to "redefine government's role" in the economy and society. This

---

[3]Francis X. Sutton, Seymour E. Harris, Carl Kaysen, and James Tobin, *The American Business Creed*, Cambridge, MA: Harvard University Press, 1956. See also David Vogel, "The Persistence of the American Business Creed," in Lee E. Preston (ed.), *Research in Corporate Social Performance and Policy*, vol. 2, Greenwich, CT: JAI Press, 1980, pp. 77–102.

[4]Robert F. Heilbroner, "The View from the Top," in Earl F. Cheit (ed.), *The Business Establishment*, New York: Wiley, 1964, pp. 1–36.

[5]George Cabot Lodge, *The New American Ideology*, New York: Knopf, 1976; and a sequel entitled *The American Disease*, New York: Knopf, 1984.

> - FREE ENTERPRISE IDEALS: PROFITS, FREEDOM, INDIVIDUALISM
> - MORE FREE MARKET, LESS GOVERNMENT INTERVENTION
> - SOCIALLY RESPONSIVE CORPORATIONS
> - SOCIALLY AWARE CORPORATE MANAGERS
> - GOVERNMENT-BUSINESS COOPERATION IN SOCIAL PROBLEM SOLVING

FIGURE 6-5. **Central elements of today's United States business ideology.**

meant greater reliance on private initiatives, reducing the role of government wherever possible, cutting back on government regulations, and generally restoring the vigor and freedom of private business.[6]

The overall shape of today's business ideology is a blend of the trends reported in these four studies. Figure 6-5 summarizes the main points. The traditional United States business belief system, which was based on pure free enterprise principles, gave way partly to the idea of socially responsive corporations run by socially aware business leaders. A larger and more active government that works in close partnership with private business has been reluctantly accepted as necessary for handling some of society's bigger problems. Corporate stakeholder groups organized by minorities, environmentalists, consumers, women, and others may place curbs and regulations on the private enterprise system, but some people believe that these should be kept to a minimum because of the costs they impose on business and the public. Above all, the business community prefers a free enterprise system based on profits and one where government intervention in business is not allowed to lower efficiency and productivity. The older ideals of freedom, equal opportunity, and the right to make one's own decisions remain at the core of today's business ideology.[7]

CENTRAL STATE CONTROL

In the Soviet Union and China—two examples of central state control—virtually all economic and social problems are the responsibility of government and party officials.[8]

Usually a government plan sets economic and social goals for one year, five years, or longer. Government officials then allocate budget money to achieve these goals. Factories, hospitals, schools, and farms strive to achieve

[6]Committee for Economic Development, *Redefining Government's Role in the Market System,* New York, 1979. For an analysis of this report, see William C. Frederick, "Free Market versus Social Responsibility: Decision Time at the CED," *California Management Review,* Spring 1981, pp. 20–28.

[7]For a more detailed account, see Gerald F. Cavanagh, *American Business Values,* 2d ed., Englewood Cliffs, NJ: Prentice-Hall, 1984.

[8]For a "classic" description of these two systems, see Barry M. Richman, *Soviet Management,* Englewood Cliffs, NJ: Prentice-Hall, 1965, chaps. 1, 5; and Barry M. Richman, *Industrial Society in Communist China,* New York: Random House, 1969, chap. 1.

production quotas set by government directive. In such a system, the government performs all the functions of a free enterprise system—deciding what will be produced; allocating resources and money to plants, offices, and farms; deciding how goods and services will be distributed to the people; and determining wages, costs, and prices.[9]

In this type of socioeconomic system, the government has to make deliberate choices about which economic and social goals to pursue. Priorities have to be assigned.

> *For many years in the Soviet Union, top officials in government and in the Communist party chose to emphasize military strength and basic industrial development in their five-year plans. Consumer goods and services were deliberately downgraded in the overall priority system. Steel, rubber, and chemicals were used to produce tanks, missiles, airplanes, and other weapons rather than to satisfy consumer desires for refrigerators, cars, and television sets. In recent years, government planners have permitted relatively more consumer goods to be produced, but even now a strong emphasis remains on military preparedness.*

Government goals can include deliberate attempts to solve social problems. For example, where a particular industry such as coal mining is known to be especially hazardous to workers, the government plan can include special allocations of money for installing safety equipment, alarm systems, and ventilation fans in the mines. Or if a certain class of workers—for example, those who manufacture steam locomotives—becomes obsolete, due in this case to the introduction of diesel locomotives, the government can channel special money to retrain these workers.

Under central state control, a political ideology usually guides government planners and party leaders in setting production targets and social priorities.[10] The official ideology may promote the broad interests of the masses of workers, or it may warn against the perils of external threats from unfriendly neighbors, or it may praise the virtues of the traditional ways unique to its own people.

> *Production goals of mainland China's economy for many years reflected Chairman Mao's ideological principles that the Chinese people should concentrate on making themselves secure from foreign attacks. The work force was exhorted to exceed production quotas in order to carry forward the Chinese people's revolution. All social goals and economic goals were determined by Chairman Mao's political ideology.*

Under such circumstances, government planners and party leaders may decide that economic production is more important than safe factories, clean

---

[9]See "How Does the Soviet Economy Function without a Free Market?" in Morris Bernstein and Daniel L. Fusfeld, *The Soviet Economy*, 3d ed., Homewood, IL: Irwin, 1970.

[10]Richman, *Industrial Society in Communist China*, pp. 46–57.

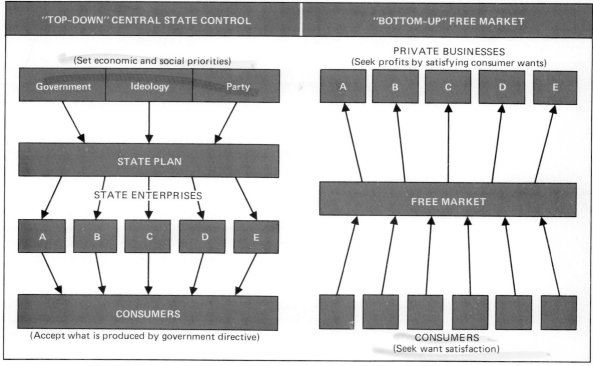

FIGURE 6-6. "Top-down" versus "bottom-up" decision making under central state control and in a free market.

air and water, and an esthetically pleasing environment. Central state control gives them the power to make such decisions. Coercion is the dominant feature of this type of socioeconomic system. Although large numbers of the population may accept the dominant political ideology, they can do little to change it if they do not like it. The government and party have a monopoly on economic and social decision making.

Figure 6-6 contrasts the "top-down" system typical of central state control with the "bottom-up" decision making in a free enterprise system. In a system of central state control, government and party planners at the top decide what and how much consumers will get, and the state-owned enterprises are ordered to produce these goods and services according to an overall plan. Consumers have no choice but to take what is decided by others at the top. By contrast, in a free enterprise system, consumers are the ones who give the orders, and private business firms produce goods and services to satisfy consumer wants. A free market is the principal difference between the two systems, allowing consumers by their purchases to direct production into channels they prefer and permitting businesses that cater to consumers to survive and make a profit.

MIXED STATE-AND-PRIVATE ENTERPRISE

Standing between the two opposite poles of free enterprise and central state control is another type of socioeconomic system that combines some elements of both of those systems. Not all, but some portion, of the industrial and financial sectors are owned and operated by the state. This may include the central bank through which the country's overall monetary policies are determined; the railroads, bus lines, and airline company; public utilities such as telephone, telegraph, electricity, water, and gas companies; and basic industries such as steel manufacturing, coal mining, nuclear power, and health care.

In spite of state ownership of these key parts of the business system, most businesses are owned and operated by private individuals and corporations. They coexist with the state enterprises and transact business according to free market principles; they make profits for their stockholders and take the normal risks of failure faced by free enterprisers everywhere.

This kind of socioeconomic system is quite popular in many parts of the world, as indicated in Figure 6-1. These countries enjoy a greater degree of political, social, and market freedom than the citizens who live under a central state control system. Political elections are open and free, and the social system tends to be pluralistic and diverse. However, when compared with free enterprise systems, the amount of market freedom is considerably less. As with all socioeconomic systems, the benefits and costs need to be balanced against each other in judging the system's worthwhileness. Some of these nations—West Germany and Japan are good examples—have achieved spectacular economic growth and productivity rates, but their record of social problem solving has not always matched their economic performance. Tokyo, for example, has one of the worst air pollution records in the world, and the Rhine River in Germany is heavily polluted with industrial by-products.

Social problems may be tackled by a combination of government initiatives, socially responsive corporations, and a politically active trade union movement. Unions are especially watchful of the welfare of their members, and often they take the lead in proposing social reforms that will enhance the quality of work life. In both France and West Germany, for example, social audits of private and state enterprises were first proposed by trade unions.[11]

---

[11]For a discussion of corporate involvement in social problem solving in Europe, see the following three articles in Lee E. Preston (ed.), *Research in Corporate Social Performance and Policy*, vol. 2, Greenwich, CT: JAI Press, 1980; Meinolf Dierkes, "Corporate Social Reporting and Performance in Germany," pp. 251–289; Francoise Rey, "Corporate Social Performance and Reporting in France," pp. 291–325; and Keith MacMillan, "Corporate Social Responsiveness to the Unemployment Issue: A British Perspective," pp. 327–352. An update may be found in Meinolf Dierkes and Ariane Berthoin Antal, "Whither Corporate Social Reporting: Is It Time to Legislate?" *California Management Review*, Spring 1986, pp. 106–121.

MAJOR CHANGES OF THE 1980S

As mentioned earlier, socioeconomic systems change. During the 1980s, some of the world's most important nations began to shift their position on the scale shown in Figure 6-1. Some moved away from central state control to greater reliance on market forces. Others shifted in the opposite direction by nationalizing key industries. These changes are obviously of great interest to the advocates of free enterprise, on the one hand, and socialist or centralized state systems, on the other hand. Since these two systems are locked in an intense competition for superiority and public acceptance among the world's peoples, any indication that one system is proving to be more effective than the other would attract much attention. China and France are especially interesting examples of socioeconomic systems in transition.

China: Sliding toward Free Markets?

As the world's most populous nation, with a history that spans hundreds of centuries, China occupies a position of great importance in today's world. For most of its history, China's socioeconomic system was a combination of feudal agriculture, merchant trading, and diverse political systems that included powerful landed baronies and centralized governmental power wielded by emperors. Even today, most Chinese citizens live in villages and small towns rather than in big urban centers, and the social structure assigns high priority to the family.

Beginning around 1980, China's socioeconomic system experienced some remarkable changes. Mao Zedong, who in 1949 founded the Communist People's Republic of China, had made two earlier attempts to stimulate economic development. The Great Leap Forward, as it was called, occurred in 1958–1960 and was a dismal failure. Mao's Great Proletarian Cultural Revolution, launched in 1966, was an even greater disaster for the nation. China adopted a "go it alone" policy with a vengeance. Ideological purity and loyalty to the Communist regime were elevated to the status of a quasi-religion. Doctors, engineers, university professors, and many other professional and technical persons were sent to the country to help with farming chores. Plant managers were subject to the whims of unskilled and inexperienced Communist party officials and members of the youth-oriented radical Red Guards. Scientific education was severely restricted, and Chinese experts were denied opportunities to make contact with scholars in other nations. Anyone thought to have a favorable opinion of capitalism was in danger of being jailed, often being called a "capitalist roader" or a "running dog of capitalism." Deng Xiaoping, who succeeded Mao as China's leader, was himself labeled a "capitalist roader" during this period and was accused of having a "lust for foreign technology and equipment, blatantly opposing the principles of independence and self-reliance."[12] In spite of official Communist party enthusiasm for

---

[12]Quoted in Kwan-yiu Wong and David K. Y. Chu, *Modernization in China*, Oxford: Oxford University Press, 1985, p. 27.

Mao's two big economic programs, they did not succeed in their goals of converting China into a modern industrial nation.

Mao died in 1976 and was succeeded by Deng Xiaoping in 1978. Deng's attitude toward economic development and capitalism was strikingly different from Mao's antagonistic anticapitalist views. Deng and his supporters took a pragmatic view of relations with free enterprise systems. What China needed was technology, foreign capital, an infusion of up-to-date scientific and technical knowledge, and a renewal of contacts with other industrial nations. The United States, European nations, and even former archenemy Japan were invited to explore possible trade, scientific, and educational exchanges. Management know-how was sought from American business schools. Chinese students were sent to universities and technical schools in the West.

Deng also loosened a number of centralized controls. Plant managers were allowed to set their own production targets rather than take orders from government planners, and some plants were permitted to keep and invest some of their profits rather than give them back to the central government. Small entrepreneurs—for example, the owner of a noodle stand in Canton or of a small restaurant in Chongqing—no longer had to risk jail for owning property and making small profits. In the all-important countryside, farmers could raise crops and sell them in private markets, a forbidden practice that could lead to jail during the Mao regime. Deng also broke up China's single state-owned airline into five competing companies in an effort to improve efficiency and service.[13]

According to the *Wall Street Journal:*

> The aim [of Deng's 1984 economic plan] is the gradual abandonment of most Soviet-style central planning. Over the next several years, more than a million state enterprises and factories are to be cut loose from government planning and protection and will rise or fall on their own economic merit and talent. Their workers are to rise or fall along with them, no longer pacified by egalitarian wages and subsidies that keep the cost of food, housing, clothing, transportation, utilities, medical care and education artificially below what it costs to provide them.[14]

Another innovation was the establishment of Special Economic Zones along China's coast. These carefully restricted regions are reserved for foreign corporations that wish to do business in China. With government permission, multinational firms are encouraged to build factories, import the latest technology, hire Chinese workers, train managers, and export their products to the rest of the world. In return, China earns foreign exchange, increases

---

[13]"Deng's Quiet Revolution," *Newsweek*, April 30, 1984, pp. 40–55; and "Capitalism in China," *Business Week*, January 14, 1985, pp. 53–59.

[14]"Peking Turns Sharply Down Capitalist Road in New Economic Plan," *Wall Street Journal*, October 25, 1984, p. 1. For further discussion, see Rosalie L. Tung, *Chinese Industrial Society after Mao*, Lexington, MA: Lexington, 1982; and "Capitalism in China," *Business Week*, January 14, 1985, pp. 53–59.

Chinese exports, gets much-needed technical know-how, creates jobs for many of its citizens, and stimulates economic development in the general region of each Special Economic Zone.

Deng's economic reforms should not be seen as a radical swing away from China's system of central state control, nor is it likely that capitalism will replace communism there in the foreseeable future. Chinese authorities are careful to wall off their Special Economic Zones from the rest of China for fear that they will be a threat to socialism and communism, as pointed out by two authorities: "the capitalist way of thinking [is] foreign and not readily accepted as part of the Chinese process of modernization."[15] Moreover, many of China's most basic economic policies and directives are still determined and carried out through a Russian-style system of centralized planning.

Not everyone agrees, however, that China's socioeconomic system will be able to avoid taking on more and more of the characteristics of free enterprise capitalism. Another expert made this prediction: "If the Chinese leaders hold firm to their policies of the open door, political stability, and increasing productivity—together with a gradual recognition of consumer preferences—*then the rules of the game will be altered in a way that must conflict with the current structure of property rights.* Something will have to give."[16] In other words, Deng may have set forces in motion that will be hard to reverse.

Amid the uncertainties of China's future, it is possible to say that this large nation has moved perceptibly from its classic position of central state control to a position somewhat nearer the mixed state-and-private enterprise systems. In doing so, it appears to be more successful in solving some of its more pressing economic and social problems.

France: A Mixed System in Transition

The winds of socioeconomic change have not been confined to China and other systems of central state control. Two of Europe's most important mixed state-and-private enterprise systems—Great Britain and France—have undergone basic changes in the 1980s. We concentrate on France here as an example of how quickly such changes can occur and how impermanent they may prove to be.

Post–World War II France relied heavily on a type of economic planning, called "indicative planning," to organize and rejuvenate its devastated economy and social structure. Through combined government regulations, indirect controls and incentives, government subsidies, price-and-wage controls, and government ownership of key utilities and the central bank, French plan-

---

[15]David K. Y. Chu and Kwan-yiu Wong, "Modernization and the Lessons of the Special Economic Zones," in Wong and Chu, *Modernization in China*, Oxford: Oxford University Press, 1985, pp. 208–217.

[16]Steven N. S. Cheung, *Will China Go "Capitalist"?*, London: Institute of Economic Affairs, 1982, p. 58. For a contrasting view, see "Chinese Crossroads: Some Sinologists Say Reforms Will Bog Down after a Decade of Rapid Change," *Wall Street Journal*, September 5, 1986, pp. 1, 9.

ning authorities could exert considerable control over the direction of economic activities by "indicating" (rather than forcibly ordering) what seemed to be best for the nation as a whole. The bulk of France's business system remained in private hands, in spite of extensive government involvement. Under this mixed system, French production soared during the 1960s, and its rate of overall economic growth rivalled that of Japan which had become the envy of all nations.[17]

For many complicated reasons, the French economy fared worse during the 1970s, and public dissatisfaction was widespread. In 1981 French voters elected a socialist government, headed by President François Mitterrand, which favored more centralized control over the economy. Eleven major industrial groups and most of the private banking sector were nationalized, which boosted the government's share of industrial output and employment to around 25 percent of the total and to over 50 percent of industrial investment in France. Among the largest corporations—comparable to the Fortune 500 industrial companies in the United States—the state's stake rose to 48 percent of sales and employment. One-third of French exports were sold by state-owned companies.[18]

These nationalizations were supplemented by a national "industrial policy" that attempted to resurrect the steel industry, breathe new life into the electronics industry, and concentrate on sectors where French producers enjoyed competitive advantage over foreign rivals. Quite clearly, France had dramatically increased the amount of central state control in its mixed socio-economic system.

However, this socialist trend had barely been put in motion when politics threatened to reverse it. France has a multiparty electoral system, as do most mixed state-and-private enterprise societies. So French voters once again expressed their preferences in 1986 by electing a conservative government directed by Prime Minister Jacques Chirac. "Privatization" became the rallying slogan of the new conservative government, as Chirac proposed to sell off a total of 65 state-owned banks, insurance companies, and industrial concerns to private interests. In addition, the minister of industry took steps to replace government intervention and many subsidies with free enterprise principles, and he encouraged market-oriented entrepreneurs, lopped off unproductive enterprises, and established enterprise zones throughout the nation to stimulate new ventures.[19]

[17]For two views of this type of economic planning, see Stephen S. Cohen, *Modern Capitalist Planning: The French Model,* Cambridge, MA: Harvard University Press, 1969; and Vera Lutz, *Central Planning for the Market Economy: An Analysis of the French Theory and Experience,* London: Longmans, Green, 1969.

[18]*Socialist France: The New Business Environment,* Business International S. A., 1983, p. 46.

[19]"Mitterand and Chirac Take Off the Gloves," *Business Week,* July 28, 1986, p. 41; François Guillaumat, "A French Official Wants to Stop Ministering to Industry," *Wall Street Journal,* August 27, 1986, p. 15; "Come One, Come All to the Great French Sell-Off," *Business Week,* September 22, 1986, p. 46; and "France Urges Citizenry to Break with Habit, Become Stockholders," *Wall Street Journal,* November 11, 1986, pp. 1, 26.

France's see-saw movements from less government to more government and then back to less government again demonstrate three important points: (1) political democracies with multiple-party systems experience more change in their socioeconomic systems than the monolithic one-party systems of Russia and China; (2) economic and political leaders in mixed state-and-private enterprise systems have to pay close attention to the public's wishes to retain their positions of influence; and (3) business planning is more difficult where political currents shift quickly from a pro-business climate to a hostile one.

Changes in Other Nations

The 1980s proved to be a time of change for many nations. The "privatization" movement in France was matched by similar developments in Great Britain and the United States as popular movements against excessive government intervention found favor among voters.[20] Communist party general secretary Mikhail Gorbachev attempted, as had some of his predecessors, to inject new initiatives into the Soviet Union's ponderous bureaucratic economic machinery. Japan proved that close cooperation between government and private business can contribute greatly to national productivity and competitive strength in global markets. Israel began selling off some of its 189 state-owned enterprises to private groups and cutting back on government subsidies.[21] Brazil's quasi-socialist approach to government controls and planning helped that mixed economy, at least temporarily, to make big economic strides in the mid-1980s in spite of its large national debt. Taiwan's vigorous private sector became a strong competitor in world markets. Government-directed enterprises in several developing nations (for example, Brazil and South Korea) took over larger portions of world steel markets. Some nations, for example, Iran, South Africa, and Israel, found that their socioeconomic systems were dominated and distorted by military pressures.

No clear winners emerged from these transitions, no unequivocal sign that one type of socioeconomic system was superior to another, and no stampede to adopt a single pattern for world economic and social development. One way to interpret these changing currents is to see them as attempts by these societies to find a happy medium between the opposite ends of the spectrum shown in Figure 6-1. Experimentation and flexibility, constantly searching for a balance between too much government intervention and not enough government support, trying to find ways to unleash business's productivity while retaining a desirable amount of social control—these are the hallmarks of socioeconomic changes during the 1980s. Perhaps the most important lesson to be learned is that each nation needs to find its own way, based on its history, its culture, its political traditions, and its unique place in the total world community.

[20]Barnaby J. Feder, "Britain Sheds Its State Companies," _New York Times_, October 7, 1984, p. F-4.

[21]"Jerusalem Tries a Dose of Reaganomics," _Business Week_, September 8, 1986, p. 40.

GLOBAL PRESSURES AND IDEOLOGICAL COMPETITION

United States corporate managers face many of the same problems as their counterparts in other socioeconomic systems. Their job is to produce needed goods and services efficiently and in sufficient amounts to support peoples' wants and desires. But they have to do so within a social context that influences their decisions. This is as true for Chinese managers as for those in the United States or Russia or France. Although the guiding ideologies of socioeconomic systems differ, they present the managers of enterprises (whether public or private) with common problems and challenges. The manager's task in each system is to achieve an acceptable amount of production in socially approved ways. *Each system places social controls on the manager, requiring that business be done within acceptable social boundaries.*

In today's highly intensive global competition—for markets, among different socioeconomic systems, for technological superiority, and for military advantage—managers everywhere are under pressure to make their respective systems work to the fullest and most efficient levels. In these circumstances *two principles* stand out as reliable guides to business thinking, regardless of the type of socioeconomic system involved. *One principle* is the importance of keeping an open mind and a broad perspective on the good and bad points of one's own socioeconomic system, and being willing to adapt that system to new conditions when needed. *The other principle* is one that runs through this entire book: *since business activities always take place within a social context, managers must learn to consider social factors along with others as they formulate strategic plans, business policies, and action programs to reach the goals they have set for their companies.*

The decisions managers make in this kind of fiercely competitive world have impacts on employees at all levels. Those decisions can mean the difference between having a job or being unemployed. Local communities also feel the impact of corporate strategic decisions that may close down a plant due to competitive pressures. So, in one way or another, almost everyone—and not just the high-level managers in a company—are affected by these decisions. That is why the socioeconomic system that encourages the greatest amount of participation by all concerned, while allowing a maximum degree of freedom to corporate managers, is likely to produce the most satisfactory results for both business and society.

SUMMARY

Most of the world's nations organize their economic and social activities according to one of three types of socioeconomic systems: free enterprise, central state control, or mixed state-and-private enterprise. Business in the United States prefers a free enterprise system and a free enterprise ideology.

Many socioeconomic systems have changed significantly in recent years. These changes are evidence of a continuing search for the most effective way to organize business and economic operations.

Global pressures and competition among different kinds of socioeconomic systems present corporate managers in all nations with similar challenges and problems. Business everywhere is conducted within some system of social controls, which thus requires managers to plan and make decisions with these social factors in mind.

DISCUSSION AND REVIEW QUESTIONS

1. Make a list of ten nations drawn from at least three of the world's continents. Identify the dominant type of socioeconomic system present in each nation, and tell how each nation's history and recent events have contributed to the kind of system it represents today.

2. From newspapers or newsmagazines, such as the *Wall Street Journal* or *Fortune* magazine, try to find examples of how government regulation and a government and business partnership have been used to solve an economic or social problem. Based on material covered in this chapter, try to envision and describe how these problems would be handled in China or in another system of central state control.

3. The governments of China, the Soviet Union, and several European nations give strong financial support for training and preparing athletes for the Olympic Games, while the United States' Olympic athletes are supported largely by private donations and private organizations. Do you favor having the United States government subsidize the training of Olympic athletes, rather than leaving it to a "free enterprise" private approach? On what grounds could such government intervention be defended? Would it be a step away from free enterprise and toward central state control of sports?

4. Of all the various components of free enterprise ideology mentioned in this chapter, which one do you consider to be the most important and indispensable? If you were forced to give up one of these, which one would you be willing to sacrifice before the others? Give reasons for your choices.

5. Imagine the manager of an electronics factory in China, the manager of a chemical plant in France, and the manager of an automobile assembly plant in the United States. Each manager is under pressure to increase production and improve efficiency of operations. What would be the primary source of these pressures for each of the three managers in their own countries? Keeping in mind this chapter's discussion of socioeconomic systems, describe what common problems they would be likely to face, regardless of the type of system in which they conduct their operations. Explain your answers.

CRITICAL INCIDENT

Choosing a System

Picture yourself as the leader of one of Western Africa's newly emerging but relatively underdeveloped nations. You are preparing recommendations to stimulate economic and social development in your country. As you are trying to make up your mind about the most desirable way to achieve these national goals, you come across some comments made by two economic commentators in the United States. One favors reliance on the private sector, while the other seems to be bothered by the tendency to let private enterprise do things that are more properly done by government. Their comments are as follows:

> Lately a new word has entered political discourse: privatization. The idea is that private is invariably more efficient than public, that government ought to stay out of as many realms as possible, and that even where government gets involved, government should contract out tasks to private firms or give people vouchers rather than provide them services directly. President Reagan wants to sell off public lands and public dams and get the government out of the mortgage insurance, legal aid, and veterans' health businesses. . . . In local government, one sees privatized garbage collection, park maintenance, and even privately operated prisons.
>
> But there are both philosophical and practical difficulties with this conservatives' utopia. First, in certain areas of life the criteria of the private market seem inappropriate. That is because human beings are not solely economic creatures. They have social attachments, patriotic stirrings, religious commitments, family bonds, and psychological needs, some of which contradict the textbook view of economic man. It offends us, as citizens, to have national symbols auctioned off to the highest bidder.
>
> In organized society, we counterpose certain public values to those of a pure market. Some things aren't supposed to be bought and sold. . . . We Americans are not just buyers and sellers; we are also citizens.[22]

The other economic commentator has another point of view about the privatization movement:

> Privatization is actually a worldwide movement. It is best known for what has happened in Britain, where [Prime Minister Margaret] Thatcher's government has sold hundreds of thousands of public housing units as well as major publicly owned companies in aerospace, automobiles, and telecommunications. It is planning also to sell British Airways, Rolls-Royce, British Gas, and many other public enterprises.
>
> Socialist and Third World governments have climbed aboard the privatization bandwagon. Spain's Socialist government, elected in 1982, immediately nationalized a major private company. Since then, however, it has returned most of the company to the private sector and sold several other state companies. . . . [T]he tide in France is now running strongly toward privatization and deregulation. Mexico, Brazil, India, and other Third World countries have sold some public enterprises and plan to sell others. China has taken the most decisive step toward privatizing its economy. . . .
>
> The sale of government enterprises to the private sector can—and should—be carried much further. Publicly owned enterprises apparently are less efficient and less flexible than competitive private companies because they are unable to separate economic choices from political considerations.[23]

[22]Robert Kuttner, "The Private Market Can't Always Solve Public Problems," *Business Week,* March 10, 1986, p. 14.

[23]Gary S. Becker, "Why Public Enterprises Belong in Private Hands," *Business Week,* February 24, 1986, p. 20.

As you read these two sharply divergent viewpoints, you recall that your own nation has a very ancient tradition of village life with strong local political leaders and deeply respected social customs and religious commitments. But modern times require an increasing efficiency in economic production to feed a rapidly growing population that is flocking to new urban centers. You wonder if these two elements—a traditional social system and a modern economy—can be reconciled. This dilemma does not make your task of recommending steps to bring about more economic and social development any easier. Should you recommend a system based on a private free enterprise system, or would your nation be better off with a system of centralized government controls?

1. Which one of the two systems would you favor and recommend? Give your reasons.

2. If you could convince either the United States or China to give aid to your country in its development efforts, knowing that the aid would require you to adhere to that nation's socioeconomic system, to which nation would you turn for help? Justify your position, both in terms of protecting your nation's ancient traditions and promoting the greatest amount of economic development.

absence of middle class and absence of political stability

1. free enterprise system
- *more incentive for people to work and produce.*
- *certainly probably the gov't is it nearly the size of the gov't in this developing country. Therefore, it doesn't have to worry about veteran health insurance, legal aid and the like*
- *your concern - get industry started. best way to bring in established while companies*

2. If you chose the free enterprise system, you would choose to seek aid from the U.S. Additional benefits would be the U.S. market for goods produced by your country, a way to learn business management

have to have a strong gov't can't be a puppet of U.S. or abuses will occur damaging traditional society

Chapter Seven

GOVERNMENT REGULATION OF BUSINESS

The regulatory system is a primary means through which government tries to harmonize business behavior and the public interest. Many types and forms of regulation have been developed. Some work better than others, and some work well for a time but lose their effectiveness. Thus, regulation is an ever-changing system. During the 1980s a major rethinking of the regulatory system in the United States has occurred, and there is little doubt that government officials, business executives, and the public will continue to evaluate its effectiveness.

CHAPTER OBJECTIVES

After reading this chapter you should be able to

- Identify major types of government regulation
- See how the regulatory system works
- Explain why government has increased in size and scope
- Discuss the economic and social costs of government regulation
- Define and discuss deregulation

When Henry Ford organized the Ford Motor Company in 1903, his relationships with government were relatively simple. There was only one important antitrust law on the books, and his business was too small to be bothered by it. The federal government did not tax the income of the company, its employees, or its capital gains. Although rival carmakers in this country were gearing up to compete with Ford, foreign competitors were no threat. No unions were permitted in the Ford plant, and government regulations concerning wages, hours, working conditions, and safety and health were unheard of. The government exacted no payments from the company for employee retirement and pension plans for the simple reason that none existed. Nor was the fledgling automaker plagued with problems of a polluted environment, an energy shortage, or consumer complaints about auto safety, all of which in later years would bring the wrath of the government down on the Ford company. His main legal worry in those early years was a patent infringement suit brought against him by competitors, but he eventually won the suit in the courts.

By the late 1970s, Henry Ford II, the founder's grandson and chief executive officer of the company, faced a different world. He could scarcely make a move without government taking an active hand or peering over his shoulder. That single antitrust law known to his grandfather had grown into a tangle of antitrust laws and court rulings regulating competition, pricing practices, mergers, and acquisitions. Labor laws legalized unions and controlled wages, hours, working conditions, safety and health, and employee discrimination. Federal, state, local, and foreign governments levied taxes on company income, its plant and equipment, capital gains, auto and truck sales, and salaries.

Decisions about the size and weight of cars, the types of engines, and gasoline consumption rates were shared with government regulators. Still another group of government officials dealt with auto and plant emissions, effluent discharges, plant noise, and solid-waste disposal. Consumer protection laws dictated guidelines on matters ranging from safety belts to recalls for defective work to the terms of a loan to finance the auto's purchase.

Nor was this all. Henry Ford II—unlike the founder, who was a staunch believer in laissez faire—depended upon the federal government to maintain general business prosperity, stabilize the dollar, and combat both inflation and recession. Such ideas were as wild and unlikely to the older Ford as if someone had told him that his grandson would live to see astronauts walking on the moon!

The older and the younger Henry Ford have lived and managed their company in truly different worlds. What was insignificant to the one—government intervention—had become central to the other.

This chapter concentrates on the expansion of government at all levels, the major problems and costs associated with regulation, and efforts to reduce the burdens of government on business and society. This discussion is related to some of the major ideas already developed in earlier chapters, including the interactive model of business and society, corporate stakeholders, and major social challenges. One of the main features of the interactive model (see Figure 4-3) is the involvement of business with government. Part of the reason for this relationship is that corporate stakeholder groups have persuaded government at all levels to regulate business activities in order to promote or protect the interests of the stakeholders. In addition, U.S. society has frequently used government regulation as a way to reinforce the efforts of business to meet some of the major social challenges listed in Figure 1-3.

AN OVERVIEW OF GOVERNMENT REGULATION

Before getting involved in the details and specifics of the regulatory system, it is useful to have an overall perspective, particularly about the nature of regulation, various types of regulation, and how regulation actually operates.

Implementing Social Choices

Government regulation of business, in its most basic sense, is a mechanism for implementing social choices. In other words, when a society has chosen to pursue a certain goal—such as free competition in the marketplace—it may then decide that the goal can be reached only by preventing the growth of monopolies. It may further decide that monopolies can be curbed by making them illegal and by creating a government watchdog agency to monitor all business practices that may lead to monopoly. A definite sequence occurs: first, a social choice is made, then one or more laws are passed and an agency is empowered to implement the choice. This sequence leads to government regulation, not just of business alone but also of hospitals, public schools, labor unions, and others.

When we discussed alternative socioeconomic systems in Chapter 6, government regulation was mentioned as one type of socioeconomic system through which a society may choose to approach some of its social problems. As one scholar has noted:

> In all countries of the world today . . . the government has significant powers to curb and circumscribe the discretion of private entrepreneurs. Governments often constitute the single most important decision making body for a private businessman to take into account.[1]

In the United States, many different types of problems are approached through regulation. The history of regulation is long; it dates back to the very earliest actions of government. The powers of government that define regulation are derived from English common law and involve traditional government authority to establish and disestablish economic activity.[2] As we shall point out later, much controversy surrounds this development, and many sincere people question the wisdom of depending upon regulation to so great an extent. However, neither the controversial character of regulation nor its inherent complexity should be allowed to obscure the essential nature of government regulation. Basically, it is a method of carrying out certain social choices made by a society through its political and legal system.

---

[1]Yair Aharoni, *Markets, Planning and Development: The Private and Public Sectors in Economic Development*, Cambridge, MA: Ballinger, 1977, p. ii.

[2]Alfred A. Marcus, Jr., *The Adversary Economy*, Westport, CT: Quorum Books, 1985, chap. 1.

Types of Regulation

Government regulations come in several different varieties. Some are directly imposed, others are more indirectly felt. Some are aimed at a specific industry such as the airlines, while others such as those dealing with discrimination apply across the board to all industries. Some have been in existence for a long time—the Interstate Commerce Commission (ICC) was created in 1887—while others, such as the Consumer Product Safety Commission, originated in the 1970s. Economic regulation characterizes some government activities, while social goals are paramount in others.

Industry-Specific Economic Regulations

Our oldest form of regulation by government agency is directed at specific industries such as the railroads, telephone companies, and merchant shipping lines. Regulations of this type are primarily economic in nature and are deliberately intended to modify the normal operation of the free market and the forces of supply and demand. Such modification may come about because the free market is distorted by the size or monopoly power of companies, or because the social side effects or consequences of actions in the marketplace are thought to be undesirable. Under such conditions, government regulators make a conscious effort to substitute their judgment for that of the marketplace in such matters as price setting, capital expansion, quality of services, and entry conditions for new competitors.

> For example, *railroads were not permitted to raise most rates to shippers without permission from the Interstate Commerce Commission, nor could they abandon a red-ink line as a free market firm would do. Nor could telephone companies increase their charges, expand into related lines of business, or deny service to customers without first getting approval of various local, state, and federal agencies.*

In these and other public utilities, a regulatory agency asserts control over the fundamental business matters facing an industry—prices, capital investments, services offered, customers served, and profits. Although a company is privately owned and managed, the scope of its decision making is severely restricted by government regulations. Public-utility regulation is direct and close, bringing government officials and business executives into close working contact.

Some critics claim that the working relationships between regulatory officials and business executives breed a "you scratch my back and I'll scratch yours" attitude that injures the public interest. In some instances, regulatory officials may become more interested in seeing the industry prosper and grow than in ensuring that the original goals of regulation are achieved. In other instances, regulatory agencies may be asked to both regulate and promote an industry, a situation that often has proven difficult or impossible to manage effectively. This was the case, for example, facing the Atomic Energy Commission in the 1950s and 1960s, and the Civil Aeronautics Board from the 1930s to the 1970s. Both agencies were reorganized because of problems that developed.[3]

Besides public utilities, other industries find themselves the subject of economic regulation. Farmers—many of them big-business operators—have been told for many years the minimum prices they may charge for an entire range of major crops, how much land they may plant in certain crops, and whether they may expand operations. Other industries such as banking, pharmaceuticals, and foods are regulated less comprehensively, but they still face a number of stringent economic rules promulgated by government agencies and departments.

All-Industry Social Regulations

Most all-industry regulations are aimed at four major social goals: pollution control, workplace safety and health, consumer protection, and equal employment opportunity. Unlike the economic regulations mentioned above, social regulations are not limited to one type of business or industry. Laws concerning pollution, safety and health, and discrimination apply to all major institutions, including business; and consumer protection laws apply to all relevant businesses producing and selling consumer goods.

Since the 1970s, critics have thought that these social regulations have created a real problem for business because the agencies that enforce them do not assume any responsibility for the overall financial impact of their actions on firms or industries. For example, the Environmental Protection Agency has required manufacturers to install costly pollution control equipment even though jobs are placed at risk. In contrast, the Interstate Commerce Commission typically has been very careful to consider the profitability of a firm or industry, for example, a trucking or bus company, when deciding on its request for rate increases. Some people believe that agencies such as the ICC focus more concern on the health of an industry than on the effects on consumers. Others believe that disregarding the effect of regulations on an industry's economic health is equally harmful to the public interest.[4] In other words, either too much or too little regulatory concern for an industry's economic health may be harmful to the public interest.

Functional Regulations

Certain operations or functions of business have been singled out for special attention by government regulators. Labor practices, for example, are no longer left to the operation of free market forces, since government sets minimum wages, regulates overtime pay, allows unions to monopolize the supply of workers if they can do so, and often intervenes to settle troublesome and serious labor-management disputes that threaten national well-being.

Competition is another business function strongly affected by regulation. Antitrust laws and rules, discussed in a later chapter, attempt to prevent

---

[3]Marcus, op. cit.

[4]Murray L. Weidenbaum, *Business, Government, and the Public*, Englewood Cliffs, NJ: 1986, chap. 2.

monopolies, preserve competitive pricing, and protect consumers against unfair practices.

Functional regulations, like social regulations, may cut across industry lines and apply generally to all enterprises, as they do in the case of antitrust and labor practices. Or they may—as with regulations governing the functioning of the stock exchanges and the issuance of corporate securities—be confined to specific institutions such as the stock markets or the companies whose stocks are listed on those exchanges.

Figure 7-1 depicts these three types of regulations—economic, social, and functional—along with the major regulatory agencies responsible for enforcing the rules. Only the most prominent federal agencies are included in the chart. Omitted are many other federal departments, as well as similar agencies in each state and in many cities. Many indirect regulations and governmental curbs dealing with taxation, aid to education, urban renewal, and others also are excluded.

How Regulation Works

In spite of the complexity of government regulation, it is possible to grasp the essentials. We want to emphasize here (1) the legal basis of regulation, (2) the primary regulatory organs or mechanisms used, and (3) the major steps involved in making regulation a reality. Knowing each of these components provides a sound basis for understanding how government regulates business and many other aspects of our lives.

The Legal Basis

A person who is skeptical about so much government intrusion into the private sector may well ask: Where does the government get its regulatory authority? The answer is: From two sources—the common law and the Constitution.

The common law is a body of legal precedents and customs built up over many years as a result of experience, trial and error, and court rulings. It contains many commonly accepted principles, such as trial by jury, the protection of property, and the enforcement of contracts. English common law was the basis of our legal system for many years, and gave government the right to regulate human affairs in order to achieve fairness and justice.

The United States Constitution, which embodies several common law principles, is now the primary legal foundation for government regulatory activities. In one way or another, all government regulation must be justified in constitutional terms or it is not allowed to stand.

Most federal regulations today are based on four constitutional powers: (1) the power to regulate interstate and foreign commerce, (2) the power to tax and spend, (3) the power to borrow, and (4) the power to promote the general welfare.[5] These powers have been used to justify all the direct and indirect regulations shown in Figure 7-1. The courts, under our constitutional

---

[5]James Q. Wilson, *American Government: Institutions and Policies,* 2d ed., Lexington, MA: Heath, 1983, chap. 15.

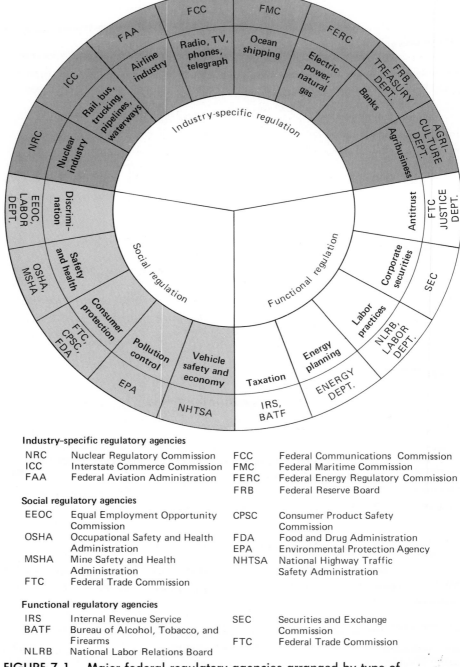

Industry–specific regulatory agencies

NRC	Nuclear Regulatory Commission	FCC	Federal Communications Commission
ICC	Interstate Commerce Commission	FMC	Federal Maritime Commission
FAA	Federal Aviation Administration	FERC	Federal Energy Regulatory Commission
		FRB	Federal Reserve Board

Social regulatory agencies

EEOC	Equal Employment Opportunity Commission	CPSC	Consumer Product Safety Commission
OSHA	Occupational Safety and Health Administration	FDA	Food and Drug Administration
		EPA	Environmental Protection Agency
MSHA	Mine Safety and Health Administration	NHTSA	National Highway Traffic Safety Administration
FTC	Federal Trade Commission		

Functional regulatory agencies

IRS	Internal Revenue Service	SEC	Securities and Exchange Commission
BATF	Bureau of Alcohol, Tobacco, and Firearms	FTC	Federal Trade Commission
NLRB	National Labor Relations Board		

FIGURE 7-1. Major federal regulatory agencies arranged by type of regulation.

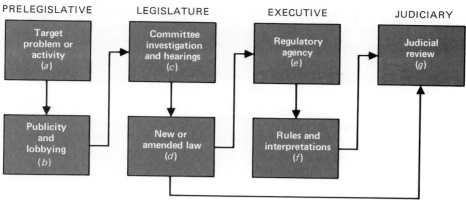

FIGURE 7-2.   Major steps in federal regulation taken by the three branches of government.

system, have generally upheld the right of the federal government to use its powers in these ways, although court interpretations are subject to modifications as society and the members of the judiciary change.

Several other constitutional provisions—for example, the implied powers, the war powers, the due-process-of-law provisions, the equal-protection clauses, and others—also are used as a legal basis of government regulation. We shall leave the details of these to legal experts. The main point to remember is that government regulation rests securely on a foundation of common law and constitutional authority.

The Regulatory Mechanism

The main lines of regulation follow closely the three branches of government—the legislative, the executive, and the judiciary, as shown in Figure 7-2. Each branch has certain responsibilities where regulation is concerned. The *legislative* branch—Congress at the federal level; state legislatures, county commissions, and city councils at other levels—is empowered to enact new regulatory laws or amend old ones.

> For example, *in 1970 Congress passed the Clean Air Act; it was amended in 1973, 1974, and 1977 (twice), and further revisions have been made in the 1980s. The Superfund Act was passed in 1980 in the last days of the Carter Administration. A 1986 revision of the law dealt with problems discovered since the initial bill was enacted by Congress. Such a process of revision and amendment is normal, as legislatures respond to the various interest groups in society that have a stake in the new regulations. These may include consumer advocates, environmentalists, and, of course, the affected business groups.*

Once a law is enacted, the *executive* branch of government becomes officially involved. It may already have been unofficially involved by lobbying for or against the legislation. A new regulatory agency—one like the Environmental Protection Agency or the Occupational Safety and Health Administration—may be created by the new law. Its task—as part of the executive branch—is to see that the provisions of a law are carried out, something it accomplishes by issuing rules and regulations that embody its interpretation of the law's intent.

The *judiciary* branch becomes active if serious disagreement arises between the regulators and those being regulated. The courts may be asked to judge the fairness or legality of the regulatory agency's rules and interpretations, or the entire law may be challenged as being unconstitutional. For example, a plumbing and heating contractor filed suit against OSHA, claiming that the agency was violating constitutional safeguards against unreasonable search when, for purposes of safety inspections, it entered a company's premises without advance notice. The courts agreed and required the agency to obtain a court order before entering a company's property.

Our aim here is to outline the structure and main steps in the regulatory system. For the most part, business executives are involved with the task of adapting to the regulations affecting their industry or firm. But executives also can anticipate regulatory trends and be proactive or interactive in the shaping of regulations. To strategically manage regulation, one must recognize that its development includes many factors, some of them rational and others irrational. Proponents of a new regulation may exaggerate their case, particularly to persuade or affect a television audience. People's fears—of nuclear accidents, toxic waste sites, or insider-trading abuses—may be highlighted by those people urging new regulations, while the businesses or other affected institutions issue soothing reassurances to the public. Politics is always present, as interest-group influence is felt by legislators concerned about the outcome of the next election, by appointed regulators, and even by the courts, whose judges are not entirely isolated from social and political currents.[6]

HOW MUCH GOVERNMENT?

In the history of America there has never been a real question of whether there would be government participation in the business system. The Constitution itself provides for certain government intervention, but it stresses minimum intervention. Nevertheless, throughout the development of the American social system the question has persisted: What kind of government intervention is appropriate, and how much? In light of today's complex social demands, the roles and responsibilities of government and other major social institutions are being reexamined.

Compared with the government in the early days of the republic, or even with the one 100 years ago, today's government is gargantuan. The government at all levels in the United States employs over 16 million people, a figure that is about equal to every man, woman, and child in the greater New York City area. These government workers vastly outnumber the total

[6]Ibid.

populations of Australia, Switzerland, or Venezuela and exceed the combined number of employees of the 200 largest United States industrial corporations.

Government spending is equally impressive. In 1984, federal, state, and local governments in the United States spent a total of $1.35 trillion, an amount that exceeds the entire industrial output of West Germany, France, or the United Kingdom. With that amount of money, you could buy more than 2 billion color television sets, 54 million luxury automobiles, or 13 million houses costing $100,000 each.

Not only is government big, but it has been expanding in recent decades, particularly since the 1930s and 1940s. For example, expenditures of the federal government were 137 times greater in 1975 than in 1929, and they increased thirteenfold between 1950 and 1980. Government spending also is growing faster than the population. Between 1950 and 1983, per capita spending increased from $464 per person to $5,400, as shown in Figure 7-3.

There is a very complex relationship between the spending of the federal government and that of state and local governments. For example, in the quarter century from 1950 to 1975, state and local governments increased their spending ten times, while federal government outlays increased over eight times their 1950 levels. And while the number of federal employees grew by 36 percent, the number of state and local government employees shot up by a whopping 180 percent! These increases, which are shown in Figure 7-4, are not independent of one another. For example, a local school may receive federal funds and hire personnel to teach handicapped children. It also may be obligated by a federal statute to initiate a dual-language program for students or support transportation for the purpose of desegregating a school system under a federal court order. Such situations are but a small example of the policy interaction between federal, state, and local governments.

During the 1980s, the Reagan administration consciously sought to reduce federal government spending by shifting many program-funding responsibilities to the state and local governments. These efforts have encountered resistance from advocates for federal funding of programs such as welfare assistance but they have generally forced state governments to assume more financial responsibility for assistance programs. The effort has produced a *shift* in spending by government but has not produced any absolute reductions. In fact, the 1988 federal budget that the administration sent to Congress was the largest in the nation's entire history.

Why Government Has Grown Bigger

How does one explain this tremendous expansion in government, especially in a nation that ranks itself at the very top of those favoring free enterprise? Several major forces have been at work, and some of these have been mentioned in earlier chapters.

Governments have taken on more functions in modern society, including many that once were performed by the private sector or not performed at all. Governments now provide retirement pay for older workers, unemployment compensation for those unable to find jobs, construction funds for

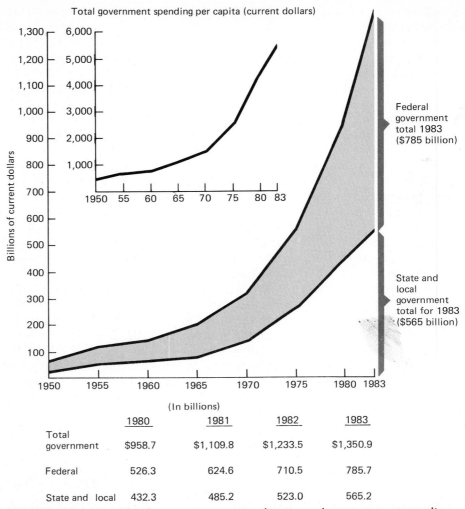

FIGURE 7-3. Growth of government expenditures and government spending per capita, 1950 to 1983, measured in current dollars. (*Source:* U.S. Statistical Abstract, *1986, table no. 442. Note: Because of data classification procedures, these figures are not the same as similar figures from the national income accounts.*)

hospitals and schools, loan guarantees for smaller businesses (or large businesses with financial troubles), insurance for companies wanting to do business overseas, and financial safeguards for investors. And this is but a small fraction of the many roles performed by government. A century ago, nearly all of these functions were considered to be either private matters not subject to government intervention or unnecessary. Today, they are considered to be necessary and often are provided best by local, state, or federal government agencies. As a result, government is the biggest spender, the biggest employer, the biggest property owner, the biggest tenant, the biggest insurer,

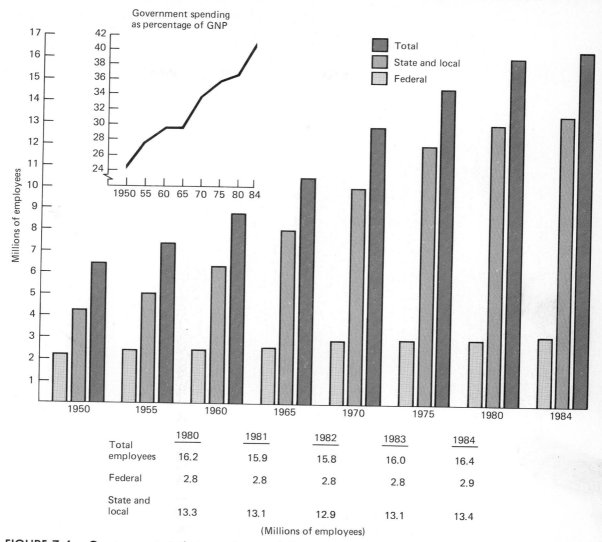

FIGURE 7-4. Government civilian employees, full- and part-time, and federal, state, and local government spending (in current dollars) as a percentage of the gross national product. (*Source:* U.S. Statistical Abstract, *1986, table no. 481.*)

the biggest lender, the biggest borrower, and the biggest customer in the free world.

Public opinion about the size of government is constantly shifting, often in response to real or proposed changes in specific programs. This is illustrated in public opinion surveys such as that shown in Figure 7-5. They indicate that between 1981 and 1987 public opinion changed concerning preferred increases or decreases in government spending on key programs. In 1987 respondents preferred to see increases in such programs as educational

Question: Do you think that spending for the following federal government programs should be increased, decreased, or left about the same?			
	1987	**1986**	**1981**
Loans and grants to college students			
Increased	46%	34%	22%
Decreased	14	20	29
Left the same	39	45	48
Day-care programs for children of working parents who can't afford to pay			
Increased	57	44	38
Decreased	8	11	15
Left the same	34	44	46
Medicaid, which provides free health care to the poor			
Increased	61	49	44
Decreased	6	9	13
Left the same	32	42	41
Medicare, which helps reduce health care costs for the elderly			
Increased	74	63	57
Decreased	3	4	3
Left the same	22	33	39
Social Security			
Increased	63	51	49
Decreased	5	6	8
Left the same	31	43	40
The military			
Increased	31	22	72
Decreased	25	34	6
Left the same	43	43	20

FIGURE 7-5. Public preferences concerning government spending. (Telephone poll of 1,505 people, "No Opinion" category omitted.) (*Source: Excerpted from "Washington Post–ABC News Poll," The Washington Post, January 27, 1987, p. A-4.*)

grants and loans, medicaid, medicare, day care, and social security but no increases in military spending.

A number of underlying forces that have moved American government toward a more active social role are discussed in the following paragraphs.

Population Increase

More people need more government, and as our nation's population grew larger it was inevitable that government also would have to expand. A big city needs more police, more fire protection, more schools, a larger sewer system, and a bigger waterworks than a small village. Over 200 million people are bound to call on government for more services than the 4 million who lived in the United States when the Constitution was adopted.

Geographic Expansion

Not only more people but also a wider area to govern causes government to grow. Our history, even into the twentieth century, has been one of geographic spread. As the frontier spread to western Pennsylvania, then to Illinois, and on beyond into the Far West and Far North, each community needed its share of laws and such vital government services as water, police protection, roads, and mail delivery.

World Events

World wars and worldwide depressions have accelerated the growth of government in the United States and elsewhere. In wartime, government is granted immense powers to mobilize people and resources, goods are rationed by government decree, and factories turn out tanks and missiles for the armed forces rather than sports cars and home computers for private citizens. During depressions, government is called on to prime the economic pump, lend money to failing businesses, and create jobs for the unemployed.

Social Complexity

Today's society—with its advanced technology, mammoth institutions, widespread suburbs, global trade systems, and international tensions—is far more complicated than the rural America of the eighteenth and nineteenth centuries. Government often steps in as a rule maker, an umpire, a mediator, and a promoter of social harmony in order to reduce social complexity to livable human terms.

Pragmatic Needs

For the most part, government has grown because we have wanted it to do certain things for us. Interest-group pluralism leads almost inevitably to this outcome, particularly when groups cannot take care of their needs by themselves and when, moreover, they can influence government to take up their cause. Our history, past and present, is full of examples.

> *Early American shipping interests persuaded the government to clear harbors, dredge channels, and build docking facilities in order to promote American trade. Farmers and merchants combined to have government build and subsidize roads, canals, and railroads to carry commercial traffic. Farming interests also lobbied for the establishment of agricultural experiment stations for conducting research on new plant varieties, farming methods, and insect and weed controls. In modern times, we see the same thing occurring, but usually on a larger scale. The airlines need reliable weather information and safe landing sites, and hence they favor government weather forecasting and government funding of airport construction. The trucking industry needs good highways to speed shipments, and the auto industry also is dependent upon good roads for its customers; so both support government investment in highways and bridges. American commercial fishing interests need protection of offshore fishing areas from foreign competition and have convinced the government to extend our national coastal claims outward to 200 miles.*

American interest groups, including business, have usually been very pragmatic and practical. Their general attitude has been: Where needs exist that cannot be met otherwise, get government to do it. As a result, the old ideological principle of laissez faire or limited government is often left behind.[7]

THE REGULATORY SYSTEM

Historians generally agree that regulation has been used to perform many tasks and to serve many different ends and purposes. Some have been economic, others political, legal, and cultural. The shapes and forms of American regulation are so numerous and diverse that inconsistencies sometimes appear. We must always remember, however, that regulation is a *tool* of government, a tool that government policymakers have used to help solve important problems throughout American history. Other nations design regulatory systems in response to their own unique problems.

The Growth of Regulation

The 1980s have been mostly an era of stable or reduced regulatory activity. But this slowing of regulatory activity is, for the most part, a reaction to the great growth of social regulation that occurred in the 1960s and 1970s. In fact, as we point out later in this chapter, government in the late 1970s and 1980s began to relax some of its tighter *economic* regulations in such industries as air transportation, trucking, telecommunications, banking, and the railroads. But for two decades, the tide of *social* regulations rose higher and higher.

Figure 7-6 shows just how extensive the growth of social regulation was during the period of greatest growth, from 1962 to 1982. More than fifty major regulatory laws were enacted by Congress, each one imposing some type of limitation on the behavior of business. The focus of these laws reflects the major political issues of the times: consumer protection, pollution control, discrimination, worker safety and health, financial security, energy conservation, and political contributions. As Congress defines new problem areas and responds to the public call for action (e.g., cleanup of toxic waste sites), specific regulatory systems are developed to deal with the problems (e.g., the Toxic Substances Control Act).

Between 1962 and 1974, nine new regulatory agencies were created, including such major ones as the Equal Employment Opportunity Commission, the Environmental Protection Agency, the Occupational Safety and Health Administration, and the Consumer Product Safety Commission. One study

---

[7]For a discussion of additional factors that contribute to government growth, see E. S. Savas, *Privatizing the Public Sector: How to Shrink Government*, Chatham, NJ: Chatham House, 1982. Savas emphasizes such matters as the vested interests of politicians, government employees, and government agencies in advocating an expansion of government to safeguard and justify their jobs; see especially chap. 2.

Year Passed	Name of Law	Year Passed	Name of Law
1962	Food and Drug Amendments	1972	Federal Water Pollution Control Act
1962	Air Pollution Control Act	1972	Noise Pollution and Control Act
1963	Equal Pay Act	1972	Equal Employment Opportunity Act
1964	Civil Rights Act	1973	Emergency Petroleum Allocation Act
1965	Water Quality Act	1973	Vocational Rehabilitation Act
1965	Cigarette Labeling and Advertising Act	1973	Highway Speed Limit Reduction
1966	Fair Packaging and Labeling Act	1974	Safe Drinking Water Act
1966	Child Protection Act (toys)	1974	Campaign Finance Amendments
1966	Traffic Safety Act	1974	Federal Energy Administration Act
1966	Coal Mine Safety Amendments	1974	Employee Retirement Income Security Act
1967	Flammable Fabrics Act		
1967	Wholesome Meat Act	1974	Hazardous Materials Transportation Act
1967	Age Discrimination in Employment Act	1974	Magnuson-Moss Warranty Improvement Act
1968	Consumer Credit Protection Act (Truth-in-Lending)	1975	Energy Policy and Conservation Act
		1976	Hatt-Scott-Rodino Antitrust Amendments
1968	Interstate Land Sales Full Disclosure Act	1976	Toxic Substances Control Act
1968	Wholesome Poultry Products Act	1977	Department of Energy Organization Act
1968	Radiation Control for Health and Safety Act	1977	Surface Mining Control and Reclamation Act
		1977	Fair Labor Standards Amendments
1969	National Environmental Policy Act	1977	Export Administration Act
1970	Public Health Smoking Act	1977	Business Payments Abroad Act
1970	Amendments to Federal Deposit Insurance Act	1977	Saccharin Study and Labeling Act
		1978	Fair Debt Collection Practices Act
1970	Securities Investor Protection Act	1978	Age Discrimination in Employment Act Amendments
1970	Poison Prevention Packaging Act		
1970	Clean Air Act Amendments	1980	Federal Trade Commission Improvements Act
1970	Occupational Safety and Health Act	1980	Comprehensive Environmental Response, Compensation, and Liability Act
1971	Lead-Based Paint Elimination Act		
1971	Federal Boat Safety Act	1981	Cash Discount Act
1972	Consumer Product Safety Act	1982	Energy Emergency Preparedness Act

FIGURE 7-6. Major social legislation enacted during the high tide of social regulation, 1962 to 1982 (*Source: Adapted from Murray L. Weidenbaum,* Business, Government, and the Public, *Englewood Cliffs, NJ: Prentice-Hall, 1986, pp. 24–26.*)

showed that the budgets of federal social regulatory agencies increased 711 percent during the 1970s, while the number of regulators working for those agencies went up 562 percent.[8]

Why Social Regulations Have Grown

Why did our society, beginning in the 1950s, turn to more and more social regulation as a way to solve some of its problems?

Part of the explanation lies in broad social trends that have occurred, not just in our society, but worldwide. First, science and technology have vastly

[8]Ronald J. Penoyer, *Directory of Federal Regulatory Agencies—1982 Update,* St. Louis: Center for the Study of American Business, Washington University, June 1982, pp. 4–5.

complicated our lives, giant institutions have sprung up all around us, relative abundance and material affluence characterize the industrial societies, and population pressures and global warfare have given existing institutions grave problems that at times appear to be insoluble. Second, as the wealthier industrial societies met many of their basic economic needs, social concerns received more attention. Belching smokestacks that once signaled jobs and prosperity became negative symbols of industrial pollution as society shifted its sights from economic problems to social goals.

A third factor was doubt that the free market could handle such problems as pollution cleanup and social justice. Critics began to charge that business was using the environment to dispose of its wastes without regard for public health or aesthetic considerations. Minorities and women believed that equal opportunity depended upon government intervention rather than upon market forces to hire, reward, and promote them. Consumers, led by such champions as Ralph Nader, allowed their frustration and disillusionment with the quality of some purchases to overcome their preference for free market solutions to economic problems, and they demanded regulatory curbs on business. Workers, too, especially those employed in hazardous occupations, spurred organized labor to lobby for a government agency to safeguard employees on the job.

A fourth contributing factor was media spotlights on such events as oil spills, civil rights confrontations, protest marches, coal mine explosions, rare industrial diseases, and poorly designed or unsafe consumer products. These televised events helped convince the general public that free market solutions were inadequate. Fifth, new pluralistic interest groups—representing environmentalists, consumers, women, minorities, older people, the handicapped, and others—sprang up, developed political muscle, and pushed through new regulatory laws. American history contained many precedents to guide these social activists, since farmers, small business, labor, public utilities, banks, and others had relied on government regulation to bail them out of difficulties in earlier times.

All these factors played a part in turning society away from market solutions and toward greater reliance on social regulation by government.

THE COSTS OF GOVERNMENT REGULATION

All social choices, including those made with the aid of government regulation, involve costs as well as benefits. As one of our famous economists has said, "There is no free lunch." Someone eventually has to pay for it. This inevitability of costs can be called the *Rule of Cost*. Simply stated, *the Rule of Cost says that all actions generate costs*. This cost rule applies in all types of socioeconomic systems, whether free enterprise or central state control.

Cost-Benefit Analysis

Since the Rule of Cost cannot be avoided, all societies try to make the benefits they want outrun the costs they must pay. This goal requires (1) well-organized and efficient institutions that can produce a steady stream of benefits at low cost and (2) a reliable method of identifying and measuring benefits and costs.

Cost-benefit analysis is a method of calculating the costs and benefits of a project or activity intended to produce benefits. If the potential costs outweigh the potential benefits, it would make sense not to undertake the project.

> For example, *when a city thinks it should upgrade its health care facilities by building a new hospital and increasing the number of doctors and nurses working there, the expected benefits must be compared with the costs that will be incurred. A cost-benefit analysis identifies all possible benefits and compares them with potential costs. In addition, the benefits and costs of various alternatives are considered, such as expanding the older hospitals in town or sending some patients to hospitals in neighboring towns. Different ways of paying the costs—through raising old taxes, adopting new taxes, issuing bonds, or encouraging a private group to build a hospital—are studied. The goal is to compare the value of all the expected benefits with all the known costs.*

Economic benefits and costs can be measured with greater ease than social benefits and costs. In business, money is the yardstick that measures business success. A cost-benefit analysis in business gives a clear answer to whether benefits do or are expected to exceed costs. A company knows how much it pays its employees, the amounts it pays for materials, and how much interest it is charged by lenders. Revenue from sales also is stated in dollar terms. If the firm's revenues exceed its costs, it makes a "bottom line" profit. This kind of cost-benefit analysis is regularly made by a business before it launches a new product or makes a new investment.

On the other hand, social costs and benefits are more difficult to calculate because many of them cannot be measured in dollar terms alone. Consider the following situation:

> *An urban housing authority decides to build a low-income housing project (a social benefit) by using recreational parkland noted for its picnic areas, lakes, and wooded lanes. The park adjoins a residential area (a social benefit) where luxurious homes are built on large, well-tended lots. Picnickers, boaters, and ecologists object to losing recreational space (a social cost) for housing (a social benefit). Wealthy residents fear traffic congestion and a loss of privacy (social costs) and a decline in property values of their homes (an economic cost).*

How can these conflicting and overlapping social benefits and costs be measured? Surely not in monetary terms alone. What is the "true value" of the relaxation and fun people have when using public parks? How much is neighborhood privacy "worth"? Is improved housing for the poor worth more? Social costs and benefits are indeed difficult to calculate with precision, but continuing public pressure for social improvements leaves no choice but to try to work out better methods for comparing social factors. That is one of the goals of social cost-benefit analysis.[9]

The Cost Problem

An industrial society such as ours can "afford" almost anything, including social regulations, if it is willing to pay the price. We paid the price of defending Western democracy during the Second World War, just as we paid huge sums for being the first nation to put astronauts on the moon. Sometimes, the benefits are worth the costs. At other times, though, a more cautious approach to society's problems may provide a better payoff in the long run. We pay for the benefits of social regulation in the following ways.

Administrative and Compliance Costs

Regulatory costs take several different forms. Most obvious are the direct costs of running the regulatory agencies, including salaries of government employees, office equipment and supplies, utility bills, and other such items. As shown in Figure 7-7, these direct administrative costs at the federal level amounted to $7.1 billion in 1985, most of it going for social regulation. Taking inflation into account, however, these regulatory costs declined 8 percent from 1981 to 1985.

But this is only the tip of the regulation iceberg. It costs money to comply with government's rules. Pollution control machinery must be bought, installed, and maintained in good working order; new hiring and training practices for disadvantaged employees have to be developed; many reports are required by the regulatory agencies, consuming much time and many employee hours. These compliance costs total over $100 billion, about $500 for every person in the United States.

Paperwork

The sheer volume of paperwork involved in regulation is astounding. The documents required to certify a car for one year would make a stack fifteen stories high. One oil company produced 636 miles of computer tape in one year's reports to a federal energy agency. Another oil company building a pipeline from California to Texas had to obtain 700 environmental and construction permits before proceeding and finally abandoned the entire project! And it has been estimated that the federal government must find 4.5 million cubic feet of storage space each year for the 2 billion pieces of paper that flow in from those firms and organizations being regulated. On a smaller scale, but one that emphasizes the problems encountered by small businesses, a Midwestern dairy with only twenty-seven employees had to submit reports to twelve different regulators.

Business efficiency is hampered by paperwork requirements, and long delays sometimes result. Approval of the environmental impact statement

[9]For a clear discussion of cost-benefit analysis, see Thomas A. Klein, *Social Costs and Benefits of Business*, Englewood Cliffs, NJ: Prentice-Hall, 1977.

AREA OF REGULATION		1970	1975	1980	1985	Percent change 1970–1980	Percent change 1981–1985
Social regulation	Budget	$ 473	$ 2,625	$ 4,939	$ 5,936	+944	+10
	Staff	9,707	52,098	66,389	55,912	+584	−12
Economic regulation	Budget	$ 327	$ 577	$ 965	$ 1,243	+195	+15
	Staff	17,954	21,908	24,106	21,595	+ 34	−6
Totals	Budget	$ 800	$ 3,202	$ 5,904	$ 7,179	+638	+11
	Staff	27,661	74,006	90,495	77,507	+227	−11
Total regulatory budget in 1970 dollars		$ 800	$ 2,300	$ 2,988	$ 2,745	+274	−8

FIGURE 7-7. **Expenditures and staffing for federal regulatory activities (fiscal years, millions of dollars, permanent full-time positions).** (_Source: Adapted from various reports of the Center for the Study of American Business, Washington University; Murray Weidenbaum, Business, Government, and the Public, Englewood Cliffs, NJ: Prentice-Hall, 1986, pp. 15–18._)

for construction of the Alaskan oil pipeline consumed five years' time. One West Coast residential builder formerly obtained a zoning approval within ninety days, but now has a specialized group within the company that works for two years in order to get the same kind of building authority.

Higher Prices and Taxes

Businesses and nonprofit organizations can "afford" such cost burdens if they have a way to offset them. But in doing so, they often pass the costs along as higher prices to others. These "hidden taxes" constitute another way the public pays for government regulations.

Taxes, too, are sometimes raised when regulations force cities to build improved water treatment systems, military posts to construct solid-waste-disposal sites, and county governments to upgrade hospitals to care for the aged.

Opportunity Costs

Almost everyone, sometimes with considerable regret, sooner or later faces the question: What could I have done with that money if I hadn't spent it in that particular way? This is the meaning of an _opportunity cost: What opportunity did I forgo by spending money one way rather than another?_

Social regulations cost money, sometimes huge sums. How might society have spent its money if it chose to have fewer social regulations? What are the opportunity costs to society for having extensive social regulations? The answers are almost as numerous as one's imagination permits.

We might have more hospitals, better and safer highways, more urban renewal, an expanded national park system, a rebuilding of deteriorating bridges, more business investment in modernizing industrial plants in order to meet foreign competition, more research on cancer and other life-threatening diseases, deeper space probes, greater aid to the poorer nations of the world, and on and on through a long list of possible ways to budget society's money.

Or if society simply chose not to spend these sums on anything, consumers might enjoy lower prices, stockholders higher dividends, workers more jobs and higher take-home pay, and taxpayers lower tax bills.

Unintended Impacts of Regulations

Some costs of government regulation are partially or totally unforeseen when the regulation is adopted. Perhaps as many as 350 foundries have been forced to close when costly environmental controls were required. In one medium-sized community in Pennsylvania, the town's major industry reduced its work force by several thousand when compelled to install equipment to control air and water pollution. One source estimated that 200,000 American jobs were lost in one year alone because of social regulations.[10]

Quite possibly the most serious impact of government regulation is on the use of capital to modernize and expand the nation's industrial base. About three-quarters of the increase in capital investment in the 1970s went for controls on pollution, health, and safety, and was therefore not available for modernization and expansion. Plant obsolescence is not the only drawback. Industrial productivity also can be lowered; one respected authority thinks that about 25 percent of our annual *increase* in productivity is lost in this way. Both outmoded plants and lowered productivity put American industry at a competitive disadvantage in world trade.

Other links in the chain of unintended consequences of regulation have been suggested. Compliance expenditures tend to favor big business over small business and sometimes create barriers to the entry of new competitors into an industry. This, in turn, might lead to bigger unions. Employee turnover rates have been increased, thus lowering business efficiency, as a result of some affirmative action rulings against seniority systems. In one case, the turnover rate went from 28 to 64 percent. Unemployment also may be raised by well-intentioned regulators. When the legal minimum wage was raised, for example, 320,000 fewer teenagers were hired by businesses that could not afford to pay the higher wages.[11]

Figure 7-8 depicts the "tree of regulation," whose branches reach higher and higher into successive cost realms.

---

[10]Willard C. Butcher, "The Stifling Costs of Regulation," *Business Week*, November 6, 1978, p. 22. The foundry estimate is in Murray Weidenbaum, "The Forgotten Consumer: Hidden Costs of Government Regulation," San Mateo, CA: National Federation of Independent Business, Public Policy Discussion Series, 1977, p. 4.

[11]The turnover figures are from Robert Leone, "The Real Costs of Regulation," *Harvard Business Review*, November/December 1977, p. 64.

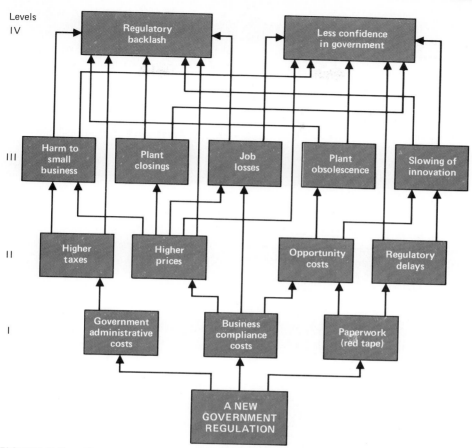

FIGURE 7-8. The tree of regulation, showing four successive levels and types of costs.

Economic and Social Trade-offs

Economic and social trade-offs occur when society discovers that its social goals involve economic costs and that its economic goals incur social costs. Figure 7-9 gives some examples. If we want cleaner and safer electric power plants (a social goal), then the added costs of installing safe, clean generators will increase utility bills (an economic cost). The Rule of Cost is at work as usual because all benefits generate costs. In this case, though, a *social* goal generates an *economic* cost. Society has to decide how much in economic terms it is willing to pay for this desirable social goal. Or in other words, how much cleanliness and safety will it trade away in order to have lower electric bills? Some families may not be concerned enough about safe working conditions or pollution to pay higher prices for electricity; others who live close to the plant or work there may feel differently.

Social Goal		Economic Cost
Clean air and water in a local community	vs.	Jobs lost when a marginal plant closes
Safe, tested drugs	vs.	Slowdown in drug production, marketing, and R&D
Cleaner, safer electric power plants	vs.	Higher home heating and cooling bills
More job opportunities for women and minorities	vs.	Higher training costs for business
Safe noise levels in factories	vs.	Cost of installing noise abatement equipment
Economic Goal		Social Cost
1 billion tons of coal per year	vs.	Increased coal-related deaths
Fast SST trans-Atlantic air travel	vs.	Increased noise and air pollution
Industrial production costs and prices kept low	vs.	More job-related deaths per year

FIGURE 7-9. Economic and social trade-offs.

Even more perplexing examples arise when human life is at stake. Should manufacturers spend their money to save lives, remembering that the added costs will probably be passed along to consumers? The question boils down to a trade-off of economic and social values. Social goals cost money.

The same kind of dilemma occurs when the pursuit of *economic* goals causes *social* costs. Sales of the Concorde supersonic airliner result in economic gain for its builders, create jobs for French and English workers, and make swift trips possible for some people. But these economic goals are achieved at a social cost: high noise levels, air pollution, and much discomfort for those living near airports. Interestingly, in France the trade-off was made in favor of the economic benefits. In the United States, however, the social costs of producing a similar supersonic plane were considered too high for the economic gains, and the trade-offs favored the social side when Congress failed to provide development funds. Politics also played a role in each nation's decision.[12]

There is no single or simple solution to the trade-off problem, because we have no socially acceptable way to equate human lives and social values with monetary values. Money can measure economic costs and benefits, but we have no comparable yardstick for calculating social costs and benefits. Most people have heard the old saying about not being able to compare apples and oranges. The same thing is true about economic and social values.

This raises the question, then, of how societies actually make the trade-off decision. The approach taken by a society will depend very largely on its basic philosophy of life, its values, and the attitude of the general public concerning the desirable balance between social and economic goals. In the United States the trade-off answers are usually reached by working through

[12]Mel Horwitch, *Clipped Wings: The American SST Conflict*, Cambridge, MA: MIT Press, 1982.

the pluralistic system, which allows both social and economic inputs to be made by all interested parties who enjoy the benefits and pay the costs.

DEREGULATION

Government regulation reached a high-water mark in the 1980s. Federal regulatory agencies spent $7.1 billion in 1985. The peak year for employment was 1980, with over 90,000 regulators working for the federal government. During the 1970s agency employees had increased 227 percent and agency budgets had gone up by 638 percent.[13]

After two decades of steady growth in government regulation, the public was ready for a change. Instead of regulation, society demanded deregulation. *Deregulation is the removal or scaling down of regulatory authority and regulatory activities of government.*

For many, President Ronald Reagan symbolized the public's revolt against government regulation, and he promised to "get government off the backs of the people." However, deregulation began even before President Reagan's election. As Figure 7-10 shows, major deregulatory laws were enacted beginning in 1975 when Gerald Ford was President and continuing through the administrations of Jimmy Carter and Ronald Reagan. These laws loosened the grip of the federal government on several industries and markets, in the following ways:

> *In the petroleum industry, all price controls on domestic oil were abolished in 1981. Prices of natural gas were gradually decontrolled, and all controls ended in 1987. A phased deregulation of commercial airlines gradually removed government supervision of rates charged, allowed airlines to enter new routes without government permission, and made mergers and acquisitions easier. The Civil Aeronautics Board, the chief airline regulator, was abolished in 1985.*
>
> *Intercity trucking companies were permitted to charge lower prices and provide wider services, and a greater number of competitors were allowed into the industry. Even among the nation's railroads—which had been tightly regulated for nearly a century—greater competition was encouraged, with some shipping rates completely deregulated. Financial institutions were granted more leeway in setting interest rates on certain types of savings deposits; thrift institutions could establish a type of checking deposit for savers; banks were permitted to pay interest on checking accounts; and the way was paved for interstate banking.*

These legislative reforms were only the first steps in a broad movement to decontrol other parts of the business system. Commercial radio broadcasting was deregulated in early 1981, and Congress relaxed the licensing process for radio and television stations. Steps were planned to promote more competition in the entire telecommunications industry—telephone service,

[13]Murray L. Weidenbaum, "Regulatory Reform: A Report Card for the Reagan Administration," *California Management Review*, Fall 1983, pp. 8–24.

Legislation	Year Enacted
Energy Policy and Conservation Act (Oil decontrol by 1981)	1975
Natural Gas Policy Act (Natural gas decontrol by 1987)	1978
Airline Deregulatory Act (Airline decontrol by 1985)	1978
Motor Carrier Act (Selected trucking decontrol)	1980
Staggers Rail Act (Selected railroad decontrol)	1980
Depository Institutions Deregulatory and Monetary Control Act (Selected banking decontrol)	1980
Garn St. Germain Depository Institutions Act (Creates federally insured money market accounts, allows S&Ls to make more commercial and consumer loans, and removes interest rate differential between banks and S&Ls)	1982
Bus Regulatory Reform Act (Allows intercity bus companies to change routes and fares)	1982
Shipping Act (Permits individual companies to offer lower rates and better service than shipping conference)	1984

FIGURE 7-10. Major deregulatory laws, 1975 to 1984.

electronic information transfer, and local and regional television broadcasting. More reliance on the marketplace and less on government guidance also characterized banking and financial services, health care delivery, workplace safety, and environmental protection. Similar attitudes and policies toward antitrust regulation were developed and are discussed in a later chapter.

Figure 7-11 summarizes some deregulatory techniques available to reduce the size and scope of government regulation. In addition to changing or repealing regulatory laws, staff and budget cuts can be made in the reg-

- Amend or repeal regulatory laws
- Reduce budget and staff of regulatory agencies
- Appoint deregulatory-minded personnel to regulatory agencies
- Impose strict cost–benefit review of proposed and existing government regulations
- Encourage regulated parties to identify burdensome, inefficient regulations
- Adopt "sunset laws"

FIGURE 7-11. Major deregulatory techniques.

ulatory agencies: at the federal level, both were reduced between 1981 and 1985. Some have, in fact, argued that financial cutbacks are the most effective method for effecting regulatory change and reform.

Other deregulation experts have emphasized the importance of another approach: "The opportunity to appoint or designate new agency heads and senior regulatory staff officials is the primary tool for placing the administration's imprint on regulatory policy."[14]

One very effective deregulatory tool was created by President Reagan in Executive Order 12291, issued in early 1981. This directive requires all federal agencies under presidential control (they issue about half of all the rules) to submit proposed new regulations to the Office of Management and Budget for a thorough cost-benefit analysis. Rules whose costs outweigh their benefits are sent back to the agency. A similar regulatory impact analysis must be made for existing rules that might cause an increase in costs or prices, whose overall impact is $100 million or more, or that might be particularly burdensome for some specific industry or the economy in general. The impact of this new system was dramatic: in one year, the number of proposed new rules dropped by 38 percent, the number of final rules approved went down by 27 percent, and the number of pages in the *Federal Register* describing new rules declined by 33 percent.[15]

Still another way to curb overactive regulatory agencies is to impose a congressional veto on any new rules the agency issues. In the summer of 1982, a new Federal Trade Commission rule that would have required dealers to disclose known defects in used cars was reversed by congressional action. However, in mid-1983 the U.S. Supreme Court declared this type of congressional veto to be unconstitutional.[16]

Another interesting type of deregulation is the "sunset law." These laws, first adopted by a number of states in the mid-1970s, provide for a periodic review and sometimes a termination of government agencies unless they can justify their existence. Colorado's 1976 law provided that one-third of its thirty-nine regulatory agencies be reviewed in public hearings every two years. In its first year, four agencies were terminated, two were merged, and another was integrated into another department. The sun had truly set on those agencies. Similar legislation was proposed in Congress but not adopted.

In spite of deregulation's general popularity, by the late 1980s public sentiment tended to support an increasing amount of government regulation in selected areas. These included tougher worker-safety rules, new environmental-protection laws, curbs on insider trading and corporate takeovers,

---

[14]Marvin H. Kosters and Jeffrey A. Eisenach, "Is Regulatory Relief Enough?" *Regulation*, March–April 1982, p. 24.

[15]Ibid., p. 22.

[16]James L. Sundquist, "The Legislative Veto: A Bounced Check," *Brookings Review*, Fall 1983, pp. 13–16. For other reports on deregulation's impact, see "Deregulating America," *Business Week*, November 28, 1983, pp. 80–96; and "Is Deregulation Working?" *Business Week*, December 22, 1986, pp. 50–55.

requirements for airline collision-avoidance equipment, and proposed drug-testing of train engineers, airline pilots, and others.[17]

SUMMARY

Government regulation of business is one way of implementing social choices by modifying the operation of the free market. Some regulations are economic and are applied to specific industries; others are social in purpose and are applied generally to all businesses; still others are called functional regulations because they are attempts to regulate particular business functions such as labor-management relations and providing financial information for investors. Government regulations of all types are based upon a legal foundation of common law and constitutional principles.

Government regulation of business has been an important feature of our socioeconomic system for more than a century. Wars, depressions, and the demands of organized interest groups have been responsible for most increases in regulation, while the general public's preference for a free enterprise system has tended to check the growth of government. Sharp increases in government regulation occurred during the depression decade of the 1930s, the war years of the 1940s, and the years of increasing social demands during the 1960s and 1970s. However, by the mid-1970s and throughout the 1980s, the pendulum swung in the other direction, toward greater reliance on free market solutions to social and economic problems. The future is likely to see a continuation of this seesawing between government regulation and free market approaches, as both business and society seek an optimum solution to major problems along with the preservation of freedoms and social justice.

DISCUSSION AND REVIEW QUESTIONS

1. From current news sources, give one example each of industry-specific economic regulation, all-industry social regulation, and functional regulation. Name the agency responsible for each regulation and show how politics may affect its actions.

2. Choose any one area of social regulation—consumer or environmental protection, or others—and present an argument supporting the use of government regulation in that area of our lives. Then take the other side and show how fewer regulations and more use of the free market might be preferable. Compare the two arguments, and evaluate your preference.

3. Assume that you, as owner of a medium-sized plant manufacturing plastic components, have just read that the federal government is proposing new regulations to protect both workers and consumers from possible health hazards arising out of chemicals used in plastics manufacturing. In writing your

[17]Laurie McGinley, "Hands On: Federal Regulation Rises Anew in Matters That Worry the Public," *Wall Street Journal*, April 21, 1987, pp. 1, 26.

congressional representative to protest, what types of added costs can you identify that may result from imposing this new regulation on your business? What alternative(s) to the new regulation can you propose?

4. If you knew ahead of time that a government-mandated testing program for new drugs would (1) possibly prevent an unknown number of deaths if a particular drug was tested prior to sale, (2) delay treatment by that drug of 100,000 persons, some of whom would die before the testing period was over, (3) indirectly increase the costs of all drugs, and (4) guarantee safer drugs in general, would you favor the government testing program or not? Discuss.

5. This chapter states, "In the United States, economic and social trade-offs are usually handled through the pluralistic system." From Figure 7-9 choose any one set of economic and social trade-offs and explain how the trade-off might be made in a pluralistic society.

6. If you were head of a task force studying ways to lighten the regulatory load on business without jeopardizing social gains made as a result of existing regulations, what three key recommendations would you want to make? Defend your choices.

CRITICAL INCIDENT

Deregulation: Short-Term or Long-Term Hazards?

The trucking industry was deregulated in 1980, increasing not only the number of trucks on the road but also the size of these trucks. By the end of 1986, statistics from across the country were in: accidents, injuries, and fatalities were all up since deregulation. Deregulation brought increased competition and has thus provided incentives for truckers to cut back on maintenance costs, ignore speed laws, and circumvent rules on hours drivers may work without resting. In addition, the larger trucks and twin trailers were almost twice as likely to be involved in accidents than smaller trucks, and three times as likely to be involved in fatal crashes than smaller trucks and passenger cars. Police, safety experts, insurance representatives, and industry officials all expressed concern over increases in safety and traffic violations.

Nationwide, the number of accidents involving interstate trucks rose 23.4 percent in two years, from 31,628 in 1983 to 39,030 in 1985.[18] The number of truck-related fatalities grew 11.3 percent in three years, from 4,065 in 1982 to 4,528 in 1985. And reported injuries rose from 25,779 in 1982 to 29,149 in 1984. Figures for individual states were equally disturbing.

Several reasons were cited for the increases in violations, accidents, and injuries. In 1986, nineteen states allowed drivers holding commercial licenses to operate the largest tractor-trailers without specialized training or road tests; most of these states did not even require a demonstration of ability. Not surprisingly, 85 percent of all truck drivers involved in accidents had never received any formal training as commercial drivers. To combat this problem, Congress passed legis-

[18]Statistics quoted on truck safety are drawn from William E. Schmidt, "Sharp Rise in Truck Crashes Prompts Action Across U.S.," *New York Times*, December 7, 1986, pp. 1, 45.

lation in October 1986 which set national licensing standards for commercial truck and bus drivers and mandated state driving tests; any state not testing its drivers risks losing federal highway funds.

Another factor contributing to increases in accidents was the ability of drivers to hold licenses issued by many different states. This allowed truck drivers to commit numerous violations without losing driving rights; by presenting a different license each time they are stopped, drivers avoid accumulating a significant number of violations in any one state, thus preventing suspension of driving privileges. Congressional testimony indicated that 30 percent of all drivers hold multiple licenses, and a National Transportation Safety Board study of 44 accidents showed that the 44 drivers held 63 licenses among them, had 98 license suspensions, were involved in 104 previous accidents, and held 456 traffic citations. The new legislation addresses this problem, by levying a civil penalty of $2,500 against any bus or truck driver found holding more than one license.

A final problem addressed by this legislation is lax maintenance standards. In Maryland, random inspections of 18,000 trucks in the first half of 1986 revealed that almost 75 percent of them had safety violations serious enough to have them taken off the road. The legislation would double, by 1989, the federal financial grants to states to increase roadside safety inspections for large trucks. In addition, because over 40 percent of big truck accidents were caused either directly or indirectly by driver fatigue, regulations limit drivers to ten hours of driving at a stretch, following eight consecutive hours of rest.

On the basis of the above statistics, one could conclude that deregulation seems to have a price in terms of safety. However, the figures may be misleading, and all the facts are not in. The airline industry, for example, was deregulated in the late 1970s. The year 1985 was a record year for airplane crashes and fatalities—almost 1,000 lives were lost. In 1986, however, large- and medium-sized passenger planes operated by United States airlines were not involved in a single fatal crash (a McDonnell Douglas DC-9 involved in a midair collision over Los Angeles cost the lives of 82 people, but the plane was operated by a foreign carrier, Aeromexico).[19] The fatal accident rate for smaller airlines was the lowest on record. The trade-offs involved in deregulation are difficult to predict or define: Will increased competition result in increased efficiency and lowered prices, or merely increased safety hazards?

1. In your opinion, is deregulation the cause of the worsening traffic safety record in the trucking industry? Give your conclusion along with the arguments pro and con.

2. Since the safety record in the airline industry actually improved in 1986 during deregulation, is it possible that other factors are the true causes of safety problems in industries such as trucking and air transport?

3. Consider a "market" or incentives approach to trucking safety. Is there a way to design incentives for improved safety that would overcome some of the temptations to lower safety standards?

[19]Richard Witkin, "Safety Record of U.S. Airlines Shows Big Gain," *New York Times*, January 13, 1987, p. A-1.

Chapter Eight

BUSINESS, PUBLIC POLICY, AND POLITICS

Business has many reasons for being active in the public policy arena and for taking a position or action on social issues. Government decisions shape the business environment in important ways and are the expression of a nation's public policies. This chapter defines the relationships between business, public policy, and politics and describes the dynamics of business and government interaction.

CHAPTER OBJECTIVES

After reading this chapter you should be able to

- Define public policy

- Outline the stages in the public policy process

- Describe why it is important for business to be involved in public policy decision making

- Understand how public policy can provide guidance to companies in meeting their social responsibilities

- Describe the relationship between business and politics, and discuss various mechanisms of political influence

*T*he relationship between business decision making and political decision making often is very complicated. Business decisions affect politics; political decisions affect business. This relationship is shown in the events surrounding product liability insurance during the mid-1980s:

> *The following scenario, according to many people in the insurance industry, is all too common: a car full of people who have been drinking careens at 10, 20, or 30 miles per hour above the posted speed limit into a utility pole. One or more of the passengers dies. The others are badly injured. Despite the fact that the driver was operating under the influence of alcohol and violating the speed limit, lawyers for the relatives of the deceased passengers still sue the town responsible for maintaining the roads on which the accident occurred, the liquor store at which the passengers purchased the alcohol, and even the company that owned the utility pole. Frequently they win.*
>
> *Under the legal rule of "joint and several liability," each of the defendants in such a suit could be forced to pay the entire claim, even if they were only 1 percent responsible for the accident. The problem is compounded by what might be called the "deep pocket" rule of jury awards in liability cases. When determining amounts to be received by people injured by products that are alleged to be unsafe or poorly manufactured, juries often award over $1 million. The combination of these two trends—assigning responsibility to any involved party capable of paying and awarding large sums to injured parties—has finally forced companies to join forces and fight back.*

Although there are those who would dispute the claim that liability suits and awards are far too many and too high, respectively, the trend has nonetheless generated a great deal of lobbying on Capitol Hill.[1] Insurance companies claimed that, given caps on liability awards, they could lower rates and provide more coverage. Thus, they exerted pressure on federal legislators to enact a federal policy limiting the size of awards.

Some observers think that insurers and manufacturers will continue to face an uphill battle in their campaign for federal product liability legislation.[2] A measure limiting noneconomic damage awards to $250,000 passed the Senate Commerce Committee in 1986, but the bill did not pass in the full Senate. The House of Representatives also failed to pass comparable legislation.[3]

This liability dilemma and the efforts of companies to petition Congress for action show that a key feature of American business life is political decision making. Issues that are complex and difficult to define and those that affect many citizens and interests are often brought to the political arena for resolution. Politics is the lifeblood of a democracy, and it has become a critical part of the interaction between business and society.

[1]William B. Glaberson and Christopher Farrell, "The Explosion in Liability Lawsuits Is Nothing but a Myth," *Business Week*, April 21, 1986, pp. 24, 25; and Joan O'C. Hamilton, Daniel B. Moskowitz and William B. Glaberson, "Liability: Business Dives for Cover," *Business Week*, February 10, 1986, p. 31.

[2]David B. Hilder, "Tort Wars: Insurers' Push to Limit Civil Damage Awards Begins to Slow Down," *Wall Street Journal*, August 1, 1986, p. 18.

[3]Ibid., p. 1.

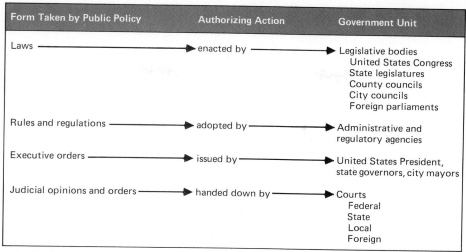

FIGURE 8-1. Major forms of public policy, authorizing action, and responsible units of government.

BUSINESS AND PUBLIC POLICY

A public policy is a plan of action undertaken by government to achieve some broad purpose affecting a large segment of the citizenry. Certainly, if federal legislation were enacted that changed liability policies or that capped awards, a large percentage of the population would be affected. Not only would the injured people face a different situation in court, but anyone seeking insurance would find the entire rate structure changed—one hopes, for the better.

> *There are many examples of broad public policies enacted by various administrations over the years. During the OPEC oil embargo, when fuel prices were skyrocketing, President Nixon imposed wage and price controls. In the mid-1970s, Gerald Ford implemented a program called Whip Inflation Now (WIN), in an attempt to stabilize the economy. During his term, President Carter imposed a grain embargo on Russia for its invasion of Afghanistan. Carter also advocated a national energy policy when the Shah of Iran was deposed and oil prices again soared.*

A public policy involves two indispensable elements: (1) action by government and (2) a goal or purpose that has an impact on the public at large.[4] In the United States, public policy takes the different forms shown in Figure 8-1. All three branches of the federal government are active in making public policy, along with state, local, and foreign governments.

[4]For a general discussion of public policy concepts, see B. Guy Peters, *American Public Policy*, 2d ed., Chatham, NJ: Chatham House, 1986; and James Q. Wilson, *American Government: Institutions and Policies*, 2d ed., Lexington, MA: D. C. Heath, 1983.

Private business firms must operate within the complex web of public policies formed by these many levels and organs of government. Doing so requires a great deal of skill and patience, and—above all—an intricate knowledge of how public policy is formed, where it comes from, and how business can be involved.

The Public Policy Process

The actual development of a new public policy—for example, one concerning a broad tax reform—is usually complex. The reason is simple: the United States is a pluralistic society, with many interest groups ready and eager to protect their own welfare, and these groups are part of a system of representative government.[5] Therefore, when a new public policy is suggested or initiated by one group in society, other groups will want to know how it will affect them.

> For example, *there was much concern over the potential effects of the Reagan administration's 1986 tax-reform plan. Two major concerns were whether individuals would be paying more or less, and how much corporations would be paying. Of course, there were varying evaluations. According to Lawrence Chimerine, president of Chase Econometrics, "If the President's tax-reform program is adopted, it would have a depressing effect on the economy and heighten the chances of a recession (in 1986)." The Administration claimed that tax reform would not hurt the economy in the short run and that capital investment would not suffer. As economist Robert Eisner put it, "No one nor any model can say that the effect of tax reform on balance, even in the short run, will be negative." Further, a Treasury Department report stated that "the effect of the proposals would be to cause real GNP to be at least 1.5% higher by 1995 than it would be under current law."[6]*

The debate about a new public policy cannot be resolved until the policy has been implemented. But questions about policy always have to be considered and debated in advance by lawmakers who try to respond to the voters who elected them to office, as well as to the many interest groups who have a stake in the proposed new public policy. Figure 8-2 summarizes the major stages or steps in this complex public policy process, and each of these will be discussed briefly.

Agenda Building

The public policy agenda consists of those major issues or problems to which officials give serious attention and upon which they feel compelled to act. Not all public issues or problems get enough attention or support to become agenda items. There are many *inputs* into the political system. Each year, people ask gov-

[5]Jeffrey M. Berry, *The Interest Group Society,* Boston: Little, Brown, 1984.

[6]Edward Mervosh, with G. David Wallace, "What Tax Reform Really Means," *Business Week,* June 17, 1985, p. 128.

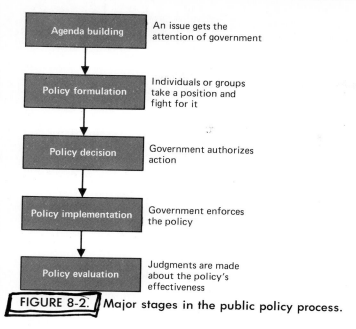

Agenda building	An issue gets the attention of government
Policy formulation	Individuals or groups take a position and fight for it
Policy decision	Government authorizes action
Policy implementation	Government enforces the policy
Policy evaluation	Judgments are made about the policy's effectiveness

FIGURE 8-2. Major stages in the public policy process.

ernment to respond to thousands of issues and problems. But response to each one is not possible. In other words, many issues do not have a chance of being converted from public concern into public policies, as the following examples illustrate:

> *Auto safety did not become a major public issue worthy of much congressional attention until the 1960s, when Ralph Nader, who was then an unknown lawyer, charged General Motors with manufacturing a car that was "unsafe at any speed."[7] Auto fatalities in the mid-1960s totaled nearly 50,000 annually, were the sixth leading cause of death in the United States, and had been climbing steadily for two decades. Although an obvious public safety problem had existed long before Nader made his charges, the highway death toll had not resulted in new public policies to reduce auto deaths by making cars safer. Not all vehicle accidents were the result of unsafe cars, but some were, and Nader's book convinced many people, both in and out of government, that government should do something to make motor vehicles safer. Twenty years later, in the mid-1980s, many states have adopted mandatory seatbelt laws as one further step toward increasing automobile safety and reducing fatalities. This action places attention on the person as well as the vehicle.*

What does it take to put a problem on the public policy agenda for action by government? As Figure 8-3 shows, several factors may be involved.[8]

[7]Ralph Nader, *Unsafe at any Speed*, New York: Grossman, 1965.

[8]For a classic discussion of agenda building, see Roger W. Cobb and Charles D. Elder, *Participation in American Politics: The Dynamics of Agenda-Building*, Boston: Allyn & Bacon, 1972; and James E. Anderson, *Public Policy-Making*, New York: Praeger, 1975, pp. 59–65.

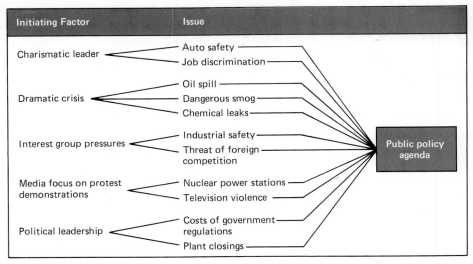

Initiating Factor	Issue
Charismatic leader	Auto safety
	Job discrimination
Dramatic crisis	Oil spill
	Dangerous smog
	Chemical leaks
Interest group pressures	Industrial safety
	Threat of foreign competition
Media focus on protest demonstrations	Nuclear power stations
	Television violence
Political leadership	Costs of government regulations
	Plant closings

Public policy agenda

FIGURE 8-3. How issues get onto the public policy agenda.

A charismatic leader like Ralph Nader or Jesse Jackson may capture enough public attention to lead a reform movement. Or in the case of environmental pollution, a dramatic crisis or even tragedy may galvanize public opinion. This occurred in Woburn, Massachusetts, in the mid-1980s, when several children contracted leukemia that was associated with local drinking water allegedly contaminated by W. R. Grace Company. In September 1986, the parents of the children settled out of court with the company. The town of Woburn then decided to sue the company because several of its wells had been contaminated and had to be closed down and water supplies had to be rerouted. In November, a referendum question on the state ballot asked voters whether or not they favored a mandatory toxic waste cleanup. The vote was overwhelmingly in favor of the proposal.[9]

The actions of an interest group also may put an issue on the public policy agenda, as the group swings into action to protect its members by advocating greater government participation. This occurred in the late 1960s when labor unions began agitating for stiffer safety regulations for industrial workers and miners. It happened again in the 1970s and 1980s when a coalition of manufacturers and labor unions advocated import controls on steel products and foreign-made cars to protect their jobs and profits.

Other initiating factors are organized protest activities and demonstrations. When featured prominently on television and in the press, they can raise an issue or problem from obscurity to national attention. Influential political leaders, from the President to senators, governors, and mayors, may pinpoint an area of public concern that has not received much attention. In doing so, they may build support for their own reelection by promising to promote a new public policy to correct the problem.

[9]Andrew J. Dabilis, "Focusing on Referendums: Ballot Questions May Spark More Voter Interest than the Races," *Boston Globe*, November 3, 1986, pp. 1, 6.

In these many ways, an agenda or list of public problems is developed, and the public policy process has begun.

It is extremely important for business to be aware of what is happening at this early stage. At first General Motors executives did not believe that Ralph Nader was very important. They did not realize that he would later arouse the attention and support of the car-buying public and influential politicians, thus increasing greatly the number of regulations imposed on auto manufacturers. Socially aware and politically alert corporations are constantly scanning the social and political environments for developments that might bring new issues onto the public policy agenda for discussion and possible government action. Of course, business itself often wants to promote its own interests by proposing new laws or advocating repeal of old ones, thereby adding items to the public policy agenda.

Policy Formulation

Getting an issue on the agenda is no guarantee that a new public policy will be developed. Before that can happen, there has to be general agreement that government action is appropriate. If that consensus cannot be achieved, the issue may die. *Business Week* reported in August 1985, for example, that several items on that year's public policy agenda were indefinitely stalled:[10]

- *Farm Programs.* The continuing recession in the farm belt was plowing under the President's hopes of drastically reducing subsidies. Only modest cutbacks would be approved.
- *Banking.* Despite concern over the wave of bank and savings and loan failures, Congress was unable to agree on changes in deposit-guarantee laws. Proposed measures would tie the insurance premiums that banks and S&Ls pay to the risk they represent.
- *Immigration.* The four-year fight for a major overhaul of immigration laws dragged on into 1986. The key stumbling blocks were what penalties to impose on businesses that hire illegal aliens and whether to legalize the status of illegal aliens already in the country.

Policy formulation occurs when interested groups take a position on some public issue and try to persuade others to adopt their viewpoint as public policy. If consensus among the participating groups can be reached, the proposed public policy moves toward the decision stage. If consensus cannot be reached, the issue may drop off the public policy agenda, or another similar effort may be made in the future to convert the agenda item into a public policy. In the cases above, the interest groups involved developed positions and fought for them but were unable to reach consensus on a government goal.

Business's stake in policy formulation is high. Lawmakers often seek the support of the business community for the policies they are trying to push through Congress, as President Reagan did in actively promoting his 1981 tax-cut policy and his 1986 tax-reform policy. The administration spent con-

[10]Ronald Grover et al., "Caught in the Crossfire," *Business Week*, August 12, 1985, p. 19.

siderable time and effort trying to enlist the support of business leaders and organizations representing business interests. Similarly, business looks to government leaders for public policies that will help businesses, as the savings and loan industry did when high interest rates and economic recession in the early 1980s threatened their stability and their survival. In both of these ways, business can and often does participate actively in helping to formulate public policy.

Policy Decision

A policy decision occurs when government actually authorizes, or fails to authorize, a course of action.

> For example, *a city council, may authorize a new bond issue to pay for building a convention center or a stadium for professional sports. Or the President may issue an executive order forbidding trade with another country. The courts—another branch of government—may hand down a decision that becomes a precedent for paying claims to victims of airline disasters.*

When these steps are taken, the government is putting into effect a new public policy or reaffirming an existing one. The policy decision occurs when a law is passed, when a regulation is adopted, when an executive order is issued, or when a court opinion is announced. The center column in Figure 8-1 illustrates types of policy decisions. Failing to act also can be a form of policy decision. If, after much debate, Congress or a city council turns down or defeats a proposed new law, it has made a policy decision.

Business normally has no *direct* role to play in policy decisions since, by definition, all the decisions are made by government officials. The influence of business and all other interest groups is felt both before and after the decision itself through lobbying and other techniques.

Passing a law, issuing a judicial opinion, or adopting a new government regulation—in other words, making a public policy decision—does not automatically mean that the public policy will be carried out. Unless someone takes steps to operationalize the decision, nothing at all may happen. This may even occur at the very highest levels of government. President Harry S. Truman was supposed to have once said: "I sit here and issue orders that things be done, and then I don't have any idea what happens to my suggestions." Congress frequently enacts laws that require government agencies to set standards or take other actions to achieve the goals that members of Congress had in mind when the policy decision was made. This requirement leads to policy implementation, the next phase in the public policy process.

Policy Implementation

Policy implementation occurs when action is taken to enforce a public policy decision.

> *When a new tax law is passed by Congress, the Internal Revenue Service sends out notices to taxpayers explaining the new law and then tries to collect what is*

owed to the government. When a President forbids trading with another nation for national security reasons, he may penalize any company that continues to do business there, thus sending a message to other companies that he is prepared to enforce the new policy.

Government regulatory agencies frequently have much leeway in implementing policies adopted by Congress. For example, the Mine Safety and Health Administration (MSHA) can decide how many mines it will inspect for safety violations, how frequently it will inspect, how carefully its inspectors will enforce the agency's rules on safety, whether fines will be levied, and how much those fines will be. Its ability to implement Congress's intentions will depend also on the size of its budget and the number of inspectors it can afford to hire. A President who is especially interested in mine safety can appoint a director of MSHA who will have a tough inspection policy and who will fight hard in Congress for large appropriations to support the agency.

At this stage, does business have a chance to influence public policy? Once a law is passed or a court decision handed down, it might seem that business would be powerless. Actually, though, business can wield significant influence in the implementation of public policy.

A company can negotiate with a regulatory agency for extending compliance deadlines, as steel companies have done concerning pollution and automakers concerning fuel economy standards. Legal steps can be taken by appealing an agency's actions to an appeals court. Or an industry may play off one branch of government against another; for example, an aggressive Presidential policy on switching industrial users of natural gas to coal may be checked by appeal to a more cautious congressional attitude.

Business has greatly improved its understanding of and participation in the formulation of public policy, especially as it moves through the executive and legislative branches at different levels of government. This understanding of how the political process works can be most beneficial to management. Rather than just reacting to laws and regulations, business can be an effective participant in implementing public policies.[11]

Policy Evaluation

The final stage of public policy may be the most important of all. *Policy evaluation occurs when the results of a public policy are judged by those who have an interest in the outcome.* Groups who initially were opposed to a policy may take an "I told you so" attitude and try to prove that it has been a bad one from beginning to end. Its supporters, on the other hand, may try to see mainly its good points and ignore the bad ones. Public policy evaluation has

[11]Alfred A. Marcus, *The Adversary Economy: Business Responses to Changing Government Requirements*, Westport, CT: Quorum Books, 1984. See also Dan H. Fenn, Jr., "Finding Where the Power Lies in Government," *Harvard Business Review*, September–October 1979, pp. 144–153.

become a big business as experts have tried to develop objective ways to measure the impacts and outcomes of various public programs.[12]

Basically, policy evaluators try to find out whether the benefits have been worth the costs incurred, and whether the same goals could have been achieved in another, more-efficient, less-expensive way. This kind of evaluation is tricky. Costs and benefits are difficult to measure, and some government agencies are reluctant to release cost data that may make the agency look bad. Also, the cause-and-effect relationships are not always clear; for example, if the economy recovers from a recession after a tax cut is enacted by Congress, did the tax cut cause the recovery or would conditions have improved anyway? It is often difficult to know the answer.

Business uses several approaches to public policy evaluation. Some companies, particularly those with public affairs or government relations departments, make their own studies of how public policies affect the company. Dow Chemical Company, for example, reported that in one year it spent $147 million complying with government regulations, including $5 million alone on the salaries and other expenses of its executives who testified on federal regulations. In other industries, a trade association such as the National Association of Manufacturers or the United States Chamber of Commerce evaluates the impact of various government programs on business costs, profits, investments, and foreign competition. Business also supports the Committee for Economic Development which issues pro-business reports either critical or in praise of various government programs and policies. Additionally, the prestigious Business Roundtable, composed of the top executives of 200 large corporations, occasionally meets directly with high-level government officials as a way of expressing the business community's view on the effectiveness of various public policies.

Policy evaluation, though the last stage in the public policy process, may actually put the whole process in motion again. Very few public policy programs are noncontroversial. A tax reduction or a drug-control law may not accomplish its intended purpose. Therefore, its evaluation may lead to changes in direction, new programs, or, in a few cases, elimination of old programs. These changes may signal the arrival of another public problem or issue that then is put on the agenda for discussion and debate, as the entire process begins anew.

In this discussion, we have divided the public policy process into its five main stages as a way of clarifying a very complicated set of activities. In actual operation, these stages often overlap and interweave with one another, creating a very complex web of government policies, programs, laws, regulations, court orders, and political maneuvers.

At any one time, something is happening in all five stages on a wide range of issues. For business or for any other interest group this means that

---

[12]For further information see Carol H. Weiss, *Using Social Research for Public Policy-Making*, Lexington, MA: Lexington, 1977; Clark C. Abt (ed.), *Evaluation of Social Programs*, Beverly Hills, CA: Sage, 1977; and Public Management Institute Staff, *Evaluation Handbook*, San Francisco: Public Management, 1980.

public policy is a constant feature of society, always present in all its stages as part of the social environment in which business operates. Knowing how to participate in that process is vital to the prosperity, survival, and vitality of business.

BUSINESS AND PUBLIC DECISIONS

Business has three primary reasons for being active in the public policy arena.

One reason stands above all others: Governments at all levels and in all regions of the world are large, powerful, and growing in size and scope of operations. The policies of these governments affect business in many ways, some good and some bad. Businesses advise government leaders on which policies they think are best, simply to defend their own interests. As one former government official remarked, "The absence of effective leadership for the business community on many public policy questions . . . means that business enterprises forfeit almost entirely to politicians."[13]

A second reason is almost equally important: There is always ongoing discussion and debate about how economic activities should be organized. The citizens of many nations now expect government to take care of needs once met through private action. Examples of these include unemployment pay for the jobless, food stamps for the destitute, financial bailouts for failing businesses, government-guaranteed pension programs for retirees, price and marketing controls for farmers, and import controls on foreign competitors. On the other hand, other interests also strive to reduce the influence and control that government has on their daily lives or business activities.

Getting "excessive government off the back of business" was one of the key components of the Reagan agenda in the 1980s; during the decade ending in 1986, many industries were deregulated. Communications, airlines, and financial services were some of the largest. And as President Reagan urged, several regulatory agencies and functions of the government also were trimmed back. The Council on Wage and Price Control was completely eliminated. Although the budgets for the fifty-five major regulatory agencies rose 1 percent between 1980 and 1984, the number of federal employees directly engaged in regulatory activities dropped from over 90,000 in 1980 to 77,500, and only five agencies increased their staffs, one stayed at the same level, and forty-nine experienced payroll cuts.

Much of the momentum for deregulation came from lobbying efforts of business; thus, a third reason for public activism is that many business goals can be promoted by keeping an eye on government and trying to shape its policies. The public policy arena is a constant tug of war. Business is always striving to further its interests, while the public is striving to protect its own, and the government is mediating on the part of both. From business's viewpoint, workable pro-business public policies might be to the betterment of

[13]John T. Dunlop, "Business and Public Policy: The Concerns," _Harvard Business Review_, November–December 1979, p. 86.

both business and society. Supporting this viewpoint is the comment of one business leader: "It is, of course, partly self-serving to look for ways to work better with government. Business leaders do that to make their companies run better and thereby make more profit. The corollary purpose, though, is to help the government work better and thereby make for a better society."[14]

PUBLIC POLICY AND CORPORATE SOCIAL RESPONSIBILITY

Well-defined public policies have another important advantage for those business firms that wish to be socially responsible. The critics of corporate social responsibility frequently say that the meaning of "social responsibility" is so vague that even a well-meaning company might have trouble understanding what it should do to be considered responsible. Others have said that business responsibility is a hit-or-miss proposition: The company whose CEO possesses a social conscience may be socially responsible, but what happens if the CEO is not interested in social problems? The bottom line of these criticisms is that corporate social responsibility is a philosophical ideal but not an operational reality. Consider the following example:

> *In 1975, in the wake of the early 1970s energy crisis, the federal government passed the Corporate Average Fuel Economy (CAFE) standards, which were designed to raise the average miles per gallon (mpg) of new cars from 14.2 in 1973 to 27.5 by 1986. The legislation allowed automakers to petition the government to reduce this standard to 26 mpg if reaching the standard was determined to be not "economically practicable." (While the difference of 1.5 mpg may seem insignificant, it can only be achieved at great expense; the average mpg has already doubled, and available technological improvements have dwindled). In September 1985 and again in January 1986, General Motors and Ford Motor Company petitioned the government to hold the standard to 26 mpg for 1986 and 1987 models, respectively. The standard was held the first time and proposed to be held the second time. Meanwhile, Chrysler Corporation was lobbying to have the standard increased to 27.5 mpg, claiming that holding the standard down allows Ford and GM to escape paying $500 million in fines at the expense of the federal deficit (thus, the economy), the consumer, the environment, and Chrysler. Opponents argued that Chrysler's motives were not at all altruistic; rather, because Chrysler already had spent the money to reach the standards, and sells mostly small cars anyway, an increase to 27.5 would cost their competitors millions, would earn Chrysler millions, and would even allow them to redevelop a large-car segment.*

Thus, definitions of "socially responsible behavior" are not clear-cut. The topic is often controversial. Companies striving to be socially responsible may need practical guidance in two areas: (1) What social goals should be pur-

---

[14]Irving S. Shapiro, "Business and Public Policy: The Process," *Harvard Business Review*, November–December 1979, p. 101.

sued? and (2) How far should a company go in its social behavior? The answers to these questions often can be found in public policy, and they provide business with valuable guidance about how to be socially responsible.[15]

As the example shows, public policy, and not the CEO alone, should help define "social responsibility" and the social goals that business should pursue. By setting up standards of social behavior, public policy also helps a company know when its activities are socially acceptable.

This public policy approach to social responsibility does not rule out any significant involvement of business in deciding whether to be responsible or not. Social directives evolve through the public policy process, and business can be very influential in determining both social goals and social performance standards if it becomes an active participant in the public policy process. Automobile manufacturers had much to say about the laws and performance standards eventually imposed on their industries. By participating early and often, business can shape public policies—and therefore corporate social responsibility—in important ways.[16]

BUSINESS AND POLITICAL SYSTEMS

Beyond participation in the resolution of specific political issues, business also can play a role in the life of the larger political system, as discussed in Chapter 6. _Politics is the means through which society makes decisions about who governs and to what ends,_[17] that is, who shall have power to make important decisions (who governs), and for what purposes and in what ways will that power be used (toward what ends). It is clear that business has a stake in the outcome of discussions of whether free enterprise, central state control, or mixed state-and-private enterprise shall prevail.

There has been a long and still unresolved debate about how politics and public policy interrelate. Marxists believe that those who control the economic system also will control the political system. Pluralists, on the other hand, think that many different interests compete for influence in the political system. Other people believe that the bureaucracy of government itself dominates the political system, and that all interests are secondary in importance to civil servants and the institutions of government. A fourth view holds that a social elite, including business leaders and others, will make key decisions without much regard to popular wishes.

It is a debate to which there is no clear answer. Individual issues often produce contradictory evidence that seems to favor one or another of these

[15]The point of view is expressed in Lee E. Preston and James E. Post, _Private Management and Public Policy: The Principle of Public Responsibility,_ Englewood Cliffs, NJ: Prentice-Hall, 1975, especially chap. 7. See also Rogene A. Buchholz, _Business Environment and Public Policy: Implications for Management,_ Englewood Cliffs, NJ: Prentice-Hall, 1982, chap. 20.

[16]Robert H. Miles, _Managing the Corporate Social Environment,_ Englewood Cliffs, NJ: Prentice-Hall, 1987.

[17]Wilson, op. cit., chap. 1.

viewpoints. The United States at the end of the 1980s remains a mostly pluralist political system. Interest groups abound, and they have an important influence on political life. Because there are so many different interests in modern America, coalitions have to be formed to advance certain ideas, specific legislation, or regulations. According to some experts, all areas of modern American political life—including legislation, regulation, and executive policy action—reflect coalition politics, which means that no interest is ever powerful enough, by itself, to determine how an issue should be resolved. It must collaborate with others.

Political parties are a vital ingredient of a pluralistic society. They represent "grand coalitions" of individuals and various interest groups who wish to promote their own welfare through political action. Although political parties are not mentioned in the United States Constitution, they nevertheless are an important part of the system of representative government. Not only do they make the electoral process possible by providing a means for nominating and supporting candidates for public office; they also serve as a rallying point for the expression of political philosophies, a way for individuals and groups to identify and work with others who hold similar ideas of how to run the government.

Business and Politics

Business and politics are different, and these differences need to be well understood if business is to be an effective participant in the public policy process. Three of the most important differences are the following:

- The primary goal of business is to produce goods and services for profit. The primary goal of politics is to allocate power among various groups in society. The politician strives to acquire the power of a public office and to hold it as long as possible. Votes and the influence of powerful allies are the lifeblood of a politician. Without these, the politician is as powerless as a business firm without profits.
- Ideally, business decisions are made by applying rational, objective, carefully calculated standards. Ideally, a new product will not be brought out nor will a capital investment be made unless business experts have considered all aspects and repercussions of such an action with great care and precision. Political decisions, on the other hand, often are made on economically irrational, emotional grounds, where hard-to-measure social and philosophical factors are involved. A city government (Detroit, for example, in the Poletown case discussed in Chapter 2), may put great pressure on a company (General Motors) to keep a plant open in order to preserve local jobs (and the votes that go with those jobs) although good business reasoning would dictate that the plant ought to be moved to another locality.
- The *primary* stakeholders in business are few in number and easy to identify: stockholders, employees, customers, and (with large corporations) financial analysts on Wall Street. The important stakeholders in politics are much larger in number and more diverse, and they place an astonishing

array of demands at the politician's doorstep. The politician has more con-
stituents to satisfy than does the business executive of even the largest
corporation. Satisfying stakeholders in politics is generally "messier" and
less precise, and it involves more contradictions and inconsistencies than
in business.

These differences between business and politics create real difficulties
and frustrations when business people enter the world of politics. One experienced government official put it this way:

> [Government administrators and business executives] have different back-
> grounds, approach issues with different time horizons, see the press and other
> media in quite different roles, and they have quite different institutional objec-
> tives and—at times—different personal values.
> Furthermore, each group sees the role of the law in society in substantially
> different ways—government, to change; business, largely to preserve. The busi-
> nessman's perspective often tends to be international, while the government
> administrator's is much more narrowly national. The two groups are also sepa-
> rated often by a gap in age and experience.
> In short, it is little wonder that business executives and government officials
> do not find it easy to communicate with one another, let alone agree about
> difficult substantive issues and values.[18]

Having observed this gap between the world of business and the world
of politics, and perhaps having suffered a bad experience at the hands of
government, some people in the business community maintain that business
should stay out of politics. Such a point of view is gradually disappearing.
Many business leaders now recognize that business survival is dependent
on political activism.

The Case for and against Political Involvement by Business

Those people who argue that business should be an active political participant
cite four main justifications shown in Figure 8-4.

- A representative political system gives business the right to express its
  views, just as other interest groups in society do. A workable pluralistic
  society depends on active participation of all groups.
- The importance of government-business relations—whether supportive or
  regulatory—requires active involvement in politics in order to safeguard
  business interests.
- Business political activity is necessary to counteract political activity by
  other groups that affect business, such as labor unions, consumerists, and
  environmentalists.
- Because of its position as one of society's central institutions, business's
  political views may at times promote the interests of other related groups,
  including workers, consumers, suppliers, and local communities.

[18]Dunlop, op. cit., p. 87.

SHOULD BUSINESS BE ACTIVE IN POLITICS?	
YES	NO
• A pluralistic right • Safeguards beneficial relationship with government • Counteracts antibusiness political activity by other groups • Business actions benefit others	• Leave politics to skilled politicians • Business is not qualified • Business power may upset pluralistic balance • Risks loss of customers and more government controls

FIGURE 8-4.   The pros and cons of business involvement in politics.

Those who argue for less political participation by business, including some business leaders, say that political action by business can lead to trouble and should be avoided for the other reasons shown in Figure 8-4. They hold the following beliefs.

- Business should stick to business and leave politics to politicians, because people in business are not necessarily qualified or knowledgeable in the field of politics and their viewpoints often are too narrow. (Of course, this may be true of other groups also.)
- Business leaders who are trained in the disciplines of the business world sometimes prove to be naive about the complexities and uncertainties of politics.
- Because of the size of many corporations, business political power may unbalance pluralism and tend to substitute a dominant private interest for the public welfare.
- Much political activity by business, particularly if it is successful, makes business a target of public criticism, causing a loss of customers and inviting even more government controls. A low-profile type of influence on government policy is more effective and less risky.

The clear trend in the 1980s has been for expanded business involvement in political debate and discussion. One rationale is self-interest:

> [I]t is imperative that corporations increase their political involvement. They can thus insure that political policy choices are influenced by the views of the private sector in general and by the corporate sector in particular. . . . In today's pluralistic society, political participation is not a luxury but a necessity and must receive top management attention and corporate resources to do it right and do it well.[19]

Other experts find the rationale in the nature of modern democracy:

[19]S. Prakash Sethi, "Corporate Political Activism," *California Management Review*, Spring 1982, pp. 32, 37.

Corporations should not, as a policy matter, be relegated to the underworld of politics but should be placed on a legal parity with other social interests and be recognized as legitimate political participants in the democratic process.[20]

Managers themselves seem to be overwhelmingly in favor of political action by business, and a 1982 public opinion poll found that 90 percent of corporate executives thought that business's political message was being heard better than five years earlier.[21] By the 1986 congressional elections, business involvement was more extensive than ever before.

Types and Mechanisms of Political Influence

Business may exercise political influence of two different types: (1) efforts are made to shape government policies, forthcoming legislation, and the actions of regulatory agencies; and (2) business tries to influence the outcome of elections. The first type deals with *governmental* politics and the second with *electoral* politics.[22]

Governmental Politics

The techniques used by business to participate in governmental politics are similar to those of other interest groups. Many large corporations place a full-time representative and staff in Washington to keep abreast of developments in government that may affect the company (this is a type of environmental scanning) and to exert influence on members of Congress and other officials. Company lobbyists may be active in city halls and state capitols also.

Smaller companies, as well as many large ones, join trade associations such as the National Association of Manufacturers or the U.S. Chamber of Commerce, where they count upon strength of numbers and a centralized staff to promote their interests with government officials. The Chamber of Commerce, for example, has a membership of 200,000 companies, has an annual budget of $60 million, publishes the most widely circulated business magazine, and has a satellite television network to broadcast its political message.[23]

The ad hoc coalition that brings diverse business groups together to lobby for or against a particular piece of legislation has proved to be effective. Defeat of proposed laws establishing a consumer protection agency in the federal government and permitting unrestricted picketing at construction sites was attributed to the work of ad hoc business coalitions, as was creation of a trigger price system to stem the flow of imported steel.

[20]Edwin M. Epstein, *The Corporation in American Politics,* Englewood Cliffs, NJ: Prentice-Hall, 1969, p. 16.

[21]*Business Week/Harris Poll,* "How Business Is Getting through to Washington," *Business Week,* October 4, 1982, p. 16.

[22]Epstein, op. cit., chap. 5.

[23]Ann Crittenden, "A Stubborn Chamber of Commerce Roils the Waters," *New York Times,* June 27, 1982, pp. F-4–F-5.

Electoral Politics

During the mid-1970s, an important court decision gave business the right to create corporate political action committees (PACs). The emergence of corporate PACs was a landmark in business involvement in electoral politics. Direct contributions by corporations to political candidates running for federal offices are forbidden by federal law, and several states place similar restrictions on corporate contributions in state elections. Since the mid-1970s, however, companies have been permitted to spend company funds to *organize* and *administer* a PAC, which may solicit contributions from stockholders and employees and then channel the funds to those seeking political office. Even companies that have organized PACs, though, are not permitted to donate *corporate* money to the PAC or to any political candidate. All donations to a company-organized PAC must come from *individuals.* Similarly, unions and other organizations may solicit contributions from members and supporters for their PACs.

The great expense of modern political campaigns, especially because of the high cost of television advertising, has made campaign financing an increasingly serious problem. Candidates need money to run effective political campaigns, and PACs have become the single most important source of funds.

The Federal Election Commission (FEC) has established rules to regulate PAC activities. For example, PACs are not allowed to give more than $5,000 to a single candidate for each election, although the winner of a primary election may be given another $5,000 for the general election. These limits were imposed on all PACs to reduce the role of concentrated wealth in determining the outcome of elections to public office.

> *But new ways are constantly being found to get around the rules. In the 1986 congressional campaigns, for example, PACs took advantage of loopholes that allowed them to spend as much as they wanted indirectly on candidates so long as they did not cooperate or consult with candidates or their campaigns. Thus, PACs spent money on television commercials, telephone banks, and mass mailings in addition to the $5,000 they were permitted to contribute directly to the candidate.*[24]

As Figure 8-5 shows, PACs have proved to be very popular with business as well as with other groups. Although corporate PACs were the most numerous, accounting for 42 percent of the total, they were not the biggest money raisers or spenders. Nonconnected organizations ranked highest in money raised and spent. Some labor unions are among the biggest contributors, although as a whole they represent only 10 percent of all PACs. During the 1970s, labor union PACs outstripped business in raising money, but in the 1980s they have fallen behind the combined efforts of corporate and trade association PACs. By the end of 1985, 3,992 PACs were registered by the

[24]"PACs Turning to Indirect Way to Aid Hopefuls," *New York Times*, November 2, 1986, pp. 1, 35.

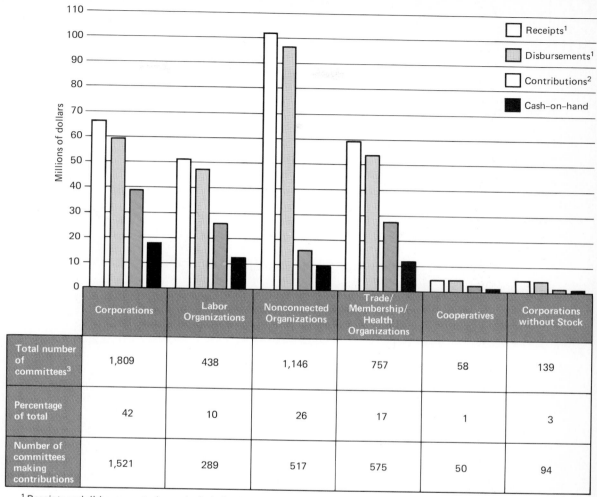

	Corporations	Labor Organizations	Nonconnected Organizations	Trade/ Membership/ Health Organizations	Cooperatives	Corporations without Stock
Total number of committees[3]	1,809	438	1,146	757	58	139
Percentage of total	42	10	26	17	1	3
Number of committees making contributions	1,521	289	517	575	50	94

[1] Receipts and disbursements do not include funds transferred between affiliated committees.

[2] Includes contributions to committees of 1984 House and Senate candidates; and all federal candidates (for House, Senate and Presidency) campaigning in future elections or retiring debts of former campaigns.

[3] Includes total number of PACs active in federal elections at any time between January 1, 1983, and December 31, 1984. Since some committees have terminated, this figure does not represent all committees active as of December 31, 1984.

FIGURE 8-5. Financial activity of PACs, 1983 to 1984. (*Source:* Federal Election Commission Record, *March 1986, vol. 12, p. 7.*)

FEC—down slightly from 4,009 in January 1985. Figure 8-6 shows the growth in the number of PACs, which peaked around the time of the 1984 elections, and has since declined in most categories.

The overall significance of PACs is not clear. Some observers worry that corporations, trade associations, and special-interest or single-issue groups will be able to wield too much influence on elections. According to these critics, officeholders who seek reelection may be "bought off" by PAC contributions, especially since election campaigning has become so expensive in

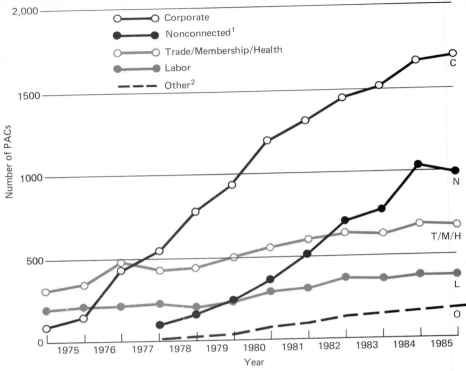

FIGURE 8-6. PAC growth from 1975 to 1985. (*Source: Federal Election Commission Record, March 1986, vol. 12, no. 3, p. 6.*)

[1] For the years 1974 through 1976, the FEC did not identify subcategories of PACs other than corporate and labor PACs. Therefore, numbers are not available for Trade/Membership/Health PACs and Nonconnected PACs.

[2] Includes PACs formed by corporations without capital stock and cooperatives. Numbers are not available for these categories of PACs from 1974 through 1976.

an electronic age. Others counter this argument by claiming that it is better to have political contributions out in the open, as required by the current law, than going back to the old system of secret slush funds.[25] The reform most frequently discussed is public financing for political candidates.

RESPONSIBLE BUSINESS POLITICS

We agree with others who say that political action by business—whether to influence government policy or the outcome of elections—is a natural outgrowth of a pluralistic society. Business has a legitimate right to participate

[25]For further discussion, see Carl L. Swanson, "Corporations and Electoral Activities: The Legal, Political, and Managerial Implications of PACs," in S. Prakash Sethi and Carl L. Swanson, *Private Enterprise and Public Purpose*, New York: Wiley, 1981, pp. 355–372; and Douglas N. Dickson, "CorPACs: The Business of Political Action Committees," *Across the Board*, November 1981, pp. 13–22.

TOP 10 MONEY RAISERS		TOP 10 CONTRIBUTORS TO FEDERAL CANDIDATES	
Political Action Committee	Amount Raised 1/1/85–6/31/86	Political Action Committee	Amount Contributed 1/1/85–6/31/86
Fund for America's Future, Inc.	$8,249,387	Realtors Political Action Committee (National Association of Realtors)*	$1,387,429
National Congressional Club	8,099,908		
National Conservative Political Action Committee	7,738,709	National Education Association PAC (National Education Association)	1,034,220
Realtors Political Action Committee (National Association of Realtors)*	4,452,939	Build PAC (National Association of Home Builders)	949,772
American Medical Political Action Committee (American Medical Association)	4,388,396	American Medical Political Action Committee (American Medical Association)	869,098
NRA Political Victory Fund (National Rifle Association)	3,155,346	Committee on Letter Carrier Political Education (National Association of Letter Carriers of USA)	839,255
Democratic Republican Independent Voter Education Committee (Teamsters Union)	2,806,109	Association of Trial Lawyers PAC (Association of Trial Lawyers of America)	803,600
Auto Dealers for Free Trade PAC	2,742,554	Seafarers Political Activity Donation (Seafarers International Union of North America)	768,956
League of Conservation Voters (League of Conservation Voters)	2,583,232	National Association of Life Underwriters PAC (National Association of Life Underwriters)	737,317
National Education Association PAC (National Education Association)	2,344,868	UAW–V–CAP (United Auto Workers)	711,470
		Democratic Republican Independent Voter Education Committee (Teamsters Union)	709,426

*The connected organizations (i.e., sponsors) of separate segregated funds are indicated in parentheses.

FIGURE 8-7.   The top ten PAC money raisers and contributors to federal candidates, January 1, 1985, to June 30, 1986. (*Source:* Federal Election Commission Record, *November 1986, vol. 12, no. 11, p. 4.*)

in the pulls and hauls of the political process, just as consumers, labor unions, minorities, and others do.

The principal danger arising from corporate political activity is that corporations may wield too much power. If that power were to "tip the scales" too much in favor of business and against the many other pluralistic interests in society, both business and society would be losers. A careful use of business influence is therefore an ideal goal to be worked for, as would also be true of union power, religious power, consumer power, or any other concentrated power that may exist in an organizational society. As we stated in Chapter 2, the Iron Law of Responsibility is always present as a reminder to all institutions to use their power in socially responsible ways or risk losing it to others. This is true of political, as well as economic, power.

SUMMARY

Public policies are government actions intended to accomplish a broad public purpose. These policies can affect business in many vital ways, thereby giving business an important reason to help develop and shape public policies that will promote a favorable business climate.

The public policy process has five major stages: agenda building, policy formulation, policy decision, policy implementation, and policy evaluation. Business is able to influence each of these stages, either directly or indirectly.

Public policies can help business be socially responsible by defining specific social goals and by spelling out the performance standards and timetables for achieving the goals.

It is possible to argue both for and against business involvement in politics, but the most widely accepted position on this issue is to recognize the legitimate right of business to exert political influence where its interests are affected, as long as its power is used responsibly and without upsetting society's pluralistic balance. In this way it can participate in the political process on the same footing as other organizations and groups.

DISCUSSION AND REVIEW QUESTIONS

1. Describe the five stages in the public policy process. From articles in *Business Week* and *Newsweek* or another current source, describe an issue that has gone through all or most of the stages in this process. Highlight any points on which the actual situation differs from the outlined process.

2. From articles in publications similar to those mentioned above, identify businesses or industries that have been slow to become involved as a certain issue was developing. What happened? How did these firms fare in comparison to those that were involved fully as the issue developed and became public policy?

3. During the 1980s, federal agricultural policy encouraged sunflower seed growers to plant such surplus crops as wheat, corn, and barley, which are protected by income- and price-support programs. As a result, there was a shortage of sunflower seeds, which are necessary for the production of polyunsaturated cooking oils. Foreign growers began to undersell American wheat, corn, and barley, and began growing sunflower seeds as a rotation crop. Evaluate the intended and unintended effects of the policy. What action might or should have been taken to assist the farmers? (Keep in mind that government action originally was taken for this very purpose.)

4. Reread this chapter's opening illustration regarding liability cap policies. Provide arguments for and against political involvement by businesses in the formulation or prevention of such a policy. What mechanisms could business use to assist in the implementation of such a policy or prevent such a policy from being implemented?

5. In the library, look up Federal Election Commission statistics from the last congressional election. Try to identify several individual PACs, including some that represent business interests, and note how much they donated to candidates in your district. What were they hoping to accomplish, and how successful do you think they were?

CRITICAL INCIDENT

Drug Testing as Public Policy?

On September 15, 1986, President Reagan signed an executive order calling for drug testing of many of the federal government's 2.8 million civilian employees. The federal government is not alone in this "crusade to clean up the nation's workforce." More than one-quarter of the Fortune 500 companies test job applicants for drug use, and a few firms have begun testing their current employees. This sudden crackdown has been foreseen for many years, as the nationwide war on drug use has been slowly shifting from focusing on drug dealers to focusing on drug users. Studies indicate that almost one-fourth of the American population has tried marijuana and 20 million people use it regularly. Between five and six million people are regular cocaine users, and half a million are addicted to heroin.

Thus, authorities have decided that the problem can best be controlled by reducing demand, rather than by attempting to control supplies and suppliers. The first and most logical or effective step, they have decided, is drug testing of workers.

Some of the arguments against drug testing are centered around employee rights versus employer rights. Those people in favor of the testing insist that the employer has the right to demand a drug-free work force because drug use reduces productivity and increases accidents and absenteeism. Opponents of the testing, however, claim that it is both unconstitutional and inaccurate. Several studies have indicated that many legal and commonly used substances can produce positive results in drug testing. Among them are nasal sprays, poppy seeds, and the painkiller ibuprofen, used in many over-the-counter aspirin substitutes. Some people even claim that the tests have a built-in racial bias due to the similarity between the chemical composition of the pigment melanin, found in high levels in blacks and Hispanics, and the active ingredient in marijuana. Finally, opponents claim that employers are not simply interested in performance but in enforcing their own brand of morality. These critics think that an employee should be able to smoke marijuana on a weekend, provided that he or she shows up and performs effectively on Monday morning.

More complex arguments are taking place on the national legislative level. Several issues are being debated, the most important being the gaps in coverage provided by the Fourth Amendment. The Bill of Rights restrains only the actions of government officials or those acting closely in concert with them. Thus, this amendment protects government employees from unreasonable searches and seizures but not private employees, because private employers have not been held subject to the strictures of the amendment. Another issue concerns the applicability of the term "administrative search" to drug testing. Administrative searches are those conducted regularly and indiscriminately for justifiable reasons—such as searches at airport departure gates. Some people claim that drug testing could not be included in this category, because it is often conducted in the absence of valid suspicions and without overriding urgency (it certainly is not as urgent as no weapons or bombs being allowed on an airplane).

Nonetheless, the Reagan administration has argued that mandatory testing is justified where employees such as airline pilots, nuclear power plant operators, and members of the military and civil defense corps are responsible for the health and safety of others. To demonstrate its commitment, the administration had the President, Vice President, and seventy-eight members of the White House senior staff participate in a "voluntary testing." Additionally, the President's Commission on Organized Crime recommended that selected groups of federal employees be tested and also suggested that government contracts not be awarded to companies that make no effort to detect and eliminate drug abuse among their workers.

1. Take this issue through the public policy process as described in this chapter and illustrated in Figure 8-2. Describe how the issue would get onto the public policy agenda, how a policy would be formulated, how a policy decision would be made and a course of action designed, how the policy would be implemented (if at all), and how it would be evaluated.

2. Explain the interest business has in this public policy decision. Why and how would business become involved? What do you think would happen to those companies that choose not to become involved, that is, not take a position on the social issue?

3. Review the ethics concepts in Chapter 3. Which ones apply to the drug-testing situation faced by employees? Using those concepts, can you say whether drug testing in the workplace is ethical or unethical? Explain your answer.

Chapter Nine

THE CORPORATION, ANTITRUST LAWS, AND THE MERGER MOVEMENT

All socioeconomic systems face the problem of deciding how much power should be held by leading enterprises, whether they are privately owned or controlled by the state. In the United States, antitrust laws have been used to curb corporate power, to preserve competition, and to achieve various social goals. However, during the 1980s a vigorous corporate merger movement raised new questions concerning corporate power; it presented public policymakers and corporate leaders with a need to reconcile corporate power, shareholders' interests, and social responsibility.

CHAPTER OBJECTIVES

After reading this chapter, you should be able to

- Understand the dilemma of corporate power in a democratic society
- Define the objectives of major antitrust laws and explain how they are enforced
- Identify business objections to antitrust laws
- Discern recent trends in United States antitrust policy
- Describe the merger movement of the 1980s and explain its significance for business and society
- Identify corporate strategies for fending off takeovers

"Corporate cannibalism" seemed to occur at a faster pace during the 1980s as big companies swallowed up other companies long familiar to the public. Gulf Oil, once one of the world's largest multinational corporations, simply disappeared when acquired by Chevron, another oil company. The same thing happened to Norton Simon Inc., producer of Max Factor cosmetics, Wesson Oil, and Hunt's tomato sauce. Its 35,000 employees were reduced to a small headquarters cadre and then to zero when the company was bought by Esmark, which was then bought by Beatrice, which was then bought by yet another group. In another series of merger deals, U.S. Rubber Company, once the seventh largest industrial enterprise in the United States, was dismantled after being acquired by Uniroyal which after being bought by its own managers, then sold off most of its own assets. Most of Uniroyal's 20,000 employees kept their jobs with other companies that bought up different pieces of the original business, while 27 top managers at Uniroyal divided up almost $7 million they made on the deal. Uniroyal's chairman received a total of $3.3 million in bonuses and a share of the breakup profits.

Sometimes the merging companies retain their own identities, and sometimes well-known brand names are preserved even when their corporate home has changed. Examples are Beatrice (Tropicana orange juice), which merged with Esmark (Playtex gloves); Quaker Oats (Quaker Oats and other cereals), which acquired Stokely-Van Camp (Gatorade); and R. J. Reynolds (Winston cigarettes), which took over Nabisco Brands (Oreo cookies). It took a court order and antitrust regulators to stop Coca-Cola from acquiring Dr. Pepper and to keep Pepsi from buying Seven-Up, on grounds that competition would be reduced in the soft-drink market.

The torrent of corporate mergers is measured by what happened during one three-year period beginning in 1983. In just over 1,000 days, 8,000 mergers and acquisitions worth $375 billion occurred. One of these was General Electric's 1985 purchase of RCA for a record price of $6.3 billion. 1985's merger deals were higher in dollar value than those struck in 1984.[1]

Doubts were raised in many quarters, not just about the economic wisdom of many of these corporate takeovers, but about the concentrated power that lay behind these decisions. Should big companies, managed by an elite corps of top executives, be allowed to exert such enormous influence over so many others in society? Do corporations have too much power? Is the influence they exercise really legitimate in a society that thinks of itself as being organized along democratic lines? Are broad public purposes being served by these large business firms?

Corporate leaders, as well as public policymakers, need to give serious attention to these questions. The answers help determine the shape and character of the United States socioeconomic system, as well as the relative amount of power and influence to be held by private business and government regulators. These questions are discussed in this chapter.

[1]"The Top 300 Deals," *Business Week*, Special Issue, April 18, 1986, p. 265; *Business Week*, July 14, 1986, p. 29; *Business Week*, October 21, 1985; and *Wall Street Journal*, August 1, 1986, p. 3.

Rank	By Sales (billions)	By Assets (billions)	By Income (billions)	By Employees
1	General Motors $96.4	Exxon $69.1	IBM $6.6	General Motors 811,000
2	Exxon $86.7	Sears, Roebuck $66.4	Exxon $4.9	Sears, Roebuck 466,000
3	Mobil $55.9	General Motors $63.8	General Motors $3.9	IBM 405,535
4	Ford Motor $52.8	IBM $52.6	Ford Motor $2.5	Ford Motor 369,300
5	IBM $50.1	Mobil $41.8	General Electric $2.3	AT&T 337,600
6	Texaco $49.3	AT&T $40.5	Amoco $1.9	K mart 330,000
7	Chevron $41.7	Chevron $38.9	Shell Oil $1.7	General Electric 304,000
8	Sears, Roebuck $40.7	Texaco $37.7	Chrysler $1.6	ITT 232,000
9	AT&T $34.9	Ford Motor $31.6	AT&T $1.6	United Technologies 184,800
10	Du Pont $29.5	Shell Oil $26.5	Chevron $1.5	Kroger 178,151
Totals	$538.0	$468.9	$28.5	3,618,386

FIGURE 9-1. The ten largest United States industrial and retailing corporations, 1985. (*Source:* Fortune, April 28, 1986, pp. 182–183. Copyright TIME Inc. All rights reserved.)

CORPORATE POWER AND LEGITIMACY

By almost any measure used, the world's largest business enterprises are impressively big, as shown in Figures 9-1 and 9-2. Size can be measured in several ways—by annual sales, assets, annual income, and employees—and a company's rank will vary depending on the measurement used. By most measures, the "big five" in 1985 were General Motors, Exxon, Mobil, Ford, and IBM. The same general pattern is seen among the biggest non–United States companies listed in Figure 9-2, where oil companies and automobile manufacturers dominate the top levels. Four of these foreign firms are state-owned, which serves as a reminder that the socioeconomic systems of many nations are a blend of private-and-state enterprises discussed in Chapter 6.[2]

[2]R. Joseph Monsen and Kenneth D. Walters, "State-Owned Firms: A Review of the Data and Issues," in Lee E. Preston (ed.), *Research in Corporate Social Performance and Policy*, vol. 2, Greenwich, CT: JAI Press, 1980, pp. 125–155.

1985 Rank	Company	Country	Industry	Sales (billions)	Assets (billions)	Net Inc. (billions)	Employees
1	Royal Dutch/ Shell	Netherlands/ Britain	Petroleum	$81.7	$74.9	$3.9	142,000
2	British Petroleum	Britain	Petroleum	$53.1	$43.6	$0.9	127,940
3	IRI*	Italy	Steel	$26.8	n/a	($0.7)	483,714
4	Toyota	Japan	Motor vehicles	$26.0	$17.2	$1.6	79,901
5	ENI*	Italy	Petroleum	$24.5	$26.8	$0.4	120,268
6	Unilever	Netherlands/ Britain	Foods, soaps, cosmetics	$21.6	$13.5	$0.7	304,000
7	Matsushita Electric	Japan	Electric machinery	$20.7	$21.5	$1.0	133,963
8	Hitachi	Japan	Electronics	$20.5	$20.2	$0.9	164,951
9	Pemex*	Mexico	Petroleum	$20.4	$36.6	$0.006	183,179
10	Elf–Aquitaine*	France	Petroleum	$20.1	$22.4	$0.7	73,000
Totals				$520.2	$276.7	$9.4	1,812,916

*Government-owned companies.

FIGURE 9-2. The ten largest industrial corporations outside the United States, 1985. (*Source: Fortune, August 4, 1986, p. 181. Copyright TIME Inc. All rights reserved.*)

The ten United States corporations shown in Figure 9-1 generated more sales in 1985—$538 billion—than the entire national output of Australia, Brazil, Canada, China, India, Italy, Mexico, or Nigeria. The employees of these same ten companies, if living together in one location, would make up the seventh or eighth largest metropolitan area in the United States—about the size of greater Boston or greater Washington, D.C. Some of the world's largest corporations are banks (Citicorp of New York and Dai-Ichi Kangyo of Japan), insurance companies (Prudential), and other financial institutions (Salomon Brothers of New York) not shown in Figure 9-1 or 9-2.

Referring to large enterprises such as these, the former president of the business-sponsored Committee for Economic Development stated:

> The model of the economy that is most relevant for both analysis and policy making is clearly one in which about 500 large firms account for the predominant share of mining and manufacturing in the United States. In most individual industries, eight or fewer companies account for an average of more than half of total sales. . . . The largest 50 banks held nearly 60 percent of commercial bank deposits as of December 31, 1979. The 50 largest insurance companies owned 78 percent of all life insurance assets as of December 31, 1979.[3]

[3]Alfred C. Neal, *Business Power and Public Policy*, New York: Praeger, 1981, p. 126.

Type of Business Firm	Number
Proprietorships (owned by one person)	10,106,000
Partnerships (owned by two or more persons)	1,514,000
Corporations (owned by stockholders)	2,926,000

FIGURE 9-3. Major types and numbers of business firms in the United States, 1982. (*Source: Bureau of the Census, Statistical Abstract of the United States, 1986, Washington, DC, p. 517.*)

These giant enterprises are by no means typical of business in the United States or other nations. The overwhelming number of business firms are owned by individual proprietors or by small groups of partners, as revealed in Figure 9-3. Only one of every five business firms in the United States is a corporation, and many of these corporations are small. For example, in 1985 the five hundredth largest industrial corporation in the United States (ranked by sales) employed only 2,250 people, and several higher-ranking companies had fewer than 700 employees. The largest firms at the top of the business pyramid are the focus of so much attention due to their size, power, and influence and not because they represent the entire business community.

Corporate Economic Power

Sheer size alone does not account for the economic significance of large corporations. Corporate power arises from the critical tasks society expects these organizations to perform. These functions as performed in the United States were described by one expert in the following way:

> Large American business corporations, although "private" enterprises, perform the great majority of essential economic tasks, which, due to their very essentiality, are in many countries undertaken by the state, either directly or through closely affiliated "public" entities. In this country, business corporations produce and distribute all forms of energy, process all ferrous and nonferrous metals and derivative products, provide air, sea, motor, and for the most part, intra-urban and inter-city rail transportation, maintain radio, television, telephone, and intercontinental satellite broadcasting services, and, finally, service virtually all of the essential financial needs of the nation.[4]

By entrusting large private corporations with all these economic functions, society has granted business much economic influence. By amassing physical assets, employing and training thousands of persons, attracting huge pools of capital, engaging in research and development on a large scale,

---

[4]Edwin M. Epstein, "Societal, Managerial, and Legal Perspectives on Corporate Social Responsibility: Product and Process," in S. Prakash Sethi and Carl L. Swanson, *Private Enterprise and Public Purpose*, New York: Wiley, 1981, p. 84. Originally published in *The Hastings Law Journal*, May 1979.

and reaching throughout the world for resources and markets, the largest corporations have become the premier economic institutions of United States society.

Corporate Political Power

We discussed the political influence of business in Chapter 8. Here, we only wish to emphasize that political influence probably increases with the size of the business firm. One long-term inside observer of the United States corporate world seems to confirm this relationship:

> Large corporations . . . have . . . moved a long way toward rivaling or surpassing the power of government on issues that are of special importance to them. . . .
> [In a sense] the large corporation becomes a piece of government. This is the real character of the large companies that constitute a major part of the economic base of this country, a nation that still contains the greatest concentration of economic power in the world. In the real economy, where companies are unrecognized parts of government, we must consider how such companies are governed and how they relate to the political structure within which they move and exercise their enormous capacity.[5]

Corporate Social Power

A corporation's social influence is felt in two kinds of ways: one is external and the other is internal.

Externally, a company's actions can influence how clean the community's air is, how adequate the local tax base is for civic improvement, whether voluntary nonprofit community agencies will be well funded, and the general tone of community relations, including local pride in community accomplishments.

A corporation's internal social influence is felt by employees who spend most of their waking hours in the service of their employer. The result, in the words of one expert, is that:

> The large corporation generally—and the megacorporation in particular—has become a social institution which embraces the thousands of human beings whose lives are affected by it and which provides an important focus for the employees' social relationships. In the more complex society, with greater mobility, the loosening of community ties, and urban anonymity, the neighborhood social unit has lost its cohesion and the corporation has assumed some of its role. . . . With the expansion of group health insurance programs, pension plans, and personal counselling services, the corporation is further strengthening the areas of its participation in the nonbusiness portion of its employees' lives.[6]

The Dilemma of Corporate Power

Neither size nor power alone is bad, when it comes to corporate performance. A big company may have definite advantages over a small one. It can com-

[5]Neal, op. cit., pp. 136, 150.

[6]Phillip I. Blumberg, *The Megacorporation in American Society*, Englewood Cliffs, NJ: Prentice-Hall, 1975, pp. 2–3.

mand more resources, often produce at a lower cost, plan further into the future, and weather business fluctuations somewhat better. Big companies make tougher competitors against foreign firms. Many communities have benefited in many ways from the social initiatives and influence of large firms.[7]

Most questions of corporate power concern *how* business uses its influence, not whether it should have power in the first place. Most people want to know if business power is being used to achieve broad public-purpose goals, values, and traditions considered to be important to the nation as a whole. If so, then corporate power is considered to be legitimate, and the public accepts large size as just another normal characteristic of modern business. Says one leading source: "Organizations are legitimate to the extent that their activities are congruent with the goals and values of the social system within which they function."[8] Another scholar points out that "a loss of legitimacy is particularly destructive to any institution, and in social systems legitimacy is perhaps the major element in the survival function."[9] Therefore, the crucial questions about corporate power are the following:

- Will corporate *economic* power be used to promote the interests of *all* the public, including small-business competitors and local communities? For example, large-scale computer systems may increase the productivity of big banks, but will this development put smaller banks at a competitive disadvantage? Or a cost-saving relocation of a plant from a New England town to Southeast Asia may bring severe economic distress to the community that is left behind.
- Will corporate *political* power be used wisely so as not to upset the pluralistic balance of power among all interest groups? Where "large corporations . . . have . . . moved a long way toward rivaling or surpassing the power of government on issues that are of special importance to them,"[10] the thoughtful business executive may express concern.
- Will corporate *social* power respect the integrity and dignity of individuals, as well as the traditions and needs of the corporation's host communities? For example, corporate drug-testing programs and sudden plant shutdowns, while considered necessary for business purposes, may be seen as unacceptable and socially undesirable by those affected.

These three basic questions assume special meaning in United States society, with its democratic traditions, representative political institutions, and strong respect for the individual. In such a society, concentrated power

---

[7]For several examples, see *1986 Social Report of the Life and Health Insurance Business: The Record of Corporate Public Involvement*, Washington, DC: Center for Corporate Public Involvement, 1986.

[8]Edwin M. Epstein and Dow Votaw (eds.), *Rationality, Legitimacy, Responsibility: Search for New Directions in Business and Society*, Santa Monica, CA: Goodyear, 1978, p. 72.

[9]Kenneth E. Boulding, "The Legitimacy of the Business Institution," in ibid., p. 89. See also Thomas M. Jones, "Corporate Control and the Limits of Managerial Power," *Business Forum*, Winter 1985, pp. 16–21.

[10]Neal, op. cit., p. 136.

of any kind—whether corporate, governmental, religious, scientific, or military—seems out of place. Reconciling corporate power with an open, free way of life is the crux of the problem. If large corporations can be made to fit into the webbing of an open, pluralistic society, their legitimacy—that is, their acceptance—will be assured.

The nation's antitrust laws, highly controversial and far from perfect, stand as a monument to our society's efforts to cope with the various dilemmas of corporate power and legitimacy. We consider them now.

ANTITRUST REGULATION

Someone once remarked that antitrust is as American as apple pie. Certainly it is an article of faith deeply embedded in the minds of many people. The antitrust laws originated in the late nineteenth century in the wake of some spectacular financial shenanigans by big-business leaders and their companies. An aroused public feared the uncontrolled growth of big business. The first antitrust laws were passed in this climate of fear and mistrust of big business.

But the story does not end there. Since those early years, other antitrust laws have been enacted and the first laws have been amended. The result is a formidable tangle of laws, regulations, guidelines, and judicial interpretations that challenge the best legal minds and present business with a good example of how government can be an adversary.[11]

Objectives of Antitrust

Antitrust laws serve multiple goals. Some of these goals—such as preserving competition or protecting consumers against deceptive advertising—are primarily economic in character. Others, though, are more concerned with social and philosophical matters, such as a desire to punish large corporations merely for being big or a nostalgic wish to return to the old Jeffersonian ideal of a nation of small-scale farmers and businesses. The result is multiple, overlapping, changing, and sometimes contradictory goals.

The most important economic objectives of antitrust are the following:

First, the *protection and preservation of competition* is the central goal of antitrust policy. This is done by outlawing monopolies, prohibiting unfair competition, and eliminating price discrimination and collusion. The reasoning is that customers will be best and most economically served if business firms compete vigorously for the consumer's dollar. Prices should fluctuate according to supply and demand, with no collusion between competitors, whether behind the scenes or out in the open. A 1983 case illustrates this feature of antitrust regulation.[12]

[11]For legal details see A. D. Neale and D. G. Goyder, *The Antitrust Laws of the United States of America: A Study of Competition Enforced by Law,* 3d ed., Cambridge, England: Cambridge University Press, 1980; and Herbert Hovenkamp, *Antitrust,* St. Paul, MN: 1986.

[12]"The FTC Redefines Price-Fixing," *Business Week,* April 18, 1983, pp. 37, 41.

Du Pont Company and Ethyl Corporation, producers of 70 percent of lead-based gasoline additives, were determined by the Federal Trade Commission to be in violation of antitrust laws, not because they secretly agreed to artificially fix prices of the additives but because they managed to "signal" each other informally about the prices they planned to charge customers. The price-signaling scheme had several features: advance announcements were made to customers of planned price increases, with an extra period granted that permitted uniform prices to develop between the two producers; contract clauses discouraged price discounts by promising each customer the lowest price given to any customer nationwide; and a uniform pricing system ignored transportation cost differences for customers in different parts of the nation. According to the FTC, this system caused artificially high prices and profits and a stifling of competition between the two producers. One antitrust expert said, "This case is about modern ways of influencing prices." Today's managers "are too smart to get caught" actually agreeing to fix prices.

A second goal of antitrust policy is *to protect the consumer's welfare* by prohibiting deceptive and unfair business practices. At first, the antitrust laws were aimed primarily at simply preserving competition, assuming that consumers would be safeguarded as long as competition was strong. Later, though, it was realized that some business methods could be used to exploit or mislead consumers, regardless of the amount of competition. Consider the following examples of unfair practices:

A company supplying plastic parts for electrical appliances bribed the purchasing agent for the appliance maker to buy the company's parts, even though they were priced higher than those made by a competitor. As a result, the consumer paid more for the appliances. This type of commercial bribery is forbidden by the antitrust laws because it takes unfair advantage of innocent consumers.

In another case, a distributor of phonograph records sent record-club members more records than they had ordered and then demanded payment, substituted one record for another in some orders, and delayed prepaid orders of some customers for several months. All these practices are considered to be unfair by antitrust authorities.

A third goal of antitrust regulation is *to protect small, independent business firms* from the economic pressures exerted by big-business competition.

For example, for forty years Congress authorized states to have "fair trade laws." These laws permitted a manufacturer of toasters, for example, to set a minimum price on its toasters sold by all retailers in a given state. Large chain stores and discount centers could not charge lower prices, even though their overall costs of operation might enable them to price the toasters lower and still make a profit. In these cases, Congress was trying to protect small retail outlets from the more efficient competition of large stores. But in 1976 Congress outlawed fair trade practices.

> *In other cases, small businesses may be undersold by larger ones because man-*
> *ufacturers are willing to give price discounts to large-volume buyers. For ex-*
> *ample, a tire maker wanted to sell automobile and truck tires to a large retail*
> *chain at a lower price than it offered to a small gasoline station. The antitrust*
> *laws prohibit such discounts to be given exclusively to large buyers unless it can*
> *be proved that there is a genuine economic saving in dealing with the larger firm.*

In promoting the interests of small business over large business in these ways, antitrust regulations disregard both competition—because big businesses are not permitted to compete freely—and consumer welfare—because big business could sell at a lower price than small firms. This inconsistency occurs because these laws serve the multiple and sometimes contradictory goals of many different groups.

A fourth goal of antitrust policy has more to do with *social and political factors* than with business and economics. A strong populist philosophy has been part of the antitrust movement from its beginning. Populists favored small-town life, neighborly relations among people, a democratic political system, family-operated farms, and small-size business firms. They believed that concentrated wealth poses a threat to democracy, that big business would drive small local companies out of business, and that hometown merchants and neighboring farmers might be replaced by large impersonal corporations headquartered in distant cities. Populists advocated antitrust restrictions on business to preserve the values and customs of small-town America. These social and political goals continue—almost one hundred years later—to affect the administration of the antitrust laws.[13]

The Major Antitrust Laws

Today's antitrust laws are the outcome of many years of attempting to make American business fit the model of free market competition that was developed during the nineteenth century. Many people have pointed out how unrealistic it is to expect a modern, high-technology, diversified, worldwide corporation to conform to conditions that may have been considered ideal a century ago when both business and society were simpler. One authority has said: "Existing interpretation of [antitrust] legislation often ignores the technological, financial, political, and social environment of the late twentieth century."[14]

Rather than trying to present all the many detailed provisions of the antitrust laws and the history of how each one came into existence, we shall concentrate here on the four main federal antitrust statutes and give a brief summary of each. States also have antitrust laws, but we shall not discuss them.

---

[13]A lucid historical account may be found in Richard Hofstadter, "What Happened to the Antitrust Movement?" in Earl F. Cheit (ed.), *The Business Establishment*, New York: Wiley, 1964, pp. 113–151.

[14]Ibid., p. 192.

The Sherman Act

Although several states enacted antitrust laws before the federal government did, the Sherman Act of 1890 is considered to be the foundation of all antitrust regulation in the United States. This law

- Prohibits contracts, combinations, or conspiracies that restrain trade and commerce
- Prohibits monopolies and all attempts to monopolize trade and commerce
- Provides for enforcement by the Justice Department, and authorizes penalties, including fines and jail terms, for violations.

The Clayton Act

Originally passed in 1914 to clarify some of the ambiguities and uncertainties of the Sherman Act, the Clayton Act, as amended, now

- Prohibits price discrimination by sellers (as illustrated by the tire maker who was forbidden to sell lower-priced tires to a chain store while selling at a higher price to a small independent store)
- Forbids tying contracts that require someone to buy a related and perhaps unwanted product in order to get another one produced by the same company (for example, Twentieth Century–Fox was fined for forcing theater chains to accept an unwanted film as a condition of showing a highly successful one)
- Prohibits companies from merging through purchase of shares or assets if competition is lessened or a monopoly is created
- Outlaws interlocking directorates in large _competing_ corporations (for example, Chevron and Mobil Oil would not be permitted to have a single person serve as a member of the board of directors of both companies at the same time)

The Federal Trade Commission Act

This act, too, became law in 1914 during a period when populist sentiment against big business was very strong. In addition to creating another government agency—the Federal Trade Commission—to enforce the antitrust laws, it prohibited all unfair methods of competition (without defining them in specific terms). In later years, the act was amended to give more protection to consumers by forbidding unfair and deceptive business practices, such as misleading advertising, bait-and-switch merchandising, and other consumer abuses.

The Antitrust Improvements Act

All the important additions made to the antitrust laws during the 1930s and 1950s (for example, the Robinson-Patman Act and the Celler Anti-merger Act) were incorporated into the three major laws as summarized above. But in 1976 Congress put a new and separate law on the books. Basically, the

Antitrust Improvements Act strengthens government's hand in enforcing the other three laws. This law

- Requires large corporations to notify the Justice Department and the Federal Trade Commission about impending mergers and acquisitions so that the regulators can study any possible violations of the law that may be caused by the merger (for example, the merger of LTV's J&L Steel division with Republic Steel was delayed by the Justice Department until two of Republic's mills were sold in order to preserve competition)
- Expands the Justice Department's antitrust investigatory powers
- Authorizes the attorneys general of all fifty states to bring suits against companies that fix prices and to recover damages for consumers

Exemptions

Not all organizations are subject to these four antitrust laws. Congress has exempted labor unions that attempt to monopolize the supply of labor; agricultural cooperatives that sometimes engage in anticompetitive behavior; insurance companies, which are regulated by state, not federal, laws; and some special small-business transactions related to national defense and cooperative research and development efforts.[15] But the great bulk of American business must adhere to the laws as written by Congress and as interpreted by regulators and the courts.

Enforcing the Antitrust Laws

The two main antitrust enforcement agencies are the Antitrust Division of the U.S. Department of Justice and the Federal Trade Commission. Both agencies may bring suits against companies they believe to be guilty of violating antitrust laws. They also may investigate possible violations, issue guidelines and advisory opinions for firms planning mergers or acquisitions, identify specific practices considered to be illegal, and negotiate informal settlements out of court.

Antitrust suits also can be initiated by private persons or companies who believe themselves to have been damaged by the anticompetitive actions of a business firm. During the 1970s and early 1980s, 95 percent of all antitrust enforcement actions—about 2,000 cases each year—were initiated by private parties, not government officials.[16]

For example, *Berkey Photo sued Eastman Kodak, charging that Kodak had (in violation of the Sherman Act) monopolized the amateur film and color paper markets, had (also in violation of the Sherman Act) unlawfully restrained trade in cooperation with General Electric and General Telephone and Electronics's*

[15]Hovenkamp, op. cit., pp. 273–276.

[16]Betty Bock, et al., *Antitrust in the Competitive World of the 1980s: Exploring Options,* Research Bulletin No. 112, New York: The Conference Board, 1982, p. 18; and Betty Bock et al., *Antitrust Issues: Are We Investing in the Future of Competition?* Information Bulletin No. 94, New York: The Conference Board, 1981, p. 19.

Sylvania unit, and had (in violation of the Clayton Act) received unlawful price discounts from those companies in purchasing flash units. A federal court jury found Kodak guilty and imposed a fine of $37.6 million for damages Berkey sustained; this amount was then trebled to $112.8 million because the laws provide for a recovery of triple damages for antitrust violations. An appeals court later modified the guilty charges, reduced the amount of the damages awarded to Berkey, and ordered a new trial on some aspects of the case.[17]

Attorneys general of the various states also may take action against antitrust violators, not only to protect consumers from price fixing (under the Antitrust Improvements Act), but also by enforcing the antitrust laws of their own states.

Finally, the courts usually have the final word in enforcement, and the outcome is never certain. Cases are sometimes tried before a jury; in one extremely complex case against U.S. Steel Corporation none of the jury members had completed high school. Sometimes a panel of judges will hear an appeal. At other times, a single judge will preside over a case that may last for years; the Justice Department's case against IBM was begun in 1969 and was finally dropped by the government prosecutors in 1982. The Supreme Court is the court of final appeal, and its opinions carry great weight. Antitrust regulators and businesses alike often appeal their cases to this final forum because the stakes are so high and the judicial precedents created by the high court are so important in the long-run development of antitrust regulation.

Figure 9-4 summarizes the main provisions of the federal antitrust laws and the major components of the enforcement process.

Business Objections to Antitrust

Much of the business community, especially big business, sees antitrust regulation as an example of unwarranted government intervention in the free enterprise system. They maintain that government has gone too far when companies must consult with antitrust regulators before merging with another company, bringing out new products before a competitor does, cutting prices to an established customer, releasing advertising copy, and putting labels on consumer products. Failure to get government approval may possibly result in antitrust action against a company. Business believes that too much of its decision making has to be shared with government regulators who do not fully understand how business works.

Another complaint of business is that the antitrust laws and regulations are too general, too vague, and too uncertain to provide a practical basis for business decision making. As proof, they cite the zigzags in both agency and judicial interpretations of the major laws, Congress's willingness to preserve competition at times but to abandon it at others, and shifting attitudes toward

[17]"Damages Voted against Kodak of $37.6 Million," _Wall Street Journal_, March 23, 1978, p. 5; _Pittsburgh Post-Gazette_, March 23, 1978; and "Berkey Photo's Victory in Kodak Suit Is Reversed," _Wall Street Journal_, June 26, 1979, p. 2.

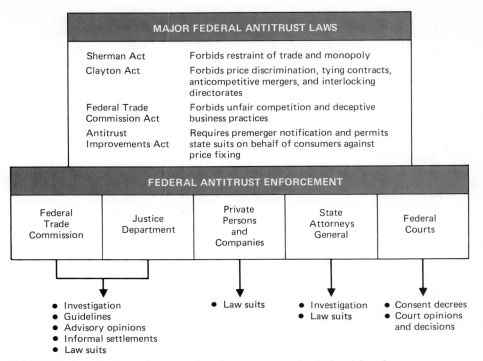

FIGURE 9-4. Antitrust laws and enforcement at the federal level.

the size and growth of large corporations that seem to be typical of different presidential administrations. Even the issuance of detailed merger guidelines by the Justice Department leaves business firms with much uncertainty because the courts, in any given case, may express differing opinions.

Still another objection is to the long delays in reaching a final decision in the courts.

> *As mentioned earlier, the government's monopoly case against IBM's data processing unit lasted thirteen years. By 1978 the company had supplied the government with over 4 million pages of documents concerning the charges; the trial transcript through the first three years when only government witnesses had been heard ran to 64,500 pages; and one government witness spent thirty-one days on the stand in 1977, his testimony alone far exceeding the length of most other trials. In the meantime, IBM's market position declined as competition for peripheral equipment increased and as Japanese producers became stronger. By the time the case was dropped, competitive conditions in the industry had changed greatly.[18]*

[18]For an account of this landmark case, see Franklin M. Fisher, John J. McGowan, and Joen E. Greenwood, *Folded, Spindled, and Mutilated: Economic Analysis and U.S. v. IBM*, Cambridge, MA: MIT Press, 1983.

One of the strongest business objections is to the bias against size per se that seems embedded in antitrust regulations. Mergers are sometimes blocked when only a tiny percentage of the market is involved. For example, in Los Angeles two grocery chains were stopped from merging, although combined they would have had only 7.5 percent of the Los Angeles market. Business argues that in cases like this one it is unable to take advantage of economies of scale that occur in large firms, and as a result it is not permitted to pass these cost savings on to the consuming public.

Key Antitrust Issues

The business community, government policymakers, and the general public have to seek answers to several key issues if the nation's antitrust laws and regulations are to serve both business and society well. We cannot discuss any of these issues in detail here, but we will identify them so that the thoughtful student may be aware of them and realize they are important policy matters affecting business.

Corporate Size

The key question here is: *Is bigness alone evidence of monopoly or a threat to competition?* In general, the courts have said that absolute size by itself is not a violation of the antitrust laws. If, however, a firm uses its larger size to take advantage of rivals through price discrimination, collusion with others, or other specific actions banned by the antitrust laws, then it may be found guilty. Corporations have grown steadily for over a century, and the antitrust laws appear neither to have prevented nor significantly slowed their growth.

Economic Concentration

The key question here is: *Does domination of an industry or a market by a few large corporations violate the antitrust laws?* Or, as some say: Should the biggest firms in each industry be broken up? Many major industries and markets are dominated by a handful of mammoth companies—examples are automobiles, tires, chemicals, insurance, copper, steel, some food products, paper, and many others. Where this kind of concentration exists, competition changes. Companies tend to compete less by underselling their rivals and more by making their products appear distinctive, by servicing their customers, by building reliability into products and parts, by developing brand-name loyalty in customers, and by advertising.

Critics claim that economic concentration eliminates effective price competition, reduces consumer choices, causes firms to grow too large to be efficient, inhibits innovation, and concentrates profits in too few hands. The best solution, they say, is to break up the giants into smaller units. Others counter by claiming that big firms have become dominant because they are more efficient, that price competition still occurs along with the other types mentioned above, that today's large firms give consumers more, not fewer, choices of goods and services, that large companies can finance more innovation than small businesses, and that profits are distributed widely to an increasing number of stockholders. Breaking up large corporations would deprive society of these benefits, say the defenders, and should not be done.

> The most spectacular corporate breakup in recent years occurred in early 1982 when the world's largest corporation, American Telephone & Telegraph Company (AT&T), accepted a court-approved settlement of the government's antitrust suit against the company. AT&T agreed to sell all twenty-two of its local telephone companies that together represented nearly two-thirds of its total corporate assets, supplied 44 percent of AT&T revenues in 1981, and accounted for 80 percent of its employees. Other parts of the giant firm were retained, including Bell Telephone Laboratories, the company's famous research facility, and Western Electric Company, which manufactures communications equipment. AT&T also kept all long-distance telephone equipment, but consumers were free to buy long-distance telephone services from AT&T competitors if they wished. In addition to breaking up the Bell system's near-monopoly control of the telephone business, the agreement was intended to create more competition in the rapidly expanding electronic information processing industry by permitting the telephone giant to enter that new line of business.[19]

Efficiency versus Competition

Another antitrust issue is efficiency versus competition. The key question here is: *Is big-business efficiency more important than preserving competition?* Many big companies claim that their large size makes possible many operating economies. Today's complex technology, far-flung markets, complicated financial systems, and transnational competition make bigness essential for survival and efficient operation. Some bigness is required to compete successfully against state-owned and state-subsidized foreign companies. Placing restrictions on today's corporate growth just to preserve a competitive ideal formed during the eighteenth and nineteenth centuries seems to make little economic sense. On the other hand, others point out that competition stands at the heart of free enterprise ideology and that small businesses, consumers, and workers should be protected against big-business expansion even though it may mean a loss of efficiency.

Corporate Mergers and Takeovers in the 1980s

The early 1980s showed an astonishing burst of corporate merger activity, as revealed in Figure 9-5. In 1984, there were 2,999 mergers or acquisitions amounting to $124.8 billion, figures that were approximately equalled in 1985. In just one of these 1985 mergers, General Electric paid $6.3 billion for RCA, making it the largest nonoil merger recorded up to that date. Other familiar

---

[19]For more details, see "The Odds in a Bell-IBM Bout," *Business Week*, January 25, 1982, pp. 22–25; and "AT&T Is Still Not off the Hook on Antitrust," *Business Week*, August 30, 1982, pp. 25, 28.

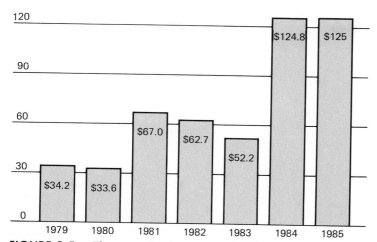

FIGURE 9-5.   The growth of mergers, 1979–1985 (in billions of dollars).
(*Source: Leonard Silk, "The Peril behind the Takeover Boom," New York Times,
December 29, 1985, p. F-1.*)

corporate names were involved in mergers that year, as shown in Figure 9-6's list of the ten largest deals. In all, there were twenty-four members of the "billion dollar club"—mergers in which at least $1 billion was paid by one corporation to acquire another. Mergers of this size continued in 1986 as thirty additional multibillion-dollar deals, totaling over $57 billion, were reported.[20]

Corporate mergers seem to occur in waves at different periods of history. The 1950s and 1960s saw much activity which culminated in 6,000 mergers during 1969. Most observers seem to agree that one factor stimulating the 1980s surge was the government's general philosophy of deregulation and a more relaxed attitude toward enforcement of the nation's antitrust laws. This philosophy and approach placed a greater degree of faith in the free enterprise system to preserve competition, protect consumers, and ensure high levels of productivity than the opposite philosophy of curbing corporate power by strong antitrust regulations. In this general climate of greater permissiveness, the number of corporate mergers ballooned.

Students of corporate mergers usually distinguish between three different types of business combinations, as outlined in Figure 9-7. *Vertical mergers occur when the combining companies are at different stages of production in the same general line of business.* For example, a rubber tire manufacturer may combine with a company owning rubber plantations and with a chain of auto parts dealers that sells the tires. Production "from the ground up" is then brought

[20]Leonard Silk, "The Peril Behind the Takeover Boom," *New York Times*, December 29, 1985, pp. F-1, F-6; and Cynthia Crossen, "Merger Activity Expected to Ease, Not Halt," *Wall Street Journal*, January 2, 1987, p. 8-B. For a detailed list of corporate mergers in 1986, see "The Top 200 Deals: Merger Mania's New Ascent," *Business Week*, April 17, 1987, pp. 273–292.

Buyer	Company Bought	Value (in billions)
General Electric	RCA	$ 6.3
Kohlberg, Kravis, Roberts	Beatrice	6.2
Philip Morris	General Foods	5.8
General Motors	Hughes Aircraft	5.1
Allied Corporation	Signal Companies	5.0
R. J. Reynolds	Nabisco	4.9
Baxter Travenol	American Hospital Supply	3.8
U.S. Steel	Texas Oil and Gas	3.7
Capital Cities Communications	American Broadcasting Company	3.5
Monsanto	G. D. Searle	2.8
Total value		$47.1

FIGURE 9-6. The ten largest corporate mergers, 1985. (*Source: Leonard Silk, "The Peril behind the Takeover Boom," New York Times, December 29, 1985, p. F-6.*)

under a single management umbrella, so it is referred to as a vertical combination. *Horizontal mergers occur when the combining companies are at the same stage or level of production or sales.* As pointed out earlier in this chapter, if two retail grocery chains in an urban market tried to combine, antitrust regulators probably would not permit the merger if the combined firms' resultant market share appeared to lessen competition in that area.

A *conglomerate merger occurs when firms that are in totally unrelated lines of business are combined.* For example, Gulf and Western (G&W), a well-known conglomerate, merged under its corporate umbrella firms that manufacture

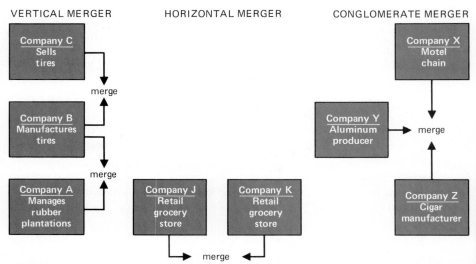

FIGURE 9-7. Three different types of corporate mergers.

pipeline equipment, auto and truck parts, cigars, chocolate candy, steel mill equipment, pantyhose, and paperback books; other units run racetracks, distribute educational films, and stage the Miss Universe and Miss USA beauty pageants! In the 1980s, G&W sold off many of these units.

Critics say that conglomerate mergers give a smaller acquired company an unfair advantage over its rivals because it can draw on the superior financial and marketing resources of the big company. Others claim that a conglomerate has the power to "subsidize" one division by allowing it to cut prices and drive its competitors out of the market, only to raise prices once the struggle is won. Various other charges have been leveled at conglomerate mergers which suggest that they violate the spirit of the antitrust laws. Defenders call attention to the virtues of the conglomerate's pooled resources from many different kinds of business experience, the diversified nature of a corporation more capable of responding to the ups and downs of the business cycle than one based on a single product or service, and the many centralized managerial, technical, and financial services that can be made available to a small business unit that otherwise would be unable to afford such aids.

Corporate Takeovers—Friendly and Hostile

People favoring corporate takeovers say that they are good for business (by increasing efficiency and making companies stronger competitors), for consumers (by delivering more and better goods at fair prices), and for stockholders (by producing maximum value for their shares of stock in the merged companies).

> A certain "synergy"—or favorable multiplier effect—is thought to occur when two companies get together under one corporate umbrella. The 1981 merger of Nabisco and Standard Brands, two food giants, took advantage of each firm's geographic, marketing, technological, and managerial expertise. Neither company was burdened with large debt, since the purchase price of $2 billion was arranged as a stock transaction based on the book value of the companies rather than on an unknown speculative estimate of market values. This meant that company officials could concentrate on long-run plans rather than scramble for short-run profits to service a huge new debt. Management turnover was much lower than usual, as care was taken to fit the two companies' management teams together in fair ways.[21]

Other combinations have not fared so well. Mobil purchased Montgomery Ward and Container Corporation in 1976 for $1.8 billion, then spent $609 million more on Montgomery Ward, while pocketing profits of only $17 million by the retailer since the takeover. In 1985 Mobil wrote off another $500 million on Montgomery Ward's assets as a probable preliminary to sell-

---

[21]"Do Mergers Really Work?" _Business Week_, June 3, 1985, pp. 90–91. For another well-managed merger, see "Burroughs Wins Praise for Handling of Sperry," _Wall Street Journal_, November 7, 1986, p. 6.

ing or spinning off the corporation entirely. Mobil's enormous losses were similar to Atlantic Richfield's $785 million loss on Anaconda Minerals and General Electric's sale of Utah International, a mining company, after six years of poor performance. In fact, in recent years one-third of corporate mergers have come apart, and some studies show that mergers and acquisitions "often result in market-share losses, skimpier profits, and, over the long haul, less money for shareholders." The bigger the merged companies and the less alike they are in product and outlook, the greater the chance that the merger will not produce good results.[22]

Takeover Tactics. When two companies combine, their stock (shares of ownership) and assets (physical, financial, managerial, and employees) are merged into one corporate identity, usually but not always with a new corporate name. For example, Nabisco and Standard Brands changed the newly formed company's name to Nabisco Brands. "Friendly" mergers occur when both companies agree to combine, and these stock and asset transactions normally cause no problem or controversy.

"Hostile" mergers, on the other hand, can create spectacular fights for control, with both sides resorting to the full panoply of takeover tactics such as the following ones:

- *Proxy fights:* A corporate "raider" or takeover specialist sometimes wages a fight for control of a corporation's board of directors and seeks one or more seats on the board. To be successful, the raider has to convince stockholders to vote for the raider's candidates. If enough stockholders cast their votes for those candidates, or if they send their "proxy" (which is a legal right to vote a stockholder's shares of stock) to the raider, the raider may be successful in putting enough supporters on the board to influence company policies without buying the company's assets or stock. In this case, an actual merger need not take place since control of the target corporation is achieved in other ways.
- *Cumulative voting:* One technique for winning seats on the board of directors is to concentrate all of one's votes on just one or two candidates instead of voting for all of those up for election. Some states permit this practice, while others do not. When T. Boone Pickens attempted to take over Pennsylvania-based Gulf Oil, he threatened to use this tactic to win seats on Gulf's board, so Gulf's board of directors reincorporated in Delaware, whose laws forbid cumulative voting.
- *Tender offers:* Most takeovers, especially hostile ones, involve offers by the takeover specialist to buy shares of stock in the target corporation. In the language of Wall Street, shareholders are asked to "tender," or formally offer, their shares of stock for sale at a price the raider is willing to pay. These tender offers can become furiously competitive, and stockholders often see the price of their stock bid higher and higher as raiders compete to win a majority of the company stock. Pickens started bidding for Gulf's

---

[22]"Do Mergers Really Work?" op. cit., pp. 88–89.

stock at a price of $65 per share, then learned of Atlantic Richfield's informal offer of $70 per share, and was finally bested by a tender offer of $80 per share by Chevron. Gulf directors turned down an even higher offer of around $87 per share proposed in a leveraged buyout by a group of its own managers.

- *Two-tier offers:* Another much-criticized technique used in corporate take-overs involves a two-tier tender offer. A corporate raider may offer to buy just over half of a company's stock at a cash price of, say, $40 per share, thereby giving the raider enough stock to control the company. Any stockholders who do not take advantage of this initial chance may then be offered a lower price, for example $30 per share, for their stock or they may get other types of securities in a swap that is not always as favorable financially. As a counter to this tactic, some corporations have put a "fair price" amendment in their charters that requires tender offers to pay the same price to all shareholders.[23]

- *Junk-bond financing:* It takes huge amounts of money to buy up one of the giant corporations, and not even the wealthiest groups have the funds to do it alone. Many of the takeovers of the 1980s have been financed by the sale of so-called "junk bonds"as a way of raising the necessary amounts. A junk bond is a bond that has a low credit rating but which carries a correspondingly high rate of return to compensate for its risky character. Many wealthy individuals, some financial investment houses, and the managers of some large pension or money-market funds are willing to take a chance on these junk bonds because the returns are so attractive. As a result, a corporate raider, in cooperation with an investment banking firm that has access to such junk bonds, can finance a big corporate takeover effort.

Takeover Defenses. Corporate managers usually resist takeover efforts for three basic reasons. Takeover battles can divert a company's top managers and planners from their important tasks of planning strategically for the company's future. When so much energy has to go into defending the company from outsiders, the day-to-day business decisions as well as the long-run strategic ones may suffer neglect. As long as managers serve in top-level posts, they have an obligation to run the company and carry out plans approved by the board of directors. Having to fight off takeover efforts only complicates an already complex job.

A second reason why top managers resist corporate takeovers is fear of losing their jobs after the merger occurs unless they are given a "golden parachute," which is a guarantee that continues their financial benefits for a number of years if they are dismissed. It stands to reason in most cases that fewer managers and other professionals and specialists will be needed when two companies are merged to form one company. Since many top managers may have spent years climbing to their present positions, they are understandably reluctant to lose out. They also may resent taking orders from

---

[23]"Girding for the Proxy Wars," *Business Week*, April 16, 1984, p. 46.

someone else in another company whose procedures and routines are different.

In addition to their own personal interests, a corporation's managers have a fiduciary or legal responsibility to the company's stockholders to make decisions in the owners' interests. A chief executive officer may therefore believe that a raider's tender offer is too low and that stockholders would not receive fair market value if they accepted such an offer. In these cases, it is best to resist. A number of takeover defenses, often called "shark repellents," are available:[24]

- *Staggered board terms:* One way to fight off an attempt to gain seats on the board of directors is to stagger the terms of board members so that fewer than a majority of the seats are up for election in any one year. Used successfully, this tactic may stretch out over several years a raider's attempt to gain a majority of the seats.
- *Super majorities:* Another way to fend off a potential takeover is to amend the corporation's bylaws to require that any offer to buy the company be approved by a very large majority, perhaps from 65 percent to 80 percent, of the stockholders. It is difficult for raiders to accumulate enough votes on their own or through proxies to achieve such a super-majority vote.
- *Nonvoting or supervoting stock:* Normally, each share of common stock issued is entitled to one vote. During the 1980s merger boom, however, some corporations created special classes of stock. Some of it had no voting rights at all, while other stocks were given more than one vote per share. By allocating these stocks carefully, a company's management could lock up most of the votes in ways that would favor its own position on merger attempts.
- *Greenmail:* If desperate enough, a management with its back to the wall and faced with a persistent raider might be willing to pay "greenmail," which is an agreement to buy back a big block of the company's stock acquired by the raider if the raider will agree to abandon the takeover effort. The offer is unfair to other company stockholders who are not paid such a premium or who may actually lose money when the company's stock falls after the raider agrees to go away.[25]
- *Increasing the company's debt:* Another last-ditch tactic is to load the company up with so much new debt that it becomes a less attractive takeover target. This might be done by borrowing huge sums of money to buy another company. It seems hard to justify this maneuver as anything more than a selfish effort by an entrenched management to protect itself, since the

---

[24]For a discussion and two illustrative case studies, see Jeffrey A. Barach et al., "Shark Repellents: Whitney National Bank, and Bendix-Martin Marietta," New Orleans: Freeman School of Business, Tulane University, 1985. For the Indiana antitakeover law discussed below, see "Justices Back State Curbs on Takeovers; Move May Deal a Blow to Hostile Bidders," *Wall Street Journal,* April 22, 1987, p. 3; and "Takeover Artists Take a Direct Hit," *Business Week,* May 4, 1987, p. 35.

[25]"The Greenmailers Learn to Play in the Shadows," *Business Week,* May 5, 1986, p. 105; and "A Flurry of Greenmail Has Stockholders Cursing," *Business Week,* December 8, 1986, pp. 32–34.

bloated debt must be serviced before any dividends can be paid to stock-holders.

- *Selling off profitable units:* One way to defeat a raider is to sell off the cor-poration's profitable units to another company, leaving behind a corporate shell containing only unprofitable businesses for the raider to inherit. In some antitakeover plans, these sales are triggered only when a raider ac-quires enough stock to control the target company.

- *Poison pills:* These plans discourage a hostile raider by allowing all share-holders in the target company to purchase stock or other securities in the proposed merged companies at a sharp discount. Some pills also permit stockholders to sell their shares to the acquired company at a premium. The poison pill is normally triggered only when a raider acquires over 50 percent of the stock of the target company. Thus, a raider may succeed in taking over a company but only after paying a premium price for the con-trolling block of stock, while other stockholders buy or sell stock at a bargain price.

- *Leveraged buyout by management:* Sometimes a company's top management group under attack from a determined raider will decide to buy the com-pany and "take it private," which means removing its stock from the stock exchanges and not allowing it to be sold to the general public. These trans-actions are usually handled through what is called a leveraged buyout, in which the managers borrow enough money to purchase the company by pledging as collateral the company's assets. If that sounds like financial magic, it is; but several such deals were consummated during the 1980s.

- *White knights:* If all else fails and a company is practically in the grasp of a hostile raider, the threatened company might be able to find a friendly buyer, known as a "white knight." This tactic was used by Gulf Oil when it seemed as if T. Boone Pickens was about to succeed in his offer to buy a majority of Gulf's stock. Gulf's board of directors made an agreement with Chevron to sell the company to Chevron for $80 per share. Gulf's top managers then bailed out in their "golden parachutes" (the CEO collected around $7 million in stock options and other benefits) and the company they had managed lost its identity and disappeared from America's cor-porate rolls.

- *State antitakeover laws:* Worried that corporate takeovers might harm their industrial base, several states have laws that restrict hostile tender offers. In a landmark case, the U.S. Supreme Court in 1987 upheld an Indiana law that prevents a bidder who buys 20 percent or more of a company's stock from voting those shares until a majority of the other shareholders approve. The effect is to delay—and perhaps eventually to scuttle—a raider's take-over attempt. Other states were expected to adopt similar laws.

The Consequences of Corporate Mergers

When the smoke has cleared from the wave of corporate mergers that began in the 1980s, what will the results be? No one knows the final story, but some preliminary results are already observable. The megamergers such as those listed in Figure 9-6 create enormously larger corporations, thus continuing a trend toward bigger and bigger business units. Successful takeover defenses entrench present management in their positions of control inside the corporation. Many employees lose their jobs when companies combine, and local communities suffer significant dislocation when a large company moves out or shifts its activities to other regions. As noted earlier, a surprising number of mergers simply do not work out as planned, which results finally in a breakup of the newly formed company after the expenditure of immense sums of money on a failed effort. Some acquired companies, often called "cash cows," are milked of their cash by the parent corporation, thus weakening that part of the newly formed company or preventing it from plowing the money back into modernization and growth.

One unfortunate result of mergers, particularly among those companies that end up with huge debt loads incurred either to finance the purchase or to ward off a takeover, is a sharp focus on short-run profits in order to pay the debt's interest charges. This often means that long-run strategic planning is made more difficult and long-run investments in improving productivity are sacrificed. Other observers have criticized the multimillion-dollar fees ($47 million in the Gulf-Chevron merger) charged by financial advisers who actively encourage megamergers,[26] as well as the huge profits taken by the raiders (Pickens made $760 million on his $1-billion investment in Gulf stock).

The results are mixed for stockholders. Share values often are driven up when a takeover struggle begins. The implication is that the company is not being managed to yield maximum value for the stockholders. In that case, shareholders would gain from a takeover.

Some companies are dismembered or badly damaged financially by takeover battles, and the stock value is diminished. A heavy debt load may burden the company with a punishing interest payment to service the debt. Valuable and profitable units of the company may have to be sold to pay off the debt, thus reducing long-run profits and dividends for stockholders. If new stock has been issued to fend off the raider, the per-share value is diluted, which results in lower dividends per share. If voting rights have been restricted by the issuance of special classes of stock, shareowners may lose some control over management. When a corporate marriage does not work out, stockholders in both companies may suffer losses.

Trends in Antitrust Thinking

As the nation moved nearer to the one-hundredth anniversary of the Sherman Act (1890), it became obvious that attitudes toward antitrust regulation of business were changing. More and more questions were raised about the relevance of these laws as guides to public policy and business behavior in an age of electronics, multinational corporations, and global competition.

---

[26]Fred R. Bleakley, "The Merger Makers' Spiraling Fees," *New York Times*, September 30, 1984, pp. F-1, F-24.

Among leading government officials, business representatives, and antitrust lawyers and scholars, the following attitudes increasingly were favored:

- Less worry about the large size of companies and about the concentrated structure of an industry or a market, and more attention to their actual impacts on competition and productivity. According to this viewpoint, if bigness or high concentration leads to more economic efficiency and lower consumer prices, it is an acceptable business practice.
- A greater tolerance of both *vertical* and *conglomerate* mergers, on grounds that the overall economic benefits outweigh any possible threat to competition. The $7.3-billion takeover of Conoco by Du Pont Company (a vertical merger), and U.S. Steel's $6.3 billion acquisition of Marathon Oil (a conglomerate merger) were not challenged by antitrust regulators.
- Continued concern about *horizontal* mergers most likely to dampen competition and harm consumers. For example, proposed horizontal mergers between Mobil and Marathon Oil, as well as between Gulf Oil and Cities Service, were blocked by the Federal Trade Commission, which feared the combinations would lessen competition in the oil industry. Price fixing and bid rigging were especially targeted for prosecution by federal authorities.
- More lenience for technological innovations by leading industrial firms, even if it gives the dominant firm an advantage over its weaker competitors. When, for example, Du Pont developed a new brightener used in paint and paper, it captured a large share of the market for brighteners. Antitrust regulators approved this development, saying that antitrust laws should not be used "to block hard, aggressive competition that is solidly based on efficiencies and growth opportunities, even if monopoly is a possible result."[27]
- Greater recognition that domestic antitrust standards sometimes penalize United States companies in global competition. Although General Motors normally captures around 45 percent of the United States car market (and therefore is watched carefully by antitrust officials), its share of the world market is only 28 percent or less, due to competition from Volkswagen, Toyota, Nissan, Renault, and others. Joint ventures and vertical mergers in the auto industry may be one way to strengthen the competitive muscle of United States companies, but such activities may be prevented by strict application of present antitrust laws. One authority has stated that "U.S. companies should be free to compete on equal terms with a German oligopoly, a French oligopoly, and a Japanese [oligopoly], whether at home or abroad."[28]
- A broadening of the focus of antitrust—from a narrow, punitive, legal attempt to curb anticompetitive behavior to a much broader policy of promoting and strengthening the competitive vigor of United States industry at home and abroad. This broader approach involves a more relaxed and

---

[27]Quoted in "The New Case for Monopolists," *Business Week*, December 15, 1980, p. 58.

[28]Economist Lester Thurow, as quoted in "Antitrust Grows Unpopular," *Business Week*, January 12, 1981, p. 92.

realistic attitude toward corporate size, concentration, mergers, and collaboration among actual or potential competitors.[29]

SUMMARY

The world's largest corporations are capable of wielding considerable influence because of the central functions they perform in their respective societies and throughout the world. Their economic, political, and social power causes some people to question the largest corporations' legitimacy, especially in societies with strong democratic traditions. In the United States the antitrust laws have been used to curb the influence of corporations and to protect consumers, small business, and others affected unfairly by corporate practices.

The merger movement of the 1980s consisted of a wave of mergers, acquisitions, and takeover attempts unprecedented in the number and size of corporate combinations. Some believed that it was good for stockholders, while others expressed concern about the long-run effects such mergers would have on both business and society. The growth in power and influence of the largest corporations tends to activate the Iron Law of Responsibility, thereby requiring business to consider social factors as well as economic ones in its decision making.

DISCUSSION AND REVIEW QUESTIONS

1. With a team of two other class members, choose one of the corporations listed in Figures 9-1 and 9-2. By examining library sources (*Fortune,* the *Wall Street Journal, Business Week, Nation's Business,* etc.), find information about the company's economic, political, and social influence. Compare the results of your team's research with what other teams of students find about other corporations. Which type of power—economic, political, or social—is the easiest to detect and describe?

2. A Chicago business executive commented as follows when asked about one famous corporate merger of the early 1980s:

> What do you tell your son to do when a bully picks on him in school? When somebody hits you, you react in kind. But sometimes these fights aren't productive, whether it's kids in school or corporate management. Shareholder and customer interest often isn't best served by takeover fights. To the extent that management allows itself to be distracted from its job, it's abdicating its respon-

---

[29]For a summary discussion of these trends, see Ernest Gellhorn, *Antitrust Law and Economics,* 3d ed., St. Paul, MN: West, 1986. More advanced treatment of these issues can be found in Robert H. Bork, *The Antitrust Paradox: A Policy at War with Itself,* New York: Basic Books, 1980; and Richard A. Posner, *Antitrust Law: An Economic Perspective,* Chicago: University of Chicago Press, 1978.

sibility. We managers need to keep our heads screwed on right. Sometimes our egos get in the way.[30]

Discuss this executive's views, pro and con.

3. When a new company called Woodlands Communications was formed to provide telephone service to residents of a new town being developed near Houston, Southwestern Bell Telephone Company, then a subsidiary of AT&T, refused to interconnect the new system to its existing lines. The Woodlands company said this violated the antitrust laws. A federal court jury agreed and awarded $18.4 million in damages to Woodlands.[31] Which antitrust laws might have formed the basis for this case?

4. Under provisions of the 1976 Antitrust Improvements Act, the Federal Trade Commission published rules declaring that any company owning $100 million in assets that planned to merge with a $10 million company would have to notify the FTC in advance and provide it with detailed financial information. In your opinion, is this rule justified as a way to protect competition and prevent monopoly, or is it an unwarranted intrusion into the private affairs of free enterprise? Discuss the pros and cons.

5. A former executive of two large steel companies, referring to "political and archaic trust-busting attitudes" of government regulators, declared that fostering competition among many small producers "doesn't relate to the times." It does not make sense, he said, for rival firms to spend large sums to build the same kind of steel mill in the same market and have "both lose money running at 50 percent" capacity. Would you agree—or disagree—that the economic efficiency of big firms is preferable to competition among many small firms? Discuss.

CRITICAL INCIDENT

To Merge or Not to Merge

"We're pleased to be tying up with them," said the president of Union Electric Steel Corporation. He was referring to Ampco-Pittsburgh Steel Corporation, which had just ended a successful effort to purchase Union Electric for $60 million. It was a strange comment for Union Electric's top executive to make inasmuch as the company's managers and a majority of its board of directors had earlier recommended accepting a competing bid from another company for only $55.5 million. But vigorous resistance by two major stockholders to this lower offer blocked Union Electric's board from getting the necessary approval.

The bidding war began when H. K. Porter, a diversified manufacturer, offered $32 per share for Union Electric's 1.5 million shares. This $48-million offer took

---

[30]"Four-Way Takeover Fight Amuses Some Spectators, Disturbs Others," *Wall Street Journal,* September 24, 1982.

[31]"An AT&T Antitrust Loss," *Business Week,* October 9, 1978, p. 56.

observers by surprise since Porter the year before had sold off its steel-related businesses, and now they seemed ready to reenter that business arena at a time when the steel industry was severely depressed. In announcing its unsolicited offer, Porter revealed that it already owned 78,636 shares of Union Electric stock, amounting to about 5.2 percent of the total.

One week later, another suitor appeared at Union Electric's door. Allegheny Ludlum Steel Corporation said it would pay $55.5 million for the company; this amounted to $37 per share. This offer specified certain conditions that would have to be met: Union Electric's board would have to give its answer the following day (although this deadline was later extended three days); the board's approval of its offer would have to be unanimous; the board would have to agree to recommend that all other stockholders accept Allegheny Ludlum's offer; Union Electric would have to reimburse Allegheny Ludlum up to $350,000 for its takeover expenses if they were not able to buy at least 51 percent of the stock; federal antitrust officials would have to approve the sale; and Union Electric's two major stockholders would have to agree to sell their stock to the acquiring company.

This last condition proved to be a stumbling block. Two nieces of Union Electric's founder held a 28.3 percent interest in the company, and a trust fund held by two banks for the nieces controlled another 12 percent. Two of the seven board seats were occupied by the nieces, who balked at accepting Allegheny Ludlum's $37 offer. They were reported to believe the offer was too low. Union Electric's stock had been trading at $29.50 per share about a week before H. K. Porter's $32 offer was made, but it had risen to $32.50 per share shortly thereafter. The other five board members were said to believe that the latest offer of $37 was fair and equitable to all stockholders as well as in the best interests of the company's employees, customers, and suppliers. In approving Allegheny Ludlum's offer, these five board members rejected the earlier offer by H. K. Porter as inadequate.

With the board deadlocked at five to two, a third bid came in from Ampco-Pittsburgh Steel Corporation. It offered a total price of $60 million, or $40 per share. The founder's two nieces agreed to sell their stock to Ampco-Pittsburgh at this price, which amounted to a total of around $17 million, not counting the trust fund holdings. The next day Union Electric's board unanimously approved the sale of the company to this third bidder. H. K. Porter's 78,636 shares brought around $3.1 million to the company that began the bidding war.

Ampco-Pittsburgh officials believed they were acquiring a company that would fit in well with its other recent acquisitions. As a manufacturer of heavy industrial products, Ampco-Pittsburgh saw Union Electric's reputation and quality production as a definite plus. "We think it's a good investment. They have a superb name in the industry. They have done a good job and maintained quality, which we think is important," said an Ampco-Pittsburgh officer.

Union Electric's book value three months earlier was $39 million, or $26 per share. The year before it earned $3.2 million, or $2.13 per share, on sales of $43 million. In the quarter prior to the bidding, its earnings were $1.2 million, or just 82 cents per share, compared with 35 cents per share for the same period the year before. These figures tended to reflect the uncertainty, instability, and generally depressed conditions that had characterized the steel industry for several years.[32]

1. In your view, did Union Electric's board of directors act in the best interests of its stockholders in this episode? What would you say if it had sold the company to H. K. Porter at $32 per share? What would you say if it had been able to sell to Allegheny Ludlum at $37 per share? Should the board have waited for a fourth possible bid from another company?

2. Was management of Union Electric doing a good job for its stockholders before the bidding began, since stock that was apparently worth $40 to the successful bidder was selling for only $29.50 on the market prior to the take-over effort?

3. What do you think about H. K. Porter's role in this transaction? It failed to gain control of Union Electric, but its initial overture resulted in a significant profit on the sale of its stock to Ampco-Pittsburgh. Was this profit justified? On what grounds?

4. In view of the higher price paid by Ampco-Pittsburgh, and knowing that the synergy claimed for this combination has not always worked out in other corporate mergers, and being aware of the depressed condition of the steel industry, do you believe that Ampco-Pittsburgh's board acted in the best interests of its own stockholders?

[32]Various news reports in the *Pittsburgh Post-Gazette* and the *Pittsburgh Press*, June 1984.

① Yes, I think it did. Although the refusal of the $37/share offer by the two nieces of the founder may have been more emotional reason rather than economic reasons. The sale of the stock netted an approximate 28% increase in profit for those that held the stock at the time the first offer was made. Fact is that when the two nieces sold their interest, the rest of the board had little choice.

② Hard to say, Ampco-Pittsburg may have only wanted certain parts of the company and may plan to sell off the rest.

③ H.K. Porter was in a win-win situation. Either outcome would benefit the company

PART 3

CORPORATE STAKEHOLDERS

Chapter Ten

STOCKHOLDER INTERESTS AND CORPORATE GOVERNANCE

Stockholders occupy a position of central importance in the corporation because they are the company's legal owners and because they expect high levels of economic performance. But the corporation is not always run solely for their benefit, so they contend with management and the board of directors for control of company policies. This chapter highlights the needs and problems of stockholders, tells of recent changes affecting their interests, and emphasizes the importance of managerial attention to this stakeholder group.

CHAPTER OBJECTIVES

After reading this chapter, you should be able to

- Understand who stockholders are, their goals, and their legal rights
- Explain the governance system of corporations
- Discuss ways of increasing the corporation's responsiveness to its stockholders
- Outline the pros and cons of employee ownership of corporations
- Show how stockholders may be hurt by insider trading and corporate takeovers

When T. Boone Pickens, a Texas oil executive, started buying up stock in Gulf Oil Corporation in the late summer of 1984, its price was about $40 per share. Several months later when he sold his Gulf stock, it was worth $80 per share. Although Pickens had started out with the intention of buying enough stock to have a major influence in Gulf's affairs, he lost out to Chevron, another oil company, which outbid him by offering a higher price. He had to settle for an estimated profit of $760 million gained from the rise in price of Gulf's stock. In his brand of Texas humor, Pickens was rumored to have said, "Shucks, I guess we lost another one." But Pickens was not alone in profiting from the takeover of Gulf Oil. All Gulf Oil stockholders who had bought stock at less than $80 per share were able to sell it to Chevron at a profit. Pickens had been largely responsible for driving the price far above its level at the time he began to buy it. He claimed that his pressures on Gulf had greatly benefited the company's stockholders and proved that Gulf's managers had not been doing a very good job of producing maximum value for the owners.

Protecting stockholder interests is complex, as revealed in another case involving two international corporations, two Middle Eastern governments, and high-ranking corporate officials in several countries. When the government-owned Kuwait Petroleum Corporation bought American-owned Sante Fe International, a private oil and gas company, it paid $51 per share. Only days before the announced purchase, Sante Fe stock was selling at $24 per share. Investigation revealed that several Middle Eastern business executives and the Interior Minister of Qatar, as well as some Sante Fe managers who had private advance information about the proposed takeover, bought Sante Fe stock at $24 and sold it at $51, thereby making huge profits. Other stockholders did not know in advance about the company's purchase and could not take advantage of the sharp rise in price, so they lost out when they sold their stock to the insiders at the lower price. This kind of "insider trading" is illegal, so the guilty persons were forced to repay their profits of $7.8 million.

These are only a few of many episodes involving stockholder concerns. In recent years, controversies have raged about "golden parachutes" for top-level managers, "greenmail" paid to corporate raiders, extravagant fringe benefits and expense accounts for executives, corporations' annual meetings being used to raise social issues, and employee ownership of corporations. This chapter discusses all of these controversial issues and others while taking a close look at the owners of stock who are one of the corporation's most important stakeholder groups.

STOCKHOLDERS

Stockholders (or shareholders, as they also are called) are the legal owners of business corporations. By purchasing a "share" of the company's stock, they become part owners of the company. For this reason, stockholder-owners have a big stake in how well their company does. The firm's managers must pay close attention to their needs and assign a high priority to their interests in the company.

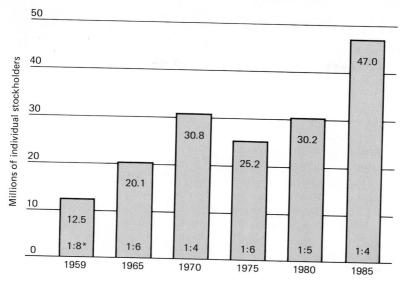

* This ratio means that 1 person out of every 8 adults is a stockholder.

FIGURE 10-1. **Numbers of individual stockholders in the United States and ratio of stockholders to adult population.** (*Source: Joyce Kalcich (ed.), New York Stock Exchange Fact Book, 1986, New York: New York Stock Exchange, April 1986, p. 56. Used with permission.*)

Who Are Stockholders?

Two types of stockholders own shares of stock in United States corporations: individual people, and institutions.

Individual Investors

As early as the 1920s, the public at large became significant holders of corporate stock. By 1970, their numbers had grown to over 30 million individuals, representing one of every four adults in the general population. Figure 10-1 charts the rise in stockholders from the late 1950s to the mid-1980s when the total was just over 47 million people. People from practically every occupational group own stock: professionals, managers, clerks, craft workers, farmers, retired persons, women who work in the home, and even unemployed adults. Almost an equal number of women and men are shareholders. In 1985 the average stockholder had a portfolio of stocks worth $6,200, and the income of a typical shareholder household was $36,800.[1]

[1]Joyce Kalcich (ed.), *New York Stock Exchange Fact Book, 1986,* New York: New York Stock Exchange, April 1986, pp. 55–58.

Type of Institution	Billions of Dollars			
	1965	1970	1975	1980
Insurance companies	$ 16.4	$ 23.9	$ 33.2	$ 65.0
Investment companies	34.7	43.1	40.5	43.2
Noninsured pension funds	37.3	70.3	106.9	219.0
Nonprofit institutions	22.3	23.6	28.5	44.5
Common trust funds	3.2	4.1	5.2	9.5
Mutual savings banks	0.5	1.4	2.4	1.5
Foreign institutions	n/a	n/a	25.1	57.5
Total	$114.4	$166.4	$241.8	$440.2
Market value of all NYSE-listed stock	$537.5	$636.4	$685.1	$1,242.8
Estimated percentage held by institutional investors	21.3%	26.1%	35.3%	35.4%

FIGURE 10-2. Major types of institutional investors and their estimated holdings of NYSE-listed stocks for selected years. (*Source: Barbara Wheeler (ed.), New York Stock Exchange Fact Book 1982, New York: New York Stock Exchange, 1982, p. 50.*)

Institutional Investors

In addition to the 47 million individuals who have direct ownership in corporations, millions more are *indirect* owners who have their money put in insurance companies, pension funds, mutual funds, churches, and university endowments. These institutions then invest their funds by buying shares of stock in corporations. Like individual shareholders, the institutions then become direct owners. The New York Stock Exchange estimates that 133 million individuals—over one-half the United States population—had an indirect ownership interest in corporations in 1980. "Generally, anyone who owns a life insurance policy, participates in a pension or deferred profit-sharing plan, has an account in a mutual savings bank, or receives a scholarship from a college endowment fund may be considered an indirect shareowner."[2] Thus, many millions of people have a direct or indirect stake in the performance of business corporations.

Since the 1960s the growth of institutional investors has been phenomenal, because more and more people have purchased insurance policies, invested in mutual funds, and joined pension funds for their retirement years. Figure 10-2 identifies the major types of institutional investors holding stocks listed on the New York Stock Exchange. In 1980 these institutions held over one-third of the value of all corporate stocks sold on that exchange. Unpub-

[2]Ibid., p. 58.

lished studies by the securities industry revealed that institutional investors were responsible for between 40 percent and 46 percent of all trading activity on the New York Stock Exchange from 1985 to 1986. Pointing out that "pension funds now own a third of the equity of all publicly traded companies in the U.S. and 50% or more of the equity of the big ones," one well-known management expert concluded that "Stock ownership has thus become more concentrated than probably ever before in U.S. history. Therefore any business that needs money—every business sooner or later—has to be managed to live up to the expectations of the pension-fund managers."[3]

Historically, an individual's holdings of stock in any one company have been small, and individual investors have had little inclination to interfere with the management of a firm. They consider themselves to be *investors* seeking a return rather than *owners* trying to control the company. However, with purchases of large blocks of stock by institutional investors comes potential power to influence corporate policies and financial health.

By the late 1970s, twenty-one of these large institutional investors had "significant voting strength" in 122 of the nation's largest companies. Altogether these corporations represented over 41 percent of the market value of all common shares outstanding. Commercial banks, investment companies, and insurance companies—big institutional buyers of stock—were therefore in a position to influence policies and decisions of the corporations whose stock they held.[4]

Because of the large influence of institutional investors in the securities markets, the Securities and Exchange Commission requires institutions holding more than $100 million in securities to disclose annually the names, types, and amounts of securities they hold and whether they can exercise the voting authority of those stocks.

Institutional Divestment for Social Purposes

University endowment funds and state pension funds—two different types of institutional investors—normally invest large sums in the stocks of "blue-chip" or high-grade corporations. Beginning in the late 1970s, the managers of these funds came under increasing pressure from students, faculty members, churches, religious orders, state legislators, and social activist groups to stop investing in the stock of any company doing business in South Africa. By the mid-1980s, eighty-four colleges and universities had "divested," or sold, the stock of companies operating in South Africa as a way of protesting that nation's system of racial separation. Half of the schools had divested fully—a sum of $267 million in stock value—and the other half had partially divested another $217 million. As Figure 10-3 reveals, the total amount of stocks held in some of these endowment funds was very large and potentially influential on corporate policy toward South African operations.

[3]Peter F. Drucker, "A Crisis of Capitalism," *Wall Street Journal,* September 30, 1986, p. 32.

[4]"Voting Power in 122 Big Firms Centered in Few Institutions," *Wall Street Journal,* January 19, 1978, p. 4.

Institution	Amount Divested (in millions)	Year
Columbia University	$ 41.7	1985
University of Minnesota	35	1985
Northeastern University	21	1986
University of Miami	17	1985
State University of New York	15	1985
Mount Holyoke	14.9	1985
Rutgers University	14.5	1985
Ohio State University	11	1985
University of Wisconsin	11	1978
Howard University	8	1978
Michigan State University	7.2	1979–1980

State or Municipal Fund	Value of Assets Affected by Divestment Policy (in millions)
New York City	$ 2,100
Los Angeles	713
San Francisco	360
Baltimore	238
Rhode Island	141
Massachusetts*	110
Connecticut*	79
Philadelphia*	57
Omaha	38
Nebraska*	28
*Divested as of 1986.	

FIGURE 10-3 Selected college and university endowment funds fully divested of South African–related corporate stock, and selected state and municipal funds with divestment policies. (*Source:* Newsweek, *April 1986, p. 18; and* Business Week, *March 17, 1986, p. 70.)*

The amounts were even larger in some state and city funds, also shown in Figure 10-3. A 1984 New Jersey law directed the manager of that state's $13 billion employee pension fund to sell all securities of companies with South African ties. The total value to be sold was $3.5 billion. Was it good for New Jersey's pensioners who were the indirect owners of these stocks? The fund's director reported a $6 million loss on the sale of some securities, increased sales expenses of $5 million, and perhaps a loss of $25 million per year by not being able to buy blue-chip stocks of leading companies. The state of California took similar action in 1986, divesting approximately $9.5 billion of South Africa–related stocks.[5]

[5]"Why Divesting Isn't Always That Easy," *Business Week,* March 17, 1986, pp. 71–72; and "California's Legislature Votes to Force Sale of Holdings Linked to South Africa," *Wall Street Journal,* August 28, 1986, p. 38. Similar pressure has been used to promote equal job opportunities for Roman Catholics in corporations doing business in Northern Ireland; see Elliott Lee, "Activist Holders Target Northern Ireland," *Wall Street Journal,* January 20, 1987, p. 12.

The basic problem faced by institutional managers is one of getting the highest possible return on the stocks they purchase—for example, to maximize the future retirement pensions of employees—while at the same time being responsive to public pressures for social change. As institutional stockholders, these funds and their managers are in a unique position to exercise their ownership rights for both economic and social goals. They face the same public expectation that all businesses do—to balance their desire to make a profit with a need to show ethical concern.

Stockholders' Legal Rights and Safeguards

In order to protect their financial stake in the companies whose stocks they hold, stockholders have several legal safeguards. Specific rights of stockholders are established by law. Legally, stockholders can influence corporate policy through the voting mechanism or, if necessary, by challenging actions of corporate officers in the courts. Stockholders have the following legal rights (and these vary somewhat among states): They have the right to share in the profits of the enterprise if dividends are declared by directors. They have the right to receive annual reports of company earnings and company activities, and they have the right to inspect the corporate books, provided they have a legitimate business purpose for doing so and that it will not be disruptive of business operations. They have the right to elect directors and to hold those directors and the officers of the corporation responsible for their acts— by lawsuit if they want to go that far. Furthermore, they have the right to vote on mergers, some acquisitions, and changes in the charter and bylaws, and to bring other proposals before the stockholders. And finally, they have the right to dispose of their stock. Figure 10-4 summarizes the major legal rights of stockholders.[6]

Stockholder Suits

If stockholders think that they or their company have been damaged by actions of company officers or directors, they have the right to bring lawsuits in the courts. These stockholder suits can be of two kinds.

If stockholders are directly and personally damaged by actions of the company's officers, they can sue in court to recover their losses. For example, if they have lost money because of insider trading by company officers or directors, they have a right to sue. Such legal actions are called _individual shareholder suits_ because they are intended to reimburse stockholders directly and personally. The stockholder personally recovers the monetary damages.

On the other hand, in a _shareholder's derivative suit_ damages are awarded to _the corporation_. In these lawsuits, disgruntled stockholders are trying to protect the corporation's assets and not just their own personal investments, as shown in the following example.

[6]For further explanation, see Francis W. Steckmest, _Corporate Performance: The Key to Public Trust,_ New York: McGraw-Hill, 1982, chap. 16, "Shareholder Rights," pp. 177–181.

- To receive dividends, if declared
- To vote on: Members of board of directors
  - Major mergers and acquisitions
  - Charter and bylaw changes
  - Proposals by stockholders
- To receive annual reports on company's financial condition
- To bring shareholder suits against the company and officers
- To sell their own shares of stock to others

FIGURE 10-4. Major legal rights of stockholders.

> *A shareholder of Allegheny International filed a derivative, class-action lawsuit against the company's directors, saying that they had wasted corporate assets and made improper business decisions. The shareholder alleged that the company maintained five corporate jets, had loaned over $32 million at 2 percent interest to some company officers and directors, and had paid excessive salaries and bonuses to executives including the CEO who allegedly received $1 million in 1984 when the company had earned only $14.9 million and was in serious financial trouble. The lawsuit was filed after the board of directors of Allegheny International had refused to sue the CEO to recover some of these corporate funds. "We gave the board the opportunity to take action itself and, by not doing so, that triggered the right of the shareholder to sue the board in the name of the company," said the suing shareholder.[7]*

Shareholder suits, according to one study, are initiated to check many abuses, including insider trading, an inadequate price obtained for the company's stock in a buyout or takeover, lush executive pension benefits, or fraud committed by company officials.[8]

Corporate Disclosure

Giving stockholders more and better company information is one of the best ways to safeguard their interests. The theory behind the move for greater disclosure of company information is that the stockholder, as an investor, should be as fully informed as possible in order to make sound investments. By law, stockholders have the right to know about the affairs of the corporations in which they hold ownership shares. Those who attend annual meetings learn about past performance and future goals through speeches made by corporate officers and documents such as the company's annual report.

[7]"Allegheny International Holder Sues Directors, Charging Breach of Duties," *Wall Street Journal,* August 5, 1986, p. 13.

[8]Thomas M. Jones, "Shareholder Suits: Good News and Bad News for Corporate Executives," *California Management Review,* Summer 1981, pp. 77–85. For additional information, see Stephen Wermiel, "Justices Upheld Investor's Right to Sue for Fraud," *Wall Street Journal,* January 25, 1983, p. 4; and Thomas M. Jones, "Corporate Board Structure and Performance: Variations in the Incidence of Shareholder Suits," in James E. Post (ed.), *Research in Corporate Social Performance and Policy,* vol. 8, Greenwich, CT: JAI Press, 1986.

Those who do not attend meetings must depend primarily on annual reports issued by the company and the opinions of independent financial analysts.

Historically, management has tended to provide stockholders with minimum information. But prompted by the Securities and Exchange Commission and by professional accounting groups, companies now disclose more about their affairs, in spite of the complicated nature of some information. A few corporations go further than required and publish financial information from the detailed "10-K" section of their official reports to the SEC. Stockholders therefore can learn about sales and earnings, assets, capital expenditures and depreciation by line of business, and details of foreign operations.

Corporations also are required to disclose detailed information about directors, how they are chosen, their compensation, conflicts of interest, and their reasons for resigning in policy disputes with management.

For example, IBM's announcement of its 1986 annual meeting gave detailed information about the twenty-one members of its board of directors, including their directorships in other corporations, the number of IBM shares they held, the salaries of board members who also were top managers of IBM, the amount and value of their stock options (a right to purchase additional shares of IBM stock), and details about their retirement benefits. To guard against charges of favoritism, the announcement also reported the amounts spent by IBM on purchases from other companies in which board members had a financial interest. Giving stockholders this kind of information reduces suspicions about how company funds are being spent and allows them to make up their own minds about the integrity of IBM's board of directors.[9]

CORPORATE GOVERNANCE

Who will govern the corporation internally is a central issue facing business. There is no easy answer to the question: Who's in charge? As Figure 10-5 reveals, several key stakeholder groups are involved. Managers occupy a strategic position because of their knowledge and day-to-day decision making. The board of directors exercises formal legal authority over company policy. Stockholders, as owners, have a vital stake in the company. Employees, particularly those represented by unions, can affect some policies. And government, through laws and regulations, also is involved.[10]

The following discussion concentrates on three of these groups: the board of directors, top management, and stockholders. Other chapters in this book deal with labor unions and government.

[9]The information is from "Notice of 1986 Annual Meeting and Proxy Statement," IBM Corporation, March 19, 1986.

[10]For a "classic" discussion of corporate governance, see Richard Eells, *The Government of Corporations*, New York: Free Press, 1962. See also Deborah A. DeMott (ed.), *Corporations at the Crossroads: Governance and Reform*, New York: McGraw-Hill, 1980; and Thomas M. Jones, "Corporate Control and the Limits to Managerial Power," *Business Forum*, Winter 1985, pp. 16–21.

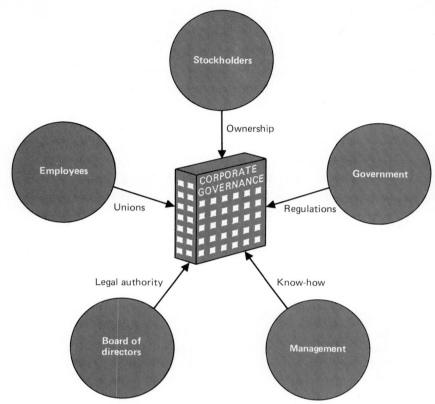

FIGURE 10-5. Major stakeholders involved in corporate governance.

The Board of Directors

The board of directors is a central factor in corporate governance because corporation laws place legal responsibility for the affairs of a company on the board. The board of directors is responsible for establishing corporate objectives, developing broad policies, and selecting top-level personnel to carry out these objectives and policies. The board also reviews management's performance to be sure that the company is well run and stockholders' interests are promoted.

A typical board consists of thirteen to fifteen members who are elected by shareholder votes. Some boards, perhaps the majority, meet only quarterly, others monthly or even more frequently. Practices vary widely, depending upon the size, type, and past history of the corporation. "Inside" boards are those whose members include a large number of high-level managers drawn from inside the company itself, while "outside" boards have a majority of members from external organizations such as law firms, universities, foundations, banks, and other corporations. In the United States, most large corporations have "outside" boards. One authoritative study estimates that "about 60 percent of all directors serving the 1,000 largest industrials are outsiders. The percentage probably rises to 75 percent for nonindustrials [for example, banks and insurance companies], but drops to 45 percent for smaller enterprises."[11] Figure 10-6 profiles the boards of 592 corporations in 1985.

Most corporate boards perform their work through committees. The *executive committee* (present in 78 percent of corporate boards) works closely with top managers on important business matters.[12] The *audit committee* (present in 97 percent) is usually composed of outside directors; it reviews the company's financial reports, recommends the appointment of outside auditors, and oversees the integrity of internal financial controls. The *compensation committee* (82 percent), also composed of outside directors, administers and approves salaries and other benefits of high-level managers in the company. The *nominating committee* (59 percent) is charged with finding and recommending candidates for officers and directors, especially those to be elected at the annual stockholders' meeting. A few corporations also have an *ethics committee* (6 percent) or a *public affairs committee* (11 percent) that gives special attention to ethical issues and social responsibility problems.

These committees, which may meet several times each year, give an active board of directors very important powers in controlling the company's affairs. In addition, when the entire board meets, it hears directly from top-level managers and has an opportunity to influence their decisions and policies. As a direct result of these strategically important powers, according to one authoritative source,

> The board can no longer play a passive role in corporate governance. Today, more than ever, the board must assume an activist role—a role that is protective of shareholder rights, sensitive to communities in which the company operates, responsive to the needs of company vendors and customers, and fair to its employees. And if directors are not willing to initiate appropriate action, we have learned from recent experience that corporate constituent groups (i.e., shareholders) will take action into their own hands and do everything within their power to protect their interests.[13]

This activist board role has exposed directors to greater risks of liability for their decisions. As court suits against board members increase, so do the costs of buying liability insurance as protection. In just one year (1985), premiums on directors' and officers' liability coverage for one group of prominent corporations went up by 362 percent, and some companies could not obtain policies at any price. These liability risks make it harder to retain existing directors, and nearly all directors (96 percent) said they would reduce

---

[11]Stanley C. Vance, *Corporate Leadership: Boards, Directors, and Strategy,* New York: McGraw-Hill, 1983, p. 51. See also Jeremy Bacon and James K. Brown, *The Board of Directors: Perspectives and Practices in Nine Countries,* New York: The Conference Board, 1977; and *The Role and Composition of the Board of Directors of the Large Publicly Owned Corporations,* New York: Business Roundtable, 1978.

[12]The figures in this paragraph are from Lester B. Korn and Richard M. Ferry, *Board of Directors Thirteenth Annual Study,* New York: Korn/Ferry International, February 1986, p. 5.

[13]Ibid., pp. 1–2.

Average number of directors on board	14
Inside directors	4
Outside directors	10
Companies with the following on board	
Women	45.0% of companies
Ethnic minority	25.4%
Employee representative	2.2%
Consumer group representative	1.7%
Major shareholder	29.4%
"Professional" director	28.2%
Average compensation of directors, 1985	
Industrial corporations under $200 million	$21.571
Industrial corporations $5 billion and over	$33,332
Average compensation, all corporations	$19,544
Average number of board meetings per year	8
Average number of hours spent annually by directors	114 (2.85 weeks)
Top-ranked issue considered by the board	
Financial results	56.3% of companies
Strategic planning	19.2%
Day-to-day operations	8.0%
Managerial succession	6.5%
Government relations	0.6%
Multinational issues	0.6%
Shareholder relations	0.4%

FIGURE 10-6. Selected facts about boards of directors of 592 United States corporations, 1985. (*Source: Lester B. Korn and Richard M. Ferry,* Board of Directors 13th Annual Study, *New York: Korn/Ferry International, February 1986. Used with permission.*)

the number of directorships held because of increased liability.[14] Shareholders in General Mills, Burroughs, Pillsbury, and other companies have voted to forfeit their right to sue directors for some forms of negligence as a way of reducing directors' liability.[15]

Despite these risks, people remain willing to serve on boards because they play a very important part in running business corporations. They are part of the governance system, and they share power with top managers and stockholders.

Top Managers

Professional managers now take the leading role in large corporations. These managers might have backgrounds in marketing and sales, or in engineering

[14]Ibid. See also "A Landmark Ruling that Puts Board Members in Peril," *Business Week*, March 18, 1985, pp. 56–57; and "The Job Nobody Wants," *Business Week*, September 8, 1986, pp. 56–61.

[15]"Companies Ask Holders to Limit Boards' Liability," *Wall Street Journal*, October 7, 1986, p. 35.

design and production, or in various aspects of financial analysis. The expanding scale and complexity of national and international business call for management specialists to guide the affairs of most big companies. The source of their power is a combination of their managerial expertise and simply being given organizational responsibility for carrying out the needed work. Being on the spot day after day and being better informed about the company's needs and opportunities mean that few other people know better than they what should be done and how and when to do it.[16]

Managers increasingly tend to consider their responsibilities as being primarily *to the company*, rather than just to the stockholders. They perceive themselves to be responsible for (1) the economic survival of the firm; (2) extending its life into the future through product innovation, management development, market expansion, and other means; and (3) balancing the demands of all groups in such a way that *the company* can achieve its objectives. This viewpoint emphasizes optimum or satisfactory profits rather than maximum profits. It considers shareholders to be just one of several stakeholder groups that must be given attention. Concerning their specific responsibilities to owners, managers today often express the belief that "what is good for the company is good for the stockholder."

Most of the time, shareholders are satisfied with management performance. They realize that running a business is not a simple matter and that managers can do a better job than the owners themselves. This point of view is true even for the big institutional stockholders who prefer not to intervene in corporate affairs, except in unusual circumstances.

Two Models of Management Influence

There are two ways to view the power and influence of top managers in governing the corporation: the traditional, legal model; and the managerial domination model.

The traditional, legal theory says that members of the board of directors are elected by the stockholders. Top managers are then selected by the board of directors and are answerable to the board for the company's performance. According to this version, therefore, the managers acting under the board's authority are supposed to promote the stockholders' interests. If they do not do so, the board can fire them. If the board does not promote stockholders' interests, board members can be voted out of their position at a stockholders' meeting. This theory of control is still recognized by the courts, although it lacks a considerable amount of reality.

The other model of corporate control says that top managers, especially the CEO, influence the board to nominate new directors who tend to give allegiance to the CEO's policies. According to a 1986 survey of nearly 600 corporations: "Board vacancies continue to be filled predominantly through recommendations by the chairman (in 81 percent of the companies) and by

---

[16]For an interesting discussion, see John Kenneth Galbraith, *The New Industrial State*, 2d ed., Boston: Houghton Mifflin, 1971, chaps. VI and VII.

Company	Number of Institutional Investors	Percentage of Stock Held	Millions of Dollars
CBS, Inc.	194	60.3	$ 2,043.5
Atlantic Richfield	455	50.8	4,791.7
Wells Fargo & Co.	161	73.8	2,034.8
K Mart Corp.	385	75.8	5,429.8
GTE Corp.	432	52.8	6,050.2
Cigna Corp.	290	77.8	3,566.8
Union Carbide	137	50.7	1,024.5
IBM	687	48.5	43,697.6
McDonalds Corp.	396	57.0	5,356.4
Firemans Fund	137	79.0	1,921.5
Chrysler Corp.	207	60.2	3,399.2
Avon Products Inc.	177	60.3	1,514.6

FIGURE 10-7. Stockholdings of institutional investors in selected corporations, 1986. (*Source:* Barron's, *September 1, 1986, p. 30.*)

other board members (in 77 percent of the companies)."[17] Since most stockholders tend to vote with management and accept their recommendations, nomination to the board is tantamount to election by the shareholders. This puts the CEO in a position to control or heavily influence the board. In addition, most corporate matters brought before the board are too complex to discuss in great detail prior to making a decision, so boards may "rubber stamp" the CEO's recommendation out of sheer necessity and on the assumption that the top cadre of managers knows what is best for the company (as they often do).

Neither theory tells the whole story, and companies vary in the relative amount of control exercised by managers and boards. As revealed in Figure 10-7, large institutional stockholders—a pension fund or an investment bank—might be able to wield much influence on top management. So can corporate takeover specialists. While top management's power is not unlimited, it is significant in most large corporations.

Stockholders

According to the theory of corporation law, the stockholders of a company have ultimate control over its policies and actions. It is easy to see why this should be true. After all, the owners have put their money into the firm and they expect to receive a return from a well-managed operation. It is therefore reasonable to believe that they should have an important voice in what the company does. As the following discussion shows, sometimes they do and sometimes they do not.

[17]Korn/Ferry International, op. cit., p. 11. This study revealed that the chairman also was the chief executive officer—in other words, the top manager—in 80 percent of these companies.

Stockholders' Annual Meetings

Stockholders' annual meetings are held for the purpose of discussing business, and to offer an opportunity for shareholders to approve or disapprove of management. Approval is generally expressed by reelecting incumbent directors, and disapproval may be shown by attempting to replace them with new ones. Where corporations are small and local, annual meetings work reasonably well. It is relatively easy to assemble most of the stockholders, and corporate business is considered and acted upon personally by at least a majority of them. But for the large corporation with thousands of owners, annual meetings are not so satisfactory. The number and wide geographical dispersion of stockholders have altered the character of annual meetings. Typically, only a small portion of stockholders attend to vote in person. Those not attending are given an opportunity to vote by absentee ballot (called a "proxy"). Most stockholders vote as management recommends by signing and sending their proxies back to the corporation, and this allows management to outvote dissident stockholders in most cases. Opposing votes seldom add up to much more than 10 percent, if that much.

Even if they were so disposed, few small stockholders are equipped financially to initiate and wage a fight for control with existing management. To unseat present management requires gathering enough voting power by proxy to outvote the incumbents. In proxy fights, the odds for success are heavily weighted in favor of present management. It is not easy to stir a group of apathetic stockholders to join the opposition. Lack of knowledge concerning issues typically leads small, uninterested stockholders to cast their lot on the side of management. Financially, too, present management has the upper hand. It may, and typically does, use both corporate personnel and corporate funds to ask stockholders to send their proxies to management. As a result, the combination of voting strength held by the board and top management allows them to perpetuate themselves and continue their policies against the wishes of some stockholders.

Shareholder Proposals

Beginning in the 1960s and gaining momentum in the 1970s, small stockholders found an effective way of making their voices heard in annual meetings. Historically it has been extremely difficult for a small stockholder to bring a proposal before an annual meeting. The right of a stockholder to attend annual meetings and vote is created under the *state laws* in which the company is incorporated. Under these laws, in order to submit a proposal to other stockholders for their consideration and action, a stockholder was required to obtain a list of stockholders from the company and then send to each a statement of the proposal. This is an expensive and time-consuming process that few stockholders are prepared to undertake.

Then in the late 1960s the Securities and Exchange Commission (SEC) amended its rules and allowed stockholders to place resolutions concerning social issues in proxy statements *sent out by the company*. Originally the SEC rules prohibited proposals that dealt with religious, political, or social issues. These rules were designed to protect management against harassment by nuisance proposals and from proposals by social reformers. This change of rules seemed to reflect a spreading belief by society that stockholders should be allowed to vote on social as well as economic questions that are related to the business of the corporation.

In 1983 the pendulum swung in the other direction when the SEC decided to place additional restrictions on the ability of stockholders, especially those holding only a few shares of stock, to introduce resolutions at annual meetings. Under the new rules, no stockholder who had owned less than $1,000 of a company's stock for a year would now be permitted to submit a resolution. Nor could more than one resolution per meeting be introduced by a stockholder. Another guideline raised the percentage of votes a resolution had to receive in order to be resubmitted in following years—5 percent (instead of 3 percent) of votes cast the first year, 8 percent (instead of 6 percent) the second year, and 10 percent the third year. Resolutions could not deal with a company's "ordinary business," since that would constitute unjustified interference with management's decisions in running the company. SEC interpretations tended to be more favorable to corporations than to dissident stockholders. Business favored these changes because they weeded out nuisance resolutions, reduced paperwork, and eliminated disorderly debates at some annual meetings.[18]

In spite of these new restrictions, shareholder activists working through the Interfaith Center on Corporate Responsibility in 1986 sponsored eighty-five resolutions dealing with ten major social issues at meetings of sixty-eight corporations. Over one hundred church groups were joined by individual shareholders and several pension funds.[19]

Since shareholder resolutions not favored by management scarcely ever garner enough votes to be adopted, what is their point? There are several answers. The annual meeting provides a forum for debating social issues. Stockholders have a legal right to raise such issues and to ask questions about how "their" company is responding to them. Management is questioned about controversial issues and has to justify its policies in public. In order to avoid the glare of publicity, an increasing number of corporations have met with dissident groups prior to the annual meeting and agreed to take action on an issue if the groups' proposed resolutions are withdrawn. Although these limited responses may amount to small victories, shareholder resolutions are one way for stockholders to make their influence felt in the executive suite.[20]

---

[18]For a detailed analysis of the new rules, see Steve Lydenburg, "A Tilt against Shareholder Democracy: The 1983 SEC Rule Changes," ICCR Brief, *The Corporate Examiner*, vol. 13, no. 7, 1984, pp. 3A–3D, published by the Interfaith Center on Corporate Responsibility.

[19]"Corporate Social Responsibility Challenges 1986," *The Corporate Examiner*, vol. 14, no. 9, 1985.

[20]For further discussion, see Lauren Talner, *The Origins of Shareholder Activism*, Washington, DC: Investor Responsibility Research Center, 1983; and David Vogel, *Lobbying the Corporation: Citizen Challenges to Business Authority*, New York: Basic Books, 1978.

INCREASING CORPORATE RESPONSIVENESS TO STOCKHOLDERS

Since a corporation's stockholders are one of its most important stakeholder groups, managers must find ways to respond to their needs and interests. Some of the most important suggestions are the following ones.

Reforming the Board

There is a growing public concern, shared by some directors themselves, that boards of directors are no longer meeting the requirements of a rapidly changing society. Critics demand that directors monitor more than just the economic performance of the companies they direct, and they question whether long-range stockholder interests are really being best served through primary concern with profit. They question whether corporations can survive if they do not place social performance at least alongside economic performance. A variety of suggestions has emerged to make boards of directors more effective and able to function better in terms of a broader concept of stockholder interest. Figure 10-8 charts the following four proposed reforms:

- *Stakeholder directors:* One popular proposal among corporate reformers is to appoint special-interest directors that represent the company's major stakeholder groups, including consumers, minorities, women, environmentalists, employees, and the general public. The objective is to broaden the corporate point of view and allow affected groups to participate significantly in corporate decision making. Figure 10-6 shows how far companies have gone in adopting this suggestion. Business is generally opposed to stakeholder directors on grounds that directors need to put the general welfare of the company before the special interests of any one group.[21]
- *Professional directors:* These directors, unlike most, would serve on a full-time basis, continuously monitoring the performance of a company's managers to ensure that policies and actions are economically effective and in compliance with the law. In 1986, more than one in four large corporations had at least one professional director on its board. See Figure 10-6.
- As mentioned previously, not many corporate boards have created *ethics committees* or *public affairs committees*, but some people think that they can be a useful way of alerting a company to external pressures and social issues. By scanning the social environment and feeding such information into the corporate decision-making process, these committees can enhance the social sophistication of a company's strategic planning.[22]

---

[21]For a discussion, see Thomas M. Jones and Leonard D. Goldberg, "Governing the Large Corporation: More Arguments for Public Directors," *Academy of Management Review,* October 1982, pp. 603–611; and Vance, op. cit., pp. 55–58.

[22]Michael L. Lovdal, Raymond A. Bauer, and Nancy H. Treverton, "Public Responsibility Committees of the Board," *Harvard Business Review,* May–June 1977, pp. 40–42ff.; and S. Prakash Sethi et al., *Corporate Governance: Public Policy-Social Responsibility Committee of Corporate Board,* Richardson, TX: Center for Research in Business and Social Policy, University of Texas at Dallas, 1979.

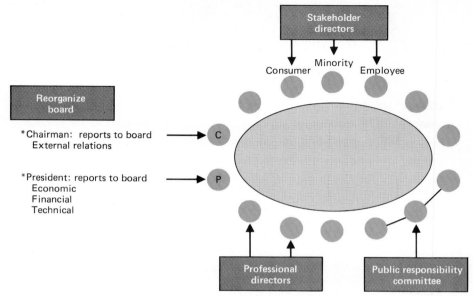

FIGURE 10-8. Proposed reforms of the board of directors.

- *Separating the board chairman and the president:* Some have recommended making a clear distinction between the duties of the board chairman and those of the chief executive or the chief operating officer, rather than combining the two in one person as done in most corporations. Under this plan, the chairman would give primary allegiance to the board and would be responsible for overseeing external relations. The company's president also would report directly to the entire board of directors, and not to the chairman as usually occurs. The president would be responsible for internal affairs, such as the economic, financial, and technical operations of the company. With this split in responsibilities, a board would have an improved chance of receiving completely candid reports about the company's external and internal affairs. By the mid-1980s, this idea had not gained much headway, since a single person still held both posts in 80 percent of companies surveyed.[23]

Federal Chartering and Codetermination

Two additional modifications in the way corporations make decisions have been advocated. *Federal chartering would have the federal government replace state governments as the chartering agent for corporations.* Advocates say that federally issued charters could specify tighter controls over corporate boards and management, for the benefit of shareholders and others. State chartering has been

---

[23]Korn and Ferry, op. cit., p. 13. For further discussion, see Courtney C. Brown, *Putting the Corporate Board to Work,* New York: Macmillan, 1976.

criticized for the different standards that exist from state to state, allowing companies to incorporate in states with the least restrictive provisions and encouraging states to lower incorporation rules to attract many companies. Opponents of federal chartering say that it would extend the power of the federal government over an already overregulated private business sector.

Labor-management codetermination would have American corporations follow the example of some West European nations in requiring labor representation on the boards of major companies. This system is called labor-management codetermination. Supporters say that this arrangement promotes a greater degree of worker loyalty to a company by giving labor an opportunity to be directly involved in decision making. Detractors doubt that the system will work in the United States, where labor-management relations have traditionally relied on a strong adversary system to work out differences.

> *The first significant breakthrough toward labor representation on a corporate board in the United States occurred in 1980 when Douglas Fraser, president of the United Automobile Workers union, became a director of Chrysler Corporation. Fraser's board membership was created under unusual circumstances. Chrysler was seeking federal assistance to avoid bankruptcy and was pressuring the union to grant major concessions in the form of lower wages and reduced benefits. Union members feared that Fraser's dual roles as UAW president and Chrysler director would weaken his tough bargaining stance. Chrysler officials worried that he would gain unfair bargaining advantage by having access to Chrysler's financial and personnel data. Fraser avoided the problem by not participating as a board member during contract negotiations. When Fraser retired as union chief, his successor took Fraser's seat on Chrysler's board.*

Figure 10-9 lists several companies that have added a significant number of worker representatives to their boards in the 1980s.

EMPLOYEE STOCK OWNERSHIP

One interesting form of stock ownership occurs when the employees of a company become its owners. *Employee stock ownership plans (ESOPs) encourage employees to invest some of their wage and salary earnings in the stock of the company where they work.* The idea is to give employees direct profit-sharing interest in addition to their wage and salary income. ESOP advocates claim that this kind of share ownership benefits the company by increasing worker productivity, reducing job absenteeism, and drawing management and employees closer together into a common effort to make the company a success. Not only do ESOP participants receive regular dividends on the stock they own, but retiring workers either take their stock from the fund or sell their shares back to the company at retirement time. Another benefit to an ESOP company—and one that has stimulated much corporate participation—is a reduction of company taxes that is linked to the amount of stock bought by the employees.

Company	Number of Employees	Percentage of Stock owned by Employees	Number of Employee Representatives on Board of Directors
Chrysler	59,000	15	1
Eastern Air Lines	37,000	25	4
Weirton Steel	8,700	100	3
Hyatt Clark Industries	1,500	100	3
Interstate Motor Freight	1,500	45	2
Pan American Air Lines	27,000	10	1

FIGURE 10-9. **Number of employee representatives on the board of directors of selected United States corporations.** (*Source:* Business Week, *May 7, 1984, pp. 152–153.*)

Beginning in the mid-1970s, ESOPs grew at an explosive pace, mostly because of new federal and state laws that encouraged their formation. From around 300 plans in 1974, they increased to more than 7,000 in 1984, and they now cover more than 10 million employees. Their annual growth rate was 10 percent in 1985; if that pace were to continue, one out of every four employees would be owners of their companies by the year A.D. 2000. From 1974 to 1985 Congress passed sixteen laws promoting ESOPs, and thirteen states added another sixteen laws of their own.[24]

When an ESOP is set up, the employee-owners normally expect to have more to say about how the company is run than employees usually do. Experience shows, however, that this does not always happen. According to one study, in over three-quarters of 150 ESOP-owned firms employees held a majority of the stock but in 38 percent of these companies they did not have a seat on the board of directors. Of the 7,000 ESOPs nationally, only 10 to 15 percent are majority owned and employees vote their stock on all issues in only 25 to 30 percent of the firms; in the others, a management-appointed trustee votes for employees. At the 70-percent employee-owned Dan River textile company, one union official said, "The company stamps its cartons with a big 'D' and 'employee-owned.' But most of the people realize that they don't own anything. They're just paying the bill for these big management people to own the company." In spite of limited employee control in some ESOPs, there is a tendency for employee ownership to draw management and workers closer together into cooperative efforts. In the great majority of the 150 firms mentioned above, employees were believed to exert important influence on company decisions and policies.[25]

[24]Corey M. Rosen, Katherine J. Klein, and Karen M. Young, *Employee Ownership in America: The Equity Solution,* Lexington, MA: Lexington, 1986, pp. 2, 15; and "ESOPs: Revolution or Ripoff?" *Business Week,* April 15, 1985, p. 94. The Rosen, Klein, and Young book is an excellent source of information on this subject, and it contains capsule accounts of many different types of ESOPs.

[25]Keith Bradley and Alan Gelb, *Worker Capitalism: The New Industrial Relations,* Cambridge, MA: MIT Press, 1983, pp. 94–95; and Corey M. Rosen, Katherine J. Klein, and Karen M. Young, op. cit, pp. 16–17. The quotation is from "ESOPs: Revolution or Ripoff?" *Business Week,* April 15, 1985, p. 94.

When employees become owners, their loyalties can be split. Should they favor paying profits to themselves as stockholders, or would it be better to plow that money back into the company for modernization? Should they demand less in wages and benefits so company costs can be lowered and profits can be higher? One union official said, "There is no way workers on a meaningful basis can be managers and workers. The interests of each group eventually clash. It just doesn't work."[26] One frustrated plant manager expressed the same sentiment: "You can't consult 480 workers every time you make a decision."[27]

In spite of such doubts, ESOPs are likely to remain a permanent part of the business landscape. Corporations favor them for the tax advantages offered; employees whose companies are financially shaky perceive them as a way to save their jobs; local communities think that ESOPs are good if they can prevent a company from moving to another location; employees who think their inputs to company policies will improve overall performance like these plans; and anyone who favors the spread of capitalist ownership supports a system that puts ownership directly into the hands of more citizens.

Research has shown that employee-owners are like other stockholders in one important respect: their highest satisfaction in being an owner comes from the prospect of earning a significant amount of money. "In a typical ESOP company, an employee making $20,000 a year gets about $2,000 more in stock." The more a company puts into the ESOP, "the more satisfied employees are—with the ESOP, with their work, and with the company in general."[28]

PROTECTING AND PROMOTING STOCKHOLDER INTERESTS

Stockholders can be damaged at times by abusive practices. On other occasions, they suffer losses because management is inefficient, careless, or puts its own needs ahead of stockholder interests. Two areas calling for special efforts to protect and promote stockholder interests are insider trading and corporate mergers.

Insider Trading

As mentioned earlier in this chapter, *insider trading occurs when a person gains sole access to information about a company's financial condition and then uses that information to buy or sell the company's stock.* Since no one else knows what an inside trader knows, it is possible to make investments or dump stock well in advance of other stockholders. If the secret information reveals that the company's stock is liable to go up when the information becomes public,

[26]"The Question for Unions: Who's in Charge Here?" *Business Week*, April 15, 1985, p. 106.

[27]*Business Week*, September 22, 1980, p. 42.

[28]Rosen et al., op. cit., pp. 44, 124, and 130–132.

then it is smart to buy the stock ahead of everyone else when its price is low. If the inside information says that the company is in trouble, then its stock is liable to drop. In that case, it is a good time to sell the stock before the bad news becomes generally known. In the Sante Fe International case cited at the beginning of this chapter, a few people knew in advance that the company's stock was going to rise in value when Kuwait Petroleum made its offer public, so they bought it at the lower price and later sold it at the higher price.

The most spectacular insider-trading scandal in Wall Street history occurred in 1986 when several individual investors and a few officers of investment banking firms were revealed to have made millions of dollars illegally through secret insider trading. By sharing confidential information about forthcoming mergers of large corporations, they were able to buy and sell stocks before the mergers were announced to the public. The leading investor in this scandal netted an estimated profit of $203 million in 1985 and 1986. In a settlement with the Securities and Exchange Commission, he paid a $50 million fine, returned $50 million in illegal profits, was barred from the securities industry for life, and faced a possible jail term. Several other involved investors were arrested for fraud, conspiracy, and violations of the securities laws. A Justice Department attorney who helped direct the investigation said:

> Insider trading is not a complex crime. It's theft. These guys are thieves. They steal information and then they fence it. It's no different than if they were stealing ice skates.[29]

Insider trading not only is illegal but also is contrary to the logic underlying the stock markets: all stockholders ought to have access to the same information about companies. None should have special privileges nor gain unfair advantages over others. Only in that way can investors have full confidence in the fairness of the stock markets. If they think that some investors can use inside knowledge for their own personal gain while others are excluded from such information, then the system of stock buying may break down because of lack of trust.

Some financial authorities think that insider trading has benefits, in spite of its unfairness to some investors. They argue that it increases the efficiency of the stock markets by getting information out quickly. Although some insiders gain an advantage over other investors, good or bad news about a corporation's stock spreads quickly through the entire market. In that way, the real value of the stock becomes apparent as soon as the word is disseminated.

---

[29]"Illegal Insider Trading Seems to Be on Rise; Ethics Issues Muddled," *Wall Street Journal*, March 2, 1984, pp. 1, 8; and "The Epidemic of Insider Trading," *Business Week*, April 29, 1985, pp. 78–92. For information and a chronology of the Wall Street scandal, see stories in *Wall Street Journal*, November 17, 1986, pp. 1, 14; November 24, 1986, pp. 2, 12; and March 30, 1987, p. 3. The quotation is from *Wall Street Journal*, December 24, 1986, p. 13.

Mergers and Takeovers

Corporate mergers and takeovers were discussed in Chapter 9, so we will only summarize here how stockholders can be affected by some of these transactions:

- *Takeover defenses:* Some of the defenses used by corporate management to fend off hostile takeovers reduce the power of shareholders. Examples are staggered terms of office for board members; multiple classes of stock with different voting rights; and requiring "super majority" votes.[30]
- *Diluted stock values:* Sometimes, a merger can dilute the earning power of existing shareholders by increasing the total number of shares outstanding; this lowers the overall value and potential earning power of each share. Some analysts thought this might have occurred when United States Steel merged with Texas Oil and Gas, because the two companies worked out an exchange of stock that increased outstanding shares from 123 million to about 257 million shares. Estimates of the drop in earnings per share ranged from 10 percent to 38 percent.
- *Greenmail:* In one famous case, financier Saul Steinberg (operating through Reliance Insurance Company) acquired 11 percent of Walt Disney stock and proposed to buy even more. Disney's board bought all of his stock back for just over $70 per share—and even paid Steinberg's takeover expenses of $28 million! The result was a profit of $297 million for Steinberg and Reliance since their purchases had been made at a range of from $51 to $65 per share. Greenmail is not illegal, but it raises two kinds of questions: Is it proper for board members and top management to spend stockholders' money to protect themselves and insulate the company from new external initiatives? Is it fair to pay a greenmail premium to make a corporate raider go away, while the rest of the company's shareholders gain nothing or even lose on the transaction? While Steinberg received $70 per share for his Disney stock, the value of stock held by others dropped from a market level of $65 to $55 the following day and to $50 a week after the announcement. He gained, they lost. Question: Was it fair?[31]
- *Golden parachutes:* Another potential abuse is the *golden parachute.* When top-level managers think that their company might be the target of a takeover attempt, they frequently persuade the board of directors to grant them *a guaranteed severance package of salary and benefits in case they lose their jobs after the takeover.* The former chairman of Revlon floated to earth under his golden parachute worth $35 million after Pantry Pride took over the company. He was joined in the skies by the others listed in Figure 10-10. The SEC chairman estimated that by 1984 over 1,000 corporations had installed similar (but less lucrative) arrangements for their top officers. Again, it is a question of fairness in spending stockholders' money for these purposes. One editorial stated, "Allowing top officers to write themselves company-

---

[30]"Why One Share, One Vote' Is On Its Way Out," *Business Week,* July 21, 1986, pp. 111–112; and Allen Michel and Israel Shaked, *Takeover Madness,* New York: Wiley, 1985.

[31]For a discussion, see J. Gregory Dees, "The Ethics of Greenmail," in Post, op. cit.

Parachutist	Company	Size of Settlement (in millions)
Michel Bergerac Chairman	Revlon	$35.0
William Granger Jr. CEO	Beatrice	6.4
David Lipson Chief financial officer	Beatrice	4.27
Leonard Goldenson Chairman	ABC	3.82
Frederick Pierce President	ABC	3.82
James Dutt CEO	Beatrice	3.8
John McConnaughy Jr. Chairman	Peabody International	3.7
Frank Grzelecki Executive vice president	Beatrice	2.57
Michael Sayres Senior vice president	Revlon	2.32
Samuel Simmons Senior vice president	Revlon	2.32

FIGURE 10-10. **The ten largest golden parachutes, 1985.** (*Source:* Business Week, May 5, 1986, p. 49. Used with permission.)

paid insurance policies in case somebody grabs off the company—or even threatens to—is an abuse of management prerogatives and a misuse of stockholder assets."[32]

In order to guard against these abuses of stockholder interests, T. Boone Pickens proposed in 1986 to establish a nationwide shareholder-rights lobbying group. Among other provisions, he favored secret ballots for stockholders voting their stock, on grounds that some institutional stockholders as well as employee-owners might be afraid to vote against entrenched management. If they did, employee-owners might lose their jobs, and pension-fund managers might lose a corporation's pension account. Others disagreed, saying that a vote "in the open sunshine" would increase the public accountability of institutional stockholders.[33]

[32]"Let's Stow Those Golden Chutes," *Business Week,* May 5, 1986, p. 132. See also Peter G. Scotese, "Fold Up Those Golden Parachutes," *Harvard Business Review,* March–April 1985, pp. 168–171, who points out that some companies have extended these "bail-out" privileges to as many as 250 upper-level managers.

[33]"From Boone Pickens, Another Popular (and Profitable?) Cause," *Business Week,* July 7, 1986, pp. 64–65. For a contrasting viewpoint, see Gary S. Becker, "Why Managers Have the Shareholder at Heart," *Business Week,* July 8, 1985, p. 14.

Another effort to protect the rights of institutional stockholders was the creation in 1985 of the Council of Institutional Investors. The Council's thirty members represent institutions and pension funds with corporate investments totaling more than $160 billion. Its "Shareholder Bill of Rights" favors equal voting rights for common stockholders; requiring majority shareholder approval of greenmail, poison pills, and golden parachutes; and fair and equal treatment of shareholders regarding tender offers.[34]

STAKEHOLDER MANAGEMENT AND THE STOCKHOLDER

Clearly, stockholders are a critically important stakeholder group. By providing capital, monitoring corporate performance, assuring the effective operation of stock markets, and bringing new issues to the attention of management, stockholders play a very important role in making the business system work. As shown earlier in Chapter 1 and Chapter 4, corporate leaders have an obligation to manage their companies in ways that promote and protect a variety of stakeholders. Balancing these various interests is a prime requirement of modern management. While stockholders are no longer considered to be the only important stakeholder group, their interests and needs remain central to successful operation of corporate business.

SUMMARY

Stockholders are the legal owners of a corporation. Millions of individuals and thousands of big institutions own corporate stock. Stock ownership confers rights to share in the profits of the corporation, to vote on important matters affecting the company, to cast votes for members of the board of directors, to sue the corporation for harm committed by its officers, and to sell one's stock.

The large business corporation is governed primarily by three groups: the board of directors which is legally responsible for company policy and general directions; the top managers who make day-to-day decisions and exert much practical control over policy; and the stockholders who may try to influence policy and corporate operations by attending the annual stockholders' meeting and by introducing shareholder resolutions to be voted on by all stockholders. Big institutional shareholders sometimes use their influence to sway corporate decisions, but generally they vote with management and the board of directors.

[34]James E. Heard, "Pension Funds and Contests for Corporate Control," *California Management Review,* Winter 1987, pp. 89–100; and "Shareholders Aren't Just Rolling Over Anymore," *Business Week,* April 27, 1987, pp. 32–33.

Today's corporate managers have many obligations to their stockholders: to manage the company efficiently so as to produce a satisfactory rate of return on stockholders' investment, to listen to the owners' viewpoints, and to deal honestly with all stockholders. Stockholders need to realize that they are only one among several important stakeholder groups and that the job of corporate management is to balance the needs and demands of all stakeholders if the corporation is to survive and prosper.

DISCUSSION AND REVIEW QUESTIONS

1. If you held shares of stock in a large corporation and thought that the company was not paying high enough dividends, what steps could you take to express your dissatisfaction? Assume that you do not want to sell the stock. Discuss.

2. Suppose the management of a company authorizes payment of a charitable contribution of $50,000 toward the building of a new hospital in the community where most of its employees live. If the $50,000 had not been contributed to the hospital, it could have been added to shareholder dividends. In your opinion, was company management acting properly as a trustee for the owners? Discuss.

3. In politics and government, the rule is "one person—one vote." But in corporations, votes are based on numbers of shares owned, and a single shareholder may cast many votes. Does this difference mean that corporate elections are less—or more—representative than political elections? Defend your answer.

4. Suppose you could choose just one of the suggested reforms of the board of directors discussed in this chapter. Which one would you prefer, and how would you defend your preference? How would you rank the others?

5. A company where you work as an hourly wage earner is owned by its employees. In the past, you have invested $2,000 of your own money to buy stock in the company, and it pays you a dividend when business is good. Now, however, the company is facing a declining market and rising costs because of general inflation. Company management is asking all employees to take an 18 percent cut in wages as a way to get the company through the difficult economic times. Your union, however, is resisting the proposed wage reduction, saying that its members are already hard pressed to meet the rising costs of living. With other members of the class, role-play your own situation as a wage earner who also is part owner of the firm. What should your position be on the requested wage cut? Which one of your roles—as wage earner or as owner—should be uppermost in making your decision? Explore all aspects of each role, including actions you might take to safeguard your own economic security.

CRITICAL INCIDENT

Handling Shareholder Resolutions

An Episcopal church group owning 15,000 shares of stock in a large metals manufacturing company introduced a resolution at the stockholders' annual meeting requiring the company to stop any expansion of its operations in South Africa. The resolution cited racial discrimination in wages and working conditions in the company's South African operations, and argued that pressure from the company would influence the South African government to change its racial policies. Management opposed the resolution, saying that it was working actively to eliminate discrimination and that failure to expand would result in financial losses for shareholders. Shareholders voted down the resolution by a resounding margin.

In another company, a group of Catholic nuns whose order owned some of the stock submitted a shareholder resolution. It asked the company to stop handing out free samples of an infant-feeding formula in developing countries. The sisters claimed that healthier breast feeding was being discouraged and that tainted water might be used to mix the formula outside hospitals. The company's management opposed the resolution and prevented it from being voted on at the annual meeting. Later, though, the company reached an informal agreement with the nuns and stopped handing out free samples.

1. In your opinion, which company management was doing the better job of promoting the interests of the owners? Justify your position.

2. When management "stonewalls" opposition to shareholder resolutions, what other courses of action are available to shareholders? List the most effective ones.

Chapter Eleven

CONSUMER PROTECTION IN THE 1980s

Business's job of serving consumers in socially responsible and ethical ways changed dramatically during the 1980s. The high tide of government-sponsored consumer protection laws was reached during the 1970s. The new deregulation philosophy of the 1980s meant that consumers in the marketplace would be expected to rely less on government and more on themselves. This shift toward greater consumer self-reliance introduced new ethical challenges and social responsibilities that had to be made a central part of business's strategic plans.

CHAPTER OBJECTIVES

After reading this chapter, you should be able to

- Explain why the consumer movement of the 1960s and 1970s occurred
- Describe the major federal consumer protection laws and agencies
- Discuss the special problem of product liability
- Show how business has responded to consumer pressures and demands
- Analyze the impact of deregulation on consumers
- Show how corporate strategic planning is affected by consumerism

Nonshattering safety glass is so much a part of modern cars and trucks that no one gives it a second thought these days. It was not always so. Alfred P. Sloan, Jr., who was president of General

Motors at the time safety glass was introduced around 1930, at first resisted putting it in some GM cars. "Accidents or no accidents, my concern in this matter is a matter of profit and loss." After being told that Ford Motor Company had begun installing safety glass in its autos, Sloan replied, "That is no reason why we should do so. I am trying to protect the interests of the stockholders of General Motors and the Corporation's operating position—it is not my responsibility to sell safety glass. . . . We are not a charitable institution—we are trying to make a profit for our stockholders."[1]

Sloan's obvious disregard for the safety of consumers who bought GM cars and trucks would certainly not go unchallenged in the 1980s. Contrast his views with what one prominent consumer activist had to say about consumer attitudes and gains in the mid-1980s:

> We now expect car makers to recall defective vehicles and repair them for free. If ads mislead us, we expect a refund. If services bought from retailers—the cleaner, the plumber—are inadequate or incomplete, we ask for and expect to receive a finished job. . . .
>
> This year's car models are twice as energy efficient as were autos of the mid-1970s. Household appliances now carry energy efficiency labels; they are far more efficient than in 1972. For example, refrigerators and freezers are 70 percent more efficient, room air conditioners 25 percent. Higher energy prices have forced businesses to conserve energy by turning to more efficient machinery and better-insulated offices and factories; private homes are now routinely built with insulation, storm windows and heat pumps. . . .
>
> More than ever before the public is alert to safety hazards and their prevention, of the health effects of lifestyle changes, of the toxicity and permanence of environmental hazards, of the pervasiveness and costs of white-collar crime, of . . . overcharging for banking, insurance, and other basic financial services, and of the legal system's mechanisms for redressing harm caused by negligence or by willful behavior.[2]

Something must have happened in the half century between Sloan's uncaring comment and the vigilant consumer attitudes and solid consumer gains described by Joan Claybrook. That "something" was the consumer movement, which sputtered along during the 1930s, was submerged during the 1940s and 1950s, but broke out with renewed vigor in the 1960s and 1970s. Its symbol and popular champion was Ralph Nader, the consumer activist, who quickly attracted as many critical barbs from business as accolades from consumers.

This chapter discusses the changes introduced by the consumer movement. Of particular importance is the impact of consumer activism on business firms and on government policies designed to protect consumers. The discussion emphasizes the increased pressures on business to develop consumer policies that are socially and ethically responsive to the needs and interests of the consuming public.

[1]Quoted in Morton Mintz, *At Any Cost: Corporate Greed, Women, and the Dalkon Shield*, New York: Pantheon, 1985, p. 252.

[2]Joan Claybrook, "The Next 15 Years," *Public Citizen*, October 1986, p. 36.

PRESSURES TO PROMOTE CONSUMER INTERESTS

As long as business has existed—since the ancient beginnings of commerce and trade—consumers have tried to protect their interests when they go to the marketplace to buy goods and services. They have haggled over prices, taken a careful look at the goods they are buying, compared the quality and prices of products offered by other sellers, and complained loudly when they feel cheated by shoddy products. So, consumer self-reliance has always been one form of consumer protection. The Latin phrase, *caveat emptor*—meaning "let the buyer beware"—has put consumers on the alert to look after their own interests. This form of individual self-reliance is still very much in existence today.

However, the increasing complexity of economic life in the twentieth century, especially in the more advanced industrial nations, has led to organized, collective efforts to safeguard consumers. These organized activities are usually called "consumerism" or "the consumer movement."

The Anatomy of Consumerism

At the heart of consumerism in the United States is an attempt to expand the rights and powers of consumers. The goal of the movement is to make consumer power an effective counterbalance to the rights and powers of business firms that sell goods and services.

Within an advanced, industrialized, free enterprise nation, business firms tend to grow to a very large size, as we demonstrated in Chapter 9. They acquire much power and influence. Frequently, they can determine prices. Typically, their advertisements sway consumers to buy one product or service rather than another. If large enough, they may share the market with only a few equally large competitors, thereby weakening some of the competitive protections enjoyed by consumers where business firms are smaller and more numerous. The economic influence and power of business firms may therefore become a problem for consumers unless ways can be found to promote an equal amount of consumer power.

Most consumers would feel well-protected if their fundamental rights to fair play in the marketplace could be guaranteed. In the early 1960s, when the consumer movement in the United States was in its early stages, President John F. Kennedy told Congress that consumers were entitled to four different kinds of protections:

1. *The right to safety:* to be protected against the marketing of goods which are hazardous to health or life.

2. *The right to be informed:* to be protected against fraudulent, deceitful, or grossly misleading information, advertising, labeling, or other practices, and to be given the facts to make an informed choice.

3. *The right to choose:* to be assured, wherever possible, access to a variety of products and services at competitive prices and in those industries in which competition is not workable and Government regulation is substituted, to be assured satisfactory quality and service at fair prices.

4. *The right to be heard:* to be assured that consumer interests will receive full and sympathetic consideration in the formulation of Government policy, and fair and expeditious treatment in its administrative tribunals.[3]

This "consumer bill of rights," as it was called, became the guiding philosophy of the consumer movement. If those rights could be guaranteed, consumers would feel more confident in dealing with well-organized and influential corporations in the marketplace.

Reasons for the Consumer Movement

The consumer movement exists because consumers believe that there is an unfair use of business power. The balance between business power and business responsibility is uneven, which results in consumer abuses such as unfairly high prices, unreliable and unsafe products, excessive advertising claims for the effectiveness of some consumer goods and services, and the promotion of some products (such as cigarettes, fatty foods, and farm products contaminated with pesticides) known to be harmful to human health. Additional reasons for the existence of the consumer movement are the following:

- *Complex products have enormously complicated the choices consumers need to make when they go shopping.* For this reason, consumers today are more dependent on business for product quality than ever before. Because many products are so complex—a personal computer or a television set, for example—most consumers have no way to judge at the time of purchase whether their quality is satisfactory. Many of the component parts of such products are not visible to consumers who, therefore, cannot inspect them even if they have the technical competence to do so. Instructions for use or care of products often are so complicated and detailed that buyers cannot understand or remember what to do. First-time computer users may spend weeks or months learning even the simplest software package—and then discover that it is not adequate for their needs. Consumers find that they are almost entirely dependent on business to deliver the quality promised. In these circumstances, business power can be used responsibly or it can be used unfairly to take advantage of uninformed consumers.
- *Services, as well as products, have become more specialized and difficult to judge.* When choosing lawyers, dentists, colleges, or hospitals, most consumers do not have adequate guides for evaluating whether they are good or bad. They can rely on word-of-mouth experiences of others, but this information may not be entirely reliable. Or when purchasing expensive items such as refrigerators, householders have not only to judge how well the items will perform but also to know what to do when they break down. The con-

[3]Quoted in David A. Aaker and George S. Day (eds.), *Consumerism: Search for the Consumer Interest*, New York: Free Press, 1971, pp. 24–25.

sumer faces a two-tier judgment problem in making purchases: First, is the product a good one? Then, what will good service cost? The uninformed or badly informed consumer is frequently no match for the seller who is in the superior position.

- *When business tries to sell both products and services through advertising, claims may be inflated or they may appeal to emotions having little to do with how the product is expected to perform.* An example was a television ad for designer jeans featuring the film star Brooke Shields, who teased viewers by asking, "Do you want to know what comes between me and my Calvins? Nothing." Another ad for fashion clothes was described this way: "A tousled blond beauty stands in the corner of a cattle pen, one finger caught between her lips, her denim bodice unbuttoned. In the next photograph she is lying down, and a man's hand is opening her shirt to reveal ample cleavage. In another shot she is dancing with a cowboy, her jean skirt ripped and her bra exposed. The jumbled black-and-white photo montage—part of a series of print-advertising campaigns for Guess fashions—is one of the latest entries in the fashion industry's era of provocation."[4] Ad-industry critics have frequently found fault with advertisements during children's television programs that feature violence, that sell sweetened cereals, or that promote toys—such as Care Bears or Strawberry Shortcake—by building program plots around the toys, thus taking advantage of young children unable to differentiate between a fictional program and a commercial advertisement.[5] Beer commercials that feature "good old boys" relaxing after work, cigarette advertisements that hint at freedom and pleasure for users, or auto advertisements that link male virility with horsepower and speed have come under attack for ignoring the negative impacts of alcohol abuse, tobacco use, and high-speed automobile deaths and injuries.

- *Product safety has often been ignored.* The symbolic beginning of consumerism in the United States was Ralph Nader's well-publicized charges about the hazards of driving the Corvair.[6] As public interest in health and nutrition grew during the 1960s and 1970s, many consumers worried about food additives, preservatives, pesticide residues left on fruits and vegetables, diet patterns that contributed to obesity, and the devastating health effects of long-term tobacco use. If the public could not count on business to screen out these possible dangers to consumers, who could they turn to for help? This question was raised more and more often, which led eventually to organized collective efforts to redress the imbalance of power between sellers and consumers.

---

[4]"Sexy Does It," *Newsweek,* September 15, 1986, p. 62.

[5]"Are the Programs Your Kids Watch Simply Commercials?" *Business Week,* March 25, 1985, pp. 53–54; "Toying with Kids' TV," *Newsweek,* May 13, 1985, p. 85; and Jeffrey Zaslow, "Children's Search for Values Leading to Shopping Malls," *Wall Street Journal,* March 31, 1987, p. 21.

[6]Ralph Nader, *Unsafe at Any Speed: The Designed-In Dangers of the American Automobile,* New York: Grossman, 1972.

Acceptance of Consumer Right	Percent Agreeing		Lack of Consumer Responsibility	Percent Agreeing
Clothing manufacturers should provide garment-care labels	100%	but	Consumers should get money back even if they do not read the label and the garment shrinks	12%
A customer overcharge should be corrected by the store	100	but	Items not charged by mistake need not be paid for	36
Costs caused by stealing should not be paid by the innocent consumer	87	but	Shoplifters would not be reported by the customer	38
			Sampling fruit and other items in a grocery store is all right	25
Instructions should be included with an item that needs to be assembled	100	but	Parts broken without reading the instructions should be replaced free of charge	20
Any item purchased should perform the function for which it was designed	99	but	A person signing a consumer-purchase contract without understanding it should not be held responsible for it	27

FIGURE 11-1. **Rights and responsibilities of consumers.** (*Source: Adapted from Rose M. Davis, "Comparison of Consumer Acceptance of Rights and Responsibilities," Proceedings, 25th annual conference, American Council on Consumer Interests, San Antonio, TX, April 25–28, 1979, pp. 68–70.*)

Despite these consumer fears and concerns, business continued to do a generally good job of serving consumers. Often, consumers themselves were at fault for not being better informed or more responsible in using the products they purchased.

In one study comparing consumer rights with consumer responsibilities, consumers were found to have accepted rights more often (96 percent) than they accepted responsibilities (74 percent). Some of the rights and responsibilities with which this study was concerned are shown in Figure 11-1. The study's author commented as follows on the significance of the findings:

> Consumers have the responsibility to offer intelligent and worthwhile suggestions and complaints when necessary to business, industry and government. Consumers have the responsibility to use information that is available in instruction booklets, owners' manuals, and use and care tags. They have a responsibility to pay their bills and to read and understand contracts before signing them. The consumer should be honest and fair in all dealings and call attention to errors that are to his disadvantage as well as those that are to his advantage. Responsible consumers should also be aware of their role and function in the economy. They should abhor waste and avoid exploitation of those who supply goods and services.[7]

[7]Rose M. Davis, "Comparison of Consumer Acceptance of Rights and Responsibilities," *Proceedings,* twenty-fifth annual conference, American Council on Consumer Interests, San Antonio, TX, April 25–28, 1979, pp. 68–70.

In other words, if business is asked to be more responsible in dealing with consumers, then consumers have a duty to exercise care in making purchases and to treat business with the same kind of responsibility they expect to find when they shop. Power and responsibility must balance on both sides of the market transaction.

Consumer Interest Groups

One of the impressive features of the consumer movement in the United States is the many organized groups that actively promote and speak for the interests of millions of consumers. One organization alone—the Consumer Federation of America—brings together over 200 nonprofit groups to espouse the consumer viewpoint; they represent some 30 million Americans. Two nonprofit organizations—Consumers' Research and Consumers Union—conduct extensive tests on selected consumer products and services and publish the results, with ratings on a brand-name basis, in widely circulated magazines. Consumer cooperatives, credit unions, and consumer education programs in schools and universities and on television and radio round out a very extensive network of activities aimed at promoting consumer interests.

The most-publicized consumer advocate is Ralph Nader, who with his associates formed the organizations shown in Figure 11-2. Public Citizen, founded in 1971, became the umbrella organization for specialized units, the main fund-raising organization, and a publishing arm for consumer publications. The Health Research Group took the lead in urging a ban on harmful color dyes used in various foods, putting warning labels on dangerous products, setting exposure limits on hazardous substances, helping consumers victimized by harmful medicines to bring lawsuits against drug companies, alerting the public to possibly dangerous medical products on the market (for example, Oraflex, Zomax, and Selacryn), and publishing an exposé of more than 600 prescription drugs whose ingredients were shown not to be effective.

The Litigation Group, formed in 1972, gives legal assistance to people who have difficulty in gaining adequate access to the court system. Consumers harmed by cancer-causing food additives, homeowners exposed to the harmful effects of insulation in their homes, or airline travelers with reservations who have been bumped from their flights have been helped by the Litigation Group. Congress Watch came into being in 1973 as a citizens' watch group to keep an eye on Congress. It lobbied against subsidies to various industry groups and has sought curbs on pesticides, unfair banking practices, and rising telephone rates. Other Nader-inspired efforts include the Tax Reform Research Group that promotes tax legislation intended to be more fair to consumers; the Critical Mass Energy Project that opposes nuclear energy and favors a conservationist approach to national energy problems; and Buyers Up, started in 1983, which negotiates volume discount prices for consumer goods and services.[8]

---

[8]For a more complete summary of the Nader network, see David Bollier, "15 Years," *Public Citizen*, October 1986, pp. 20–24, 32; and Claybrook, op. cit., pp. 34–36.

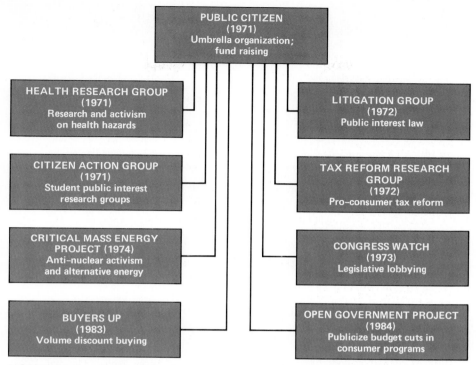

FIGURE 11-2.   Ralph Nader's consumer protection network. (*Source: Adapted from David Bollier, "15 Years," Public Citizen, October 1986, pp. 20–24, 32.*)

HOW GOVERNMENT PROTECTS CONSUMERS

The federal government's involvement in consumer affairs is extensive. During the 1960s and 1970s, Congress passed important laws to protect consumers, created new regulatory agencies, and strengthened the powers of older consumer protection agencies. These developments meant that consumers, rather than relying strictly on free market competition to safeguard their interests, could turn to government for aid.

Goals of Consumer Legislation

Figure 11-3 lists the major consumer protection laws adopted by Congress during the heyday of consumerism—the 1960s and 1970s. This surge of consumer legislation reflected three major concerns of government policymakers and regulators.

First, some of the laws were intended to provide consumers with better information when making purchases.

For example, *the Truth in Lending Act of 1968 requires lenders to inform borrowers of the annual rate of interest to be charged, as well as all related fees and service charges that may accompany a consumer loan. In the past, consumers*

Year	Law	Purpose
1960	Hazardous Substances Labeling Act	Requires warning labels on hazardous home products
1966	Fair Packaging and Labeling Act	Requires labeling of contents by name and quantity for various home products
1966	Cigarette Labeling Act	Requires a health warning on cigarette packages
1966	Child Protection Act	Bans hazardous toys and games intended for children
1966	National Traffic and Motor Vehicle Act	Establishes national safety standards for motor vehicles
1968	Consumer Credit Protection Act	Requires full disclosure of credit information on consumer loans and installment buying
1969	Child Protection and Toy Safety Act	Broadens the coverage of the 1966 act and defines some hazards more clearly
1970	Public Health Smoking Act	Bans radio and television advertising of cigarettes and strengthens warning label
1970	Federal Deposit Insurance Act, as amended	Limits credit card loss to $50, requires consumer access to credit files, and prohibits unsolicited issuance of credit cards
1972	Consumer Product Safety Act	Creates the Consumer Product Safety Commission with broad power to protect consumers from hazardous products
1974	Real Estate Settlements Law	Requires disclosure of all costs to buyers in real estate deals
1975	Magnuson–Moss Warranty Act	Requires clear language on warranties and clarification of the warranty's coverage
1977	Equal Credit Opportunity Act	Prohibits various types of discrimination by credit institutions

FIGURE 11-3. Major consumer protection laws, 1960s and 1970s.

had sometimes been misled by the "fine print" in the loan papers they signed and ended up paying far more than they realized or could afford. Armed with full information, consumers can make better decisions about the wisdom of borrowing or buying on credit.

Other examples of better consumer information are mandatory labels telling buyers how much it costs to operate home appliances or how to care for clothing, clearer or more specific warranties and guarantees, warnings on products that are dangerous to health, and Federal Trade Commission efforts to police deceptive advertising.

A second aim of consumer legislation is to protect consumers against possible hazards from products they may purchase.

Under current legislation of this type, drugs must be proved safe and effective before they can be marketed, flammable fabrics are limited in usage, unsafe toys can be recalled, efforts are made to eliminate spoiled and contaminated meat and poultry from sale to the public, warning labels are required on cigarette packages and advertisements, and lead-based paint has been banned from widespread use.

Other nations have similar consumer protection laws. In 1983 Israel banned advertising of tobacco products on radio and television and in theaters, public transport, and outdoor signs, and prohibited celebrities, people younger than 40, or anyone wearing sports clothes or uniforms from appearing in tobacco advertisements. Norway and Italy have similar laws.

A third goal of government in protecting consumer interests is to work toward competitive pricing.

Three of Cleveland's largest supermarket chains, accounting for over 70 percent of the area's grocery business, were charged with fixing food prices. The U.S. Department of Justice brought criminal conspiracy charges against the stores and some of their executives, and store customers brought a class action suit to regain money lost by all the stores' customers when charged too much. Two of the chains agreed, in an out-of-court settlement, to repay $20 million to the people of northeastern Ohio, with each resident receiving twenty $1 coupons for buying food at the stores. The other supermarket chain agreed to pay $1.5 million to a charity fund. In addition, the stores and their executives received fines and probations upon pleading ''no contest'' to the criminal charges. The presiding judge said he hoped the settlement would infuse a new competitive vitality into the Cleveland supermarket industry.[9]

Prior to the deregulation of some industries, a few government agencies maintained anticompetitive pricing policies for some businesses. A prime example was the airline industry that was permitted by regulatory authorities to set air travelers' rates artificially high, a practice discontinued when the industry was deregulated. Prices charged by railroads and intercity bus lines continued to be held above competitive levels by regulatory agencies in the early 1980s, while other prices—such as those on natural gas—were gradually decontrolled.

[9]Martin Sloane, "Consumers Win Price-Fix Settlement," *Pittsburgh Post-Gazette,* July 21, 1982, p. 21.

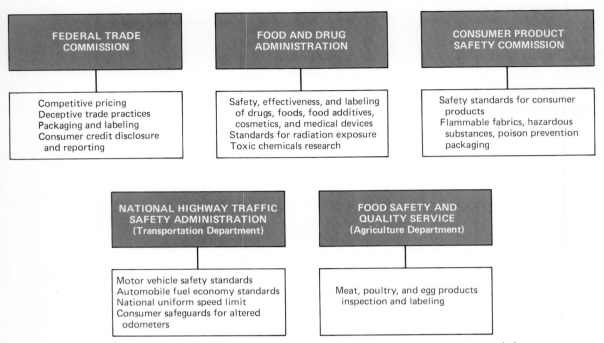

FIGURE 11-4. Major federal consumer protection agencies and their main responsibilities.

Consumer legislation has therefore followed closely the ideal principles of a free enterprise economy: maximum information for the buyer so that rational consumer decisions can be made, some guarantee that goods and services will perform as expected, and fair prices established through competition among profit-seeking businesses.

Major Consumer Protection Agencies

Looking out for consumer interests has become an important part of government activity at local, state, and federal levels. Large cities, as well as county governments in urbanized areas, may have a department of consumer affairs whose job is to promote consumer education and to act as a channel of investigation and mediation when disputes arise between consumers and companies. In some states—New York is a good example—the state attorney general oversees a special division created to safeguard consumers against harmful acts by business.

While state and local activities on behalf of consumers are important, by far the most significant government intervention in consumer affairs occurs at the federal level. Federal laws and enforcement agencies affect more consumers and attract greater media publicity than state and local efforts. Figure 11-4 depicts the principal consumer protection agencies that operate at the federal level, along with their major areas of responsibility. The oldest of the five is the Food and Drug Administration and its predecessors which, along with the Department of Agriculture's meat and poultry inspection programs, date back to the first decade of the twentieth century. The Federal Trade Commission, as noted earlier, was established in 1914 and then given additional powers to protect consumers during the 1930s. Two of the agencies—the Consumer Product Safety Commission and the National Highway Traffic Safety Administration—were created during the great wave of social regulations in the early 1970s.

These five major agencies are authorized by law to intervene directly into the very center of free market activities, if that is considered necessary to protect consumers.

> For example, *car manufacturers can be and have been told what types of safety features to build, what fuel performance levels to achieve, what kinds of antipollution devices to install, and what information about prices must be posted on cars for sale. Advertisers are given strict guidelines for writing advertising copy and staging televised commercials. Drug companies and food processors are instructed what may and may not be added to products or said on labels. Toy manufacturers can be ordered to withdraw toys from the market and make refunds to purchasers.*

In other words, consumer protection laws and agencies substitute government-mandated standards and the decisions of government officials for decision making by private buyers and sellers.

Consumerism during the Carter Administration

Presidential candidate Jimmy Carter made a strong appeal to consumers during the 1976 election campaign, and when he assumed office in early 1977 he appointed several consumer activists to important posts in the regulatory agencies. As a result, government policy swung sharply to their point of view. A consumer advisor to President Carter, reflecting on her experiences in those years, said, "One of the biggest achievements [of the consumer movement] was getting consumer activists into government jobs. They became known and recognized as [being] in the consumer corner. They became trusted people in the public mind."[10]

As a result of this interventionist attitude by government, the late 1970s marked the high tide of the consumer movement. By that time, consumers had a three-tier protectionist system in place: (1) traditional self-reliance (the *caveat emptor* approach); (2) private consumer advocacy groups and organizations, such as those organized by Nader; and (3) a pro-consumer government regulatory apparatus. The Carter administration's pro-consumerist policies continued the presidential support that had begun with President Kennedy and the consumer bill of rights. Consumerism peaked at that point.

[10]Esther Peterson, quoted in Bollier, op. cit., p. 24.

A business may be legally liable to consumers when

Privity of contract is applied to the manufacturer as well as retailers and distributors

Warranties—express or implied, full or limited—grant rights to purchasers

Injury to a consumer is caused by a product or service

FIGURE 11-5. Three types of legal liability to consumers.

During the more conservative 1980s, consumer activists found it more difficult to influence public policy—partly because they had already won many of the big battles, partly because business was more ready to negotiate and compromise on the remaining issues, and partly because the Reagan administration believed that consumers' needs could best be promoted in deregulated markets rather than through more laws and regulatory rules.[11]

Product Liability: A Special Problem

In today's complicated economy, consumers' relationships with products they use and relationships with producers of those products are much more complicated and abstract. It is no longer reasonable to expect consumers to share the responsibilities for product performance as they once did. The burden of responsibility has been shifted to the producer. Although many businesses have attempted to assume much of the responsibility through money-back guarantees and other similar policies, consumers have thought that this is not enough and have demanded that business assume a larger burden of responsibility. The result has been a strengthening of product liability laws and a softening of court attitudes toward consumer claims. Walls protecting producers from consumer lawsuits have crumbled, and there has been a dramatic increase in product liability suits.

Traditionally consumers had little legal recourse against producers of faulty products. The common legal defenses available to producers were the doctrine of privity of contract, warranties, and the doctrine of strict liability in tort. All three, now modified in favor of consumers and summarized in Figure 11-5, are discussed in the following sections.

Privity of Contract

The doctrine of *privity of contract* stressed direct contractual relationships and held that producers could avoid responsibility for product failure if a product was purchased from someone other than the manufacturer. This meant that

---

[11]"Consumer Groups Try to Keep Earlier Gains as Their Power Wanes," *Wall Street Journal,* December 31, 1986, p. 1.

injured consumers could sue only the person from whom they purchased a defective product—not the producer. The dealer could then sue the wholesaler and so on up to the manufacturer. In the economy of the early 1800s, this doctrine probably made a great deal of sense. But as the distance between consumer and producer widened and as products passed through longer and more complex channels of distribution, the strength of this defense has been dissipated through court decisions. The landmark decision was rendered in 1916.

> MacPherson purchased a new Buick from a local automobile dealer. Shortly thereafter defective wooden spokes in a wheel collapsed, and MacPherson was injured as a result. He sued Buick. The company claimed that MacPherson had purchased the car from a dealer and not from Buick and therefore Buick had no obligation to him. The judge ruled that Buick had been negligent because the wheel had not been inspected before it was put on the car. He further ruled that Buick was responsible for defects resulting from negligence, regardless of how many distributive firms were in between.

This legal philosophy has been expanded since the MacPherson decision. Today an injured consumer can sue any or all people in the chain of distribution. In general, the courts have reasoned that through advertising and labeling, manufacturers make a variety of representations about a product. The manufacturer intends and expects the product to be purchased and used in accordance with representations of performance and assurances of quality. Therefore, when a consumer purchases the product and that product fails to live up to express or implied representations and thereby causes injury to the purchaser, that purchaser has the right to be reimbursed for the injury.

Warranties

There are two kinds of warranties—express and implied. When a product is offered for sale, the seller makes claims for its characteristics. Claims that are explicitly stated by the seller are *express warranties*. Representations on a warranty card that the parts of a product will not fail within ninety days from the time of purchase are examples of express warranties. Not all express warranties are on the warranty card. Statements on labels, wrappers, packages, and in advertising also are express warranties.

More troublesome for sellers is the question of *implied warranties*. Courts have held that simply by selling a product to a customer the seller implies that the product is fit for the ordinary use for which it is likely to be used. The landmark case in the area of implied warranty occurred in 1960.

> In this case, Claus Henningsen purchased a new automobile that he and his wife drove around town for several days. Then, when driving out of town, the steering mechanism failed, and Mrs. Henningsen crashed into a highway sign and then into a brick wall. She sustained injuries and the car was a total loss. Henningsen went to court. The automobile company claimed that Henningsen had signed a

disclaimer when he bought the car and this limited the liability of the company to replacement of defective parts. The court held that the company could not avoid its legal responsibility to make automobiles good enough to serve the purpose for which they were intended.

Congress attempted to clarify warranty provisions by passing the Magnuson-Moss Warranty Act in 1975. The law, administered by the FTC, requires manufacturers, retailers, and importers to specify whether warranties they voluntarily issue are full or limited, says that terms must be spelled out in clear language, and gives consumers the right to sue if warranties are not honored.

Strict Tort Liability

A *tort* is a civil wrong that sometimes results in injury to a person. Within the last few years courts have increasingly taken the position that manufacturers are responsible for injuries resulting from use of their products. One result has been a rapid rise in the number of personal injury and product liability law suits—from 3,300 in 1977 to over 8,000 in 1981.[12] The trend is not confined to the United States; member nations of the European Economic Community have tried to establish uniform standards and limits on product liability claims. Small companies are especially vulnerable to lawsuits and may be driven out of business by sky-high liability insurance rates.[13]

Under existing court interpretations, it is not necessary for consumers to prove either negligence or breach of warranty by the producer. Nor is the consumer's contributory negligence an acceptable defense by the manufacturer. If a product is judged to be inherently dangerous, manufacturers can be held liable for injuries caused from use of the product. And strict liability extends to all who were involved in the final product—suppliers, sellers, contractors, assemblers, and manufacturers of component parts.

The following case illustrates the extent to which manufacturers can be held liable today:

Ford Motor Company and Goodyear Tire & Rubber Company were sued by the mother of a driver killed in the crash of a Mercury Cougar automobile that had been traveling more than 100 miles per hour when a tire failed. Court records established that the driver's blood tested far in excess of the established standards for intoxication. However, a federal district court, later upheld by an appeals court, ruled that both companies were liable for the death and must pay damages to the mother. Ford had argued that it had no duty to warn the owner against tire failure, that it had not manufactured the tire, and that the car's driver was guilty of contributory negligence by being intoxicated.

[12]"The Widening Shadow of Product Liability," *Chemical Week,* February 3, 1982, p. 44.

[13]Sanford L. Jacobs, "Changes in Products Liability Jeopardize Small Companies," *Wall Street Journal,* November 30, 1981, p. 29; and T. Lewin, "Insurers Balking on Company Losses," *New York Times,* March 30, 1983, p. 1.

The appellate court said:

> The sports car involved here was marketed with an intended and recognized appeal to youthful drivers. The 425 horsepower engine with which Ford had equipped it proved a capability of speeds over 100 miles per hour, and the car's allure, no doubt exploited in its marketing, lay in no small measure in this power and potential speed. . . . It was to be readily expected that the Cougar would, on occasion, be driven in excess of the 85 miles per hour proven maximum safe operating speed of its Goodyear tires. . . . Consequently, Ford cannot escape its duty either to provide an adequate warning of the specific danger of tread separation at such high speeds or to ameliorate the danger in some other way.

In this case, a company (Ford) was held liable for damages caused by use of a product (the Goodyear tire) it did not even manufacture and where the user was clearly irresponsible due to intoxication. However, the court went on to point out that the car itself was potentially hazardous and that Ford had a responsibility "for its own active role in the assembly of the unreasonably dangerous composite product, the Cougar automobile."[14]

Courts have even held business firms liable for injuries to children not yet born and workers harmed by asbestos materials even though the companies did not know about the health dangers.

> *In the first case, a pregnant mother who took a drug called DES to prevent a miscarriage found out later that it caused cancer in her daughter; a subsequent operation on the adolescent child then rendered her unable to have children of her own. The court rejected the drug manufacturer's claim that it could not reasonably have foreseen such a risk to the child, saying that the manufacturer did not test the drug on laboratory animals prior to marketing it.*
>
> *In the second case, the asbestos companies were held liable for damages, in spite of their claims that they did not know of the dangers of working with asbestos and therefore could not have warned their employees; the court said they had not invested enough money in research to discover such health hazards. The judge in this 1982 case also said this about spreading the burdens of liability: "Spreading the costs of injuries among all those who produce, distribute, and purchase manufactured products is far preferable to imposing it on the innocent victims who suffer illnesses and disability from defective products."[15]*

(Notice the ethics principles involved in these two cases and in the judge's comments: the *ethical rights* of consumers to safety were given higher priority than the companies' *utilitarian* costs; and the *just and fair* way to distribute the burdens of these tragedies was to require the companies to

---

[14]Insurance Institute for Highway Safety, *Status Report,* vol. 15, no. 14, September 17, 1980, p. 6.

[15]"Unsafe Products: The Great Debate over Blame and Punishment," *Business Week,* April 30, 1984, p. 104; and Michael deCourcy Hinds, "A Move to Stem Liability Cases," *New York Times,* October 2, 1983, p. F-12.

compensate the victims. Figure 3-5 in Chapter 3 is a useful way to review these ethics principles and to see how they can be applied to cases of product liability.)

Business Efforts to Reform the Product Liability Laws

Faced with an increasing flood of liability suits, business has lobbied for changes in laws and court proceedings. Since the early 1980s, bills have been introduced in Congress that would establish the following principles in liability suits:

- *Set up uniform federal standards for determining liability.* This would reduce a company's exposure to repeated trials on the same charges in many different states, and it would lower legal costs for companies and help them develop a uniform legal strategy for confronting liability charges in court.
- *Shift the burden of proving liability to consumers.* They would have to prove that a manufacturer knew or should have known that a product design was defective before it began producing the item for consumption. Under present law and judicial interpretations, a company is considered to be negligent if a product injures the user, and it is up to the company to prove otherwise.
- *Eliminate some bases for liability claims.* Products not measuring up to a manufacturer's own specifications—for example, *poorly made* tires that blow out at normal speeds—could be the basis for a liability claim, but the vast majority of liability cases go further and blame *poorly designed* products or *a failure of the manufacturer to warn of dangers.* The DES-injured child described above most likely would not have been able to recover damages if the proposed law had existed then, nor would the asbestos workers have been able to sue on these grounds.
- *Severely curb the expanded privity of contract adopted by court rulings.* No longer could consumers seek compensation for their injuries by suing retailers, distributors, or others unless it could be proved that they, along with the manufacturer, also were negligent.
- *Allow judges, not juries, to determine punitive damages.* Currently, the size of damage awards is commonly determined by the jury that hears the testimony during the trial, and these jury awards may be very large. When three people were killed in the crash of a Ford Pinto, a jury assessed Ford Motor Company $125 million in damages; later a court reduced the award to $3.5 million. The new law would have judges, not juries, determine the amount of punitive damages, which would greatly reduce these awards.

Under strong pressure from both business lobbyists and consumer groups, Congress in 1985 failed to enact these reforms. Business efforts to reform the liability laws were strongly supported by insurance companies who sometimes found themselves facing multimillion-dollar settlements and who raised the premiums on all forms of liability insurance. These added insurance costs then put heavy burdens on many companies, especially small ones in competitive markets. The Florida legislature, attempting to deal with excessive damage awards and rising insurance rates, adopted a new law that limits noneconomic (i.e., pain and suffering) damages to $450,000 and reduces insurance rates. North Carolina and Hawaii took somewhat similar steps. These reform measures were unpopular with insurance companies who said that they would probably have to stop writing liability policies in those states, thus depriving companies of even that protection against the risks of manufacturing products that might injure consumers.[16]

POSITIVE BUSINESS RESPONSES TO CONSUMERISM

The consumer movement of the 1960s and 1970s demonstrated to business that it was expected to perform at high levels of efficiency and reliability in order to satisfy the consuming public. Because business did not always respond quickly or fully enough, consumer advocates and their organizations turned to government for protection. On the other hand, much effort has been devoted by individual business firms and by entire industries to encourage voluntary responses to consumer demands. Some of the more prominent positive responses are discussed next.

Consumer Affairs Departments

Many large corporations have created consumer affairs departments, often placing a vice president in charge. These centralized departments normally handle consumer inquiries and complaints about a company's products and services, particularly in cases where a consumer has not been able to resolve differences with local dealers. Some companies have installed consumer "hot lines" for dissatisfied customers to place telephone calls directly to the manufacturer. Experienced companies are aware that consumer complaints received internally by a consumer affairs department can be handled more quickly, at lower cost, and with less risk of losing goodwill than if customers take a legal route or if their complaints receive widespread media publicity.

Arbitration

Some companies have established arbitration panels that are given authority to settle disputes between customers and the company. In these cases, specially appointed arbitrators who are not related to either party in the dispute make final decisions.

[16]David B. Hilder, "Tort Wars: Insurers' Push to Limit Civil Damage Awards Begins to Slow Down," _Wall Street Journal_, August 1, 1986, pp. 1, 14. This article contains a state-by-state summary of actions taken to reform liability laws. See also an interesting discussion by Jane Bryant Quinn, "Cutting Back Verdicts," _Newsweek_, July 7, 1986, p. 44.

General Motors, Ford, Chrysler, and many foreign auto importers "now sponsor some kind of local umpire system that will handle knotty warranty, product, service, or sales problems when the customer cannot get satisfactory redress from the company or dealer."[17] Automakers find that many complaints—from 40 to 85 percent—can be resolved without going to an arbitration panel. They also have learned that these referee programs reduce consumer dissatisfaction and improve the industry's image.

Consumer Action Panels

Consumer Action Panels (CAPs) have been formed by some industries, and they go one step beyond Better Business Bureaus in resolving consumer complaints. Dissatisfied customers are encouraged to work out the problem at the local level, then by writing to the manufacturer, and finally by contacting a CAP. Those who work with CAPs claim a large measure of success for the system; the Major-Appliance Consumer Action Panel, for example, reported that 90 percent of complaints were resolved before the CAP was involved. CAPs have been organized by carpet and rug manufacturers, the furniture industry, automakers, and insurance companies.[18]

Product Recalls

Beginning in the mid-1970s, product recalls by companies became a more frequent way of dealing with consumer dissatisfaction. A product recall occurs when a company, either voluntarily or under an agreement with a government agency, takes back all items found to be dangerously defective. Sometimes these products are in the hands of consumers; at other times they may be in the factory, in wholesale warehouses, or on the shelves of retail stores. Wherever they are in the chain of distribution or use, the manufacturer tries to notify consumers or potential users about the defect so that they will return the items. A recalled product may be repaired or replaced or destroyed, depending upon the problem.

Not all recalled products are actually found to be defective. Chrysler once recalled 1.3 million Dodge Aspens and Plymouth Volarés to check on a front-end suspension problem but found that only 13,000—just 1 percent—of the cars had this kind of trouble. Another problem is the low response rate for some recalled items, which can run as low as 5 percent (although up to 90 percent may be recorded in other cases).

The four major government agencies responsible for most mandatory recalls are the Food and Drug Administration (FDA), the National Highway Traffic Safety Administration (NHTSA), the Environmental Protection Agency (EPA) (which can recall polluting motor vehicles), and the Consumer Product Safety Commission (CPSC).

---

[17]"Detroit's Tonic for Lemon Buyers," *Business Week*, April 4, 1983, pp. 54–55; and Leslie Maitland, "Arbitration Plan Set for Defects in G.M. Cars," *New York Times*, April 27, 1983, p. 1.

[18]Arch W. Troelstrup and E. Carl Hall, *The Consumer in American Society*, 6th ed., New York: McGraw-Hill, 1978, pp. 468–470.

Company	Item	Estimated Cost (in millions)	Year
Recalls Involving Alleged Defective Products			
Firestone Tire & Rubber Co.	Radial 500 tire	$135	1978
Parker Brothers	Riviton construction set	$ 10	1978
Procter & Gamble	Rely tampon	$ 75	1980
Volkswagen AG	Audi-5000 automobile	n/a	1987
Recalls Involving Tampering and Contamination by Individuals			
Johnson & Johnson	Tylenol capsules	$100	1982
Johnson & Johnson	Tylenol capsules	$150	1986
Smith–Kline–Beckman	Contac, Teldrin, and Dietac capsules	$ 8–10	1986
Bristol Myers	Excedrin, Datril, and Bufferin capsules	n/a	1986

FIGURE 11-6. Some major product recalls.

Figure 11-6 lists some of the most important and well-publicized recalls of the 1970s and 1980s. Of these, Procter & Gamble's (P&G) Rely tampon, Firestone's Radial 500 tire, and Johnson & Johnson's Tylenol (twice recalled) are perhaps the best known. Deaths were reported in all three cases, but the circumstances were strikingly different. Firestone denied any responsibility for its faulty tires—it insisted that they were misused by drivers—but eventually it was forced by a government agency to recall them. P&G's Rely tampon was associated with a little-known rare disease called toxic shock syndrome (TSS), and the company acted quickly to take its product off the shelves and to alert women to the possible danger. Later studies failed to prove either a specific link between Rely and TSS or that Rely was more to blame than other similar tampons. The makers of Tylenol acted even more promptly to remove all supplies from stores and to destroy all stocks when deaths occurred from capsules that had been poisoned. Later the company abandoned Tylenol capsules altogether, saying they could not be made tamper-proof.

Figure 11-6 also shows that some recalls are the result of defective products, while others are necessary because corporations and their consumers are attacked by individuals who hold grudges or are deranged mentally. When 250,000 Audi 5000 autos were recalled in early 1987, it was because the cars accelerated suddenly and unexpectedly because of an alleged defect in the automatic transmission.[19]

[19]"Audi Problems with Sudden Acceleration May Not Be Over, Despite Recent Recall," *Wall Street Journal,* January 20, 1987, p. 31. For another example, see Laurie McGinley, "U.S. Says GM Didn't Give Its Customers Adequate Warning about Safety Defects," *Wall Street Journal,* April 6, 1987, p. 23.

An outstanding example of socially responsible decision making is the voluntary recall by Parker Brothers of its toy construction set after two children choked to death on some of the parts. The company was under no pressure from government safety agencies and was thought to be in the clear legally, but it quickly recalled the sets. These instances were well-publicized, but it is probably true that many more recalls are undertaken quietly and voluntarily by smaller companies wishing to avoid legal difficulties, wanting to retain customer goodwill, or desiring to avoid the negative aspects of mandatory recalls.

THE IMPACT OF DEREGULATION ON CONSUMERS

When deregulation of the business system began in the late 1970s and then picked up steam during the eight years of President Ronald Reagan's administration, consumers made some gains, but they also suffered some losses. On the positive side, greater competition in the airline industry, in telephone communication, and among banks and other financial institutions, gave consumers more choices of some services, lower prices on some items, and higher returns on some of their savings. On the negative side, some of the big corporate mergers permitted by antitrust regulators threatened to reduce competition in some markets, thereby posing the possibility of higher prices; and such consumer watchdog agencies as the FTC scaled back enforcement of some consumer protection rules.

Deregulation in general meant that the consumer would have to depend more on self-reliance and consumer advocacy groups and count less on government protectionist laws and regulations.

In this climate of deregulation, many consumer advocates worried that the gains made during the heyday of the consumer movement would be lost. By the mid-1980s, however, these fears seemed somewhat exaggerated, for the following reasons:

- All of the consumer protection laws adopted during the 1960s and 1970s remained in place. Congress showed no inclination to roll them back, even in the face of the product liability crisis discussed earlier. Although the Reagan administration filled consumer agencies with deregulation-minded appointees (just as the Carter administration had earlier filled them with pro-consumerists), and although agency budgets were reduced, the agencies themselves were not abolished and, in fact, they continued to function.

  In other words, a *consumer protection infrastructure—consisting of the laws and agencies discussed in this chapter and shown in Figures 11-3 and 11-4*—had been created during the 1960s and 1970s and it continued to be a baseline to guide dealings between consumers and business firms during the 1980s. This infrastructure helps to resolve questions of product safety, effectiveness, reliability, legal recourse when harmed, provision of adequate purchasing information, and maximizing free choice by consumers.

- In addition, the consumer movement has been remarkably successful in making a lasting impact on both the consuming public and business. A heightened consumer consciousness has emerged. Consumers are more aware of their rights, better informed about what can be done to protect themselves, and more willing to stand up and be counted. Business, too, has heard the consumer message and reacted positively. Consumer advocacy organizations are more militant and more effective in lobbying for consumer gains.

The result was rather remarkable—and considerably less threatening than consumer advocates had feared. A better-educated, more-aware consuming public has permitted the deregulation approach to work in the interests of both consumers and business. But it has done so *only* because the consumer protection infrastructure created by the consumer movement has remained intact as a guide for consumers and as a check on potential and actual abuses of consumer rights and needs.

These combined developments growing out of consumerism and deregulation, moved United States society toward *freer* markets but not toward completely *free* consumer markets. The result is nearer to a mixed state-and-free enterprise model, with a government-sponsored protectionist infrastructure that allows the bulk of consumer decisions to remain in the hands of private buyers and sellers. (A review of Figure 6-1 in Chapter 6 would be helpful in understanding this relationship.)

STRATEGIC IMPLICATIONS OF THE CONSUMER MOVEMENT

When corporations plan strategically, they are required to think about the kind of company they want to be, the kind of basic mission they see themselves carrying out, the kind of markets they want to serve, and the organizational structure most effective for achieving the company's goals. The consumer movement has affected corporate strategic planning in two basic ways.

First, in order to attain their long-run strategic goals, corporate planners and policymakers have learned to assign high priority to the things consumers expect—high-quality goods and services, reliable and effective products, safety in the items they buy, fair prices, legal recourse if they are not well-served by business, and marketing practices (such as advertising) that do not threaten important human and social values (such as the health of children) or promote undesirable values (such as pornography). These consumer expectations can no longer be ignored by companies planning production, developing new products, or entering new markets. If they are ignored, the best laid strategic plans are almost bound to fail.

Second, because of extensive deregulation, corporate planners during the 1980s have been safe in assuming that a larger role is being played by free market forces in setting consumer priorities and in serving their needs. However, they also have been aware of the continuing existence of government regulations, watchdog agencies, and consumer advocacy organizations acting as a check on business decisions, plus the generally greater consumer sophistication created by the consumer movement. Corporate strategic planning, therefore, has had to be conducted with an awareness of these two levels of consumer interest—one expressed through free market–type purchases and the other consisting of government-sponsored consumer protections. To overlook either one of these levels of consumer activity in planning a corporation's future would be risky, either because market opportunities might be missed or because legal penalties might be imposed.

A corporate mission that encompasses these broad consumer interests, plus an organizational structure open to communicating with and responding to many diverse consumer needs, is the combination most likely to promote socially responsible and ethically aware strategic planning.

The most likely future consumer challenges for business are in the professional services area. The demand for more and better health and medical-care services will increase as the population ages. Educational services will be given a boost by the advanced societies' increasing commitment to more sophisticated technical and scientific approaches. Legal services, already much in demand, are likely to expand as the litigious (legally protective) character of many societies increases. All kinds of urban and municipal services—law enforcement, transportation, recreation and entertainment, urban redevelopment and planning, architectural and landscape engineering, maintenance of public facilities—are another expanding frontier of consumer demand. The combination of an aging population and greater diversity in family patterns creates more need for welfare and retirement services.

While not all business firms will be a direct part of this expanding service economy, few of them will escape its influence. For that reason, the strategies developed for tomorrow's corporations will need to be based to an important degree on an awareness of these emerging consumer demands.

SUMMARY

Consumers are a vitally important stakeholder group requiring the close attention of business managers. The consumer movement of the 1960s and 1970s attempted to give the consuming public greater protection. Many new consumer laws were passed, and new regulatory agencies were created to look out for the interests of consumers. Consumer activists founded many "watchdog" organizations to fight for consumer rights. The consumer movement reached its "high-water mark" in the late 1970s when it received strong support from the federal government.

The deregulation movement of the 1980s shifted the focus of consumer protection to private self-reliance, although the basic consumer protection infrastructure of laws, regulations, and agencies remained intact.

The business response to consumerism, although sometimes negative, has been generally positive. Corporate strategic planners realize that their plans must give high priority to satisfying an aroused and aware consuming public. Consumer services of all kinds are likely to be the area of greatest consumer demand in the foreseeable future, so business planning needs to take this trend into consideration in charting its own course.

DISCUSSION AND REVIEW QUESTIONS

1. Select two advertisements for consumer goods from newspapers, magazines, or television. Evaluate and compare them in terms of how well they provide reliable information that would help consumers make buying decisions.

2. Identify three examples in which you, friends, or family members have been dissatisfied with purchases of goods and services. Was the disappointment because of (a) unfair actions by the seller, (b) careless buying behavior by the purchaser, or (c) the complex nature of the items purchased? What remedies were available for the buyer?

3. Business's efforts to reform the product liability laws, discussed in this chapter, are a good example of business participation in the public policy process, which is discussed in Chapter 8. After reviewing Figure 8-3 in Chapter 8, identify which stages in the public policy process are illustrated by these business efforts to change the product liability laws. At which one of these stages does business appear to be? What strategy could business adopt to move to a more favorable stage?

4. Consumers are protected by three types of legal provisions: a broadened privity of contract, warranties, and tort (injury) liability laws. Review the Ford Cougar/Goodyear Tire case discussed in this chapter, and show how each of these three legal devices might have been involved. As a consumer, which one of the three would give you the greatest protection? As a manufacturer, which of the three might cost you the most in legal claims? With other members of the class, discuss the issue of responsibility in this case: Do you side with the court decision that the two companies were responsible, or do you believe that the driver (and her parents and friends?) should bear some of the responsibility?

5. Some studies show that the response rate on some product recalls is very low—3 to 6 percent. In one case, only 6,000 items were returned out of a possible 186,000. Should business continue to have a responsibility to consumers who fail to respond to recall notices? Discuss the pros and cons.

CRITICAL INCIDENT

Searle's Copper-7 and Tatum-T

In early 1986, G. D. Searle & Company of Chicago, a subsidiary of Monsanto Corporation, announced a voluntary withdrawal from the market of its Copper-7 and Tatum-T intrauterine devices (IUDs), used by women for contraceptive purposes. It decided to stop selling the products because of the high cost of defending the company against lawsuits brought by users who complained of infections and sterility caused by the IUDs. At the time of withdrawal some 775 lawsuits had been filed, and most observers thought that still more would occur in future years as complications developed in some users. Company officials estimated that approximately 1 million of these two IUDs were in use.

Withdrawing these two items from the market all but eliminated IUD sales in the United States. A. H. Robins Company, maker of the Dalkon Shield, another IUD, had stopped selling its product in 1974 when a torrent of lawsuits were brought against the company, alleging hazards similar to those associated with Searle's two IUDs. Ten years later, Robins declared itself bankrupt due to an overwhelming number of legal actions and potential settlements running into billions of dollars.

Of the 33 million women who practice birth control in the United States, authorities estimate that about 7 percent, or 2.3 million, tend to be IUD users. About one-third of the rest use the birth control pill, and another one-third rely on sterilization for either partner. For women beyond 35 years of age, the IUD meets a unique need, because the health risks of the pill increase at that age while women remain fertile and often bear children through their 30s and early 40s. IUDs also may be favored by younger women who smoke or by women with high blood pressure, both of whom are at risk through use of the pill. Sterilization may be avoided by some women who still want to bear children, and abortion is rejected by many women as a birth control procedure. Placing contraceptive responsibility on the male partner is another option.

As the supply of IUDs in the United States dwindled, some women traveled to Canada where Searle's Copper-7 and Tatum-T were still being sold and where product liability lawsuits are not as big a problem for companies. The other major manufacturer of IUDs in Canada is Ortho Pharmaceutical Ltd., a subsidiary of Johnson & Johnson. Both companies insist that their products are safe, a position apparently not disputed by the United States Food and Drug Administration, which continued to approve them for sale. Planned Parenthood, a nonprofit organization that promotes birth control, refers IUD users to its Canadian affiliates, and United States doctors send patients to Canadian doctors whom they know. Since these IUDs need to be replaced every three years, it was estimated that the number of United States consumers going to Canada for this purpose would increase in the future. This way of obtaining a needed consumer product would favor those who could afford the trip, raising the likelihood that abortions might increase or that less reliable methods of birth control would be used by those with more limited incomes. The only remaining IUD sold in the United States was manufactured by

Alza Corporation of Palo Alto, California, but its annual production for United States customers was estimated to be only 50,000, far fewer than total consumer demand.

Exporting Searle's two IUDs might not allow the company to escape lawsuits brought in the United States, according to some product liability lawyers. A company representative stated that Searle did not condone the practice of its former United States customers going to Canada. The company announced in early 1986 that it was thinking about selling its entire foreign IUD business operation to others.[20]

1. Imagine that you are presiding as chairman of the board and CEO at Monsanto's annual stockholders' meeting. A group of stockholders called Women Consumers United has proposed a stockholders' resolution requiring Monsanto's Searle unit to start selling the Copper-7 and the Tatum-T again. They argue that they and other women like them are being deprived of a needed product that has been approved by government regulators, approved by prominent birth control organizations, and routinely prescribed by millions of United States doctors. Withdrawing the IUDs from sale in the United States has discriminated against women, they charge, and has given unfair advantage to affluent consumers who can afford to travel to Canada for a replacement. What would be your reply?

2. At that same stockholders' meeting, imagine that another group of stockholders called Women Injured by IUDs has proposed a resolution requiring the company to stop selling the Copper-7 and Tatum-T worldwide. They argue that Searle's products caused pain and suffering for hundreds of women and that continued sales would only make matters worse for women customers. They say that it is unethical to sell a hazardous product in foreign nations which has been taken off the market in the United States. Additionally, they predict that hundreds of new lawsuits will be brought against both Searle and Monsanto, thereby lowering the value of their stock and threatening the financial viability of both companies. What would be your reply?

3. Following the annual stockholders' meeting, you and your top officers schedule a meeting with Monsanto's and Searle's strategic planning staffs to chart a course for the two companies over the next five-year period. Everyone at the meeting is looking to you for leadership, particularly regarding the role to be played by Searle's IUD production in the two companies' future. What guidelines would you want to suggest that would (a) secure the companies' future markets, (b) reduce liabilities, (c) serve the greatest number of customers, and (d) be socially responsible and ethically proper?

[20]See Peggy Berkowitz, "Canada Attracts U.S. Women Seeking IUDs," *Wall Street Journal,* September 11, 1986, p. 37; "Did Searle Close Its Eyes to a Health Hazard?" *Business Week,* October 14, 1985, pp. 120–122; and "Searle's Troubles Give Alza Its Big Break," *Business Week,* February 24, 1986, pp. 123–125.

Chapter Twelve

EMPLOYEES AND LABOR UNIONS

Employees have a big stake in corporate decisions and policies, so business managers and supervisors have to give careful attention to the human element in the workplace. Labor unions representing employees face new challenges to stem membership losses and to recruit a younger, more mobile, and more diverse labor force. Business, government, and employees are finding new, exciting ways to meet the new needs and demands of today's jobs and careers.

CHAPTER OBJECTIVES

After reading this chapter, you should be able to

- Understand the development, purposes, and recent changes in labor unions
- Know how government regulates labor-management relations
- Describe the changing composition of today's labor force
- Explain the increasing importance of women in the work force
- Discuss ways to improve job safety, make work more satisfying, and reduce job discrimination

*D*uring the 1980s, corporations have had to cope with an increasing array of social and human problems. Employees are demanding new kinds of on-the-job and off-the-job support. The labor force is younger, more women work, social attitudes toward work have changed, and new laws protect employees' interests.

When one of Drexel Burnham Lambert's vice presidents was reassigned from his New York office to Los Angeles, his wife had a problem. She was reluctant to give up her job in retail sales management with the same company; and both spouses had family and friends in New York. So, what did the company do? It arranged a series of job interviews for her with several southern California companies. As a result, a savings and loan association in Beverly Hills appointed her vice president and investment department manager. Several other well-known corporations—Procter & Gamble, General Mills, Minnesota Mining and Manufacturing (3M), and Cargill—offer similar help to two-career couples faced with the "trailing spouse" problem. Management-relocation firms report that 60 percent of corporate moves involve dual-career couples; by 1990, it is expected to rise to 75 percent.

A woman who sold advertisements for a small New Jersey newspaper took disability and vacation time when she gave birth to a daughter. She assumed that her job would be waiting for her when she returned but discovered that the only opening offered was a different job at half the pay. For failing to accept the new job, she was fired. If she had been working in Sweden, she (or her husband) could have received forty weeks of paid leave, plus additional unpaid leave until her daughter was eighteen months old. In cases like this one, a union official said, "I don't see the question of parental leave as [just] a women's issue, and neither does this union. It's a family issue."

AT&T, the giant telecommunications company, agreed in negotiations with the Communications Workers union to fund a training program to teach new job skills to their employees faced with a more and more sophisticated technological work environment. Today's young employees want and need such retraining if they are to keep up. One labor organizer said, "Workers under 35 are looking for growth, upward mobility, training in new skills. People 40 and above, they're mainly concerned with job security."

Employees, unions, and corporations faced new challenges in the 1980s. Labor unions lost members in droves. Blue-collar and white-collar employees were laid off when their companies could not keep up with increasing competition or when jobs were moved overseas. Women and minorities encountered job discrimination in spite of protective laws. Many businesses were pushed to the wall by foreign competition. In this climate of crisis and economic pressure, the human element in work became both more important and more difficult to satisfy. Many business leaders realized that the future of their companies depended on having an up-to-date, skilled, satisfied group of employees. This chapter discusses this social challenge and the various ways business has interacted with this vitally important stakeholder group.

LABOR UNIONS: HISTORICAL ROLE AND NEW DIRECTIONS

Employees constitute one of business's most important publics. When things go wrong in the workplace, a company can suffer large losses. If work is not performed well, customers may complain and turn to other firms for goods and services. If a climate of distrust exists between management and labor, there may be continual trouble, many grievances on both sides, strikes, and even violence on occasion. Under these conditions, productivity may drop to dangerously low levels, threatening the firm's profits and eventually leading to job losses or possibly a plant closure as more efficient and productive competitors win business away from the troubled company. So both business and employees have a stake in working toward labor peace and cooperative arrangements that minimize controversy and lead toward labor-management harmony.

Labor unions in the United States have occupied an important place in the relations between business and employees for over a century. In some industries—transportation, construction, and primary metals manufacturing—the majority of employees are union members. Because union membership is so uneven from industry to industry, generalizations must be handled with caution. But it remains true that labor unions historically have been a major force in shaping the dialogue between business and employees.

Union Philosophy and Goals

The economic goal of a labor union is to enroll all employees in an office, plant, company, industry, trade, or profession in order to monopolize the supply of labor. With monopoly control and the legal authority to represent the employees in collective bargaining, a union can have a powerful influence on wages, fringe benefits, working conditions, and other company policies. Not many unions ever attain this monopolistic goal, but some do exercise enough control to exert critical power over a company or industry. Unions have been exempted from prosecution under the antitrust laws that forbid monopolization and attempts to monopolize.

Although economic power is a primary goal of labor unions, it is not the only one. Broader social functions have always been an important part of labor union activity, including a concern for health care, recreational opportunities, and identification with other employees as coworkers who face similar problems and who share similar values. Some white-collar unions—for technical or engineering personnel or airline pilots, for example—help develop a sense of professional status and identity that has psychological as well as social meaning for their members.

The basic political philosophy of the American labor movement has long been moderate rather than radical. Rather than trying to overturn the capitalist system through state ownership, American labor unions have accepted capitalism as a legitimate economic system. Within that system, they try to maximize economic gain for their members. Unlike Western Europe and other parts of the world, labor unions in the United States are not organized into political parties.

Government Regulation of Labor-Management Relations

A remarkable trait of labor-management relations since the 1930s has been the prominent role played by government. The labor market is no longer a free market subject just to the undisturbed forces of supply and demand.

This situation came about rather abruptly in the 1930s when Congress enacted a series of laws giving organized labor more power than it had ever enjoyed before and swinging government influence over to the side of labor unions.

The federal government's role, from that time to the present, has been to act as a referee in labor-management relations, establishing and enforcing the rules of the bargaining game. The free labor market was modified by creating certain minimum conditions and extending various rights to workers that could not be changed by bargaining. These included a legally established minimum wage, a standard number of hours in the workweek before overtime pay began, unemployment insurance, a retirement pension system (Social Security), and compensation for injuries suffered at work (initiated in the early twentieth century).

After government lays down the rules, however, it generally steps back and allows labor and management to bargain privately. Long and nationally disruptive strikes may bring government into the negotiating process as a mediator to speed up a settlement or to establish better communication between the two sides. But in general, both labor and management prefer to bargain as private parties, with as little government intervention as possible.

Labor Laws and Government Agencies

Using its constitutional authority to regulate interstate commerce, the federal government has become the major regulator of labor-management relations. But state governments also have important powers to regulate labor relations, especially the right to guarantee individual workers some protection against unfair influence from unions.

Today's federal laws provide the following broad guidelines for regulating the conduct of both business and labor:

- Employees are legally guaranteed the right to organize and join labor unions and to bargain collectively with employers. Employers must deal with these legally constituted labor organizations.
- Labor and management are prohibited from engaging in unfair practices. For example, both must bargain in good faith, which means that they must sincerely try to reach agreement. Also, an employee cannot legally be fired for being a union member, nor can a union bring pressure on one company by boycotting another firm that supplies goods or services to it (a secondary boycott).
- Unions are required to submit annual financial reports to the Secretary of Labor, to conduct fair elections, and to govern themselves according to democratic rules.
- When labor disputes threaten national health or safety, the federal government may intervene in an attempt to resolve the differences.

The primary agency for overseeing the rights and responsibilities of labor and management is the National Labor Relations Board (NLRB), created in 1935. This board supervises elections among employees to determine union

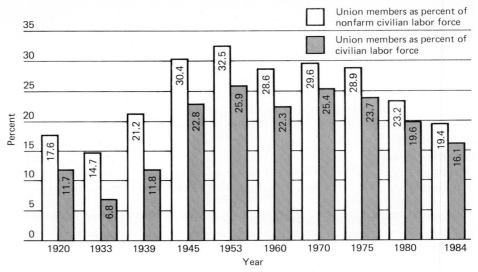

FIGURE 12-1.   Union membership trends in the United States. (*Source: Leo Troy and Neil Sheflin, Union Sourcebook: Membership, Structure, Finance, Directory, West Orange, N.J.: Industrial Relations Data Information Services, 1985, pp. 3–10.*)

representation and enforces the ban against unfair practices by employees and employers. Another agency, the Federal Mediation and Conciliation Service, was established in 1947 to help prevent or minimize work stoppages by acting as a neutral mediator when management and labor cannot agree. The U.S. Department of Labor is charged with administering various laws having to do with minimum wages, overtime provisions, and discrimination.

Union Growth and Decline

By the mid-1980s, the union movement in the United States seemed to be in serious trouble. Total membership had dropped to 18.3 million members by 1984, down from the 1975 all-time high of 22.2 million. While the size of the labor force continued to go up, unions were not able to keep pace. There are two ways to measure union success in signing up members, as shown in Figure 12-1, and both of them show a decline beginning around the mid-1950s. Only 16.1 percent of the total labor force carried union cards in 1984; and fewer than one of every five nonfarm workers (19.4 percent) were members.[1] Most experts predicted continued losses through the end of this century, and many union leaders knew that they were in a fight for survival.

What happened beginning around the mid-1950s to reduce the attractiveness of labor unions as a way of protecting employees' interests? The answer is a complicated one, but certain major forces have eroded union power in significant ways.

[1]Leo Troy and Neil Sheflin, *Union Sourcebook: Membership, Structure, Finance, Directory*, West Orange, N.J.: Industrial Relations Data and Information Services, 1985.

Economic Changes

By the mid-1950s, white-collar *service* workers made up the largest portion of the labor force, and they were more difficult to organize into unions than blue-collar manufacturing employees. Unlike the blue-collar workers, they tended to think of themselves as candidates for promotion into the ranks of supervisor or manager, so they shunned union membership. The insatiable demand of consumers for more varied services—travel, education, recreation, legal services, health care, and government services—made this shift toward a service economy inevitable. No longer were blue-collar workers the mainstay of the economy, although they had been the backbone of the unions' organizational successes of the 1930s, 1940s, and 1950s.

The need for higher levels of productivity led businesses to substitute technology for human workers—electric-arc steel furnaces for open hearth workers; coal-digging machines for pick and shovel miners; or tractors, cotton-picking machines, and harvesting combines for farm hand workers.

Three other economic forces played a big role. Foreign competition became intense by the late 1970s in such industries as oil, autos, steel, copper, aluminum, chemicals, tires, and other older "smokestack" industries which had always been the core of union strength. As a result of such competition, massive layoffs occurred and unions lost many dues-paying members. The deregulation of several industries, discussed in Chapter 7, hit some unions hard; an example is the Teamsters Union where competition caused by deregulation eliminated many trucking companies and reduced union membership. Adding to the unions' troubles was the recession of the early 1980s. Bad times always tend to erode union membership, as workers lose jobs, have less money for union dues, and are willing to work for lower nonunion wages.

Management Opposition

Labor-management relations in the United States have always been adversarial, with each side trying to outmaneuver the other. Managers have never been comfortable with any interference in their decision making, whether from unions or government. They prefer maximum flexibility in determining what their employees should do on the job and how they should do it. Union work rules that limit certain jobs to certain classified workers—for example, painters who are not permitted to perform simple carpentry tasks—or seniority rules that promote or retain workers with the most service regardless of their competence are strongly opposed by management. To escape such restrictions, business has taken a number of steps that have tended to weaken union power and influence.

Among the most successful tactics is to stay a step ahead of unions in providing good working conditions, high wages, and fringe benefits such as health-care plans, retirement plans, paid vacations, and similar economic benefits. IBM has headed off unionization at its installations by such a tactic and by cultivating a feeling of closeness among employees.

Since 1914, the company has successfully used management practices to treat workers like family. IBM is a top-paying employer in the computer industry. The company provides country clubs for some employees and nurtures the family spirit at picnics and intramural sports events. Employees who disagree with their managers' appraisals of their work can appeal to the chairman and be heard in a grievance process known as "Open Door."[2]

This approach has been so successful for IBM that one labor official declared, "Getting union representation at IBM is the labor equivalent of putting a man on the moon."

"Human resource management"—which stresses employee participation, increased communication between managers and employees, and a whole range of new employee needs such as child day-care centers, flexible working hours, and job rotation—has simply outflanked the unions in many companies. Studies show that such companies enjoy greater flexibility in making decisions (because they do not have to share decision making with union officials), lower labor costs, and more efficiency due to less on-the-job conflict, greater trust between management and employees, and fewer restrictive work rules.[3]

Also contributing to lowered union membership has been the tendency of many corporations to close down older facilities in the industrial North and open up new ones in the Sunbelt states of the South and the Southwest where union strength has never been as great. During the 1980s, many United States jobs were "exported" to foreign countries whose wage rates were even lower. Such moves drained the strength of unions by reducing their ranks and forcing them to seek new members in regions far less easy to organize.

Unfavorable Public Opinion

The general public's opinion of many aspects of labor unions and their leaders, summed up in Figure 12-2, is unfavorable. A majority of the public approves of labor unions in general and has done so since the mid-1930s, and most people also think that unions are good for the general public. Nearly three out of every four Americans surveyed say that unions improve wages and working conditions for their members. But the rest of the picture is bleak. Unions and their leaders do not have the confidence of the public; they are believed to score poorly in ethical and moral practices; they are thought to be too powerful; and they are blamed for inflation, for stifling individual initiative on the job, and for driving some companies out of busi-

---

[2]"Family Feud: IBM Dissidents Hope for Increased Support as Work Force Is Cut," *Wall Street Journal*, January 13, 1987, pp. 1, 18.

[3]Thomas A. Kochan, Harry C. Katz, and Robert B. McKersie, *The Transformation of American Industrial Relations*, New York: Basic Books, 1986, chaps. 3 and 4.

Do you approve or disapprove of labor unions?		
1985	Approve 58%	Disapprove 27%

Percentage of the public expressing a great deal of confidence in the leaders of the following institutions (1985).		
	Organized Labor	Major Companies
1985	13%	17%
Average, 1966–1985	15	24

Public ratings of the ethical and moral practices of the following organizations (1985).		
	Excellent or Good	Fair or Poor
Labor union leaders	23%	65%
Average workers	74	25
Corporate executives	39	47
Small business proprietors	76	21

FIGURE 12-2. **The public image of labor unions and labor leaders.** (*Source: Selected data from various public opinion polls reported in Seymour Martin Lipset, "Labor Unions in the Public Mind," in Seymour Martin Lipset (ed.),* Unions in Transition: Entering the Second Century, *San Francisco, Calif.: Institute for Contemporary Studies, 1986, pp. 287–322.*)

ness. This kind of public image obviously increases the difficulty of attracting new members to unions. It also lessens labor's power at the polls and weakens its chances of getting favorable labor laws passed.[4]

Concession Bargaining

From its weakened position in the mid-1980s, the labor union movement could look back to the heyday of the 1940s and 1950s with considerable disappointment and even bitterness. Hard-won gains made earlier had to be given back, which was called "concession bargaining." Some of these losses included wage freezes or wage cutbacks, early retirement, giving up cost-of-living wage adjustments, shorter paid vacations, reduced health care, less generous pensions, fewer work rules favorable to employees, and less job security generally. Some unions were able to offset these losses by gaining seats on a company's board of directors or sharing decision making with managers or restructuring jobs to give workers more say in how tasks were to be done.[5]

[4]For a good summary of many public opinion polls about labor unions, see Seymour Martin Lipset, "Labor Unions in the Public Mind," in Seymour Martin Lipset (ed.), *Unions in Transition: Entering the Second Century,* San Francisco: Institute for Contemporary Studies, 1986, pp. 287–322.

[5]James A. Craft, Suhail Abboushi, and Trudy Labovitz, "Concession Bargaining and Unions: Impacts and Implications," *Journal of Labor Research,* Spring 1985, pp. 167–180.

THE CHANGING LABOR FORCE: NEW FACES, NEW VALUES, NEW DEMANDS

Today's labor force, whose support and loyalty are sought by both business and labor unions, is vastly different from what it was thirty years ago at the height of union power. Women have flooded into the workplace in such large numbers that 45 out of every 100 employees are women. Blacks, Asian Americans, Hispanics, and other ethnic minorities now have job opportunities that were denied to them for many years. In addition, today's work force is young, because the baby-boomers of post-war America have reached mature working years. Single-parent families are more common, as divorce rates have zoomed and society has become more accepting of divided families; and many of these families are headed by women who need jobs to support themselves and their children. For white-collar managerial and professional people, a dual-track career (which means having more than one significant career during one's working life) has emerged as an entirely unexpected development, partly as a result of corporate cutbacks forced by increasing market competition. No longer able to count on staying with a single company or even a single line of work for their entire career, these mid-level workers have a changing array of needs and demands. Still another difference between employees of the mid-1950s and those of today is the increasing number of public sector workers—those who work for local, state, and federal governments.[6]

Women at Work: Opportunities and Issues

The United States economy created 20 million new jobs between 1975 and 1985, and two-thirds of them went to women. Working women in the United States now number over 53 million. They are dominant in the fast-growing service sector, holding 60 percent of those jobs. Only Sweden among the world's industrial nations has a higher proportion of its female population in the labor force—80 percent compared with about 54 percent in the United States.[7]

Many of today's working women are married, have children, and are the sole head of their family. They have special needs for good jobs with good pay. Over half (52 percent) of married women now work, and working mothers commonly return to their jobs after bearing children. Eight out of ten working women are of child-bearing age, with some 90 percent becoming pregnant sometime during their working years. While greater opportunities exist for women, many live below the poverty line—13 million in the mid-1980s.

---

[6]"Beyond Unions," *Business Week*, July 8, 1985, pp. 72–77.

[7]"Women at Work," *Business Week*, January 28, 1985, pp. 80–85.

Day-care child centers, parental leaves to care for newborn children, flexible work schedules, relocation assistance for two-career families, pay equity, and equal advancement opportunities have been added to the list of employee needs by working women.[8]

New Initiatives by Labor and Management

Because of the growing diversity in America's work force, both labor and management have had to rethink their policies and devise new strategies for gaining the loyalty of employees.

Labor Union Initiatives

Hit hard by jobs and members lost to foreign competition, recession, new technology, and nonunion workers, labor unions have fought back in a number of ways. Their bargaining demands now include a range of issues important to the new work force, according to a report in the *Wall Street Journal:*[9]

> More and more, unions are bargaining, lobbying, and going to court to press for such family-related goals as child care, maternity and parental leave, pay equity, and flexible work arrangements. Bread-and-butter issues of wages, health and pension benefits, and job security still are priorities. But unions are also responding to the new concerns of a work force in which, increasingly, both the husband and wife have jobs and in which, according to some surveys, women are even more interested than men in joining unions.

In unions traditionally dominated by men, reforms have been slow, but where the concentration of women workers is high—for example, in the services, among garment workers, and in the public sector—the pressures for change are greater. The United Steel Workers union negotiated agreements with Bethlehem Steel and Inland Steel to establish joint union-management committees to survey employees' child-care needs. Auto workers and electric workers won child-care-related projects at Ford Motor, General Motors, and Sperry Corporation.[10] With women accounting for half the total increase in new union members, and where one of every three union members is a woman, these new programs are necessary if unions are to be responsive.

Unions also make appeals to the burgeoning service workers—clerical workers, insurance agents, keypunchers, nurses, teachers, mental health aides, computer technicians, loan officers, auditors, and salespeople—by treating them as professionals and catering to their special needs. Many of these nonunion workers experience on-the-job stress from working with new

[8]"Business Starts Tailoring Itself to Suit Working Women," *Business Week,* October 6, 1986, pp. 50–54.

[9]Cathy Trost, "More Family Issues Surface at Bargaining Tables as Women Show Increasing Interest in Unions," *Wall Street Journal,* December 2, 1986, p. 66.

[10]Ibid.

forms of technology. Others fear the health effects of computer video display terminals. Some service workers want additional training for better jobs and protection against arbitrary job assignments.[11]

Unions have taken many other initiatives, too. They have traded fewer jobs in the plant for seats on a company's board of directors. Or they have agreed to job cuts in return for stock ownership in the company. Some have accepted wage cuts for more say in how work is done. An example of labor's adaptability and willingness to experiment occurred at LTV Corporation in Cleveland:[12]

> *To compete in the expanding market for corrosion-resistant steel used by auto-makers, LTV wanted to build a new high-tech electrogalvanizing facility as part of its Cleveland works. Doing so meant changing union work rules and practices that dated back to the 1930s. LTV's threat to build the new facility elsewhere, probably in a nonunion region, spurred the union to accept these changes. In 1984, the United Steel Workers union agreed to a radically new kind of contract to govern the new plant. Workers were to receive salaries rather than hourly wages, and these salaries were to be lower than the industry average. However, a bonus system tied to productivity, quality of work, total output, and work attendance would increase employee income significantly. Work rules were greatly simplified; workers gained a voice in major decisions, including hiring and firing. Younger workers were picked on the basis of their willingness to learn new skills and work as a team. All workplace decisions were to be made by consensus, with workers having far more authority and responsibility than in the older-style steel mills.*

Whether these labor union initiatives will be able to stem the continuing loss of members is not clear. Most experts believe not. But the unions' new flexibility and greater awareness of social and economic pressures may slow the pace of their decline and make them more responsive to the needs of people in the workplace.

Management Initiatives

Business has matched, and in some cases outdone, the unions in trying to meet employee needs.[13]

> *One pharmaceutical maker, Merck & Co., opened a child-care center for its employees, allowed employees (many of whom were parents) to begin work at any time from 7:00 A.M. to 9:30 A.M., and let some working parents do their jobs at home after a maternity leave. Workshops were held and a counseling*

---

[11]Cathy Trost, "Unions Court People in Service-Type Work to Stem Fall in Ranks," *Wall Street Journal*, September 19, 1986, pp. 1, 12.

[12]"LTV Steel Knocks the Rust Off Its Labor Relations," *Business Week*, December 23, 1985, pp. 57–58.

[13]"Business Starts Tailoring Itself to Suit Working Women," op. cit.

service was available on how to balance the demands of family life and work. The Conference Board estimated that 2,500 companies were providing some form of child care in 1985.

IBM reached out beyond its own company to establish a nationwide corporate network for referring employees to community child-care facilities. Around 16,000 children have been referred, and the company's annual budget for this program is reported to be $2 million. In addition, IBM has supported a nonprofit group that has trained 5,000 new providers to care for 13,000 children. One of IBM's managers of employee services said, "The rising number of women among our employees is leading us to consider things that didn't seem important before."[14]

Recognizing the problems that can accompany an aging population, companies such as Travelers, Mobil, Consolidated Edison, and Ciba-Geigy help employees care for elderly relatives by sponsoring "eldercare" seminars and counseling services. In another age-related move, McDonald's started a "McMasters" job-training program in Maryland for senior citizens when it could not find enough young people to fill its needs.[15]

More and more companies are turning to worker participation programs in order to improve productivity and help meet competitive pressures. An increasing number of lower-level employees—and not just a supervisor or a trouble-shooting manager—are being sent into the field to solve customers' special problems. For example, Westinghouse Electric sent thirty hourly workers who produce subway generating equipment to New York to see how their work looked in action. As a result, one employee said, "There's a difference between putting wires into a black box and riding the product through the South Bronx." After these on-the-spot experiences, employees tend to be more careful about the way they do their work, thus helping to retain valuable customers and saving jobs in the long run.

Profit-sharing plans are springing up more frequently as another way to increase worker productivity. Cummins Engine extended its profit-sharing plan, which was formerly reserved for its executives, to all of its 13,000 employees, and the company believes it has boosted profits by making workers more conscious of quality and costs. The Profit Sharing Research Foundation of Chicago estimates that there were 430,000 profit-sharing programs in American business in 1984.[16]

As yet another way of coping with competition and caring for employees simultaneously, work-sharing plans have been used. The idea is to spread the available work around among employees instead of firing some of them, thus giving all workers more job security. In these systems, employees work a four-day week and then collect unemployment compensation for the fifth

---

[14]Ibid.

[15]*Wall Street Journal,* September 12, 1986, p. 1.

[16]Ed Leefeldt, "Profit-Sharing Plans Reward Productivity," *Wall Street Journal,* November 5, 1984, p. 27.

day. In Motorola's semiconductor plant in Phoenix, work sharing has affected about 15 percent of the 13,000 employees since 1982.[17]

These newest innovations have been added to earlier ones such as quality circles, job redesign, and flextime. A quality circle is a small group of employees and supervisors who meet to discuss ways of improving the quality of work done in their unit. A single company may have many quality circles located in plants and offices throughout the enterprise; Honeywell, for example, was reported in 1980 to have more quality circles—130—than any corporation outside Japan, where quality circles originated.[18] Managers say that quality circles improve employee morale, strengthen teamwork, and lead to better human relations, as well as improve product quality. One electronics firm employing 46,000 workers estimated its gains from quality-circle improvements at $13.3 million for one year, at an added cost of only $2.7 million.[19]

In job redesign, attempts are made to make the work more interesting and more meaningful to individual workers, and more under their control. Flextime permits workers to set their own hours of starting and quitting a day's work, just as long as they put in the expected number of hours during the day.

JOB SAFETY AND HEALTH

Much industrial work is inherently hazardous because of the extensive use of high-speed and noisy machinery, production processes requiring high temperatures, an increasing reliance on sophisticated chemical compounds, and the nature of such work as underground and undersea tunneling, drilling, and mining. Accidents, injuries, and illnesses are bound to occur under these circumstances. Minimizing them has become a major national priority in recent years.

An aroused and alarmed labor movement mounted a campaign in the late 1960s for stronger federal legislation to protect employees at work. The resulting new laws and government agencies have thrust the issue of employee safety and health into the forefront of social problems facing employers.

Occupational Safety and Health Administration

The Occupational Safety and Health Administration (OSHA), which was created by Congress in 1970, quickly became one of the most controversial of all the government agencies established in the great wave of social legislation during the 1970s. Congress gave OSHA sweeping powers over employers, requiring them to provide for each employee a job "free from recognized hazards that are causing or likely to cause death or serious physical harm."

---

[17]"Shorter Workweeks: An Alternative to Layoffs," *Business Week*, April 14, 1986, pp. 77–78.

[18]Robert R. Rehder, "What American and Japanese Managers Are Learning from Each Other," *Business Horizons*, March–April 1981, pp. 63–70.

[19]Hirotaka Takeuchi, "Productivity: Learning from the Japanese," *California Management Review*, Summer 1981, pp. 5–19.

Unannounced job-site inspections by OSHA were authorized, although a later court ruling required OSHA to obtain a court-approved search warrant before entering a plant without permission. Employers found in violation of OSHA safety and health standards can be fined and, in case of a willful violation causing the death of an employee, jailed and fined.

In addition to OSHA, Congress also created the Occupational Safety and Health Review Commission (OSHRC) to hear appeals of OSHA charges against employers, and the National Institute for Occupational Safety and Health (NIOSH), which conducts research on workplace hazards and ways to offset them. Three other government agencies are active in this field. The Department of Health, Education, and Welfare (later divided into the Department of Education and the Department of Health and Human Services) initiated a program to warn 6 to 8 million workers of possible health risks from on-the-job exposure to asbestos; the Environmental Protection Agency has worked with OSHA to protect coke-oven workers from noxious fumes; and the Mine Safety and Health Administration has special authority to safeguard miners.

Business has criticized OSHA as being too costly a way to safeguard employees. Small businesses in particular have a difficult time carrying the paperwork burden required by OSHA's rules. Other companies object to the high cost of redesigning machinery and production processes, saying that these expenses would far outweigh any tangible or marginal benefits in increased safety and health for workers. Employees themselves often have refused to wear required safety goggles, earplugs, respirators, and other special equipment intended to protect them from harm—but if they were to be injured while _not_ wearing such items, the _employer_, not the employee, would be subject to penalty.

Other critics have said that enforcing OSHA regulations over a wide range of industries is difficult. OSHA inspections are infrequent, fines for violations are quite small—averaging about $16 per violation in most cases—and OSHA inspectors rarely report all violations.

Labor unions charged that the Reagan administration was lax in enforcing OSHA rules, but Reagan supporters maintained that job safety should be left largely to private initiatives undertaken by employers and employees. In 1983, OSHA issued a "right to know" rule requiring companies to disclose to their employees the names and possible health risks of chemicals used in the workplace. Critics claimed that the new rule is much too weak. Some twenty states have enacted similar but tougher legislation. Pennsylvania's right-to-know law requires labeling the chemical contents of every container in the workplace, compiling data on all hazardous materials, and posting warnings of potential dangers to employees.

EQUAL EMPLOYMENT AND AFFIRMATIVE ACTION

Working to achieve equal employment opportunities is an important social priority for major institutions in the United States. Taking affirmative action to overcome job discrimination is required by law for most of these institutions, including business. This area of employee relations is another one calling for positive responses and initiatives if business is to continue its evolution toward social responsiveness and public approval.

Job Discrimination

Like many other social problems facing business, employee discrimination became the center of national attention in the 1960s and 1970s. The civil rights movement focused on the exclusion of blacks from equal opportunities in education, public accommodations, and jobs. The women's movement, dormant for some decades, stirred itself and began once again to seek equal rights for women, including job rights. Older employees, physically and mentally handicapped workers, various ethnic minorities, and members of some religious groups maintained that they had suffered discrimination related to work.

The origins and causes of discrimination against these groups are too numerous and complex to discuss here, but one observation holds true across all groups. In one way or another, the discrimination they experience is embedded in the cultural value systems and long-standing historical conditions of society. This point is important in considering possible remedies for workplace discrimination, and it may help to avoid superficial theories about who is to "blame" for these practices. The truth is that no one group in our society—business included—is responsible for the prevalence of discrimination, nor is it likely that one solution is possible. When social problems of this complexity and duration occur, the only feasible and practical approach is a many-sided one that involves all principal institutions. Human culture and long-standing traditions have created tensions among groups that are not easily or quickly dissipated. Long-term solutions tend to be the rule in these circumstances.

Job discrimination is obviously at odds with the ideological principle of equal opportunity for all individuals. This principle has long been an important part of American society's ideals, and it has been an inspiration for many disadvantaged groups throughout American history. Today the goal of equal opportunity for all individuals is the main philosophical justification of attempts to eliminate discrimination in the workplace.

Government Policies and Regulations

Beginning on a major scale in the 1960s, United States Presidents issued directives and Congress enacted laws intended to improve equal employment opportunities. The most important of these executive orders and laws are shown in Figure 12-3. These government rules apply to most businesses, educational institutions, nonprofit organizations, state and local governments, labor unions, and government contractors in the following ways:

- Discrimination based on race, color, religion, sex, national origin, physical or mental handicap, or age is prohibited in all employment practices. This includes hiring, firing, promotion, job classification and assignment, compensation, and other conditions of work.

Laws	
Equal Pay Act Required equal pay for similar work.	1963
Civil Rights Act Created EEOC. Outlawed job discrimination by race, color, religion, or national origin.	1964
Age Discrimination in Employment Act Outlawed job discrimination against persons forty to sixty-five years of age.	1967
Equal Employment Opportunity Act Strengthened enforcement powers and expanded jurisdiction of EEOC. Outlawed sex discrimination.	1972
Education Amendments Act Prohibited job discrimination against employees and students of educational institutions. Expanded coverage of Equal Pay Act.	1972
Vocational Rehabilitation Act Required affirmative action for handicapped persons by government contractors and other companies.	1973
Executive Orders and Guidelines	
Executive Order 10925, President Kennedy Prohibited job discrimination by government contractors.	1961
Executive Orders 11246 and 11375, President Johnson Required written affirmative action programs by most government contractors.	1965, 1967
Revised Order No. 4, OFCC, Department of Labor Required results-oriented affirmative action, with goals, timetables, and statistical analysis.	1970

FIGURE 12-3. Major federal equal job opportunity laws and executive orders.

- Government contractors must have written affirmative action plans detailing how they are working positively to overcome past and present effects of discrimination in their work force.
- Women and men must receive equal pay for performing similar work.

During the 1970s and early 1980s, regulators and courts used a results-oriented approach to these laws. In other words, a company would be considered in violation of the law if a statistical analysis revealed that its jobs were out of line with the proportions of whites and blacks or men and women potentially available for such work. If a company had only one woman engineer out of a total of 100 engineers but statistics showed that women engineering graduates made up 10 percent of all engineers, the company would be risking a charge of job discrimination for not hiring enough women engineers. In most cases, the courts said that good intentions were not enough and that business must produce tangible results in overcoming discriminatory employment patterns.

In the mid-1980s, however, the Supreme Court began to favor another interpretation. In 1982, it declared that a person charging another with a civil rights violation would have to prove that there was an actual intention to discriminate. In 1984, it also ruled that job seniority could not be set aside just to protect the jobs of minorities or women when an employer had to lay workers off because of bad economic times, even if it meant that white men with seniority kept their jobs and blacks and women were let go. Such special preferences could be given only to those individuals who could prove that they were victimized by deliberate racial or sexual bias.

The three major agencies charged with enforcing federal equal employment opportunity laws and executive orders are the following:

- The Equal Employment Opportunity Commission (EEOC), created in 1964 and given added enforcement powers in 1972. EEOC, which may go to court if necessary, is primarily responsible for enforcing provisions of the Civil Rights Act of 1964, the Equal Employment Opportunity Act of 1972, the Equal Pay Act, and the Age Discrimination in Employment Act.
- The Office of Federal Contract Compliance Programs (OFCCP) in the Department of Labor. OFCCP monitors compliance of government contractors with equal employment opportunity executive orders issued by the President, including affirmative action plans.
- The Department of Education enforces equal opportunity laws and orders that have special applicability to educational institutions.

Alternative Approaches to Equal Employment Opportunity

Federal legislation has imposed responsibilities upon business to eliminate discrimination and equalize employment opportunities for all. Companies have responded in several ways. Some companies have adopted a posture of *passive nondiscrimination,* under which all decisions about hiring and promotion are made without regard to race or sex. This posture focuses on the present and future and does not consider the past. It does little to overcome past discrimination that leaves many potential employees unaware of present opportunities.

Another approach to ending discrimination is *affirmative action.* Under this approach, companies make every effort to ensure that employment opportunities are highly visible and to seek minorities, women, and others for employment. While this approach enlarges the number of applicants, hiring and promotion decisions most often are made on the basis of qualifications for the job.

A third approach is *affirmative action combined with preferential hiring,* which not only tries to expand the number of people from whom to choose, but also gives preference to women and minority groups in hiring and promotion. This approach was upheld in 1979 for preferential hiring of blacks and again in 1987 when the U.S. Supreme Court ruled that public (as well as private) employers may initiate voluntary affirmative action plans to correct a "manifest imbalance" in the proportions of women and men in their work force, as long as the rights of other workers are not "unnecessarily trammeled."[20]

A fourth approach is to establish *employment quotas.* Unlike affirmative action with preferential hiring, which does not establish any particular numbers of disadvantaged who must be hired and/or promoted, quotas establish specific numbers or proportions as a hiring goal.

Businesses that have not responded affirmatively to equal employment-opportunity laws often find themselves faced with expensive back-pay settlements. The landmark court judgment came in 1973, when AT&T was ordered to pay $15 million in back pay to women and minorities, plus an estimated $50 million yearly to adjust wages and promotions for those groups in the company. Since then many other companies have made similar court-ordered settlements for bias against minorities and women. One such case occurred in 1983 when General Motors agreed to a $42.5 million program to hire more women and minorities over a five-year period. The EEOC had charged the company with discrimination in 1973. GM pledged to hire higher percentages of women and minorities in various job categories and to spend $15 million to provide scholarships for GM employees and family members to attend colleges and technical schools.

Not all companies are opposed to affirmative action programs, because they are helpful in tracking their own progress in providing equal job opportunity. When the Reagan administration proposed to drop rules requiring federal contractors to set affirmative action goals and timetables, General Electric, AT&T, and IBM said that they would continue to use the system because it was useful. Hewlett-Packard revealed that goals and timetables had helped it measure the rise in minority employment (from 7 percent in 1966 to 18 percent in 1986) and female employment (from 39 percent in 1966 to 42 percent in 1986).[21]

The Unfinished Job Opportunity Agenda

As the end of the 1980s approached, American society and the American business system obviously had much to do if the ideal of equal job opportunity was to be fully realized. Significant gains were made during the 1960s and 1970s as a result of changed laws, changed attitudes, and sincere efforts by both business and government. But workplace discrimination persisted and took the following major forms:

• Both women and blacks who had gained professional, managerial, and technical jobs often found themselves stuck at relatively low levels of responsibility and authority. Promotions came slowly, if at all. Lingering racist and sexist attitudes, often unconsciously held by their coworkers, sometimes meant that they were passed over for advances or interesting assignments. By not being part of a company's informal social networks, golf

[20]Stephen Wermiel, "Supreme Court, in 6–3 Vote, Backs Hiring Goals to Correct Sex Bias," *Wall Street Journal,* March 26, 1987, p. 3.

[21]*Wall Street Journal,* September 3, 1986, p. 1.

Women's Earnings for Each Dollar Earned by Men	
Year	Earnings (in cents)
1955	63.9
1960	60.8
1965	60.0
1970	59.4
1975	58.8
1980	60.2
1983	63.8

FIGURE 12-4. The wage gap between men and women in the United States, 1955–1983. (*Source: U.S. Bureau of Labor Statistics as reported in* National NOW Times, *March-April 1985, p. 9.*)

outings, fishing trips, or neighborhood gatherings, they were easily overlooked or bypassed. Women executives continued to be mistaken for secretaries, and black executives arriving for an appointment made by telephone could face a surprised or even untrusting reception. One woman vice president who broke through some of these barriers said, "I beat all of them [her male colleagues] at poker and most of them at gin, and I catch my share of fish." Many black executives were assigned to staff functions rather than line jobs that could lead to higher levels of responsibility. A black corporate officer said, "You can still manage to count those of us who have significant profit-and-loss responsibility on your fingers and toes."[22]

• The wage gap between women's pay and men's pay persisted. Figure 12-4 shows that on average women earn around 60 cents for each dollar a man earns. This ratio has remained very stable since the 1920s. The difference persists partly because the jobs available to many women are low-skilled, do not require advanced education, and require fewer years of experience than many jobs going to men. Another reason is related to social customs and traditional attitudes that have discouraged women from entering advanced educational programs to prepare themselves for professional and managerial jobs. The same kinds of discriminatory attitudes are found in the workplace, where women frequently are shunted into low-paying jobs that traditionally have been filled by women. Companies can help reduce the wage gap by revamping their job classification and pay policies to avoid this kind of discriminatory practice. A 1984 study predicted that the wage gap would be narrowed significantly—perhaps to a 25 percent difference—by the year 2000 because of increased numbers of women entering the job market with college degrees, improved skills, and lengthening work experience records.[23]

[22]"You've Come a Long Way Baby—but Not as Far as You Thought," *Business Week*, October 1, 1984, pp. 126, 130–131; "Progress Report on the Black Executive: The Top Spots Are Still Elusive," *Business Week*, February 20, 1984, pp. 104–105.

[23]James P. Smith and Michael P. Ward, *Women's Wages and Work in the Twentieth Century*, Santa Monica, Calif.: Rand, 1984.

Paying men and women on the basis of *comparable* work was proposed during the 1980s as a partial solution to the wage gap. Dissimilar jobs requiring the same general level of skill and training—secretary and carpenter, or practical nurse and correction officer—would be paid the same. This plan would be a step beyond the Equal Pay Act, which requires equal pay for men and women doing *similar* work.

- Minority joblessness, particularly among young people, continued to be one of the most difficult problems to solve. "Neither the Great Society of the '60s nor the jobs programs of the '70s made any difference. Today, blacks, Hispanics, and other minorities are worse off than ever. Black unemployment is 15%, or 2.3 times the white rate. The Hispanic rate is 11.2%, or 1.75 times that for whites. Both multiples are higher than in 1980. And among teenagers, the rates are 21% for Hispanics and 41% for blacks."[24]

THE NEED FOR A STAKEHOLDER PARTNERSHIP

Most of the problems discussed in this chapter are social problems, not exclusively business ones. This means that business needs to reach out to other institutions for help in combatting job discrimination, making the workplace safer, making work attractive and meaningful, and respecting the rights of employees. Where employees have voted to have a union represent them, business needs to work with that union. Where elected officials have passed laws to protect employees, business needs to work within the law and cooperate with government agencies. Where there is no union or where problems arise for which the law provides little or no guidance, business needs to accept employees as one of its important stakeholder groups and must consider their needs carefully.

If business is to meet its strategic goals in socially responsive and ethically responsible ways, while coping with increased competition at home and abroad, it must work in harmony with a wide range of stakeholders. A partnership between business and all of these stakeholders, including employees, is the most effective way to guide the affairs of a modern business firm.[25]

SUMMARY

Because employees are one of business's most important stakeholder groups, management must pay close attention to their needs. During the 1970s and 1980s, the American labor force experienced many changes—different attitudes toward work, more women workers, more two-career couples, greater proportions of minorities, younger employees whose goals differed from older workers, and other big changes. Both management and labor unions

[24]"The Forgotten Americans," *Business Week,* September 2, 1985, pp. 50–55.

[25]Donald N. Scobel, "Business and Labor—From Adversaries to Allies," *Harvard Business Review,* November–December 1982, pp. 129–136.

struggled to keep pace with these new employees and their needs. Top-priority items continued to be adequate pay, satisfying work, equal job opportunities, safety on the job, and innovative programs to match the needs of the changed labor force. Leading business corporations have recognized the importance of working closely with employees and other stakeholders to attain their strategic goals.

DISCUSSION AND REVIEW QUESTIONS

1. Review the major reasons why labor unions have had difficulty maintaining their membership rolls in recent years. What importance does this development have for business? What importance does it have for employees of business (whether they are union members or not)?

2. Commenting on a sex discrimination case against Sears, Roebuck (which was won by the company), a woman who had been an expert witness said after the trial, "American culture, not merely employer discrimination, reinforces traditional roles for women. Insisting that employer discrimination is the only significant factor in explaining the low numbers of women in certain jobs threatens to cripple the cause of working women, not advance it. To focus exclusively on discrimination is to ignore and hence excuse a host of social failings—many of them more important than employer discrimination."[26] Discuss this statement, and tell whether you accept it or not. What "social failings" can you identify that might be responsible for keeping women in traditional roles and jobs?

3. If a company for which you worked resisted the efforts of employees to improve the quality of work life there (for example, by establishing quality circles and allowing flextime), what arguments could you make in support of such improvements? How might the company, as well as the employees, benefit?

4. Suppose that you are a nonsmoker but work in an office where several others smoke. All employees in this company are members of a union that represents them in collective bargaining. You are aware that secondhand smoke from burning cigarettes has been reported to be a health hazard, so you are concerned that your fellow employees' smoking habits may be endangering your own health. When you appeal to your supervisor for a no-smoking rule, she (who also is a nonsmoker) refuses to do so on grounds that smokers as well as nonsmokers have rights. "Besides," she says, "the evidence is not clear-cut on the actual health hazards from secondhand smoke." In situations such as this, what responsibility should the union have for making the workplace a safe and healthy one for all employees? What responsibility should the office management have?

---

[26]Rosalind Rosenberg, "What Harms Women in the Workplace," *New York Times*, February 27, 1986, p. 31.

5. One proposed solution to the problem of high joblessness among teenage blacks is to permit companies to pay them less than the federal minimum wage. It is argued that many small- and medium-sized businesses which cannot afford to pay the minimum wage could provide jobs at these lower wage levels. Unions generally have been opposed to this proposal, while business generally has approved. What arguments can you make for and against this proposal? Thinking back to earlier chapters in this book, do you think the plan would be socially responsible? Would it be ethical? Would it help business to meet its strategic goals?

CRITICAL INCIDENT

General Motors' Saturn Contract: Bonanza or Folly?

"You must be kidding. You mean this is a guaranteed lifetime job? There's no boss breathing down my neck to get the work done? I get a salary instead of hourly wages—and a bonus, too? And did you say that our union has a say in all decisions including ones made by the top manager of the plant? Come on, you must be putting me on. I may be dumb but I'm not crazy!" At General Motors' planned Saturn automobile plant in Tennessee, this might well be the reaction of a newly hired worker. The contract between GM and the United Automobile Workers (UAW) union is a radical departure from past practices.

The Saturn plant, to be built in 1989, will produce a new small car called the Saturn. By using the most up-to-date technology available, GM hopes to meet and beat strong competition from Japanese automakers who can produce a small car for about $2,000 less than United States companies. Much of the Japanese cost advantage is due to higher labor costs in the United States. So the Saturn labor contract gives workers only 80 percent of average pay in the auto industry. Other cost savings for the company are fewer restrictive union work rules and simplified job classifications. In exchange, the plant's workers are given a big voice in running the plant plus a guarantee that 80 percent of the workers will have their jobs for life unless the plant is forced to close because of "severe economic conditions" or "catastrophic events."

In the plant where the production work is done, work units of six to fifteen workers elect a leader from their own ranks. The team decides who will do the various jobs, and each work unit will be responsible for meeting production schedules, staying within budgets, controlling absenteeism, handling safety and health matters, and even deciding on vacation schedules for team members. This kind of cooperative teamwork between workers and plant management extends all the way up to the highest levels of authority in the plant, including employee membership on a top-level strategic-planning advisory committee. Quite clearly, the old "top-down" system of management is to be replaced by one that encourages unusual amounts of "bottom-up" employee participation.

Not all union officials were happy with the new Saturn contract. They feared the loss of seniority rights and wondered if salaries (instead of hourly wages) paid to blue-collar workers would convert them away from loyalty to the union. The president of one union local said, "If the union climbs into bed with the company, you don't have checks and balances [that will protect the workers]." Another union official countered that point of view by saying, "We're providing an opportunity to do things in a different fashion."

There was general agreement, though, among most observers that the Saturn labor contract was path-breaking. Management advocated an astonishing amount of employee participation in running the plant. The union shared decision-making power in unprecedented ways while insuring job security for four out of five employees. One labor relations executive declared, "This will set the standard for 1987 bargaining and beyond."[27]

1. If you were president of a union local of the United Automobile Workers, would you recommend approval of the Saturn contract? What would be your main arguments for or against approval? What would you say to a long-time union member who told you that he did not want to give up his seniority rights? What would you say to a woman union member who said that she believed that work units composed mostly of men would not pay enough attention to the needs of women workers? What would you say to a member who took the position that production levels and costs were management's problems, not the union's?

2. If you were plant manager of one of General Motors' conventional auto plants where a "top-down" system of management concentrated decision making in the hands of a small group of managers and where workers were expected to follow orders, would you favor adopting a Saturn-like plan in your plant? What would be your main arguments either for or against the plan? What would you say to a long-time manager who feared that his job would be threatened by a new system of consensus management? What would you say to a black manager who had worked his way up to a position of considerable authority who told you that he believed that his authority might be undermined by this new system?

3. As a potential auto buyer who might one day be interested in buying a Saturn, would it matter to you whether your auto was produced by a traditional kind of GM auto plant or by this new worker-participation plant? Would it matter to you whether your small car was produced in the United States by American workers or in Japan by foreign workers? Discuss the various issues involved.

[27]"A New Labor Era May Dawn at GM's Saturn," *Business Week*, July 22, 1985, pp. 65–66; "How Power Will Be Balanced on Saturn's Shop Floor," *Business Week*, August 5, 1985, pp. 65–66.

Chapter Thirteen

THE INDIVIDUAL AND THE CORPORATION

American society has a long tradition of respecting the individual person. But American society also has a high regard for the large business corporation and for the high standard of living the corporation has provided for most citizens. At times, these two respected elements of American society come into conflict, which presents disturbing issues and problems to both business and society.

CHAPTER OBJECTIVES

After reading this chapter, you should be able to

- Discuss the legitimacy of organizational influence on individuals
- Understand issues of organizational loyalty
- Present ideas for and against whistle-blowing
- Analyze questions of privacy on the job
- Describe the problems of work-related substance abuse and testing

Business organizations raise a number of issues about the rights of people and protection of their interests. Consider the following situations and the questions they raise about individuals' rights.

When a plant employee left at the end of a day's work, his pockets were bulging so much that security guards at the plant gate stopped him. The guards were informed that the worker had been wandering away from his normal work station *and through parts of the plant that made radios and tape players. Since the plant had been suffering serious inventory shortages, the guards felt justified in searching him for stolen equipment. When the employee shouted, struggled, and tried to run away, they caught him and looked through his clothing. They found nothing that did not belong to the worker. Later, the employee sued the company for assault, false imprisonment, and slander and was awarded $27,000 in damages.* Question: *Should the company's private security guards have used their authority to stop and search this employee? Was it fair to the innocent worker?*

Richard Parks, an engineer working for Bechtel Corporation to clean up the damaged nuclear power plant at Three Mile Island, Pennsylvania, noticed that risky shortcuts were being used in some of the cleanup operations. Quality control tests were not always being conducted. An untested crane was lifting heavy pieces of equipment that might have ruptured the reactor's containment vessel if it had failed, thereby endangering workers and the general public. After months of unsuccessfully trying to get these problems corrected by Bechtel's management, Parks reported his concerns—"blew the whistle"—at a news conference. The following day, Parks was suspended from his job, with pay. Four months later, he was reassigned to a job in the Mojave Desert. Within a half year he was dismissed. Questions: *Was the company's treatment of Parks justified? Was Parks justified in blowing the whistle on Bechtel?*

ENSERCH Corporation began testing its cafeteria workers for the AIDS virus in 1985, fearing that if a food service employee were infected with AIDS, the disease might be transmitted to others. Although no evidence existed at the time that AIDS could be contracted through food or beverages, the company insisted that it was a reasonable precaution to take. Employees found to have AIDS were placed on indefinite leave of absence. Questions: *Was this company policy justified? Does the policy override the rights of employees with AIDS in favor of employees without AIDS?*[1]

These three illustrations show how the interests of corporations and individuals can clash. In such cases, which should come first—the corporation or the individual? What are the proper relationships between individual persons and business corporations? Corporations can seem massive, powerful, impersonal, machinelike, demanding, and not always sympathetic to the needs of individuals. On the other hand, some individuals can be unreasonable, troublesome, uncooperative, and demanding. They too can be unsympathetic to the needs of corporations.

This chapter discusses some of the troubling issues and problems that can arise between individuals and corporations. Finding ways to approach and resolve such questions is part of the job of today's corporate managers.

---

[1] For further details on these three illustrations, see Robert J. Nobile, "Employee Searches in the Workplace: Developing a Realistic Policy," *Personnel Administrator*, May 1985, p. 92; William McGowan, "The Whistleblowers Hall of Fame," *Business and Society Review*, Winter 1985, pp. 31–33; and Frank E. Kuzmits and Lyle Sussman, "Twenty Questions about AIDS in the Workplace," *Business Horizons*, July–August 1986, p. 40.

LEGITIMATE CORPORATE INFLUENCE: HOW MUCH? WHAT KIND?

Every organization develops policies and boundaries for performance. If the organization and an employee define the boundaries differently, then organizational conflict is likely to develop. This conflict can be sufficient to interfere with cooperation and job performance. If, for example, employees think that it is legitimate for management to control the personal telephone calls employees make from work, they may dislike the interference with their freedom on this matter, but they are unlikely to develop serious conflicts with management about it. If, however, employees think that personal calls are their own private right, then this issue may become a center of conflict with management.

This same type of reasoning applies to any person or group with which the organization deals. As long as there is agreement on the legitimacy of influence among the parties, each should be satisfied with the power balance in the relationship.

A Model of Legitimacy of Organizational Influence

Research about legitimacy of organizational influence has led to the model shown in Figure 13-1. The research covered labor leaders, business managers, air force managers, university students, and men compared with women. In the model, the two key variables are conduct on the job or off it, and conduct that is job-related or not job-related. As shown in the model, there is agreement on high legitimacy when conduct is on the job and job-related.

Legitimacy tends to become less accepted as an act's connection with the job becomes more hazy. If an act is performed in the job environment but is not job-related, such as playing cards during lunch hours, usually only moderate legitimacy is supported, depending on the situation. Sometimes, however, even an indirect relationship is enough to justify legitimacy if the connection with the job or with organizational goals is strong.

A publisher of health magazines, for example, prohibited on-the-job smoking in any of its buildings, including offices, bathrooms, and meeting rooms. It stated

Type of Conduct	Job–Related	Not Job–Related
On-the-job	High legitimacy	Moderate legitimacy
Off-the-job	Moderate legitimacy	Low legitimacy

FIGURE 13-1. Model of legitimacy of organizational influence on employees.

that smoking employees who were seen by visitors gave the company a negative image, because its publications emphasized health and nonsmoking. It also stated that there were increasing complaints from nonsmoking employees who were concerned about their own health. Employees who continued to smoke were treated as a disciplinary problem.[2]

Off-the-Job Conduct

With regard to off-the-job conduct, we can begin with a general statement that a business cannot use its power to regulate employee conduct off the job. Certainly when the conduct is not job-related, there is little reason for the employer to become involved. On the other hand, some activities off the job may affect the employer, so questions of organizational influence arise. A basic guideline is that *the more job-related and the more publicly visible one's conduct is when off the job, the more support there is for organizational influence on the employee.*[3]

> For example, *because of public visibility, an automobile company vice president was required to drive a company-made car, rather than a competitor's product. On the other hand, an assembly worker was not required to drive a company product, but all workers were encouraged to do so by publicity and large company discounts on automobile purchases.*

There are, however, many hazy situations in which interpretations become difficult. For example, what kinds of controls should be applied to off-the-job conduct of an employee living on company property at an oil-pumping site and on twenty-four-hour call? Even when an employee has left company property and is not on call, the boundaries of employer interest are still not fixed. Consider the angry employee who waited until the supervisor stepped outside the company gate and then struck the supervisor several times in the presence of other employees. In cases of this type, arbitrators consistently uphold company disciplinary action because the action is job-related. In the United States at least, the organization's jurisdictional line is clearly functional, related to the total job system and not the property line.

ORGANIZATIONAL LOYALTY AND BONDING

Many of today's companies, in order to meet their long-term strategic goals, are having to lay off many employees. This move is sometimes called "down-

---

[2]"Health Book Publisher to Ban Smoking on Job," *Pittsburgh Press*, March 7, 1982, p. A–15. It is estimated that in 1980 employee smoking cost employers over $47 billion as a result of employee sickness, absenteeism, extra insurance, and other costs; see Donald C. Kent, Martin Schram, and Louis Cenci, "Smoking in the Workplace: A Review of Human and Operating Costs," *Personnel Administrator,* August 1982, pp. 29ff.

[3]Daryl G. Hatano, "Employee Rights and Corporate Restrictions: A Balancing of Liberties," *California Management Review*, Winter 1981, pp. 5–13.

sizing" or "restructuring" or "demassing." Whatever its name, it occurs because companies are subject to pressures from foreign competition, deregulation, corporate takeovers, technological change, or downswings in the business cycle. Having fewer employees means a slimmer and more efficient operation, with fewer layers of bureaucracy. Costs are lower, communication lines are shorter, and productivity may rise.

The price often paid for these corporate gains is a great loss of employee loyalty. The loyal ties between company and worker have been the backbone of productivity, since employees identified their own future with the company and were willing to work hard for themselves and their company. As one expert has said, "The attachment of the individual to the goals of the corporation was very important. It served the long-run needs of the corporation." Company loyalty was a kind of unwritten social contract between employees and their employer.[4] Now, all that seems threatened by a different kind of corporate need to survive in increasingly competitive world markets, as employees are laid off or encouraged to retire earlier than they had planned.

> *A steelworker laid off for the third time in less than five years said, "I'll never feel loyalty for a company again." One employee in his late fifties said, "I was hurt. After thirty-four years with the company, I was surprised that it came down to an economic relationship between the two of us. I thought I was in a family kind of thing." Another described her experience this way: "It was like some unseen hand that came down from on high. People are freaked out and anxious. I've never seen anything like it."[5]*

These comments reflect an understandable type of bitterness and disappointment, but others seem satisfied, particularly if they are able to land a comparable job with another company or go into the consulting business for themselves. And three out of four middle managers declared that companies treated their employees fairly when they lost their jobs. Nevertheless, two-thirds of these same managers in mid-1986 reported feeling less loyal to their company than they did ten years earlier.[6]

Another interesting test of company loyalty occurred when the manager of a convenience store was told to sell sexually explicit magazines. He refused on grounds of his religious principles and because he was concerned about the magazine's effects on marriage relationships and the exploitation of women. Although the manager had been twice named district manager of the year and won other performance-related awards, he was fired for not following company orders. The manager's loyalty and bonds to his religious and social principles were greater than his loyalty to the company.[7]

[4]"The End of Corporate Loyalty?" *Business Week*, August 4, 1986, pp. 42–49.

[5]Ibid., p. 42.

[6]Ibid., p. 49.

[7]George W. Cornell, "Now-Jobless Couple Place Principles above Paychecks," *The Arizona Republic*, December 20, 1986, p. D-3.

Employment-at-Will: A Fading Doctrine?

Although company loyalty has traditionally created a bond between employees and their companies as long as workers were doing their jobs, the law customarily has permitted employers to fire an employee "at will," especially if there was no written contract and no specific legal prohibition such as racial discrimination. Of course, employees have been free to quit their jobs also. The ability to break this bond between company and employee carried advantages for both parties. Companies could expand or contract their work force to fit the volume of business they were doing. Employees were free to better themselves if they could, without being stuck in one job or in one company for their entire life.

Big changes are now occurring in the employment-at-will doctrine. No longer can companies simply call someone in and say, "You're fired." In addition to laws protecting workers against discrimination on grounds of race, sex, religion, physical or mental handicap, color, national origin, or age, a growing network of laws now makes it difficult for companies to be arbitrary in dealing with individual employees.

> *An example occurred in a series of lawsuits filed in California against Atari, the computer and game manufacturer. One case claimed that employees were allegedly told for a two-year period that their jobs were secure while actually the company was making plans to shift much production (and their jobs) to foreign plants. Another said that Atari employees allegedly were persuaded through false promises not to seek other jobs at a time when the company was experiencing a financial crisis. Then when the company was sold to Commodore International, most of the employees who had stayed with the company throughout its crisis were laid off. Both groups of employees thought that they had been wrongfully discharged. They were challenging their employer's right to "fire at will."*[8]

About half of the states have laws declaring that employees cannot be fired for disobeying a company order that violates public policy. An example would be an environmental control engineer who refused to shut off the pollution control machinery in order to save money for the company. Another would be a sales manager who would not go along with a price-fixing scheme. Neither employee could be fired "at will" for upholding public policy against the company's wishes and orders.

The public policy trend is being expanded into other situations to protect an employee from arbitrary termination. The burden of proof is shifting from the employee to the employer. This trend symbolizes a changing relationship between corporations and individuals. Employment-at-will once symbolized business's ability to deal flexibly and even arbitrarily with individual employees. But society has stepped in to restrict unjust dismissal by private

---

[8]David A. Bradshaw and Linda Van Winkle Deacon, "Wrongful Discharge: The Tip of the Iceberg?" *Personnel Administrator*, November 1985, pp. 74–76. See also "Beyond Unions: A Revolution in Employee Rights Is in the Making," *Business Week*, July 8, 1985, pp. 72–77.

employers. In doing so, it seems to be strengthening the bonds that exist between corporation and individual.

Blowing the Whistle on an Organization

Sometimes the loyal bonds between a company and an employee are strained to the breaking point, especially when a worker thinks that the company is doing something wrong or harmful to the public. When that occurs, the employee "blows the whistle."[9] *Blowing the whistle occurs when an insider reports alleged organizational misconduct to the public.* Generally, employees are not free to speak out against their employer because there is a public interest in allowing organizations to operate without harassment from insiders. Organizations face countless ethical issues and internal conflicts in their daily operations. Choices must be made where there are many opinions. Mistakes are made, and waste does occur, but usually corrective action is taken. If employees, based on their personal points of view, are freely allowed to expose these issues to the public and allege misconduct, the organization may be thrown into turmoil and be unable to operate effectively.

On the other hand, there may be situations in which society's interests override those of the organization, so the employee may feel an obligation to blow the whistle. Examples where blowing the whistle may occur are willful and widespread embezzlement, fraud, restraint of trade, or other illegal activities, especially when there is an attempt to cover up the misdeeds after discovery. In these situations there often is public support for blowing the whistle. Also, if an employee is fired for blowing the whistle, the courts in some instances permit the employee to sue for damages. In other selected situations, state law may protect the employee from discharge.

> *Two cases illustrate such legal actions. Rockwell International settled out of court with a former employee who claimed he was fired after reporting contract mischarges on a space shuttle contract. Terms of the settlement were not revealed, but the whistle-blower had sued for $14 million in damages. In another case, a New Jersey jury ruled that Mobil Corporation had unfairly fired one of its experienced research biologists. She had insisted that the company should report two toxic chemical accidents at one of its installations. She received $425,000 in compensatory and punitive damages.*[10]

When whistle-blowing occurs, both management and the courts tend to use criteria such as the following to determine if the employee's interests should be protected:

Whether the issue is of legitimate public concern

[9]Alan F. Westin (ed.), *Whistle-Blowing! Loyalty and Dissent in the Corporation,* New York: McGraw-Hill, 1981.

[10]Associated Press report from Fullerton, California, "Rockwell Settles with Fired Employee," *Pittsburgh Post-Gazette,* October 13, 1983, p. 12; and Alan L. Otten, "States Begin to Protect Employees Who Blow Whistle on Their Firms," *Wall Street Journal,* December 31, 1984, p. 11.

Impact of the disclosure on harmony among workers

Choice of words and manner of their expression

Damage to the organization's reputation

Truth or falsehood of the disclosure

Reason for the disclosure

Nature of the audience receiving the disclosure[11]

The costs of whistle-blowing are high for both the company and the whistle-blower. The company "gets a black eye" whether it wins or loses. It also spends much time and money defending itself and may damage general employee morale by seeming to be unsympathetic to legitimate concerns expressed by employees. The whistle-blower also suffers: "Even if he ultimately wins, the costs can be high: money spent for attorneys and living expenses while the case drags on, mental anguish, ostracism by former co-workers who resent his 'betraying the team.' And, even if he wins, his career at the company and perhaps in the industry may be over."[12]

To avoid these costs for both company and employee, many companies have become more receptive to employee complaints. They establish hotlines that employees can use to report dangerous or questionable company practices. Others use ombudsmen who can act as neutral judges and negotiators when supervisors and employees disagree over a policy or practice. Confidential questionnaires are another device to encourage potential whistle-blowers to report their concerns before they become a big issue. In these ways, progressive corporations attempt to lessen the tensions between company and individual and thus balance the confidence and trust between the two.

Trade Secrets and Job Mobility

An area of both legal and ethical difficulty is the maintenance of a firm's trade secrets in a mobile society in which professional employees frequently move to a better job with another company. The organization certainly has a right to protect its trade secrets and other proprietary data that it may have spent much time and effort in developing. On the other hand, individuals have rights to seek employment elsewhere and use their abilities in their new jobs. These conflicting rights make it difficult to establish controls that effectively protect trade secrets.

In serious cases, a firm may go to court to protect its trade secrets.[13] An

---

[11]Tony McAdams, "Speaking Out in the Corporate Community," *Academy of Management Review,* April 1977, pp. 196–205. See also Frederick A. Elliston, "Anonymous Whistleblowing: An Ethical Analysis," *Business and Professional Ethics Journal,* Winter 1982, pp. 39–58.

[12]Otten, op. cit. For other examples, see Myron Glazer, "Ten Whistleblowers and How They Fared," *The Hastings Center Report,* December 1983, pp. 33–41; and McGowan, op. cit.

[13]An example of a court case is William M. Carley, "IBM Wins Tough Trade-Secrets Ruling against Two Ex-Workers Accused of Theft," *Wall Street Journal* (Western ed.), December 1, 1982, p. 7.

example is an employee who steals and sells secret documents not ordinarily accessible to the employee. In normal relationships the better approach is to develop prior agreements mutually satisfactory to both parties. Some firms set up part-time consulting arrangements following employment, but these are available only if the employee does not work for a competitor during this period. Others provide stock options that are lost if an employee joins a competitor within a certain time period after resigning. For example, do you consider the following option program to be an effective one?

> *An electronics company has a stock option plan available to key professional employees in exchange for their agreement that they will not ''be directly or indirectly engaged in, . . . or have any material investment or any other material interest in, any business that is competitive with the business of the Company'' for a period of one year after leaving the company. Exceptions are made in the case of merger and other special situations.*

RIGHTS OF PRIVACY

Rights of privacy primarily refer to protection from organizational invasion of a person's private life and unauthorized release of confidential information about a person. Employees, customers, and others believe that their religious, political, and social beliefs are personal and should not be subject to snooping or analysis. The same view applies to personal acts and conversations in locations such as company lavatories and private homes. Exceptions are permitted grudgingly only when job involvement is clearly proved, and burden of proof is on the company. For example, it may be appropriate to know that a bank teller is deeply in debt as a result of betting on horse races, or that an applicant for a national credit card recently was convicted for stealing and using credit cards. On the other hand, does a creditor really need to know the maiden name of the applicant's spouse's mother?

Modern technology and life-styles have brought about new and significant developments such as computer data banks, personal credit card purchases, and more variety in life-styles. These developments have made people more concerned about their privacy. In turn, corporations have been encouraged to revise their privacy policies; for example, they may decide to reduce confidential information about employees.

> *An example is IBM Corporation, which has streamlined its application blanks and personnel files so that substantially less information is required.[14] The company no longer asks about employment of spouse, relatives working at IBM, or even the applicant's former address. In addition, information is not sought on nervous disorders, mental illness, or arrest records, although criminal convictions*

---

[14]Frank T. Cary, ''IBM's Guidelines to Employee Privacy,'' *Harvard Business Review*, September–October 1976, pp. 82–90; and Walton E. Burdick, *IBM's Experience with Developing and Administering Employee Privacy Practices* (pamphlet), Armonk, NY: International Business Machines Corporation, 1982, pp. 1–36.

during the last five years are required to be reported. Personality and intelligence tests are not used. Age is not requested on the application blank, but it is required in connection with benefit programs after a person is employed.

Policy Guidelines Relating to Privacy

General policy guidelines have been developed for maintaining individual privacy in organizations.[15] These guidelines help build a protective barrier to prevent loss of a person's privacy.

- *Relevance.* Only necessary, useful information should be recorded and retained. Obsolete information should be removed periodically. This is the policy IBM was following in the example mentioned earlier.
- *Notice.* There should be no personal data system that is unknown to an affected person.
- *Fiduciary duty.* The keeper of the information is responsible for its security.
- *Confidentiality.* Information should be released only to those who have a need to know, and release outside the organization normally should be with the person's permission.
- *Due process.* The person should be able to examine records and challenge them if they appear to be incorrect.
- *Protection of the psyche.* The person's inner self should not be invaded or exposed, except with prior consent and for compelling reasons.

Major areas where privacy is involved are shown in Figure 13-2. These areas will be discussed in more detail.

The Polygraph

The *polygraph* (lie detector) is one instrument whose legitimacy is often questioned, and some states regulate its use.[16] Science has determined that conscience usually causes physiological changes when a person tells a significant lie. Based on this information, the polygraph was developed. Business claims ample reasons for using the polygraph because its losses from employee theft are substantial.

In the banking industry, whose losses are well documented, internal losses increased tenfold in ten years and are five times the losses from external crimes. In retail stores, internal theft is at least five times larger than shoplifting losses. For all businesses, internal theft is more than $50 billion a year and is growing

---

[15]Employee viewpoints are reported in Paul D. Tolchinsky and others, "Employee Perceptions of Privacy: A Field Simulation Experiment," *Journal of Applied Psychology,* June 1981, pp. 308–313; and Richard W. Woodman and others, "A Survey of Employee Perceptions of Information Privacy in Organizations," *Academy of Management Journal,* September 1982, pp. 647–663. See also David W. Ewing, "Due Process: Will Business Default?" *Harvard Business Review,* November–December 1982, pp. 114–122.

[16]For both sides of the issue see Gordon H. Barland, "The Case *for* the Polygraph in Employment Screening," and David T. Lykken, "The Case *against* the Polygraph in Employment Screening," *Personnel Administrator,* September 1985, pp. 58–65.

Threats to Rights of Privacy	
■ Lie detectors	■ Surveillance devices
■ Disease testing	■ Computer data banks
■ Genetic testing	■ Confidential records
■ Medical examinations	■ Junk mail
■ Control of alcoholism	■ Junk telephone calls
■ Control of drug abuse	

FIGURE 13-2.   Business activities that involve rights of privacy.

fast. In many instances it is so large that it threatens the survival of a business. An insurance firm estimates that one-third of business bankruptcies result from internal theft. About 350,000 workers are arrested each year for theft.[17]

The large losses from theft usually must be passed to customers in the form of higher prices, so business claims that it is acting in the public interest when it uses the polygraph to screen people away from theft-prone activities.

For example, *a convenience food chain says that use of the polygraph permits it to abolish various audits and controls that would otherwise be oppressive. This arrangement gives employees more freedom from surveillance and leaves them free to work in whatever manner is most productive. Similar reasoning applies to a jewelry chain that uses the polygraph on job applicants and has found that between 10 and 25 percent fail the test. The ones that pass the test benefit from less controls and more freedom, and customers benefit from lower costs, so the company says that the public interest is served in two ways.*

Employees and unions often object to the polygraph. They say that it invades their privacy by probing their innermost feelings and that test errors (often 5 to 10 percent) may cause job loss for otherwise qualified employees. Even though an examinee usually may refuse a test, refusal may lead to suspicions that reduce a person's chances of getting or keeping a job. Employees especially object to having to prove themselves innocent, that is, taking a test routinely even when no theft has been discovered or no evidence points to them as thieves. They object less to a specific test about a specific known theft of major proportions. In this situation they may welcome a test to take the pressure of suspicion off them.

Since there are strong objections to the polygraph, some firms use instead written psychological tests that seek to predict employee honesty on the job. One testing firm reported that it had 2,000 company clients in the mid-1980s, and another said that it typically sells about a million honesty

[17]Richard J. Tersine and Roberta S. Russell, "Internal Theft: The Multi-Billion-Dollar Disappearing Act," *Business Horizons,* November–December 1981, pp. 11–20; and "Bankruptcies Are Linked to Thieving Employees," United Press International News Release, *The Arizona Republic,* November 15, 1981, p. C-10.

tests each year to hotel chains, clothing shops, convenience stores, and other companies whose employees regularly handle merchandise or large sums of cash.[18] Written tests are less objectionable to employees than a polygraph test, and they tend to be less costly ($9 as compared with $40 to $50). However, some employees object to the written tests, and test errors do occur as with the polygraph.

Considering all factors, the basic issue concerning tests of job honesty is the conflicting needs of the employee (primarily privacy and fairness) and the needs of the corporation and society (primarily for protection from job theft). There is no easy solution, but in all instances employers should carefully balance the interests of both parties to ensure fairness to both. If an examination is given, the information that is gained should not be reported to third parties except with the employee's permission.

Medical Examinations

Although medical examinations may invade privacy, the relationship of physician and patient is such a private and privileged one that medical tests of employees usually are permitted. The health and safety of the patient and others may be involved. Other issues are costs of insurance and potential liability for accidents and permanent health damage; so there are good reasons for medical examinations. Normally a manager may require an employee to take a medical examination to determine both physical and emotional fitness for work.

After a medical examination is made, the employer has an obligation to keep the records confidential in order to protect the privacy of the patient. Neither records nor information from them can be released to others unless there are suitable medical or job reasons. There also is an obligation not to conceal from the employee any significant illness that is discovered.[19]

Sometimes there are difficult, conflicting points of view about medical examinations.

> For example, *Fred Gates, a supervisor at a package delivery firm, thought that Martin Schneider, a delivery truck driver, was intoxicated when he reported for work. Schneider claimed that he was sober and ready to drive. Gates insisted that Schneider should take a blood test to determine the alcohol content of his blood, but Schneider refused, claiming that a blood test was an invasion of his privacy. In this situation a number of conflicting issues were involved, such as Schneider's safety, public safety, company liability for accidents, company reputation if an accident was caused by driver intoxication, Schneider's rights to privacy, and the company's rights to order a physical examination to determine fitness for work. What would a responsible decision be?*

[18]Susan Tompor, "More Employers Attempt to Catch a Thief by Giving Applicants 'Honesty' Exams," *Wall Street Journal* (Western ed.), August 4, 1981, p. 15; "Can You Pass the Job Test?" *Business Week*, May 5, 1986, p. 48; and Paul R. Sackett, "Honesty Testing for Personnel Selection," *Personnel Administrator*, September 1985, pp. 67–76.

[19]Mitchell S. Novit, "Physical Examinations and Company Liability: A Legal Update," *Personnel Journal*, January 1982, pp. 47–53.

Treatment of Alcoholism

Related to medical examinations is the treatment of alcoholism. This condition presents major medical and job problems; therefore, employers need to develop responsible policies and programs to deal with it without endangering rights of privacy. It is estimated that as many as 10 percent of employees have alcoholic tendencies and that they cost employers billions of dollars annually in absenteeism, poor work, and related costs.

Sometimes the job environment may contribute to an employee's alcoholism, but more often than not the employee's personal habits and problems are the major contributor. In some instances employees are well on the road to alcoholism even before they are hired. Regardless of the causes, an increasing number of firms are recognizing that they have a role to play in helping alcoholics control or break their habit. One reason is that the firm and employee already have an ongoing relationship on which they can build. A second is that any success with the employee will save both a valuable person for the company and a valuable citizen for society. A third reason is that the job tends to be a favorable environment for helping an alcoholic recover, because a job helps an alcoholic retain a self-image as a useful person in society.

Successful corporate programs treat alcoholism as an illness, focus on the job behavior caused by alcoholism, provide both medical help and psychological support for alcoholics, and protect the privacy of the patient.[20] As shown in Figure 13-3, the company demonstrates to alcoholics that it wants to help them and is willing to work with them over an extended period of time. A nonthreatening, no-job-loss atmosphere is provided; however, there is always the implied threat that alcohol-induced behavior cannot be tolerated indefinitely. For example, if an employee refuses treatment, then the employer has little choice other than dismissal if incompetent behavior continues.

Drug Abuse and Drug Testing

Abuse of drugs other than alcohol, particularly hard drugs such as heroin and cocaine, may cause severe problems for both employers and employees. The United States Chamber of Commerce estimated in the 1980s that drug and alcohol abuse costs employers $60 billion yearly in lost time, lowered productivity, medical costs, accidents, absenteeism, and theft of company property. The risks to life and property are especially large in some jobs, such as airline pilots, school bus drivers, nuclear power plant operators, surgeons, or investment analysts handling large accounts for others.

In order to screen out drug users from job applicants, many leading corporations—perhaps as many as 40 percent—have initiated drug-testing

---

[20]Counseling for alcoholic employees is discussed in Steven H. Appelbaum, "A Human Resources Counseling Model: The Alcoholic Employee," *Personnel Administrator*, August 1982, pp. 35–44. Assistance programs for alcoholism are discussed in Richard J. Tersine and James Hazeldine, "Alcoholism: A Productivity Hangover," *Business Horizons*, November–December 1982, pp. 68–72. Legal aspects are analyzed in Louis K. Obdyke IV, "Employee Intoxication and Employers' Liability," *Personnel Administrator*, February 1986, pp. 109–114.

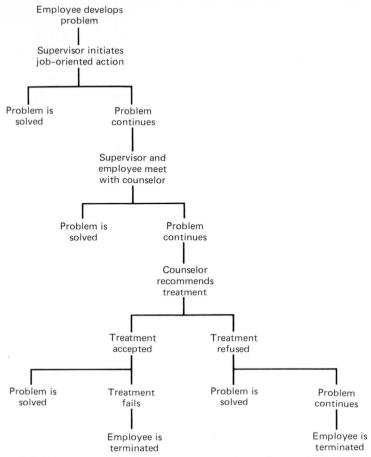

Employee develops
problem
|
Supervisor initiates
job-oriented action

Problem is
solved

Problem
continues

Supervisor and
employee meet
with counselor

Problem is
solved

Problem
continues

Counselor
recommends
treatment

Treatment
accepted

Treatment
refused

Problem is
solved

Treatment
fails

Problem is
solved

Problem
continues

Employee is
terminated

Employee is
terminated

FIGURE 13-3.   Program for treatment of employee alcoholics and drug abusers.

programs. Some of these same companies also randomly test employees, particularly if drug use has the potential for affecting job performance. A vice president of Kidder, Peabody, a New York investment bank, described his company's program this way:

> Our program consists of policy statements and a lot of communication: manager-awareness training, employee-assistance programs. And, yes, testing—of new hires, and just recently we began unannounced testing of current employees too.
>
> We want to create a workplace mentality where people say, "If I work at Kidder, I don't do drugs." I see our workers accepting that objective, and I believe it's due to an umbrella of programs. It wouldn't be happening just with testing, but testing gives our program teeth.
>
> Our program isn't designed to get rid of people. We invest a lot of money to find people and train them. And what we want to do is influence them toward working in our way, which is drug free.[21]

[21]Michael Waldholz, "Drug Testing in the Workplace: Whose Rights Take Precedence?" *Wall Street Journal*, November 11, 1986, p. 35.

Much of the controversy about workplace drug testing concerns the privacy rights of employees. Testing procedures are very personal, and some people think that they are demeaning to individuals, even those who use no drugs. Others say that many people who never use drugs have their privacy invaded to catch the few who are users. From a legal point of view, a corporate employee's right to privacy is narrowly defined, since Constitutional privacy protections apply to actions taken by federal government officials and not by private citizens or firms. According to court rulings, the possession and use of illegal drugs are not considered to be fundamental rights protected by the Constitution, so drug testing would not necessarily be a violation of a person's right to privacy.[22]

The other big concern over drug screening is that the tests are not always accurate. A false reading will jeopardize the job and future career of an innocent employee. By the mid-1980s the most widely used tests were approximately 90 to 95 percent accurate, but that could produce faulty results in about 5 or 10 tests out of every 100 given. New York state laboratory regulators determined that testing errors were made by 66 percent of the laboratories selling drug-testing services in the workplace.[23]

Faced with problems like these, what do the most progressive corporations do? According to one expert, they adopt the following kinds of commonsense procedures:

1. All employees and job applicants should be informed of the company's policy regarding drug use.
2. The program should be presented in a medical and safety context, e.g., drug screening will help improve the health of employees and help ensure a safer workplace.
3. The drug detection program should be clearly explained to all employees. It should be distributed in writing to all employees.
4. The drug policy, and the possibility of testing, should be included in all employment contracts.
5. Employees should be given advance notice that drug testing will be a routine part of their employment.[24]

AIDS in the Workplace

The disease known as Acquired Immune Deficiency Syndrome (AIDS) became a major public health problem in the United States during the 1980s. Since at the time, it was contagious, incurable, always fatal, and predicted to spread rapidly, many persons were alarmed. A question arose whether

---

[22]Robert T. Angarola, "Drug Testing in the Workplace: Is It Legal?" *Personnel Administrator*, September 1985, pp. 79–89.

[23]"Can You Pass the Job Test?" op. cit., p. 50; and Walt Bogdanich, "Labs Offering Workplace Drug Screens in New York Have Higher Error Rate," *Wall Street Journal*, February 2, 1987, p. 5.

[24]Angarola, op. cit., p. 84. Also see Peter B. Bensinger, "Drugs in the Workplace," *Harvard Business Review*, November–December 1982, pp. 48–60; and Jan P. Muczyk and Brian P. Heshizer, "Managing in an Era of Substance Abuse," *Personal Administrator*, August 1986, pp. 91–103.

AIDS victims should be permitted to work alongside fellow employees or whether job applicants with AIDS should be refused employment.

Although the legal situation in early 1987 remained in a state of flux while medical and legal authorities struggled with the complexities of the disease and its treatment, opinion seemed to support certain key principles for dealing with AIDS in the workplace:[25]

- AIDS victims are handicapped people who have a right to their jobs as long as their illness does not interfere with job performance. The same would be true of an employee with any serious illness such as cancer. Legal experts believe that those with AIDS qualify as handicapped persons under the Vocational Rehabilitation Act of 1973, which requires government contractors and recipients of federal funds to make "reasonable accommodation" for workers with handicaps. In a related case, the U.S. Supreme Court ruled in early 1987 that employees who have some contagious diseases are protected by this law if their coworkers are not at risk as a result of workplace contacts.
- Employees should not be tested for the presence of the AIDS virus, partly because it would be an invasion of privacy, partly because the available tests are frequently inaccurate, and partly because the tests do not reveal whether a person having AIDS antibodies will ever develop the disease.
- According to guidelines issued in 1985 by the U.S. Department of Health and Human Services, since AIDS cannot be contracted by casual and normal workplace contacts, employees with the illness should not be segregated from others nor should they be restricted in performing jobs for which they are qualified.
- National surveys of business firms show that few of them have developed special AIDS policies but they tend to approach the problem on a case-by-case basis. Most firms think of AIDS as they do other serious illnesses. This general lack of written policies will probably change as more is known about the disease and its treatment.
- Companies where employees have become alarmed about working with AIDS-infected workers have developed programs and seminars to educate the work force about AIDS and have trained supervisors and managers to be sensitive to the special concerns of both healthy employees and those unfortunate enough to be ill with AIDS. Companies have sometimes arranged a job transfer for an employee whose fear of AIDS exists, while other companies have resisted this kind of action.

Genetic Testing

Two developments have presented employers and employees with yet another issue where business necessity and individual freedom can come into

[25]For more discussion, see Mary P. Rowe, Malcolm Russell-Einhorn, and Michael A. Baker, "The Fear of AIDS," *Harvard Business Review*, July–August 1986, pp. 28–29, 34–35; Frank E. Kuzmits and Lyle Sussman, "Twenty Questions about AIDS in the Workplace," *Business Horizons*, July–August 1986, pp. 36–42; John Aberth, "AIDS in the Workplace," *Management Review*, December 1985, pp. 49–51; and "A Victory for AIDS Victims," *Newsweek*, March 16, 1987, p. 33.

conflict. One of these developments is newly acquired knowledge of genetics—the hereditary components of our physical makeup. The science of genetics can now reveal how a person's inherited makeup may dispose one to good health or to susceptibility to certain kinds of illness. This new knowledge has appeared at a time when workers in all kinds of businesses are increasingly concerned about the health effects of hazardous substances present in the work environment. This second development—a heightened health awareness—has combined with the first development—genetic knowledge—to thrust genetic testing into the limelight.

Genetic testing is any attempt to use the science of genetics to understand the links between our inherited makeup and certain illnesses. Although genetic testing is in its infancy, a limited number of testing techniques have been developed to help identify some genetically based human illnesses. Sickle-cell anemia is one such genetic disorder that can be detected by genetic testing. Others include cystic fibrosis (the most common form of genetically based disease), Type A hemophilia (a blood-clotting disorder), and PKU (which causes mental retardation in children). There are even simple testing kits intended to help individuals tailor their nutrition and fitness activities to genetic traits revealed by the tests.[26]

Genetic testing can occur in two different forms. *Genetic screening is used to identify persons who are susceptible to certain genetically based illnesses.* The goal of genetic screening is to single out individual persons or groups of people who have certain genetic traits. *Genetic monitoring, on the other hand, is used to identify substances that are capable of causing damage to the genetic makeup of people.* The goal of genetic monitoring is to single out, not people, but harmful substances. Genetic *screening* is a test performed directly on a specific individual, and it therefore raises a question of whether an individual's privacy and freedom are being violated. Genetic *monitoring* is a test used to identify the presence of some potentially harmful substance in the workplace.[27]

Because the technology of genetic testing is so new, not many companies have adopted it, although no present laws prevent it. Critics fear the widespread use of *genetic screening* could result in discrimination against individuals or groups with certain inborn tendencies to illness. By screening out these persons, companies would save considerable sums of money on health costs and would reduce absenteeism caused by illness. For example, blacks are known to be more genetically susceptible to sickle-cell anemia than whites. Tests for this disorder among some of its black employees were made by Du Pont Corporation in the early 1970s. Objections were raised by some employees who believed the company might use the test information in making decisions about job assignments or the availability of health insurance. Du Pont, as well as Dow Chemical who used similar tests, discontinued the testing. Out of 366 companies surveyed by the Office of Technology Assessment, only five corporations reported current use of genetic screening, but twelve others said they had resorted to it in the past twelve years, and eight-

[26]"The Giant Strides in Spotting Genetic Disorders Early," *Business Week*, November 18, 1985, p. 82. For several other examples, see "The Gene Doctors," *ibid.*, pp. 76–80.

[27]Thomas H. Murray, "Genetic Testing at Work: How Should It Be Used?" *Personnel Administrator*, September 1985, pp. 91–102.

een companies said they had taken actions based on their genetic screening. Included in these actions were health warnings to affected employees, transfers to other jobs, providing personal protection devices on the job, and installing engineering controls to reduce workers' exposure to chemicals.[28]

Genetic monitoring, on the other hand, is less threatening to employees' rights to privacy and to jobs. It acts as an early warning system for any group of employees exposed to a potentially dangerous chemical. When Johnson & Johnson discovered that ethylene oxide, a gas used to sterilize medical supplies and equipment, may have caused genetic damage in some of its workers, it discontinued all use of the chemical at one of its plants. The United States Occupational Safety and Health Administration also tightened up exposure standards after tests in a number of companies confirmed that genetic harm was being done by the chemical.[29]

These two emerging technologies of genetic testing pose ethical questions of privacy and the possible uses of test results. Since companies are under constant pressure to lower their costs and to be economically productive, they can be expected to use genetic testing to promote these purposes. But business also is expected by society to be ethical and responsible to its employees, protecting their rights and privacy wherever possible. So a balance is needed between these two kinds of business goals. As one expert said, "When there is some, but not conclusive, evidence that workplace exposures are hazardous, the principal problem will be finding a balance between harm to individuals on the one hand and cost to producers and consumers on the other. But that is a balance worth trying to strike."[30]

Surveillance Devices

Surveillance devices especially are used to observe shoplifting and theft. A simple device is the curved mirror seen in some retail stores. Another is a television camera mounted on a wall or ceiling. There also are more sophisticated electronic devices. Since the shopper is in a public place, these devices normally are not considered an invasion of privacy as long as they are used for the purpose intended. Similar reasoning applies to secret surveillance of public places to provide evidence of illegal behavior. For example, in the following situation could the robber properly claim that privacy was invaded?

A statewide banking system installed hidden cameras that could be secretly activated during bank robberies. When the bank had pictures of the robbers in four unsolved robberies, it published close-ups of them in newspaper advertisements throughout the state. The next day one of the pictured men walked into a police station and gave himself up, saying that after seeing his picture in the paper he thought that he could not hide any longer.

---

[28]Murray, op. cit., p. 94.

[29]Ibid., p. 100.

[30]Ibid., p. 102.

Hidden surveillance of private places, such as dressing rooms in a clothing store, employee locker rooms, and lavatories, usually is considered an invasion of privacy. Exceptions sometimes are made in the case of a compelling public interest, such as detection of illegal behavior. People are even more sensitive about unknown electronic bugging of conversation. It almost always is considered an invasion of privacy.

Computer Data Banks and Confidential Records

The development of computers with massive capacity to store and recall information has caused people to be concerned about improper storage and release of personal information. Organizations need information about people in order to perform their functions, but rights of privacy must be judiciously balanced with the organization's right to know. Policies to balance these rights are typically based on three principles reported by the federal Privacy Study Commission in 1977:

1. *Minimize intrusiveness on the individual.* Seek only information that is necessary for the activity involved.

2. *Maximize fairness.* Allow people to see records about themselves and to challenge inaccurate records.

3. *Maintain a high level of confidentiality.* Information released to others should be governed by stringent corporate policies and government laws.[31]

With regard to employee records, some states regulate their use, and a majority of companies have policies for controlling them.[32] Generally they follow the principles of the Privacy Commission. Special care is taken when employee information is requested by outsiders, because substantial questions of employee privacy arise. An example is employee records requested from a former employer by a possible future employer.

With regard to federal data banks, the United States Privacy Act of 1975 governs their use. In general, many problems of data bank privacy remain, and both government and employers have a long way to go before people feel confident that their data bank privacy is secure.

Invasion of the Privacy of One's Home

It has been said that a home is each citizen's own private castle, and an area of increasing irritation at home is the large amount of unsolicited mail, often called "junk mail." Much unsolicited mail is advertising from business, but a large amount comes from nonprofit organizations asking for gifts or trying to convey their points of view.

Government also sends some unsolicited mail, such as announcements of public university training programs for management. Producers of unso-

[31]W. Lee Burge, "Privacy in the Information Society," *Business,* January–March 1982, pp. 52–54.
[32]Hermine Z. Levine, "Privacy of Employee Records," *Personnel,* May–June 1981, pp. 4–11.

licited mail claim that as long as recipients have the right to throw junk mail into a wastebasket there is no invasion of privacy. However, citizen complaints persist on the basis that the citizen's private time is consumed in separating unwanted mail from wanted mail.

There also are special situations that threaten privacy more directly. For example, unsolicited obscene mail definitely may invade the psyche, shock the recipient, and cause emotional upset; therefore, a federal law permits the recipient to file a form that requires the mailing firm to remove the individual's name from its mailing list. According to this law, which was upheld unanimously by the Supreme Court in 1970, the obscenity of any piece of mail may be determined by the recipient. For example, a householder who was tired of junk mail objected to department store advertising on the basis that it showed women in underwear. The Post Office Department agreed that the law allows an individual choice on this matter without relation to generally accepted community standards.

A related issue is unsolicited telephone calls, often called "junk telephone calls." These usually are made for advertising or selling purposes. Citizens object because the call interferes with whatever they are doing and may require them to go to another room to answer the telephone. Traditionally these calls have been by individuals so that a back-and-forth conversation can occur, but automated equipment is available that can deliver recorded sales pitches to thousands of homes daily. The equipment even calls unlisted numbers, so junk calls, if abused by business, could become worse for citizens than junk mail.[33]

THE INDIVIDUAL-ORGANIZATION RELATIONSHIP

As shown in Figure 13-4, the relationship of an individual to an organization is a mutual social transaction, and mutual obligations arise out of the relationship. This mutual relationship deteriorates if either party fails to act ethically and responsibly toward the other. An advanced civilization in which individuals have relative freedom is built upon ethical, responsible action by its individuals as well as by its organizations. For example, individual theft from the organization is as irresponsible as organizational theft from the individual.

An individual—whether an employee, a customer, a client, a competitor, or a private citizen without any direct connection to a company—is a potential corporate stakeholder because a corporation's actions may have an important effect on any given individual person. Many of these links between corporations and individuals involve ethical issues. Some have an impact on the company's attempts to reach its long-run strategic goals. Most of the issues discussed in this chapter require a mutual respect between individuals and corporations and a willingness to work together cooperatively to reach mutually acceptable solutions. This kind of partnership has a good chance of

[33]Timothy K. Smith, "Dial 'N' for Nuisance," *Wall Street Journal*, February 24, 1986, p. D-42.

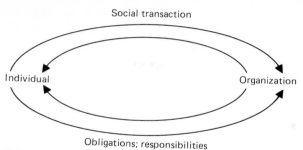

FIGURE 13-4. **The mutual individual-organization relationship.**

producing decisions and policies that are both ethically sound and strategically sensible.

SUMMARY

In the business-individual relationship the rights and interests of both parties
need to be protected. Two areas of concern are organizational influence and
rights of privacy. An aid to thinking in this area is a model of legitimate areas
of organizational influence. Two key variables in the model are whether conduct is on the job or off it, and whether conduct is job-related or not. Special
issues concern blowing the whistle on an organization and job mobility in
relation to trade secrets.

Some areas that raise issues of rights of privacy are the polygraph, written tests to predict honesty, genetic testing, medical examinations, treatment
of alcoholism and drug abuse, surveillance devices, computer data banks,
confidential records, and junk mail and telephone calls. A number of useful
policy guidelines are available for maintaining rights of privacy. In the final
analysis, both the individual and the organization need to act ethically and
responsibly with each other to maintain an effective relationship.

DISCUSSION AND REVIEW QUESTIONS

1. Review the three examples at the beginning of the chapter. How would
you respond to the issues in each episode? Give reasons for your responses.

2. Describe the employment-at-will doctrine and tell why it is being replaced
in some parts of the business system. Do you agree that restrictions should
be placed on this practice? What are the pros and cons of doing so?

3. Imagine that you are a research analyst working in the laboratory of a
private firm that does a large volume of contract work for the U.S. Department of Defense. The laboratory director has come to you with a request that
you certify as safe a certain chemical that is to be used by military personnel
to clean their weapons. Your own laboratory tests lead you to believe that

the chemical can cause genetic damage if there is prolonged contact with the skin or if its concentrated fumes were to be inhaled. Previously, you had reported your findings to your coworkers and to the laboratory director. The director tells you that a negative test result of the kind you have discovered might cause the laboratory to lose future contracts from this very lucrative source. What would you do in this situation? Would you blow the whistle? Are there other actions you could take? Discuss the possibilities.

4. Suppose upon graduation that you were offered a job with a company that pays twice the amount you had expected to get from your first job. However, the company's policy is to test all job applicants for drug and alcohol usage, for genetic traits, and for the presence of the AIDS virus. Once hired, random testing will be conducted on all employees, and you will be expected to sign a statement that the company can dismiss or reassign you depending on the test results. Would you take the job? Tell why or why not.

5. Review the ethical concepts of utility, rights, and justice in Chapter 3 of this book. Using those concepts, tell whether you think polygraph testing is ethical or unethical.

CRITICAL INCIDENT

Energy Electric and Gas Company[34]

The State Board of Public Utilities allows Energy Electric Company to record calls to service representatives for purposes of "training, retraining, supervisory assistance and/or measurement of service levels." The company has attached microphones to the telephones and, after a period of adjustment, the microphones record only telephone conversations. These are recorded a full twenty-four hours a day, because the company says that "in any kind of emergency situation it is important to have a record of the call, the time it was made and what the person said." In one instance, after a customer complaint, the company replayed a tape and disciplined an employee for poor service.

Eventually the employee union appealed to the state board saying that recording of *all* telephone calls, which presumably included even personal calls, violated the privacy of service employees. The union also claimed that monitoring calls for company purposes required only a sampling of them, not all-day recording.

1. Explain why employees tend to think that their privacy is being invaded by recording of all telephone conversations.

2. Recommend policies for the company that would balance the service, training, and public relations needs of the company with the rights to privacy needed by service employees.

[34]Adapted from Lynn Asinof, "These Workers Wish Their Bosses Wouldn't Listen to Them So Much," *Wall Street Journal* (Western ed.), August 9, 1982, p. 15.

Chapter Fourteen

THE COMMUNITY AND THE CORPORATION

When business has a good relationship with its community, it makes all the difference in the quality of that community's life and in the successful operation of the business firm. Communities look to business for civic leadership and for help in coping with urban problems, while business expects to be treated fairly and in supportive ways by the local community. In the 1980s, industrial relocations and plant closings have created special problems to be solved through joint efforts of business and community groups.

CHAPTER OBJECTIVES

After reading this chapter, you should be able to

- Understand the links between business and community
- Explain ways business has responded to community problems and needs
- Discuss community impacts of plant closings and strategies for coping with such problems
- Describe the goals, strategies, and beneficial results of business contributions to the community
- Demonstrate that social partnerships between business and the community are needed to resolve today's community problems

Hershey, Pennsylvania, is known to many people as "Chocolate Town" because it is the home of the famous candy company founded in 1903 by Milton Hershey. Until the early 1970s, an outsider might have had trouble distinguishing between the company and the town. For many years the chocolate firm had provided jobs for most of the townspeople, shoveled snow from city streets, and paid for lighting the streets. The founder also built free public golf courses and rose gardens, a large community center, an orphanage, and an amusement park that held free band concerts on Sundays. In the earliest days, there were no city taxes since most city services were provided by the candy company, and until the mid-1970s township records were kept in the office of a Hershey employee who was on the township board. Jobs at the chocolate factory were easy to get if you were a local citizen.

These paternalistic ways began to change around 1970 when Hershey Foods encountered stiffer competition in the candy-bar market.[1] More time had to be spent on company business and less on running the town. The parent company's CEO said, "Hershey was paradise, it was fantasy land, but it wasn't the real world. Confound it, in the real world, the choices are you either run a good business or you go out of business. It's that simple." Snow removal was turned back to the city, the band shell was torn down, the rose gardens began to charge admission, and the community center was turned into a company office building.

Resentment ran high against this reversal. One long-time employee at the chocolate factory said, "They used to care about serving the people but now they're just after the buck. And this town is getting to be just like anyplace else." Another said, "You used to get a break if you lived in this town, especially if you worked for the company. Now you're just the same as Joe Blow."

Others thought the changes were good for the town. The township manager, speaking in 1985, said, "There's no question about it, the community has become diversified. I've been here since 1974, and every year that 'company town' image fits less and less." The editor of the local newspaper noted another interesting change in the town's culture: "My daughter graduated from high school last year and, of her five best friends, one was Pakistani, another was Japanese and a third was from Czechoslovakia. It was fantastic." Financial analysts on Wall Street also supported the changes, believing that the company would prosper more if it broke away from its traditions and expanded into new products and markets.

This story of one town's changing relationship with a major business firm captures many of the issues that arise between businesses and the cities and communities in which they conduct operations. The gains are obvious when town and company draw close together. A company must have some home base and a sympathetic local citizenry with a government that wants it to succeed. Most communities need the jobs, the economic stimulus, the philanthropic contributions, and the many voluntary services that a healthy business provides.

[1]For additional details and the quotations used here, see Betsy Morris, "Hershey, Pa., Accepts Weaning from Firm with a Bit of Remorse," *Wall Street Journal*, February 23, 1982, pp. 1, 27; and "Medical Center Changing 'Chocolate Town' Image," *Pittsburgh Post-Gazette*, October 21, 1985, p. 6.

These town-and-community relationships are the subject of this chapter. They illustrate vividly the interactive nature of business and society relationships, as well as the need for collaboration, cooperation, and partnership arrangements.

COMMUNITY RELATIONS

The community discussed in this chapter is an organization's area of local business influence. It often includes more than one political community, for political boundaries do not necessarily follow economic and social boundaries. A major company in a metropolitan area may have as its community the central city and nine satellite cities. Another company may be located in a rural area having three surrounding cities as its community. A public utility has a separate community for each of the local economic areas it serves. In all cases, both company and community have a mutual dependence that is significant economically and socially.

The involvement of business with the community is called community relations. Community relations in the 1980s are quite different from those of 50 or 100 years ago. The urban landscape in which business is conducted is undergoing enormous changes. Technological advances and massive population shifts, not just in the United States but throughout much of the industrial world, are putting pressures on both business and society. Community relationships are sometimes strained, as in Hershey. Business decisions have become more complex, even as the impact of those decisions has loomed larger in the life of many communities. Keeping their community ties alive, well, and relevant is a major task for today's businesses.

Limited Resources Face Unlimited Community Needs

Almost any community has a multitude of social needs that requires far more resources than are available. *This situation requires that choices be made with regard to priorities.* In some instances the community decides the priorities, but in many instances business management faces the hard choice of determining priorities for use of its limited resources. Further, in all cases, once management has decided to help serve a need, it must still decide how much of its resources can be applied to that need. This means that any action management takes will result in some dissatisfaction from those who get no help and from those who do not get as much help as they want. It is impossible for business always to "do the right thing" and "come out smelling like a rose."

Figure 14-1 illustrates the large variety of expectations that communities have of business. The figure reports some of the major requests made of a large manufacturer in a Midwestern city. There were artistic, educational, and charitable requests serving both special groups and the community as a whole. The company agreed to support all these requests, and its work with them consumed hundreds of days of employee time and thousands of dollars of company resources. Mean-

Requests Made
• Assistance for less–advantaged people
• Support for air and water pollution control
• Support for artistic and cultural activities
• Employment and advancement of minorities and women
• Assistance in urban planning and development
• Support of local health care program
• Donation of equipment to local school system
• Support of local bond issues for public improvements
• Aid to community hospital drive
• Support of local program for recycling to conserve scarce resources and prevent pollution
• Executive aid for local United Fund
• Company participation in "get out the vote" campaign

FIGURE 14-1. Community requests made of a manufacturer during a year.

while the company was required to meet its primary obligation of serving customers competitively throughout the nation.

Small and Large Business Compared

Studies show that both large and small businesses, whether they are local firms or branches of large firms, tend to be active in community affairs.[2] There are strong pressures for corporate social involvement, so community involvement has become a part of most corporate life-styles. Business leaders believe that they are reasonably successful in community affairs.

Large businesses usually have more public visibility in community affairs, but small businesses are vitally involved in setting general community standards.[3] The conduct of appliance service people, automobile salespeople, and retail proprietors has a significant influence on the quality of life in a community, regardless of what IBM Corporation does at the national level. If these small businesses take advantage of their customers and oppose civic improvements, the community's quality of life will deteriorate. If they take an opposite approach, the quality of life will improve, regardless of what business giants decide to do nationally.

We can speak of small-business people as Lincoln spoke of the common people: "God must have loved them because he made so many of them." Approximately 95 percent of all business firms have fewer than twenty employees. In most communities there are so many small-business people that

[2]John Reeder, "Corporate Social Involvement at the Local Level," in Jeffrey C. Susbauer (ed.), *Academy of Management Proceedings,* Mississippi State: The Academy of Management, Mississippi State University, 1978, pp. 256–259.

[3]See Philip M. Van Auken and R. Duane Ireland, "Plain Talk about Small Business Social Responsibility," pp. 1–3; and James J. Chrisman and Fred L. Fry, "Public versus Business Expectations: Two Views on Social Responsibility for Small Business," pp. 19–26; both articles in the *Journal of Small Business Management,* January 1982.

diverse viewpoints may be expected. This fact sometimes interferes with unified effort for civic improvement. It is difficult to get them all going in the same direction. But most of all, because they individually control their business practices, small-business managers and their personal values are much more directly and obviously involved than large-business managers. The large organization makes decisions based on established policy, but the small one usually decides according to the proprietor's personal views.[4]

On the other hand, the large business has its negative aspects also. Although its business practice may be more consistent, its community interest is frequently more detached. One reason is that the larger firm's sales area usually extends far beyond the community, even if its only office is in the community. In contrast, the small retail or service business depends on the local community as its primary market.

Decentralized Branches

Another reason that community detachment develops in large firms is that many of them have decentralized branches. The result is that the firms have an interest in many communities rather than one. Although they have many operational locations, they have only one headquarters where top management can be directly contacted for major support of community projects. Managers in the branches come and go as they move through the promotion ladder of the total organization. It is difficult for them to have the same interest in the community that a small retail proprietor has, because their relationship to the community is different. Therefore, their decisions have to be based more on policy than on personal interest, and that policy is centrally determined, often without recognition of the peculiar needs of each community. This condition makes it desirable for central headquarters to give local managers broad leeway to make community-related decisions. Even when these decisions seem to be exceeding the bounds of policy, there may be justifiable local reasons for them.

Headquarters policies emphasize branch economic performance, frequently giving minimum attention to social performance. Branch managers act accordingly, often trying to squeeze out a few more dollars of economic performance while depleting human and community assets. To avoid this unfortunate tendency, headquarters management needs to include in its branch-appraisal process an evaluation of social as well as economic performance. Unless social measures are genuinely valued by headquarters, branch management will be tempted to give them little attention.

Offsetting the personal detachment that branch executives may have is the fact that they do represent additional resources brought to a community from outside. They also can call upon headquarters for specialists to aid in civic planning. They can even call for economic support in special cases, beyond what a local business might be expected to contribute. They bring to communities a high quality of leadership that may be in short supply locally.

[4]For a discussion see Daniel J. Brown and Jonathan B. King, "Small Business Ethics: Influences and Perceptions," *Journal of Small Business Management,* January 1982, pp. 11–18.

Perhaps more important, they bring a steady stream of new leaders with fresh ideas. The branch managers have broad experience and a viewpoint far beyond local provincialism. They can expand community horizons and help a community adjust to changing world conditions.

Business People in Civic Affairs

Business people often seek participation in civic affairs. Almost every museum board, development committee, or other civic group has business people among its members. Many business people become involved in community service because their company encourages them to do so and because they also have strong personal drives to serve their community. As human beings, they have the normal altruistic drives that most other people have. They also want their community to be a better place for their families to live.

Community Support of Business

The relationship of business and community is one of mutual interdependence. It is a social transaction in which both parties need to be fair and supportive for the relationship to be successful. Each has obligations to the other, because each has social power to affect the other. The power-responsibility equation applies to both to remind them that success is a matter of mutual support, rather than opposition.

Types of support that business normally expects from a community are shown in Figure 14-2. In general, business expects fair treatment, and it expects to be accepted as a participant in community affairs because it is an important part of the community. It also expects full community services such as water supply and police protection. Finally, it will be encouraged to remain in the community and grow if there are appropriate cultural, educational, and recreational facilities for its employees.

If community citizens, labor organizations, or the government abuse business or take advantage of it, then success for both business and the community becomes more difficult. This lack of support may take many forms. The following individual company incidents illustrate the nature of the problem:

- One city required a proposed new factory in the city limits to install its own water main for a mile along city streets. The management declined and built in a neighboring city.
- Another city harassed a retail store with parking and beautification requirements, which took months of public hearings. The publicity generated community opposition to the store; sales deteriorated; the store closed; and a proposed new department store declined to enter the community.
- A striking example of tax policies contributing to a plant closing is an incident that occurred in Lackawanna, New York. Bethlehem Steel's average taxes per ton of shipments from its Lackawanna mill were five times higher than at the company's five other major steel plants. The company objected to what it thought were arbitrary property tax assessment increases, especially since the company estimated that it paid 73 percent of total property

> **Community Services Desired by Business**
>
> - A cultural and educational environment that supports a balanced quality of life for employees
> - Adequate family recreational facilities
> - Complete public services, such as police and fire protection and sewage, water, and electric services
> - Taxes that are equitable and do not discriminate for or against business
> - Open acceptance of business participation in community affairs
> - A fair and open public press
> - An adequate transportation system to business and residential areas (for example, suitable public transportation and well-maintained streets)
> - Public officials, customers, and citizens who are fair and honest in their involvement with business
> - In general, a cooperative problem-solving approach in working with mutual problems

FIGURE 14-2.   Areas of desirable community service and support for business.

taxes in Lackawanna. Bethlehem sued the city for tax inequity and won a settlement and retroactive tax cuts. Eventually because of many factors the Lackawanna plant was closed, but observers thought that the city's un-cooperative tax policies were one of the major reasons.[5]

The desirable combination of business-community mutual support is shown in Figure 14-3. As shown by point *C* and the shaded area in the figure, both business and community leaders need to develop attitudes that support each other's interests as well as their own. Often they think primarily of their own needs, as represented by point *A* for business and point *B* for the community. The result is that they fail to understand each other's problems and fail to develop adequate cooperation for problem solving. In the long run in this kind of situation both business and community are likely to lose.

PLANT CLOSINGS AND SOCIAL RESPONSIBILITY

By the early 1980s plant closings and relocations became so numerous and disruptive of life in some communities that a new wave of criticism was directed at business firms that made these decisions.

> *One group of Episcopal bishops, referring to "the present tidal wave of economic dislocation," declared that they "know of no more sinister power and threat to the human community than that flowing from corporate structures which remove control of resources and decision-making from the people most affected." They urged "new avenues of cooperation and localism in order to avoid the destructive consequences of an economic life that places little value in community."[6]*

---

[5]John Strohmeyer, "The Agonizing Ordeal of a One-Company Town," *Business and Society Review*, Summer 1985, pp. 45–49.

[6]Bohdan Hodiak, "Bishops Decry Misuse of Corporate Power," *Pittsburgh Post-Gazette*, September 6, 1982, p. 4.

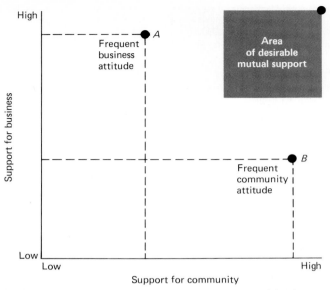

FIGURE 14-3.   Business and community need high mutual support for each other.

These plant closings are a result of the many forces mentioned in earlier chapters of this book—sharper foreign competition, corporate takeovers that result in consolidations of production facilities, obsolete technology being replaced by newer forms of labor-saving technology, production being moved to low-wage regions of the world, deregulation that increases the pace and intensity of competition, the invention and substitution of new materials (such as plastic and ceramic auto parts) for older ones (such as steel), and a constant push to find ever-more-efficient ways to produce goods and services.

Whatever the reasons are, serious problems can result when plants close. For employees, jobs are lost, perhaps as many as 38 million during the 1970s alone.[7] For the local economy, a negative ripple effect spreads to other businesses in the area. For local governments, tax revenues decline.

• The human impacts can be devastating. Research shows that displaced workers seldom manage to find new jobs as good or as well paying as the ones they lose when a plant closes. Single-income families may be so hard hit that home mortgage payments cannot be met; and homes may be sold at sheriff's sales to meet back taxes. Sometimes pension benefits and health-care insurance are lost. Older workers, minorities, and women suffer more than other groups of displaced workers, taking longer to find new jobs and receiving lower pay when they do. Family tensions build up as former breadwinners lose their self-esteem, parents worry about caring for their

[7]Archie B. Carroll, "When Business Closes Down: Social Responsibilities and Management Actions," *California Management Review*, Winter 1984, pp. 125–126.

children, and children are deprived of basic necessities. Divorce rates increase, depression and mental illness rise, suicides become more frequent, alcoholism and drug abuse multiply, and child abuse and spouse abuse occur more readily.[8]

- Some communities, especially one-company towns, can no longer provide even the most basic services. When U.S. Steel began closing some of its older western Pennsylvania mills in the late 1970s, the assessed property values in some towns dropped by one-third. In 1980, the company's taxes accounted for one-fourth of the budget in Clairton, Pennsylvania, but by 1983 they accounted for only 10 percent. Wage taxes also dropped due to massive layoffs of steelworkers, and the city exhausted its borrowing power. Finally, police and firefighters were dismissed. By late 1985 and with only $3,000 in the bank, Clairton city officials could not pay insurance premiums, electric bills, or interest on borrowed money. Much the same thing happened when Wheeling-Pittsburgh Steel Company declared bankruptcy and closed some of its plants. In one of the affected towns, some streetlights were removed from service, heat in the municipal building was turned off, city workers were furloughed, and all city services were curtailed severely.[9]

These human and community problems have not been confined to the older industrial regions. California's Silicon Valley has been squeezed by foreign competition, and Texas and other oil-producing states in the mid-1980s have felt the impact of falling world oil prices.[10]

Available research identifies five major groups involved in plant closing-and-relocation decisions: (1) company management; (2) unions; (3) affected employees; (4) the community; and (5) local, state, and federal governments.[11]

Company Management

Managerial policies and attitudes vary from company to company. In some cases, ample advance notice is given, and management makes an effort to find new jobs for displaced employees, as well as to work with local citizens' groups and municipal officials to ease the impact of a closing. At other times,

[8]Angelo J. Kinicki et al., "Toward Socially Responsible Plant Closings," *Personnel Administrator,* June 1987, pp. 116–128.

[9]From various reports in the *Pittsburgh Post-Gazette,* December 29, 1983; August 28, 1985; and September 16, 1985.

[10]See Michael W. Miller, "Silicon Slump: California's Valley Is Not Immune to Imports, Plant Closings, Layoffs," *Wall Street Journal,* reprinted in *Pittsburgh Post-Gazette,* July 30, 1985, p. 9; and "Port Arthur: How a Boom Town Is Turning into a Backwater," *Business Week,* February 4, 1985, p. 67.

[11]The following discussion is based mostly on Jeanne P. Gordus, Paul Jarley, and Louis A. Ferman, *Plant Closings and Economic Dislocation,* Kalamazoo, Mich.: W. E. Upjohn Institute for Employment Research, 1981. See also U.S. Department of Labor, *Plant Closings: What Can Be Learned from Best Practice,* Washington, DC: U.S. Government Printing Office, 1982; and Archie B. Carroll, op. cit., pp. 125–140.

little or no advance announcement is made by a company that does not want to be pressured to reverse its decision, and the company may offer little aid to employees, the union, and community groups.

An example of the former type of policy was Brown & Williamson's plan to close one of its facilities in phases over a three-year period; the plan called for giving more than eighteen months' advance notice (which was called for in its union contract), relocating many employees, and providing separation pay, health and insurance benefits, and vocational training to those laid off. On the other hand, National Car Rental gave its workers only three weeks' notice of an indefinite closing of a local facility and did not inform employees until more than a year later that the closing was permanent; nor did the company coordinate its efforts with the union or provide training for displaced workers.[12]

Unions

Union reactions also vary considerably. Very few union contracts—fewer than one in three—contain provisions protecting workers in case of a plant closure, such as guaranteed transfer to another job with the same company or severance pay when permanently laid off. Generally speaking, a union's first move is to try to reverse management's decision to relocate or to close; if that fails, the union may pressure the company to delay its decision, transfer workers to other plants, and grant generous layoff payments. Sometimes a union will help form a coalition of various community groups that have a stake in the closure.

Affected Employees

Employees faced with job loss suffer a variety of fates. Lucky ones are able to move to another job with the same company but in a different location. Older workers, women, ethnic minorities, and those with little formal education have the most difficult time finding work; many join the ranks of the hard-to-employ. Some are retrained and enter a new skill or craft. One mill worker with twenty years of experience at one job in one company simply refused to accept reality, saying, "I think it's going to open again." Even those who find new jobs often end up with lower pay, have less desirable jobs, and lose their seniority.

Figure 14-4 shows that top managers and displaced employees do not always agree on the proper actions to be taken when plants close. Both groups did agree that counseling and seminars focusing on expected problems are a top priority, and advance notice was thought to be important also. Overall, those who had lost jobs wanted to be given information about what they would face and how they might be helped to find new jobs. Neither group put an emphasis on severance pay, employee ownership, or payments to the community to assist local recovery.

[12]Kinicki, op. cit.

Actions	Rankings (mean scores)*	
	CEOs	Displaced Employees
• Provide counseling services to employees and their families	1 (3.37)	1 (4.28)
• Provide seminars on what problems to expect after a plant closes	2 (4.31)	2 (4.31)
• Teach job–search skills	3 (4.69)	8 (7.04)
• Provide warning to employees long before the closing	4 (4.83)	3 (4.32)
• Provide job transfers	5 (5.63)	7 (6.92)
• Give a presentation on how community agencies can assist employees after the closing	6 (5.85)	4 (5.31)
• Provide constant communications to clear up rumors during the closing period	7 (6.14)	6 (6.03)
• Assist employees in contacting employment agencies	8 (6.30)	5 (5.98)
• Provide severance benefits	9 (7.60)	9 (7.06)
• Continue health benefits up to one year after termination	10 (7.73)	10 (7.15)
• Provide employees an opportunity to buy out the firm	11 (9.06)	11 (10.19)
• Provide lump–sum payment to local community to finance economic redevelopment	12 (11.55)	12 (10.54)

*The lower the mean score, the more important the item is considered to be.

FIGURE 14-4.   What actions should be taken when a facility is closed? Opinions of 145 chief executive officers and 125 displaced workers. (*Source: Angelo J. Kinicki et al., "Toward Socially Responsible Plant Closings,"* Personnel Administrator, Exhibit 3. Reprinted with permission from June 1987 issue of *Personnel Administrator,* copyright 1987, The American Society for Personnel Administration, 606 Washington Street, Alexandria, VA 22314.)

The Community

Although some communities have effectively pulled themselves together to reverse, slow down, or eventually adjust to a plant closing, research demonstrates that many are ineffective in responding to such a crisis. The ripple effects of a closure touch many community groups—merchants may suffer loss of sales, school systems may lose students and part of their tax base, local governments may experience lower revenues, and charitable organizations begin to see a bigger load of needy persons. The most successful strategies for coping with these new pressures on community life involve a well-coordinated program to counsel employees about their future prospects, a retraining program for those losing their jobs, and the use of government aid to reduce the short-term economic shock and to rebuild the economic base by attracting new businesses to the area. In a few cases, as discussed in an earlier chapter, an entire community may buy the threatened plant and operate it as a community enterprise.

Local, State, and Federal Governments

Local governments generally mirror the concerns and activities of the other groups mentioned above. Some state legislatures have adopted or discussed new laws requiring a company to give advance notice—anywhere from sixty days to one or two years—before a plant closes. Similar laws have been proposed but not adopted at the national level. Some would require businesses closing a plant to pay compensation to a community, give severance pay to employees, and give employees and the community first opportunity to buy the threatened facility. Some Western European governments require early notification, provide job training and job search assistance, and often require community compensation payments. Business has tended to oppose these protective laws because they restrict the freedom of managers to redirect company resources to their most efficient uses in the competitive marketplace.

When polled about desirable actions that could be taken by local communities or state governments to deter plant closings, a majority of corporate officials favored the following steps:

Property tax reductions

Worker-compensation changes

State income tax reductions

Worker retraining programs

Creation of enterprise or high-tech zones

These managers were strongly opposed to plant-closing laws that require advance notice or specific payments to displaced workers and their communities.[13]

As we have noted many times in this book, business's task in society is twofold: to use economic resources prudently and productively, and to be responsive to other broad social and human needs. Closing a plant or moving its operations elsewhere, while disruptive to one community, may bring important benefits to another one. It may at the same time increase the productivity of the company and enable it to create new jobs and be a stronger competitor. In considering the impact of plant closings, a community should

[13]James J. Chrisman, Archie B. Carroll, and Elizabeth J. Gatewood, op. cit., September–October 1985, p. 30.

Business Responses

- Improving urban and suburban development
- Neighborhood housing rehabilitation
- Technical assistance to municipal government
- Aid to minority enterprise
- Easing relocation and pollution impacts

FIGURE 14-5.   Selected business responses to urban needs.

not lose sight of management's economic responsibilities, and corporate managers should do what is possible to ease community problems created by these often-painful decisions.

BUSINESS'S RESPONSE TO URBAN NEEDS

Business initiatives, particularly when linked in partnerships with public institutions, have helped improve the quality of urban life in a number of different ways, as summarized in Figure 14-5.

Improving Central Cities and Suburban Development

Unlike the older and often neglected poorer areas, the central business district of most United States cities has not suffered from neglect. During the 1960s, 1970s, and 1980s, business has helped transform the business district into a collection of shining office buildings, entertainment facilities, fashionable shopping centers, conference centers, and similar urban amenities. In spite of these developments, many downtown areas have become forbidding and inhospitable places, lacking diversity, coherence, and a human touch, as well as experiencing high crime rates.[14]

Through extensive planning, planners are trying to control development, so that the central business district will again become a friendly, human, cohesive whole. Some of the ingredients are open spaces devoted to fountains, small plots of grass, trees, outdoor sitting areas, arcades, a variety of attractive stores, outdoor cafés, and theaters; and encouraging more people to live in the city.

Obviously, American cities cannot be rebuilt overnight. The rebuilding must occur a little at a time. But most cities are formulating long-range plans that attempt to relate, coordinate, and control rebuilding efforts. Most rebuilding and modernization in central business districts is being accomplished through cooperative efforts of federal government, city government, and private capital.

[14]Paul Goldberger, "The Limits of Urban Growth," _New York Times Magazine,_ November 14, 1982, pp. 46–68.

Waterfront developments have been successful in cities such as Baltimore and Toledo. In Toledo, the catalyst for capitalizing on waterfront possibilities was a private corporation, Owens-Illinois. The company, when faced with a decision on locating its new headquarters building, decided to remain in Toledo but only if the city came up with a comprehensive plan for waterfront development. An Owens-Illinois executive explained, "You have to have a total conceptual plan that is specific enough yet general enough to allow for contingencies. The role of the public sector is different from what it was in the past—it has to be a partner with the private sector in risk-taking. . . ." As part of the renewal plan, Owens-Illinois purchased a 10-acre site from the city and erected a thirty-two-story headquarters building and an adjoining plaza near the waterfront. Other companies and organizations did likewise, and they were followed by new hotels, a portside festival marketplace, and a waterfront park. Planners and developers hoped to add waterfront housing, condominiums, museums, ethnic markets, marinas, and other features.[15]

Sometimes, the rush of business development can be a problem, as Nashville, Tennessee, demonstrates:

Tennessee state officials were highly successful in drawing new businesses to the Nashville area. Nissan, the Japanese automaker, built its first United States assembly plant in nearby Smyrna; and forty other Japanese companies are located in Tennessee, accounting for about 10 percent of Japan's total investment in the United States. General Motors' Saturn plant is to be just 30 miles south of Nashville, and American Airlines planned a regional hub at the Nashville airport. Citicorp established an insurance-services division, and other insurance companies and banks expanded operations to Nashville. The metropolitan area's population was expected to increase by 40 percent in just fifteen years.

Whether all this booming growth could be kept orderly worried many local citizens and business leaders. Their concerns were put simply by a Nashville resident: "How do you grow and keep it clean?" Obviously, the business firms that were partly responsible for creating new jobs and contributing to general economic growth also had to think about the impact these developments would have on local traditions and on the quality of urban life there.[16]

Being aware that rapid business growth, although welcome, can also be troublesome, General Motors sought to avoid a public backlash in building its Saturn plant in the tiny hamlet of Spring Hill, Tennessee. It planned to surround the plant with a white wooden fence like those used in neighboring farms and to build earthen bunkers to shield the plant from nearby roadways. An old estate that was much admired by local citizens was spared, as was a

---

[15]Clarke Thomas, "New Bustle in Toledo at Its Old Waterfront," *Pittsburgh Post-Gazette,* January 10, 1986, pp. 1, 6. See also Paul Goldberger, "Baltimore Marketplace: An Urban Success," *New York Times,* February 18, 1981, p. A-18; and "A Rush to Redo the Waterfront," *Business Week,* February 11, 1980, pp. 108, 111.

[16]Timothy K. Smith, "City on the Move: Nashville Is Booming and a Little Worried How It Will Turn Out," *Wall Street Journal,* January 7, 1987, pp. 1, 13.

bird haven sheltering a species rare in the area. The Saturn development plan worked out with local authorities called for the plant to be owned by the county. For that reason, General Motors was to pay no property taxes, but it contributed $7.5 million to local government in 1986, about half that amount in 1987 and 1988, and additional annual sums afterward.[17] In taking these community-oriented steps, GM displayed a sensitivity to local conditions and values that is part of good stakeholder management.

The congestion and other problems that accompany metropolitan growth are not limited to a few exceptional cases. Office building has mushroomed in many suburban areas; almost two-thirds of new office space built in 1985 was in the suburbs. Community backlash can and does occur as business expands into outlying metropolitan areas. In the San Francisco suburb of Walnut Creek, local citizens voted to bar large-scale office buildings and retail projects until traffic congestion was relieved.

Business is attracted to the suburbs for a number of reasons. One is to escape the crowded conditions of the central city. Others are related to technological and social changes. Computers and sophisticated electronic communications permit some operations to be shifted away from central headquarters. Some companies recruit women workers who sometimes are more easily hired when not having to commute long distances from their homes. Young professionals often prefer to work in suburban locations that are new, attractive, and close to organizations and facilities that offer an interesting life-style.

Business's role in urban and suburban development is a mixed one. Job creation, tax revenues, and the many services provided by business are welcomed as positive contributions by most communities. But they do not like the congestion, ugliness, and crime that also result. One planning consultant called the new suburban complexes "linear junkyards." To avoid community backlash and an anti-growth public attitude, business leaders will need to take positive steps, often with the cooperation of elected officials, to balance business growth with a high quality of community life.[18]

Neighborhood Housing Rehabilitation

Life and health insurance companies have taken the lead in programs to revitalize neighborhood housing through organizations such as Neighborhood Housing Services (NHS) of America. NHS, which is locally controlled, locally funded, nonprofit, and tax exempt, offers housing rehabilitation and financial services to neighborhood residents. It coordinates its activities with top officials in the federal government who are concerned with policies and programs affecting the urban setting. Low-interest loans are arranged for

[17]Dale D. Buss, "GM's Saturn Venture Strives for Acceptance in Tennessee," *Wall Street Journal,* November 25, 1986, p. 31.

[18]See "Back to the Suburbs," *Business Week,* April 21, 1986, pp. 60–62; and "Shallow Roots: New Suburbs Tackle City Ills while Lacking a Sense of Community," *Wall Street Journal,* March 26, 1987, pp. 1, 22.

homeowners, city government agrees to make improvements in the neighborhood, and residents come together for planning and communication.

Technical Assistance to Municipal Government

In a number of cities, business has spearheaded programs to upgrade the quality of local government. It provides special advice and technical expertise on budgeting, financial controls, and other management techniques. Business know-how in these matters can inject vitality and efficiency into government systems that often are overburdened, underfinanced, and obsolete.[19]

Aid to Minority Enterprise

In addition to programs to hire and train urban minorities for jobs in industry, private enterprise has extended assistance to minority-owned small businesses that must struggle for existence in the inner cities. Long-standing historical factors place these minority businesses at a great economic disadvantage. They do business in one of society's most dubious economic locations, where high crime rates, congestion, poor transportation, low-quality public services, and a low-income clientele combine to produce a high rate of business failure. Large corporations, sometimes in cooperation with universities, have provided financial and technical advice to minority entrepreneurs and have helped launch programs to teach managerial, marketing, and financial skills. They also have financed the building of minority-managed inner-city plants, and sponsored special programs to purchase services and supplies from minority firms.[20] These initiatives have given significant help to some minority entrepreneurs who otherwise might have failed. However, the private sector can be expected to contribute only a portion of the total effort needed to overcome decades of neglect and discrimination.

BUSINESS GIVING

Since 1936 the federal government has encouraged corporate giving for educational, charitable, scientific, and religious purposes. The incentive for such giving is the current Internal Revenue Service rule permitting corporations to deduct from their income all such gifts that do not exceed 10 percent of the company's before-tax income (prior to 1982 the allowable deduction was 5 percent). In other words, a company with a before-tax income of $1 million could contribute up to $100,000 to nonprofit community organizations devoted to education, charity, science, or religion. The $100,000 in contributions would then reduce the income to be taxed from $1 million to $900,000, thus saving the company money on its tax bill while providing a source of income

---

[19]For a good example, see "Running a City like a Business," *Business Week,* June 2, 1980, p. 100.

[20]For a discussion of the problems encountered by some of these inner-city plants, see "Why Few Ghetto Factories Are Making It," *Business Week,* February 16, 1987, pp. 86, 89.

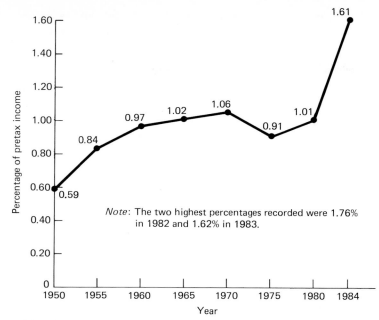

FIGURE 14-6. Corporate contributions as a percentage of pretax net income for selected years. (*Source: Linda Cardollo Platzer,* Annual Survey of Corporate Contributions, 1986 Edition (for Calendar Year 1984), *New York: The Conference Board, 1986, p. 25.*)

to the community agencies. Of course, there is nothing to prevent a corporation from giving more than 10 percent of its income for philanthropic purposes, but it would not be given a tax break above the 10 percent level. Gifts given by business partnerships and individually owned firms (proprietorships) are governed by individual income tax laws and are not usually deductible as business expenses.

The courts have ruled that charitable contributions fall within the legal and fiduciary powers of the corporation's policymakers. Some opponents have argued that corporate managers have no right to give away company money that does not belong to them. According to this line of reasoning, any income earned by the company should be either reinvested in the firm or distributed to the stockholders who are the legal owners. But the courts have taken the position that corporate contributions are one additional way in which companies link themselves to the broader interests of the community, thereby advancing and strengthening the company rather than weakening it.

As shown in Figure 14-6, average corporate giving in the United States typically has been far below the 10 percent deduction now permitted. It has been close to 1 percent of before-tax income since the early 1960s but increased sharply in the early 1980s. The percentage varies somewhat from year to year, depending primarily on business profitability and public needs.

A few large corporations, many of them headquartered in the Minneapolis–St. Paul metropolitan area, have pledged to give 5 percent of their pretax income.[21] Even at the national average of 1 percent giving, substantial amounts of money are channeled to community organizations. In 1986, total corporate contributions were $4.5 billion.[22]

A substantial number of business gifts are not recorded in these figures, because they are handled separately. Several examples are as follows:

- Routine gifts of products and services for local use often are recorded as advertising expenses.
- Gifts of employee time for charity drives and similar purposes usually are not recorded separately.
- Costs of soliciting and processing employee gifts, such as payroll deductions for the United Fund, usually are not recorded.
- Recorded gifts of depreciated property and equipment may substantially understate its value to the organization that receives it.

A number of businesses (58 percent of those surveyed in one study) have established foundations to handle their contributions. By 1980, between 35 percent and 40 percent of all corporate giving was channeled through company-sponsored foundations. This approach permits them to administer their giving programs more uniformly and objectively. It also provides a central group that handles all requests. This procedure is usually not used for minor local contributions in order to avoid red tape and permit some local autonomy.

Reasons for Business Giving

There are several reasons for business gifts, and Figure 14-7 ranks those reasons that were considered to be "very important" by a group of 229 large corporations surveyed in 1980 and 1981.[23] Giving is frequently justified as an *investment* that benefits business in the long run by improving the community, its labor force, the climate for business, or other conditions affecting business. A gift to a hospital building fund is rationalized in this way because it should create better health care in the community. Gifts for education are considered to be means of improving the labor market or expanding the economy, thereby increasing a firm's potential market.

Another basis for giving is to consider routine local gifts as an *operating expense* of doing business. Gifts of this type are thought to provide public relations or advertising returns and are treated like any other public relations

---

[21]"Foundations of a Better Society?" *Industry Week,* April 20, 1981, pp. 50–51.

[22]Janice C. Simpson, "Charitable Donations Surged to Record $87.22 Billion in 1986," *Wall Street Journal,* May 12, 1987, p. 32.

[23]John J. Siegfried and Katherine Maddox McElroy, "Corporate Philanthropy in the U.S.: 1980," Working Paper No. 81–W26, Columbia Center for Law and Economic Studies, December 1981, p. 19. For further discussion, see Kathryn Troy, *The Corporate Contributions Function,* New York: The Conference Board, 1982.

Reason	Percent of Firms Believing Reason Is Very Important
Corporate responsibility	83.8
Improve health and welfare environment	56.2
Improve cultural environment	47.6
Improve quality of labor force through education	45.4
Maintain viability of private not-for-profit sector	35.8
Enhance public image	27.5
Encourage other contributions	26.2
Improve efficiency of charities	21.4
Improve employee morale	16.0
Support independent research	9.2

FIGURE 14-7. Reasons considered very important for corporate contributions.
(*Source: John J. Siegfried and Katherine Maddox McElroy, "Corporate Philanthropy in the U.S.: 1980," Working Paper No. 81-W26, New York: Columbia Center for Law and Economic Studies, December 1981, p. 19. Used with permission.*)

expense. Examples are gifts of food products to a local charity or souvenirs to visiting school students.

A third philosophy assumes that a corporation is a citizen of the community in the same way that a person is, except that it has greater resources than most citizens. As a citizen it has a duty to support *philanthropy* without regard to its self-interest, which is what an individual usually does. The philanthropic approach can create problems. Unless it is governed by carefully formed policies, it may bind the corporation to support requests without careful screening simply because it has no policy reason to say no. Since the corporation has money in the bank and since philanthropy is one of the noblest qualities of civilized people, how can it refuse its needy neighbors? As we have said before, business people are human and are likely to act that way. They feel concern for their community and are partly motivated by philanthropic ideals.

Another assumption is that some corporate gifts take on the characteristics of *taxes*. Since it is the prevailing opinion that corporations should be good citizens, helpful neighbors, and human institutions, the community comes close to imposing some types of gift giving on the corporation as a kind of unofficial tax. The gifts are a cost of doing business. They are given to retain public approval for the business. In effect, business is saying that public attitudes make the cost of not giving greater than the cost of giving, so business feels compelled to "pay the tax."

Regardless of whether gifts are considered to be an investment, an expense, a philanthropy, or a tax, most of their costs are probably passed on to consumers, because giving in the long run becomes a cost of doing business. If this viewpoint is valid, then the fifth reason for giving is that business is acting partly as agent and *trustee* for the community, receiving funds and distributing them according to community needs. In its trusteeship role business responds to various stakeholder claims in its community, and one of

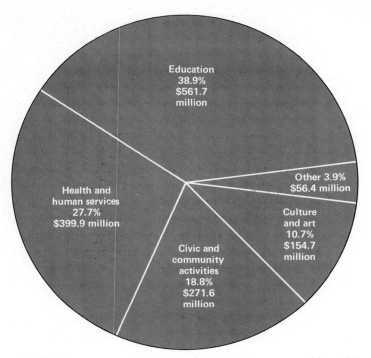

FIGURE 14-8. Distribution of contributions reported by 415 companies. (*Source: Linda Cardillo Platzer*, Annual Survey of Corporate Contributions, 1986 Edition (for Calendar Year 1984), *New York: The Conference Board, 1986, p. 19.*)

these responses is gifts to those whose claims are perceived as being either legitimate or so powerful that they threaten the business if not satisfied. Thus, both legitimacy of claim and power of claimants are considered when making a decision concerning corporate giving.

Gifts to Education

About 39 percent of corporate gifts is used to support education, as shown in Figure 14-8. This proportion of giving to education shows that business has a serious interest in upgrading the education of citizens and potential employees. Gifts include scholarships, research grants, capital grants for buildings, endowed professorships, and outright grants for general expenses. (Educational payments for present employees are recorded separately as a fringe benefit cost.)

Business aid to education is typically justified under the investment philosophy of giving. It is considered to be an investment in educated citizens, in advancing technology that business uses, in building a better community, and in a better public climate for business. All these objectives can be related to business's long-range well-being.

One sensitive policy decision is whether to give to educational institutions where there is significant hostility toward the business system. Most firms are cautious in this situation but may continue giving to support free inquiry.[24]

A related issue has arisen on some campuses where college endowment funds have divested the stocks of companies doing business in South Africa. In retaliation, several corporations have withdrawn their financial support of divesting colleges and universities. FMC Corporation ended its grants to six schools and indicated that it might take similar action against others. Marathon Oil cut off gifts to the University of Minnesota, four California universities, and other institutions in Michigan, Wisconsin, Iowa, and Arizona. Other big companies, including General Motors, IBM, and Xerox, have refused to penalize colleges and universities in these ways.[25]

Gifts for Artistic and Cultural Activities

Throughout the centuries, art has been heavily dependent on some form of patronage for support. Pharaohs, nobles, the church, and the state have all provided patronage. Traditionally in Europe, deficits are made up by state subsidies. In the United States wealthy persons have supported cultural activities; but with greater tax restrictions on accumulation of wealth, this source has declined, which requires a broader base of support to be found. Cultural organizations have sought support from business and, in small amounts, from today's larger middle class. About 10 percent of the business gift dollar now goes for cultural activities, and the list of business donors to operas, art shows, symphonies, and ballets gradually is expanding.

Business justifies its cultural gifts as an investment in a better quality of life in the community. As shown in Figure 14-9, gift giving improves quality of life in a number of ways as it flows through the system. For example, it increases satisfaction of employees with their community, provides a better place for their children to grow up, and encourages intellectual and emotional growth of employees. Familiarity with the arts may make better managers, by broadening their outlook, improving their sensitivities to the external environment, and helping them become more adept at perceiving social change.[26]

In spite of these benefits, some members of the art world have criticized a tendency of corporations to focus their support on spectacular "blockbuster" traveling exhibits, from which they gain much favorable publicity, while

[24]For arguments for and against these types of gifts see Robert H. Malott, "Corporate Support of Education: With Strings Attached," and Louis W. Cabot, "Corporate Support of Education: No Strings Attached," *Harvard Business Review*, July–August 1978, pp. 133–144.

[25]Dennis Kneale, "Firms with Ties to South Africa Strike Back at Colleges that Divest," *Wall Street Journal*, December 10, 1986, p. 33.

[26]Peter G. Scotese, "Business and Art: A Creative, Practical Partnership," *Management Review*, October 1978, pp. 20–24. For the practical side of arts contributions, see Martin E. Segal, "Business Can Benefit by Giving to the Arts," *Wall Street Journal*, January 11, 1982.

Community Effects
• Improved recruiting and retention of employees
• Increased satisfaction of employees with their community
• Better place for children to develop
• Encouragement of employee growth
• Broaden management, more sensitive to the environment and change
• Improved chances for community growth, which provides more customers
• Higher-quality labor pool
• Reduced tax burden
• More balanced community

FIGURE 14-9. Possible community effects of business gifts for artistic and cultural activities.

slighting other forms of needed financial aid to museums and fledgling experimental artists. Another criticism is that corporate financing of art shies away from controversial subjects that may deal with sex, violence, religion, or political issues. In some cases, pressure is brought to bear on an art institution by a corporate sponsor; this happened when city museums in New York who were the recipients of grants from Philip Morris Corporation received a strong letter from the company urging them to oppose pending city legislation that would limit smoking in public places.[27]

Leaves of Absence, Volunteer Staffing, and Matching Grants

A unique approach to gift giving is letting employees have leaves of absence for community service. Usually the employee's salary is either partially or wholly continued during this period of public service. Sometimes the employee's leave is without pay, but even in these instances the business makes a sacrifice because it foregoes the employee's services and may suffer delay in some of the work with which the absent employee is involved. For many decades businesses have granted short leaves of several weeks for work on special community projects such as the United Fund. This approach has given community projects valuable services that they could not otherwise have secured on a short-term basis. Several hundred IBM employees have taken social service leaves, often at full pay, to teach in colleges with predominantly minority enrollments.

Volunteer staffing of community agencies has been growing in recent years, as companies encourage their employees to devote some of their own time to helping others. According to one authoritative study, Levi Strauss pioneered this approach in the early 1970s by creating Community Involvement Teams that "work actively to identify community needs and creative solutions." Other companies allow employee-volunteers to recommend their agency for special company grants. Still other plans encourage employees to

[27]"A Word from Our Sponsor," *Business Week*, November 25, 1985, pp. 96–98.

contribute to community needs by matching these individual grants with company funds.[28]

Corporate Giving in a Strategic Context

One way to stretch the corporate contributions dollar is to make sure that it is being allocated and used strategically to meet the needs of both recipient and donor. A strategy of mutual benefits is one of the major themes of this book. More companies are thinking about their giving in this way.

> *Chevron Corporation tries to allocate its annual $20 million in contributions along strategic lines. From the 3,000 requests it receives each year, the company sets a limited number of specific target agencies to receive the bulk of its gifts. High-priority areas have included education, environmental quality, and support for economically and socially disadvantaged groups, youth, and the elderly. Contributions to these groups are part of Chevron's program to stay in touch with grass-roots developments likely to affect the company's operations. Links are made also to the corporation's larger business plans for operations around the world. For example, when a new facility is to be built, the managers in charge of corporate contributions identify how the new operation will affect the local community and what the company might require from the community. Environmental improvements might be made before construction begins. The result is an improved image and greater acceptance by the community. Company officials also think that it reduces the size and expense of a government bureaucracy that otherwise might have to deal with such problems.[29]*

One group of scholars pointed out that strategic philanthropy occurs in two forms. "Strategic process" applies a "professional business approach to determine the goals, budgets, and criteria for specific grants." Chevron takes this approach. "Strategic outcome" emphasizes the links between corporate contributions and certain business-oriented goals—such as introducing a new product—or providing needed services to employees—such as child-care centers—or maintaining positive contacts with external stakeholder groups—such as Asian-Americans—that had exerted pressure on the company in the past and might again in the future. Chevron's attempts to stay in touch with grass-roots organizations are an example of this approach. The most popular of these two approaches among companies surveyed was strategic process—in other words, the one that treats corporate giving in a businesslike manner.[30]

[28]For several examples, see Lee Burke, Jeanne M. Logsdon, and Martha Reiner, *Profiles of Community Involvement Programs in the Greater San Francisco Bay Area*, Berkeley, CA: Center for Research in Management, January 1986.

[29]"Thinking Strategically: Chevron Sets the Pace in Corporate Giving," *Business International*, January 18, 1985, pp. 17, 22–23.

[30]Lee Burke, Jeanne M. Logsdon, and Martha Reiner, "Corporate Philanthropy: Linking Social Responsibility and Strategic Management," presented to the annual meeting of The Academy of Management, Chicago, IL, August 1986. For a similar view, see Timothy S. Mescon and Donn J. Tilson, "Corporate Philanthropy: A Strategic Approach to the Bottom-Line," *California Management Review*, Winter 1987, pp. 49–61.

THE NEED FOR PARTNERSHIP

In few areas of society is the need for a partnership between business and government more apparent than in dealing with community problems. As one leading group of business executives has said:

> Whether growing or contracting, young or old, large or small, in the Frost Belt or Sun Belt, America's urban communities possess the resources of an advanced and affluent society: highly educated and skilled individuals, productive social and economic institutions, sophisticated technology, physical infrastructure, transportation and communications networks, and access to capital. Developing this potential will require cooperation. . . . Public-private partnerships are a source of energy and vitality for America's urban communities. . . .
> In fashioning local partnerships, there is no substitute for the judgment and leadership of individuals who live in a community, are knowledgeable about its people and institutions, and care about its future.[31]

This last point is worth emphasizing. Many problems are "people problems" involving hopes, attitudes, sentiments, and expectations for betterment of the human condition generally. Neither government nor business can simply impose solutions or be expected to find quick and easy answers to problems so long in the making and so vast in their complications. Grassroots involvement is needed, where people are willing and able to confront their own needs and work to fulfill them through cooperative efforts and intelligent planning. In that community-oriented effort, government and business can act as facilitators, contributing aid and assistance where feasible and being socially responsive to legitimately expressed human needs.

SUMMARY

There is a mutual interdependence between business and its community that requires mutual support from both for effectiveness. Communities need the jobs, specialized skills, executive talents, and the resources that business can provide. Business needs cooperative attitudes in local government, basic infrastructure services, and a feeling that it is a welcome member of the community. Under these circumstances, much can be accomplished to upgrade the quality of community life.

The range of business-community relationships is extensive, giving business many opportunities to be socially responsible. Careful handling of plant closings, planning operations to minimize urban and suburban congestion,

---

[31]Committee for Economic Development, *Public-Private Partnership: An Opportunity for Urban Communities*, New York, 1982, pp. 1, 7.

and strategically placing corporate contributions are a few of the ways business can have a positive impact on the quality of community life.

DISCUSSION AND REVIEW QUESTIONS

1. Identify one or two prominent business firms in your hometown or your college town and compare their community relations with those of the Hershey Foods Company as described in the opening paragraphs of this chapter. In what ways are these relationships helpful to your community? In what ways are they supportive of the business firm? What changes would you recommend in order to benefit both community and firm?

2. An advertisement appearing in the *Wall Street Journal* carried this headline: "Cut Manufacturing Costs Up to 50% in Mexico: Seminars Tell You How!" The ad told readers—mostly business people—that their firms could save up to $20,000 per manufacturing assembler by moving their United States operations to Mexico. Companies were told that, in addition to being able to hire lower-wage employees, they could buy state-of-the-art high-tech components from Far East manufacturers at a cost saving of up to 30 percent.[32] Comment on the significance of this type of ad for employees and communities in the United States. What issues of social responsibility, if any, does it raise? If you were the owner of a company that could save the advertised amounts, would you move your operations to Mexico, even if it meant closing your United States plant? Defend your answer.

3. One recent urban study stated: "Once a city has begun to lose population and jobs, its decline often becomes self-reinforcing, because each loss creates conditions that encourage further losses. . . . Urban decline is not a self-correcting process, but usually tends to get worse rather than better. [For that reason], market forces alone cannot cope with urban decline."[33] Comment on this statement from the viewpoint of the business community of a Frost Belt city that is losing population. What steps can be taken by local business to offset such decline?

4. Suppose you are a stockholder attending the annual shareholders' meeting of your company and the following proposal is made: "No corporate funds of this corporation shall be given to any charitable, educational, or other similar organization except for purposes directly related to the business of the company." Would you vote for, or against, this proposal? Give arguments to support your vote.

5. Review this chapter's discussion of strategic corporate philanthropy. Then discuss which one of the two strategic approaches—strategic process or strategic outcome—would be likely to produce the greatest amount of socially responsible behavior by companies.

[32]*Wall Street Journal*, August 28, 1986, p. 21.

[33]"What's Ahead for the Cities?" *The Brookings Review*, Fall 1982, pp. 27–28.

CRITICAL INCIDENT

This Land Is Your Land, This Land Is My Land?

"This is not a third-world country. This is the panhandle of Texas." "Corporate Phillips," meaning Phillips Petroleum Company, should not be allowed to "push Texas Americans around." So said a Houston lawyer hired by a group of citizens of Phillips, Texas, to help them fight an eviction order to leave their homes.

The tiny town with a current population of 1,500 was established some sixty years ago by the company to house its refinery workers. In the intervening years, the refinery had expanded—most recently in 1978—until the residents were living in the shadow of the huge refinery with its tanks of volatile liquids. In 1980 a huge explosion at the refinery leveled the town's two churches and damaged most houses in town. A company official declared, "If the refinery were being built today, houses would not be built there." The company admitted, though, that safety was not the only reason it wanted the houses vacated—it might need the land for future expansion of the refinery.

Although homeowners owned their houses, Phillips Petroleum owned the land they stood on. In earlier times, the company owned the entire town including the houses, had built a park and a swimming pool, and even repaired the streets. In the 1950s it sold the houses but not the land to its workers. Each homeowner now paid Phillips Petroleum $18 land rent each month plus $9 for trash collection. A local cattle company also owned some of the lots and had been negotiating with the homeowners to sell them the land on which their houses stood. But the oil company bought the cattle company and now wanted to reclaim all the land and had ordered all homeowners to leave.

Townspeople were upset about the deal offered them by the company. Fewer than half had accepted the corporation's plan to give each homeowner a free plot of land in a neighboring town plus paying them $3 to $4 per square foot to help defray the cost of moving their houses to the new location. Opponents said it was not enough and that many families could not afford the additional cost of moving. Others said that they did not want to move regardless of what the company would pay because they liked small-town living and had lived nowhere else for their entire lives. For them, the company had no right to force people to give up their birthplace.

Faced with losing their homes, a group of citizens formed the Phillips Homeowners Association. It was this group that called in a colorful lawyer from Houston known as Racehorse Haynes. He told the group, "They might whup us fair and square, but they better bring lunch." Townspeople were split on what to do. Those who favored accepting the company's offer were called "company men," while those opposed were labeled "radicals."[34]

1. Compare the situation in Phillips, Texas, with the one described at the beginning of this chapter concerning Hershey, Pennsylvania. Which town

---

[34]Robert Reinhold, "Oil Company Town, Facing Eviction, Digs In for Legal Battle," *New York Times*, February 23, 1986, p. 22.

illustrates the better relationships between company and community? How do you account for the differences?

2. Using Figure 14-3 in this chapter, plot the position of business-community relationships in Phillips, Texas, at three different times: at the town's founding 60 years ago; during the 1950s when workers bought their homes; and at the time the company sent eviction notices to the homeowners.

3. What solution do you recommend in Phillips, Texas? Assume that the company wants to act in a socially responsible way and would prefer to avoid a costly legal battle that might damage the company's public image.

DO ARTICLE   FEAR OF FARMING , The Economist 5-12-90

① When Phillips, Texas was founded, the relationship between the town and the Company was probably very similar to the Hershey Corporation - Hershey PA relationship. The situation in Hershey is probably a better relationship at this time than the relationship that exists between Phillips & the TX community. Hershey's cutbacks in community support curtailed activities which the majority of the remaining American citizens located elsewhere in the country supported with their tax dollars. The cutbacks where not as devestating as relocating an entire community.

In both cases, the community assistance provided by both firms illustrated good will towards the community on the part of the corporation. However, while both of the corporations actions where related to business motives (ie increased competition), Phillips also saw a need to remove people from a potentially dangerous situation. The people who did not want to move where reacting emotionally and where not thinking of the possible harmful effects posed by living so close to a refinery.

③ The company should try to emphasise a common sense attitude, stressing the possible dangers that exist regardless of how well managed the refinery is.

DO ARTICLE — FEATS OF FARMING, The Economist 5-12-90

4

MANAGING IN A
TURBULENT WORLD

Chapter 15

BUSINESS AND MEDIA RELATIONS

Media institutions—television, radio, newspapers, magazines, films, and books—have become enormously important elements affecting the relationships between business and the general public. Business frequently complains that the media give an inaccurate and unfair view of business, thereby complicating its task of establishing good relationships with its many stakeholders. This chapter discusses business and media relations, the social responsibilities of the media, and media strategies used by business.

CHAPTER OBJECTIVES

After reading this chapter, you should be able to

- Describe the general outlines of the media industry
- Explain basic economic factors governing the media
- Describe government regulation of the media
- Identify critical social issues surrounding media operations
- Outline corporate media strategies
- Understand social responsibility guidelines for the media

The television image was vivid and dramatic. The network reporter was standing in the middle of a runway at the busiest airport in the United States. He held aloft a small bolt that was about 4 inches long. One just like it had been found on the very runway from which his broadcast was originating. Then, in a voice that rang with muffled tragedy and irony, he told his prime-time news audience that this tiny bolt which was designed to hold one of the mammoth airliner's engines to the wing had apparently failed and was a possible cause of America's worst aviation accident. Just hours earlier, an American Airlines DC-10 had crashed while taking off from Chicago's O'Hare Airport, killing all passengers and crew members. In homes all over the United States, viewers could draw their own conclusion about who was probably responsible for the crash.

Many months later, a careful government investigation revealed that the bolt had nothing to do with the accident. The engine tore loose from the wing because of improper maintenance procedures that had weakened the engine's supports. For the bolt manufacturer, this finding was good news, for it meant that the company was not liable for the accident. However, the reporter's dramatic, on-the-scene conclusion left millions of television viewers convinced that the bolt manufacturer was to blame for this tragic loss of life. No one knows how many of the original audience were around several months later to hear the rather dry investigative report that cleared the company.

This episode is all too typical of the damage that can be done by emotional, sensational, and inaccurate reporting of news affecting business. Dramatic impact is all-important to the media because exciting news attracts viewers and readers who are the targets of the media's commercial ads. High viewer ratings are the lifeblood of television, just as large circulation is essential to newspapers and magazines and just as big audiences are necessary for a Hollywood film to become a blockbuster. When drama, excitement, and entertainment begin to displace factual accuracy in both news reporting and in documentary presentations, the media flirt with trouble.

This chapter discusses the major media and the impact they have on business and society. Because of television's central importance, the discussion emphasizes its role. The chapter also demonstrates what business firms can do to develop media strategies that improve their own interactions with the media and with society.

THE MEDIA IN THE 1980S

The media assume many forms, as shown in Figure 15-1. Taken together, they create a vast communication network responsible for sending millions of messages to the public on a daily basis. Most people have multiple, overlapping media experiences because they read daily newspapers, listen to the radio, subscribe to magazines, buy and read books, attend the theater, see motion pictures, and enjoy listening to a wide range of musical recordings.

Television broadcasting on a big scale began shortly after the Second World War. It became enormously popular during the 1950s and is now the

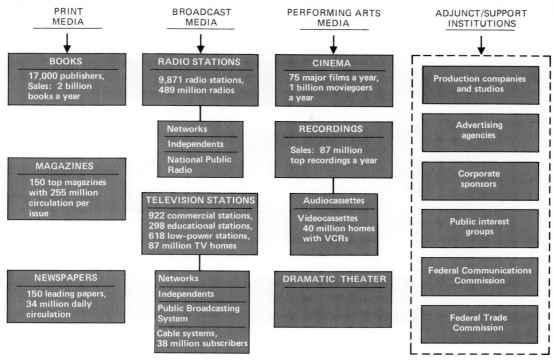

PRINT MEDIA	BROADCAST MEDIA	PERFORMING ARTS MEDIA	ADJUNCT/SUPPORT INSTITUTIONS

BOOKS
17,000 publishers,
Sales: 2 billion
books a year

RADIO STATIONS
9,871 radio stations,
489 million radios

CINEMA
75 major films a year,
1 billion moviegoers
a year

**Production companies
and studios**

Networks
Independents
**National Public
Radio**

RECORDINGS
Sales: 87 million
top recordings a year

**Advertising
agencies**

MAGAZINES
150 top magazines
with 255 million
circulation per
issue

TELEVISION STATIONS
922 commercial stations,
298 educational stations,
618 low-power stations,
87 million TV homes

Audiocassettes
Videocassettes
40 million homes
with VCRs

**Corporate
sponsors**

**Public interest
groups**

NEWSPAPERS
150 leading papers,
34 million daily
circulation

Networks
Independents
**Public Broadcasting
System**
**Cable systems,
38 million subscribers**

DRAMATIC THEATER

**Federal Communications
Commission**

**Federal Trade
Commission**

FIGURE 15-1 Major types of media in the United States.

premier medium of communication in the United States and throughout much of the world. By the mid-1980s, 98 percent of United States homes—a total of 86 million "TV homes"—had at least one television set, and over 48 million had two or more sets.[1] More homes have television sets than refrigerators or bathrooms.

Figure 15-2 shows average television viewing time. The average United States citizen sees more than thirty hours of television programming each week, and the television set in an average home was on for over seven hours each day during the 1984–1985 television season.

Some especially popular television programs reach into millions of homes. Figure 15-3 lists the top twelve television programs through 1985 and the number of households seeing the programs. On these occasions, the majority of the adult population of the United States is simultaneously sharing the images, viewpoints, and emotions—whether fictional, factual, or commercial—projected onto their television screens. Television's ability to touch the lives of its viewers, perhaps briefly through a single program or through sustained average viewing time, is of great significance in the media world. By employing sight and sound, and by being continuously and conveniently present within the home (unlike films that require going to a thea-

---

[1]*The World Almanac, 1986,* New York: Newspaper Enterprise Association, 1985, pp. 359–366; and "Media Current Analysis," *Standard & Poor's Industry Surveys,* 1987, p. M-41.

	Hours, Minutes per Week
Average, all persons	30:38
Women	35:19
Men	29:04
Teenagers, female	21:37
Teenagers, male	23:19
Children, ages 2 to 5 years	28:20
Children, ages 6 to 11 years	26:34

(*Source*: *World Almanac, 1986,* New York: Newspaper Enterprise Association, 1985, p. 366.)

FIGURE 15-2   Average television viewing time. (*Source: World Almanac, 1986,* New York: Newspaper Enterprise Association, 1985, p. 366.)

ter), television is able to reach and affect more people and to do so more effectively and lastingly than other media.[2]

MEDIA BUSINESS IN THE UNITED STATES

Media enterprises tend to be large, with lucrative earnings, as shown in Figure 15-4. Several of these companies are among the largest corporations in the nation. Their earnings run into millions of dollars. However, not all media companies are large, since some of them, such as local newspapers, specialize in serving relatively small markets or audiences.

The overwhelming majority of media in the United States are privately owned. They are businesses trying to make a profit. They must find and serve an audience that is willing and able to buy or receive the media's messages. Without such a receptive market, no media business can make a profit or continue to operate. The ways of finding and keeping that audience vary among the media.

- Book publishers, record companies, and video- and audiocassette makers generally sell to the customer through retail outlets and through book and record clubs. The source of income for these publishers is the sales price of the product.
- Other media—radio, television, newspapers, and magazines—rely heavily on advertising revenues for their income in addition to direct sales to the consumer, and that tends to be the key to finding and keeping an audience. *Their programs or the content of their magazines and newspapers must attract and hold an audience long enough for advertisers to get their commercial messages across to potential customers.* Newspapers and some magazines receive significant revenues from subscriptions and newsstand sales but remain heavily dependent on advertising for their financial stability.

[2]Marshall McLuhan, *Understanding Media: The Extensions of Man,* 2d ed., New York: McGraw-Hill, 1964, chap. 31.

Program	Year	Network	Households
M*A*S*H Special	1983	CBS	50,150,000
Dallas	1980	CBS	41,470,000
Super Bowl XVII	1983	NBC	40,480,000
Super Bowl XVI	1982	CBS	40,020,000
Super Bowl XIX	1985	ABC	39,390,000
Super Bowl XVIII	1984	CBS	38,800,000
The Day After	1983	ABC	38,550,000
Roots	1977	ABC	36,380,000
Thorn Birds	1983	ABC	35,990,000
Thorn Birds	1983	ABC	35,900,000
Thorn Birds	1983	ABC	35,400,000
Super Bowl XIV	1980	CBS	35,330,000

(*Source*: *World Almanac, 1986,* New York: Newspaper
Enterprise Association, 1985, p. 367.)

FIGURE 15-3   **Top television programs through 1985.** (*Source: World Almanac, 1986,* New York: Newspaper Enterprise Association, 1985, p. 367.)

Television as a Business

Television advertising has made the commercial sponsor an important element in United States society, as noted by one experienced industry participant:

> The television sponsor has become semi-mythical. He is remote and unseen, but omnipresent. Dramas, football games, press conferences pause for a "word" from him. He "makes possible" concerts and public affairs broadcasts. His "underwriting grants" bring you folk festivals and classic films. Interviews with visiting statesmen are interrupted for him, to continue "in a moment." . . .
> A vast industry has grown up around the needs and wishes of sponsors. Its program formulas, business practices, ratings, demographic surveys have all evolved in ways to satisfy sponsor requirements.
> . . . sponsorship is basic to American television.[3]

Advertisers spend about $20 billion annually for commercial messages on television. The programs they underwrite must attract a large viewing audience if these expenditures are to be justified. This necessity puts television stations and production companies on notice. If they wish to sell advertising time, their presentations must appeal to the broadest range of desires and interests to be found in the general consuming public. Mass audiences require mass appeal. Programs that cater to highly specialized or minority interests run the risk of being turned off by most viewers. Some critics of the television industry say that the unfortunate result of commercial sponsorship is programming that caters to the widest and lowest common denominator of public taste. However, the basic fact remains: the sponsor

[3]Erik Barnouw, *The Sponsor: Notes on a Modern Potentate,* New York: Oxford University Press, 1978, pp. 3, 4.

Company	Types of Media	Gross Revenue (billions, 1986)	Net Income (billions, 1986)
CBS	Network TV, network radio, TV and radio stations, records, music video, magazines, books, software, data bases	$4.7	$.189
Capital Cities/ ABC	Network TV, network radio, TV and radio stations, cable TV programming, newspapers, books, periodicals, data bases	4.1	.181
Time Inc.	Magazines, books, cable TV, TV programming	3.7	.376
Times Mirror	Newspapers, books, cable TV	2.9	.408
Warner Communications	Motion pictures, home video, records, books, magazines, cable TV	2.8	.163
Gannett	Newspapers, TV and radio stations, outdoor advertising	2.8	.276
Walt Disney	Motion pictures, home video, Disney Channel	2.4	.247
MCA	Films and programs for TV, home video, and theater; books	2.4	.155

(*Source*: *Moody's Handbook of Common Stocks*, New York: Moody's, Spring 1987.)

FIGURE 15-4   Selected media companies. (*Source: Moody's Handbook of Common Stocks,* New York: Moody's, Spring 1987.)

demands a large audience, and that requires television stations to tailor their presentations to assure large viewing audiences.

The main segments of the United States television system are depicted in Figure 15-5. Broadcasting stations depend very largely on production companies to create programs, especially the most popular ones shown during the prime evening viewing hours. These production companies work directly with advertising agencies who often provide the ideas and general themes they want to feature in their clients' ads. The ad agencies, in turn, are in close contact with their corporate clients whose money is the ultimate source of funding for the advertisements produced. The commercial broadcasting station earns its revenues by selling time slots for the presentation of these advertisements.

Cable television has become the nation's "direct pay" system of broadcasting. Rather than relying primarily on advertising revenues, most cable systems earn their profits by charging customers a monthly fee. Although more than 1,000 cable systems accept advertising, this source accounts for less than 5 percent of gross revenues of cable systems generally.[4]

---

[4]For details and recent developments regarding cable television, see "Deregulation a Plus for the Cable Industry," *Media Current Analysis,* op. cit., pp. M-22–M-26; and Vernone Sparkes, "Cable Television in the United States: A Story of Continuing Growth and Change," in Ralph M. Negrine (ed.), *Cable Television and the Future of Broadcasting,* London: Croom Helm, 1985, pp. 15–46. For television in other nations, see *Television and Cable Factbook,* Stations Volume, no. 52, Washington, D.C.: Television Digest, 1984; and Negrine, op. cit., chaps. 2–8.

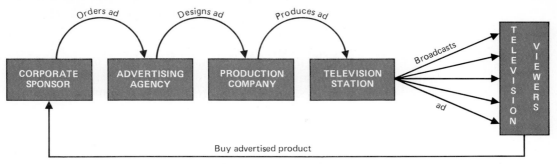

FIGURE 15-5   Major components of the commercial television system.

Government Regulation of Television

Constitutional guarantees of free speech and a free press, which are discussed later in this chapter, mean that government regulation of television is severely limited. The two main regulatory agencies are the Federal Communications Commission and the Federal Trade Commission.[5]

Federal Communications Commission

The Federal Communications Commission (FCC) was created in 1934 to regulate radio broadcasting, and its powers were extended later to include television broadcasting. However, the FCC was specifically forbidden by the Federal Communications Act of 1934 to censor broadcast programs. While it cannot regulate program content, the FCC does have some powers over the orderly day-to-day operation of stations; it makes certain that they operate in accordance with "public interest, convenience, and necessity." Since broadcast channel space is limited in any given geographic region, the FCC oversees the granting of broadcast licenses and supervises the renewal or revocation of these licenses.

The main programming control exercised by the FCC is over program content that is considered to be indecent, obscene, or profane. For example, the use of profane four-letter words or the description of explicit sexual functions or activities has been restricted by the FCC. Much controversy occurs when these regulations are imposed because broadcasters usually argue that their Constitutional rights of free speech are threatened or denied by such restrictions.

The "prime-time access rule" was adopted by the FCC in the 1970s. It requires network stations in the fifty largest TV markets to allow one hour of programming to originate from local stations. The intention was to en-

[5]For a fuller description, see John R. Bittner, _Broadcast Law and Regulation_, Englewood Cliffs, NJ: Prentice-Hall, 1982; and Stanley M. Besen, Thomas G. Krattenmaker, A. Richard Metzger, Jr., and John R. Woodbury, _Misregulating Television: Network Dominance and the FCC_, Chicago: University of Chicago Press, 1984.

courage creative local programming and to give independent producers a market for their programs during early evening hours.

Another programming regulation governs broadcast time devoted to candidates for political office. If the views of one candidate are broadcast, then all competing candidates must be permitted equal time to reply. However, newscasts, news interviews, and news conferences mentioning or featuring political candidates are exempted from the rule, as are political debates between candidates. The reason is that these programs are considered to be news events rather than one-sided political views of the candidates. Broadcast stations also must allow candidates running for federal elective offices—the Senate, House of Representatives, and the Presidency—the right to purchase time to broadcast their political messages.[6]

The FCC's ''Fairness Doctrine'' that deals with on-air presentation of controversial issues of public importance is discussed later in this chapter.

Federal Trade Commission

The Federal Trade Commission (FTC), which was created in 1914 to safeguard consumer interests, has jurisdiction over broadcasting of advertisements that are found to be untruthful, misleading, or deceptive. One famous case occurred when it was discovered that a television ad gave a bowl of soup a more attractive image when marbles were placed in the bottom of the soup container, thus pushing the vegetables up to the surface and making it appear that the soup contained a misleading amount of vegetables. The FTC banned the ad as misleading and deceptive.

Media Mergers in the 1980s

The media world was caught up in the same wave of mergers and acquisitions that took the rest of the corporate world by storm in the 1980s. Sales, mergers, and buyouts of all media properties announced in 1985 amounted to over $30 billion. Over 1,800 radio and television stations with a value of $5.7 billion changed hands that year.[7] Some of these mergers posed troubling questions about the freedom and independence of the press.

The National Broadcasting Company (NBC) was purchased by General Electric Corporation (GE) as part of GE's acquisition of RCA for a price of $6.3 billion. The American Broadcasting Company (ABC) was bought by Capital Cities for $3.4 billion and became known as Capital Cities/ABC. And CBS (the Columbia Broadcasting System) was taken over by Lawrence Tisch and other financial interests. In each case, staff was pruned sharply by the new owners, writers at CBS went on strike for an extended period, some well-known media figures were fired, and general cost-cutting measures were

---

[6]Bittner, op. cit., chap. 4.

[7]''Media Current Analysis,'' op. cit., p. M-20. See also Michael Cieply and Peter W. Barnes, ''Bigger Screens: Movie and TV Mergers Point to Concentration of Power to Entertain,'' *Wall Street Journal*, August 21, 1986, pp. 1, 12.

taken. Fears arose that the independence and effectiveness of the networks' news divisions would be threatened by these new policies. Veteran journalists worried that smaller staffs would mean less news coverage and fewer informative documentary programs, that an excessive concern for lower costs might override the thoroughness required for adequate news reporting, and that network news divisions might feel front-office pressures to avoid or downplay news programs and reports critical of top-level management and the corporate owners.

During a 1987 Congressional inquiry into the mergers, some members of Congress questioned the ability of the media, especially the broadcast news media, to retain their independence if continually faced with the possibility of being taken over by outside interests who held or favored a limited view of current events and public policies.[8]

CRITICAL MEDIA ISSUES

The nature, size, and influence of the media have created several pivotal and highly controversial issues. All of these issues raise questions about business's social and ethical responsibilities. They do so in two ways. As discussed earlier, the media themselves are businesses, and they are expected to adhere to the same social responsibility principles that apply to all other businesses. The same thing is true of companies that buy advertising time in the media for their commercial messages and the advertising agencies and production companies that design and produce the ads. They are not exempt from social and ethical obligations to the general public. Perhaps in no other area of business and society relationships does it become so clear that business actions and policies can have such an enduring and significant impact on the quality of life and on a society's fundamental values. Four of the most critical media issues are discussed next.

The Image Issue

The image issue is about the way people and social groups, including business, are depicted by the media.

Although all the media are capable of projecting false or misleading images of people and social groups, much of the criticism is directed at television. As one authority said of television entertainment, "These shows are registries of symbols, central bulletin boards on which the looks of social types get posted."[9] The following examples illustrate some of the problems.

[8]Bob Davis, "Hearings in House On Network News End in a Dispute," *Wall Street Journal*, May 1, 1987, p. 20; and Dennis McDougal, "Lawmakers Seek New TV Controls," *Los Angeles Times*, May 1, 1987, pp. 1, 24.

[9]Todd Gitlin, "The Image of Business on Prime Time Television," *California Management Review*, Winter 1984, p. 64.

Media Images of Business

One of business's strongest complaints about the media is that business activities and business people frequently are portrayed in unflattering, negative ways. For example, the Media Institute studied 200 episodes from the top fifty entertainment programs during the 1979–1980 television season and reported that two out of three TV businesspeople were portrayed as foolish, greedy, or criminal. Over half of all corporate chiefs in these programs committed illegal acts ranging from fraud to murder.[10]

Prime-time television programs such as *Dallas* and *Dynasty* present business executives as ruthless, greedy, and self-centered with little or no social conscience. Only rarely are business leaders shown to be engaged in socially useful or economically productive activities.

Ironically, the media images of business that appear in entertainment programs are designed and produced by business, paid for by other businesses whose ads make the programs possible, and broadcast by media companies that are themselves businesses.

Some companies have fought back when shown in a negative light by media presentations.

Illinois Power was one such company. It was featured in a 60 Minutes *program that emphasized cost overruns in the construction of nuclear power plants, especially in a plant being built by Illinois Power. The company claimed that the* 60 Minutes *presentation was grossly unfair and damaging to the company's reputation. A public affairs official said, "The show was simply devastating to us. . . . We began getting hate telephone calls minutes after the broadcast. The next day, Monday, more than three times as many shares of our stock were traded in a single day than ever before, and the stock price dropped by more than one dollar. And our employee morale hit rock bottom. We knew we had to do something, and fast."[11]*

Fortunately, the company had made its own videotapes as 60 Minutes *interviewed its executives. It used these tapes and additional facts taken from official government records to answer the* 60 Minutes *charges. Entitled "60 Minutes/ Our Reply," it compared what was shown on network television with the actual films made of the interviews. One* 60 Minutes *interview that lasted ninety minutes was edited to show only two-and-one-half minutes that told Illinois Power's side of the story. Several statements* 60 Minutes *made about the company and its cost structure were revealed by the full videotape to be false and misleading. The Illinois Power videotape was widely distributed and became a well-known symbol of corporate efforts to offset negative and unfavorable media images of business.*

---

[10]Leonard J. Theberge (ed.), *Crooks, Conmen and Clowns: Businessmen in TV Entertainment*, Washington, D.C.: The Media Institute, 1981.

[11]Quoted in Frank M. Corrado, *Media for Managers: Communications Strategy for the Eighties*, Englewood Cliffs, N.J.: Prentice-Hall, 1984, p. 86.

Several other companies, including Kaiser Aluminum, Exxon, and Shell, have actively counteracted false and misleading media presentations of complex issues and business actions.

Media Images of Other Groups

Business has not been the only group to complain about its treatment by the media, as illustrated by the following examples.

- One of the best-known image problems is the way women have been depicted in television commercials as married homemakers and mothers intent on buying products that will somehow please their husbands and contribute to family happiness. A floor that shines like a mirror, dishes that sparkle, plumbing that flushes and drains instantly, and various over-the-counter nostrums that treat a frightening range of bodily ills—all are shown to be welcomed eagerly by a witless and largely helpless female who also is dependent on men to repair the home's appliances, mow the lawn and trim the shrubs, and "bring home the bacon" at the end of *his* day's office work. By the mid-1980s, Madison Avenue ad agencies were struggling to escape these traditional images, as were writers and producers of popular television programs. According to the *Wall Street Journal*, "With only a few exceptions, the traditional housewife mother has disappeared from television programs, too. . . . [S]tay-at-home moms, once a television staple, have been replaced by single women, divorced mothers, female detectives with unemployed husbands and divorced women sharing homes." One network official said, "Good old mom doesn't stay home and be good old mom anymore."[12]
- The National Commission on Working Women said, in a 1986 study, that television programs consistently misrepresent older women. They are underrepresented in numbers; their TV marital status is usually single although in real life most over-50 women are married; in TV shows their wealth is grossly exaggerated compared to their actual real-life income; and whereas less than 2 percent of women of any age are corporate top managers, on TV 75 percent of older women are shown to be running multi-million-dollar corporations. The study concluded that, "TV's older women live in an artificial world that is unrecognizable to the average older woman viewer."[13]
- Another study of prime-time television shows during the 1980–1981 season revealed that Italian-Americans were unfavorably depicted. One out of six Italian-American television characters was a criminal and "a majority made obvious grammatical errors, could not comprehend standard English words

[12]Bill Abrams, "TV Ads, Shows Struggle to Replace Bygone Images of Today's Mothers," *Wall Street Journal,* October 5, 1984, p. 27.

[13]Gary Deeb, "The Older Woman: Life's Rosy on the Tube, but Not in Real Life," *Pittsburgh Post-Gazette,* August 23, 1986, p. 34.

or phrases, or used broken English. The 'dese, dem and dose' school of broken English was a recurring motif, as was the use of 'ain't' and double negatives."[14]

- Black people have long criticized films, radio, and television for ignoring blacks almost entirely or for presenting negative images of black behavior. During the 1950s and 1960s, blacks were rarely seen on television and practically never in commercials. Later when they began to appear, the characters they played tended to reflect traditional racial stereotypes. Black actors appeared less frequently than whites, and the roles they played were minor and involved less time on screen than others.[15]

Most observers agree that the greatest harm done by these social stereotypes and negative images is their influence on children, whose values, attitudes, and understanding of life are significantly influenced by television, films, and radio. A study sponsored by Action for Children's Television (ACT), made the following observation: "As a representation of some of the real changes taking place in the status of women in society, children's television provides a distorted mirror, with outdated models for young children." ACT reached the same conclusion regarding blacks, Hispanics, and other ethnic minorities: "Commercial children's television can only be seen as a major barrier in the battle for recognition of and respect for ethnic groups in this country."[16]

The Values Issue

The values issue is about the power of the media to shape social attitudes and values.

The values issue is closely related to the image issue just discussed, but more is involved because values are one of the basic determinants of human behavior and social attitudes. Most of us acquire our values from early family experiences, from observing and imitating the behavior of friends and authority figures (parents, teachers, and other role models), and from the trial-and-error process of growing up and learning to live with other people. The media, especially radio, films, and television, are now recognized as new value-shaping forces in society. That gives them an importance that goes far beyond their ability to inform, to entertain, and to promote the sale of goods and services. As a value source, the electronic media tend to act as parent, school, church, peers, and Ann Landers all rolled into one. In the Television Age, that little screen defines for millions of viewers "what life is all about."

Materialism is one value that gets a big boost from the media. Commercial messages bombard listeners, viewers, and readers with opportunities to

[14]Associated Press report in the *San Jose Mercury*, May 21, 1982, p. A-2.

[15]Robert M. Liebert, Joyce N. Sprafkin, and Emily S. Davidson, *The Early Window: Effects of Television on Children and Youth*, 2d edition, New York: Pergamon, 1982, chap. 7; F. Earle Barcus, *Images of Life on Children's Television: Sex Roles, Minorities, and Families*, New York: Praeger, 1983, Part 3; and Frank Mankiewicz and Joel Swerdlow, *Remote Control: Television and the Manipulation of American Life*, New York: Times Books, 1978, chap. 4.

[16]Barcus, op. cit., pp. xiii, 65, 114, 115.

live "the good life" if only they will buy the advertised products. As one television beer ad put it, "It doesn't get any better than this." Another one urged the audience to hurry and buy its brand of beer because "You only go around once." A dazzling array of goods and services, including luxury cars, exotic vacation trips, stylish clothing, expensive appliances, and cash prizes, are regularly shown and won during contest shows. The effect (and purpose) of this steady drumbeat of material display is to attract a viewing audience and to stimulate consumer demand for these and similar goods and services. While the media do not necessarily *initiate* or *begin* the cycle of consumer materialism—which, as noted previously, is probably a combination of family influence, peer pressure to conform, and learning the traditional pathways to adulthood in our society—the media surely encourage and support the value of material consumption. Their programs, films, and commercial images show materialism to be a desirable social value, embraced by those who have succeeded in life.[17]

But more than materialism is involved. It is possible that other values can be inculcated or reinforced through the media. Violence as a way of solving a problem is one. The relationship between televised violence and behavior remains a controversial subject. However, most studies report a connection between viewing television violence and acting out aggressive behavior. Not all children are susceptible to this kind of influence; researchers have concluded that TV violence has a large effect on a small percentage of children viewers but only a small effect on a large percentage of children. Some cases have been recorded of children and adults committing crimes of violence after seeing similar acts in television shows. Studies also have revealed that the rate of teenage suicides increases following television presentations about suicide, even when the programs are an attempt to prevent such suicides by encouraging public discussion of the issue.[18]

Since the media apparently can influence the acceptance and acting out of aggression, as well as other values, what can or should business do about it? Some business executives and their companies take a very strong stand on this issue. One such company is Quaker Oats. As early as 1971, the company identified violence on television as a troubling social issue that could harm corporate advertisers. As a result, Quaker Oats developed guidelines prohibiting commercial sponsorship of programs portraying violence or antisocial behavior.[19] Other major corporate advertisers have followed Quaker's lead.

Aware of the value-shaping power of television, some educational groups have experimented with programs that teach socially acceptable

[17]For a discussion, see Gitlin, op. cit., pp. 64–73.

[18]For a discussion, see Liebert et al., op. cit., chaps. 4 and 5. For an early report on violence in various forms of media, see Otto N. Larsen (ed.), *Violence and the Mass Media,* New York: Harper & Row, 1968. The suicide studies are reported in Jerry E. Bishop, "Rise in Suicide by Teen-Agers Is Noted in Wake of TV Programs on the Subject," *Wall Street Journal,* September 11, 1986, p. 12.

[19]Louis Banks, "Taking on the Hostile Media," *Harvard Business Review,* March–April 1978, p. 127.

"positive" values and attitudes. The popular children's programs *Sesame Street* and *Mr. Rogers' Neighborhood* are examples. However, critics argue that television should not be used deliberately to socialize children because the "systematic use of television entertainment to influence children is undoubtedly a subtle but effective type of brainwashing. Now that we *can* harness the potential power of television to influence children, the question of whether we *will* remains."[20] On the other hand, it can be argued that commercial television already *does* shape values, and since it is not possible to be "neutral" about values, the real question is *which* values should be promoted.[21]

The Fairness and Balance Issue

The fairness and balance issue is about how the news media report events, particularly business activities that are being discussed in this chapter.

    The Media Institute, a probusiness organization that analyzes media treatment of the news, has charged that television coverage of business news is generally unfair to business and does not give viewers enough information to make rational decisions about controversial issues such as nuclear power and the oil crisis of the 1970s. An example was described by another observer when a Senate subcommittee held hearings on the oil industry and oil imports:

> For seven days the committee heard what a Texaco spokesman termed "anti-industry" witnesses. These witnesses were extensively covered by the [*Washington*] *Post*. [Then] the pro-industry witnesses were heard. Not a single line of their testimony was reported. The score for the *Washington Post* was: anti-industry days, 300 lines; pro-industry days, 0. The business newspaper, *The Wall Street Journal*, ran only one story on the entire hearing, which covered thirteen days.[22]

    One reason for inadequate media business reports, which is acknowledged by many media people, is that few reporters are well trained in financial and business matters.

    Another reason sometimes given is that most journalists tend to be liberal in their social and political outlook, although this point is disputed by others. One national survey of journalists and business executives found that half of the journalists identified themselves as liberal while 70 percent of the executives classified themselves as conservative. Sixty-one percent of journalists expressed a preference for the Democratic Party, and 87 percent of executives preferred the Republican Party. In the Presidential elections of 1972, 1976, and 1980, large majorities of journalists voted for Democratic candidates,

---

[20]Liebert et al., op. cit., p. 211.

[21]For a discussion of the issues, see Kenneth E. Goodpaster, "Should Sponsors Screen for Moral Values?" *Hastings Center Report*, December 1983, pp. 17–18.

[22]Scott M. Cutlip, "The Media and the Corporation: A Matter of Perception and Performance," in Craig E. Aronoff (ed.), *Business and the Media*, Santa Monica, Cal.: Goodyear, 1979, p. 139.

while business executives voted overwhelmingly for the Republican candidates.[23]

However, the question of media bias is a complex one. One well-respected study of representative households in the United States demonstrated that three out of five people believe the news media are biased in their treatment of business. But of those who thought the media are biased, half said the media are biased *in favor* of business and half believed the media are biased *against* business. People who were already favorably disposed toward business tended to see media bias against business, while those seeing bias in favor of business began with an unfavorable attitude toward business.[24]

Further indication that "bias is in the eye of the beholder" comes from a 1982 public opinion poll that asked upper-level business executives their opinions of news media reporting of business activities. Television news was roundly criticized for being antibusiness by three out of four executives, but radio, newspapers, news magazines, and business magazines were thought to be either probusiness or neutral in their reports. Those executives who saw the greatest amount of antibusiness reporting were from industries that had been in the public spotlight as a result of public policy controversies.

Although media representatives may square off against business on specific issues, they do not question the fundamental principles of free enterprise. As noted in one study of newspaper editors:

> The newspaper business editors surveyed are not only positively disposed toward capitalism in an absolute sense; as a group they are more favorably disposed toward capitalism than is the general public. . . . [T]he generalized perception that the news media are biased against business (and capitalism) is probably too simplistic and requires further research and refinement.[25]

Another well-qualified television observer said, ". . . if television is unkind to businessmen, it is scarcely unkind to the values of a business civilization. Capitalism and the consumer society come out largely uncontested."[26]

The Fairness Doctrine

As one way of trying to assure that all sides of an issue are made available to the public, the FCC developed and enforces the "Fairness Doctrine." The

[23]Fred J. Evans, "Management and the Media: Is Accord in Sight? The Conflict Surveyed," *Business Forum*, Spring 1984, p. 18. For a related discussion, see Stanley Rothman and S. Robert Lichter, "Media and Business Elites: Two Classes in Conflict?" *The Public Interest*, Fall 1982, pp. 117–125.

[24]Robert A. Peterson, George Kozmetsky, and Isabella C. M. Cunningham, "Perceptions of Media Bias Toward Business," *Journalism Quarterly*, Autumn 1982, pp. 461–464.

[25]Robert A. Peterson, Gerald Albaum, George Kozmetsky, and I. C. M. Cunningham, "Attitudes of Newspaper Business Editors and the General Public Toward Capitalism," *Journalism Quarterly*, Spring 1984, p. 65.

[26]Gitlin, op. cit., pp. 69–70.

doctrine consists of rules requiring broadcasters who air controversial topics of broad public interest to give opponents an opportunity to respond. It also permits a person who is attacked or criticized in the media an opportunity to reply. This rule is not the same as the "equal access" rule discussed earlier, which requires political candidates to be given equal media time to promote their views to the voting public.

The Fairness Doctrine has been used by opponents of nuclear power to tell their side of the story after programs favorable to nuclear power plants have been broadcast. Stations also have been required to provide broadcast time to consumer groups who opposed media-advertised rate increases for public utilities. The idea in all such cases is to give the listening or viewing public both sides of an issue of public importance so they can make up their minds without unbalanced influence from the interested parties.

The broadcasting industry has opposed the Fairness Doctrine as an unwarranted restriction of their First Amendment free-speech rights of expression. The original reason for the doctrine was the need to prevent a handful of licensed stations from abusing their power to influence the public. But opponents say that this condition no longer exists, because greater numbers of stations and an increasing diversity of broadcast technology now bring many diverse points of view to the public. As one veteran observer of the industry said, "Just count the number of newspapers in your city and compare it to the number of cable channels on your TV set. . . . If a broad exchange of views is your goal, it had better be done on television."[27] Still others say that the doctrine actually diminishes the amount of broadcast time devoted to important public issues because stations know they will be forced to provide opponents an opportunity to reply.

In the deregulation climate of the 1980s, the FCC's chairman advocated elimination of the Fairness Doctrine, and a 1986 federal court ruling stated that the doctrine was not required by law but was only a discretionary power of the FCC. In August 1987, the FCC voted to abolish the Fairness Doctrine, but the doctrine's supporters hoped that Congress would reinstate the rule by making it a law.[28]

The Free Speech Issue

The free speech issue is about how to find a balance between the media's Constitutional right to free expression and business's desire to be fairly and accurately depicted in media presentations, as well as to present its views on controversial public issues. (Of course, the free speech issue also affects other groups in society, but our discussion focuses on business.)

The press in the United States is a "free press," meaning that it operates under explicit Constitutional protections. The First Amendment to the Con-

---

[27]Thomas Garbett, "The Issue of Issue Ads," *Public Relations Journal*, October 1986, p. 33.

[28]Bob Davis, "Senate Clears Way for Fairness Doctrine Covering Broadcasting to Be Made Law," *Wall Street Journal*, April 22, 1987, p. 14; and *Wall Street Journal*, August 5, 1987, p. 29.

stitution says, in part, "Congress shall make no law . . . abridging the freedom of speech, or of the press. . . ." State governments also are prohibited, under the due process clause of the Fourteenth Amendment, from passing laws that impair free speech or interfere with a free press. Although these Constitutional provisions are subject to continual interpretation and reinterpretation by government regulators, by the courts, and by general public opinion, their fundamental meaning does not change through time. Constitutional free-press guarantees mean that the privately owned, profit-seeking media are free to print, broadcast, and distribute messages to the general public without getting authorization from government officials.

Defenders of the media say that freedom of expression, even when the result is negative or unfavorable to business, is a vital part of maintaining a free and open society. As one author stated, "The services of the media as advocate and adversary are considered to be among the most important in the democratic scheme and probably are the chief reasons for the free-press guarantee of the First Amendment."[29]

Another media scholar defended the media's searching inquiry about business conduct in this way:

> If business could conduct its affairs in a society that had a controlled press, the only news that would be made public would be that presently found in house organs, annual reports, company brochures, and speeches by executives. Management could comfortably go about its business without revealing anything that might in any way be legally damaging. But the qualities of our society and the protection of public interest which all of us—business executives as well as reporters—hold especially dear would be jeopardized.[30]

The contrasting business point of view is that the media's right to free speech is not the same as an ordinary citizen's right of expression. The media are enormously influential in shaping public attitudes toward business. For example, a single episode of *60 Minutes* can be very damaging to a company's reputation, particularly when an edited script or tape omits a vital part of the company's viewpoint. When the media disseminate messages to the public, those messages cannot be called back. They enter the public domain where they create impressions, encourage certain attitudes, and inculcate various values. *Therefore, business says, the media have an overarching responsibility to be fair, balanced, and accurate in their portrayals of business if they are to be justified in retaining their Constitutional rights to freedom of expression.*

Another free-speech issue occurs when corporations try to express their opinions on controversial questions of public policy, such as the size of the national debt or import restrictions. Government regulators and the United States Supreme Court have ruled that "commercial speech"—that is, the kind that appears in commercial advertisements—is not protected by the First

---

[29]Lester A. Sobel (ed.), *Media Controversies*, New York: Facts on File, 1981, p. 15.

[30]David Finn, "The Media as Monitor of Corporate Behavior," in Aronoff, op. cit., p. 125.

Amendment guarantee of free speech. The three major television networks have therefore usually refused during the prime-time viewing period to run "public issue" advertisements from corporations because they believe the Fairness Doctrine would require them to give free air time to groups holding opposing views. However, most other media, including cable television, independent broadcasting stations, radio stations, newspapers, and magazines, accept public-issue advertisements from corporations.

CORPORATE MEDIA STRATEGIES

To be effective in communicating with the public—which means getting the corporation's viewpoint across to key stakeholders—companies can take action on three fronts.

Managing Public Affairs and Public Relations

The most fundamental media strategy for any corporation is to design and manage an effective public affairs and public relations program. Chapters 4 and 5 in this book describe the major features of the public affairs function in today's socially responsive corporations. As pointed out in those chapters, an effective public affairs approach includes social awareness through environmental scanning, a proactive or interactive social strategy, an issues-management approach, the use of stakeholder mapping and analysis, active participation in the public policy process, and an open attitude toward the company's major stakeholders and the changing social scene. When a company has done these things, it has taken the first important steps to communicate with a wide range of audiences. On the other hand, a company that waits until a public-issue crisis, such as a chemical spill, is on its hands has waited too long. By then it is too late to learn how to deal with outsiders, and the company probably will be unable to get its position clearly stated and understood.

Once a company has developed and implemented a strong public affairs program, it can turn its attention to specific relations with the media on a variety of issues that may arise from time to time. It can then view the media as a positive force that enables the company to communicate with the public. A well-run public relations program prepares and sends out through the media a steady stream of positive messages to its key stakeholders such as stockholders, the financial community, and customers. These positive messages, along with the relationships they establish with external groups, can help counteract negative or inaccurate media reports and impressions.

Advocacy advertising is another way to get a corporate viewpoint into the media. The most famous example is Mobil Corporation's vigorous and sometimes provocative advocacy ads on a broad range of public issues; they appear in national-circulation newspapers as statements of the company's views which frequently are at odds with editorial opinions and government policies.[31]

Crisis Management

Crisis management is another approach that has proved effective for some companies. *Crisis management generally means that a company has created an internal task force or some similar group to devote full time to handling any serious crisis that may arise unexpectedly.* A media-contact person is a key member of the crisis management team, and contingency plans are made beforehand on how media relations are to be handled during the emergency period.

A good example of effective crisis management is seen in Johnson & Johnson's handling of the Tylenol poisoning episodes in 1982 and 1986.

> *Johnson & Johnson's CEO created a crisis management team consisting of top managers, including the vice president of public relations. In addition, personnel at several levels of the company set aside their normal duties and did what was necessary to recall the capsules. The company hired an outside firm to help it with media relations, and during the days immediately following the deaths of several poison victims the company launched a vigorous effort to give the public full details.*

A contrasting example of ineffective crisis management and poor media relations occurred during the Bhopal disaster in India when thousands were killed and injured by a chemical leak at a plant owned by Union Carbide Corporation.

> *Because the accident occurred so far from company headquarters in Connecticut and because communication was very difficult due in part to the chaos and confusion caused by the accident, the company tended to be overly cautious in its relations with the media. An impression was created that the company was not being forthright about the accident's cause or the company's accountability. Its hasty action in sending Union Carbide's CEO to Bhopal to give immediate relief to the victims proved to be a public relations mistake when Indian authorities arrested him and advised him to leave the country for his own safety. By not having an effective crisis management team ready to respond to an emergency of this magnitude and by not dealing effectively with the media, Union Carbide lost credibility with the public.[32]*

[31]See "Mobil Oil Corporation: Advocacy Advertising," in Rogene A. Buchholz, William D. Evans, and Robert A. Wagley, *Management Response to Public Issues*, Englewood Cliffs, NJ: Prentice-Hall, 1985, pp. 186–199. For another comprehensive case study, including many samples of advocacy ads, see "Bethlehem Steel Corporation: Advocacy or Idea/Issue Advertising Campaign," in S. Prakash Sethi, *Up Against the Corporate Wall*, 4th ed., Englewood Cliffs, N.J.: Prentice-Hall, 1982, pp. 162–205.

[32]For other examples and a general discussion, see Marion K. Pinsdorf, *Communicating When Your Company Is Under Siege: Surviving Public Crisis*, Lexington, Mass.: D. C. Heath, 1987; Ian I. Mitroff and Ralph H. Kilmann, *Corporate Tragedies: Product Tampering, Sabotage, and Other Catastrophes*, New York: Praeger, 1984.

Media Training for Employees

A third step corporations can take to develop successful relations with the media is to give media training to executives and others in the company who are likely to have contact with the media.

Media training is necessary because communicating with the media is not the same as talking with friends or coworkers. As a company representative, an employee is normally assumed to be speaking for the company or is expected to have special knowledge of company activities. Under these circumstances, the words one speaks take on a special, "official" meaning. In addition, news reporters sometimes "ambush" an executive, asking penetrating or embarrassing questions and expecting instant answers. Even in more deliberate news interviews, the time available for responding to questions is limited to a few seconds. Moreover, facial expressions, the tone of one's voice, and "body language" can convey both positive and negative impressions.

Many large corporations, such as Mobil, General Motors, and Bank of America, routinely send a broad range of their employees to special courses to improve their media skills. Media communication experts generally give their clients the following advice:

- Resist the temptation to see reporters and journalists as an enemy. It is better and more accurate to accept them as professionals with a job to do. Most of the time, their main interest is to get information that will help them write a news report.
- Resist the temptation to avoid the media. It is better, even in the most difficult situations, to establish positive contacts with media representatives. Withdrawing into a shell of silence tends to generate suspicion that the company has something to hide.
- "Honesty is the best policy" tends to be the wisest long-run media strategy. Not only does this attitude create a positive impression but it avoids embarrassment at a later time if new and different information becomes available to the company or the media.
- Employees facing the media should be well informed about company actions and policies and determined to put that point of view across, rather than falling victim to a reporter's or an interviewer's own agenda.[33]

When *media training* is linked with *crisis management* and *an institutionalized public affairs and public relations function*, a company has an improved chance of managing its affairs with the media in positive, rewarding ways that will benefit the firm's overall strategies and goals.[34]

[33]Mary Munter, "Managing Public Affairs: How to Conduct a Successful Media Interview," *California Management Review*, Summer 1983, pp. 143–150; and "Learning to Shine in the Limelight," *Business Week*, July 7, 1986, pp. 88–89.

[34]For a discussion of corporate strategies for coping with media coverage of product liability lawsuits, see Christopher P. A. Komisarjevsky, "Trial by Media," *Business Horizons*, January–February 1983, pp. 36–43.

SOCIAL RESPONSIBILITY GUIDELINES FOR THE MEDIA AND MEDIA SPONSORS

The public expects the media to exhibit a high level of social responsibility for two basic reasons.

The first reason is the awesome power of the media to influence culture, politics, business, social groups, and individual behavior. Media technology reaches into every corner of society and into the inner recesses of human consciousness. No other form of technology is so subtle and insidious in influencing human affairs.

Social and ethical responsibilities also arise from the potential clash of commercial motives and society's traditional values. The media's need for high ratings and large circulation figures may at times allow cherished human and social values to be overridden, ignored, or diminished.

The media's great potential for being a positive force in society is most likely to be realized if the media and their commercial sponsors try to observe the following social responsibility guidelines.

- Balance media power with an equal amount of responsibility in all presentations. This broad relationship between power and responsibility is summed up in the Iron Law of Responsibility, which was described in Chapter 2. It applies with particular force to the media because they wield such potentially great influence on social values and individual behavior.
- Seek and present the truth accurately and professionally, while striving for a balanced view of controversial issues and events.
- Protect and preserve the privacy and dignity of individuals who are the subject of media coverage. The public's "right to know" needs to be balanced against the price paid by individuals whose privacy and personal dignity may be threatened by media presentations.
- Portray professional, social, and ethnic groups accurately, avoiding unfavorable stereotypical images that damage such groups' social acceptability. This principle applies to media images of business, as well as to those of ethnic minorities, religious groups, and others.
- Present the full spectrum of human values typical of a society, rather than emphasizing a narrow band of values that tends to distort social reality. Choices among a society's values can then be made with greater intelligence by the people themselves, instead of allowing the media to substitute their judgment for the public will.

SUMMARY

The media occupy a place of great significance in United States society. Collectively, they form a communication network that is capable of exerting great influence on public opinion, major institutions, and individual behavior. As a result of their influence and their Constitutional right of free speech, the media have a social and ethical obligation to be fair, accurate, and balanced.

One way that companies can offset some of the negative and inaccurate information about business that is found in the media is to establish comprehensive public affairs programs, crisis management capability, and media training of employees. Media relations then become an integral part of a company's strategy for coping with its environment and achieving its overall mission.

DISCUSSION AND REVIEW QUESTIONS

1. Why does this chapter say that television "is now the premier medium of communication in the United States?" Do you agree with the statement? Give your reasons.

2. Discuss media economics, and tell how commercial advertising, size of the media audience, and programming or publishing standards work together to determine program or media content. What is your response to the charge that the popular media must cater to the lowest common denominator of public taste in order to be economically successful?

3. Form teams of three or four students and observe prime-time television programs and commercials for one evening. Report to the class on the images of women, minorities, people of foreign origin, and business people that were protrayed in those programs and ads. Also indicate the general impressions conveyed about various occupations (including business), social values, violence, and other aspects of society. Tell whether these images and impressions seemed to be accurate and realistic. What is your group's overall judgment about these media images and their social impact?

4. Choose a presentation from any of the following media—radio programs, newspaper or magazine articles, music recordings, rock video, motion picture films, or theatrical drama—and identify the values that seem to be represented and promoted by the program, the music, or the article, as well as any commercial ad that may be part of the presentation. In your judgment, are the media messages about these particular values aimed at specific groups in society? What conclusions can you draw about their impact on society generally?

5. Tell how the Iron Law of Responsibility might be applied to the media. To what extent can the corporate media strategies discussed in this chapter help a company adhere positively to the Iron Law?

CRITICAL INCIDENT

All in Favor of a Bigger Public Debt, Please Say "Aye"

The television commercial produced by W. R. Grace & Co. was entitled "The Deficit Trials, 2017 A.D." It was described, in part, by the company's director of corporate advertising as follows:

Set three decades in the future, in a once majestic public hall, a haggard and remorseful old man faces an adolescent prosecutor and a rag-tag jury of youngsters, all intent on learning why nothing was done generations ago to protect them from the ravages of deficit spending.

"It was all going to work out somehow," explains the old man, "but no one was willing to make the sacrifices."

"Maybe so," says the youthful prosecutor, "but the numbers speak for themselves. In 1986, for example, the national debt had reached $2 trillion. Didn't that frighten you?"

The old man shrugs helplessly and asks, "Are you ever going to forgive us?"[35]

When Grace attempted to buy commercial time to screen the ad on the three national television networks, the company was turned down. The networks said the Grace ad fell into the category of controversial public issues, thus obligating the networks to provide free time for opposing points of view to be expressed. It was, according to the networks, the job of news professionals, not private corporations, to deal with controversial issues on national television.

Grace then purchased time for showing the ad on independent stations, cable systems, and on syndicated programs; and a group of 122 independent television stations even agreed to air the commercial as a public service and free of charge to the company. However, Grace wanted to reach network prime-time audiences which accounted for a much larger percentage of television viewers.

In adhering to the Fairness Doctrine, the networks were protecting themselves as well as their affiliated stations from complaints of unfairness and unbalanced programming. Additionally, they expressed the view that companies able to pay the large expenses of television advertising might gain an unfair advantage over those with opposing viewpoints who could not pay to have their messages broadcast. But Grace questioned this line of reasoning by pointing out that the ad was not considered to be controversial: "So far as we know, not once in the 10 months this commercial has been aired has anyone requested time to respond. Is the Grace ad controversial? Apparently the public doesn't think so."

Responding to the uproar that resulted from their rejection of the ad, CBS and ABC relented and agreed to run the ad, provided some changes were made. A phrase was dropped that alluded to a proposed Constitutional amendment requiring a balanced budget, which was a highly controversial matter that had generated considerable public discussion in Congress. CBS broadened its policy on issue ads to allow their acceptance if the ads did not express "explicit or implicit advocacy."

Grace's opinion was summed up in these words: "Democracy depends on citizens' having access to a free marketplace of ideas. We recognize and respect the First Amendment rights of the networks, and all we hoped was that they would respect our First Amendment rights to speak out." Another corporate executive agreed, saying that ". . . the objective of an informed audience making its own decisions in its own best interest is thwarted [by the networks' refusal to show the ad]. The public is the loser."

[35]"The Issue of Issue Ads," _Public Relations Journal,_ October 1986, pp. 30–33, 42–43. All other quotations appearing in this critical incident are from this article.

1. Assume you are an official at the NBC network who can decide whether or not to accept the modified Grace ad. Would you agree to run the ad? Consider the pros and cons, and then give reasons for your decision.

2. Review the question of commercial free speech that is raised by this critical incident. In your opinion, should Grace's "First Amendment rights to speak out," as they called them, be honored by the networks? What are the issues that need to be considered?   Yes

3. Imagine a situation in which a vitally important national-defense weapons system could be built only by increasing the national debt. Under those circumstances, would the Grace ad be likely to generate groups opposed to its underlying message of no deficit spending? If so, would the networks be justified in rejecting the ad on grounds of the Fairness Doctrine?

Chapter Sixteen

SCIENCE AND TECHNOLOGY: SOCIAL IMPACTS, ETHICAL BURDENS

Business is one of the major institutions through which new forms of science and technology are introduced into society. Computers and television alone have had huge impacts on people's lives, and genetic engineering promises many other changes that may improve as well as carry risks for the quality of life. Business's strong interest in improving productivity through scientific and technological innovations thus creates many difficult human problems while simultaneously enhancing the general quality of life in society.

CHAPTER OBJECTIVES

After reading this chapter, you should be able to

- Describe major features of technology
- Understand five major phases of technological and social development
- Identify the technological characteristics of an electronics-based society
- Assess the economic and social consequences of technological change
- Discuss business's need to consider the social and ethical impacts of technological change

Technology shows two sides to most societies. One side is highly beneficial and promising, as revealed in the following examples. By the mid-1980s the most technologically advanced societies had learned to:

- Store 4 million bits of information on a one-quarter-inch computer chip.
- Reshape genetic material to produce hormones, drugs, and new strains of plants and animals.
- Find deep-lying mineral deposits by three-dimensional computer imaging and space satellite transmissions.
- Double the productivity of some factories by use of automated robots and computer-guided assembly lines.

The other side of technology is sometimes threatening to individuals and society.

- The jobs of more than 40 million United States employees were affected by computer-based technology by the mid-1980s; some jobs were eliminated while others required more complex training; many traditional managers had a hard time adjusting to these new high-tech systems.
- One of the largest Middle Eastern oil-producing nations feared a religious and tribal backlash against the rapid modernization that was part of that country's industrialization.
- When a genetic engineering firm proposed to field-test an artificially produced genetic strain intended to reduce frost damage on crops, it was opposed by citizen activists who feared the possible long-term negative effects on the environment.

Civilization is in its greatest age of technological breakthrough, and both business and society are in the midst of a massive task of absorbing technology on a scale never before experienced. Technological change has become the *norm* instead of the exception. Because business has successfully applied new technology in the past, we expect that it will do so again, but this expectation should not blind us to the magnitude of the job. The statement from *Through the Looking Glass* is almost a truism for organizations in a technological society: "It takes all the running you can do, to keep in the same place."

This chapter discusses some of the characteristics and effects of technological change and business's involvement with it. Modern technology has given business new powers, but also new responsibilities, such as managing a more complex system and using technology in a way that enhances the quality of life.

ABUNDANT TECHNOLOGY

Throughout history technology has pressed onward like a glacier, overturning everything in its way and grinding all opposition into dust. Its unrelenting power has overcome all who tried to stand in its way. In early nineteenth-century England, for example, a band of unhappy workers known as *Luddites* challenged the Industrial Revolution by roaming the countryside, smashing machinery and burning factories. From their narrow viewpoint, machines were enemies taking away jobs and freedom and harming people. But the Luddites were soon overcome by the benefits brought by the same machinery they opposed. Their movement failed, much the same as their more modern successors did, such as the glassblowers who opposed glassmaking machinery. And we know now that they were largely mistaken about the broader significance of industrial technology. Though the Industrial Revolution created new and serious human problems for some people in society, it was a great advance in the history of civilization.

Technology continues to grow because of people themselves. Human beings, having tasted the fruit of knowledge, cannot suppress their desire for it. They forever seek to expand knowledge of their environment, probably because of the excitement of learning and their belief that more knowledge will help them control their environment.

Features of Technology

The dominant feature of technology is change and then more change. Technology forces change on people whether they are prepared for it or not. In modern society it has brought so much change that it creates what often is called *future shock,* which means that change comes so fast and furiously that it approaches the limits of human tolerance and people lose their ability to cope with it successfully. Although technology is not the only cause of change, it is the primary cause. It is either directly or indirectly involved in most changes that occur in society.

> *The computer is an example of fast change and the future shock that results from it.*[1] *In the forty years from the 1940s into the 1980s the computer dramatically changed business practice and required large numbers of people to learn new skills. Progress was astounding. Costs were halved and speed was doubled again, again, and again. One industry executive has estimated that if the automobile industry had made similar progress during those forty years, it would be able to offer a Rolls-Royce for $2.50 with a rating of 2 million miles per gallon of gasoline. Other industry executives estimate that in the next ten or twenty years computer performance could increase another 100, 500, or even 10,000 times.*

Another feature of technology is that its effects are widespread, reaching far beyond the immediate point of technological impact. Technology fans out through society until every community is affected by it. Its shock waves push their way into even the most isolated places. People cannot escape it. Even if they move to a mountaintop, it is still there, represented by airplanes and satellites flying overhead, radio signals moving with the speed of light, and industrial contaminants in the air.

---

[1]"Computing for Business in the 1980s," *Fortune,* June 5, 1978, unpaged special section.

An additional feature of technology is that it is self-reinforcing. As stated by Toffler, "Technology feeds on itself. Technology makes more technology possible."[2] This self-reinforcing feature means that technology acts as a multiplier to encourage its own faster development. It acts with other parts of society so that an invention in one place leads to a sequence of inventions in other places. Thus, invention of the wheel led rather quickly to perhaps a dozen or more applications. These applications, in turn, may have affected fifty other parts of the system and led to several additional inventions that similarly influenced society as multipliers.

> *The automobile serves as an example. It could not have been invented much earlier because hundreds of inventions had to precede it, such as improvements in metallurgy, vulcanization of rubber, electrical generation for spark plugs, and refining of crude oil. Once these inventions existed, the automobile almost had to be invented, because there was a market for faster transportation than horses and bicycles and for more individualized transportation than the faster trains offered.*
>
> *When the technological breakthrough of the automobile did occur, its effects were pervasive throughout society. It has a profound effect on the whole ecological system. It changed the living habits of people, including their buying habits, the location of their homes, their independence, and their patterns of courtship. It increased the number of supermarkets and helped create drive-in movies. It expanded land areas allocated to roads, increased traffic to wilderness areas, and added pollution to the air. By means of the truck, it altered shipping patterns and manufacturing locations. Hardly any area of society remained untouched by the automobile.*

The same principle holds for the computer, for television, for organ transplant technology, for genetic engineering, and for many other forms of modern science and technology. Once started, they spread their effects widely and persistently throughout society.

Business Applies Technology

As soon as new knowledge exists, people want to apply it in order to reap its benefits. At this point business becomes important, because *business is the principal institution that translates discovery into application for public use.* Printing, manufacturing, housing, education, and television are all dependent on business activities to make them work productively. Society depends on business to keep the stream of discovery flowing into useful goods and services for all people. Less-developed nations have learned that scientific discoveries mean very little to them unless they have competent business systems to produce for their people what science has discovered. In a similar manner, developed nations have learned that their progress stops unless they operate an innovative business system that translates technological developments into useful goods and services for their people.

[2]Alvin Toffler, *Future Shock,* New York: Bantam, 1971, p. 26.

Technology	Phases in the Development of Technology	Approximate Period of Dominance in U.S.	Activity	Primary Skill Used
1	Nomadic–Agrarian	Until 1650	Harvests	Manual
2	Agrarian	1650–1900	Plants and harvests	Manual
3	Industrial	1900–1960	Builds material goods	Manual and machine
4	Service	1960–1975	Focuses on providing services	Manual and intellectual
5	Knowledge	1975–	Abstract work	Intellectual and electronic

FIGURE 16-1   Phases in the development of technology in the United States.

Phases of Technology and the Social Systems They Create

Looking at technology in a very general way, five broad phases of technology have developed, as shown in Figure 16-1. One phase at a time tends to dominate the work of a nation, and in so doing it has a major influence on that nation and creates its own distinct type of social system. Nations tend to move sequentially through each phase, beginning with the lowest technology and moving higher with each step, so the five phases of technology roughly represent the progress of civilization throughout history. Although one phase of technology tends to dominate a nation's activities at a particular time, other phases often will be practiced at the same time. The five phases are discussed in the following paragraphs.

Nomadic Society

In a nomadic society people live primarily by hunting, fishing, picking berries, and otherwise taking what nature has provided. Rather than producing more by planting and cultivating, they merely take what is available. They use a crude technology of spears, fishing hooks, and baskets, but their technology is poorly developed. Often they move as nomads to wherever a good natural harvest is available.

Agrarian Society

Eventually an agrarian society may develop in which people grow plants and raise animals for specific uses. *An agrarian society is one in which agricultural activities dominate work and employ the largest proportion of the labor force.* Most nations in the modern world still are primarily agrarian. More than 50 percent of their labor force is busy providing food for the population. These nations tend to remain at an agrarian level until they can develop enough productivity to release many of their labor force from the farm and employ them in other productive occupations.

Industrial Society

In the 1800s the United States began moving toward an industrial society, and it was clearly industrial by the early 1900s. *An industrial society is one in which the building and processing of material goods dominates work and employs the largest proportion of the labor force.* It is the natural result of the great Industrial Revolution, which originated in Britain, and it symbolically represents the materialism that social critics sometimes condemn.

When a nation progresses from an agrarian to an industrial technology, dramatic changes usually occur, as they did in the United States. Large factories develop because of economies of scale, and a large labor force is required. This new type of enterprise also makes management more necessary and important. People move off the farms and into the cities for higher wages, and congestion and pollution develop. Both the factories and the cities require large amounts of new capital, which leads to emphasis on capital formation. In addition, the changed living conditions, greater affluence, and new material goods produce new life-styles. Indeed, the move from an agrarian to an industrial society substantially changes a social system.

Service Society

Business was so successful in applying technology in factories that by the 1960s the United States became the world's first service society, sometimes called a postindustrial society.[3] The United States made remarkable technological progress by moving in less than one century from an agrarian to an industrial to a service society!

A service society is one in which the majority of the labor force is employed in industries, such as retailing, banking, health care, and insurance, that provide non-product values (service), rather than in direct production work, such as manufacturing, farming, and construction. In the United States, 70 percent of the working population works to provide services of one type or another, and services account for approximately one-half of gross national product and each family dollar spent.[4] In a service society the production of material goods is no longer the primary user of labor or the central economic and social problem.

Although no one can be sure what long-run changes a service society will bring, some possible changes can be mentioned based on preliminary experience with it. Until recently, it was thought that a service society's productivity would decline because much service work is labor-intensive and difficult to mechanize. By the mid-1980s, however, business was pouring millions of dollars into high-tech investments in the service sector, and these were expected to boost productivity sharply, perhaps by 2.5 percent annually. One knowledgeable observer said, "There is a revolution going on in

[3]This development was first discussed comprehensively by Daniel Bell, *The Coming of Post-Industrial Society,* New York: Basic Books, 1973, chap. 2. For a later analysis, see Alvin Toffler, *The Third Wave,* New York: Bantam, 1981.

[4]Daniel Bell, "The Third Technological Revolution," *Business Quarterly,* August 1982, pp. 33–37; and James D. Robinson III, "A Full Partnership for Services," *Business Week,* June 29, 1982, p. 15.

the service sector, in some ways akin to the U.S. industrial revolution of the last century."[5] Just how this revolution is occurring can be seen from the following illustrations.

> *Part of the job of running a national magazine distribution service is to tell magazine publishers how many of its magazines remain unsold when the next edition appears on the newsstand. In that way the distributor can be given credit for the unsold items. Recording such information by hand, even when using an electronic calculator, can be very time-consuming. One Philadelphia-based distributor installed 80 laser scanners, similar to those used in grocery stores, in its offices around the nation. The unsold magazines are passed across the laser scanner, doing the work in a fraction of a second and then filing the information for mailing to the publisher. The work is done quicker, more accurately, and with fewer employees, thereby increasing productivity.*
>
> *Similar gains were achieved by TRW's Electronics & Defense Sector division when it installed a computerized graphics design system. Engineers there were able to produce two to four times as many drawings with the new system as they had done previously by hand. Other gains were in the higher quality and reliability of their work, made possible by designing, simulating, and integrating the plans of different engineers working on different parts of a complex network.*

In fact, some expect gains of this kind to give the service sector a decided edge in productivity gain in future years. One experienced expert believes that "each $1,000 invested per service worker in the new technology is twice as productive as the same $1,000 invested per industrial worker in machine tools or conveyer belts." By 1990, he predicted that this advantage will double again.[6]

Knowledge Society

Knowledge is such a distinct phase of technology that, when it dominates a nation's work activities, it creates a different type of social system. *A knowledge society is one in which the use of knowledge and information, rather than manual skill, dominates work and employs the largest proportion of the labor force.* "Work becomes abstract, the electronic manipulation of symbols."[7] Examples of people in knowledge jobs are news editors, accountants, computer programmers, and teachers. Even the surgeon, who must use a delicate manual skill, is primarily working from a knowledge or intellectual base. Examples of knowledge industries are newspaper publishing, television, education, book publishing, telecommunication, and data processing.

It is estimated that the United States became the world's first knowledge society sometime in the 1970s. Since no nation has ever reached this tech-

[5]For this quotation and the following two examples, see "A Productivity Revolution in the Service Sector," *Business Week*, September 5, 1983, p. 106.

[6]Ibid.

[7]Shoshanah Zuboff, quoted in Jeremy Main, "Work Won't Be Same Again," *Fortune*, June 28, 1982, pp. 58–61, 64–65.

nological goal before, there are no specific guidelines learned from the experiences of others, but its effects are likely to be massive. As people move from manual work to information processing and intellectual work, there are substantial changes in life-styles, education, recreation, and living conditions.

A knowledge society's technology is primarily electronic in nature and is heavily dependent on the computer and the semiconductor silicon chip. The power of these devices rests on their ability to process, store, and retrieve large amounts of information with very great speed. By the early 1980s, technical advances had made possible a new generation of the microprocessor—called a computer on a chip—with vastly greater computing power than those that were first developed in the early 1970s. Intel Corporation, which pioneered the microprocessor, said that it could pack the power of a large mainframe computer on just three thumbnail-size silicon chips.[8] That opens up new areas of human work to computer applications, such as automated office workstations and robots that can recognize and learn to work with different parts on an assembly line. One source predicts that United States industry will have 100,000 factory robots by 1990 and that electronic workstations in offices and plants will increase from 4 million in the early 1980s to 25 or 30 million in 1990.[9]

Systems like these will indeed create "the factory of the future." As one authoritative source said, "With the integration of computer-aided design, computer-aided engineering, and computer-aided manufacturing, an order that comes in on Monday could be ready for shipment on Tuesday morning. The part would be designed on a video screen, automatically analyzed for performance and producibility, then electronically shipped off to an automated system on the shop floor." Although this picture might be more ideal than real in many present business locations, it suggests the potentialities for greatly increasing the competitive strength of United States businesses. As one expert put it, "I don't see any other hope for maintaining the industrial base and thus the standard of living in America."[10]

Another important difference concerning work appears in a knowledge society. In an industrial society, employees must go to a central location—an office, a factory, a laboratory, or a shop—where raw materials and machinery are combined with human skills to produce material products. But knowledge work, unlike industrial work, involves the manipulation of ideas and abstract symbols, not physical materials. So knowledge work can be performed in any location where the necessary information can be made available. Knowledge work can be brought to employees, rather than bringing the employees to a central workplace. The result is the emergence of telecommuting, a new work-at-home routine that taps labor pools not otherwise available to business.

For example, *Control Data Corporation installed computer terminals in the homes of 60 professional and managerial employees and allowed them to work*

[8]"A Mainframe on Three Chips," *Business Week*, March 2, 1981, pp. 116, 118.

[9]Main, op. cit., pp. 58–59.

[10]"High Tech to the Rescue," *Business Week*, June 16, 1986, p. 101.

there. Other companies have done the same for clerical and secretarial staff members. Walgreen, McDonald's, and Mountain States Telephone & Telegraph put terminals in the homes of handicapped personnel who could write computer programs without having to leave their homes. Nearly all 600 employees of one computer software firm work at home, and half of them use company-installed computer terminals.[11]

Telecommuting lowers a firm's real estate costs, provides more flexible work schedules for employees, reduces energy and transportation costs, and taps new sources of talented labor. One industry expert has predicted that as many as 10 million workers—nearly 10 percent of all jobs in the United States—may be telecommuting by the mid-1990s.[12] By 1986, telecommuting technology—office computers, portable computers, modems, electronic mailboxes, personal copiers, and overnight mail—made telecommuting possible for some 7 million Americans.[13]

Another energy- and time-saving way to bring information to employees is through the videoconference, which also is made possible by electronic technology.

Atlantic Richfield, a leading oil company, initially linked eight of its regional centers by means of a satellite network and planned to expand the system further. Two-way video teleconferencing among the company's managers in different locations eliminated the need for many time-consuming, energy-expensive trips. The system also provides electronic mail service, transmission of documents, and computer-to-computer data transfers. An overall saving of 20 percent of travel costs was predicted for the new communications network.[14] *Other companies have used videoconferencing to gain a competitive edge. Boeing linked executives, designers, and pilots together through four video centers to reduce production time on its 757 airliner. A Boeing executive said, "No other aircraft maker has developed video to this extent, so the timeliness of our decisions gives us a competitive advantage."*

A variation on the videoconference is the use of satellite networks to beam one-way messages from a central location—e.g., a company headquarters—to several receiving stations where customers view the program and telephone their orders in to the company. One Merrill Lynch satellite program experienced a 35 percent order rate from an audience of 30,000 potential customers; as a result the firm then planned to install the system in all 500 of its sales offices.[15]

These technological innovations are only a small part of a broad and potentially revolutionary social transformation occurring in many institutions

[11]"The Potential for Telecommuting," *Business Week,* January 26, 1981, pp. 94–103.

[12]Ibid.

[13]"These Top Executives Work Where They Play," *Business Week,* October 27, 1986, pp. 132, 134. For some of telecommuting's drawbacks, see Clare Ansberry, "When Employees Work at Home, Management Problems Often Arise," *Wall Street Journal,* April 20, 1987, p. 21.

[14]"ARCO's $20 Million Talk Network," *Business Week,* July 7, 1980, pp. 81–82.

[15]"Videoconferencing: No Longer Just a Sideshow," *Business Week,* November 12, 1984, pp. 116–120.

throughout the postindustrial world. Alvin Toffler has called this period of broad-scale social change "the Third Wave."[16] The First Wave of social change came with the rise and dominance of agriculture, a period that lasted from 8000 B.C. to A.D. 1650–1750, which indicates the time that phase dominated in the United States (see Figure 16-1). The rise of industrial civilization signaled the beginning of the Second Wave, which reached a peak in the mid-1950s, according to Toffler. The Third Wave is typical of all high-technology, service-oriented, knowledge-based societies. In each of these three major eras, human institutions and values have been shaped by underlying technological systems. The movement of society from one major period to another often is painful and confusing, owing to the lag that occurs between people's accustomed ways of thinking and acting and the new conditions created by new forms of technology. We examine some of the economic and social effects of Third Wave technology in the following sections.

SOME ECONOMIC EFFECTS OF TECHNOLOGY

Higher Productivity

Perhaps the most fundamental effect of technology is greater productivity in terms of both quality and quantity. This is the main reason that most technology is adopted. In a hospital the objective may be qualitative, such as maintaining life with electronic monitoring equipment regardless of costs. In a factory the objective may be quantitative in terms of more production for less cost.

> *An example is General Electric's highly automated locomotive plant in Erie, Pennsylvania. Before being equipped with computers, robots, and other advanced machines, it took sixty-eight skilled machine operators sixteen days to build one locomotive motor frame. The new factory can produce a frame in one day, with no human workers at all—except someone to take the frame away when the computer is satisfied with the work.*[17]

Automated factories are made possible by computers and the extensive use of robots that can perform many work functions, such as welding, spray painting, assembling parts, and machining operations. Even before a factory begins production, computer-aided design (CAD) systems can design and test new products on a computer screen, thus eliminating the need for blueprinting and the production of prototypes. United States business firms,

---

[16]Toffler, op. cit. For a similar view of social trends increasingly typical of advanced societies, see John Naisbitt, *Megatrends: Ten New Directions Transforming Our Lives*, New York: Warner, 1982.

[17]William D. Marbach et al., "The Factory of the Future," *Newsweek*, September 6, 1982, p. 69. For other examples, see Otto Friedrich, "The Robot Revolution," *Time*, December 8, 1980. pp. 72–83.

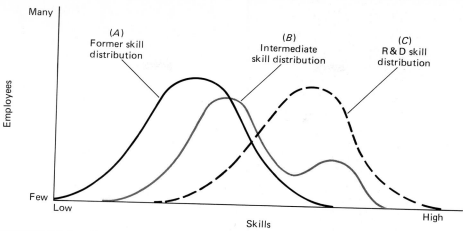

FIGURE 16-2 Changes in the skill distribution in a business required by advances in technology.

faced with increasing competition from abroad, are expected to invest growing amounts of money in these "factories of the future" by 1990. Their survival may depend on it. As one business executive said, "U.S. business has three choices in the '80s: automate, emigrate—or evaporate."[18]

Upgraded Job Skills

With the advance of technology, jobs tend to become more intellectual and otherwise upgraded. The job that once required a day laborer now requires a skilled crane operator, and the job that formerly required a clerk now requires a computer expert. A generation ago the typical factory had a range of skills approaching curve A shown in Figure 16-2. This curve was shaped like the normal curve of intelligence among people. Being matched to people, it suggested that an adequate supply of labor would be available at all levels of business in the long run.

In modern business the curve has moved toward the right, higher in skill, as shown in curve B. And in many organizations the skill distribution has become biomodal, as shown by the second top on the curve. Many scientific and professional people are required in research, development, planning, and other specialized work, creating the secondary bulge toward the skilled end of the scale.

Curve C represents the skill distribution that is developing in firms oriented toward research and development. Even though these firms manufacture products for sale, much of their effort is devoted to development and to building a small number of complex products. In some of these firms the number of engineers, scientists, and college graduate specialists exceeds the total number of other employees.

[18]Ibid.

The nature of technology is that it creates jobs that many people are not yet prepared to fill. The bargain that technology strikes with workers is to take away one job and offer them another one, usually requiring higher ability, for which they may not be qualified. It places a burden of training and education on the employee, the firm, and the nation. The poorly educated, the aged, and other marginal employees are the first to be dislocated, but they are usually the ones least able to adjust. Society faces the immense task of motivating and aiding these persons, for without help they become the long-term unemployed and the "untrainables."

More Scientific and Professional Workers

The increased number of intellectual workers represented by curves *B* and *C* in Figure 16-2 has placed new responsibilities on business for managing the creative spirit, which is sometimes called "maverick management." Historically, scientists have worked in small laboratories at their own pace, usually in an academic setting, but more and more they are working for big organizations, both private and public. Most certainly they perform best in a work culture different from that of the assembly line.

Creative and intellectual workers expect relatively high job freedom. They are motivated by opportunities that offer change, growth, and achievement. They are less motivated by expectations of higher formal authority than by their own professional interests and perceptions of opportunities. Their orientation is *cosmopolitan,* toward their profession and the world outside their organization, rather than *local,* depending primarily on the reward structure of the firm itself. Although they are a part of the company work culture, they are just as much a part of a separate scientific culture operating beyond their organization's boundaries. Under these conditions they may have an organizational rootlessness that tends to increase job mobility.

Business is adjusting its supervisory practices to meet needs of intellectual workers. Some companies have established dual promotion ladders so that distinguished technical people can rise to ranks and receive salaries that are equivalent to those of managers. Flexible work schedules are allowed. Profit sharing is provided to give creative persons a financial stake in the ideas they create and to discourage their rootlessness. Attendance at professional meetings and writing professional articles are supported. In further response to intellectual workers' cosmopolitan interests, they are allowed to teach part time or are given special assignments.

Technostructure

Scientific and other specialized workers make up the *technostructure* of modern organizations and exert much influence on decision-making processes. This condition exists regardless of the pattern of authority shown on the organization chart. According to John Kenneth Galbraith the technostructure "embraces all who bring specialized knowledge, talent, or experience to group decision-making. This, not the management, is the guiding intelligence—the brain—of the enterprise."[19] Technostructure is a convenient term, although a broad one, for emphasizing the pervasive influence of technology and specialization in organizations.

Since the majority within the technostructure of most organizations are likely to be technically trained persons, care must be taken to assure that they do not become a _technical elite_ dominating business and social decisions. They are the experts concerning the technical feasibility of their proposals. Their expertise in this area cannot be questioned, so they may become impatient with people who stand in the way of a technically feasible project. However, their expertise may be the factor that limits their broader view of social effects. Business managers, therefore, have a responsibility to assess pluralistic views _within_ the firm, as well as viewpoints from stakeholder groups outside the firm, when making decisions about the use of technology. Decisions concerning technological changes are broad social decisions rather than narrow technological decisions. This requires socially responsive decision making by socially conscious managers.

More Emphasis on Research and Development

As technology has advanced, research and development (R&D) has become a giant new activity in organizations. _Research_ concerns the creation of new ideas, and _development_ concerns their useful application. Effective management of R&D is important because R&D brings social benefits through increased productivity. With the world's exploding population and the needs of less-developed nations, society requires the material and social gains that R&D can provide. Society also depends on R&D to find ways to reduce pollution and otherwise improve the quality of life. Just how rapidly R&D has grown is depicted in Figure 16-3.

R&D has become so important in some companies that it is ranked along with production and sales as a primary activity. No longer do companies only produce goods and sell them. With accelerated technology, many companies now develop goods, produce them, and sell them. Research and development becomes a major department, having as many employees as either production or sales. Its salary budget is similarly large, and it assumes an active voice in the councils of top management. The traditional industrial order of priorities may shift from production to R&D. The assumption is that new products must be developed in order to keep abreast of competition and that if something useful can be developed, production and sales will follow normally. R&D, therefore, becomes the key to market leadership in many situations. A number of companies can show that 25 to 50 percent of their revenues today are from products not even produced ten years ago.

Capital Requirements

Another effect of technology is its insatiable demand for capital. Large amounts of capital are required to build the enormous production systems

---

[19]John Kenneth Galbraith, _The New Industrial State_, Boston: Houghton Mifflin, 1967, p. 71.

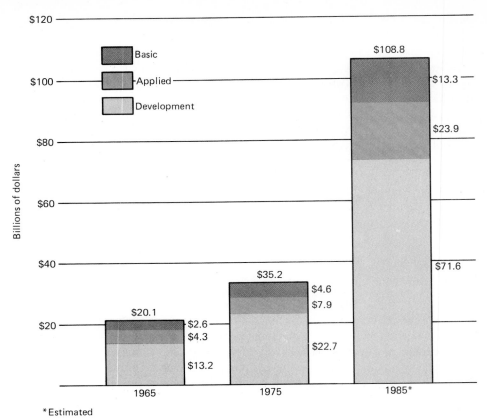

FIGURE 16-3   Domestic R&D spending in the United States, 1965, 1975, 1985. *(Source: "Funding Research: An Overview," Wall Street Journal, November 10, 1986, p. D-5. Used with permission.)*

that save labor time and provide other benefits of technology. At the turn of the century, an investment of $1,000 for each worker often was adequate in a factory, but modern investments in pipelines and petroleum refining exceed $200,000 for each worker.

Capital needs become staggering when considered in terms of new jobs. Assuming a moderate average investment of only $30,000 for each worker and using forecasts of 20 million new jobs needed in the United States in fifteen years, *$600 billion* of new capital is needed. This figure does not include expenditures for capital replacement to keep the existing labor force employed. These developments require business to generate large amounts of capital and engage in more long-range planning and budgeting for capital use. It also is necessary for government to establish public policies that encourage business to generate adequate capital for needed jobs.

SOCIAL CONSEQUENCES OF TECHNOLOGICAL CHANGE

Technological advances bring both benefits and costs to society. Over long historical epochs, human society has been carried to supreme heights of material progress and accomplishment by technology and by technology's handmaiden, science. The five phases of technological development summarized in Figure 16-1 illustrate the progressive steps toward material betterment that human society has taken. Economic growth—driven by the engine of technological progress—has conferred wide benefits on humankind: supporting larger populations at higher levels of living; extending individual life spans; and expanding a whole range of human potentialities for both individuals and entire societies. Various fields of endeavor—medicine and health care, engineering, transportation, communication, computational analysis, and many others—exhibit obvious progress and improvement of technique.

Social Costs

However, in the same way that a lifesaving antibiotic may have side effects, technology also has social side effects. When they are negative, they become social costs. From society's point of view these social costs need to be calculated in the cost-benefit analysis of every proposed technological change. Very often some of these social costs are overlooked because the persons who work with technology do not think broadly enough of its social effects. However, even among the broadest thinkers, these effects frequently are not predictable. There is not even agreement concerning whether some technological changes will result in net social costs or social benefits.

Technology assessment is a useful technique that seeks to provide feedback about technology's effects and to try to anticipate the unintended, indirect, and possibly harmful effects of new technology. The Office of Technology Assessment was created by Congress in 1972 to undertake studies of this type in projects involving government funding.

A fact frequently overlooked is that technology can be used to correct side effects that exist. It is not unidirectional; it can be corrective as well as causative. For example, technology does cause pollution; however, technology also can be used to reduce pollution from both machine and human activities. Technology does contribute to urban blight, but it can be used to increase beauty and make it easier for people to live in cities. It already has done so. For example, the smoke from one electric generating plant serving 100,000 homes is much less than the smoke from fireplaces in a similar number of homes in earlier days—and it can be better controlled. Further, the waste from one city sewage plant is much less damaging than the waste, odors, and disease in cities without sewer facilities.

Biotechnology—A New Scientific Frontier

A good illustration of the problems associated with new scientific and technological breakthroughs is the emerging field known as "biotechnology" or "genetic engineering." Neither of these terms is very precise, but in general they refer to a cluster of new techniques that enable scientists to combine knowledge from various areas of science—such as biochemistry, genetics, microbiology, ecology, recombinant DNA, and others—with practical applications in medicine, industry, farming, and other areas of human life.[20] Some of the results are truly startling and revolutionary, as the following examples illustrate.

> *Newly engineered forms of bacteria have been introduced into experimental crops to protect them from herbicides that are used to control insect damage. Other genetically engineered crops include soybeans with a built-in immunity to diseases, wheat designed for the special needs of commercial bakers, and tomatoes with traits that make them especially suitable for canning. Growth hormones are used to promote animal growth and production; one estimate claims that this technique might increase United States milk production by 20 percent. By stimulating growth by these artificial means, commercial farmers could save vast sums of money on feed costs. Another company has engineered changes in a bacterium that clings to the roots of crop plants to increase its ability to convert nitrogen into food for the plant.*
>
> *Still other advances combine science and technology to perform tasks that improve human judgment. Computers now direct fertilizer spreaders to read a soil map and change the nutrient mixture as they roll across farmland; the savings are expected to be from $5 to $15 per acre in reduced fertilizer costs and increased crop yields. Another computer-directed system uses sensors buried in the soil to calculate the precise amount of irrigation water and fertilizers needed; by preventing overwatering and overfertilizing, the farmer reduces costs and increases productivity.[21]*

No one doubts the *end-use benefits* of these new scientific and technological advances. The trouble comes when the economic and social consequences are calculated. Boosting milk production by using growth hormones is fine, but it may force from 10 percent to 25 percent of dairy farmers out of business since fewer farms will be able to produce all the milk needed. The congressional Office of Technology Assessment predicted in 1986 that about 1 million farms—in other words, nearly half the total in the United States—would disappear by the end of the century, leaving only 50,000 large farms to produce three-quarters of foodstuffs. So the small farmer may vanish from the social scene, the victim of a scientific revolution intended to improve the quality of life for all.[22]

Other fears involve environmental dangers. While herbicide-resistant crops promise higher yields by clearing weeds, their availability may lead to showering the land with an even greater load of chemicals. Environmentalists

[20]Henry I. Miller and Frank E. Young, "Biotechnology: A 'Scientific' Term in Name Only," *Wall Street Journal,* January 13, 1987, p. 32.

[21]For these and other examples, see Wendy L. Wall, "Here a Chip, There a Chip. . . ," *Wall Street Journal,* November 10, 1986, pp. 31D–32D; and "Biotechnology Down on the Farm: The Coming Cornucopia," *Business Week,* September 15, 1986, pp. 180–184.

[22]Wall, op. cit.

Issue	Approve (%)	Disapprove (%)	Not Sure (%)
Use of genetic engineering to cure people with fatal diseases	64	24	12
Pre-employment genetic testing by employers	11	86	3
Employer's refusal to hire someone shown by genetic testing to be susceptible to a serious disease	15	82	3
Employer's right to use genetic test results to bar employees from certain kind of jobs	35	61	4
Life and health insurance companies' use of genetic test results to refuse to insure persons likely to develop a fatal disease later in life	21	75	4

FIGURE 16-4   Public attitudes toward genetic engineering and business uses of genetic testing. (*Source: Adapted from "Business Week/Harris Poll: It's OK to 'Play God'—within Limits,"* Business Week, *November 18, 1985, p. 85. Used with permission.*)

claim that herbicides potentially dangerous to human health have leaked into the water tables of many major farm states.

But the biggest worries surrounding biotechnology and genetic engineering focus on the uncontrolled release of these human-produced genetic forms into the environment where they may cause unpredictable harmful results. For example, an engineered bacterium intended to build disease immunity into a plant might also accidentally kill off a beneficial insect. Nature's sometimes tightly knit ecological systems could possibly be upset and irreversibly damaged by infiltrating them with human-engineered genetic units. Although the bulk of United States scientists appear to favor continued experiments and carefully controlled environmental uses of genetically engineered materials, the controversy is likely to continue. Figure 16-4 reveals that the general public also is on the side of pushing ahead with genetic engineering but that it wants strong curbs on the possible uses of these new techniques.

The biotechnology revolution has produced environmental activists strongly opposed to many of these innovations favored by business. One of the best known is Jeremy Rifkin—some of his critics call him a Ralph Nader clone!—who has successfully tied up a number of proposed experiments by bringing lawsuits against government regulators and genetic engineering firms. He and others have formed coalitions of various stakeholder groups, ranging from members of the Humane Society who oppose genetic engineering on animal genes, to religious leaders who object to using human reproductive cells for such experiments. Rifkin answers his critics by saying, "I'm asking the fundamental economic, social and ethical questions that should be asked first, rather than waiting for the damage."[23]

---

[23]"Rifkin's Vow: 'We Will Not Be Cloned,' " *Business Week,* May 26, 1986, p. 56. See also *Conservation Exchange,* Winter 1986–1987, for a discussion of the pros and cons of biotechnology.

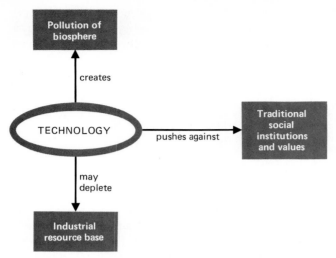

FIGURE 16-5   Three major factors capable of limiting technological development.

Restraints on Technological Growth

Students of technology have identified three major factors that may limit technology's ability to contribute positively to society, as depicted in Figure 16-5.

- *Pollution.* Pollution is an unavoidable consequence of industrial production since waste by-products are produced along with useful things. In addition, many consumer items—for example, automobiles—are themselves responsible for much pollution; and sooner or later, all manufactured goods wear out and are discarded as useless.

  The biosphere—the land, air, water, and natural conditions on which all life on earth depends—can absorb and recycle many of these industrial contaminants without harm to plants or animals. But the biosphere is not an infinite sponge. Its absorptive and recycling power may be overtaxed when a single society concentrates its industrial technology and industrial products too densely in one region. The Los Angeles urban area frequently exhibits this kind of environmental overloading when industrial operations and automobile emissions clog the air. It is even conceivable, as some observers have thought, that the globe's ability to industrialize its poorer regions is limited by the load of pollutants that would then be injected into the biosphere. One answer to this potential obstacle to further technological development is to invent and use new and less polluting forms of technology and energy.

- *The industrial resource base.* A second factor limiting technological growth is the possible depletion of the world's industrial resource base. This base is composed mainly of minerals, various forms of energy, water supplies, a skilled labor force, and human knowledge. Some studies have questioned whether the globe's supplies of reasonably priced minerals, energy, and water are sufficient to support unlimited industrial and technological expansion.

Two offsetting forces, however, give a brighter picture of the future. Technological ingenuity keeps finding ways to dig deeper, explore more surely, retrieve minerals more economically, and use what is found more efficiently. The other positive force is human knowledge itself, which one observer has said is the only part of the industrial resource base that keeps expanding with no apparent finite limits.[24] Finding imaginative ways to harness that human knowledge to new and more economical forms of technology is a likely path to the future.

- *Social institutions.* A third factor limiting technology is social values and institutions that may be inconsistent with the full productive potential that is present in technology.

  An example is seen in Western Australia where aborigines prevented two international mining companies from drilling for oil at a spot considered sacred by the tribal group. According to their tribal legends, the spirit of a giant sacred serpent lies sleeping under the ground where the oil was discovered. Australian labor unions supported aboriginal demands to halt drilling by boycotting the site and threatening to blacklist all other mining operations of the two companies. Anthropologists estimate that Western Australia may have as many as 200,000 sacred sites like this one, thereby posing a considerable problem for mining and drilling operations there.[25]

Many societies, perhaps most of those that adopt modern technology, encounter similar but less dramatic problems in arriving at a fit between their traditional social institutions and the routines dictated by new technology.

BUSINESS RESPONSIBILITY FOR TECHNOLOGICAL CHANGE

In a broad general sense, business has served as society's designated agent responsible for developing new technology. Whether one thinks of Henry Ford's Model T car or today's microprocessor chip, private enterprise has led the way in introducing new technology for human use. In the United States, the public has expected and wanted business to perform this function; and it has praised business for enriching and elevating human life and experience in all the material ways made possible by technology: higher living standards,

---

[24]Carl H. Madden, *Clash of Culture: Management in an Age of Changing Values*, Washington, D.C.: National Planning Association, 1972, pp. 20–28, 48–60. See also Julian L. Simon, *The Ultimate Resource*, Princeton, N.J.: Princeton University Press, 1981.

[25]"The Spirit of a Serpent Stalls a Mining Project," *Business Week*, October 27, 1980, pp. 69, 73. For a similar episode, see Geraldine Brooks, "Giant Mining Project in Papua New Guinea Is Beset by Calamities," *Wall Street Journal*, April 24, 1985, pp. 1, 27.

the creation of jobs, greater leisure time, and an apparently inexhaustible cornucopia of new products and services. For taking the technological lead, business has been rewarded with profits, growth, and general social approval.

In one important sense, business has only responded to expressed or potential public demands for more and better technology. In a free enterprise society, people register their wants through the marketplace, voting with their purchasing dollars. These free market demands have encouraged business to push for ever greater technological growth through the introduction of new products and services. The enormous popularity and demand for today's many electronic inventions—whether video games, videodiscs, pocket calculators, personal computers, or digital recordings—illustrate the powerful dynamics of combining modern technology with a free enterprise system.

At times, these technological advances have occurred pell-mell and with little foresight for long-term consequences.

> For example, *when technologically superior trucks, buses, and airlines cut deeply into the freight and passenger business of railroads, entire towns such as Altoona, Pennsylvania—a large rail center—suffered severe economic decline. Or when new surface mining equipment made coal recovery in the western regions of the United States more profitable than the deep mining that was typical in the southern and eastern regions, many parts of Appalachia were thrust into deeper poverty than they had ever known.*
>
> *At the same time, helter-skelter, unplanned urban sprawl can accompany rapid economic buildup brought on by the newer forms of electronic technology. California's Silicon Valley, home of the revolutionary computer chip, is a good example of headlong economic development that presses hard on environmental resources and brings on many serious urban problems.*

These problems may seem unique to our technological age but they are not. Adjusting society's institutions and people to new technology is an ancient problem.

> *Long ago, many farmers resisted the use of iron plows instead of wooden ones, believing that the metal would contaminate the soil and ruin the crops. More recently, the automobile was considered by some persons to be a less genteel and refined mode of transportation than the horse and buggy; the same snobbish attitude developed toward ready-to-wear clothes when compared with tailor-made ones. And many people today express both fear and hostility concerning the computer, just as others did a few years ago when telephone companies switched home dialing systems to digits from a combination of letters and digits.*

The major difference in adjusting technology and institutions in the 1980s is in the scale, magnitude, and speed of the needed adjustments. Worldwide competition and enormous productivity gains pose the possibility of massive unemployment in several industrial nations. Retraining needs for displaced workers are far greater than they once were. The economic and social dislocations appear to be more painful, more long-lasting, and more resistant to satisfactory solution.

What are business's responsibilities in a time of rapid and sometimes disruptive technological change? Now that the Pandora's box of technology has been opened, it cannot be closed again. There is no turning the technological clock back to a more serene era.

Instead, society seems to be sending three kinds of signals to the business community.

- One message is that society wants new technology to be introduced with greater care and more foresight. For example, premarket testing of drugs, safety guidelines for genetic engineering projects, and government regulation of chemical waste disposal can safeguard individuals and society.
- Another emerging development is the idea of a compensatory payment or other type of support by business that would help individuals, groups, or communities readjust their lives when damaged by technological changes. Examples of such help include industrial retraining programs for technologically displaced employees; advance notification to employees and local communities when plants are to be closed; compensation payments to communities and severance pay to laid-off employees; and acceptance by multinational firms of some sacrifice in economic efficiency in order to strengthen national security and preserve jobs at home instead of shifting operations to the lowest-cost foreign location. When business firms take these kinds of steps, they build confidence in society that the social costs of new technology will be widely shared rather than resting on just a few persons or groups.
- Perhaps less clearly perceived—but vitally necessary—is an emerging understanding that technology is far too central, far too important, and far too complex in its consequences to be entrusted to any single institution in society. Business has pioneered the creative development of much technology, just as government has led the way in sponsoring the technology of national defense. Society has much to gain from both, as well as much to think about in terms of their respective social costs. Universities, labor unions, nonprofit institutions, professional groups, and many local communities have made distinctive contributions to technological advance. All of these groups and institutions are technological stakeholders, each with an interest in the outcome of society's great adventure in technological achievement.

The idea of a broad institutional partnership for humane technological advance belongs in the thinking of business leaders, as well as in the minds and actions of all those in society who have a stake in the technological future.

SUMMARY

When we begin to see the intricate relationships of technological developments to one another and to many institutions, we realize that technological change is not a simple creation of business alone. Business responds to market demands and is rewarded for technological innovations. Business is perhaps the primary agent for introducing technological change, so it has major responsibilities for using technology effectively.

Technology leads to enormous social changes where it is allowed to develop freely. Its evolution over the centuries has produced five distinctive phases, the most recent being a knowledge-based society dependent increasingly on electronic technology.

The overall results of technology are both positive and negative. Since rapid technological change can disrupt the lives of individuals and communities, society expects business to use care in introducing new technology and to consider the interests of all groups who have a stake in the technological future.

DISCUSSION AND REVIEW QUESTIONS

1. By consulting library sources, obtain a list of the member nations of the United Nations. By referring to brief descriptions of these nations in encyclopedias or similar reference books, try to classify UN member nations as belonging to one of the five phases of technology discussed in this chapter. In which phase of technology are most of the member nations found? Should efforts be made to move each member nation to the next higher phase? Why or not? What role should business play in such efforts?

2. Identify two major problems that are characteristic of each of the five major phases of technology discussed in this chapter. What can business do to help overcome these characteristic problems? Be as specific as you can. Consult library references, if necessary.

3. What do you consider to be the three most favorable effects of technology (a) in the whole society and (b) in your local community? Explain why you chose each. Do likewise for the three most unfavorable effects.

4. Laws have been proposed that would require a company to provide severance pay, relocation job guarantees, or job retraining for any employee discharged because of automation. Would such laws benefit—or penalize—the affected business firms? What effects would such laws have on technological developments? Which groups in society would bear the economic and social costs of such legislation?

CRITICAL INCIDENT

GENES versus Genetic Engineering

As president of a hypothetical genetic engineering firm, imagine that you have just received the following letter:

Dear Ms. President:

I represent a group known as the Group to Eliminate New Experiments in Science (GENES), which has a number of chapters in the United States and a rapidly growing membership from all walks of life, including science. At our recent national convention, a resolution was adopted that opposes all types of genetic engineering, including the kind of work your firm is doing.

We believe that you and your scientific staff cannot improve on nature and should not try to do so. To us, you are tampering with and trying unsuccessfully to imitate Divine intelligence. Human beings are not prepared either psychologically or morally to handle the kind of power conferred by this brand of science. We fear also that "engineered" microorganisms will escape from your laboratories into the environment and possibly cause unfortunate and irreversible damage to healthy living things, including ourselves and our children. The same bad effects may well occur when the altered genetic materials you use in industrial applications come into contact with employees, customers, and the general public. Overall, we think you are using the biosphere in unwise ways, just for the sake of making a profit for your stockholders.

GENES recently purchased 10 shares of stock in your company and plans to offer some suggestions at the next annual stockholders' meeting for restricting your work in genetic engineering. I would be pleased to hear from you before that time. As stockholders, we believe you have an obligation to respond to our viewpoints. As members of the public, we think you should consider the risks your firm is creating through this new form of technology.

The letter was signed by someone identifying himself as a professor of biochemistry at a leading university.

1. As president of the firm, how would you respond to this letter? Would you answer it, ignore it, or wait to see what happens at the annual stockholders' meeting? What corporate strategy could be developed for dealing with GENES?

2. In your own personal opinion, are the members of GENES just another version of the nineteenth-century Luddites (described in this chapter), opposed to new technology because it threatens society's traditional ways of doing things? Discuss.

3. What can business firms like this one do to reduce public concerns and fears about the new technological and scientific advances that occur in a knowledge society?

Chapter Seventeen

ECOLOGY, ENVIRONMENT, AND BUSINESS

Strong public interest in preserving nature's ecological balance and a clean, healthy environment means that business must constantly strive to achieve these goals for society. At the same time, business is expected to produce needed goods and services at reasonable prices. The task for corporate and public policymakers is to find socially acceptable ways to meet both ecological and economic goals.

CHAPTER OBJECTIVES

After reading this chapter, you should be able to:

- Explain how business and ecology are related to each other
- Understand how environmental pollution became a major national issue
- Summarize the main features of United States environmental protection laws
- Describe how environmentalism changed in the 1980s
- Review the continuing problems of environmental pollution

*I*n the early morning hours of November 1, 1986, a fire broke out in a Basel, Switzerland, warehouse owned by Sandoz AG, a major manufacturer of drugs and chemicals. The building was filled with over 1,000 tons of insecticides, herbicides, and fungicides, all potent chemicals used widely in farming and many other applications. Fire companies did not reach the blaze until it was well under way because the warehouse had no alarm system and no automatic sprinklers. Soon the tons of water used to contain the fire overflowed catch basins and began to cascade into the Rhine River, carrying 300 tons of poisonous chemicals into one of Europe's major waterways. The effects were devastating for humans and for the river's animal life. As the 40-mile chemical slick floated down the Rhine to the North Sea, it destroyed marine life and threatened the water supplies of dozens of cities and villages. The balanced ecological life-support system of the river was seriously damaged, perhaps for many years. Six days after the fire, a makeshift containment system holding still more chemical wastes gave way, spilling the equivalent of 2 tons of mercury into the river. When Sandoz officials held a meeting to explain the accident to local Swiss citizens, they were pelted with dead eels and water bottles by protesters. The company's stock value fell 16 percent on the Zurich Stock Exchange, and tighter government regulations were predicted to be one result of the accident.[1]

Earlier in 1986, the world's worst nuclear accident had captured the attention of the entire globe. The Soviet Union's nuclear power plant at Chernobyl, located a few miles north of the large Russian city of Kiev, ran out of control. The results were even more devastating and widespread than the Rhine River tragedy. A nuclear reactor caught fire and burned out of control for several days, spewing out an immense amount of radiation that was carried by winds across several Western European nations and eventually around the entire globe. Radiation fallout was so intense in neighboring countries that milk supplies and many farm products were dangerously contaminated. A number of persons, most of them Chernobyl workers or local firefighters, died of radiation poisoning contracted while trying to contain the fire. Hundreds more were hospitalized; thousands of people living within an 18-mile radius of the Chernobyl plant were permanently evacuated from their villages, which were part of a deserted and radioactively "hot" zone. Kiev residents were cautioned to remain indoors and take other precautions to protect themselves from the risks of radiation overdoses. Several thousand persons throughout the world were expected to contract cancer in future years as a result of the Chernobyl disaster.

What these tragic events symbolize is a major collision between industrial technology and nature's ecological systems. Agricultural chemicals, nuclear power, and the many other advances made possible by modern science and technology bring enormous benefits to humankind. But the human price and the pressures on the earth's ecological systems are sometimes unacceptably high. Finding a balance between industrial benefits and life-sustaining ecological systems is another major challenge facing business managers, government policymakers, and society generally.

---

[1]"The Blotch on the Rhine," *Newsweek*, November 24, 1986; Margaret A. Studer, "Swiss Never Thought Sandoz Disaster Could Happen in Their Orderly World," *Wall Street Journal*, November 13, 1986, p. 33; Terence Roth, "Chemical Firms in Germany Face Scrutiny," *Wall Street Journal*, November 11, 1986, p. 36.

THE ECOLOGICAL CHALLENGE

Ecology is the study of how living things—plants and animals—interact with one another and with their environment. The ecological challenge occurs when wastes created by human productive activities cannot be readily absorbed into the environment without causing harm. These wastes—for example, strip mining wastes or the emissions from power plants—are produced directly by industrial operations. Other wastes—for example, automobile exhausts and discarded rubbish—are created by using the goods and services produced by industry. When these wastes are injected into the environment—air, water, open spaces, human communities—they can upset the long-established natural rhythms, cycles, and interrelationships that support plant, animal, and human life.

The ecological challenge requires business to formulate long-run company strategies that (1) make the most efficient use of scarce industrial resources, (2) reduce wastes that pollute the environment, and (3) keep industrial production within the limits set by nature's ecological systems.

HISTORICAL PERSPECTIVE ON POLLUTION

Pollution needs to be seen in its historical perspective in order for it to be understood with a balanced view. It is not something new to the twentieth century. People have dumped their trash into the soil and water since the beginning of civilization. Archaeological excavations show the trash of several civilizations (not generations) dumped one on top of the other. Smoke from household fires has polluted the air since the Stone Age. Citizens of early Rome complained that soot from fires dirtied their clothes, and London was described in 1660 as covered with "clouds of smoke and sulphur."

Natural Pollution

Nature itself pollutes the air. Dust storms toss dirt and debris into the air, natural forest fires cast a pall of smoke over mountain valleys, and lightning creates certain chemical compounds. The pollution from volcanoes is phenomenal and puts modern pollution clearly in perspective. The 1980 eruption of Mount St. Helens in the state of Washington spewed 1.3 billion cubic yards of ash and rock into the air, which was enough material to fill 162.5 million dump trucks. One hundred square miles of forestland were burned or polluted, as were fisheries, streams, and lakes.

Although pollution has existed for many centuries, it was usually of minor significance. Since 1700, however, three additional causes have arisen that have fundamentally altered the seriousness of pollution. They have upset the delicate balance of nature that allowed people to live comfortably in their environment. They are the Industrial Revolution, a higher standard of living, and the population explosion. All of these have contributed to a related problem, the excessive use of polluting forms of energy. In more recent years, a fourth factor—social value changes associated with technologically advanced societies—has focused greater attention on environmental issues.

The Industrial Revolution

A primary cause of air and water pollution has been the Industrial Revolution. Its factories spread first across Britain and then the rest of the world, with smokestacks belching contaminants into the air. Industry requires energy, much of which is secured from incomplete combustion that releases pollutants of various types. The complex chemical processes of industry produce undesirable by-products and wastes that pollute land, water, and air. Its mechanical processes often create dust, grime, and unsightly refuse. More recently, the Agricultural Revolution as an adjunct of the Industrial Revolution has produced overkill with pesticides, herbicides, chemical fertilizers, refuse from cattle-feeding "factories," and other unpleasant conditions.[2]

One major result of the Industrial Revolution is production of manufactured chemicals that biodegrade slowly or that have cancer-causing potential. As long as nature can biodegrade waste, such as a fallen tree trunk, the waste does not create a long-run problem. However, modern science has created complicated wastes that may take years to biodegrade, so the accumulated waste becomes a burden on the environment. Nuclear wastes also can be dangerous, because they degrade slowly for decades or centuries.

Other chemicals are shown to increase the rate of cancer when the chemicals contact the human system in high concentrations or for prolonged periods of time. In addition, laboratory experiments have shown that some chemicals cause cell mutations, so they are suspected as cancer agents. The result is that business and government must be extremely careful to verify the safety of these products before releasing them for general use.

A Higher Standard of Living

Industrialization has raised the standard of living enormously. As people consume more, their consumption tends to create more wastes. The more elegant their tastes for food become, the more garbage and other refuse they produce. The more they buy, the more paper and packaging are required, most of which becomes refuse. When they buy a car, they travel more and the engine they use leaves more airborne pollution. As they travel, they leave a trail of debris such as cans, bottles, and wrappers.

It is a fact that the real economic output of the United States grew about as much from 1950 to 1980 as it did in the three centuries from the time the Pilgrims landed in 1620 until 1950! And pollution tended to increase at somewhat the same pace. Meanwhile the earth's capacity to recycle wastes remained substantially unchanged. The result is that normal and moderate

---

[2]Philip M. Boffey, "20 Years after 'Silent Spring': Still a Troubled Landscape," *New York Times*, May 25, 1982, pp. C-1, C-7; and "Silent Spring Revisited?" *Newsweek*, July 14, 1986, pp. 72–73.

increases in the standard of living in the last few decades have created an ecological crisis.

The Population Explosion

The ultimate time bomb in pollution is a speedup in population growth. Population growth is not the result of a higher birth rate, because the birth rate is declining in many parts of the world. Instead, population is expanding because people live longer, primarily as a result of economic and medical progress.

Each additional person adds pollutants to land, air, and water, although the amount of these vital natural resources remains the same. The result is more intensive pollution of these existing resources, unless people take steps to reduce pollution. In the year 1900 in the United States, for example, about 3 million square miles accommodated less than 80 million people. By the 1980s, this area, and the air and water that go with it, had to accommodate over 200 million persons. It should therefore not be surprising that the environment is becoming more polluted.

Changes in Social Values

High-consumption, technologically advanced societies tend to undergo important shifts in social values. With a more secure economic foundation and rising standards of material living for most people, such societies turn their attention to other matters. Leisure time is available for recreation, hobbies, creative expression, and related outlets. Freed from around-the-clock work routines, people can be more concerned about health, nutrition, exercise, and outdoor enjoyment generally. They also may give more attention to voluntary work in their own communities and may join a variety of groups that promote a higher quality of life locally and regionally. Their political interest and involvement tends to be higher, too, particularly where community life is concerned.

These subtle shifts in behavior and attitude probably are symbolic of underlying value changes occurring in society. In turn, the changes have a powerful effect on people's attitudes toward the environment. More concern is expressed about industrial pressures on the natural environment; wilderness areas and open spaces are considered worth preserving; and all kinds of actual or potential threats to ecological balance and human health get more attention. These new attitudes and values powered the environmental movement of the 1960s and 1970s and raised the public's consciousness about the importance of their natural surroundings.

The Environmental Movement of the 1960s and 1970s

Even in an age of electronics and video images, books still have the power to capture and express profound human meanings and yearnings. Rachel

Carson's 1962 *Silent Spring* was such a book.[3] This best-seller symbolized the renewal of public concern about the environment. Carson, a biologist, wrote forcefully of her scientific alarm about the widespread, reckless use of pesticides, particularly DDT. Continued heavy use of such chemicals, she believed, posed a direct, long-term threat not just to the target insects but to all the animals that belonged to interwoven food chains in nature; eventually, the effects would be felt by humans themselves. She feared a future time when the sounds of nature would be muted, even silent, if the relentless rain of chemicals continued apace.

Silent Spring galvanized environmental activists who began pressuring private business as well as government agencies. Actually, there has long been an interest in protecting the rivers, forests, and wilderness areas of the nation. Beginning in the late nineteenth century, states, cities, and the federal government passed laws to control the dumping of wastes into rivers, lakes, and inland waterways; and some communities tried to control smoke emissions and to find suitable ways to dispose of refuse. Conservationists, as they were first called, since around 1900 have been active in preserving natural areas and finding ways to conserve natural resources and croplands. Some of these far-sighted conservationists, encouraged by the support of President Theodore Roosevelt, led early fights to establish the national parks in the western states, while others worked with farmers to halt land erosion.[4]

Organized environmental groups sprang up during the 1960s and 1970s, quickly learning confrontational and legal tactics to oppose actions they thought were detrimental to the environment. By the late 1970s some twenty-four environmental "public interest" groups were in existence. The most important and successful were the New York–based Environmental Defense Fund and the Natural Resources Defense Council, the Sierra Club's Foundation and Legal Defense Fund headquartered in San Francisco, and the National Wildlife Federation with headquarters in Washington, D.C. Environmental activists helped block construction of a large power plant in Utah, stopped oil drilling in the Palisades area near Los Angeles, and supported the government's ban on widespread use of DDT and other toxic chemicals. Environmentalists did not win all the time, though; for example, a counter-environmentalist group, the Pacific Legal Foundation of Sacramento, brought suit against the Environmental Protection Agency to permit the use of DDT in combatting the tussock moth in thousands of acres of Pacific Northwest timberland, an action approved by the EPA in spite of opposition by western environmentalists.

However, the biggest accomplishment of the environmental movement of the 1960s and 1970s was a structure of laws and agencies whose basic purpose was to protect the environment from a variety of possible dangers.

---

[3]Rachel Carson, *Silent Spring*, Boston: Houghton Mifflin, 1962.

[4]For American historical views of the environment see Duke Frederick, William L. Howenstine, and June Sochen (eds.), *Destroy to Create: Interaction with the Natural Environment in the Building of America*, Hinsdale, Ill.: Dryden, 1972.

ROLE OF GOVERNMENT

Government has a major role in pollution control. It has strong capabilities for setting priorities, general policies, and minimum standards for environmental quality. It also can provide economic incentives to encourage businesses, communities, and regions to reduce pollution, and it can offer legal and administrative systems for resolving disputes about pollution.

Often business firms favor government standards because they realize that a cleaner environment can be accomplished only by joint action of all firms. If only one company acts to reduce pollution, the environmental improvement may not be evident, and the remaining pollution will continue to give even the nonpolluting firm a poor public image. Further, the nonpolluting company will have a competitive disadvantage because of the cost of its control equipment. Clearly, this is a situation requiring government standards.

Major Environmental Laws and Agencies

Figure 17-1 summarizes the major environmental laws enacted by Congress in the 1960s, 1970s, and 1980s. These command-and-control techniques represented movement away from an unregulated market system. In adopting these laws, Congress was responding to strong public concerns and pressures to save the environment from further damage. Public opinion polls taken regularly since the 1960s consistently show that a strong majority of the public favors environmental protection, so these new laws expressed the general public's preference for environmental action.

Accompanying these laws were new regulatory agencies and a strengthening of the powers of some existing government departments. Figure 17-2 diagrams the principal types of pollution and shows the jurisdictional authority of several major federal agencies and departments.[5]

Environmental Protection Agency (EPA)

As shown by Figure 17-2, EPA is obviously the nation's main pollution control agency. It was created in 1970 to coordinate most of the government's efforts to protect the environment. It sets standards for air and water quality, controls the use of toxic substances including pesticides, monitors radiation levels, oversees solid-waste and noise control programs, and even becomes involved in safeguarding food through its pesticide and toxic substances controls. EPA's research program helps expand knowledge of pollution problems and possible technological controls. All in all, it is intended to be the public's advocate for a livable environment.

---

[5]A fuller description of these and other federal agencies can be found in the *United States Government Manual 1986/87,* Office of Federal Register, Washington, D.C.: U.S. Government Printing Office, 1986.

Year	Law	Purpose
1969	National Environmental Policy Act	Created Council on Environmental Quality to oversee quality of the nation's environment.
1970 & 1977	Clean Air Act as amended	Established national air quality standards and timetables.
1972	Noise Pollution and Control Act	Defined noise limits and standards for certain equipment.
1972	Water Pollution Control Act	Established national goals and timetables for clean waterways.
1972	Pesticide Control Act	Registration of and restrictions on pesticide use.
1974	Safe Drinking Water Act	Authorized national standards for drinking water.
1974	Hazardous Materials Transport Act	Regulated shipment of hazardous materials.
1976	Resource Conservation and Recovery Act	Regulated hazardous materials from production to disposal.
1976	Toxic Substances Control Act	Established national policy to regulate, restrict, and (if necessary) ban toxic chemicals.
1977	Surface Mining Control and Reclamation Act	Established standards for stripmining and land restoration.
1980 & 1986	Comprehensive Environmental Response, Compensation, and Liability Act (Superfund)	Established superfund and procedures to clean up hazardous waste sites.
1987	Clean Water Act amendments	Authorized funds for sewage treatment plants and waterways cleanup.

FIGURE 17-1   Leading environmental protection laws.

Nuclear Regulatory Commission (NRC)

Created in 1974 as a successor to the Atomic Energy Commission, NRC licenses and regulates nuclear facilities and materials, including their possible impacts on the environment. It is often a target of groups protesting the licensing and building of nuclear power plants.

Occupational Safety and Health Administration (OSHA)

OSHA, created in 1970, enters into the pollution picture when it attempts to make the work environment safer for employees by controlling emissions from production processes and chemicals used by workers. It has, for example, opposed the use of coke oven sheds intended to reduce *external* air

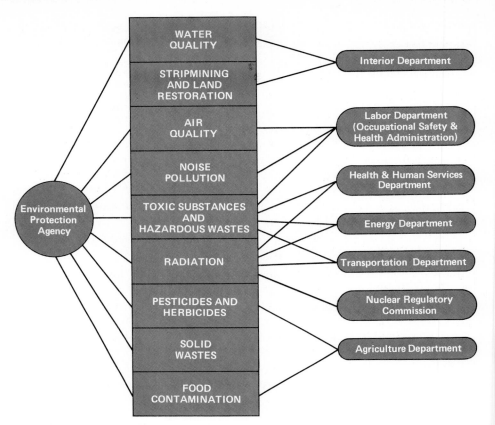

FIGURE 17-2   Regulatory and monitoring jurisdiction of major federal pollution control agencies.

pollution because they increase pollution *inside* the plant where the workers are. OSHA also has clashed with EPA concerning dust controls in grain elevators; EPA opposes venting the dust outside, while OSHA wants it reduced inside to protect workers and to reduce the risk of dust-induced explosions.

Other Government Departments

Several other government departments house various research or regulatory organizations responsible for a portion of the federal government's watchdog role. The Department of Health and Human Services has a special mission of monitoring the health effects of toxic substances and radiation exposure. The Interior Department polices water quality and surface mining, including restoration of stripmined areas, and it administers the endangered species program to protect wildlife. The Transportation Department has regulatory powers regarding the transport of hazardous materials. Nuclear waste problems and issues fall within the jurisdiction of the Energy Department. And the Department of Labor, in addition to housing OSHA, also oversees operation of the Mine Safety and Health Administration.

Council on Environmental Quality (CEQ)

CEQ does not appear in Figure 17-2 because it is not, strictly speaking, a regulatory agency, although it does play an important role. It was established in 1969 to formulate and recommend national policies regarding environmental improvement. Its annual reports to the President contain a wealth of environmental information, and the Council has been a strong advocate of continued progress in cleaning up the environment. Perhaps its most important and controversial function is to oversee the environmental impact statements required when federally assisted projects pose a potential threat to the environment.

Regional, State, and Local Agencies

Under the United States system of federalism, state and local governments share pollution control powers with the federal government, although federal regulations ·and laws are paramount in case of disagreements among regulators. In a typical state, there is a state department of environmental control; some counties have special bureaus to monitor and enforce controls; and many cities have ordinances regulating solid-waste disposal, noise, and other kinds of pollution. Where special pollution problems occur across state lines, regional authorities are sometimes created to encourage cooperation and effective regulation.

Ways of Applying Government Controls

Government applies pollution controls in a variety of ways, because the situation is too complex for just one approach to work. In order to cover different pollutants, kinds of pollution sources, economic conditions, and technological features, government needs to use its full arsenal of "social motivators" for environmental improvement.

The regulatory approaches most likely to produce results are incentives, environmental standards, pollution charges, and buying and selling pollution rights.

Incentives for Environmental Improvement

The government may offer various types of incentives to firms who reduce their pollution. Sometimes these incentives work toward standards that may eventually be required. At other times they work for any improvement. For example, the government may decide to purchase only from those firms that meet certain pollution standards, or it may offer aid to those that install pollution control equipment. Tax incentives for pollution control equipment (such as faster depreciation or tax credits) also may be used.

The major advantage of incentives is that they encourage voluntary improvement without the stigma of governmental force. They allow different industries and businesses to proceed at the pace that is best for their individual situation. Further, some businesses may be encouraged by incentives to go beyond the minimum standards of compliance that a regulation would have been able to achieve. The main disadvantage of incentives is that what is voluntary may not be accomplished at all.

Environmental Standards

Another type of pollution control is environmental standards. These standards are established by legislative action and applied by administrative agencies and courts. One type of standard is an *environmental-quality standard*. In this instance the specified environment is permitted to have only a certain amount or proportion of pollution, such as a certain proportion of sulfur dioxide in the air. Polluting sources then are required to control their emissions to maintain the area's standard of air quality. EPA has legal authority to set this type of ambient air quality standard for several different kinds of pollutants considered dangerous to public health and property, as well as similar water quality standards.

A second type of standard is an *emission standard*. For example, the law may specify that the permissible release of fly ash from a smokestack is 1 percent of the ash generated by the plant. Then each business is required to install fly-ash-control equipment that removes at least 99 percent of the fly ash. Emission standards, with some exceptions, are usually set by state and local regulators who are familiar with local industry and special problems caused by topography and weather conditions.

To sum up, *federal* regulators decide how clean the air and water should be by establishing environmental-quality standards. *Local* regulators then impose direct emission controls on polluting sources in order to achieve the federally mandated standards.

An advantage of environmental standards is that they are enforceable in the courts; therefore, there is greater assurance that their requirements will be met than through the use of incentives, which are voluntary. Further, they are usually across-the-board standards applicable to all, and so general compliance in society is assured. A disadvantage is that in order to apply the standard to all businesses fairly, the lawmakers may so water down the standard and fill it with exceptions that it is not effective. A further disadvantage is that the law is only as good as the administrative agency enforcing it. A number of sound laws have been weakened by poor administration. Another disadvantage is that across-the-board standards may cause inequity and suffering because each business faces a different pollution control problem. Older, less efficient plants especially face problems because it is costly to renovate them, and a new nonpolluting plant may not be justified because of capital costs or market conditions.

The Bubble Concept. In order to ease compliance with environmental rules while still protecting the public, government regulators in 1979 introduced the "bubble concept." A large industrial plant has many potential sources of pollution from numerous smokestacks, manufacturing processes,

Percentage of Pollutant Removed	Cost of Removing an Additional Pound of Pollutant (cents)
40	2
60	4
80	7
90	10
95	15
99	40

FIGURE 17-3   Marginal cost schedule of pollution cleanup in a hypothetical company. (*Source: Adapted from Allen V. Kneese and Charles L. Schultze,* Pollution, Prices, and Public Policy, *Washington, D.C.: Brookings, 1975, p. 88.*)

and pipes that discharge liquid by-products. At one time, environmental rules required that each one of these pollution sources conform to mandated standards. However, under the bubble concept, regulators treat an entire plant as if it were surrounded by an invisible plastic bubble and they measure only the total pollution coming out of the top of the bubble. This means that one or more smokestacks or discharge pipes may emit more pollutants than the law allows, just so long as the entire plant's total emissions do not violate air and water quality standards.

An example of how this system works and how much it can save in pollution control costs comes from a manufacturer of pressure-sensitive tapes and labels. Pollutants are given off in several stages of manufacturing, particularly in the coating and drying processes. An EPA-approved bubble plan allowed the company to restrict these emissions at some points but not at each and every point in the production run. Total emissions were kept within legal bounds, and the company saved $500,000 per coating line.

By 1984, EPA had approved forty-six bubble plans at an estimated saving of over $200 million in pollution control costs. Another $500 million in savings were expected from 150 state-approved bubble projects.[6]

Pollution Charges

Another type of pollution control is establishment of *pollution charges*. Each business pays fees for the quantity of undesirable waste that it releases, and the fee varies with the amount of waste released. The result is, "The more you pollute, the more you pay." Figure 17-3 illustrates how a fee or tax on pollution can be used to encourage polluters to clean up. If a pollution charge of 10 cents were imposed on each pound of pollutant released into the environment, a company would find it profitable to remove 90 percent of the pollutant because the cost of removal is less than the pollution charge up to that point. The company would choose to let the remaining 10 percent pollute the environment, since the cost of removing it would be greater than the

[6]Council on Environmental Quality, *Environmental Quality*, 15th Annual Report, 1984, pp. 61–63.

pollution charge. If the charge were raised to 15 cents, the company would find it profitable to remove 95 percent of the pollutant. In other words, a pollution charge can be set high enough to accomplish any desired degree of pollution removal.[7]

Pollution charges are based on the proposition that market mechanisms are a better form of control than extensive standards that require a large and costly enforcement bureaucracy. Sufficiently high charges must be put on pollution to discourage its release. Then each firm is allowed to work out its own least-cost relationship for waste release or abatement according to its own special set of circumstances.

The principal disadvantage of pollution charges is expressed by critics as "a license to pollute." It does not seem consistent with environmental philosophy to allow people to pollute even when they pay a charge for doing so. Further, some critics fear that charges will be so low that present polluters will continue. Another disadvantage is that for some types of pollutants it may be difficult to compute charges, and so this approach may not be effective.[8]

Buying and Selling Pollution Rights

A fourth regulatory approach allows pollution to be controlled by applying the free market principle of buying and selling the right to pollute. Although it sounds contradictory to environmental goals to allow someone to buy the right to pollute, this approach may work as well as other methods and save money at the same time.

> *An example comes from efforts to control the amount of lead released into the air from lead-based gasoline.[9] In late 1982 the EPA told major refiners to limit the amount of lead in each gallon of gasoline to 1.1 grams. However, those refiners able to produce gasoline with even less lead—say, 0.85 grams—could sell or trade this lead-pollution saving to another refiner whose gasoline might contain 1.25 grams. The overall effect on air quality would be the same as if each refiner had met the legal standard of 1.1 grams, provided, of course, that they produced approximately the same volume of gasoline for consumers.*

A similar principle guides a "mitigation banking" project of Tenneco LaTerre, an oil and gas producer in Louisiana's coastal wetlands. Saltwater intrusion threatens the delicate ecological balance of this area, which also is a prime region for energy resources. Oil and gas production requires the building of canals, but these canals permit saltwater to invade freshwater areas. Working with federal and state regulators and private conservationists,

---

[7]This illustration is a paraphrase of Allen V. Kneese and Charles L. Schultze, *Pollution, Prices, and Public Policy,* Washington, D.C.: Brookings, 1975, p. 89.

[8]A large collection of articles dealing with pollution charges may be found in Congressional Research Service, *Pollution Taxes, Effluent Charges, and Other Alternatives for Pollution Control,* Washington, D.C.: U.S. Senate Committee on Environmental and Public Works, 1977.

[9]"Why Refiners Bought the EPA's Lead Rule," *Business Week,* November 1, 1982, pp. 33, 37.

Tenneco LaTerre agreed to a plan of protecting and improving the swamp-lands in advance of canal dredging and filling operations. It then "banks" these ecological improvement credits and uses them to offset future damage caused by its search for energy in the wetlands. For this innovative plan, Tenneco received the National Wildlife Federation's Corporate Conservation Award in 1984.[10]

This offset policy operates on a barter or trading principle, rather than actual buying and selling, but the basic idea of swapping pollution debits and credits is the same. Supporters claim that all of these market-oriented policies—bubbles, sales of pollution rights, air pollution banks, offsets—can accomplish government-supervised environmental goals more efficiently, at greater savings, and with less government red tape than other methods.

THE COSTS OF POLLUTION CONTROL

One of the central issues of pollution control is its cost. The question is: Can the nation afford to clean up the environment and keep it clean? The answer is not simple and tends to vary from group to group.

During the early days of the environmental movement, pollution control expenditures by some companies were punishingly high. Hardest hit were the older "smokestack" industries—such as copper and steel, petroleum and coal, paper manufacturers, chemical companies, and electric utilities. As shown in Figure 17-4, some of these industries spent from 10 percent to nearly 20 percent of their total plant and equipment budgets on pollution controls. Industry leaders pointed out that these large expenditures did not contribute anything to a company's output or to its overall productivity. Money spent for pollution control might make the air and waterways cleaner, but it did not help the "bottom line" where profits are measured. For older, marginal plants, these expensive systems could be the "straw that broke the camel's back." In the mid-1970s, the Council on Environmental Quality reported that 107 plants employing over 20,000 persons had named pollution control spending as a significant reason for closing their doors. Another source believed the job losses were closer to 200,000. In Montana, the Ana-conda division of Atlantic Richfield was forced to close one of the nation's oldest copper smelters when faced with a pollution control bill exceeding $400 million.

Cleaning up the environment and keeping it clean carries a big price tag. The Environmental Protection Agency estimated that pollution controls would cost private industry $329 billion from 1981 through 1990. In 1983 alone, business spending on pollution control was $62 billion, and since 1972 these current-dollar costs have increased by 15 percent each year. Car owners paid $11 billion more to buy and operate their vehicles in 1983 because of emission control systems and the added cost of unleaded gasoline. Business's capital spending on pollution controls amounted to 2.6 percent of the nation's

[10]"The Delicate Balance," *Tenneco*, a publication of Tenneco, Inc., Autumn 1984, pp. 1–6.

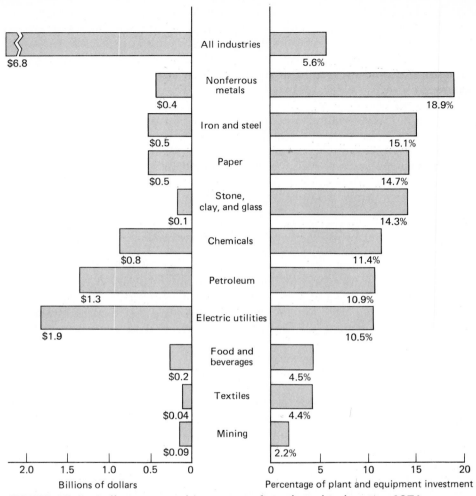

FIGURE 17-4   Pollution control investment for selected industries, 1976.
(*Source: Council on Environmental Quality,* Environmental Quality—1977: *Eighth Annual Report, Washington, D.C.: U.S. Government Printing Office, 1977, pp. 324–325.*)

gross national product in 1983, with future increases expected. However, when inflation is taken into account, overall pollution control spending by business, government, and consumers leveled off in the first half of the 1980s.[11]

   In addition to direct dollar costs, jobs may be lost, productivity may decline, prices of many products may be higher, some plants may be forced to close, and some companies are placed at a disadvantage when competing with foreign companies whose nations do not have such stringent pollution controls.

[11]"Pollution Abatement and Control Expenditures, 1980–83," *Survey of Current Business,* March 1985, pp. 18–22.

As these cost issues loomed larger and larger, business leaders began to fight back against overzealous environmentalists who were ready to accept the benefits of pollution control but seemed to ignore or downplay the costs involved. The result was a blunting—a slowing down, not a halt—of the drive to clean up the environment. Advocates of the slowdown asserted that society should take stock of what it was spending each year and think about whether that money could be spent better on other public purposes or be returned to the tax-paying public in the form of lower taxes.[12] By 1980, this view was sufficiently widespread to be one of the contributing factors to the election of Ronald Reagan as President, who advocated a general rollback of government regulations and an easing of environmental controls.

ENVIRONMENTALISM IN THE 1980s

1980 was a watershed year for environmental protection in the United States. The Reagan administration played down the role of the federal government as an environmental watchdog. Newly appointed environmental officials took strong and sometimes provocative stands on environmental issues that alienated many environmentalists and alarmed big segments of the general public. Ironically, public concern and opposition became so great that it powered a renewed interest in environmental protection and filled the coffers of environmental public interest groups with a flood of donations.[13] In spite of these developments, though, the Reagan administration's emphasis on less government involvement in all spheres of American life reduced the active role government had played in the environmental movement of the 1960s and 1970s. Other factors were at work also to change the character of environmental activism in the 1980s, as discussed in the following sections.

Progress in Controlling Pollution

After more than a decade of efforts to clean up the nation's environment, the Council on Environmental Quality (CEQ) reported in 1984 that these efforts had produced definite progress. Federal standards for clean air had been achieved for four of the six major pollutants regulated by the Environmental Protection Agency: solid particulates (dust, soot, etc.), sulfur dioxide, nitrogen dioxide, and lead. Ozone and carbon monoxide levels, although still too high, were trending downward. Urban areas such as Los Angeles and Houston, which experience heavy automobile traffic along with weather conditions that aggravate the problem, continued to report excessive levels of ozone and carbon monoxide. The use of unleaded gasoline contributed a great deal to the general cleanup, as shown in Figure 17-5. The CEQ predicted in 1984 that national goals for cleaner air would be completely achieved by

---

[12]For a general discussion of this view, see Murray L. Weidenbaum, *Business, Government, and the Public*, 3d ed., Englewood Cliffs, N.J.: Prentice-Hall, 1986.

[13]Andy Pasztor, "Environmentalists Switch Tactics," *Wall Street Journal*, April 13, 1984, p. 50.

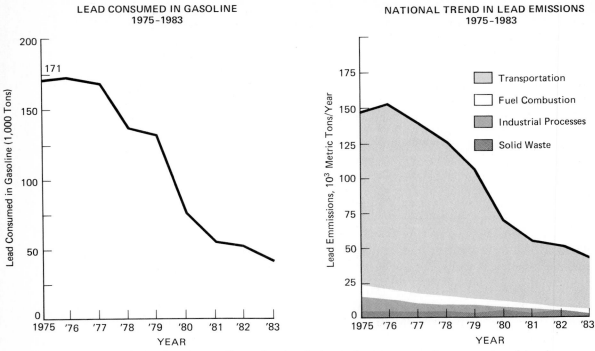

FIGURE 17-5   **Effect of unleaded gasoline consumption on national lead emission levels.** (*Source: Council on Environmental Quality*, Environmental Quality, *15th Annual Report, 1984, pp. 51 and 52.*)

1990, due largely to the emission controls required for new motor vehicles and to the phaseout of older cars and trucks.[14]

The water-quality story was not as bright. About the best that could be said is that the deterioration of the nation's rivers and lakes had been halted. Surveys indicated that some areas continued to suffer from excessive dumping of pollutants into rivers, streams, and lakes, while other waterways were experiencing a remarkable comeback from near ruin. Whereas in the 1970s, much of the pollution had come from industrial sources, by the 1980s attention had shifted to public sewage-disposal systems. Concern also was growing about the chemical contamination of groundwater supplies—the deep underground aquifers that are the source of drinking water for many of the nation's communities. In early 1987 Congress authorized $18 billion in grants and loan funds to help pay for sewage-treatment plants, plus an additional $2 billion to clean up lakes, rivers, and estuaries and to help states find ways to curb runoff pollution from urban and rural land.[15]

---

[14]Council on Environmental Quality, op. cit., pp. 11–13. However, for a report on continuing problems, see Robert E. Taylor, "Despite Nearly 2 Decades of Federal Efforts, Many in the U.S. Still Breathe Unhealthy Air," *Wall Street Journal*, April 6, 1987, p. 48.

[15]Ibid.; and Robert E. Taylor, "Senate Votes 86–14 for Clean Water Act, Joining House to Override Reagan Veto," *Wall Street Journal*, January 5, 1987, p. 48.

Controversy continued also about how to dispose safely of the heaps of solid waste—for example, 250 million tons in 1986—generated by modern life. Many municipal landfills were reaching capacity. Proposals to incinerate solid wastes met with opposition from groups and communities who raised questions about the air pollution that incineration might cause.[16] One plan to burn these wastes at sea was rejected by government authorities who were uncertain about the effects on the ocean's ecology.

In spite of continuing pollution problems, the nation's inhabitants could say by the mid-1980s that they were breathing cleaner air and enjoying more environmentally stable waterways than had been true in 1970. These gains were a result of the new laws and agencies created in the early 1970s as well as a heightened environmental awareness on the part of citizens and business firms.

The Pressures of the New Global Competition

By 1980 global competition was heating up, putting severe pressures on the older "smokestack" industries. For that reason, productivity has become more important than ever if these industries are to stay afloat in the new competitive environment. Some of the new competitors are companies in nations with weaker pollution controls—and therefore lower costs—than the United States. This new competitive situation tends to put a damper on the drive for added environmental protection, since business firms and elected officials more frequently have to choose between of a cleaner environment and saving the jobs of workers. Legislative battles for environmental laws have become more prolonged and divisive. The coalitions of environmental activists, progressive business leaders, politicians who are concerned about the environment, and alarmed communities are not so easily formed as in the 1960s and 1970s. Although the general public continues to favor environmental protection, there is a growing awareness that competition, productivity, and jobs also must be considered.

Environmentalism's "Third Stage"

By far one of the most interesting changes during the 1980s was a shift in the strategies and tactics of major environmental protection groups. An example of this new approach comes from the executive director of the Environmental Defense Fund (EDF):

In the late 1970s the country's largest investor-owned utility, Pacific Gas & Electric Co. [PG&E], had plans to build $20 billion of large coal and nuclear power plants [in California]. The company thought those plants were indispensable to California's economic health; many others thought they were unbearable impositions on California's environment. An EDF team—a lawyer, an economist, and a computer analyst—developed a package of alternative energy sources and

[16]Bill Paul, "Burning Trash Is Becoming Big Business," *Wall Street Journal*, October 13, 1986, p. 6.

conservation investments, including cogeneration, voltage controls and utility-financed insulation and efficiency improvements.

EDF ultimately persuaded PG&E to adopt the plan. Why? Because it not only met the same electrical needs, but also meant lower prices for consumers and higher returns to PG&E stockholders through a package so innovative it had never been on any utility's drawing board. Today, PG&E is even paying to lease the EDF computer model that showed how. The alternatives made every one of the proposed large power plants unnecessary.[17]

This cooperative "let's work together" attitude of the 1980s began to replace the older confrontational "they're wrong–we're right" attitudes of the 1960s and 1970s. Instead of lawsuits and legislative battles, environmental disputes tended to be worked out directly through negotiations. Environmental mediation became a "growth industry;" in 1977 only nine disputes were mediated, but by mid-1984 more than 160 were settled through negotiations. One prominent environmentalist said:

> We are learning to trust each other. It's a slow and necessary process. Environmentalists and industrialists for too many years have considered one another as natural adversaries. Both sides have been far too doctrinaire, far too determined to create winners and losers. Now is the time to pursue positive options that will produce winners from both the economic development and environmental protection perspectives. We must chance cooperation in our pursuit of environmental success lest we stay mired in combat and stalemate.[18]

To put teeth into this philosophy, a number of innovative steps were taken by business leaders and environmentalists.

- The National Wildlife Federation created the Corporate Conservation Council, a forum of fifteen top corporate executives who meet four times each year to discuss important environmental issues.
- Beginning in 1982, the Conservation Foundation sponsored meetings of pesticide producers and conservation groups to discuss the impact of pesticides in the Third World.
- The National Water Alliance, which includes corporations, conservationists, and knowledgeable professionals, was formed in 1983 to develop a national policy on water use, water pollution, and treatment of polluted water sources.
- One of the most interesting initiatives of the "new environmentalism" was the creation of Clean Sites, Inc. (CSI) in 1984. With the Conservation Foundation leading the way, a coalition of chemical industry leaders and leading environmentalists established CSI as a private, nonprofit organization. Its task is to clean up many of the nation's hazardous waste dumps through combined private and public efforts. It works closely with the Environmental Protection Agency by encouraging private corporations to accept

[17]Frederic D. Krupp, "New Environmentalism Factors in Economic Needs," *Wall Street Journal*, November 20, 1986, p. 26.

[18]Jay D. Hair, "Conciliation: Charting a Future without Rancor," *Conservation Exchange*, National Wildlife Federation, July 1985, pp. 1, 8.

financial responsibility for part of the cleanup costs rather than taking an adversarial stance and forcing the EPA to take legal action that might delay efforts for many years. EPA's director said, "We need bridging institutions like this one to link people of good will on all sides of difficult, emotion-laden public issues that normally produce only gridlock."[19]

THE REMAINING ENVIRONMENTAL TASKS

As the late 1980s approached, several environmental problems remained on the nation's agenda. Many of the massive pollution sources had been brought under control by reducing smokestack emissions, automobile and truck emissions, and the careless dumping of industrial pollutants into the waterways. The remaining problems frequently were more difficult—and more costly—to solve.

Controlling Toxic Substances

Modern science and chemistry have contributed much to material comfort and have made possible a dazzling array of products for consumers as well as advanced production processes for industry and agriculture. The great majority of the estimated 70,000 chemical substances sold each year, and the approximately 500 new chemicals introduced annually, pose no threat to the human environment.[20] Some materials, though, are highly toxic when there is prolonged exposure.

> _H. J. Heinz Company, one of the nation's three major baby-food makers, announced in 1986 that it would no longer buy crops treated with a dozen chemicals that might carry risks for infants. Use of these compounds by farmers was legal at the time of the Heinz ban, but the company stated it did not want to risk the health of infants by exposing them to pesticide residues. The potential hazards are greater for infants, who consume far higher levels of fruits and vegetables for their body weight than do adults. The Environmental Protection Agency was in the process of studying the possible health risks associated with these materials. A company spokesperson said, "A lot of these chemicals are going to be found to be safe, but we don't know which ones. We feel it is a very conservative position [we are taking]." The two other large baby-food manufacturers did not follow Heinz's lead._[21]

Public concern about such health risks led Congress to adopt the Toxic Substances Control Act of 1976 and to strengthen federal laws restricting the

[19]"A Pragmatic Partnership Geared for Action on Derelict Dumps," _Chemical Week,_ June 6, 1984, pp. 10–11.

[20]Environmental Protection Agency, Office of Research and Development, _Environmental Outlook 1980,_ Washington, D.C., 1980, chap. 11.

[21]"Heinz to Restrict the Use in Baby Foods of Crops Treated with Some Chemicals," _Wall Street Journal,_ November 7, 1986, p. 11.

manufacture and use of agricultural chemicals. Chemical manufacturers are required to notify the EPA prior to commercial production of a new chemical substance, and they may be required to perform tests to verify its safety. Rules about labeling the product and how and where it is to be used are permitted by the law.

Hazardous Waste Disposal and Cleanup

Any industrial society has to find ways to dispose of waste materials that are a natural by-product of manufacturing. Studies show that only about 10 to 15 percent of industrial refuse can cause death, serious illness, genetic damage, or birth defects if not disposed of carefully. The most frequently found offenders are an electrical insulating compound known as PCB, various pesticides, and heavy metals such as mercury, cadmium, and lead.[22] Unfortunately, only about 10 percent of these hazardous wastes are safely dumped each year, and many old dump sites filled with these and other dangerous wastes pose a direct threat to human health.

To encourage a nationwide cleanup of hazardous waste dumps, Congress in 1980 passed the Superfund Law, known officially as the Comprehensive Environmental Response, Compensation, and Liability Act. The original "superfund" was a $1.6 billion trust fund that would help pay for the cleanup effort. It was financed by a special tax on manufacturers of petrochemicals and toxic organic chemicals and on oil importers, but the law also required those responsible for hazardous conditions to do the cleaning up and to pay restitution costs to those affected. In 1986 Congress authorized a fivefold increase in the Superfund to a five-year total of $9 billion, financing it this time with a broad-based tax on corporations as well as special taxes on chemical producers and crude oil producers.

Congress extended the Superfund Law in response to growing public concern about the penetration of hazardous materials into the environment. By 1984, over 19,000 hazardous waste sites had been identified, with an additional 6,000 expected to be found by 1986. The most threatening ones were put on the EPA's National Priorities List (NPL). By 1985 the NPL was expected to include over 750 extremely dangerous cleanup sites.[23] One such location was in Massachusetts where a 70-acre landfill some 75 feet deep was filled with cancer-causing chemicals that were leaking into local groundwater supplies. Authorities estimated a total cleanup of this one site alone would cost $1.6 billion—the total amount spent on all such cleanups since 1980.

The biggest immediate danger from these waste disposal sites is possible contamination of groundwater. The Council on Environmental Quality found that three of every four sites on its National Priorities List posed threats to groundwater supplies, over half were in danger of contaminating surface

[22]For data on hazardous wastes, see *Environmental Outlook 1980*, pp. 516–522. For a discussion, see Ed Magnuson, "The Poisoning of America," *Time*, September 22, 1980, pp. 58–69; and Winston Williams, "Saving Face and Cleaning Up," *New York Times*, March 13, 1983, pp. F-1, F-2, F-17.

[23]Council on Environmental Quality, op. cit., pp. 177–178.

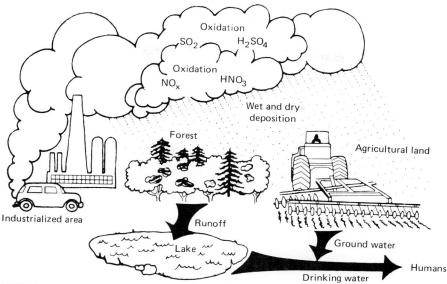

FIGURE 17-6 Formation and fallout of acid rain. (*Source: Adapted from Environmental Protection Agency, Office of Research and Development,* Environmental Outlook 1980, *Washington, D.C., 1980, p. 199.*)

waters, and one of every five polluted the air. Even more alarming was the fact that over 6 million persons were drinking water from wells located within 3 miles of the NPL waste dumps.

Acid Rain

Another kind of environmental danger is acid rain. Acid rain falls when nitrogen and sulfur oxides in the atmosphere combine with naturally occurring water vapor to form a dilute solution of nitric acid and sulfuric acid. Acid rain has been falling on the earth for millions of years because rotting vegetation and evaporating seawater have released the oxides that generate the problem. The Office of Technology Assessment has estimated that natural sources are responsible for between 20 and 40 percent of the problem in the United States. The other 60 to 80 percent is generally thought to come from the smokestack emissions of coal-burning industrial plants and from motor vehicle exhausts, as depicted in Figure 17-6.

Environmentalists claim that acid rain—which at times has the acidity of vinegar or lemon juice—kills fish in lakes and streams, stunts forest growth, threatens soil fertility, corrodes municipal water systems, and defaces statues, monuments, and buildings. Nearly half of Canada, much of the northeastern part of the United States, and portions of Scandinavia and Germany experience high levels of acid rain. Canada fears the long-term effects on its $1-billion sport-fishing industry and its $22-billion-a-year forestry industry.

If the power plants and other industrial installations that burn high-sulfur coal switched to more expensive low-sulfur coal, or if they installed smokestack controls, they would be forced to charge higher prices for electricity and other products. After putting scrubbers on two of its power plants, one large Eastern electric utility estimated it would cost up to $500 million more to equip all of its plants with similar controls. Also, coal miners in some parts of the country would suffer job losses, while others might gain. Complicating the entire picture is uncertainty about the precise extent to which industrial pollutants contribute to acid rain. However, the authoritative National Academy of Sciences reported that sulfur dioxide emissions from industrial sources produce acid rain and that acid rain harms the environment.[24]

Faced with these prospects, the governments of Canada and the United States agreed to a plan to improve the technology of coal burning, thereby reducing the amount of harmful pollutants spewed into the air. Government and industry would split the plan's $1-billion cost over a five-year period. Planners estimated that up to 90 percent of the emissions that cause acid rain would be eliminated at the source.

High-Tech Pollution

In the mid-1980s, it came as a surprise to learn that pollution could be a problem even for the seemingly cleaner high-tech industries. In California's Silicon Valley, underground storage tanks for solvents used in producing electronic components were found to be leaking chemicals into local drinking-water sources. The EPA proposed to add nineteen of these trouble spots to its National Priorities List for quick cleanup, and the involved companies agreed to fund voluntary cleanup operations costing at least $70 million.

High-tech pollution was not limited to the outside environment. Inside the plants, workers were sometimes exposed to dangerous acids, solvents, and gases necessary for producing silicon chips and microprocessors. In spite of company efforts to insure employees against overexposure, injuries sometimes occurred. Thus, in these ways society paid a price for the marvels that were made possible by the electronics revolution.[25]

STRATEGIC GUIDELINES FOR BUSINESS ACTION

Ecological issues can be condensed into a few basic guidelines for business. As society's major economic institution for production of goods and services, business cannot ignore the natural environment. It must live in harmony with nature. In order to do so, it needs to observe the following guidelines:

- To reduce pollution to the extent that is economically and technically reasonable.

---

[24]"Who'll Stop the Acid Rain?" *Newsweek*, March 24, 1986, p. 60; and Robert E. Taylor, "Acid-Rain Damage to Lakes Minimal, EPA Advisers Find," *Wall Street Journal*, March 26, 1987, p. 41.

[25]David E. Sanger, "Worries Over Toxins Grow in Silicon Valley," *New York Times*, November 10, 1984, p. 1.

- To design future facilities and activities for ecological harmony. Included is an obligation to create better ways to live in harmony with the environment.
- To respond meaningfully to ecological concerns expressed by stakeholders and the general public.

In this situation society needs to be cautious that it does not become overzealous and excessive in its demands for virtually zero ecological effects from business activities. Almost any human activity has an ecological impact. The idea is not to prevent activity, but rather to assure that activity is in harmony with nature so that nature's powers of self-restoration will maintain a clean and livable environment.

SUMMARY

Ecology is concerned with the relationships of living things and their environments. As a contributor to pollution, business is involved in society's ecological problems. These problems are complex, and their solution requires many trade-offs between economic production and a cleaner, safer environment.

Pollution control became a high social priority in the United States during the 1970s. In the 1980s environmental cleanup continued to receive strong public support, and there was evidence of increasing cooperation between business and environmentalists. However, the cleanup task is far from over and will continue to be a challenge for business during the remainder of the twentieth century.

DISCUSSION AND REVIEW QUESTIONS

1. In 1960 few people had ever heard about ecology, but by 1980 it had become a common household word. How do you account for this relatively rapid rise in public consciousness about ecological relationships?

2. Suppose that a group of environmentalists proposes to a board that governs a city-owned convention center that the board deny use of the center's facilities to any business or business group that "contributes to ecological imbalance." The group specifically mentions strip mines, chemical manufacturers, automobile firms, and petroleum companies, especially any company that has been found guilty of illegal dumping of hazardous wastes. You chair the governing board and also are vice president of a local chemical plant that produces industrial chemicals. How would you respond to the proposal?

3. Assume that you and your family live within "polluting distance" of an electric-power-generating station that burns high-sulfur coal and also has a nuclear power reactor. Would you favor pollution charges as a way to control the company's pollutants? How would you feel as a company stockholder? As an employee? As a user of electricity? Discuss the different points of view.

4. Suppose a new supply of a low-cost but highly polluting energy were discovered. Assume it could free us forever from dependence on foreign sources of energy, could double the average person's standard of living, but would require destruction of large areas of undeveloped wilderness lands in this country. Pollution deaths from this new energy source are estimated at 50,000 per year. Would you favor developing and using this new form of energy? Discuss the pros and cons.

5. Which of the following groups should pay for cleaning up the environment and keeping it clean: Carmakers whose cars pollute the air, or car owners who drive them? Microprocessor-chip manufacturers who discard toxic wastes, or consumers who buy computers and other devices that rely on microprocessors? What would be a fair way of allocating the cost burdens?

CRITICAL INCIDENT

Ozone—the Earth's Solar Shield

Picture yourself as the director of a hypothetical task force composed of representatives from the major United States manufacturers and industrial users of chlorofluorocarbons (CFCs). These chemical compounds are used as refrigerator and air conditioner coolants, as solvents and cleaners in electronics manufacturing, and in making insulation and padding material, and foam packaging for such uses as fast-food throwaway cartons. Some of the companies represented on your task force are Du Pont Company (the nation's largest CFC maker), Allied-Signal, Kaiser Aluminum & Chemicals, Pennwalt, York International (producer of air conditioners), and several industrial users of CFCs such as IBM, General Motors, Ford Motor, and Digital Equipment.

The hypothetical task force has been formed by these companies to develop recommended guidelines concerning future production and use of CFCs. Several scientific studies have concluded that CFCs are partly responsible for a thinning out of the earth's layer of naturally occurring ozone. The ecological function of this stratospheric ozone layer is to screen out strong ultraviolet rays from the sun, thereby protecting life at the earth's surface. Without this protective screen, humans would experience more skin cancers, eye cataracts, and dysfunctions of their immune systems; many food crops would be destroyed; certain forms of aquatic life would die; and weather cycles might be drastically altered.

Complicating the task force's job is some degree of scientific uncertainty. CFCs are not the only chemical compound capable of depleting the ozone layer. Bromines, used widely in fire extinguishers, also produce the same effects. Some scientists believe that volcanic eruptions spew out sulfur compounds and other particles that are partly responsible. Still others say that solar cycles and sunspots may be involved. It is even possible that purely isolated stratospheric conditions deplete ozone in limited areas, thereby exaggerating the presumed worldwide effects.

In spite of these complexities, some things seem reasonably certain. The ozone layer has thinned out since the problem was first noticed in the mid-1970s. CFC producers agree that their product is partly responsible. Sales of CFCs worldwide are increasing after a drop in the late 1970s following a ban on spray-can use of

CFCs in the United States. The fastest-growing uses of CFCs are in car air conditioners, insulation, and fast-food packaging. Once injected into the environment in these forms, CFCs cannot be prevented from eventually finding their way into the stratosphere. A complete worldwide ban imposed today would still lead to decades of continued leakage of CFCs into the air from present uses. One other certainty is the expected increase in skin cancers, perhaps as many as 40 million additional cases and up to 800,000 cancer deaths by 2075. Substantial curtailment of CFC usage would cut these risks by 90 percent.

The manufacturers on your task force sell $750 million of CFCs annually, and this amounts to about one-third of world production. Some of the demand comes from developing nations whose citizens want more refrigerators, air conditioners, automobiles, and other CFC-using products. Most European producers did not stop using CFCs as spray-can propellants in the 1970s. Obviously, United States manufacturers are reluctant to restrict their sales if foreign makers remain free to meet the increasing demands. Competitive pressures like these led CFC producers from twenty-four nations to meet in Geneva, Switzerland, in late 1986 to try to agree on ways to cope with this ecological threat.

Finding substitute materials for CFCs is not easy. Du Pont ended its research program in 1980 after discovering that alternatives would be uneconomical to make, would lead to costly manufacturing redesign, and might create additional toxicity problems for producers and users. By 1986, though, a company official said, "We have been rethinking our position." Automakers were looking to chemical companies in the United States, Germany, and Japan to develop alternative coolants for air conditioners.

After several months of work, your task force is to meet soon to draft its list of recommendations and guidelines. As task force director, you are expected to take the lead.[26]

1. What are the main recommendations and guidelines you can suggest for the task force?

2. What position can the task force take that will be socially responsible while still protecting the economic interests of CFC manufacturers, their stockholders, and their employees?

3. Who should pay for the research and development needed to find less environmentally damaging substitutes for CFCs? Should it be the CFC producers, the automakers, and others who use CFCs in their products, or the end-use consumers (car buyers, fast-food consumers, and others)?

4. What would you say to a member of the task force who said that no action should be taken at the present time because of scientific uncertainty about the precise role of CFCs in causing ozone depletion? Could you argue that taking action now would be less costly for the industry in the long run, as well as being more ethical? What would that argument be?

[26]Barry Meier, "Ozone Demise Quickens Despite '78 Ban on Spray Propellant; New Curbs Debated," _Wall Street Journal_, August 13, 1986, p. 23; "Ozone: Industry Is Getting Its Head Out of the Clouds," _Business Week_, October 13, 1986, pp. 110, 114; Barry Meier, "Hard Choices Await Industry as Ozone-Layer Fears Rise," _Wall Street Journal_, December 2, 1986, p. 4; and New York Times News Service, "Ozone Loss May Double Skin Cancer," reprinted in _Pittsburgh Post-Gazette_, November 5, 1986, p. 5.

Chapter Eighteen

GLOBAL BUSINESS AND SOCIAL POLICY

Modern business is increasingly global in character. Global corporations face great complexities and challenges in the international business environment. The necessity of dealing with two or more governments increases the political uncertainty for business. The large size and market power of multinational enterprises also pose serious challenges to government and managers. Moreover, the social infrastructure of a host nation influences a multinational company's conduct, creating social issues and ethical dilemmas that affect global strategic plans.

CHAPTER OBJECTIVES

After reading this chapter, you should be able to

- Illustrate how business has become increasingly internationalized
- Describe the influence that foreign governments and intergovernmental relationships have on multinational enterprise
- Analyze the influence multinationals can have on a host nation's socioeconomic structure
- Describe how the economic and social environment of a host country can affect the operations of a multinational
- Analyze how the public in a multinational's home country can influence that company's subsidiary operations in other countries
- Define questionable payments and discuss the impact of the Foreign Corrupt Practices Act on the operations of multinationals

Most large businesses can no longer consider just one country as their entire sphere of operations; increasingly, corporations operate in, and conduct business with, many other countries. Managers cannot create or implement policies without considering the impact of their actions on the countries in which they do business.

For example, environmentalists and government officials around the world have criticized the World Bank for providing loans for many development projects that are rapidly destroying the world's tropical rain forests and the hundreds of living species they house. The Polonoroest project in Brazil, an effort to pave a 500-mile highway and an extensive web of secondary roads in the Amazon jungle to open the Amazon Valley to agriculture and industry, is credited with some of the most serious deforestation problems to date. The World Bank has loaned more than $450 million to the developers, and millions of acres of tropical rain forest have been destroyed.

Polonoroest was supposed to be a showcase of environmental responsibility. Special loan provisions required that certain areas be protected as natural reserves, certain areas be left to tribal groups, health measures be enacted to protect the local Indians, and soil areas that are deemed unsuitable for settlement or agriculture be left uncleared. However, critics claim that both the World Bank and the Brazilian government grossly mismanaged the project. According to an attorney with the Natural Resources Defense Council, extensive violations have resulted in "an ecological, human, and economic disaster of tremendous proportions. . . . [I]ntended protected natural areas and Indian reserves have been invaded by spontaneous settlement, now out of control, and in one such area . . . the threatened tribe recently took a dozen settlers hostage in a desperate attempt to force the government to protect its lands."[1]

Pressure has been exerted from various sources to force the World Bank to take a more socially and environmentally responsible position in lending to land developers. In 1985, an international consortium made up of representatives from the World Bank, the World Resources Institute (a Washington, D.C.–based environmental think tank) and the United Nations, developed a global strategy to save the tropical forests. The United States government also has taken action, and Congress has initiated action calling for denial of foreign aid to projects that would result in further deforestation.

Environmental writer Edward Flattau suggests, however, that reform in environmental policies will have to come from the countries themselves, and then rub off on the World Bank. "These multinational banks are heavily laden with bureaucrats who hail from the countries obtaining the loans," he said. "And these foreign governments have a disproportionately large role in dictating the terms of the loans they receive. If these governments happen to be environmentally insensitive, the banks are unlikely to do anything about it."[2]

[1]"Conservation Foundation Letter," November–December 1984, p. 5.

[2]Ibid., p. 6. (Original quote: *Statesman Journal*, Salem, Ore., July 8, 1983.)

This problem well illustrates the complexity of international business relationships and responsibilities. Governments are directly dealing with one another in an attempt to finance important projects and develop a global environmental policy. The operations of developers are influenced by the actions of both the host country (Brazil) and by the actions of international bodies (the World Bank). And the social environment of the host country has been threatened to the point where, in one instance, local citizens actually took settlers hostage to force the government to protect their lands. These three basic issues—governmental relationships, economic needs, and socio-cultural pressures—form a framework for understanding the situation facing global organizations.

INCREASING INTERNATIONALIZATION OF ENTERPRISE

Modern business relationships are increasingly global in nature. Only a few decades ago, the opportunities for global operations were limited. International communications systems were much slower; travel and shipping were slower and much less practical. In the United States, sizeable profits could be made without the trouble and cost of operating in other countries.

This is no longer the case. Today, people get to virtually any place on the globe in a day or less, and international communication is almost instantaneous. It is possible to manage and control operations in many countries simultaneously, and it can be done effectively and profitably. Resources are sometimes more plentiful and less costly in other countries; labor may be cheaper, taxes may be lower. In some cases it is even beneficial if the weather is better.

The developing nations are among the fastest-growing markets in the world, which is another factor that has caused many companies to take their business abroad. However, some feel that the American business community has not competed effectively for its share of these new markets, which are vital to our ability to sustain growth that will create more jobs in the future. During the 1980s, the Reagan administration consistently emphasized the need for private sector participation in furthering the development process, and the Overseas Private Investment Corporation (OPIC), created by an act of Congress in 1961, has intensified its efforts to increase investment flows to the developing world and increase the entry rate of smaller businesses into international markets.[3]

Development of Multinational Enterprise

International business has changed in character over the years. The first "international businesses" consisted of national companies that operated one plant, or a few mines, in another country. This type of company viewed its

[3]Craig A. Nalen, "The Role of Private Investment in Third World Development," *Columbia Journal of World Business*, Twentieth Anniversary Issue 1966–1986, Fall 1986, p. 62.

home nation as its major area of operations, and it looked to this home nation as the major source of its capital, markets, managerial talent, and even legal system for security and justice. It was *ethnocentric* in the sense that its standards were based upon its home nation's customs, markets, and laws. The ethnocentric "international" company operated on two premises: first, it assumed that all managerial practices that were successful in the home country would be equally successful in other countries of operation; second, it assumed that management should be supplied by the home country, while operating employees should be provided by the host nation.

Modern international businesses have found they must adopt a less ethnocentric approach to be successful on a global basis. These businesses consider the world, not just the home nation, as their "primary" area of operations. They are *geocentric* in outlook, adapting their practices to different national cultures and environments while continuing to maintain worldwide identity and policies. They develop leadership among all nationals and truly seek to use the best people for all jobs regardless of their country of origin.

> *Companies such as IBM, Exxon, Ford Motor, Digital Equipment, and Citicorp are among the many examples of firms with truly international management staffs. American Standard, Inc., headquartered in the United States, is a worldwide producer and distributor of plumbing fixtures, building supplies, and commercial products. At least eight of the vice-presidents located in the company's headquarters have been foreign-born. And there are over twenty foreign-born department managers reporting directly to the headquarters vice-president.[4]*

Challenges of Going Abroad

Expansion beyond national boundaries is much more than a step across a geographical line. It is also a step into different social, educational, political, and economic environments. As we have illustrated in previous chapters, even businesses operating in only one country cannot operate successfully without taking into consideration a wide variety of stakeholder needs and interests. Anything the company does to achieve its business purpose must respect the business-government-society relationship: it must act within the laws of the nation, and its behavior must be considered acceptable and safe by affected groups in the society.

This dynamic relationship is compounded on the international level. Multinational firms not only must compete with national firms in the national market and conform, overall, to the policies of the corporate headquarters (and, by implication, the laws of the home country); they also must compete with firms in a completely different market and conform to the customs, cultures, and laws of the host societies of each foreign subsidiary. Quite frequently, this creates conflicts. Managers of the foreign subsidiary may find themselves forced to choose between following the host country's laws or customs and following the corporation's headquarters' policies.

[4]"American Standard's Executive Melting Pot," *Business Week*, July 2, 1979, p. 92.

Consider the example of the British book publisher's representative, whose sales territory was the entire continent of Africa.[5] This representative sold textbooks to governments that purchased them for public school systems. As the sales representative explained it, "each country is different. In some of them, we work through local agents who receive a commission on each sale. In other countries I deal directly with a government representative. In one country I deal with the minister of education, who makes the final decision. He requires that we pay him personally a sales commission of 8 percent (some sales amount to more than $100,000). Our company and all our competitors pay the 8 percent. In some other nations the percentage is lower or higher."

Though such a practice would be considered bribery in Britain, the representative stated that in Africa it was simply "the custom of the country. If we refused, our books would not even be considered, so we would sell nothing. We have to follow the customs of each country. If we try to tell them how to do business, they ignore us." Further, he stated that "there would be bribery only if we paid him more than 8 percent in order to influence his decision unfairly. This is an open transaction known to all people in the trade. As long as we pay the same rate as the others, no book company has an unfair advantage."

Thus, the international business environment is extremely complex and problematic. The business-government-society relationship defined in earlier chapters applies individually to each subsidiary in each foreign country and to the multinational as a whole. The complexity of these relationships is illustrated in Figure 18-1. Each multinational firm must develop appropriate strategies and policies for working with these complexities.

GOVERNMENT AND POLITICAL ISSUES

The operation of international business is affected by governmental and political dynamics on two basic levels. First, in the broadest sense, business operates in an environment largely dictated by the relations between governments. If the governments of two or more countries are in conflict, business and trade between them, even between companies in a parent–subsidiary relationship, may be prevented or inhibited. Second, even in an atmosphere of normal or friendly relations between governments, international companies and their subsidiaries must consider their host governments as powerful political forces. A host government has the power to influence, control, or completely take over the operations of a company operating on its soil.

Intergovernmental Relations

The relationships between governments have a great impact on international business. Certainly, if two countries are at war, there will be no trade between

[5]This information was derived from a personal interview between one of the book's authors and a sales representative of a British book publisher.

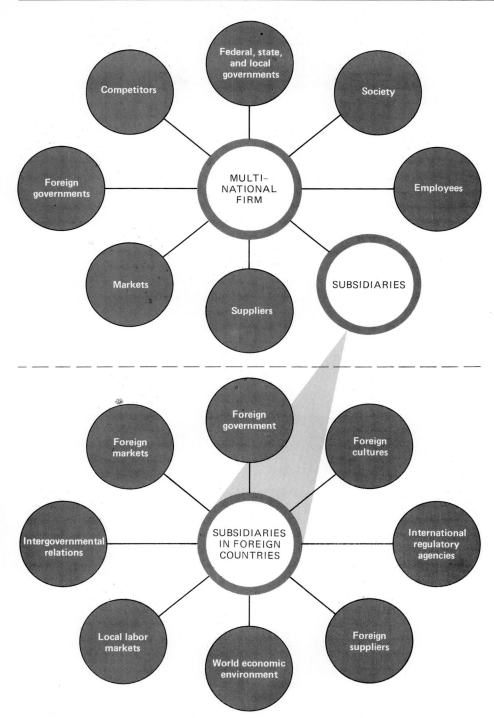

FIGURE 18-1   International business-government-society relationships.

them. But even in the absence of major conflicts, the nature and volume of international business activity are to some degree regulated by the state of intergovernmental relations.

> Consider trade relations between the United States and two other leading world powers: China and the Soviet Union. Diplomatic relations were established between the United States and China in 1979, during the Carter administration. Though China is a socialist nation and practices a planned economy, it also allows some flexibility for market forces. Since that time, two-way trade has expanded at an average rate of 44 percent, and bilateral trade topped $6 billion by 1984.[6] In less than a decade, economic relations have developed to conform with the fundamental interests of the two countries.
>
> On the other hand, trade between the United States and the Soviet Union has been much weaker, though given many more years to develop. After the Nixon–Brezhnev summit in 1972, which produced major grain and maritime trade agreements, estimates of future trade levels were extremely high. The White House issued a statement at the signing of the United States–Soviet Trade and Economic Agreement on October 12, 1972, which included a projection that total trade in the next two years would triple what it had been three years earlier.[7] Initially, American exports rose eightfold, and trade rose sixfold. Trade in later years, however, has been quite sluggish. Imports of Soviet goods have never been more than half of United States exports to the Soviet Union and in most cases are much less. In addition, after 1976, the increases in United States exports to the Soviet Union leveled off and in many cases dropped. Grain had accounted for the largest portion of United States exports, but after the Soviet invasion of Afghanistan and the ensuing grain embargo initiated by the United States, it dropped off by almost half and did not exceed its 1976 volume until 1984. Exports of machinery and transportation equipment were roughly one-sixth in 1984 what they had been in 1976.[8]

What accounts for these declines? A mutual distrust has existed between the United States and the Soviet Union for several decades. It is compounded by the efforts of those highly opposed to the Soviet Union to use trade—or a withholding of trade—as a weapon to punish it. The low volume of machinery exports signifies this best: "For a (large) number of vocal critics, there should be no trade at all. In their minds is the thought that just as the scrap metal sold to the Japanese prior to the bombing of Pearl Harbor came back to haunt the United States, so the sale of even conventional ma-

[6]Jia Shi, "Future Prospects for Broadening U.S.–China Economic and Trade Cooperation," *Columbia Journal of World Business*, Twentieth Anniversary Issue 1966–1986, Fall 1986, p. 57; also, Richard H. Holton, "Marketing and the Modernization of China," *California Management Review*, Summer 1985, pp. 33–45.

[7]U.S. Department of Commerce, "U.S.–Soviet Commercial Agreements 1972: Text, Summaries and Supporting Papers," Washington, D.C.: U.S. Government Printing Office, 1972, p. 75.

[8]Marshall I. Goldman, "U.S.–Soviet Trade: What Went Wrong and What About the Future?" *Columbia Journal of World Business*, Twentieth Anniversary Issue 1966–1986, Fall 1986, pp. 45–48.

- Pre-investment screening
- Incentives
  Tax holidays
  Import privileges and tariff exemptions
- Subsidies
  Assistance in plant construction or the training of employees
  Low-interest loans
- Guarantees by the host government
  Loan guarantees
  Investment insurance
  Guarantees of currency convertibility or repatriation of dividends and capital
- Tariff protection and/or local monopolies
- Promotion (advertisements, overseas investment centers, etc.)
- Regulations, licensing requirements, laws, to achieve various objectives
- Tying of licenses, permits, privileges, to desirable actions by an investor
- Persuasion, personal contacts, on-site visits

FIGURE 18-2   **Policy tools to shape and regulate foreign investment.** (*Source: William A. Stoever, "The Stages of Developing Country Policy Toward Foreign Investment," Columbia Journal of World Business, Fall 1985, p. 4.*)

chinery to the Soviet Union may some day be used against us in the same way."[9]

Foreign Government Influence over Multinationals

Even in an atmosphere of healthy trade and friendly relations the government of a host country has much power and authority to influence the actions of multinationals and "visiting" business. This influence can be understood in terms of the degree of impact on the business. The mildest type of influence is essentially *bureaucratic*. When a multinational firm enters another nation, it is usually subject to a variety of ownership regulations, controls, licenses, and foreign exchange rules imposed by the government. Even in the absence of malice on the part of the host government, this web of restrictions can be complicated if the government itself is unstable and bureaucratic and if it has inconsistent policies.

A second and more deliberate or manipulative type of influence that a host government may wield involves *sanctions and enticements*. A host country can derive many benefits from foreign investors, such as technology transfer and training, increased employment, and increased local productivity. On the other hand, because of the potential power of the multinational, many host governments fear that their sovereignty may be in jeopardy. Thus, the host government may use a variety of policy tools to shape and regulate foreign investment, attempting simultaneously to lure investors and prevent excessive manipulation by these investors. Examples of these tools are listed in Figure 18-2.

[9]Ibid., p. 46; see also Bill Keller, "Joint Ventures, Russian Style," *New York Times,* January 6, 1987, pp. 1D–6D.

Ideally, a government will utilize policy tools to increase the development and well-being of the country. However, according to William A. Stoever, a researcher in foreign investment, "host governments in developing countries have often driven away potential investors by demanding too many benefits in relation to what the countries could offer in return. . . . In addition, host countries have on occasion changed their terms towards investment projects after the projects were already in place."[10] In a similar sense, the host nation might implement policies that protect its national firms and put multinationals at a disadvantage.

> For example, *a multinational automobile manufacturer contracted with a local firm to supply automobile batteries, which turned out to be of inadequate quality and not according to specifications. The engineers from the assembly plant discussed the problem with the local supplier, explaining what could be done to correct the problems. While they waited for the local firm to produce the improved batteries, they arranged to use imported ones.*
>
> *However, instead of working to correct the problems, the local battery supplier worked with the government to secure a high tariff on imported batteries so that they would not be competitive with local batteries. The government chose to secure special protection for an inferior local product rather than to assist the visiting firm in its efforts to help the local supplier improve the product.*

The country in question was misusing its policy tools and making itself unattractive to foreign investors. However, some countries, whether by accident or design, have tended to increase their demands on foreign investors at a pace roughly corresponding to increases in their ability to attract investors. This practice is a better balanced use of policy tools. A framework for analyzing the stages of evolution in foreign investment policy has been created and is illustrated in Figure 18-3.

In the most serious cases, a host country might exert power of a *possessive* nature on multinationals. In some nations, especially with regard to basic industries, the government may insist on being a partial owner of a foreign business. In situations of sudden social upheaval or changes in government control, a country may nationalize, or expropriate, the assets of a company or plant. That is, the government will take ownership and control of the property and may or may not pay for what it takes. This can be very costly to the multinational. For example, in one year alone, between 1959 and 1960, Cuba nationalized $1.5 billion in United States assets.[11] There are several extreme examples such as this one, but the overall level of expropriation between 1960 and 1976 was roughly 4.4 percent of the 1976 total stock value of wholly and partially owned foreign firms in less-developed countries plus

---

[10]William A. Stoever, "The Stages of Developing Country Policy toward Foreign Investment," *Columbia Journal of World Business,* Fall 1985, p. 3.

[11]A classic discussion of this problem can be found in Franklin R. Root, "The Expropriation Experience of American Companies," *Business Horizons,* April 1968, pp. 69–74; see also Dennis Encarnation and Sushil Vachani, "Foreign Ownership: When Hosts Change the Rules," *Harvard Business Review,* September–October 1985, pp. 152–160.

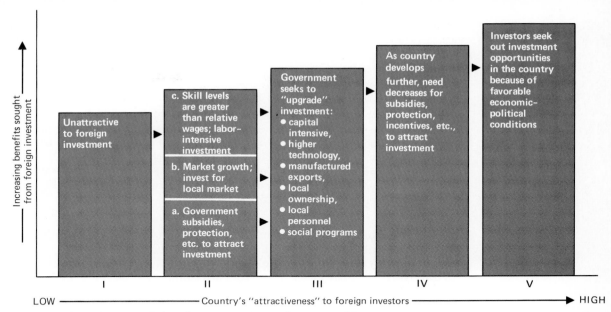

FIGURE 18-3   Stages of developing country policy toward foreign investment.
(_Source: Adapted from William A. Stoever, "The Stages of Developing Country Policy toward Foreign Investment," Columbia Journal of World Business, Fall 1985, p. 5._)

the value of seized assets.[12] The risk of nationalization is a strong deterrent to multinational firms in nations with a history of nationalization such as Algeria, Argentina, Chile, Cuba, Iraq, Libya, and Peru, or in nations with unstable governments or with a hostile attitude toward private business.

Political risk insurance, which covers a firm in the event that its assets are seized or trade contracts broken, became very popular in the early 1980s. The dollar volume of political risk coverage grew 50 percent annually between 1980 and 1984, but then it leveled off. One reason was the size of the claims made; Lloyds of London paid out $20 million in 1984 after Sudan failed to pay off a debt. After a rash of similar claims against Mexico, Venezuela, and Nigeria, insurance companies cut by 30 to 40 percent the amount of political risk insurance they are willing to write.[13] The Overseas Private Investment Corporation (OPIC) is a government corporation that insures United States companies against certain types of political risks but not all.

With risks still high and insurance harder to come by, multinationals must take other measures to protect their interests—and assets. One way to do this is by organizing operations so that the cost-benefit relationship is beneficial to the host nation. One study revealed that foreign firms can reduce

[12]F. N. Burton and Hisashi Inoue, "Expropriations of Foreign-Owned Firms in Developing Countries," _Journal of World Trade Law_, September–October 1984, p. 398.

[13]John Paul Newport, Jr., "Risky Business," _Fortune_, August 5, 1985, p. 71; see also J. Daniels et al., "U.S. Joint Ventures in China: Motivation and Management of Political Risk," _California Management Review_, Summer 1985, pp. 46–58.

- Complex operations that are above the normal operating abilities of the local labor force
- Much plant production sold to other plants of the same company
- Over 40 percent of production exported to other nations
- Management team consisting of less than 50 percent of foreign nationals
- Being of only minor strategic importance to the host nation
- Being small or moderate-sized
- Aggressive management contact and communication with influential host nationals in government

FIGURE 18-4 **Conditions that give a multinational company bargaining power to reduce political intervention in a less-developed host nation.** (*Source: Developed from data in Thomas A. Poynter, "Government Intervention in Less-Developed Countries: The Experience of Multinational Companies," Journal of International Business Studies, Spring–Summer 1982, pp. 9–25.*)

intervention in general by maintaining certain conditions, as listed in Figure 18-4.[14] In general, the firm develops conditions that give it strength and independence so that it has effective bargaining power with the government. It avoids large size and strategic importance when possible. Then it makes sure that influential government officials understand its strong position. In sum, the firm "manages" its political risk vulnerability.

When nationalization does occur, an equal or greater loser sometimes is the expropriating nation itself. It can only nationalize property. It cannot nationalize managerial skills, technical know-how, international markets, and the many benefits that multinational business offers a nation. The multinational business may be needed because a *multiplier effect tends to develop and spread management skills, labor skills, capital, technology, and market opportunities in the nations in which it operates.*

MARKET AND ECONOMIC ISSUES

A multinational enterprise in a foreign country is itself a political force, having the power to affect, positively or negatively, the country in which it is operating. Because operating on an international level often requires very large amounts of capital and other resources, international firms tend to be economic giants. The sales of the world's largest corporations rival the gross national product of many less-developed nations. Such powerful multinational firms are certainly subject to the implications of the Iron Law of Responsibility (which was discussed in Chapter 2).

Multinational Economic Influence in Foreign Countries

Multinational companies have a powerful effect on the nations that host their subsidiaries and branches. These companies have the power to employ, or

---

[14]Warnock Davis, "Beyond the Earthquake Allegory: Managing Political Risk Vulnerability," *Business Horizons*, July–August 1981, pp. 39–43. See also Mark Fitzpatrick, "The Definition and Assessment of Political Risk in International Business: A Review of the Literature," *Academy of Management Review*, April 1983, pp. 249–254; and John Fayerweather, "Four Winning Strategies for the International Corporation," *Journal of Business Strategy*, Fall 1981, pp. 25–36.

not employ, hundreds of local people. They can support or compete with local businesses, buying their products or blocking them out of the market. They can strengthen or weaken the nation's economy. They can enhance the socioeconomic infrastructure by building roads, schools, hospitals, and housing, or they can restrict use of all of their resources to their own operations.

> *There are numerous examples of the negative impact companies have had on their host nations. In many developing nations, a multinational has built a plant, drawn peasants and farmers from the countryside, and thus disrupted the social structure of the people. Then when the plant is closed because of political unrest in the country, a change in the company's strategy, or some other reason, the people are let go, and they have no means to support themselves. Even companies whose operations involve only marketing rather than on-site production can have a profound effect on the people who buy their product. Nestlé, for example, was criticized for its marketing of infant formula in the developing world. Because the successful use of the formula was dependent on the availability of sanitary water and the ability of mothers to afford a regular supply of the formula, conditions that often were not met in developing countries, many infants became sick and died from malnutrition or infections.*

It is evident that a multinational business should develop strategies and policies that respect the "economic sovereignty" of any country in which it chooses to do business, as well as try to understand the nature and strength of the economic environment of this country to determine what types of activity it can or cannot support.

Economic Environment

Business is so thoroughly involved in the economic life of a nation that several books would be required to discuss the international economic environment. There are high interest rates, capital shortages, unstable economic systems, and restrictions on repatriation of profits. All are important issues, but three—inflation, trade, and debt—are the most central problems of the international economic environment.

Inflation

For several decades, inflation was the single most critical issue facing the world's economies. A high level of inflation creates so much instability and social unrest that it restricts business's capacity to operate successfully.

> *The United States in the 1960s and 1970s had inflation that reduced the value of the dollar more than one-half, but between 1980 and 1985 high inflation was all but conquered in most Western and industrial countries (though the cost was a greater-than-expected economic slowdown). In other countries, however, currency has been cut to one-hundredth or even one-thousandth of its value since 1940, as reflected by cost-of-living indexes. What used to cost one unit of currency now costs 1,000 or more: in other words, an ice-cream cone that originally cost 20 cents would now cost 20,000 cents, or $200.*

The countries suffering the highest levels of inflation in the first half of the 1980s were Argentina, Brazil, Israel, and Bolivia, with monthly peaks (at an annual rate) of 2,500 percent, 400 percent, 2,000 percent, and 20,000 percent respectively. Only by instituting severe inflation-cutting measures was Argentina able to reduce its inflation rate to 100 percent, Brazil to 20 percent, Israel to 20 percent, and Bolivia to 50 percent. Argentina and Brazil were able to increase industrial output at the same time, and Bolivia and Israel were able to keep unemployment increases to under 2 percentage points.[15]

With high inflationary conditions, such matters as capital investment, inventory policy, sales policy, and cash discounts are substantially affected. An entire year's profit could be wiped out by currency depreciation or some other condition external to the firm. Typical "good management" through long-range planning is very difficult, and even regular operations can be disrupted.

Since inflation weakens confidence in money, it often causes capital to flee from the inflated country to one with a more stable currency. This condition increases capital shortages and further limits business and national development. The many possible constraints[16] on productive enterprise in developing nations have led some people to believe that certain nations tend to use their resources less effectively because their socioeconomic infrastructure is not supportive of development.[17] When multinational businesses consider entering a nation, they need to be able to assess this infrastructure so that their decisions will be strategically sound.

Trade

Another aspect of the economic environment that heavily influences international business is the balance of trade. In the most basic sense, the country that imports much more than it exports is in a weaker position than the country that exports much more than it imports. Trade goes on at varying levels between all nations in the world, and because each country's trade balance differs from country to country, the web of international trade relationships and the overall import-export balance are almost impossible to define accurately.

Following World War II, global trade increased steadily until 1980, at which time it leveled off. This was mostly because of the onset of a worldwide recession, the first since the Second World War. By the mid-1980s, the recession had eased, and international trade increased as the economies of the

---

[15]"Hyperinflation, Taming the Beast," *The Economist*, November 15, 1986, p. 55; see also Alan Riding, "Brazilian Debt Crisis Flames Again," *New York Times*, February 16, 1987, pp. 43, 48.

[16]A study of constraints is reported in Richard W. Wright, "Comparative Management in a Dynamic Setting: Empirical Research in Chile," *Organization and Administrative Sciences*, Winter 1976–1977, pp. 1–20.

[17]Jacques Delacroix, "The Export of Raw Materials and Economic Growth: A Cross-National Study," *American Sociological Review*, October 1977, pp. 795–808.

United States, Western Europe, and other regions improved. However, economic recovery is unevenly distributed around the world. Many Third World countries are struggling with enormous debts, high interest payments, and austerity measures that make it difficult for them to compete or survive in the worldwide economy and that depress their ability to purchase foreign goods. Nations such as Mexico, which depended heavily on oil revenues, suffered greatly when oil prices dropped from $30 per barrel to less than $15 per barrel.

Though smaller, less-developed countries are at an obvious disadvantage, even larger, highly developed countries can have trade deficits. In the mid-1980s, for example, the United States had a trade deficit that reached $174 billion. The strong dollar made imports cheaper to sell in the United States and American-made goods more expensive to sell abroad. The result was pinched economic growth at home and the loss of jobs all across industrial America. According to one estimate, the United States economy by the end of 1984 had 2 million fewer jobs—1.5 million in manufacturing—because of the strong dollar.[18] Many in industry and in government began taking steps to alleviate the problem by tackling both the federal budget deficit and the trade deficit. As explained by one analyst:

> There have been discussions among representatives of leading free world governments on what actions should be taken to bring the value of the dollar down. Some steps have been taken by central banks, intervening in exchange markets. There have been calls, too, for another international monetary conference, which would be the first since Bretton Woods in 1944. Also encouraging is the proposal . . . for initiatives to achieve greater world economic stability through innovative new programs to aid debtor nations and developing countries. . . . To address the problems with the United States and world economies, we . . . must achieve a balanced role for America in world manufacturing and business . . . that assumes that the U.S. is part of an interdependent world economy.[19]

Debt

A third problem affecting multinational business operations is international debt. At the end of 1985 Third World debt neared $1 trillion, and many of the countries with severe inflation problems (Argentina, Brazil, Mexico, and Israel) were also some of the heaviest borrowers. Though rescheduling of debt repayments helped to alleviate some of these problems, it was widely agreed that the health of the United States economy would greatly affect recovery and growth efforts in debtor nations. Therefore, many became deeply concerned in spring 1985, when the United States became a debtor to the world for the first time since World War I. By early 1987, United States indebtedness—the difference between all known foreign holdings of equity and debt in the United States and similar American investments abroad—

[18]Monroe W. Karmin with Robert F. Black, "Where Surge of Imports Is Hitting the Hardest," *U.S. News & World Report*, May 6, 1985, pp. 45–46.

[19]Colby H. Chandler, "A Vision for America's Role in a Balanced World Economy," *Columbia Journal of World Business*, Fall 1986, pp. 13–14.

exceeded $200 billion. If these trends continue, not only will the United States economy and standard of living suffer, but the whole indebted world will struggle to recover. Thus, economic and market issues have a powerful impact on the conduct of international business.

SOCIAL INFRASTRUCTURE ISSUES

The third major factor affecting multinational operations is the social environment. The multinational enterprise must understand and take consideration of two social environments when operating between countries. One is the social environment of the host nation; all international operations must operate within its constraints. The other is the social environment of the home nation itself; the multinational firm's operations abroad must be sanctioned by the home-country society.

Social Infrastructure of the Host Nation

Four major aspects of the social infrastructure directly affect foreign business operations in a host nation: variations in culture, social overhead costs, public acceptance, and educational overhead costs.

Variations in Culture

The widespread variation in culture among people and nations makes each operating situation unique, creating both opportunities and problems. There are important variations in social factors such as human resource development, environmental protection, employment of women, and corporate giving.[20] Sometimes these variations are so unusual that they stretch the creativity of the multinational company.

> The Intercontinental Hotel Unit of Pan American Airways had an opportunity to construct an Intercontinental Hotel in Mecca, the Moslem religious capital that is off-limits to non-Moslems. The firm did not have enough qualified Moslem engineers and construction managers available, so a creative solution to the problem was required. The firm stationed its non-Moslem construction engineers and project supervisors outside the city, where they watched construction on closed-circuit television and communicated by radio and telephone with Moslem work crews.[21]

> The amount of difference between any two social systems is called cultural distance, and in many situations it may be substantial. As concisely stated by a

[20]Lee E. Preston et al., "Comparing Corporate Social Performance: Germany, France, Canada and the U.S.," *California Management Review*, Summer 1978, pp. 40–49; and Vern Terpstra, *The Cultural Environment of International Business*, Cincinnati: South-Western, 1978.

[21]"Holy Hotel," *Forbes*, July 1, 1977. p. 10.

When Entering a New Nation	Percent Expressing Difficulty	When Returning to One's Home Nation	Percent Expressing Difficulty
Adjustment problems related to:		Adjustment problems related to:	
Personnel and labor philosophies	73	Insufficient decision-making authority	93
Quality control	51	Less responsibility than abroad	80
Language	51		
Currency fluctuations	51		
Foreign work attitudes	50		

FIGURE 18-5   Major adjustment difficulties reported by employees when entering another nation or returning to their home country. (*Source: Developed from data in "When the Overseas Executive Comes Home,"* Management Review, *August 1982, pp. 53–54, based on a survey of approximately 100 managers by Korn/Ferry International.*)

citizen of an Asian country, "We are two days and 200 years distant from Washington."[22] Extensive cultural distance sometimes makes it difficult for employees to adapt to foreign assignments. They may experience *cultural shock (also called culture shock)—the disorientation and insecurity caused by the strangeness of a different culture*—when they first take an assignment in a foreign country. They may become psychologically upset and unable to perform effectively, because their surroundings appear so unfamiliar and chaotic. As shown in Figure 18-5, they especially have difficulty adjusting to different philosophies, quality control, language, currency, and work attitudes.

> *Several studies of expatriate assignments indicated that incidences of expatriate failure in United States multinationals are sometimes as high as 30 to 40 percent. Most of the failures were attributed to two primary factors: one, the family situation (the spouse and/or children do not like living in the foreign country for personal or professional reasons); and two, a lack of relational skills, that is, the inability of the expatriate to adapt to the different cultural environment.*[23]

However, a different culture is not social chaos. It is a systematic structure of behavior patterns, probably as systematic as the culture in the employee's home country. It can be understood if the employee has a receptive attitude. Expatriate managers must be able to adapt to the new culture and integrate the interests of the two or more cultures involved. There are several

---

[22]Quoted by Jose de Cubas, "Let's Call 'Time,'" *Columbia Journal of World Business,* November–December 1967, p. 7.

[23]Rosalie L. Tung, "Corporate Executives and Their Families in China: The Need for Cross-Cultural Understanding in Business," *Columbia Journal of World Business,* Spring 1986, pp. 21–25. See also Robert Shuter, "Know the Local Rules of the Game," *New York Times,* November 2, 1984, p. 2F.

actions that firms can take to reduce cultural shock and increase expatriates' ability to succeed in the foreign assignment.[24] Four useful actions are

- *Careful selection*: choosing employees who are low in ethnocentrism and who have an interest in living in another nation;
- *Assignment to culturally compatible areas*: adjustment to new surroundings is easier if employees, especially on their first assignment, are sent to nations that have some similarity to their own. Figure 18-6 illustrates clusters of nations that are socioculturally compatible or similar;
- *Predeparture training*: training employees and their spouses regarding the culture, general environment, and language of the country where they will be living;
- *Orientation in the new country*: adjustment is encouraged after arrival if employees are assisted in finding housing and learning their way around, literally and figuratively.

Social Overhead Costs

Social overhead costs are public and private investments that are necessary to prepare the environment for effective operation of a new business. When a business establishes a major operation abroad, it may find that support facilities such as schools, hospitals, roads, and public utilities either are not available or are in such short supply that efficient operation of business is prevented. Essentially, the economic and social infrastructure is inadequate for the new operation. The whole system must be upgraded, and this results in substantial social overhead costs as well as additional start-up time.

> *An example is Marcona Mining Company, which opened a new iron ore mine in Peru on the western edge of the Andes Mountains. Although the mine was near the Pacific Ocean, it was in an uninhabited desert region, because prevailing winds deposit most of their moisture on the other side of the Andes.*
>
> *In this desolate area (the nearest major city was eight hours by road) it was necessary for the company to build a completely new city for its workers and support personnel. The company built streets, houses, schools, stores, and utilities. It was necessary to build a hospital, employ physicians and nurses, and bring water to this desert region.*
>
> *In addition, a complete port had to be built, including the harbor itself, since there was no natural harbor. Specialists for all of these support facilities were employed from several nations of the world.*
>
> *These new facilities primarily were social overhead costs that amounted to tens of millions of dollars. The entire community with its complex economic and social infrastructure was required for the mining venture to operate successfully.*

[24]For one discussion, see Faneuil Adams, Jr., "Developing an International Workforce," *Columbia Journal of World Business*, Twentieth Anniversary Issue 1966–1986, vol. 20, no. 4, pp. 23–25. Interesting examples of how Japanese workers are adapting to the United States are found in Isabel Wilkerson, "Influx of Japanese Changing Face of Midwest," *New York Times*, February 15, 1987, pp. 1, 26; and Bernard Wysocki, "Japanese Executives Going Overseas Take Anti-Shock Courses," *Wall Street Journal*, January 12, 1987, pp. 1, 18.

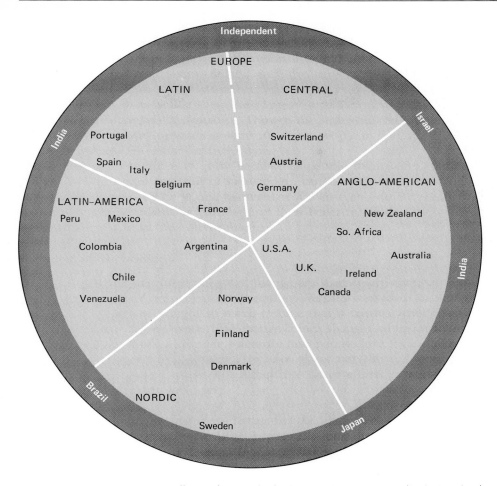

Note: India appears near two nonadjacent clusters: Anglo–American and Developing (Latin American).

FIGURE 18-6 Sociocultural clusters among selected industrial nations. (*Source: Simcha Ronen and Allen I. Kraut, "Similarities Among Countries Based on Employee Work Values and Attitudes,"* Columbia Journal of World Business, *Summer 1977, p. 94.*)

Public Acceptance

Not only must a multinational business live up to different standards in each country, but it also must be prepared to meet these standards with more perfection than national businesses are expected to do. As an outsider and guest, it is less accepted than local businesses. Nationalism, love of one's own people, and desire to protect national businesses make both government and local citizens more critical of foreign business. They know that a foreign company's whole loyalty—or its primary loyalty—is not to their economy and their people. They accept it less than national businesses and are quick to criticize it.

> *One example of this is Bayer Company's Mexican subsidiary, which was closed by the Health Secretariat for alleged pollution. Even though the company claimed it complied with all local pollution laws, it was summarily closed. An analyst concluded that Bayer was selected as a "pollution scapegoat" for public exhibit because it did business with a local firm that had pollution problems.*[25]

Multinationals should, however, make an effort to respect a host country's culture and social systems. This should be the case even if the host country is highly developed and not susceptible to the influence of foreign companies.

> *For example, Kikkoman Corporation, headquartered in Tokyo, Japan, has developed a credo or statement of principles for all of its operations in foreign countries, including the United States. "In order to create a friendlier world,"* says Yuzaburo Mogi, the company's managing director, *"I believe we need many types of cultural exchanges. Kikkoman believes that soy sauce marketing is the promotion of the international exchange of food culture." Kikkoman has developed a policy for maintaining "harmony" with society and the local community. According to Mr. Mogi, "It is needless to say that a foreign concern should try to prosper* together *with society and the local community in order to promote the success of the entire operation."*
>
> *Kikkoman tries to carry out the following commitments in its Wisconsin plant: they are committed to employing as many local people as possible; they try to participate in local activities and events, and contribute to society through their business activities; they try to avoid the "Japanese village" stereotype by advising their Japanese employees to spread themselves among the community rather than living in ethnic groups; they try to do business with many local companies, rather than with Japanese companies; and they delegate most authority to local management and try to avoid a "remote-control situation with letters or telephone calls from Japan."*[26]

Other situations are more difficult, especially when the fundamental value systems of the host country and the home country differ greatly from one another. Examples occur when United States multinationals do business in South Africa, Libya, or various Middle Eastern nations. Where religious, social, or political systems of two nations vary widely, multinational corporate managers sometimes must choose between loyalty to home standards or gaining host-country acceptance by adhering to local values.

Educational Overhead Costs

A characteristic of many nations is a lack of qualified persons to serve the advanced economic needs of the nation. This condition may be aggravated

---

[25]Cited by Jeffrey Leonard and Christopher J. Duerksen, "Environmental Regulations and the Location of Industry: An International Perspective," *Columbia Journal of World Business,* Summer 1980, pp. 63–64.

[26]Yuzaburo Mogi, "The Conduct of International Business: One Company's Credo—Kikkoman, Soy Sauce and the U.S. Market," *Columbia Journal of World Business,* Twentieth Anniversary Issue 1966–1986, Fall 1986, p. 94.

by a "brain drain," in which skilled workers emigrate to other nations that seem to offer better opportunities. When there are major shortages of managers, scientists, and technicians, these deficiencies limit business's ability to employ local labor productively and diminish the economic attractiveness of the nation.

In the absence of sufficient human resources, people with needed abilities are temporarily imported, while major training programs prepare local workers. In fact, the lending of trained workers to a nation may be of more lasting benefit than the lending of capital because of the multiplier effect by which the trained workers help develop qualified nationals, who then become the nucleus for developing more nationals in an ever-widening circle of self-development.

> For example, *one German manufacturing multinational had difficulty recruiting enough skilled machinists and toolmakers to satisfy its ultrafine product tolerances. To develop an adequate long-run supply of skilled labor, it established a three-year apprentice program with thirty students. The cost was about $80,000, including wages, for each student in the program. When the students graduated, they became both workers and trainers to help others meet the company's exacting standards.*

In some nations educational facilities are inadequate for economic expansion. There are shortages of schools and equipment for them. In turn, there are not enough qualified teachers to supply an expanded educational system; thus, either existing universities must be expanded or new ones established to train teachers. Economic and social growth require a steady supply of qualified human resources.

Social Environment of the Home Nation

The second major environmental consideration in multinational operations is the social environment of the home nation. The public in the home nation will be watching the company's actions abroad; if it finds some policy or method of operation unacceptable, it will pressure the company to change.

> *Perhaps the most prominent example during the mid-1980s concerned the situation in South Africa. The South African government had enforced for decades a system of apartheid, under which black people were segregated in the workplace and in everyday life from the white population. Finding this system abhorrent, many civil liberties and human rights groups, as well as government officials and private citizens, exerted pressure on businesses with operations in South Africa. For years, businesses were pressured to challenge apartheid or cease conducting trade with South African companies and the government.*
>
> *In 1986, the United States Congress enacted economic sanctions against South Africa. Many major companies sold or closed their South African operations. General Motors sold its plant to a local management and investment group; IBM, Eastman Kodak, Coca-Cola, and other large concerns also pulled out.*

In the case of South Africa, an almost worldwide consensus has been reached; very few nations or public interest groups support the South African system of apartheid. Even those who lobby in the United States for South African interests do not directly defend apartheid. Rather, some people claim that disinvestment would mean a loss of jobs for thousands of black workers employed by United States multinational companies—that disinvestment would hurt the very people it proposes to help.

Many situations are less clear than that in South Africa. When a social consensus has not been achieved and the public in the home country is divided about what companies should do in another environment, management is forced to contend with many conflicting pressures.

> For example, *General Foods over the years has built a reputation of being a socially responsible firm. The company has made many efforts to respond to social pressures and has a minority employment record, for example, that is quite good. In the early 1980s, however, the company came under great pressure for its policy of buying coffee, its biggest product, from El Salvador and Guatemala. Some of the revenue from the sale of Salvadoran and Guatemalan coffee goes to those governments, which have been criticized for their widespread human rights violations. In response to a 1983 stockholder petition to try to stop the company from buying coffee from these two major sources, a General Foods executive said, "We believe that the plea is clearly improper in that it seeks to have a business corporation act independently as a prime agent of political change in these countries."[27] Nonetheless, this pressure for the company to find other sources of coffee beans could have a significant effect on its business operations in the United States and abroad.*

Thus, even companies that make a sincere effort to be socially responsible on the international level are not immune to societal pressures on the home front. Together, the social, economic, and political environments of both the home and host nations will affect all business strategy, operations, and social policies of the multinational firm.

VALUE CONFLICTS AND THE ISSUE OF QUESTIONABLE PAYMENTS

Conflicts between the home and host nations in the multinational business environment arise for many reasons, some of which have been discussed in this chapter. The complexity of international business operations makes it difficult to manage, control, or mediate these conflicts. Thus, measures taken to "police" political, social, and human value conflicts between countries and multinationals are limited. In extreme cases, these conflicts may lead to government trade embargoes, harassment of business, bombing of business properties, kidnapping of managers, and protests by partisan groups. Value

[27]Mary Ann Fiske, "General Foods Roasted Over Coffee Buying Policy," *Business and Society Review,* Spring 1984, pp. 19–21.

conflicts are the most difficult to manage due to their subjective nature and the emotional intensity surrounding them. Consider the following examples:

- A computer manufacturer is refused an export license for sale of an advanced computer to Russia because of its possible military use
- Arab nations boycott firms with business ties to Israel
- A foreign firm's plant manager is kidnapped by a political terrorist group

Often, business is caught in the middle of these conflicts as it tries to conduct normal business in different political and social systems.

Questionable Payments

One of the most persistent issues, and one that relates directly to business practice, is the issue of questionable payments. This issue arises primarily because of differences in customs, ethics, and laws among the nations of the world. *Questionable payments by business are those that raise significant ethical questions of right and wrong in the host nation or other nations.* It is easy to condemn all questionable payments as unethical bribes, but real situations are not that simple. There are several different types of payments and a variety of situations, so decisions about right and wrong are rarely clear-cut and easy.

Political payments, bribes, responses to extortion, sales commissions, and expediting payments are five of the most common forms of questionable payments. *Political payments* might be made to continue a certain party in office or to ensure the election or reelection of a friendly candidate. A *bribe* is money or something of value given to someone in power in order to influence materially that person's decision in favor of the giver compared with others. Bribes might be given to obtain contracts, licenses, tax concessions, or any number of other benefits. When a business feels forced to pay money in an effort to protect itself—for example, to prevent the levying of an increased export tax or the cancellation of a franchise—it is responding to *extortion.* This is usually the case only for firms with extensive business in a given nation, firms with much to lose by not complying. *Sales commissions* are not intrinsically questionable unless the commission is paid to a government official or a local power broker, or unless the payment is exceptionally large. *Expediting payments,* also called fix, dash, tea money, grease, squeeze, and sticky handshake, are payments normally given to lower-level officials to guarantee the prompt, efficient, and cooperative execution of normal duties. These are generally accepted in many parts of the world, but they are considered unethical and illegal in the United States if made to government employees.

The Foreign Corrupt Practices Act

The Foreign Corrupt Practices Act regulates questionable payments of all United States firms *operating in other nations.* It was passed in 1977 in response to disclosure of a number of questionable foreign payments by United States corporations. The law has the following major provisions:

- It is a criminal offense for a firm to make payments to a foreign government official, political party, party official, or candidate for political office to secure or retain business in another nation.
- Sales commissions to independent agents are illegal if the business has knowledge that any part of the commission is being passed to foreign officials.
- Government employees "whose duties are essentially ministerial or clerical" are excluded, so expediting payments to persons such as customs agents and bureaucrats are permitted.
- Payments made in situations of genuine extortion are permitted.
- In addition to the antibribery provisions that apply to all businesses, all publicly held corporations that are subject to the Securities Exchange Act of 1934 are required to establish internal accounting controls to assure that all payments abroad are authorized and properly recorded.

It can be seen that the basic purposes of the law are (1) to establish a worldwide code of conduct for any kind of payment by United States businesses to foreign government officials, political parties, and political candidates, and (2) to require appropriate accounting controls for full disclosure of the firm's transactions. The United States law applies even if a payment is legal in the nation where it is made. The idea is to assure that United States businesses meet United States standards wherever they operate.

Advocates of the law say that the reputation of the United States is affected by business conduct so the law is necessary to assure ethical conduct. The law should encourage businesses from other nations to improve their conduct, since they will not need to make payments in order to compete on equal terms with United States businesses. The law also may reduce corruption in foreign governments, and it should improve disclosure to corporate stockholders.

Critics of the law say that it is an ethnocentric attempt by the United States to apply its ethical standards in other nations, regardless of their laws and customs. And since it is an extraterritorial application of national jurisdiction, it may be wrong.[28] Independent nations want to control their own destiny and have a right to make their own choices; so business-government customs will continue as usual in these nations. The result is that some United States businesses have a competitive disadvantage when seeking foreign contracts and may be tempted to make covert questionable payments to protect themselves.

In the mid-1980s, business began lobbying in Washington for amendments to the Foreign Corrupt Practices Act. Most agreed that the antibribery and record-keeping provisions should be clarified, but there was significant

[28]Mark Pastin and Michael Hooker, "Ethics and the Foreign Corrupt Practices Act," *Business Horizons*, December 1980, pp. 43–47. For a contrasting point of view, see Thomas Goldwasser, "Don't Make Foreign Bribery by U.S. Firms Easier," *Wall Street Journal*, October 1, 1986, p. 28.

Question: Do you favor or oppose these proposed changes in the Foreign Corrupt Practices Act?			
	Favor (%)	Oppose (%)	Not Sure (%)
Reduce detailed record keeping on all business transactions	68	25	7
Allow payments to foreign officials when they speed up or unblock routine government actions	65	26	9
Make the law more specific as to who in a foreign country legally can receive such payments	64	30	6
Eliminate the criminal penalties for violating the accounting sections of the law	46	44	10
Ease United States executives' accountability when they delegate an agent to make payments	42	52	6

FIGURE 18-7   How business wants the law changed on foreign payments (Based on a Survey of American business executives). (*Source: Adapted from "The Antibribery Act Splits Executives,"* Business Week, September 19, 1983, p. 16.)

opposition to easing the liability of an executive responsible when an agent makes a payment. Opinions are divided over whether Congress should eliminate criminal penalties for violations of the accounting provisions, as shown in Figure 18-7.

THE CHALLENGES OF DOING BUSINESS ABROAD

The basic lessons of this chapter should now be obvious. Multinational business operations are surely one of the most challenging tasks ever undertaken by private enterprise. Doing business abroad is inherently complex because of cultural differences and the complicated network of governmental, political, ideological, and economic relationships found in today's competitive global system. As far as corporate management is concerned, these international complexities are simply added to the six fundamental social challenges normally faced at home (see Chapter 1).

However, we do not suggest that business should shun the opportunities presented by doing business abroad. As discussed in earlier chapters of this book, the economic welfare of many nations is promoted by international trade. The poorer as well as the richer regions of the world need the goods and services that multinational corporations can produce. Companies themselves can make handsome profits while serving these global needs, and many MNCs count on foreign transactions for a substantial portion of their overall income. Multinational companies have become one of the world's major institutions linking nations together. They provide channels through which technology, ideas, and people can flow from country to country. They have the ability to stabilize societies and to make life more secure for many people. They operate better in a world at peace; thus, they favor peaceful relations in the regions where they do business.

The fundamental challenge to multinational corporations is similar to that faced by domestic companies: *All business firms are challenged to manage their affairs in ways that serve both primary and secondary stakeholders. In other words, they must strive to meet economic as well as social goals. The Iron Law of Responsibility applies on the international scene as well as at home, meaning that all businesses need a strategy that is responsive to society's expectations or they risk losing their power and influence to other institutions and groups in society.*

SUMMARY

Nations of the world want to develop their economies and to make more productive use of their human and natural resources. Multinational business is a change agent that serves these needs. When a business firm enters another nation, it tends to be more effective when it can be responsive to the environment of its host. Responsiveness requires managers who are culturally aware, sensitive to local issues, and capable of developing flexible policies that are compatible with a host nation's needs.

Multinational companies are increasingly challenged by the international environment. More industries are becoming global in nature, with competitors from many nations pursuing cost-efficient business strategies. This places pressure on the economic power of multinational firms, as they are forced to shift production and other operations in response to competitive pressures. Further, governments of both home nations and host countries expect that multinational companies will obey their laws and be good corporate citizens. At times, the expectations of home and host countries can be in conflict, causing severe pressures for the companies involved.

DISCUSSION AND REVIEW QUESTIONS

1. Reread the opening illustration concerning the World Bank and the Polonoroest project. Then find an example in current sources such as *Business Week* or *Fortune* that also illustrates the complexities of international business relationships. In what ways does the relationship between governments or countries affect the situation? How does the relationship among foreign and national businesses affect the situation?

2. Choose a Third World country that is developing rapidly and determine which types of businesses are likely to locate there. Prepare an analysis for a hypothetical company in one of these industries, and explain how it would best set up a plant, office, or marketing operation in this country. How should its practices be amended to take into consideration local political, economic, and social conditions?

3. Consider the reverse situation to number 2 above. Assume that a Japanese electronics manufacturer is about to open a plant in the United States. Prepare a report outlining the key economic and cultural "facts" about the United States that the company should understand if it is to succeed.

4. In late 1986, the U.S. Commerce Department threatened to levy a countervailing duty on imports of Canadian softwood lumber to appease American lumber producers who claimed their Canadian competitors were unfairly subsidized by low government timber fees. The Canadian government succumbed to United States pressure and levied a 15 percent tax on softwood lumber exports to the United States. Canadian lumber industry officials denounced their government. Describe the dynamics between business, government, and economic conditions in this situation.

5. The Foreign Corrupt Practices Act imposed restrictions on the payment of bribes and "questionable payments" by employees of United States multinational companies. Assume that you are plant manager in another nation for such a company. An important shipment of spare machinery parts is on board a freighter in the harbor. Delays threaten to force a closing of the plant, but a harbor agency official has told you he could speed up the off-loading. You believe him, but also know the company's policy is not to pay anything of value that would be considered a bribe. What decision would you make and why?

CRITICAL INCIDENT

Pullout in Honduras[29]

On May 5, 1983, 289 woman workers of the Hondbra factory in Honduras' free trade zone reported to the factory early in the morning, as usual. When they arrived, they found the factory doors closed. The company's management was nowhere to be found. Some of the women walked into the factory office and discovered a brief telex from Angelo Sanguedolce, executive vice president of NCC Industries whose subsidiary, Crescent Corset, owned Hondbra. The telex read: "To all employees of HONDBRA S.A.: I have to inform you with regret that because of the economic situation of our enterprise and the failure of our endeavors to sell the company in Puerto Cortes, we are forced to close the factory. I should like to thank you for all your cooperation during these years."

The women went home, most of them to six or eight children and no husband to help support them. With no unemployment or welfare benefits available to carry them over, and few prospects for alternative work, most of the women faced a grim future. "We had no idea this could ever happen," said one. "It has left us in a terrible situation."

Crescent Corset, itself a wholly owned subsidiary of NCC Industries, a multinational garment concern, was responsible for forcing these Honduran women

[29]Adapted from Anne M. Street, "Multinationals Square Off Against Central American Workers," _Business and Society Review,_ Winter 1985, pp. 45–49.

out of work indefinitely. NCC is the twelfth largest United States company in the design, manufacture, and sale of women's lingerie.

NCC has left a trail of situations similar to the one in Honduras just described. In 1979, the company had opened a nonunion shop in Honduras, which by May of 1980 was operating at top capacity. In 1982, it contracted with Triumph International to buy goods from that firm and its affiliates who manufactured primarily in the Far East using cheap nonunion labor. In 1980, citing "political unrest which escalated costs and reduced production," NCC closed its unionized plant in El Salvador with virtually no warning, throwing several hundred employees out of work. In January 1982, the company closed its subsidiary in Zacatecas, Mexico, citing unreasonable labor demands. In its 1982 annual report, the company wrote: "During 1981, labor problems at the [Mexican] plant caused major operational and financial problems throughout the company's operations." Five hundred women lost their jobs. Then in January 1983, a unionized shop in Puerto Rico was closed down; again, labor problems were blamed, and 125 jobs were lost. With NCC's last unionized shop closed, the International Ladies Garment Workers Union (ILGWU) decided to challenge the American company under United States law dealing with unfair labor practices.

In a lawsuit against NCC brought by the ILGWU before the National Labor Relations Board, Angelo Sanguedolce, NCC's executive vice president, was called to testify. Sanguedolce cited an incident in the Salvadoran plant in which workers occupied the plant and held management hostage for several hours. Claiming that Honduran workers at the Hondbra factory were planning similar unrest, he said management agreed to "get everybody out of there, and we closed the plant. . . . [W]e just took everything out of there, we got as much as we could get." The women told a very different story. They claimed the union and management at the Hondbra factory had always had good relations and that the workers put up with much more than they should have. The former union president at Hondbra stated that "they wanted to lay off 100 workers without compensation and they did fire some. We never went on strike or (slowed down). . . . We never behaved badly." A former manager supported these statements, but the union did not win the lawsuit.

1. What considerations might have led NCC Industries to originally open the Hondbra factory in Honduras? How were these factors related to NCC's business strategy?

2. What concerns might the Honduran government have had in originally permitting the Hondbra factory to open? How were these factors related to the government's goals and objectives?

3. What influence, if any, should the Honduran government have had in NCC's decision to close Hondbra? Should the government have the power to approve plant closings?

4. If you were a loan officer at an international bank, what criteria would you use to evaluate a loan application from NCC to establish a new factory in another developing nation?

Chapter Nineteen

CORPORATE STRATEGY FOR A CHANGING WORLD: A SUMMARY

In managing today's business corporation, a broad social perspective is indispensable. Corporate strategies need to take account of the demands and needs of corporate stakeholders while continuing to adhere to the corporation's central economic mission. In this chapter, we review and summarize the major features of corporate social responsiveness and corporate social strategy.

CHAPTER OBJECTIVES

After reading this chapter, you should be able to

- Identify three levels or dimensions of corporate social responsiveness
- Review specific social actions that the public expects business to take
- Understand how social partnerships can contribute to corporate social responsibility
- Relate your own career goals to the major themes of this book

From the opening paragraph of this book, we have described a world that places many demands on business. These demands come from many different points of the social compass—from employees, government regulators, consumers, environmentalists, charitable and educational organizations, ethnic groups, city officials, foreign governments, and even entire communities. At times, these stakeholder claims threaten to overwhelm the calm, rational logic of the business manager whose traditional job has been to produce for economic purposes alone. The demands often are excessive and irrational. As a result, some people ask: Should business try to be socially responsible by acting on the many petitions it receives from the public?

Our answer is that business has little or no choice. Social involvement is inevitable. Business operates in a complex environment in which business, government, and society are interdependent. Social demands are here to stay, even though specific topics will come and go. At one time, the public may want to place curbs on multinational corporations doing business in South Africa or limit the size of megacorporations formed through mergers or takeovers. The next year, a fear of technological unemployment may occupy great attention. And the following year may see rising social concern about workers' privacy rights or unsafe disposal of toxic wastes. Rarely are stakeholder groups satisfied that their demands have been fully met or that business has helped enough. Among all the uncertainties of business life, this kind of environmental pressure seems destined to persist.

The key question is not *whether* business should respond but *how* business should respond and *what goals* it should pursue. Social responsiveness is essential. The central management challenge is knowing how to strike a balance between the competing demands of stakeholders and the business firm's economic, profit-seeking goals. For this task, corporations need well-crafted *strategies* that include both business *and* social goals.

AN OVERVIEW OF THE BOOK'S MAIN IDEAS

This chapter reviews and re-emphasizes the ideas and approaches that make corporate social responsiveness attainable by business and indispensable for society.

Foremost among these ideas is the concept of *corporate social responsiveness*—the ability of business to interact positively and humanely with its surrounding social environment. A second perspective is the broad framework of *major social challenges* that is a constant companion of business in the modern world. Those challenges have created an agenda of *social issues and public expectations* that must be incorporated into business's strategic thinking. One theme in particular stands out from the others: the need for *social partnerships* between business and society that can give practical meaning to the concept of corporate social responsibility.

Figure 19-1 (which also appears in the book's Introduction) serves as a guide for this final overview and summary. It diagrams the major ideas and themes of the book. It demonstrates how the major topics are related to each other and how, when grouped together, they illustrate **the modern theory of the socially responsive corporation.** That theory requires corporations to become skilled in **environmental analysis** and to integrate social factors into **corporate strategic plans.** A company's decisions and policies will be more likely to succeed when they are based on a thorough knowledge of all affected **corporate stakeholders.** Among management's most **challenging environ-**

THE SOCIALLY RESPONSIVE CORPORATION

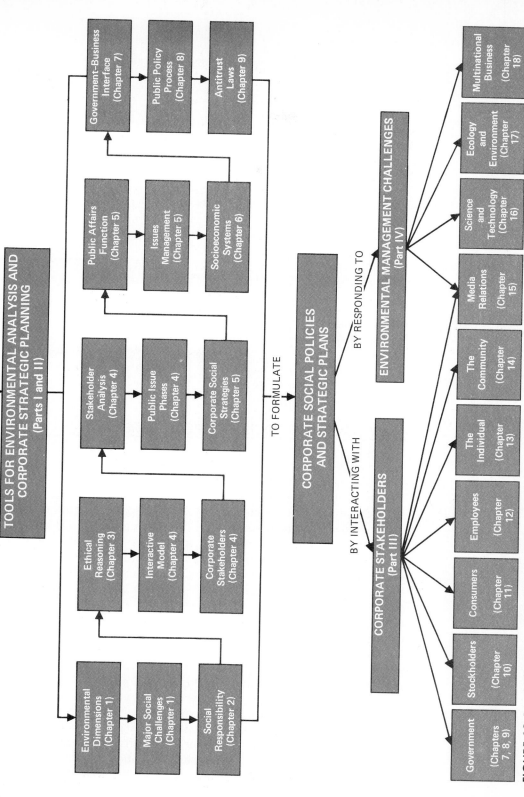

FIGURE 19-1. A diagram of the book's major ideas and themes.

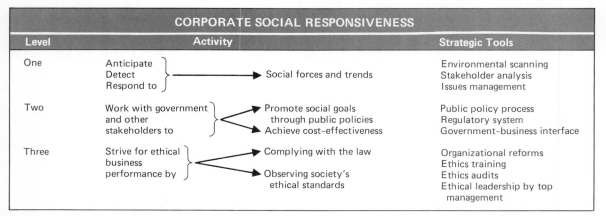

FIGURE 19-2.   Three levels of corporate social responsiveness.

mental tasks are managing science and technology, working for ecological balance, and overseeing multinational operations.

All of these matters are discussed as a way of helping each individual student reach conclusions about the role of business in society that are meaningful and satisfying from both a personal and a professional point of view.

STRATEGIES FOR SOCIAL RESPONSIVENESS

Figure 19-2 illustrates three different levels on which companies respond to the social environment. On level one, an individual company organizes itself to anticipate, detect, and respond to the social forces and trends that bear immediately on its operations, as well as those that might become important in the future. The techniques of environmental scanning, stakeholder analysis, and issues management are used for these purposes.

On level two, business works with government officials and stakeholder groups to help formulate public policies about social issues and problems. Because these public policies are a blend of the views of many interested groups in society, they provide general guidance to business as it responds to social demands. They help individual companies determine the goals and directions of their own social policies. A prime business interest at level two is working for cost-effective government programs, thereby reducing excessive cost burdens on business and the general public. For these purposes, business needs a thorough knowledge of the public policy process, the governmental and regulatory system, and the government-business interface.

On level three, a socially responsive business firm tries to improve its ethical performance by complying with society's laws and observing society's ethical standards. The firm's managers integrate society's legal and ethical standards into their own decisions and into their company's strategic plans. The tools used to improve and monitor ethical performance include various organizational reforms, ethics training, ethics audits, and strong ethical leadership by top management.

These traits of socially responsive corporations closely parallel other models developed by social analysts. Alvin Toffler speaks of "the multipurpose corporation," which is

> . . . no longer responsible simply for making a profit or producing goods but for simultaneously contributing to the solution of extremely complex ecological, moral, political, racial, sexual, and social problems.
>
> Instead of clinging to a sharply specialized economic function, the corporation, prodded by criticism, legislation, and its own concerned executives, is becoming a multipurpose institution.[1]

John Naisbitt also takes note of the broadened role of "the participatory corporation." Internally, these modern corporations are being restructured to allow greater employee participation in workplace decisions and "are seeking a new role externally by participating more and more actively in the political and social world at large."[2]

"Vanguard Management" is another way of expressing the same idea. According to James O'Toole, Vanguard corporations exhibit four basic traits. First, they practice stakeholder management. Second, they exist to "provide society with the goods and services it needs, to provide employment, and to create a surplus of wealth (profit) with which to improve the nation's general standard of living and quality of life. In this view, profit is the means, not the end, of corporate activity." Third, they are committed to continuous learning. Finally, the Vanguard companies "attempt to be the best at everything they do" and have the moral courage to maintain their standards. O'Toole believes that the central challenge facing these corporations is to help society achieve a condition of social justice.[3]

Still other commentators reinforce the notion that the modern corporation's very existence depends more and more on ethical awareness and social responsiveness. Some say business must go "beyond the bottom line" in its management practices,[4] and others argue that ethical skills and practices must be made an integral part of corporate decision making.[5]

Few observers of the corporate world doubt any longer that society is rapidly transforming many business practices and values. A corporation's social strategy today must be based solidly on top management's understanding of these social changes if the company is to survive and perform its economic mission.

[1]Alvin Toffler, *The Third Wave,* New York: Bantam, 1981, chap. 18.

[2]John Naisbitt, *Megatrends: Ten New Directions Transforming Our Lives,* New York: Warner, 1981, pp. 175–188.

[3]James O'Toole, *Vanguard Management: Redesigning the Corporate Future,* Garden City, N.Y.: Doubleday, 1985. The quotations are on pp. 41 and 49–50.

[4]Tad Tuleja, *Beyond the Bottom Line: How Business Leaders Are Turning Principles into Profits,* New York: Facts on File, 1985.

[5]Robert C. Solomon and Kristine R. Hanson, *It's Good Business,* New York: Atheneum, 1985.

- ● ACHIEVING ECOLOGICAL BALANCE
- ● IMPROVING BUSINESS AND SOCIAL PRODUCTIVITY
- ● ACKNOWLEDGING THE HUMAN ELEMENT IN WORK
- ● BALANCING ETHICS AND ECONOMICS
- ● RESPONDING TO GLOBAL PRESSURES, DEMANDS, AND NEEDS
- ● DESIGNING SOCIAL PARTNERSHIPS

FIGURE 19-3. Major social challenges to business.

AN AGENDA OF SOCIAL ISSUES AND PUBLIC EXPECTATIONS

Most of the social pressures brought to bear on business in the past three decades can be classified into one or more of the six social challenges listed in Figure 19-3. Again and again these themes appear in discussions of business's social responsibilities. They express the public's ideal goals for business in a complex world. "Do these things," the public seems to say to business, "and you shall have our blessing. Ignore them and you shall merit our disapproval." The themes define the comprehensive tasks that lie ahead for socially responsive business firms. In the following sections, we review each theme as a way of drawing together the separate strands of the book's chapters into a cohesive picture of business's remaining social responsibilities.

Theme One: Achieving Ecological Balance

The public wants business to find a workable balance between industrial production and nature's limits. To meet this broad social challenge, business is expected to take the following steps:

- Reduce harmful environmental impacts to the minimum level consistent with economic costs, available technology, and maintaining the standard of living.
- When threatening situations do arise, act quickly and openly to prevent or alleviate human suffering and environmental damage.

Theme Two: Improving Business and Social Productivity

The public wants business to increase the efficiency with which it converts both economic and social inputs into economic and social outputs. The result would be improved productivity for business firms and for society as a whole. To meet this broad social challenge, business is expected to take the following steps:

- Manage employees in creative and humane ways, involving them in workplace decisions, in order to increase their productivity.
- Work cooperatively with labor unions and government agencies to reduce costs, develop flexible work rules, and reform public policies to encourage technological innovations.

- Introduce new technology with due care for possible negative impacts on people, communities, and valued traditions.
- Involve community leaders in discussions of options that could affect the health and welfare of the communities where business is done.

Theme Three: Acknowledging the Human Element in Work

The public wants business to protect the human dignity and individual freedom of its employees while continuing to harness their skills for productive work. To meet this broad social challenge, business is expected to take the following steps:

- Improve the quality of work life, reduce on-the-job hazards, and encourage equal employment opportunities for all groups.
- Settle union-management differences legally, within the framework of collective bargaining, and with minimum disruption to economic life.
- When plants must be closed or relocated for economic reasons, provide tangible, practical assistance to employees and to their communities.
- Encourage employee participation in job planning and job design, protect employees from unwarranted invasions of privacy, recognize each employee's individuality and worth as a person, and provide a reasonable amount of job security and retirement security.

Theme Four: Balancing Ethics and Economics

The public wants business to achieve both high economic performance and high ethical standards, respecting both and slighting neither. This social challenge is a particularly broad one, cutting across many fields of business endeavor. To meet this broad social challenge, business is expected to take the following steps:

- Exercise ethical responsibility toward all corporate stakeholders, remembering the Iron Law of Responsibility, which in the long run requires power to be used responsibly.
- Institutionalize ethics into the operating procedures of business firms so that they may base decisions partially on the ethical principles of utilitarian cost-benefit, human rights, and social justice.
- Preserve the social justice involved in various government programs and public policies while working for cost effective ways to solve such problems.
- Use corporate economic, political, and social influence to promote broad public-purpose goals, values, and traditions, not just the interests of business alone.
- Protect the interests and rights of corporate stockholders as owners and as suppliers of capital.
- Respect the rights of employees, customers, suppliers, competitors, and local communities, shielding them from harm that may result from company actions.

- Accept a responsible role in preserving and developing cities as livable centers of civilization, while minimizing the disruptive impacts on them of economic decisions.
- Through philanthropic contributions, provide aid to nonprofit organizations as one way to enrich community life.
- Show respect for the rights of future generations by being prudent in the use of scarce industrial resources.
- Design production processes to minimize negative ecological influences.
- Consider the potentially disruptive impact of new technology on cultural values and ethical traditions, minimizing these effects where possible.

Theme Five: Responding to Global Pressures, Demands, and Needs

The world's peoples want business to be aware of and responsive to the development problems of the entire globe, especially the poorer nations burdened with large populations and widespread poverty. To meet this broad social challenge, business is expected to take the following steps:

- Produce needed goods and services and sell them at fair prices on open and free international markets.
- Purchase raw materials, goods, and services from the less-developed nations at fair prices and in reasonable proportions.
- Invest private capital in less-developed nations to assist the process of economic development there.
- In multinational operations, demonstrate respect for the rights, economic needs, varying cultural traditions and values, and the ecology of host countries.
- Participate in the implementation of public policy in the nations in which business operates.
- Consider the impact of foreign operations on markets, jobs, and communities at home, balancing economic gains against the human costs of economic dislocation.

Theme Six: Designing Social Partnerships

The public wants business to work toward more cooperative relationships with a wide variety of pluralistic interest groups, including governments and labor unions, for the purpose of solving important social problems. To meet this broad social challenge, business is expected to take the following steps:

- Rely on decentralized decision-making approaches that involve all interested parties and affected groups.
- Substitute cooperative problem-solving approaches for the conflict that often prevails in government-business and labor-management confrontations.
- Promote social responsibility through joint action with government and other community groups rather than proceeding in isolation and in piecemeal fashion.

THE NEED FOR SOCIAL PARTNERSHIPS

The above agenda of social issues sends two kinds of messages to business: (1) society needs business's help in solving some of its most serious problems; and (2) business can best preserve its legitimacy—that is, it can gain public approval—by being responsive to society's needs.

In extending a helping hand to society, business leadership needs to reach beyond the conflict and adversarial relations that have been all too typical of business's interface with external groups. The problem arises from several quarters:

> _Hostility, bad feelings, and mutual lack of trust often accompany government regulatory activities. Social activist groups also have generated a large share of the negative atmosphere that surrounds some business and society relationships. Examples abound: attacks on the nuclear power industry, on weapons manufacturers, on firms that do business in South Africa, on firms that fail to do business with minority enterprise suppliers, and other criticisms that perpetuate a negative and hostile climate between business and its critics. Adding to the problem have been the actions of the mass media, who frequently have found it advantageous to emphasize the sensational, emotional, and conflictual elements of these struggles between business and its social stakeholders._

Adversary relations, conflict, and competition among society's pluralistic groups are not easily or lightly set aside. Many people believe they are an essential part of a complex society, guaranteeing that all viewpoints will be heard and considered. Besides, say others, competition and conflict—for example, in labor-management relations—are the traditional way of doing things in this society: Why change now? Still others point out that competition is one of the pillars of a free enterprise system, and nothing should be done to weaken competition.

The most compelling argument for going beyond a purely adversarial approach to one that involves widespread collaboration among competing groups is the following: _The magnitude, complexity, and seriousness of today's social problems outrun the ability and skills of any one group—when acting alone—to do enough._ Some examples are the following:

> _Global competition in automobiles, steel, textiles, wheat, sugar, poultry, microprocessors, robots, and many other products exposes many local communities to unexpected and disruptive shifts in economic and social life. How can one small farming community in Kansas—or one computer-chip manufacturer in California's Silicon Valley—be expected all by itself to offset economic developments occurring halfway around the globe? In a similar fashion, the pricing and production practices of major oil-producing nations may seriously impair economic and social development in rich and poor nations alike. Still other social problems clearly transcend regional and national boundaries: industrial pollution, a shrinking resource base, and energy scarcities are complex global problems. None of these problems can be successfully resolved if each affected firm, farm, industry, or nation attempts to "go it alone."_

Under these circumstances, new approaches tend to emerge. Social partnerships are formed. These partnerships draw together groups that traditionally have been adversaries. When facing complex problems whose solution requires cooperation, the groups agree to work together to find an acceptable answer. A great deal of compromise is required from all participants. The final result may not be completely satisfying to any of the partners, but it tends to meet the minimum needs of all. Quite frequently, the partners come from both the private and public sectors of society, and such arrangements are usually called "public-private partnerships." When government and business cooperate in solving some important problem, they are operating on the basis of the public-private partnership principle.[6]

Government and Business: Developing a Cooperative Interface

Although collaboration between the two is sometimes difficult, prickly, and distasteful, government and business have a long history of supporting each other.

Government depends heavily on business in a number of ways. About one-third of federal income is derived from business taxes. Business also serves as the government's tax collector by withholding income taxes, social security taxes, sales taxes, and excise taxes. Government draws extensively on business's technical expertise and managerial know-how for many government-financed projects, and many business executives and professionals serve directly in government posts or as advisors to governments at all levels. In an odd way, business—by being a prime target of government regulators— becomes an important source of government employment because of the need for regulatory personnel to keep an eye on business. Still other government workers are employed to promote, subsidize, protect, and purchase goods and services from business. These supportive links with business obviously strengthen government.

But cooperation has two sides, and business traditionally has benefitted handsomely from its relationships with government at all levels. Courts enforce contracts, protect private property, and extend due process of law to businesses as well as to individuals. State and local governments pave the way for companies to conduct business by issuing certificates of incorporation or licenses. These legal grants to operate tend to reassure the public that minimum standards have been met, thereby instilling confidence in private business. The federal government has built a business infrastructure that makes a free enterprise system possible: a monetary system, standard weights and measures, roads and airports, weather services, zoning laws, traffic controls, water supplies, sewage disposal, and other essential services.

Other kinds of support provided to business include direct and indirect cash subsidies, loan guarantees, tax benefits and concessions to encourage companies to locate facilities in certain states or communities, and—perhaps

[6]For a thorough discussion, see Sandra A. Waddock, "Public-Private Partnership as Social Product and Process," in James E. Post (ed.), *Research in Corporate Social Performance and Policy*, vol. 8, Greenwich, Conn.: JAI Press, 1986, pp. 273–300.

the most direct form of support—government purchases of goods and services from private business. In 1984, federal government purchases amounted to $747.4 billion.

All of these supportive and mutually advantageous links suggest strongly that the government-business interface in the United States is already one of extensive collaboration and accommodation. However, it would be naive—and perhaps even a bit risky—to expect or advocate an end to all adversarial interfacing between government and business. An arm's-length relationship, where each party respects the viewpoints and needs of the other, may be healthier. In that way, business influence would not override the broader public interest, nor would the dead hand of government bureaucracy be allowed to stifle business initiative and know-how. The outcome might be an accommodation of each to the other and a compromise representing a blend of private business interest and broad public interest.

Speaking of the potential gains from a partnership approach, the former president of the Committee for Economic Development said:

> . . . [T]he traditional adversary relationship between big business and government deprives the country of counsel and support from corporate, labor, and other private sector leaders who could greatly improve the policy-making process, the policies that result from it, and their adoption and implementation. . . .
>
> One of the greatest contributions that executives of large companies can make is uniting national policies with the organization and management of programs to carry them out. The capacity of large companies in this respect is transferable when people in business and in government can work as partners instead of, as is usually the case, as antagonists.[7]

Designing Other Social Partnerships

Extending the cooperative principle to additional corporate stakeholders produces other types of social partnerships.

> When major automobile companies successfully appealed in the early 1980s to auto industry labor unions for cost-cutting contract concessions in order to meet vigorous foreign competition, the partnership principle was at work. Jobs were saved, a home-based industry was strengthened, and car buyers enjoyed more choices in the marketplace.
>
> In 1981 a coalition of steel companies, labor unions, federal regulators, and environmentalists pressured Congress to give the steel industry an additional three years to comply with costly pollution-control regulations. The coalition's goal was to allow steelmakers to use more capital for modernization, which also would contribute to cleaner air in the long run. Here again is the partnership principle in action, bringing together traditional adversaries for the purpose of achieving common goals that would be unattainable otherwise.[8]

[7]Alfred C. Neal, *Business Power and Public Policy*, New York: Praeger, 1981, pp. 157–159.

[8]"Steel's Unlikely Allies to Help It Buy Time," *Business Week*, June 1, 1981, p. 35.

> *As insurance companies have worked with neighborhood groups and local governments to rehabilitate rundown and blighted neighborhoods, social partnerships have emerged. Frequently these coalitions outlast the rebuilding project to become a voice for other matters affecting the community's welfare.*[9]
>
> *Since the mid-1960s, many business firms have worked with government agencies and minority groups to train and place the hard-to-employ. Government grants have covered some of the training costs, businesses have provided on-the-job training, and minority groups have set hiring and training goals, encouraged the participation of minority persons, and lobbied both business and government for financial support. Collaboration among these three groups has produced tangible results in jobs and new skills. During the 1980s, similar partnership programs were aimed at joblessness and retraining needs created by industrial relocation and new forms of technology.*[10]

These examples illustrate the growing popularity and acceptance of the partnership principle as a way of confronting and solving complex social problems. Such partnerships, which in earlier times were only experimental, are now better established in corporations and in government. They have become another tool of both corporate strategic policy and of government public policy.

Social Partnerships and Corporate Social Responsibility

The central feature of all these partnership arrangements is a cooperative attitude that is developed among organizations whose goals, purposes, and values may differ greatly. Many of the successes scored thus far in the area of social responsibility are the work of groups who found ways to achieve sufficient harmony among themselves to address serious problems without abandoning their respective values and beliefs. Business frequently has yielded decision-making autonomy over pollution control, employment opportunities, job safety, consumer protection, and other matters to coalitions of business firms, government agencies, environmentalists, labor unions, civil rights groups, and others. In doing so, it has not lessened—and perhaps has strengthened—its status as society's central institution. Nor have the competing members of these coalitions gained all they desired. The nation's air and water remain considerably contaminated with industrial by-products, women and minorities continue to suffer job discrimination, and preventable industrial accidents still occur. What *has* happened is tangible movement toward resolving some of society's major problems. In these cases, business

---

[9]For a discussion, see C. William Verity, Jr., "Community Partnerships: An Insurance Policy for the Nation," *Response*, March 1982, pp. 19–20. Each issue of *Response*, which is published by the Center for Corporate Public Involvement in Washington, D.C., describes a wide variety of social partnerships initiated by the nation's life and health insurance companies. This center began issuing public reports on that industry's social programs in 1973.

[10]*Business Impact on Training the Disadvantaged: Issues and Findings*, Washington, D.C.: National Alliance of Business, 1982. For several examples of partnerships formed during the 1980s under the auspices of the federal Job Training Partnership Act, see Waddock, op. cit.

has yielded to social pressures without allowing social demands to overwhelm the essential economic mission of business.

The future of corporate social responsibility lies in these directions. Social partnerships are a way to link social needs to business purposes, modifying but not destroying business, and permitting business to participate fully as one member of a coalition serving broader goals and purposes than those of business alone. At the same time, corporate stakeholders throughout society learn to appreciate and depend on the many positive benefits of a profit-seeking business system fully aware of its social obligations.

THE STUDENT, THE EXECUTIVE, AND THE CORPORATE FUTURE

As the end of this book—and your course—approaches, it is natural to wonder what it all means to you personally and professionally. How can all of this information, all of the concepts and tools, all of the complex issues and challenges discussed here make a difference in your own life and especially in your business career? We believe that every reader deserves to know just how these ideas can affect his or her future, so we would like to give our answer to this extremely important question: What difference does it make to know these things?

What This Book Means for Executives

A corporation is a curious kind of human institution. We sometimes speak as if it is a tangible object that can be seen and touched. We say that IBM or Nissan or Lloyds of London *entered* a new market with a new product or *relocated* a plant from one country to another. In our imagination, we invoke pictures of these giant institutions actually performing tasks as if they were real persons. But "the corporation" is not a person, and it cannot be understood by thinking of it as a person. Rather, a corporation is a very complex human institution embedded in a richly configured environment. It is a form of organized, collective human action. As such, it has a declared purpose, pursues tangible goals, boasts of a tradition, and has an identifiable culture. It is this kind of human institution that business managers seek to direct and control. But can it be done? Or can it be done successfully?

At any one time, events within a corporation are driven by *inertia*—by the accumulated forces that are in motion and that have brought the company to its present position. This inertia—this tendency to stay on the same track—is a result of the company's past history, its major successes and failures, and its institutional customs and habits. Viewed this way, a corporation may seem to have a life of its own that is quite independent of the people in it. It may appear to be moving along a path determined by uncontrolled (or even uncontrollable) forces, almost like a charging rogue elephant or a loose cannon rolling wildly across the decks of a fighting ship in rough seas.

What is called "corporate strategic planning" is an effort by managers to gain control of these inertial forces and events, in order to direct a corporation toward consciously chosen goals. Rather than allowing past events to determine where the company will go and how it will get there, top managers chart new directions and then work to reach their new goals.

We believe that well-informed and socially aware executives can strengthen corporate strategic planning by applying environmental knowledge and new tools of environmental analysis in their own companies. New human purposes, goals, and aspirations can be breathed into the corporate shell. The collective human actions that are the substance of corporate life need not run out of control nor be limited to narrow economic or technical purposes. *Our main message throughout this book is that corporate strategic planning has a greater chance of success—and the corporation is more likely to be accepted by the public—when business executives are aware of the broad social environment and when they apply this environmental knowledge to their companies.* Including these new environmental perspectives in corporate strategic plans not only increases the effectiveness of a corporation's economic performance but also serves society's broader humane purposes and aspirations.

So, to the question, "Can environmentally sophisticated executives make a difference?" we say "yes." They can help lead their companies toward goals that are rewarding for both business and society.

What This Book Means for the Student

What can we say to the student who plans, but has not yet experienced, a significant business career? How does a knowledge of business-and-society relationships and of environmental analysis help such a student who may be many years away from having major management responsibility and influence? We suggest three answers to these questions.

First, the more a student knows about business before starting a career, the more likely it is that his or her career choice and preferred job specialization will be appropriate and satisfying. Every employee goes through a "break-in" period in a new job and in a new company. You learn not just the technical demands of your particular job but also how to get along with fellow workers. Another thing to be learned is how your job specialty fits in with other jobs and with the overall goals of the company. *The more you know about your company, including its environmental links with stakeholders and the demands they make, the better you will be able to perform your own job and to help the company achieve its goals.*

Second, many of today's students will, in fact, be tomorrow's corporate managers and business leaders. Although some of the specific environmental problems to be faced in the future will be different from those now in the news, the basic model of business-and-society relationships developed in this book will almost certainly be the same. Business will continue to operate within a complex web of social interactions and environmental pressures. Today's student gets a head start on tomorrow's leadership responsibilities by learning at the *beginning* of his or her business career that environmental analysis is an indispensable tool of the professional manager.

A third answer is that a young college graduate does not have to wait for some remote future time before being influential in business. Each individual counts *now*. Having a job in a corporation—whether it is a large well-known company or a small local one—means that you are part of one company's "organized, collective human action." You can have influence on your fellow workers by your interpersonal skills. You can affect the company's productivity by the way you do your job. You can help your company decide whether it will do business ethically or unethically by the standards of conduct you observe. You can help create the company's public image by your behavior on and off the job. Finally, you can help determine how well the company discharges its social responsibilities to others by being responsible and acting with integrity in your own work. Your future and the future of the corporation are partly in your own hands. You need not wait. It begins now.

Finally, whether you are a practicing executive or a student planning your professional future, your business career is only a part of your life. Each of us also is part of a larger existence lived in society with others—in our families, in our churches and synagogues, among our friends, in our local communities, and as members of humanity at large. This book has urged that a concern for this larger human realm be placed at the center of business decision making and corporate strategic planning. If that can happen—and we believe each business participant has the *potential* ability to make it happen—then business will serve broad human purposes that enrich living for everyone.

SUMMARY

The social world places multiple demands on business. As a result, many business firms have learned and applied the techniques of corporate social responsiveness. They interact positively with social forces and trends, they help formulate public policies, and they integrate ethics into their decisions, policies, and actions.

Six major social challenges help define business's main social tasks. These challenges create an agenda of social issues and public expectations concerning business's behavior. Many of society's perplexing social problems can and should be approached by using social partnerships that allow social purposes and business goals to be advanced together, rather than sacrificing either one to the other. In these ways, corporate social responsibility is more likely to be achieved while at the same time permitting business to perform its economic role in society.

Young college graduates as well as mature business executives who read this book can make a difference in how business firms operate in today's and tomorrow's society by being active, socially aware professionals determined to bring their environmental knowledge to bear on business decisions and policies.

DISCUSSION AND REVIEW QUESTIONS

1. Assume you are chief executive officer of hypothetical Corporation X and you want to increase the corporation's social responsiveness at all three levels shown in Figure 19-2. Identify two specific actions that could be taken at each of the three levels that would make Corporation X socially responsive. Refer to Chapters 3, 4, 5, 7, and 8 for ideas.

2. Review each of the six major social challenges discussed in this chapter and in Chapter 1. In your opinion, which one of these challenges has been met most successfully by business firms in the United States? Refer to relevant chapters in this book to illustrate your views.

3. This chapter identifies many specific steps that the public expects business to take in order to be socially responsible. What are the major obstacles encountered by business in trying to be responsive to these social demands? Refer to relevant chapters in this book to support your answer.

4. By referring to any one of the chapters in Parts Three and Four of this book, describe two specific steps that both business and government can take to promote greater cooperation between them to solve some social problem described in the chapter you selected.

5. Consult recent issues of news magazines and newspapers for examples of a business firm working with other groups in a cooperative partnership role. Was the outcome a positive one for business? Did it help society solve a problem? Could the problem have been approached in another, more effective way? Comment on the general usefulness of social partnerships as a way of promoting an effective long-run strategy for a corporation.

CASE STUDIES IN CORPORATE SOCIAL POLICY

Beneficial Builders is a major subdivision home builder in southern California. During the last fifteen years it has developed seven large subdivisions in the Los Angeles area. Its policy is to buy large tracts of land on the edges of suburbs and build good-quality, low-cost homes for working families. In order to keep costs low, Beneficial Builders uses only a few house plans in each subdivision, enabling it to precut lumber and subassemble walls, door frames, windows, cabinets, and other house parts in its shops. There are several variations of the front, or "elevation," of the houses, so that the houses are not identical in appearance.

A shopping center and 800 homes had been planned for the Hills East subdivision, located in high foothills 50 miles east of Los Angeles. Over 700 homes had been built and sold when heavy winter rains started. After the ground had been thoroughly soaked, an unprecedented 12-inch rainfall occurred on Monday night in the foothills just above the subdivision. A stream that drained these foothills ran through the center of Hills East. In planning this subdivision, Beneficial Builders recognized that heavy thunderstorms did occur in the area, so it widened and straightened the stream bed according to a plan approved by county engineers.

The rain sent torrents of water down the steep stream bed at an estimated 30 miles an hour. It appeared that the stream bed was adequate until the fast, high water uprooted a giant eucalyptus tree on the edge of the stream and carried it ⅓ mile to a highway bridge. The tree lodged against the bridge and held fast, soon collecting other debris until it blocked an estimated 60 percent of the streamflow. The lake created behind the bridge soon flooded a few homes, and even worse, it caused a major streamflow over a low spot in the highway 100 yards from the bridge. This overflow could not return to the stream bed, so it continued down a street for several blocks, horizontal to the stream but one block away.

Soon there was a torrent of raging water 3 to 5 feet deep in this overflow route. Homeowners were awakened suddenly about 5:30 A.M. by the sound of water running through their houses and cars crashing against carports and house walls. Water rose about 3 feet in over twenty-five houses, and occupants had to flee to roofs or to a second story if they had one. Walls and doors were torn away, but no house was swept from its foundation. Two persons were swept away by the current and drowned.

In a few hours the flood subsided, leaving a jumble of automobiles, uprooted trees, furniture, and house parts. Forty houses and thirty-five automobiles had damage estimated at $850,000. National Guard, civil defense, armed services, and city police helped restore order and provided trucks to haul away debris. Light showers continued, but the stream was back in its bed, and no further flooding was predicted. All utilities including water were disrupted, and none of the damaged homes could be occupied.

Glen Abel, president of Beneficial Builders, heard of the flood early in the morning and drove directly to his subdivision. He talked with public officials on the scene and with dazed and shocked residents. Although some were understandably bitter, there was no evidence that they thought the flood had been caused by poor design of the subdivision. Their homes had received the same heavy rains that hit the foothills, so they knew the rainfall was torrential. A flood victim described his experience to Abel as follows: "When I woke up, the water was leaking through the walls at the joints. We all started picking things off the floor so they wouldn't get wet, and then there was a crash as the water broke a plate-glass window and an outside door.

"The furniture started to float on top of the water, and big pieces like our dresser fell over. I knew then that we had to get out, but I didn't know how or where to go.

"I started to the boys' room, but before I got there the bedroom wall gave way and they came floating right by me out into the yard, both in their beds. I started after them, sort of swimming. Finally I reached one of the boys, still on his bed, and I handed him up to my neighbor on the roof of his house. I just handed him up; the water was so high, I didn't stand on a ladder or anything. Somebody else reached my other boy and put him on a roof.

"My house is still standing and the roof is good, but most of the walls are gone. I really don't know how it all happened, because you couldn't see anything in the dark."

Abel checked with city street engineers at the bridge, and they reported that the stream bed had proved large enough to hold the flood and that there was no overflow except that caused by the blocked bridge. On the basis of these discussions and all other evidence he had, Abel concluded that the subdivision drainage design was sound and that his firm had no liability for the damages.[1]

Although no company liability was evident, Abel was nevertheless distressed by suffering caused by the flood. He felt sure that these wage-earning residents, most with young families, were not financially prepared to cope with losses this large.

From a business point of view, Abel recognized that even though the Hills East subdivision was nearly sold out, any remaining sales would be handicapped by publicity about the flood. He reasoned that many persons would not be able to repair their homes, which would leave eyesores of wrecked buildings until mortgage settlements were made. He expected that various types of lawsuits and legal entanglements would develop among homeowners, automobile insurers, real estate mortgagors, chattel mortgagors (furniture and appliances), finance companies, and others.

While on the scene Abel checked with city engineers and determined that they would work with civil defense and National Guard truckers to clear all debris and return furniture to homes. The city would rebuild streets. Abel also worked with officers of the Hills East Community Improvement Asso-

---

[1]Weeks later a special engineering report requested by the city council and made by city engineers concluded that the flood was an "act of God" and that no negligence was evident.

ciation to arrange for flood victims to live temporarily with neighbors. The improvement association was a voluntary community group encouraged by Beneficial Builders when the first home buyers moved to Hills East.

Later that afternoon Abel returned to his downtown office several miles from Hills East in order to discuss with his associates what might be done for the flood victims. They considered asking the state governor for state flood aid, but delayed for two reasons. First, they felt that government aid should be requested only when all private and public self-help, such as the American Red Cross, was insufficient. Second, government aid would probably require much red tape and delay, and action was needed now.

They were discussing what direct action Beneficial Builders might take when Arch Smith, the union business agent for Beneficial workers, arrived and asked whether the union might help. He said that he had talked informally with several union leaders and could guarantee 200 volunteer carpenters and other selected skilled workers all day Saturday and Sunday to repair all structural damage to houses, if someone would supply materials, equipment, and supervision.

After extended discussion, Beneficial executives and Smith decided they would take direct action to repair all flood damage with donated labor and materials, provided Apex Lumber Company would donate lumber and building materials. Apex was considered the key to this plan, for lumber was the main building material needed. If Apex agreed, Abel and Smith believed that all lesser services would "fall in line." Apex was one of the largest building suppliers in the West, and it had been the principal supplier of Beneficial Builders since Beneficial Builders was organized.

If Apex accepted, the following plan would be used. All services would be donated. All homes would be restored to approximately their original condition, except for furniture and household supplies. A newspaper release would announce that the restoration was a joint effort of businesses, unions, and community agencies. Appeals for help would be made privately through existing groups; there would be no public appeal playing upon emotions and possibly leading to disorganized action. Unions would provide sufficient skilled labor (an estimated 200 workers) for ten hours daily on Saturday and Sunday and the following weekend if necessary. Beneficial Builders would provide supervision, shop services, and construction equipment (worth an estimated $50,000 wholesale). Apex would provide all building materials (worth an estimated $75,000 wholesale). Community agencies would be asked to supply unskilled labor (about 100 workers). Other groups employed by Beneficial Builders to construct its subdivisions would be asked to donate services, such as plumbing and electrical work, appliance repair, landscaping, and painting. All services except painting would be donated for the forthcoming weekend so that homes would be livable on Monday. Painting would be donated the following two weekends. The Red Cross or some other service agency would be asked to provide food and coffee for all volunteer labor.

Abel and Smith were convinced that 95 percent of the repairs could be made in one weekend because of the fortuitous circumstance that Beneficial's shops had completed cutting and assembling all components for the last fifty houses in the Hills East subdivision on the Friday before the flood. These components provided a ready-made inventory matching most of the houses destroyed. In the few instances where necessary items were not assembled, Abel promised to work his shops overtime to assure that all needed precut materials and subassemblies would be delivered to the carport of each home by 6:00 P.M. Friday. This procedure probably would delay by ten days the completion of the remaining fifty houses because new lumber would have to be cut and assembled. Some persons who had bought one of these fifty houses might be inconvenienced or have added expenses if they had already promised to vacate their present residence and move to Hills East on a certain date, believing that their homes would be available at that time.

By the time Abel and Smith completed their plans, it was 7:30 P.M. They telephoned Abe Silver, southern California manager of Apex Lumber, at his home near Los Angeles. When he learned the purpose of their call, he agreed to an appointment in his home at 9:00 P.M. that evening.

At 9:03 P.M. Abel and Smith rang the doorbell of Silver's palatial home.

DISCUSSION QUESTIONS

1. By the end of the case what strategic and policy decisions, if any, concerning social responsiveness have already been made by (a) Abel, (b) Smith, and (c) Abel and Smith together? Specifically state these decisions and then state the probable reasons for each.

2. At the end of the case what strategic and policy decisions need to be made by Silver and others? Specifically state them. Do Abel and Smith appear to have a plan for influencing these decisions? Discuss.

3. Who are the different stakeholders and what are their different expectations in this situation?

4. What are the probable costs and benefits (including risks and rewards) of involvement in this situation by (a) Beneficial Builders, (b) the union, and (c) Apex Lumber, if Silver decides to become involved? Are the results of involvement, as a whole, likely to be better or worse than noninvolvement? Answer separately for each major group involved, and specify why.

5. If you were Abel, Smith, or Silver when the three meet in Silver's home, what would you say and do? Role-play the 9:00 P.M. meeting of Abel, Smith, and Silver.

Twice within a four-year period, one or more poisoners placed cyanide in capsules of Extra-Strength Tylenol sold as over-the-counter (o-t-c) medications for pain relief. These tainted capsules killed seven persons in 1982 and one person in 1986. Tylenol's manufacturer, Johnson & Johnson, is a leading health care products firm, and at the time of both poisonings Tylenol was one of the company's major and most successful products.

When these two poisoning episodes occurred, the company faced crises of enormous ethical and financial proportions. With human lives at stake, swift decisions were needed to prevent further deaths. But with millions of dollars also at stake, company officials realized that a false step or a bad judgment could jeopardize not only Tylenol but also the company's financial future and the jobs of its employees. Few management challenges have been so filled with frightening possibilities as the ones that unfolded in Chicago in September 1982 and in New York's Westchester County in February 1986.

Johnson & Johnson: A Brief History

Johnson & Johnson began operations in 1886 in New Brunswick, New Jersey, and was incorporated in 1887. The company pioneered the concept of an antiseptic surgical dressing, based on the work of Sir Joseph Lister, an English surgeon. Over the years the company grew in size by broadening its array of products for the health care market. BAND-AID, one of its best known and most widely used products, was introduced in 1921.

The company pursued a vigorous strategy of growth by acquisition as well as internal development of new products and businesses. New product lines included baby care products, feminine protection products, birth control products, ethical surgical products, hypodermic needles and syringes, prescription drugs, veterinary drugs, kidney dialysis products, and other health care products.

Simultaneously with product line expansion and diversification, the company began to expand internationally. Johnson & Johnson in 1982 was a worldwide family of 150 companies, based in 50 countries, whose products were sold in 149 nations.

In 1959, the company acquired McNeil Laboratories, Inc., a producer of prescription pharmaceuticals. In keeping with the spirit of decentralization generally prevalent in the company, McNeil was operated as an autonomous division. McNeil was the manufacturer of the Tylenol line of o-t-c analgesics.

---

[1]The portion of this case dealing with the 1982 Tylenol crisis was prepared with the research and drafting assistance of Vasudevan Ramanujam. Sources include several articles appearing in the *Wall Street Journal*, the *New York Times*, *Advertising Age*, *Chemical Week*, *Business Week*, *Newsweek*, *Fortune*, and *Chemical Marketing Reporter* during the months of October and November 1982 and several months in 1986. These sources are cited in the case narrative only when useful for verifying specific figures or quotations, company information, and similar items. Two Johnson & Johnson publications were used: "Brief History of Johnson & Johnson" and "The Tylenol Comeback," both available from the company.

The parent company was known as a maker of quality products serving the needs of society. Its commitment to quality products and its strong consumer orientation were handed down from the company's early founders. The following legend appears on a large bronze plaque in the company's New Brunswick headquarters:

> We believe our first responsibility is to the doctors, nurses, and patients, to mothers and all others who use our products and services. In meeting their needs, everything we do must be of high quality.

The above quotation was a part of what the company called its "credo" philosophy. In looking back over their own conduct in the face of the Tylenol tragedy, company officials credited this "credo" for guiding their actions and decisions during the 1982 crisis.[2]

The First Tylenol Crisis: 1982

The first five Tylenol-related deaths occurred on Thursday, September 30, 1982, in three Chicago suburbs. That morning Johnson & Johnson learned of three of the deaths from a reporter of the *Chicago Sun-Times*, who, in turn, had heard about them from the Cook County (Illinois) medical examiner's office. Within forty-eight hours, the roster of victims rose to seven, all from the Chicago area.

The Company's Response

Johnson & Johnson's response to the bad news was swift and direct. Within hours of learning of the Chicago deaths, the company announced a recall of all 93,400 bottles of Extra-Strength Tylenol in the implicated MC2880 lot, which had been manufactured in McNeil's Fort Washington, Pennsylvania, plant and distributed to thirty-one Eastern and Midwestern states. This decision was made quickly, even though tests on samples of the same lot did not reveal any contamination, suggesting that the poisoning may not have occurred in manufacture. By noon that day, the firm had dispatched nearly half a million Mailgrams to physicians, hospitals, and wholesalers, alerting them to the danger. A press staff member and several scientific and security people were flown to Chicago by corporate jet to assist in the investigations. A laboratory was set up outside Chicago and staffed with thirty chemists to help the authorities analyze samples of Extra-Strength Tylenol.[3] It placed an additional 500 salespersons from two of its pharmaceutical divisions on call

---

[2]"The Tylenol Comeback," New Brunswick, N.J.: Johnson & Johnson, p. 4.

[3]However, local authorities appeared to have been reluctant to release the suspected samples to the company, leading to one of the few skirmishes between the company and the investigators. In another instance, an attorney for McNeil objected when Chicago authorities broadened the recall to include other forms of Tylenol in addition to extra-strength capsules. See the *"Wall Street Journal*, October 4, 1982, pp. 3, 16.

to help recall the Tylenol shipments. By late evening the company also offered a $100,000 reward to anyone who could give information leading to the arrest and conviction of "the person or persons responsible for the murders." All advertising and promotion of Tylenol was suspended. One of the company's two plants that manufactured Tylenol capsules was idled.

The recall was expanded by the following day to include one more batch of 171,000 bottles that had been manufactured in Round Rock, Texas, since the death of the latest victim was traced to a capsule from that batch. However, the worst was yet to come. An apparently unrelated case of strychnine-contaminated Tylenol that almost killed a man in Oroville, California, prompted the company to extend the recall to *all* Tylenol capsules, both regular and extra-strength. Production of the capsules was temporarily halted. On October 5, 1982, within a week of the first of the Tylenol deaths, the company was beginning to pull back the product and was considering destroying the entire stock. Some 31 million bottles with an estimated retail value of $100 million were involved. The decision to recall all Tylenol was considered by the company for four days and was no doubt hastened by the California incident. The after-tax impact was expected to be approximately $50 million. On the following morning, cyanide was discovered in Tylenol capsules in the apartment of a Philadelphia student who was thought to have committed suicide some seven months earlier.

The company stated that its first reaction was to protect the public and inform them about rapidly unfolding developments. The recalls seem to have been decided on almost as a matter of course. In fact, according to *Fortune*, James E. Burke, the chairman of Johnson & Johnson, had wanted to announce a total recall of all Extra-Strength Tylenol from the very beginning, but, surprisingly, the FBI and the Food and Drug Administration (FDA) had advised him against premature recall on the grounds that such an action might "cause more public anxiety than it would relieve."[4] Early during the crisis, Burke said, "It's important that we demonstrate that we've taken every single step possible to protect the public, and that there's simply nothing else we can do."[5] At that point, the company said they were not thinking about the future of the brand. Another Johnson & Johnson executive declared, "We've been trying to put out the fire. We really haven't thought about how to rebuild the house."

In its effort to protect and inform the public, the company undertook a number of other voluntary steps. A conscious decision was made not to place any warning ads in newspapers but to respond only to press calls. In the first week of the crisis, toll-free lines were established to respond to inquiries concerning the safety of Tylenol. Through November, more than 30,000 phone calls had been handled through this medium. The company made it a policy to respond to every letter from consumers about Tylenol. By late November, some 3,000 responses had been sent.

[4]"The Fight to Save Tylenol," *Fortune*, November 29, 1982, p. 48.
[5]*Wall Street Journal*, October 4, 1982, p. 16.

Rebuilding the Tylenol Name

While the above steps were of a firefighting nature, the company soon began to plot a strategy for reestablishing the embattled Tylenol name. A seven-member crisis management team of key Johnson & Johnson and McNeil executives began to meet twice daily to make decisions on rapidly developing events and to coordinate companywide efforts.

At the time of the crisis, Tylenol was the leading o-t-c analgesic, with an estimated 37 percent share of the $1.2 billion a year market. From modest beginnings in the mid-seventies, when it held a 10 percent share of a much smaller market, Tylenol was carefully nurtured to its dominant position by shrewd and sometimes hard-hitting marketing techniques. By 1982 Tylenol had far outdistanced its nearest competing brands. Figure 1 gives estimated market share data on those brands.

Tylenol had been positioned as a safe and effective alternative to aspirin, and the company claimed it to be free of the unpleasant side effects that some aspirin users experienced. For many years it was promoted heavily among doctors and hospitals before a concerted program of advertising and promotion directly aimed at the end user was begun. This change of approach was mainly in response to the heavy advertising and promotion campaigns launched by competitor Bristol-Myers for its own nonaspirin painkiller, Datril. In the marketing battle that ensued, Tylenol emerged the clear winner. Tylenol's spectacular success over the years was attributed to its image as a safe and effective product and to the trust and support it received from the medical community, the retail trade, and, of course, the final consumer. Advertising had clearly played a major role in the process of building up this overwhelming level of trust and support. In 1981, Tylenol alone accounted

FIGURE 1
ESTIMATED MARKET SHARES OF THE OVER-THE-COUNTER ANALGESIC INDUSTRY PRIOR TO THE TYLENOL CRISIS.

Company	Product	Market Share(%)	
Johnson & Johnson (McNeil Consumer Products Company Division)	Tylenol	37	
American Home Products	Anacin	13	
	Anacin-3		1
Sterling Drug	Bayer Aspirin	11	
Bristol-Myers	Excedrin	10	
	Bufferin	9	
	Datril	1	
All others		18	

Source: Chemical Week, November 3, 1982, p. 30.

for an estimated $43 million of advertising expenditures, the largest in the analgesics field.[6]

The critical question facing Johnson & Johnson and McNeil in the days immediately following the crisis was, "To what extent had the Chicago incidents damaged the product's image, and how long would it take to repair that damage, if it was at all possible to do so?" To many experts the brand's prospects appeared very dim, in view of its association with death. But the company remained strongly committed to the Tylenol name. The options of dropping the line or reintroducing it under another name were never seriously considered.

To gauge the shifting public perceptions in the weeks following the crisis, the company commissioned a series of opinion polls. The polls revealed that both the brand and the company were getting a lot of potentially negative publicity, the effects of which could not be estimated with confidence. However, a large proportion of the respondents did not appear to be blaming the company for the poisonings, and as time passed, more and more of the regular users were expressing a willingness to return to the fold. By the fifth week after the tragedy, this figure rose to 59 percent. When asked if they would buy Tylenol in a tamper-resistant package, as many as 77 percent of regular Tylenol users answered positively.[7]

In the wake of the crisis, sales of Tylenol fell sharply, by as much as 80 percent, according to some estimates. At the same time, sales of aspirin and other competing brands of nonaspirin pain relievers were beginning to surge. In the face of such adverse circumstances, the company mounted a carefully planned campaign of communication and packaging modifications in an effort to win back the public trust it was losing. It began by sending some 2 million pieces of literature to doctors, dentists, nurses, and pharmacists, the groups that had most contributed to making Tylenol the success it was. The fact that the company had not been the source of the poisonings was strongly emphasized in the communications.

Throughout the crisis, employees of the company had shown a strong sense of commitment and high morale. Hundreds of them volunteered to work around the clock without extra pay, and many were staffing the phone lines to answer as many calls as possible. To help maintain that morale, the company also undertook an internal communications program. This included writing letters to all employees and retirees, keeping them updated on important information and thanking them for their continued support and assistance. Four videotaped special reports were prepared and distributed or shown to employees.

Before the crisis, the company had generally been known for its low-key profile and tight-lipped approach to dealing with press and public inquiries. The crisis changed that policy. The press became a close ally of the company,

---

[6]*Chemical Week*, November 3, 1982, p. 33.
[7]See *Advertising Age*, November 15, 1982, p. 78, and October 11, 1982, p. 78.

especially in the first frenzied days, providing the company its most accurate information on various developments. The company praised the efforts of the broadcast community, which had been instrumental in getting Tylenol commercials off the air in a matter of hours after news of the first deaths.[8] In a reversal of the company's traditional policy, company executives made several appearances on television, including *60 Minutes, The Phil Donahue Show, ABC Nightline, Live at Five,* and others. Interviews were freely granted to business journals and periodicals, such as *Fortune* and the *Wall Street Journal.* In short, every effort was made to "get the word out," to use the company's own phrase.

The press praised Johnson & Johnson's quick action, citing it as an example of corporate responsibility. The *Wall Street Journal* declared:

> Johnson & Johnson, the parent company that makes Tylenol, set the pattern of industry response. Without being asked, it quickly withdrew Extra-Strength TYLENOL from the market at a very considerable expense . . . the company chose to take a large loss rather then expose anyone to further risk. The anti-corporation movement may have trouble squaring that with the devil theories it purveys.

The *Washington Post* equally admired the company's actions in the face of adversity:

> Johnson & Johnson has effectively demonstrated how a major business ought to handle a disaster. From the day the deaths were linked to the poisoned TYLENOL . . . Johnson & Johnson has succeeded in portraying itself to the public as a company willing to do what's right regardless of cost.[9]

While Tylenol advertising still remained off the air, Johnson & Johnson beamed a series of trust-building messages to the American public during October and early November. These sixty-second messages featured Dr. Thomas Gates, medical director of McNeil, who assured consumers that the company would do everything possible to maintain the trust and support of the public, and it also alerted them to the fact that the company planned to reintroduce Tylenol capsules in new tamper-resistant packaging.

The company hastened to be the first in the market with improved tamper-resistant packaging for its Tylenol products, even though new regulations on the packaging of o-t-c products were still being debated by the Food and Drug Administration (FDA) and the Proprietary Association, the trade association of the o-t-c products industry. On November 11, 1982, a new safety package, with three separate safety seals, was demonstrated at a video conference, broadcast via satellite, and simultaneously aimed at thirty cities and attended by some 1,000 reporters and news media representatives. In that conference the chairman of Johnson & Johnson reaffirmed his com-

[8]*Advertising Age,* October 11, 1982, p. 78.
[9]Both press passages are quoted in Johnson & Johnson, "The Tylenol Comeback," p. 8.

pany's continuing commitment to the Tylenol name, referring to the commitment as a "moral imperative."

The company's polls had revealed that 35 percent of Tylenol users had thrown away their supplies of the product when news of the crisis broke. To make good their loss and to help overcome their reluctance to using the product again, the company placed special coupons in newspapers nationally that could be exchanged for a free bottle of any Tylenol product. A toll-free number also was established for this purpose. Consumers could call and a coupon would be sent in the mail for a free bottle of Tylenol.

The company was fully aware that while a beginning had been made, restoring Tylenol's market share to its precrisis level of 37 percent was still a formidable task. In one interview, the chairman of McNeil stated that he expected Tylenol's share for the next reporting period to be in the 5 to 10 percent range.[10] In that interview, it also was revealed that in a four-city survey where Tylenol had a 27 percent market share before the tragedy, grocery scanning data showed that the brand's share fell to 6.5 percent the week after the poisonings but had rebounded to 18 percent. By the end of 1982, Tylenol had regained first place among analgesics, with 29 percent market share.

The Cost Impact

In addition to the toll of human lives, the Tylenol tragedy had a profound cost impact on the company in the short term. Just prior to the crisis, Johnson & Johnson's stock had been trading on the market at $46.125. Immediately following the crisis, it fell by as many as 7 points before eventually stabilizing in the mid-40s.

The costs directly associated with the recall of the capsules translated into a $50 million write-off against the company's third-quarter profits. In percentage terms, this represented a 26 percent drop in net income. Fourth-quarter domestic income declined by more than $25 million compared with the same period in 1981, and industry observers believed the drop was due to the Tylenol incident.

The company decided to absorb the costs of the improved packaging, estimated to be 2.4 cents a bottle. Since price increases were ruled out as a matter of company policy and may not have been practical anyway, these costs would continue indefinitely. The costs of the coupon campaign were estimated between $20 million and $40 million. The dealer discount program also added to the overall costs. Johnson & Johnson estimated that the cost of all these actions could run as high as $140 million.

The company also was faced with three lawsuits shortly after the deaths in Chicago. However, some observers believed that since it appeared that the company was not responsible for the poisonings and could not reasonably have foreseen them, no damages could be won in court.[11]

---

[10]_Advertising Age_, November 15, 1982, p. 78.
[11]_New York Times_, October 7, 1982, p. B-12; and _Chemical Week_, October 13, 1982, p. 17.

Other intangible costs to the company were difficult to estimate. For many weeks the Tylenol crisis occupied the key executives of the company on a full-time basis. The day-to-day operations of the other divisions of the company were left to others. What effect this had on their performance, if any, remains uncertain.

Government Regulatory Responses

The first actions of a regulatory nature were taken by local and state officials, who issued warnings and orders of their own. Stores began to remove stocks of Tylenol in response to these warnings. At first the FDA issued a warning related only to the first implicated lot, but as news of more deaths followed, implicating other lots, the warnings were extended to Tylenol capsules in general. The FDA also sent its inspectors to McNeil's Fort Washington, Pennsylvania, plant, to collect samples, review batch records, and to investigate manufacturing processes. The agency's nineteen laboratories began collecting and testing some 40,000 Tylenol samples. It was expected at that time that some 2,100 FDA employees would assist in the testing. Over the weeks that followed, some 8 million capsules were analyzed, of which 75 were found to contain cyanide. The major question for the agency was to determine quickly if the cyanide had been introduced into the capsules during the manufacturing process, at a later point in the distribution chain, or at retail stores.

Chicago's mayor went on the air to urge citizens not to take any Tylenol. The sale of Tylenol was banned in the state of North Dakota, and Colorado ordered stores to withdraw all Tylenol capsules, while Massachusetts retailers were directed to remove all Tylenol products. Warnings also were issued by health officials in New York. Similar actions were taken in foreign countries as well.[12]

Soon initiatives for regulating safety packaging of all o-t-c products were taken. On October 4, the Cook County Board voted unanimously to require all o-t-c drugs and medicines to carry manufacturers' seals. The ordinance was to take effect in ninety days, and required a seal of plastic, paper, metal, or cellophane, which restricts air into the product, and when broken, would be evident to an observer or consumer. Mayor Byrne also proposed an ordinance to the City Council that would, after hearings, require protective sealings on all o-t-c products.

There was some concern that piecemeal local and state regulations would proliferate. The federal government was irked by the precipitate actions of local authorities in Chicago, which some believed had been politically motivated, because county legislators were facing reelection soon. The FDA was ordered to enact an emergency packaging code that would require manufacturers to introduce interim bottle seals within ninety days. Industry and government officials had announced earlier that they would work together to develop federal regulations requiring tamper-resistant packaging for all drugs sold without a prescription. It was anticipated that such regulation would

[12]*New York Times,* October 2, 1982, p. 21, and October 6, 1982, p. A-24.

take time to draft and implement, since no single, simple solution would be uniformly applicable to all products. Also, the industry association believed that individual companies should have sufficient flexibility in choosing packaging methods or options. A later meeting of industry representatives concluded that tamper-resistant packaging was feasible for drug items. As a first step, a tamper-resistant package was defined as "one that can reasonably be expected to provide visible evidence to consumers if the package is tampered with or opened."[13]

While the industry association and the FDA both appeared to favor some form of packaging regulation, one economist expressed doubts about the costs and benefits of such regulation. In an article in the *New York Times*, he argued that the costs of such regulation would far exceed the benefits, and the consumer would pay more for drugs.[14] Some expressed more pragmatic concerns, namely that seals and other elaborate protective measures might render the package harder to open by arthritics, who were among the major users of pain relievers.

Competitor and Industry Responses

Competitive reactions varied. Many competitors asserted that they had no intentions of exploiting the company's misfortunes. However, the actions of some told a different story. Major retail chains such as Walgreen in Chicago were approached by the representatives of Johnson & Johnson's competitors with offers to fill the shelf space vacated by Tylenol.[15] American Home Products, maker of Anacin, Anacin-3, and Arthritis Pain Formula, and normally low-key and press-shy, called a rare press conference to announce plans for increased production of its nonaspirin pain relievers. The company also announced plans for newer formulations of its Anacin-3 brand.[16] Although American Home Products declined to disclose whether it planned to step up advertising support for its products, one report alleged that the company was trying to pick up the air time released by Tylenol. The company responded with a statement that it was not AHP's policy to capitalize on the misfortunes of its competitors.[17]

At Bristol-Myers, whose Datril had suffered badly when Johnson & Johnson battled it head-on with heavy advertising of Tylenol, company officials would not discuss any plans. It acknowledged a surge in demand for Datril and stated that the company was looking into new packaging for all its analgesic products. The company ran coupons for Bufferin and Excedrin in a number of national newspapers during the first week of the Tylenol crisis.

[13]*Chemical Week*, October 13, 1982, p. 16; *New York Times*, October 6, 1982, p. A-1; *Wall Street Journal*, October 8, 1982, p. 17.

[14]Paul W. MacAvoy, "F.D.A. Regulation—At What Price?" *New York Times*, November 21, 1982, p. F-3.

[15]*Wall Street Journal*, October 5, 1982, p. 22; *Chemical Week*, November 3, 1982, p. 30.

[16]*Advertising Age*, October 18, 1982, p. 82.

[17]*Advertising Age*, October 11, 1982, p. 78; *Chemical Week*, November 3, 1982, p. 30; and *Fortune*, November 29, 1982, p. 49.

What made these advertisements unusual was their placement on late-news pages, not in the usual food-shopping sections. A company representative claimed that the company was simply doing "business as usual."[18] Seemingly opportunistic moves also were made by Richardson-Vicks, which ran consumer ads for the first time for its newly acquired Percogesic brand.

The Search for the Killer

Finding the Tylenol poisoner was not easy. One suspect was convicted and given a ten-year jail term for trying to extort $1 million from Johnson & Johnson after the poisonings took place; his wife had formerly worked for Tylenol's maker. Another person who had been employed in a store where some of the poisoned capsules were found was imprisoned for the 1983 slaying of a man he believed had identified him to the police as a Tylenol suspect. Authorities were not convinced that either of these suspects was the actual Tylenol killer. A police official said, "This is an unusually tough case. There's little physical evidence. The victims and the tainted bottles show no pattern. And the motive is unclear. It's enormously frustrating."[19]

The Second Tylenol Crisis: 1986

By early 1986, Tylenol was once again the premier over-the-counter (o-t-c) pain reliever, with a 35 percent share of the annual $1.5-billion market. It was Johnson & Johnson's most profitable single brand, bringing in $525 million in revenues. Extra-Strength Tylenol, the type that had been involved in the Chicago killings, accounted for about one-third of those revenues.· Overall, the company's recovery had been remarkable.

The Poisoning and Early Management Response

On the evening of February 8, 1986, a 23-year-old woman living in Yonkers, New York, took two Extra-Strength Tylenol capsules from a brand-new package and went to bed. When she did not appear for breakfast and lunch the next day, relatives went to her room and found her dead. The cause of death was cyanide poisoning. Investigating police found three other cyanide-tainted Tylenol capsules in the same bottle. The bottle had been purchased at a nearby A&P grocery store.

The first public reaction was, How could this have happened again, since all Tylenol containers had been triple-sealed after the Chicago experience? The mystery only deepened when it was learned that the Yonkers bottle had indeed been triple-sealed in the approved manner. The finding led to an early theory that the poison had been put in the capsules during the manufacturing process, but this theory apparently would not hold up under more careful investigation that was to come later.

---

[18]*Advertising Age,* October 11, 1982, p. 78.
[19]*New York Times,* February 21, 1986, p. A-11.

When the cause of death was announced on February 10, Johnson & Johnson's chairman, James Burke, who had guided the company through the 1982 crisis, ordered continuous monitoring of consumer sentiment about Tylenol products. He also cancelled all Tylenol capsule advertising after seeing an ad for the capsules on the same newscast that announced the cause of the victim's death. Although shocked by the reappearance of poison, this time in the safety-sealed packages, company officials tended to believe that it was an isolated incident.

Then came the real shocker. On February 13, Frank Young, head of the Food and Drug Administration (FDA), whose staff had been examining Tylenol that was pulled from stores in the Yonkers area, told Burke that a second container of cyanide-laced Extra-Strength Tylenol had been found in a Woolworth's store only two blocks from the A&P store where the first bottle had been bought. Burke replied, "Frank, that is the worst news you could give us."[20] The poisoned capsules in the second container showed evidence of tampering—the logo printed on the capsule halves was misaligned—but the outer and inner seals appeared to be intact. Again, it seemed that the cyanide must have been introduced during manufacture before the safety seals were secured.

To make things even more complicated, investigators discovered that the two containers were produced in different locations at different times. After the safety seals were affixed, the two bottles had been stored at the same storage facility but at different times. Within a day, the FDA revealed that the cyanide in both of the contaminated bottles appeared to have come from the same source, but it did not match the cyanide found in Tylenol capsules during the 1982 crisis.

The Recall

Spreading public alarm caused the FDA to warn consumers not to use Tylenol capsules for the time being, and ten states banned their sale. Inside Johnson & Johnson, officials were reading the results of polls showing that customer loyalty was beginning to fade as the "single local incident" theory looked less plausible. Other market research revealed that 36 percent of the public believed the tampering came from inside the company, which was a contrast with the 1982 episode when the vast majority concluded that an outsider had been to blame.

Burke created a six-member crisis management team. It included the two top managers from Johnson & Johnson and from McNeil Consumer Products Company (the maker of Tylenol) plus Johnson & Johnson's general counsel and its vice president for public relations. The team was advised by the public relations firm of Burson Marsteller.

The day following the FDA chief's phone call to Burke, the crisis management team decided to suspend production of Tylenol capsules. Saying that "[t]his is an act of terrorism, pure and simple," Burke offered a $100,000

[20]*Newsweek,* March 3, 1986, p. 52.

reward for information leading to the arrest and conviction of the poisoner. The company also announced that it would give a refund or a new bottle of Tylenol tablets or caplets to customers wishing to exchange their Tylenol capsules. More than 200,000 people responded to the offer. Simultaneously, Johnson & Johnson's stock price fell $4 per share to $47.75.

With capsule advertising and production suspended and public confidence waning, a spirited debate broke out among top company officials about next steps to take. Burke himself told reporters later that some of the meetings were punctuated with "yelling and screaming." Managers from McNeil Consumer Products Company, the maker of Tylenol, argued that the company should try to ride out the storm since only two tainted bottles had been found and since surveys showed that 52 percent of capsule users wanted the company to keep producing them. They also feared the financial impact on the McNeil division if more drastic action were taken. However, Burke concluded that "there is no tamperproof package [and there] is never going to be a tamperproof package." If a third poisoned package were to turn up, "Not only do we risk Tylenol, we risk Johnson & Johnson."[21]

Eight days after the Yonkers death, on February 16, the company decided to recall all Tylenol capsule products and to abandon the use of capsules entirely for all of its o-t-c products. The decision was announced to the public the next day. These actions would cost the company an estimated $150 million in 1986.

The case took another puzzling turn in late February when the Federal Bureau of Investigation (FBI) reversed an earlier opinion that the tampering probably occurred in the manufacturing process. An FBI official said, "Previously undetected signs of tampering have now been discovered using sophisticated scientific examinations. Our examinations have further determined it was possible to invade the bottles after packaging was complete without detection through conventional means of examination." This finding applied to both bottles containing the poisoned capsules.[22]

Tylenol's Recovery

"To date [mid-1986], our recovery looks very strong," said McNeil's vice president of marketing. Just five months after the tampering, Tylenol had recovered 90 percent of its previous market share. In fact, discontinuing the capsule form apparently had not damaged the company as much as some had feared. Immediately after the poisoning death, Tylenol sales dropped by $128 million, but $48 million of these sales had been regained by late April. One reason for the quick recovery was the availability of caplets as an alternative to capsules. Johnson & Johnson's caplets had been on the market since 1984 and already accounted for nearly one-fourth of all Tylenol sales. When the capsules were recalled, McNeil's plants went on a crash program to increase production of caplets, spending $20 million for new equipment. In the

[21]Ibid.
[22]*New York Times*, February 27, 1986, p. 20.

switchover from capsules to caplets, which caused the encapsulating machinery to be idled, no McNeil employees were furloughed.

Doctors and hospitals continued to recommend Tylenol to their patients, and McNeil's sales force managed to convince 97 percent of their top accounts to maintain shelf space for Tylenol products. One year after the Yonkers poisoning, Johnson & Johnson claimed it was once again the leading seller of o-t-c analgesics.[23]

Copycat Tampering

A major reason why public authorities are wary of nationwide recalls of suspect drugs is the fear of encouraging further tampering and creating consumer panic. It did not take long for "copycat" episodes to emerge.

A Nashville, Tennessee, man was found dead on February 23 of a massive dose of cyanide. A bottle of Extra-Strength Tylenol containing one capsule was found under his bed. Investigators said the bottle and capsule revealed traces of cyanide, but they were unwilling to say that his death was caused by taking poisoned Tylenol.

One of the most bizarre episodes occurred in March when Smithkline Beckman Corporation withdrew Contac, Teldrin, and Dietac capsules from the market after rat poison was found in some of these products. Police then arrested a former stock brokerage clerk who allegedly hoped that the poisoning threat would force down the price of Smithkline stock, thus enabling him to make a profit by trading in stock options. He was convicted and jailed in October.

Other copycats followed. In May, the Walgreen drugstore chain removed all Anacin-3 capsules from its shelves, following the death of an Austin, Texas, man whose body contained cyanide. An opened bottle of Anacin-3 that had been bought at Walgreen's Austin store showed signs of tampering. Bristol-Myers ordered a nationwide recall of Excedrin capsules after two deaths in the Seattle area were linked to the cyanide-tainted painkiller. Like Johnson & Johnson, Bristol-Myers was expected to replace capsules with caplets at an estimated cost of $10 million.

The tampering was not limited to drugs. IC Industries' Accent flavor enhancer had to be removed from Texas stores after someone claimed that he had placed cyanide in six cans. A similar call forced General Foods to clear the shelves of sugar-free Jello in four supermarket chains in four states.

Nor was tampering confined to the United States. In Japan eight people had died in 1985 after drinking juice that had been mixed with a weedkiller, and boxes of chocolate had to be recalled after being dusted with cyanide. The previous year, animal-lover activists in Britain who were opposed to using animals for tooth-decay research forced a recall of Mars candy bars after claiming some were poisoned.[24]

---

[23]"Tylenol Begins Making a 'Solid Recovery,' " New Brunswick, N.J.: Johnson & Johnson, 1986; and *New York Times*, February 8, 1987, p. 35.

[24]*Fortune*, March 31, 1986, p. 62.

Gerber Foods dug in its heels and refused to recall baby food after a receiving a rash of reports that glass shards were found in over 200 bottles in at least thirty states. In fact, Gerber sued the state of Maryland for ordering retailers in that state to withdraw Gerber's strained peaches from sale. As with Johnson & Johnson, it was Gerber's second contamination crisis; in 1984, it had voluntarily recalled over a half million bottles of juice at a considerable financial loss. Believing the company was being victimized by fraudulent claims of contamination, Gerber's CEO said, "When we tried to quiet the press with an unjustified recall [in 1984], it didn't work. So why should we do it again? It's our decision not to keep this media event going. We have found no reason to suspect our product. I suppose we could get on television and make that statement every day. But generally, the sensational gets covered, and the unsensational does not."[25]

The Industry Response

Where capsules were concerned, sentiment throughout the o-t-c analgesic industry tended to favor Gerber's hard-nosed stand rather than Johnson & Johnson's more cautious approach of banning capsules. American Home Products, maker of Anacin-3, decided to stick with capsules. So did Smithkline Beckman, whose Contac cold capsules had been contaminated with rat poison. Smithkline's consumer products division president said, "We looked for a way to improve the relative safety of the capsule and found one; the others decided they couldn't. One of us could be wrong, or we could both be right. It will be interesting to watch. We take our responsibility for public safety very seriously." However, the company also offered Contac customers a choice of caplets or capsules.[26]

Both the FDA and the Proprietary Association, a trade association for nonprescription drug makers, opposed a general ban on capsules. The FDA's chief officer said, "If we banned capsules the problem of tampering wouldn't go away. It would probably occur in other product forms which are just as vulnerable."[27] Some consumerists disagreed, citing the spate of capsule contamination cases already on the record as evidence of the need for even greater caution. They wondered if the FDA, as one of the federal government's main consumer protection agencies, was not working too closely with an industry that it was supposed to be regulating in the public interest.

One defensive tactic favored by the Proprietary Association was to offer rewards for information about tamperers. More than $1 million was set aside for this purpose, and it paid a $200,000 reward to a stockbroker who reported the trading activities of the clerk who had put rat poison in Contac capsules.

Federal antitampering laws were strengthened after the 1982 Tylenol episode; tampering with food, drugs, or cosmetics can lead to a maximum penalty of life imprisonment and a $250,000 fine, and a hoax can land a

[25]*Business Week*, March 17, 1986, p. 50.

[26]*Wall Street Journal*, July 31, 1986, p. 23.

[27]*Wall Street Journal*, May 30, 1986, p. 2.

person in jail for five years. However, of more than 100 tampering investigations undertaken by the FBI from 1984 to early 1986, only four convictions were obtained; sentences were relatively light, ranging from five-years' probation to five years in jail.[28]

DISCUSSION QUESTIONS

1. Do you consider Johnson & Johnson's voluntary recall decisions to be acts of corporate social responsibility? Why or why not?

2. Product tampering has been called "corporate terrorism." What corporate strategies can you recommend for reducing this kind of terrorist attack?

3. Identify the ethical issues involved in product-tampering episodes. To what extent are companies such as Johnson & Johnson obligated to take ethical actions to protect their customers, even if doing so causes financial losses to stockholders or threatens employees' jobs?

4. What is the role for public policy in the area of product tampering? Assess the actions of government authorities—local, state, and federal—in the Tylenol poisonings, and tell whether you believe they acted properly and in the public interest.

5. Relations between the news media and business corporations are not always congenial, but they were in both Tylenol episodes. What factors produced this good relationship? Do those factors provide a basis for improving media-and-business relationships in general? Discuss the possibilities. Gerber Foods seemed to blame the media for the problems it had with complaints of broken glass in some of its products. Evalute the contrasting media attitudes and media strategies of these two companies.

---

[28]*Fortune*, March 31, 1986, p. 62.

DRESSER INDUSTRIES AND PIPELINE POLITICS[1]

On August 23, 1982, Robert E. Tron found himself in a situation for which there was no known precedent or easy solution. As the President of Dresser-France, an American subsidiary in France, he had contracted in 1981 with Creusot-Loire, a nationalized French firm, and Machinoimport, a Soviet trading agency, to deliver equipment destined for use in a major Russian pipeline project. Between 1981 and 1983, however, global politics had intervened with the following results:

> *The United States, home of Dresser Industries, the parent corporation of Dresser-France, had issued an embargo against shipment of U.S. pipeline technology to the Soviet Union. The ban purported to include all pipeline equipment manufactured by any firm that used U.S. technology anywhere in the world.*
>
> *Representatives of the French government had delivered a requisition to Mr. Tron which directed him to ship three compressors which stood ready for loading onto an awaiting Soviet freighter.*

Each government had threatened severe punishment for noncompliance with its directive, and Tron found himself between the proverbial "rock and a hard place." If he followed the directive put forth by the U.S., he would be subject to imprisonment in France for violating a directive issued by the French government. If he followed the French directive, Dresser Industries would be subject to severe penalties, and Tron would have to consider himself responsible for violating a directive issued by the United States. Caught in the crossfire among three of the most powerful countries in the world, all of the company's options at this stage seemed fraught with dangers and potential disaster.

To understand the complex relationships between actors in this drama, and to understand the motivations behind the actions of each, it is important to understand the nature of each actor and the nature of their conflicting interests. Dresser Industries, the American parent of Dresser-France, had certain profit motives, certain social motives, and certain responsibilities to the U.S. government. Dresser-France had a different set of motives and responsibilities, as did the French and American governments themselves. All of these motives and interests were being played out in a changing political environment, with the result being the tight-wire standoff in late August of 1982.

Dresser Industries

In 1981, Dresser Industries operated 500 profit centers in 100 countries and employed 57,000 people. Its decentralized management structure encouraged decision making at the lowest practical levels in the organization.

[1]This case was prepared by Janet Murphy and Michelle Poirier under the direction of James E. Post. Copyright © Public Affairs Research Program, Boston University School of Management. Used with permission.

Pipeline equipment was produced in Dresser's Energy Processing and Conversion Industry Segment, one of five major divisions of the corporation. Compressors for gas pipelines were the primary product line of the segment; together with the related line of pumping equipment, they accounted for 60 percent of the segment's $900 million sales in 1981. Sales to Europe and the Soviet Union made up the largest part of the segment's exports at 14 percent.

The company's corporate goal was stated as "maximizing returns to shareholders through long-term stock price appreciation and rising dividend payments." The philosophies and policies that support the company's primary goal were outlined in Dresser's 1981 Annual Report:

> Business philosophy—To conduct Dresser's affairs in a responsible manner . . . by working to improve the quality of life of our employees and the communities in which we operate . . . and by understanding and meeting our customers' needs.
>
> Operating philosophy—To position the Company as a leading supplier to those essential industries that find, produce, transport, and process the vast quantities of petroleum, natural gas, and coal required for an energy-reliant world.
>
> Organizational philosophy—To develop an effective and manageable organization that provides continuity of experience and innovative entrepreneurship—the primary requirements for coping with an increasingly complex business environment.
>
> Social concerns—During the fiscal [year] 1981, the Company and its affiliated foundations made charitable contributions totaling over $3 million, primarily in the areas of education, health and welfare, and social services.

The company's attitude toward international trade had been spelled out in Dresser's 1979 Annual Report:

> Throughout much of the world, rising economic and social expectations present new opportunities for business growth. With these new opportunities have come new responsibilities for Dresser—to the host countries and their economic, political and social institutions and to our shareholders whose investment provides the means to pursue new profit opportunities.
> The Company believes that it acts in a responsible manner by providing quality products, conducting its affairs with honesty and integrity under the laws of each host country, and working to improve the quality of life in all areas in which it operates.

John V. James, chairman and chief executive officer, was no stranger to either business or political disputes, with a record of outspoken views and aggressiveness on important issues. In 1978, President Carter attempted to block export of oil and gas exploration equipment to the Soviet Union. Mr. James publicly called the move "sheer idiocy," arguing that it would "hand American export business to foreign competitors on a silver platter."

Clearly, Dresser Industries had very clear motives and interests prior to the crisis in 1982. The company had an interest in maintaining its leading position as a supplier in the petroleum, natural gas, and coal industries. Dresser also intended to realize its goals in a socially responsible manner, respecting the needs of its customers, its employees, the local communities surrounding its plants, and the governments of its various host countries. Dresser-France shared the same overall business philosophy, but its interests and responsibilities differed because of its location in a foreign country, its product structure, its dependence on its parent for technical information, and France's dependence on it for jobs and revenues.

Dresser-France

Incorporated as a French company in 1956, Dresser-France was acquired by Dresser Industries' Lichtenstein branch in 1971. The French office employed about 800 people in a depressed section of Le Havre. Another 390 were employed in associated or subcontracted firms. During 1981, the company contributed between $50 million and $75 million in worldwide sales of compressors and pumps.

Dresser-France was solely a manufacturing operation. It was completely dependent on American divisions in New York and Texas for engineering designs and plans. Robert E. Tron, President and General Manager of Dresser-France, explained:

> Like other foreign subsidiaries or licensees of Dresser Industries that manufacture compressors, Dresser-France is dependent on the Dresser Clark Division of Dresser Industries for product development, design and application. Dresser Clark is located in Olean, New York. Compressors are extremely complex pieces of equipment. Each customer has particular performance requirements (usually expressed in terms of gas inlet conditions, gas discharge conditions, and gas quality). A critical task in the construction of a compressor is product design and application—that is, the selection or design of the impellers, bearings, seals, and other components that will satisfy the customer's requirements in the most efficient manner. Dresser Clark performs at its Olean facility product design and application for Dresser-France, and, in doing so, relies heavily on computer programs developed for this purpose. In most cases, Dresser Clark also provides the manufacturing drawings required for the construction of the compressors, and Dresser Clark's facility in Olean sometimes provides certain components that cannot be manufactured by Dresser-France.

Dresser Clark also was the division to which Dresser-France reported, the relationship to the Lichtenstein office seeming to be a legal and financial formality.

Dresser-France was scheduled to add a line of drilling rigs during 1982; they were projected to account for 30 percent of sales within one year. The technology for rig manufacture was to be delivered from Dresser's Ideco Division in Beaumont, Texas. Compressor sales were expected to account for 64 percent of 1982 business.

Thus Dresser and its subsidiary in France had similar and compatible overall goals but different interests and motivations pertaining to their individual positions. The governments of France and the United States also had different interests and motivations, but all of these differences might never have caused the companies or government any troubles had it not been for rapid changes occurring in the political environment.

Political Background

On Sunday, December 13, 1981, the military forces of the Polish government, with full support of the Polish Communist Party, declared martial law and seized the reins of control. Within days, as many as 20,000 people had been arrested or interned. The target of the dragnet included anyone who was regarded to have been in an influential position with respect to the populist Solidarity union—from union leaders and activists to journalists, artists, writers, and intellectuals. For over a year, the Solidarity union had been gaining in domestic strength and international support. As the political crackdown proceeded, civil and union rights were suspended, labor strikes were broken, and cities were occupied by Polish tanks and troops.

While there was no direct military involvement in the coup by Soviet forces, Russian troops and equipment were present in the country and speculation ran strongly that Soviet influences were instrumental to the takeover. NATO allies progressed slowly and individually in applying economic and diplomatic pressures against the Soviets and the Polish government. Poland had long been an important trading partner of the Western bloc, and previous attempts to use trade sanctions to apply pressure after Soviet interventions in Czechoslovakia, Hungary, and Afghanistan had not proven effective.

President Ronald Reagan took the most stringent steps against the Polish and Russian governments, quickly applying a series of sanctions and issuing condemnations against those governments. On December 23, in a nationwide broadcast, he announced curbs on Poland's credit and trade privileges and warned the Soviet leadership that continued or escalated suppression of the Polish people would endanger U.S.-Soviet relations:

> The Polish Government has trampled underfoot solemn commitments to the U.N. Charter and the Helsinki accords. It has even broken the Gdansk agreement of August 1980, by which the Polish Government has recognized the basic right of its people to form free trade unions and to strike.

The December Embargo—Stage One

One week later, stating that the Soviet Union "does not understand the seriousness of our concerns and its obligations under both the Helsinki Act and the U.N. Charter," the President expanded pre-existing controls and outlined a set of specific sanctions against the Soviets. The practical intent of this effort was to bar the sale or shipment of U.S. refining equipment and technology to the Soviet Union.

President Reagan imposed the measures on behalf of the United States without the supportive consensus of the allied European nations. For six months, the U.S. administration urged its allies to join in pressuring the U.S.S.R. to ease the situation in Poland. But as the months passed, the motivating forces behind the sanctions were eclipsed by issues surrounding the embargo's target—the Soviet gas pipeline under construction from Siberia to Western Europe.

The Urengoy-Uzhgorod Pipeline

Since mid-1981, the Soviet Union and seven Western European nations had been negotiating the details of one of the biggest construction projects in history. Two pipelines from northwestern Siberia were to deliver between 1.2 and 1.4 trillion cubic feet of natural gas per year to West Germany, France, Italy, Belgium, Austria, Spain, Switzerland, and West Berlin. Costing between $10 billion and $15 billion, the first pipeline was projected to run 3,700 miles in length (four times that of the Alaskan pipeline) and was to begin deliveries in 1984. Estimates of Soviet gas deliveries ranged between 5 and 30 percent of future West European demand.

More than a source of future energy supplies, however, the pipeline project was of vital immediate concern to the leaders of Western Europe; the bulk of the equipment for the project was to be sourced from European manufacturers. In a time of deep and widespread economic recession, the pipeline contracts meant hundreds, perhaps thousands, of jobs. Eager for the opportunity, the governments of Europe offered generous lines of credit and heavily subsidized interest rates on pipeline contracts. By late 1982, it was estimated that European banks had financed about $4 billion in pipeline contracts at interest rates as low as 7.8 percent. Peter Gehring of the West German economic ministry stated:

> We would have been able to survive very comfortably without the Soviet natural gas. The pipeline contract was dictated by pure misery—jobs were the main consideration.

Beyond this, the European nations, and also Dresser-France, had to keep in mind Russia's contract right to impose 5 percent penalties for breached agreements.

Still, the Reagan administration objected to the pipeline project on two principal grounds. First, it feared the potential resource dependence of its allies on its most formidable global adversary. Second, the uses to which the Soviets could put annual hard currency sales revenues of between $7.5 billion and $12 billion caused hard-line Washingtonians to blanch. It was their opinion that the Soviet economy was on the brink of complete collapse. Accordingly, favorable trade allowances and future guaranteed income might help the struggling giant to regain a competitive economy.

The June Amendment—Stage Two

The December embargo measures had limited practical impact on the pipeline's progress. While American firms complied with the terms of the directive by stopping all exchange of oil- and gas-related technology with Soviet buyers and suppliers, their European associates were able to continue and complete contracted obligations. In most cases, the licenses and engineering specifications pre-dated the imposition of the embargo. In other cases, the European suppliers found alternative means to meet their contractual requirements.

In early June 1982, the NATO leaders and Japan held a summit at Versailles. President Reagan again asked the other world leaders to form a united front in the embargo, as the situation in Poland had shown no signs of relief. Prime Ministers Helmut Schmidt (W. Germany) and Pierre Trudeau (Canada) argued openly for normal trade relations with the Soviet Union.

At the close of the round of talks, the participants agreed to tentative cooperative measures on several of the more important issues; among the agreements was one by the French and British leaders to cut back on concessionary credits to the Soviet Union. Further, the allies called for "commercial prudence in deals with the Soviet bloc." The U.S. promised to forestall further efforts to block the pipeline.

On June 18, however, to "advance reconciliation in Poland," President Reagan announced that, through an amendment, the embargo on oil and gas technology would be extended to foreign subsidiaries of American companies using such technology under American license. The administration invoked its powers under the Export Control Act of 1979 to issue regulations effective June 22. The *New York Times* noted:

> The President's decision was seen by Administration officials as a major victory of Pentagon and White House officials who favor intensified economic warfare against the Soviet Union. It was a stunning defeat for the State Department and Treasury Department officials who argue that the sanctions will only alienate American allies without really harming the Soviet Union.

It was in this hectic, politically charged environment that Dresser and Dresser-France became caught in an international catch-22. The parent company and its subsidiary essentially became pawns in an international power struggle.

Dresser's Pipeline Crisis

On September 28, 1981, Dresser-France entered into a contract with Creusot-Loire to supply 21 gas pipeline compressors for the Siberian project. Valued at between $18 and $20 million, the contract called for delivery of equipment and related services to Machinoimport, a Soviet trading agency. Payments were to be made through Creusot-Loire as purchaser. Dresser-France notified the U.S. Commerce Department of the contract, as they were obliged to do under existing regulations. The Commerce Department made no objections.

By the time that President Reagan announced the first stage of the Soviet embargo, the French subsidiary already had the technical information it required to complete the full order. On December 31, the day following the President's order, Dresser Industries notified its French office that no further advice or assistance would be forthcoming regarding the Soviet contract. Robert Tron immediately ordered that all such correspondence en route from the United States be intercepted and returned unopened. Manufacturing operations continued at the Le Havre plant.

The President's order prohibiting the delivery of U.S. technology and commodities to Dresser-France, while having no effect on the manufacture of the compressors for the Soviet pipeline, was considered to have a severe impact on the company's ability to carry out its other contracts and on its ability to acquire future contracts. In Tron's judgment, "the impact would be so severe that Dresser-France would be obliged to cease all operations within the next few months."

When President Reagan extended the embargo to cover foreign subsidiaries in June of 1982, Tron was immediately advised to cut back on all expenses associated with the Soviet deal and to stop all deliveries as of June 22; he took hasty action to comply with the directives. Although three compressors stood ready for packing and loading with the shipping agent, the agent was ordered to stop work and hold shipment. And in the Le Havre plant, where eighteen compressors were under construction, material orders were cancelled, personnel reassigned, and sub-contractors advised to halt related work. The customs documents for the three completed compressors were withdrawn and cancelled on July 20. Dresser-France had done all it could to comply with its American directives.

Tensions between the allied nations over economic and trade policies escalated, fueled in large part by the pipeline embargo. The European nations had hiked interest rates on loans to the Soviets, in accord with the Versailles agreement, and considered the broadened American embargo to be an unreasonable interference with their economic affairs. Some viewed it as a challenge to national sovereignty.

The situation was rapidly approaching a flashpoint when, on July 21, Evan Galbraith, the American ambassador to France, warned that executives of U.S. subsidiaries could face criminal prosecution and fines if they were to violate President Reagan's orders.

European reaction to the ambassador's statement was swift and bitter. A high-ranking French official warned that "a progressive divorce" was taking place between the U.S. and its West European allies. "We no longer speak the same language," he affirmed, adding that the U.S. "seems totally indifferent to our problems." Prime Minister Schmidt of West Germany commented that "the embargo is a serious matter, affecting not only the interests of European nations, but their sovereignty."

On July 22 the French government issued a communiqué rejecting the Reagan embargo:

> The Government wishes to make it clear that the Urengoy gas pipeline construction contracts concluded by French companies must be honored.
>   The deliveries scheduled for 1982 will therefore have to be effected at the appropriate time. The Government cannot accept the unilateral measures taken by the United States.

The West German, Italian, and British heads of state quickly followed with statements of support for the French position. The European Community filed a protest with the U.S. Department of Commerce on August 10. Citing international law, they stated that the June amendments represented "an unacceptable interference with the affairs of the European Community."

Dresser-France, on the same day, received a directive from Jean-Pierre Chevenement, the Minister of State for the French Ministry of Research and Industry. The message stated:

> [The French Government] wishes that the contract made by your company for the construction of the Urengoy gas pipeline be carried out and that you keep the Government informed of the arrangements you will be making in this respect. [The Government] reserves the possibility to take any administrative or statutory measures that its decision may make necessary.

Still under direct orders from Dresser Industries to refrain from work, Tron did not comply with the French directive. He reconfirmed with his shipping agent that delivery of the three finished units was not to take place. On August 17, 1982, he wrote the French Minister of State that he had been advised by counsel that neither the French communiqué of July 21, 1982, nor the letter of August 10, 1982, constituted a binding order of the French government and that shipment of the pipeline compressors would raise serious questions under United States law. Tron also informed him that he had instructed the packing company not to release the compressors for shipment to the Soviet Union.

Monday morning, August 23, Tron was summoned to the office of the French Ministry of Research and Industry. There, Minister Chevenement served him with a Requisition Order for Services. The order cited a 1959 French law which empowered the government to requisition the services of a private company when such a move was necessary for national interest.

Tron was advised by French legal counsel that the order was legal, binding, and enforceable by fine and imprisonment.

There was not a corporate executive in the world who would have wanted to be in Tron's shoes at that point, regardless of what his salary was. It was a classic no-win situation: either course of action would bring legal punishment or sanctions from the government of one country or the other. Beyond the legal and economic aspects, Tron also had a moral dilemma to consider. The directives from the U.S. were based on the notion of national security; he could be accused of compromising the United States' position as a superpower if he violated its directive. On the other hand, the directive from France was based on the notion of France's national sovereignty and economic well-being as well as on the idea that normal trade relations with the Soviet Union were crucial to world peace and European safety. Thus he also could be accused of compromising France's economic and sovereign position if he violated its directive. Tron explained his decision:

> I concluded that the officers and employees of Dresser-France, including myself, were no longer capable of independent managerial direction in respect of the compressor shipments but were legally bound to comply with the order of the French Government. I concluded that it was not within my power to adhere any longer to the directives I had received from Dresser Industries not to permit delivery of the compressors nor perform additional work on the contract.

Edward R. Luter, Dresser's vice president for finance, showed tacit support for Tron's decision:

> We're between a rock and a hard place. As an American company, we fully intend to obey the U.S. law. But it is our position that our French subsidiary is a French company that must obey the laws of that country. We dearly hope the matter can be resolved diplomatically between the two governments. I don't see any other way to get us off the hook.

On August 24, 1982, Dresser-France's three compressors stood packed and ready for loading on a Le Havre, France, dock. Loading was postponed to the following day to allow time for clarification of Dresser's legal obligations.

On August 25, the American news media reported that the Commerce Department would issue a 30-day denial order against Dresser-France if the impending shipment took place. A denial order would cut the company off from all incoming trade with all United States firms and was probably the strongest sanction among Administration options. Counsel for Dresser-France was unable to get the Commerce Department to confirm the media reports. Loading the finished compressors was postponed for another day.

At 9:00 A.M. on August 26, legal counsel for Dresser-France hand-delivered a letter to the U.S. Commerce Department in Washington, requesting information on the Department's intentions and asking that they have an opportunity to respond before action was taken against the company. They received no response.

Under heavy escort of French police, the three compressors at Le Havre were loaded onto the Soviet freighter *Borodine*. At 2:30 P.M., 35 minutes after having been informed of the compressors' shipment, the Commerce Department announced a denial of trade privileges against Dresser-France and its primary contractor, Creusot-Loire.

Legal Issues

The legal standings of the participants in this confrontation were a source of intense friction and confusion throughout its unfolding. Many observers felt that President Reagan stood on shaky grounds in extending the terms of the Export Control Act to foreign subsidiaries and licensees; certainly the affected nations felt that their own sovereignties were compromised by the President's act. Additionally, the regulations supporting the act had never before been put to the test of full implementation. It was generally accepted, however, that the Commerce Department was required to give notice of possible violation to offending companies and then conduct an investigation of the charges before imposing corrective measures. These procedures are in line with the basic American right of due process.

In the month that followed the compressors' shipment, Dresser-France appealed to the Commerce Department's International Trade Administration and, again, to the U.S. District Court to set aside the denial order. Neither route provided any relief. On September 17, the *Wall Street Journal* reported that Dresser-France had been stricken from the bidding lists of several international engineering companies because the company had been cut off from its technological resources. In October, the company lost its contract for Australian drilling rigs—the new product line that was to have accounted for 30 percent of sales in the coming year.

During the same period, the U.S. administration began to waffle on its embargo policies, although the new initiatives were to have no bearing on Dresser-France's dilemma. With turbine shipments by John Brown Co. (a British firm) looming, the Secretaries of Commerce and of State pressed for less severity in sanctions imposed by the President. On September 1, the embargo sanctions were modified for future infractions and were made retroactive; denial orders were henceforth to be applicable to oil and gas technology only. Eight days later, however, these modified sanctions were broadened to cover subsidiaries of foreign firms; twelve of Creusot-Loire's subsidiaries were, therefore, placed under the oil and gas denial order with their parent. Less than three weeks later, the Commerce Department again modified its guidelines, releasing eight of the twelve French subsidiaries from its denial order.

By early October, United States subsidiaries and foreign firms and their subsidiaries in France, Britain, Italy, and West Germany were under denial orders from the U.S. Commerce Department. Tass, the Soviet news agency, reported that the Siberian pipeline was now 15 percent complete.

Edward R. Luter, Dresser Industries' senior vice president for finance and chief corporate spokesperson for the pipeline problem commented on the company's options at the height of the dilemma:

> We talked about everything. In fact, our president of Dresser-France considered resigning and just walking away from it. The attorneys said it would be a futile act because you're not going to stop the shipments whatever you do. Had he gone to jail, they would have taken the compressors and shipped them anyway.
>
> We called State, Commerce, everyone in Washington who was working on this. They did nothing. We asked them what we could do—"Do you want us to ask the French government to delay this thing while you discuss it?"—and they said no.
>
> [A Federal court decision to overturn the administration's sanctions] could take Reagan off the hook, if [it] said you don't have the authority to do this, you're invading the sovereignty of another nation. We just wished Reagan could have gotten himself out of the corner he painted himself into.
>
> The U.S. no longer has a lock on technology. If the Russians don't order from us, they'll order it from the French, Italians, Japanese. They'd just love to do it.

DISCUSSION QUESTIONS

1. What could or should the United States government have done during the unfolding crisis? Should Tron have been placed in the final decision-making position?

2. What were Dresser's political objectives? What were the political objectives of the United States? How did they differ and come into conflict?

3. Could Dresser Industries have foreseen the problems that occurred? Discuss this in terms of the timing of the events and of the use or nonuse of environmental analysis.

4. What should be the strategy of an international company in the oil or energy industry? Did Dresser conform basically to the strategy you recommend?

5. What foreign policy responsibilities does such a company have? Whose flag, so to speak, should a subsidiary or division located in a foreign country fly?

MOBIL'S RUN AT MARATHON[1]

On October 30, 1981, Mobil Oil Corporation initiated an attempted hostile takeover of the Marathon Oil Company. The company offered to pay $85 a share—$20 higher than the New York Stock Exchange (NYSE) listing—for approximately 67 percent of Marathon's shares. Mobil's acquisition strategy at this time was a two-part process. At the first stage, Mobil offered $85 a share for 40 million Marathon shares. If the shareholders tendered at least 30 million of the 60.1 million shares outstanding or held in reserve, then Mobil would proceed with the second stage, where it would acquire the remaining shares for thirty-year debentures valued at $85 a share.

Mobil's interest in Marathon was understandable. The company wanted to acquire Marathon's oil reserves, especially the Yates Field. Considered by Marathon to be the "crown jewel" of its holdings, this West Texas oil field held the largest oil reserves in the United States outside Alaska. While most domestic fields have a life span of nine years, it was estimated that the Yates Field could produce 125,000 barrels a day for the next twenty-six years. In addition, by combining its own marketing and service operations with Marathon's, Mobil could gain an extensive competitive edge in several states in the Midwest.

Marathon's Response

Top management at Marathon responded immediately by filing for a 10-day temporary restraining order on November 1 in Cleveland's Federal District Court. On November 3 Marathon also filed an antitrust suit, claiming that a Mobil takeover would lessen oil industry competition in the Midwest. And on a broader front, Marathon began to lobby legislators in Washington and the Midwest in an effort to marshall political support against the oil merger.

At the same time, Marathon directed its financial advisors, First Boston Corporation, to actively solicit friendly suitors for immediate entry into the takeover battle. First Boston began "calling everybody"—a broad cross-section of American industry including both large and small corporations. There was no contact, however, with other oil companies so as not to damage credibility of Marathon's antitrust suit against Mobil. Oil-industry veterans speculated that if Marathon won its antitrust suit against Mobil, the oil giant would retreat from the takeover battle. A court decision against Mobil would also signal a "hands off" policy to other oil companies. However, should Marathon lose, industry observers predicted open warfare in the competition for Marathon. Gulf Oil Corporation and Texaco, Inc., had already expressed interest in acquiring Marathon if they were invited to bid.

In a move to further protect itself against Mobil, Marathon modified its $5-billion credit line to enable the company to purchase up to $2 billion of its own stock. This announcement by Marathon spurred additional speculation

[1]This case is adapted from James E. Post, *Anatomy of a Merger: Mobil's Run at Marathon*, Boston: Boston University, Public Affairs Research Program, 1986. Used with permission.

that Marathon was positioning itself to initiate a hostile takeover. Indeed, on October 28, Marathon had entered a bid for Husky Oil of Alaska. Other analysts viewed the modification of the credit line as precautionary. A Marathon spokesperson commented that "the borrowing is being made so that if Marathon were to decide at some future date to use all or a portion of the funds, it would be in a position to do so promptly."

In Washington, congressional representatives publicly expressed concern over the possible Mobil-Marathon merger. Representative Paul D. Simon (D, Illinois) assailed the Department of Justice for its lack of reaction to the merger trend. In a letter to William F. Baster, head of the department's antitrust division, he asked the department to block Mobil's takeover of Marathon and dampen "the present climate of merger mania." Representative Clarence Brown (R, Ohio) introduced legislation in the House to require Cabinet-level review of the continuing trend of takeover attempts of midsize domestic oil companies by major international oil companies. Rep. Brown also expressed concern over the Justice Department's inactivity with regard to the merger trend.

The temporary restraining order against Mobil, scheduled to expire on November 11, was extended by Federal Judge John M. Manos until Tuesday, November 17. Pending the antitrust hearing scheduled to open in Cleveland, Mobil was permitted to accept shares for payment. For the first time since November 1, Mobil and Marathon were now allowed to communicate with the public on the takeover issue. Also, by November 12, Marathon shares closed at $84 on the NYSE.

During these first few weeks, Mobil opened preliminary discussion with the Federal Trade Commission (FTC) in an effort to gain government antitrust clearance. In the wake of congressional calls for an investigation, Mobil brought a "hold separate" agreement drafted by lawyers from both the FTC's Bureau of Competition and Mobil. The terms of the November 11 draft agreement were as follows:

1. Mobil agreed to ensure the "existence of Marathon as a readily identifiable and separate competitor" for up to 180 days after Mobil had complied with the Securities and Exchange Commission (SEC) request for more data.

2. Marathon's assets would not be consolidated with Mobil's nor would Mobil require Marathon to transfer any assets or change its policies.

3. Marathon's present business organization, staff, and structure would be preserved, and Mobil promised to give the FTC staff at least 72 hours' advance notice "of termination of employment of any Marathon officer."

If the agreement was accepted by FTC Chairman James C. Miller III, Mobil would be able to proceed with the Marathon purchase while undergoing FTC investigation into the takeover bid.

The contents of the draft were released by Representative Mike Oxley (R, Ohio) in Washington, D.C. Although he stated that he received a copy of the draft while at Marathon headquarters in Findlay, Ohio, he neither confirmed nor denied that he received the material from Marathon officials. On November 13 Representative John D. Dingell (D, Michigan), Chairman of the Oversight Subcommittee of the House Energy and Commerce Committee, announced hearings on the Mobil-Marathon merger. He also requested a copy of the "hold-separate" agreement from the FTC.

On November 14 the FTC asked for additional information from Mobil, thereby delaying clearance of its takeover proceedings for ten days following delivery of the new information to Washington. If the FTC did not file an antitrust suit within that ten-day period, Mobil would be free to proceed with the Marathon purchase.

During this period of time the Ohio legislature passed a bill intended to block Mobil's bid for Marathon or any other similar takeover proceeding for an Ohio-based petroleum company. The bill was sent to Governor Rhodes for his signature. Rhodes, who would be an advocate for Marathon throughout the takeover battle, signed the bill. The legal significance of this bill was unknown, however, as its conflict with the federal antitrust laws had not been resolved. A federal court in Columbus was asked to review the constitutionality of Ohio's law.

Judge Manos opened hearings November 17 on the antitrust suit filed by Marathon against Mobil. Marathon's lead counsel, Patrick F. McCartan, attempted to extend the arguments beyond antitrust issues to include the projected socioeconomic impact of the merger. McCartan characterized Findlay, Ohio, as a one-company town, financially dependent on the Marathon Oil Company. Judge Manos refused to consider issues beyond the legal parameters of the antitrust laws.

U.S. Steel Enters

On November 19, U.S. Steel announced that it had entered a bid of $6.4 billion in the takeover battle for Marathon Oil. The nation's number-one steelmaker reported that the acquisition was part of its strategy of continuing diversification away from steel.

Officials from U.S. Steel and Marathon approved the offer of purchase of at least 30 million Marathon shares, or 51 percent of the oil company's common shares outstanding, for $125 a share. The tender offer was scheduled to expire on December 17. The stock market reacted favorably to U.S. Steel's entry into the takeover race. Marathon's stock skyrocketed and closed at $104.25.

The U.S. Steel–Marathon merger agreement contained two clauses known as "lock-up" options. These options give certain privileges to the acquiring company by the takeover candidate. They are designed either to reduce the attractiveness of a hostile takeover effort or to thwart continued pursuit of the merger by the unfriendly company. Marathon's agreement with U.S. Steel specified that U.S. Steel had the option (1) to purchase Marathon's oil and mineral interests in Yates Field in Texas for $2.8 billion only if control of Marathon was won by a third party, and (2) to purchase 10 million treasury shares of Marathon at $90 each. The shares had been authorized for release but had not yet been issued.

Reactions

Marathon employees were jubilant at the announcement. As the third largest block of shareholders, they could expect to realize a substantial profit if they tendered their stock to U.S. Steel. A local stockbroker stated that "people in here are making tons of money, bundles of money." Indeed, there were more people ready to buy Marathon stock than to sell it at this point. Signs at the Findlay headquarters which read: "Marathon Says Eat Your Heart Out, Mobil" and "Mobil Found Out How We Feel, So Now We're Going with U.S. Steel" were further evidence of employee approval. Billboards around town headlined "Welcome U.S. Steel." This enthusiasm was not only the result of Marathon stock price gain, however. Harold D. Hoopman, Marathon's president, announced that U.S. Steel was committed to "maintaining our operations intact under the direction of Marathon's management with headquarters in Findlay, Ohio. We've been assured by U.S. Steel that Marathon will remain a vigorous competitive force in the oil industry."

The steelworker unions, on the other hand, expressed suspicion and concern despite U.S. Steel chairman David Roderick's declaration that the Marathon merger would not curtail capital investment into modernization of existing plants: "Our investments in those operations will continue as planned." One steelworker at U.S. Steel's Homestead Works in Pittsburgh emphatically stated:

> The Marathon deal is a slap in the face to us. You'd think with all the cash U.S. Steel's got they could at least buy two electric furnaces and a continuous caster, but this leaves nothing for steel.

The U.S. Steel tender offer faced mixed reactions from industry analysts as well. Most observers agreed that the scope of the diversification move was without industry precedent, although steelmakers had been diversifying since the early 1960s to offset declining profitability. Robert Crandall, a senior fellow at the Brookings Institution, stated: "They realize that if they're to grow, the growth certainly isn't going to be in the steel industry. I think it's a healthy sign." Others, however, such as a Gulf Oil executive, indicated some skepticism:

> Here you've got a company in an industry that professes to be cash poor ready to spend $6 billion to buy into an entirely different industry. What I want to know is how does this investment produce another pound of steel?

Some Wall Street analysts expressed concern that the high interest rate that U.S. Steel would have to pay for the borrowed funds needed to purchase Marathon would eliminate Marathon's earnings for at least the first two to three years. Others speculated that U.S. Steel would have to sell some assets in order to carry the interest burden of $800 to $900 million a year. Manufacturers of capital equipment used in steelmaking were cautious in their comments: "U.S. Steel's priorities have shifted and we haven't been expecting massive investments in new production facilities."

Congressional reaction was sharp and critical, particularly on the part of Ohio legislators. Rep. Brown flatly stated: "U.S. Steel might better have used its money investing in steel mills." Senator Howard M. Metzenbaum (D, Ohio) stated that while he supported U.S. Steel over Mobil, he was concerned about the merger. He maintained that the liberal treatment that the steel industry was receiving from Congress, in terms of tax incentives and lenient pollution control laws, was meant to enable the industry to regain its competitive position in a market now dominated by the Japanese and the Germans. He pointed out that the purchase of Marathon with these funds "won't help the steel company to compete more effectively, won't add one drop of oil to our nation's resources, and won't help in any way to alleviate the nation's economic ills."

The U.S. Department of Commerce, a pivotal actor in the steel industry's bid for protection against imported steel, declined to comment on the merger. For some time, the steel industry, and particularly U.S. Steel, had been actively lobbying for duties on subsidized foreign steel and penalties on foreign steel being sold below fair value. In light of U.S. Steel's entry into the Marathon takeover battle, some observers believed that the industry's campaign to convince the government that it was suffering because of the unfair trade practices of foreign steelmakers might now suffer a credibility gap.

Despite the agreement for a friendly takeover by U.S. Steel, Marathon officials announced that they would proceed with the antitrust suit against Mobil as planned. Takeover professionals believed that the U.S. Steel–Marathon merger would ultimately succeed only if Mobil's efforts were defeated on antitrust grounds. Because of this, Marathon was seeking a permanent injunction against the Mobil takeover.

In the Cleveland federal court, Judge Manos heard conflicting opinions with regard to the legitimacy of the antitrust suit raised by Marathon. Marathon called Frederick Scherer, a professor at Northwestern University, to testify on their behalf. Scherer supported Marathon's statement that a Mobil takeover would severely curtail competition in the sale of gasoline products. He stated that the key issues involved the impact on local and state share of the market (SOM). On that basis, he concluded that the Mobil-Marathon merger would violate the Justice Department's market share guidelines in twenty-four of thirty-six cities and in three of seven states where the two companies competed. Mobil, however, claimed those definitions of the "market" were too narrow. It contended that the national market was the only relevant index.

Other antitrust specialists noted that market share was only one aspect of antitrust analysis. Factors to be considered included the market shares of others, whether those shares had remained static or had changed significantly over time, and whether there were high barriers to entry in the industry under investigation. Specialists cautioned that the Justice Department's guidelines were just that—indications as to when the department may file an antitrust suit.

Attorneys for Marathon also claimed that a Mobil-Marathon merger would eliminate the independent gasoline retailers. A study of Mobil retail practices revealed that the giant had a history of withholding gasoline products from nonbrand outlets, while a large portion of Marathon gas was sold to independent dealers. However, Mobil's president, William P. Tavoulareas, assured the court that the merger would not eliminate Marathon's practice of supplying gasoline to the nonbrand outlets.

Mobil Falls Short

Mobil announced on November 23 that its tender offer of $85 a share had fallen short, by 7 million, of its first stage goal of 30 million shares. However, the oil giant did not drop out of the bidding for Marathon. Analysts speculated that Mobil would raise its tender offer to become competitive with U.S. Steel's bid. Experts believed that many traders were positioning themselves to take advantage of what would probably be an upward revision of Mobil's initial tender offering.

In Washington Congress heard testimony against the Mobil-Marathon merger by off-brand dealers. At a joint hearing of the House and Senate Commerce Committees, Jack A. Blum of the Independent Gasoline Marketers Council made a statement expressing concern for Midwest gasoline price competition in the event of a merger:

> The nonbrand independent station is the cutting edge of price competition. Because low prices attract customers and build volume, nonbranded independents constantly test the price-volume relationship by selling at the lowest price at which they can operate profitably.

His statement was reinforced by Ohio's Attorney General, William J. Brown: "Off-brand gasoline service is an important check against the major oil companies." He expressed fear that a Mobil-Marathon merger would drive gasoline prices up in the Midwest, particularly without the checks and balances imposed by the off-brand dealer. He also made note of the "trigger effect" of a Mobil-Marathon:

> I share the view of many who think that this unwelcome takeover by Mobil could well set off a "domino effect," whereby many mid-size oil companies are eliminated by the large, international energy giants.

Closing arguments made to Judge Manos in Cleveland's Federal District Court also made mention of the trigger mechanism. Marathon attorneys reported that a Mobil takeover might set off a wave of oil company takeovers. Patrick F. McCarten, counsel for Marathon, stated: "The trigger can be pulled right here in Cleveland if this acquisition is permitted to proceed." McCarten also projected that a Mobil takeover would eliminate many independent dealers. Sanford N. Litvack, Mobil's chief counsel, contested Marathon's arguments by stating that even if Mobil were to discontinue supplying the independents, they could easily obtain gasoline supplies elsewhere.

Judge Kinneary Halts U.S. Steel's Bid

On November 24 Mobil obtained a ten-day restraining order preventing U.S. Steel from proceeding with its takeover bid for Marathon. U.S. Steel also was temporarily restrained from exercising the lock-up options granted by Marathon. The order was granted in Federal District Court in Columbus, Ohio, by Judge Joseph Kinneary. The preliminary injunction was scheduled to expire on December 4 unless extended. A hearing was scheduled for December 3.

U.S. Steel and Marathon were clearly unhappy with the decision. The preliminary injunction gave Mobil a powerful new weapon in the takeover battle. In particular, the injunction gave Mobil the time it needed to close the gap between its initial bid and U.S. Steel's.

In a related development U.S. Steel announced that it was negotiating a $2-billion increase to its existing $3-billion bank line of credit. Observers speculated that it was positioning itself to respond to an increase in Mobil's tender offer.

Mobil made another interesting move as well. Herbert Schmertz, Mobil's vice president for public affairs, confirmed Wall Street reports that the company was buying U.S. Steel stock! The amount purchased was small, however, amounting to less than 1 percent of U.S. Steel's common stock. Analysts speculated that the Mobil move was more of an intimidation than a serious takeover threat. However, one respected Wall Street banker characterized Mobil's move as "arrogant" and "anything but beyond the realm of possibility." A substantial stake in U.S. Steel might enable Mobil to drop its bid for Marathon and exchange its U.S. Steel shareholdings for the Yates Field or reserves. Other investment bankers dismissed the move, saying it was not a serious threat to U.S. Steel. As one observer commented: "Do I believe Mobil's going to buy U.S. Steel? No. They're just flexing their muscles. I don't think it means much."

A United Steel Workers local in Pittsburgh went to court to force U.S. Steel to disclose its capital spending plans for plants in Western Pennsylvania. Union officials expressed concern that the Marathon acquisition would preempt plans for modernization of area steel plants. The capital spending information was included in an application to the Environmental Protection Agency (EPA) requesting a three-year delay in carrying out an earlier cleanup agreement. The agreement required that U.S. Steel comply with government air and water quality standards by 1982. However, in early 1981 Congress passed a bill that granted the steel industry a three-year delay. Delays were to be granted on a case-by-case basis, and U.S. Steel's application for an exception or "a stretchout" for its plant in the Monongahela Valley in Western Pennsylvania had not yet been approved by the EPA.

The capital spending plan submitted to the EPA required that money that was not spent on pollution control equipment had to be invested in modernization. In requesting the plans, union officials stated that they wanted to investigate just how serious U.S. Steel was in its commitment to the industry. Said Ron Weisen, president of USW Local 1397, which represented the Homestead works:

> Either U.S. Steel intends to modernize steel or it doesn't. If it doesn't intend to rebuild mills it allowed to rot, why are we allowing them to lower pollution standards?

Staughton Lynd, an attorney for the local, commented that U.S. Steel's "recent action with Marathon suggested the company intends to run the Monongahela Valley plants into the ground and then walk away."

The Plot Thickens

On November 27, Mobil announced that it would raise its bid for Marathon to $126 per share for at least 51 percent of the company's stock. The company also threatened to withdraw its bid if the federal court in Columbus did not invalidate the lock-up options in the Marathon–U.S. Steel agreement. The announcement was intended to put pressure on Marathon's shareholders, the company's management, and the federal court.

Judge Kinneary opened the hearing in Columbus the same day and heard Mobil's attorneys charge that U.S. Steel and Marathon had entered into a "sweetheart deal" which made it impossible for Mobil or any other company to acquire Marathon stock at a profit. This, according to Mobil's lawyers, was a "blatant conspiracy" and an "unlawful course of action." Marathon's attorneys responded that the deal with U.S. Steel was an honest one, and U.S. Steel's attorneys claimed that the bid for Marathon reflected their company's desire to become substantially involved in the oil and gas business. Hence, the lock-up options were of great value to U.S. Steel and a legitimate contract existed, not the conspiracy that Mobil claimed.

A few days later, Judge Kinneary ruled that U.S. Steel could resume its solicitation of Marathon stock. On the same day, Judge Manos in Cleveland ruled that Mobil's bid to acquire Marathon violated the antitrust laws. In a seventeen-page opinion, Manos said the crucial question was the impact of Mobil's takeover on competition in gasoline marketing in states where Marathon and Mobil both had sizeable market shares. In Illinois, Indiana, Michigan, Ohio, Tennessee, and Wisconsin this would result in combined market shares that violated previous antitrust precedents. Further, Manos expressed concern that allowing Mobil to continue its bid would encourage other oil giants to join the bidding and trigger more takeovers.

Mobil executives were disappointed, while Marathon's management celebrated the two decisions. The celebration proved to be premature. Mobil moved quickly on two fronts. First, it appealed Judge Manos's decision to a federal Court of Appeals. Second, it moved to counter the market share objection raised by Judge Manos by bringing in a new partner, the Amerada-Hess Corporation. The plan was for Mobil to sell Marathon's marketing and refinery operation in the Midwest to Amerada-Hess, whose operations were confined to the East Coast of the United States. Thus, a new competitor would actually enter the Midwest, while Mobil got what it most desired, the Yates Field oil reserves.

Pressures mounted on stockholders, executives of all the companies involved, and dozens of law firms, advisors, and investment bankers assisting the primary players. It became clear that the final outcome would be determined by the federal courts and the Federal Trade Commission.

The FTC acted first. On December 8, it announced that it would act to prevent Mobil's takeover of Marathon because of the market effects of the merger on gasoline retailing in the Midwest. The FTC did not comment on the possibility of Amerada-Hess's acquisition of the Midwest marketing operations, but it made clear its opposition to Mobil's expansion in the Midwest. Mobil made no comment.

The next day, however, Mobil informed the FTC and the Justice Department that it would purchase between 15 percent and 25 percent of U.S. Steel. The action signified Mobil's intention to get the Yates Field reserves, even if they had to buy U.S. Steel to do it. Some observers believed that this action was actually Mobil's admission that it could not acquire Marathon directly. Critics charged that it would cost Mobil $600 million to acquire the U.S. Steel shares, a sum that would be better invested in exploration for new reserves. But Mobil's chairman retorted: "Don't tell me there's a cheaper way of buying oil reserves. There's no cheaper way." U.S. Steel said that it would not be intimidated by Mobil or coerced into abandoning its plans to acquire Marathon.

On December 23, the Federal Court of Appeals issued rulings that favored Marathon and U.S. Steel. Mobil refused to concede and filed a last-resort appeal with the United States Supreme Court. The following days were filled with legal maneuvers, all designed to keep Mobil's slim chances alive. As the New Year dawned, however, it was clear that Mobil had lost its bid for Marathon. The final act occurred at 12:01 A.M. on January 7, 1982, when a U.S. Steel executive in Pittsburgh called a bank official in New York and told him to proceed with the payout of $3.75 billion for a block of Marathon shares which the bank held for willing sellers as a result of the tender offer. Marathon Oil became a subsidiary of U.S. Steel, and Mobil Oil was left to ponder its next moves. Should it try to acquire U.S. Steel? Should it try to acquire another oil company with substantial reserves? And if it were to pursue any company, should it do so in a friendly or a hostile way?

DISCUSSION QUESTIONS

1. What strategic interests did Mobil Oil and U.S. Steel each have in their attempts to acquire Marathon Oil? In what ways did these strategic interests affect the interests of other stakeholders?

2. What obligations did Marathon Oil's board of directors have to the company's various stakeholders? As the contest for the company continued, did the stakeholders remain the same? In what ways did the board of directors have to change its priorities?

3. Discuss the decision of Judge Manos to reject socioeconomic arguments in evaluating Mobil's takeover bid. Why did he insist on confining the discussion to the antitrust issues of competition and market share? Should merger and acquisition attempts be evaluated on grounds other than competition and direct economic effect?

4. Discuss the efforts of the United Steel Workers to learn about U.S. Steel's capital spending plans. Should a company's employees be entitled to know longer-term investment plans? Should a company's stockholders have access to such information? What policies should a socially responsive management pursue when it is considering a diversification move?

5. Should the federal government intervene to prevent unfriendly takeovers such as Mobil's attempt to acquire Marathon or to encourage friendly takeovers to create economic efficiencies? Should Ohio be permitted to take action to prevent the acquisition of companies located in the state by out-of-state firms? Develop a detailed recommendation for your state legislator as to what considerations should guide a merger and acquisition decision of this type.

"Not since the days of Prohibition has a law been so widely flouted by the public. I think it ought to be repealed."

"But think of the lives it saves, even if not everyone obeys the law. I think we should keep it and try to make it work."

So the argument went in the mid-1980s as the American public debated the pros and cons of the controversial 55-miles-per-hour (mph) speed limit law. It was a debate that involved several highly charged issues and questions of national importance: a shockingly high vehicular death toll; national vulnerability to pressure from foreign oil producers; state versus federal control of the nation's highways; citizen compliance with an unpopular law; technological capabilities (in autos, trucks, and radar detectors) inconsistent with the law's intent; the "wide open" Western states pitted against the Eastern seaboard states; and government restrictions on the freedom of individuals and businesses. Here, all rolled into one simple law were vital issues of public policy, national energy independence, social responsibility, personal freedom, and the role of law in society.

The nation's experience with the 55-mph speed limit unfolds in two main phases, the first from 1973 to 1982, the second from 1983 to 1987.

55 MILES PER HOUR—THE FIRST DECADE (1973–1982)

In December 1973, the United States Congress passed a law requiring all fifty states to establish a speed limit of 55 miles per hour on roads and highways. Failure of a state to do so could result in loss of some federal funds used for building and maintaining highways in that state. Three months later, all states were in compliance and had posted signs and directed highway patrols to enforce the new speed limits. Some grumbling was heard from trucking lines and bus companies, as well as from companies heavily dependent upon truck transportation for their supplies and for shipping goods to market. But by and large the general public seemed to favor this newest of many government regulations that had appeared during the 1960s and early 1970s.

The 55-mph speed limit was imposed in the wake of the Arabian oil embargo, which began in October 1973. The Arabian states belonging to the Organization of Petroleum Exporting Countries (OPEC) refused to sell crude oil to any industrial nations that they believed were supporting Israel or were generally sympathetic to Israel's policies. Industrial economies in North and South America, Western Europe, and parts of Asia (especially Japan) were immediately faced with the serious problems of keeping homes heated, factories running, and transportation systems operating. Arabian oil made up a large proportion of total oil supplies in many of these nations. Without that oil, entire economies could be seriously harmed. Almost overnight, the oil spigots were turned off, thereby threatening widespread chaos throughout the Western industrial world.

Although the oil embargo dramatically demonstrated the vital dependence of the West on Arabian oil, there had been earlier warning signals that the world's petroleum supplies perhaps were inadequate to meet expanding global demands. In the United States during the summer months of 1973, long lines often formed at gasoline stations, some stations simply ran out of gasoline and closed at night or on weekends, and the "See America First" campaign that had urged motorists to do their traveling here rather than in foreign nations began to falter. Utility companies that had promoted the sale of gas and electric appliances shifted their advertising messages toward conservation and energy saving. Manufacturers of the luxury-class travel vans saw sales drop drastically, as consumers became more economy-minded.

On into the autumn months of 1973, before the oil embargo was imposed, gasoline supplies remained tight. "Gasless Sundays" became common. The President and several state governors called for voluntary reductions in highway speeds as one way to conserve fuel, particularly as the colder months brought on an increased demand for heating oil for homes, offices, and factories. Car pools and greater use of mass transit facilities were advocated. Bumper stickers urged readers to "Save Energy, Shower with a Friend."

On April 29, 1974, the oil embargo was lifted, but oil-producing nations now charged far more for crude oil than in preembargo days. In the summer of 1973, the price per barrel of imported oil was $2.41. One year later it ranged from $11.25 to $12.64, approximately five times higher. So even though the spigots had been turned on again, oil cost a great deal more.

On a worldwide basis, demand still exceeded available supplies, with the prospect that eventually the industrial world would have to find other energy sources to replace the steadily and rapidly dwindling global oil reserves. President Nixon announced a national goal of achieving energy independence for the United States by the mid-1980s. The process of granting permission for developing the rich oil fields of Alaska's North Slope, which had been held up for years by the concern of ecologists, was speeded up. The time was obviously ripe for any and all actions that could either increase oil supplies or lead to a more efficient use of available oil. It was in this overall context of alarm and national concern over energy supplies that the 55-mph speed limit was accepted.

Saving Fuel by Driving Slower

In 1973 between one-fifth and one-fourth (22.5 percent) of all United States imports of petroleum came from Arabian countries.[1] An interruption in the supply of that much oil could easily throw the economy into chaos. Actually, the United States had been steadily increasing its dependence upon imported oil since the mid-1950s, as revealed in Figure 1.

All forms of transportation taken together consumed slightly over half

[1]American Petroleum Institute, *Monthly Statistical Report,* vol. 2, no. 12, December 1978, p. 3.

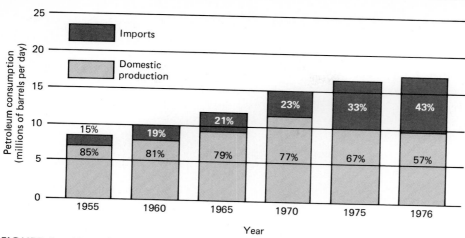

FIGURE 1. United States petroleum consumption, by source, 1955–1976.
(*Source: U.S. Department of Transportation, "Automotive Fuel Economy Program," First Annual Report to the Congress, January 1977, p. 6.*)

of all the oil used in the United States, as shown in Figure 2, with motor vehicles burning up some 44 percent of the total. Quite clearly, any steps that could be taken to reduce gasoline consumption by cars, trucks, and buses would make the nation less vulnerable to interruptions in oil supplies. In the long run, such conservation would lessen United States dependence on foreign oil.

Lowering the speed limit was only one of a number of conservation measures proposed. Others included the adoption of Daylight Savings Time throughout the nation on a year-round basis, car pooling and van pooling by commuters, gasless Sundays, greater use of mass transit in urban areas, and fuel economy requirements for newly produced automobiles.

The idea of reducing speed limits across the nation had been talked about since the summer of 1973, well before the embargo. But no one knew at the time just how much gasoline could be saved by this measure. In the fall of 1973 the United States Department of Transportation (DOT) estimated that a speed limit of 50 miles per hour would reduce national gasoline demand by about 3 percent. In adopting the 55-mph limit, the United States Congress apparently acted more on faith and the seeming logic of "the lower the speed, the less gasoline burned" than on solid evidence. Very few reliable studies existed at the time to guide national policymakers.

By the summer of 1975, the National Highway Traffic Safety Administration (NHTSA) admitted that actual savings were only 1.1 to 1.8 percent of total gasoline consumption.[2] Later studies, though, seemed to confirm the original prediction that reduced driving speeds lowered gasoline demand by approximately 3 percent.

---

[2]Ezio C. Cerrelli, "The Effect of the Fuel Shortage on Travel and Highway Safety," NHTSA Technical Report, DOT HS-801 715, August 1975, p. 49.

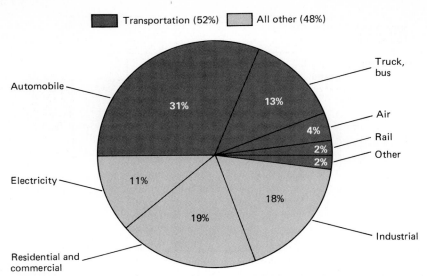

FIGURE 2. United States petroleum consumption by sector. (*Source: U.S. Department of Transportation, "Automotive Fuel Economy Program," First Annual* Report *to the Congress, January 1977, p. 8.*)

While these percentage figures seem small, the amount of gasoline saved was more impressive—3.6 billion gallons per year. If everyone had complied with the speed limit laws, savings would have amounted to 5.7 billion gallons each year. For 1977 that would equal over 38 gallons per motor vehicle. Even at the lower actual savings of 3.6 billion gallons, enough would have been conserved to run the entire motor vehicle fleet of the nation for two weeks. At 1977 gasoline prices of about 70 cents per gallon, that would have been $2.4 billion that motorists would not have had to spend for gasoline.[3]

Does Driving Slower Really Save Gasoline?—The Evidence

One of the earliest controlled tests undertaken by the DOT to determine the effect of speed on gasoline consumption rates was published in October 1973, the month the Arabian boycott began.[4]

> Twelve cars of various makes and weights were driven over two highways near Washington, D.C. All of the test cars were 1970 or later models that had been driven at least 3,000 miles. Only one was tuned before the tests began. On the average, the twelve cars burned over 8 percent more gasoline when increasing speed from 40 to 50 miles per hour, over 11 percent more when going from 50 to 60 miles per hour, and over 17 percent more by speeding up from 60 to 70 miles per hour. Three of the cars were more efficient in consuming fuel at 50 miles per hour than at 40 miles per hour, but none of the twelve was more

[3]U.S. Department of Transportation, *55 MPH Fact Book*, September 1978, p. 7.

[4]E. M. Cope, *The Effect of Speed on Automobile Gasoline Consumption Rates*, U.S. Department of Transportation, October 1973.

Speed	AVERAGE MILES PER GALLON		
	Passenger Cars and Motorcycles	Combination Trucks	Buses
Under 50 mph	19.93	5.05	9.43
50–55 mph	19.05	4.57	7.54
55–60 mph	18.05	4.20	5.70
60–65 mph	16.95	3.79	4.47
Over 65 mph	15.65	3.15	3.84

FIGURE 3.   Estimated average miles per gallon, by type of vehicle for different speeds of free-flowing highway travel, 1972 and 1975. (*Source: "Fuel Savings Aspects of the 55 M.P.H. Policy," National Highway Traffic Safety Administration, n.d. Mimeographed.*)

economical of gasoline usage at speeds higher than 50 miles per hour. The test also revealed that tuning a car can lead to significant gasoline savings, since the one car that was tuned up burned an average of almost 12 percent less gasoline at all speeds than it did prior to tuning.

Continuing studies by the DOT emphasized the steady erosion of fuel economy as motor vehicle speeds increase. Figure 3 compares average miles per gallon for three different types of vehicles. For example, a passenger car that speeds up from 50 to 55 miles per hour to over 65 miles per hour gets almost 18 percent less fuel to the mile at the higher speed. A tractor-trailer truck that whooshes by at over 65 miles per hour has reduced its fuel efficiency by almost one-third over what it would have been at 50 to 55 miles per hour. A bus increases its rate of consumption by a whopping 50 percent by driving over 65 miles per hour!

Truckers complained when the 55-mph speed limit was first imposed, saying that their trucks' motors were designed to be more efficient at higher speeds. The DOT responded with a number of road tests of tractor-trailer trucks.

One test carried out in Virginia demonstrated that truck speeds of 60 miles per hour consumed 12.5 percent more diesel fuel than a speed of 50 miles per hour. In another test, the well-publicized "Double Nickel Challenge" offered thirty-two independent owner-operators of trucks an opportunity to prove they could get as many or more miles per gallon at higher speeds than at the 55-mph limit. They drove their trucks on two 45-mile trips around an oval track in East Liberty, Ohio. One trip was at 55 miles per hour and the other at a higher speed selected by the truck driver (the highest average speed used was 66 miles per hour). Six of the thirty-two trucks proved they could get slightly better mileage (an average of just over 4 percent) at the higher speeds, while the other twenty-six trucks saved an average of 14 percent in fuel consumption by driving at 55 miles per hour.[5]

[5]E. M. Cope, *The Effect of Speed on Truck Fuel Consumption Rates*, U.S. Department of Transportation, August 1974; and U.S. Department of Transportation, *55 MPH Fact Book*, pp. 15–16.

In addition to these government tests, private transportation companies began to show interest in the possibilities of saving significant amounts of fuel by reducing speeds.

> United Parcel Service tested two of its trucks, finding that the new legal limit of 55 mph saved 1¾ miles per gallon when compared with a speed of 65 mph. On this basis, the company's fuel bills could be reduced by almost 25 percent by having its drivers adhere to the 55-mph limit.[6]
>
> Continental Oil Company (Conoco), with a fleet of 200 tractors and 400 trailers that operated over 25 million miles each year, found that it could save 1.2 million gallons of diesel fuel in a single year by adopting a variety of new practices. Conoco drivers were required to obey the 55-mph speed limit, and trucks were equipped with radial tires, fuel-efficient diesel engines, fan clutches, and aerodynamic shields.[7]
>
> In 1978, the Trailways bus company discovered that it could save 3 million gallons of fuel per year that cost $1.5 million by installing speed governors on its highway buses. Before the 55-mph speed limit was adopted, Trailways buses had been adjusted for a maximum speed of 76 miles per hour. The hardware for the governor cost the company $170 per bus plus five hours of labor for installation. Claiming a payback of less than three months on this investment, the company stated, "There is no single system or device that can achieve such astronomically large fuel savings or return on investment in such a short period of time." Additionally, the company believed its public image as a technical innovator and a responsible corporate citizen would be improved by promoting the lower speeds mandated by the law.[8]

Confronted with this kind of evidence, the trucking industry softened its opposition to the new speed limit law. The American Trucking Association, representing most large trucking concerns, and the Teamsters Union, representing many over-the-road truck drivers, gave official approval to the lower speeds. So did the American Bus Association and the American Automobile Association.

The Costs of Saving Fuel

Major opposition to the speed restrictions came from smaller independent owner-operator truckers who claimed that competition forced them to make as many trips as possible in the shortest time period. Their livelihood depends upon higher speeds, regardless of the greater amount of gasoline consumed. In the summer of 1979, the Independent Truckers Association, whose members include many independent owner-operators, demonstrated against higher fuel prices and the 55-mph speed limit, saying the combined effects were ruinous to their business. A similar protest about speed restrictions was

---

[6]United Parcel Service, *Fuel Economy Speed Test Report (55 MPH vs. 65 MPH)*, October 27, 1977, pp. 1–2.

[7]Brian Taylor, "Making 55 MPH Pay," *Commercial Car Journal*, January 1979, pp. 103–105.

[8]Trailways Inc., "Road Speed Governor Program: 55 MPH Information Brief," n.d. (Mimeographed.) In early 1980, a new management at Trailways, claiming the governors frequently malfunctioned, ordered their removal and reset bus engines to a top speed of 63 to 64 mph. See Insurance Institute for Highway Safety, *Status Report*, February 19, 1980, p. 5.

made in early 1983 when independent truckers opposed increases in gasoline taxes and highway user fees.

Other truck and bus drivers, including some working for the big transportation companies, complained that the lower speed limit penalized them when a shipment or scheduled bus trip was delayed in getting away from the loading dock or bus station or by a breakdown en route. Illegal speeds under those conditions were the only way to save a perishable cargo or to maintain a contracted delivery schedule. Joining these opponents of the 55-mph limit were many citizens of Western states where the "wide open spaces" between cities encourage high-speed highway travel. These critics claimed that boredom and monotony, not to speak of driver impatience at the loss of valuable time, were not worth the gasoline savings achieved at lower speeds.

An economist criticized the 55-mph limit on three grounds. First, the overall savings were less than predicted and marginal at best—perhaps only 1 to 2 percent of gasoline consumption. Second, truckers, commuters, bus passengers, and vacation travelers had to spend more time on the road, thereby wasting valuable time that otherwise could be converted into higher profits, more time for commuters to spend at home or at work, or more leisure activities for vacationers.

A third reason to doubt the worth of the lower speed limit, according to this critic, was that an equal or greater amount of fuel could be saved by other, less expensive methods. These might include tuning up the engines of all cars on the road, which would save an estimated 5 percent of gasoline demand; switching more drivers to smaller, fuel-efficient cars—a switch of only 4 percent would save more than is saved by the 55-mph limit; or encouraging the widespread use of radial tires and proper tire pressures.[9]

Saving Lives by Driving Slower

Congress was persuaded to lower the national speed limit as a way of saving fuel during a national crisis. In doing so, it also saved many lives—more than anyone had believed possible.

In the years after World War II, automobile, truck, and bus accidents had become one of the nation's major sources of death. In the peak year of 1972, 56,300 people were killed in motor vehicle accidents. This was the fifth leading cause of deaths in the United States, ranking behind heart disease, cancer, stroke, and pneumonia. Motor vehicle accidents killed over 2½ times the number of persons who were murdered. Yearly road deaths also outstripped all United States fatalities in the Vietnam war (46,376) and the Korean war (34,000).

Soon after the new 55-mph speed limit was adopted in late 1973, state police bureaus around the country began reporting a remarkable falloff in highway accidents, deaths, and injuries. By the end of the year, deaths had dropped by an astonishing 9,393, or 16.8 percent, the largest annual reduc-

[9]Charles A. Lave, "The Costs of Going 55," *Newsweek*, October 23, 1978, p. 37.

tion since the onset of reduced driving and gasoline rationing during World War II. As revealed in Figure 4, the annual fatality rate, which makes allowances for additional miles actually driven each year by the general population, also went down in 1974. Clearly, something very dramatic was happening to reduce the yearly toll of dead and injured on United States highways.

Motor vehicle accidents in 1974 also were down by some 5 percent, and injuries by 7 percent. Very severe injuries were reduced by 10 percent. These accident and injury figures suggested that the accidents that were continuing to occur were less severe, causing fewer injuries and deaths than previously.

Slower speeds were believed to be primarily responsible for the improved safety on the roads. Speeds had been slowly increasing over the years until 1973, the first year of pinched fuel supplies. The average highway speed of unimpeded vehicles in 1973 was 65 miles per hour. In 1974, the figure dropped to 57.6 miles per hour, a decrease of 11 percent. The percentage of vehicles exceeding 55 miles per hour on rural interstate highways went from 89 percent to 65 percent, and the percentage exceeding 60 miles per hour from 72 to 29 percent.

Lower average speeds result in fewer accidents and injuries for several reasons. Driver reaction time can be important in avoiding a potential accident; higher speeds reduce the amount of such time available. Stopping distances lengthen dramatically with faster speeds. Additionally, a more uniform flow of highway traffic, with most vehicles moving at approximately the same speed, reduces the chances of accidents. Impact damage is considerably less at lower speeds, thus increasing the probability of survival in the event of a crash. Cars and trucks also experience less friction on tires and parts, and drivers suffer less nervous tension, at lower speeds.

In spite of these gains, the American motoring public began driving somewhat faster beginning in 1975. Speeds crept up slowly in a majority of the states. In 1976 thirty-four states recorded increased average speeds; in 1977, forty-one had higher averages. As speeds increased, the number of traffic deaths began to climb again—by 1.8 percent in 1976 and by another 4.7 percent in 1977—and the long decline in the vehicle fatality rate leveled off (see Figure 4). Clearly, highway speeds, increased travel, and traffic deaths were interrelated.[10]

Notwithstanding this close connection between speed and deaths, several other factors also were at work. Studies undertaken by the National Safety Council concluded that the reduction of speed was actually responsible for only about one-third to one-half of the saved lives.[11] With the gasoline shortages of 1973 and 1974, travel was reduced, so fewer vehicles were on the roads. Travel on the high-speed interstate roads was particularly down, and that was where the most severe accident and injury rates are normally recorded. Because of gasless Sundays and general fuel shortages, fewer peo-

---

[10]U.S. Department of Transportation, *55 MPH Fact Book*, pp. 8–11.

[11]National Safety Council, "Council Tells Factors behind Traffic Death Drop," September 17, 1974. (Mimeographed news release.) See also Vincent L. Tofany, "Speed Does Kill; 55 Saves Lives," *USA Today*, January 20, 1983, p. 10A.

Note: The fatality rate is the number of fatalities
per 100-million vehicle–miles driven.

FIGURE 4.   United States highway fatality rate, 1960–1985. (Source: Adapted
from Insurance Institute for Highway Safety, Status Report, September 9, 1986, p. 5.)

ple engaged in recreational driving, thus dropping the average occupancy
rate of automobiles. So when an accident occurred, it tended to affect fewer
passengers than before. Night driving, which is generally more dangerous
than daytime travel, also was off. Seat restraints, the redesign of car interiors,
improved tire standards, and highway redesign also helped.

Even with all these qualifications, the 55-mph speed limit appeared to
be saving at least 4,500 lives each year. In Georgia, highway officials credited
the limit with reducing interstate highway fatalities by 53 percent during the
period from 1974 to 1976 and by 31 percent even after average driving speeds
began climbing in 1977.[12] In addition, medical authorities pointed out that
spinal cord injuries were reduced about 65 percent and some 90,000 serious
head injuries that might have led to epilepsy were prevented. The National
Safety Council claimed that an increase of the speed limit from 55 to 65 or
70 miles per hour would have resulted in 5,200 to 7,800 more deaths in 1978
than actually occurred. The DOT stated flatly that "The 55 mph speed limit
is . . . perhaps the most important safety measure in modern times."[13]

The safety gains associated with the 55-mph speed limit were so impressive that one observer, the president of the Insurance Institute for Highway Safety, advocated that all automobiles be designed and built to operate
at a speed close to the limit of 55 mph. This "socially responsible" automobile
would thus relieve car manufacturers of the potential legal liability of pro-

[12]Insurance Institute for Highway Safety, *Status Report,* February 17, 1982, p. 6.
[13]U.S. Department of Transportation, *55 MPH Fact Book,* p. 11.

ducing and selling vehicles that might not be capable of protecting their occupants in crashes. In a closely related move, the National Highway Traffic Safety Administration began studying the feasibility of requiring all commercial interstate vehicles to be designed so they could not exceed 57 miles per hour. This latter proposal was first put forward by the Trailways bus company, which, as noted above, installed speed governors on its entire fleet of buses.[14]

An Expensive Way to Save Lives?

Some critics of the 55-mph speed limit pointed out that emotion about traffic deaths distorts our view of this government-imposed restriction on the freedom of drivers. Surely, they say, saving lives is important and admirable. But what does it cost us?

One such critic said that time is money and that the 55-mph speed limit was wasting immense amounts of time for those who drive. He calculated that this traffic slowdown wasted about $6 billion worth of travel time each year for the American public. If the reduced speeds saved 4,500 lives annually, then it was costing about $1.3 million to save one life. He asked:[15]

> Is this a bargain, or are there other social policies that might save more lives for less money? Well, it has been estimated that placing a smoke-detector in every home in the U.S. would save about as many lives in total as the 55-mph limit, and would cost only $50,000 to $80,000 per life saved; or more kidney-dialysis machines could save lives for only about $30,000 per life; or additional mobile cardiac-care units cost only about $2,000 per life saved; and there are even a great number of highway improvements that can be made, through reducing roadside hazards, which cost only about $20,000 to $100,000 per life saved. At a cost of $1.3 million per saved life, the 55 mph limit is hardly a bargain.

55-MPH—TAKING ANOTHER LOOK (1983–1987)

National and world conditions in the mid-1980s were not what they had been in 1973 when this new public policy was adopted. The global oil famine had become, at least for a while, a global oil glut. Oil prices had plummeted, leading to severe economic adjustment problems for oil-producing nations and for portions of the United States' Southwest. Conservation measures had taken hold, with the result that national attention shifted away from concern about energy supplies.

Another change had occurred when Ronald Reagan became President in 1980; his administration wanted to "get government off our backs" by reducing regulatory restrictions of all kinds. In the opinion of some administration supporters, the 55-mph speed limit was a perfect example of the government stepping too far into the personal lives of people.

---

[14]Insurance Institute for Highway Safety, *The Highway Loss Reduction Status Report,* vol. 14, no. 4, March 8, 1979, pp. 5–7.

[15]Lave, op. cit., p. 37.

One of the biggest tests of the law, however, was whether the citizenry obeyed it. Surveys showed that most highway drivers exceeded the speed limit. They were encouraged to violate the law by lax enforcement and trivial fines in some states. But public attitudes and driver behavior were not consistent; public opinion polls year after year recorded a large majority (as high as 58 percent in January 1987) in favor of retaining the 55-mph limit.

It was in this climate of shifting forces and unclear signals from the public that Congress began debate on the Federal Highway Act of 1987. The act contained a provision to raise the national speed limit.

Still Saving Lives and Fuel

Proponents of keeping "55" pointed out that 20,000 lives had been saved since 1974. The National Research Council and the National Academy of Sciences estimated that lower speed limits continued to save from 2,000 to 4,000 lives each year. Projections of additional deaths resulting from raising the limit ranged from 300 to 1,000 per year, plus an expected increase in serious injuries. As shown in Figure 4, the nation's highway fatality rate continued to decline, as it had done since passage of the Motor Vehicle Safety Act and the Highway Safety Act in the mid-1960s. If the nation had continued to experience the highway death rates of the mid-1960s, over 100,000 driving fatalities would have occurred in 1985.[16]

The United States was not the only nation to reduce driving speeds by passing new laws. Denmark, Finland, France, Sweden, New Zealand, Canada, Australia, and England experienced significant drops in fatality and injury rates after imposing lower limits. After a comprehensive study of international experience with speed limit laws, one authoritative source reported that "in all cases, when reductions in the posted speed alter driver behavior, lives are saved and injuries averted. The reverse is generally true as well—increases in posted speeds increase the frequency and severity of accidents."[17]

In addition to being a life saver, "55" was saving 167,000 barrels of oil each day in the mid-1980s, according to the National Research Council. The nation's annual fuel bill was lower by $2 billion, even though many drivers exceeded the legal limit of 55 mph. With full compliance, even greater fuel savings would have been possible.

The Main Arguments for Raising the Speed Limit

The advocates for higher speed limits attacked "55" on several fronts, but three arguments were uppermost.

Noncompliance

The simple truth was that most drivers were not complying with the posted speed limit. On rural interstate highways, fully 75 percent of vehicles were

[16]Insurance Institute for Highway Safety, _Status Report,_ September 9, 1986, pp. 1–2.
[17]Insurance Institute for Highway Safety, _55 Speed Limit,_ February 1987, p. 2.

clocked at over-55 speeds in 1985. The *Wall Street Journal* reported that the "55 speed limit is widely ignored by drivers and police charged with enforcing it." Two U.S. Senators from Western states said, "No law in this country has been broken and ridiculed more since the days of Prohibition." "Why shouldn't we bring back some common sense and reality on this issue?" Traffic surveys also revealed that over half of the drivers in thirty-seven states violated the legal limit of 55 mph.[18]

One big aid to some speeders was the radar detector, which had become increasingly popular, especially among tractor-trailer drivers. The detectors were prohibited in Virginia, Connecticut, and the District of Columbia. Studies showed that about one of every four drivers traveling in excess of 70 miles per hour was using a radar detector.[19]

Lax enforcement also encouraged speeding. One state official estimated that for every speeder caught, 22,000 others got away; from the speeder's point of view, these odds were far more favorable than the odds in playing the popular state lotteries offered by a number of states. Fines for speeding ranged from $100 in Ohio to $5 in some Western states, although surprisingly there was little correlation between size of fine and speeding behavior. A study by the National Research Council found that the real deterrent to speeding was the visible presence of enforcement efforts and the fear of being stopped.[20] In some states, a subtle political factor tended to soften enforcement efforts, because a state could lose federal funds for highway construction if more than half of its drivers exceeded the national speed limit. Police officers in some states felt pressures to "look the other way" so that their highway departments would not be penalized.

Wasted Time

Many drivers considered "55" an enormous waste of valuable time, particularly when good road and weather conditions invited high speeds. Collectively, United States drivers spent about 1 billion extra driving hours each year, or an average of seven hours per driver per year. On a trip-by-trip basis, it amounted to about two or three minutes per trip, but on a long road journey these average times gave little comfort to drivers who wanted to reach their destinations more quickly than the legal speed limit allowed.

Speed Is Given Too Much Credit for Saving Lives

Some people questioned the close link thought to exist between speed and highway deaths. They pointed to the fact that average driving speeds had been increasing since the mid-1970s but in that same period the fatality rate for drivers declined in most years. This relationship suggested that other

---

[18]For the quotes, see *Wall Street Journal*, February 4, 1987, p. 12, and March 19, 1987, p. 10. See also "Does Speed Kill?" *Newsweek*, July 21, 1986, p. 14.

[19]Insurance Institute for Highway Safety, *55 Speed Limit*, February 1987, p. 4, and *Status Report*, March 14, 1987, p. 1.

[20]*Newsweek*, op. cit.

factors must have been responsible for saving some lives. Some states had passed mandatory seat-belt and child-restraint laws, while others had mounted campaigns against drunk driving that included tougher penalties. Automakers had improved safety design, especially in the car's interior, and safer highways were being built. Of course, seat belts, child restraints, and safer car interiors could save lives only in case of an accident, which could still be caused by illegal speeding. Just how much additional safety could be attributed to these nonspeed factors was not clear, but it was reasonable to believe they were helping to reduce traffic deaths and injuries.

The Energy Specter

During the congressional debate on raising the speed limit, not much attention was given to the original problem that led to a limit of 55 mph. But the specter of a national energy shortage was present in the minds of some who remembered the 1973 oil embargo and the second oil shock that accompanied the Iranian revolution of 1978.

The nation had fallen far short of its announced goals of energy independence. By 1984, oil imports were rising again and, according to some estimates, would probably account for half of domestic consumption by 1990. If that were to happen, the United States would once again be vulnerable to a sudden stoppage of foreign oil. Domestic oil production also was down, partly because of weakening oil prices and partly because world demand was off. Some oil companies preferred to acquire oil reserves by merging with reserve-rich competitors rather than drilling new wells, and the prospect of making more profits abroad also contributed to a fall in United States production. Efforts to switch from foreign oil to greater reliance on nuclear power were hampered by cost overruns, regulatory routines, and environmental and safety concerns. Relying on abundant supplies of coal and new synthetic fuels to provide national energy self-sufficiency was undermined by low oil prices and reduced government funding of synthetic fuel projects.[21]

The oil-producing countries of OPEC that had been so powerful during the 1970s seemed helpless in the face of tumbling oil prices in the mid-1980s when a barrel of oil brought as little as $11 (down from a 1981 peak of $36 per barrel). A combination of economic recession in several nations, conservation practices in the industrial nations, the use of alternative energy sources, and a buildup of non-OPEC oil production drastically cut demand for OPEC oil.

CONGRESSIONAL ACTION AND EARLY PUBLIC RESPONSE

Meanwhile, back in Washington, Congress was struggling with passage of the highway appropriations bill. After much legislative maneuvering, the House of Representatives voted, on March 19, 1987, to allow states to raise

[21]*Wall Street Journal*, April 21, 1985, p. 6.

the speed limit on rural portions of interstate highways to 65 miles per hour. The House vote was close—217 in favor and 206 opposed. Four days later, the Senate approved the House bill by a margin of 60 to 12. As expected, President Reagan vetoed the bill, saying that he approved raising the speed limit but was opposed to the costly "pork barrel" road projects included in the legislation. The House of Representatives then overrode the veto by a vote of 350 to 73, and on April 2 the Senate did likewise by a margin of 67 to 33. The Federal-Aid Highway Act of 1987, including the higher speed limit provision, became law on April 2, 1987.

By the following month, about twenty-seven states had moved to raise the speed limit, and another handful were considering similar action. It was thought that a half dozen states in New England and on the Eastern seaboard were not likely to raise the speed limit on their portion of the interstate network.

DISCUSSION QUESTIONS

1. Consider the various ways in which different kinds of businesses are affected by the 55-mph speed limit. For example, what are the costs and benefits of the speed limit for large trucking companies? For petroleum producers and refiners? For gasoline stations? For small independent owner-operators of trucks? For car manufacturers? For companies and stores that depend on trucking for a large proportion of their transportation? How do these various costs and benefits compare with the costs and benefits to society at large?

2. In imposing the 55-mph speed limit, Congress chose the regulatory route to solving a national problem. Are there alternative ways to accomplish the same goals (saving fuel and saving lives) by relying more on the free market and less on government regulation? How would these alternatives work?

3. Identify the stages of the public policy process as they occurred from 1973 to 1987. Tell what actions business firms could have taken at each of these stages to promote their own interests. Would these actions have benefited the public as well as the business firms? Explain.

4. Identify and discuss the ethical issues involved in this case study. Demonstrate how an ethical analysis would use utilitarian reasoning, rights reasoning, and justice reasoning. Which mode of reasoning do you believe is the most appropriate to apply to the question of a national speed limit?

Atlantic Richfield Company is a major producer, refiner, and marketer of petroleum and other minerals. Its Anaconda subsidiary was incorporated as a separate company in Montana in 1895. It steadily grew to become one of the world's leading producers and refiners of copper. It also produced other minerals such as gold, silver, lead, and zinc, often as by-products of its copper mines. By the 1970s it also was the leading U.S. producer of brass mill products and a major producer of aluminum. In the late 1970s Anaconda was merged into Atlantic Richfield Company, a major petroleum company.

Throughout much of its history Anaconda has been a major mining company and employer in the state of Montana. Its primary operations were concentrated in the towns of Anaconda, which proudly carried its name; in Butte, about 25 miles distant; and in Great Falls, over 150 miles away, where it had a refinery. Strong ties developed between the company and its communities, because they substantially depended upon it for jobs and the prosperity of their economies.

The mining history of the Butte area began in 1864 when gold was discovered on Butte Hill. Several years later a copper lode was discovered in the Anaconda Mine, which eventually developed into the well-known Anaconda Company. The company grew rapidly and by 1927 controlled most of the mines in the area. All mining was underground until the Berkeley open pit mine was started in 1955. The pit was located in the town of Butte, and as it developed it consumed four neighborhoods, seven schools, and a major city park. However, the company supported many town services that taxpayers normally would pay, so townspeople and the company worked together in relative harmony.

In 1980 a worldwide oversupply of copper developed. Prices soon declined to 70 cents a pound or lower. Since experts estimated that U.S. mines needed a price of 90 cents to $1.50 to break even, the U.S. mines faced a severe cost-price squeeze that made operation of their mines uneconomical. Reasons included:

1. A worldwide economic recession that reduced demand for copper.
2. Technological change that reduced demand for copper, such as aluminum alloy automobile radiators and optical fiber telephone cables instead of copper ones.

[1]Sources include Eric Morgenthaler, "Butte, Mont., Strives to Revive Economy as Copper Jobs Fade," *Wall Street Journal* (Western ed.), July 13, 1982, pp. 1 and 20; Maria Shao, "U.S. Copper Industry Is Being Devastated by Its High Cost as Well as by Recession," *Wall Street Journal* (Western ed.), September 16, 1982, p. 50; Lydia Chavez, "When Arco Left Town," *New York Times*, July 25, 1982, p. F15; "Arco Unit to End Copper Mining in Butte, Mont.," *Wall Street Journal* (Western ed.), January 10, 1983, p. 5; Atlantic Richfield Company, "Notice of Annual Meeting of Shareholders and Proxy Statement," Los Angeles, March 16, 1981 and March 16, 1982, company news releases, and the company's annual and quarterly reports to stockholders.

3. Opening of large new mines in less-developed nations that increased the supply of copper. Examples are Chile, Peru, Zambia, Indonesia, and Zaire.

4. Tendency of less-developed nations to operate their mines with government support, regardless of low copper prices, in order to keep labor employed and to export copper to pay for much-needed purchases abroad.

5. Lower-grade copper ore in the United States than in most other nations, making the ore costly to extract.

6. Stricter environmental regulations in the United States that were more costly than in most other nations.

7. Higher labor costs than in less-developed nations. For example, U.S. copper miners often earned $25,000 to $30,000 or more a year plus fringe benefits, compared with $1,000 to $5,000 a year in less-developed nations.

8. Older, more costly mine facilities, smelters, and refineries in the United States compared with newer, more productive facilities in several nations.

As a result of the conditions just described, the U.S. share of world copper production declined from 35 percent in 1950 to 19 percent in 1981. Experts predicted that the U.S. copper mining industry was in a long-range secular decline and probably would not make a major recovery when the worldwide recession ended. The Anaconda Company was required to adjust to this secular decline along with other U.S. copper mining companies.

Anaconda's problems were especially severe in Montana where its facilities were old, unproductive, and not in compliance with environmental regulations. Costs of retrofitting its old smelter to comply with environmental requirements were estimated to be in excess of $400 million and not economically feasible. Since the company was the largest employer in both Butte and Anaconda, it knew that any major reductions in its mining operations would have a significant impact, be a major community relations issue, and be closely monitored by various groups.

On several occasions beginning in 1979 Anaconda hinted that it might have to close its outdated and expensive seventy-five-year-old smelter in the town of Anaconda, but it appeared that most residents refused to believe that this long-established smelter would close. Finally on September 29, 1980, in simultaneous announcements in Helena (the state capital), Los Angeles (Atlantic Richfield headquarters), and in Washington, the company announced the indefinite closing of its smelter. The approximately 1,000 employees who were to be laid off were not working at the time because of a nationwide copper strike.

The announcement sent shock waves through the community. The company attempted to reduce layoff dislocations by giving a number of special benefits, often more than the union contract required. The combined benefits gave each employee approximately a year of normal take-home pay so that employees would have one year to adjust. Benefits included lump sum severance pay, a year of paid medical insurance, supplemental unemployment benefits, and supplemental retirement benefits until age sixty-two for employees taking early retirement. The company also helped employees search for other jobs but was largely unsuccessful in the depressed local area.

For the community the company gave over 50 acres for a park and several million dollars (equivalent to about one year's taxes for the town) to a community adjustment fund.

Early in 1981, in apparent reference to the smelter shutdown, certain shareholders announced that they intended to present the following policy proposal at the annual meeting of shareholders of Atlantic Richfield Company, on May 5, 1981. A proposal requires an affirmative vote of a majority of voting shares represented at the meeting in order to be approved.

Shareholder Proposal regarding a Policy on Plant Closings

The following proposal has been submitted by seven religious organizations and one individual:

"WHEREAS, Atlantic Richfield has a reputation for high standards of social responsibility and accountability;

"WHEREAS, an Atlantic Richfield subsidiary, The Anaconda Copper Company, announced on September 29, 1980, that it was indefinitely closing the company's copper smelter in Anaconda, Montana, and its refinery in Great Falls, Montana;

"WHEREAS, the Anaconda Smelter was the major industry in Anaconda, Montana, employing about 1,000 workers out of a population of almost 10,000 and providing about 50% of the local county's tax revenues;

"WHEREAS, advance notice of plant closings enables affected workers and their families to plan for future needs, and enables affected municipalities to develop alternative employment and financing plans in light of anticipated losses in industrial base and tax revenue;

"WHEREAS, the social and psychological consequences of abrupt and unannounced plant closings include higher rates of alcoholism, suicide, domestic violence and divorce, to which churches, among other institutions, must respond;

"WHEREAS, American corporations generally are seeking greater productivity from their employees, and productivity is related to employee perception of company concern for their welfare;

"WHEREAS, companies are increasingly recognizing their responsibilities to communities where they have operations, particularly in times of economic hardship.

"THEREFORE BE IT RESOLVED that the Shareholders request that the Board of Directors of The Atlantic Richfield Company, adopt a written policy with procedures for the permanent or indefinite closing of its plants and other facilities, in light of the effects such closings have on employees and surrounding communities. Issues such as the following should be considered in the development of this policy to minimize the impact of economic dislocations:

—advance notice to employees, communities, and local and state governments
—retraining and reassignment of the affected workforce
—planning for conversion of facilities to alternate uses or employee ownership
—cooperation with and possible compensation for local communities"

Shareholders' Statement in Support of the Proposal regarding a Policy on Plant Closings

As church shareholders, we are concerned about the anguish and economic hardship which workers and their families are experiencing as a result of plant closings. We are also concerned that our company's operation be as creative and responsible as possible, for all those with a stake in its successful management.

In the case of the closing of our subsidiary's smelter and refinery in Montana, no advance notice was given and no cooperative planning was done with other institutions now trying to cope with its consequences, which affect some 82% of Anaconda, Montana's primary and secondary employment. Certainly ARCO is not the only company faced with plant closings, for whatever reasons, and, although we focus on the apparent inconsistency between our company's actions in Montana and its generally positive reputation, we are aware of the environmental and economic constraints involved.

We do not question the "why" of the plant's closing, but rather the "how," or the methods involved. Given the significant social benefits gained by a policy of reasonable advance notice and contingency planning for communities affected by such closings, we feel that adoption of the policy is clearly in the best interest of our company.

The Board of Directors' Statement in Opposition to the Shareholder Proposal regarding a Policy on Plant Closings

It is the intent of the Board of Directors that Atlantic Richfield be an exemplary corporate citizen, which certainly includes a concern for the welfare of its employees and the communities in which they live. Such a policy is both ethically and economically sound. The Board believes that this concern has been evidenced throughout the Company's extensive operations.

Anaconda Copper Company, a unit of Atlantic Richfield, intensively studied the feasibility of continuing operations at its Anaconda, Montana copper smelter and Great Falls, Montana copper refinery for a number of years and had disclosed many times, commencing at least as early as July 1979, that plant closure was an alternative being considered.

The decision to suspend operations was made after investigations and research disclosed that no option to retrofit the existing smelter or build a new one could meet two essential requisites; namely, economic feasibility and compliance with existing environment, health and safety laws and regulations. The decision was made on September 29, 1980 in time to meet a commitment date to the Montana State Board of Health to disclose plans for the smelter. This was communicated to employees and the public that same day.

When the decision was finally reached, the Company made special efforts to minimize the impact on the employees and communities affected. The Company developed special generous severance allowances for employees not eligible for retirement. Early retirement programs were supplemented. For example, hourly employees received a substantial lump sum severance payment, enhanced supplemental unemployment benefits for one year and, those retiring, a contract monthly payment as a supplemental retirement benefit until age 62. An aggressive program to place employees in other jobs is continuing. Also, the Company has contributed $5,000,000 to a "community readjustment fund" to be administered locally. The Company is assisting local public officials in attracting new businesses into the impacted communities. The foundry has been converted to employee ownership and alternative uses of other facilities are being investigated.

The Company consistently takes thoughtful steps to minimize the impact of closing facilities which are no longer viable. The Company, unfortunately but necessarily, will experience occasional closure of facilities and, more often, opening of new plants. The impact of these events on employees, communities and the Company is likely to be different for each occurrence. The Company's policy is to deal with individual situations as they arise on a case-by-case basis. The Board of Directors believes that this is an appropriate policy and that a more formal one with written procedures should not be adopted. The proposal would not improve the existing plant closure procedures of the Company, which it considers to be ethically sound, and could impair the flexibility of the Company to handle each situation as it occurs.

The Board of Directors urges you to vote AGAINST the shareholder proposal regarding a Policy on Plant Closings. Proxies solicited by the Board of Directors will be so voted unless shareholders specify otherwise.

The shareholder proposal was rejected by 97.19 percent of the votes cast at the meeting.

The worldwide recession and low copper prices continued in 1981, and Anaconda stated it had losses of $60 million in its Montana copper operations that year. During the year it indefinitely closed its main Berkeley pit mine in Butte, laying off several hundred employees. They were given extra supplemental employment benefits for one year, encouraged to retire with a supplemental retirement benefit until age sixty-two, and helped to find other jobs including those in other Anaconda locations.

The main mine remained closed at the beginning of 1982, and many local people believed it would not reopen for years, if ever. Many also criticized Anaconda for its large layoffs. Only 750 Anaconda employees remained, mostly working at the East Berkeley pit, which was still open. The Butte-Anaconda area was depressed, and town leaders began trying to lure other industries in order to build a more diversified job base. One local resident commented about Butte's situation, "Now it's just like a child becoming an adult. Now we will have to go out and earn our own living." In effect, no longer could the town depend on Anaconda Company to provide jobs.

For the May 4, 1982, annual meeting a group of shareholders made the following proposal:

BE IT THEREFORE RESOLVED that the shareholders request the Board of Directors to have prepared a written report for the shareholders by September 1982 to include the following information:

1. A list of any anticipated full or partial closing involving 100 or more employees of any of the corporation's facilities for 1982 through 1987;
2. A list of facilities where production will be expanded or started-up to replace that of the closed facilities for 1982–87;
3. Management's position on:
   a. Providing advance notice of one year before any total or partial closing, as defined above;
   b. Giving workers and local community first option to buy facilities and mineral rights, where they are involved, when facilities are being closed;
   c. Giving priority in the location of new facilities to areas in which a facility has been or will be closed.

Information directly affecting the competitive position of the company may be omitted and funds expended in preparing this report shall be limited to amounts deemed reasonable by the Board of Directors.

The proposal was defeated by the shareholders at the annual meeting. Other metal companies also made large layoffs and plant closures during the 1980–1982 period, and the metal recession continued into 1983. Early in January, 1983, Anaconda announced that it would indefinitely close operations at the East Berkeley pit on June 30. The move would eliminate 700 jobs and leave a staff of only about 50 Anaconda employees in Butte, down from about 3,000 employees a few years earlier. Anaconda said the closing was not permanent, but it did not know when its operations would reopen in the area. In effect, this move closed all of Anaconda's copper mining operations in Montana, where the company once dominated the state's economy and politics. This latest move was another blow for depressed Butte, which once was the center of copper mining in the United States.

Separately the Arco Metals division of Atlantic Richfield announced in January that it was reducing its Columbia Falls, Montana, aluminum refinery to 40 percent capacity. About 350 employees would be laid off from a work force of 900. The company said it expected the refinery to resume normal operating levels when the economy recovered.

In 1985 Atlantic Richfield Company announced a major restructuring of the corporation. As a part of this restructuring the company announced that it would "sell or otherwise dispose of all of its remaining noncoal operations conducted by its Anaconda Minerals division." On September 10 the company signed a contract for sale of its Columbia Falls aluminum plant to a newly formed Montana Aluminum Investors Corporation that was headed by a former Atlantic Richfield vice president. The investors' group planned to keep the plant in operation in order to retain jobs in the Columbia Falls area.

On September 23 Atlantic Richfield announced the sale of its Anaconda Minerals properties to Washington Corporation. The sale included about 40,000 acres of land, water rights, mineral rights, the Butte Water Company, and the active mining and concentrating operations in Butte. It did not include the Anaconda Smelter properties, which did not meet Environmental Protection Agency standards, or the storage pond in Deer Lodge Valley. In the announcement of the purchase the buyer expressed appreciation to Anaconda Minerals Company for helping find a Montana buyer that it believed capable of resuming mining operations, and for offering its assistance during the transition period. However, the buyer added that at the present price of copper and other minerals from the mine, "significant changes in costs for energy, labor and management wages and benefits, taxes, smelting, and freight must occur before the economics will be in place to allow the Butte operation to open." Also the relationship of the Environmental Protection Agency's toxic-waste superfund to the mine must be clarified.

Atlantic Richfield's financial statements for 1985 reported that the sale of its Anaconda Minerals properties resulted in losses of more than $100 million after income tax benefits.

DISCUSSION QUESTIONS

1. What strategies and policies did Atlantic Richfield and its Anaconda division appear to have in managing the decline of their mining operations in Montana? Specifically state the strategies and policies, if any, and explain the probable reasons for each. Discuss how socially responsive these strategies and policies were.

2. With reference to the Anaconda case discuss what obligations a socially responsive company may have when it closes a facility in a community in which it has been the dominant employer for decades.

3. Discuss each of the layoff benefits given by the company in the Anaconda-Butte area, including the stakeholders that the benefit served and the probable effectiveness of the benefit. How socially responsive was each benefit mentioned? Discuss.

4. Should the state or federal government intervene
   a. to prevent plant shutdowns such as those at Anaconda and Butte (for example, impose copper import duties to make imported copper costlier than the cost of copper produced in the United States), or
   b. to protect laid-off employees more than normally (for example, government payments for free training for new jobs, salary during training, and moving expenses to new job locations when jobs are available)?

5. Develop in detail an effective mining company policy for working with communities and employees during plant closures, both temporary and permanent.

BIRTH OF THE SUPERFUND[1]

On November 24, 1980, the United States Senate passed a bill which provided for a $1.6-billion fund to be used to finance the cleanup of hazardous waste dumps in the United States. The so-called "superfund" was to be provided by contributions from the chemical industry and the government, with the former contributing 87.5 percent and the latter 12.5 percent. On December 3, the House of Representatives passed an identical bill by a vote of 274 to 94. With this action, the Congress officially made toxic waste cleanup a national goal. Within weeks, President Carter would sign the new law and the United States would embark on a national toxic dump-site cleanup.

The birth of the superfund involved years of controversy, lobbying, debate, and struggle. Chemical firms had been arguing that they should not have to contribute to the fund: after all, most of the sites targeted for cleanup were abandoned. Industry representatives claimed that it was unfair to hold the chemical industry liable for the mistakes of those who came before them. Government representatives held the opposing viewpoint: they were not willing to use public funds to clean up the waste dumps created by companies that profited from the cheap and irresponsible disposal of their production refuse. Public interest and environmental protection groups were not primarily concerned with who paid for the fund. They pressed strongly for the establishment of a fund and the cleanup of the dump sites.

The issue emerged gradually over a period of years. Various interested parties (chemical firms, public interest groups, environmental protection groups, and government agencies and representatives) all voiced their opinions and flexed their political muscles in an arena characterized by rapid change. Each attempted to use the political process to achieve its goals and the tools of power and influence at its disposal to force the others to agree to its conditions or plans. When the smoke cleared, there was still a certain amount of ambiguity over who was the "winner."

Environmental and public action groups "won" in the sense that a fund bill was passed and a national commitment was made to clean up dump sites. The government "won" in the sense that the chemical industry was forced to contribute the lion's share of the fund: 87.5 percent. And the chemical industry "lost" in the sense that it was forced to provide the bulk of the $1.6 billion, although each chemical firm's portion of that contribution might be quite small in comparison to earnings. Ironically, the industry as a whole may have benefited from an improved public image as a result of the cleanup efforts.

---

[1]This case was adapted with permission from John F. Mahon, *The Politics of Toxic Waste: A Study of Political Strategy*, Boston: Boston University, Public Affairs Research Program, 1987. Quotations in the case are from the original manuscript.

CHEMICALS, PUBLIC CONCERN, AND REGULATION

The chemical industry has long been an important force in the United States economy. The top chemical producers include not only chemical firms, but oil, mining, steel, and tire firms as well. The vitality of the industry is tied to industrial development. As the U.S. economy has grown, chemical industry sales growth and profits have been larger than the average in manufacturing over the span of several decades.

The chemical industry's prosperity faced several serious challenges in the 1970s and 1980s. The most important and influential of these were increasing worldwide competition, escalating raw materials prices, decreasing supplies, and increased public scrutiny and government regulation.

The raw materials problem is perhaps the most serious. Chemicals are derived from such natural products as petroleum and natural gas. These are called "feedstocks." Petroleum is becoming scarce and relatively expensive. Natural gas, although readily available, will not sustain chemical producers in the United States forever. Substitutes for these feedstocks, such as coal, are available and will certainly play a major role in the industry during the next thirty years. But each substitute is expensive and presents environmental concerns.

Increased public scrutiny is also a serious concern. During the 1970s, prominent episodes of environmental contamination by toxic substances endangered human lives and threatened natural resources. The most notorious of these episodes included the dumping of mercury in Lake St. Clair; PCBs in the Hudson River; kepone in the James River; carbon tetrachloride in the Ohio River; and HEXA-OCTA in the Ohio River. These episodes were newsworthy, and stories of dead fish, destroyed cattle, possible health hazards to humans, sewage-treatment-plant breakdowns, and drinking-water warnings have become familiar.

These incidents have had a great direct impact on the chemical industry and the public's perception of it. Opinion research undertaken for Monsanto in the late 1970s showed that the public continued to identify the chemical industry as the prime contributor to air and water pollution problems. Seventy-one percent said that waste from chemical plants was the greatest pollution hazard, greater than hazards from all other industries. Other surveys indicated that the chemical industry's public image ranked lowest of thirteen industries surveyed. In 1979, the industry spent more than $10 million on advertising to restore polish to its tarnished image.

These perceptions had a grave impact on the industry. During the period 1970–1980, there was a tremendous increase in regulation of the industry. Some regulation was attributable to strong public interest lobbies, and some was a clear reflection of the industry's loss of public confidence and the felt need for increased protection of the environment.

Three notable pieces of legislation were passed in 1970: the National Environmental Policy Act, the Occupational Safety and Health Act, and the Clean Air Act. The Environmental Protection Agency (EPA) was established to protect the nation's environment. This agency brought fifteen different federal offices dealing with pollution under single management, whose administrator reported to the President.

In 1976, the Toxic Substances Control Act was passed over bitter chemical industry opposition. This far-reaching environmental law gave the federal government broad control over chemicals. The EPA is granted the authority to approve or deny clearance for any chemical agent before it enters the market, and it has power to control existing chemicals if they are shown to be unreasonably hazardous. The Resource Conservation and Recovery Act (RCRA), also enacted in 1976, created a federal hazardous materials disposal program for land disposal of the 3 to 4 billion tons of materials discarded each year.

BEGINNINGS OF THE SUPERFUND

The beginnings of the idea of a superfund can be traced back to 1973. In that year, the petroleum industry began seeking federal legislation in the area of oil spills in order to achieve a dollar limit on liability and to obtain relief from various conflicting state statutes that existed at this time. The proposed oil spill fund provoked thought on the entire problem of hazardous spills. As other environmental laws were passed, the issue of hazardous wastes repeatedly entered the discussion and eventually moved to the top of the agenda.

Superfund's legislative roots can also be traced back to the Resource Conservation and Recovery Act (RCRA) of 1976. The General Accounting Office, a U.S. agency that audits federal programs, released a report in December 1978 on the administration of RCRA. "Inadequate disposal practices in the past have caused harm to humans and the environment many years after sites have closed," the report said. In many cases, site ownership was transferred or relinquished, making legal liability and responsibility difficult to establish and causing cleanup costs and remedial costs to be passed on to taxpayers. "A federal fund is needed to address the liability problem," the report concluded.

Starting in late 1978, meetings were held between Congress, the EPA, and the Chemical Manufacturers Association (CMA), the industry's major trade association, to discuss a possible bill for hazardous wastes. At these meetings the EPA laid out the government's position and asked the industry for its inputs. At that time, the CMA's first position was that the government should fund all cleanup costs. This was later modified to suggest a one-third split among the industry, the federal government, and state and local governments. Finally, the industry said they thought they could contribute 40 percent of the total cost. Edmund Frost, general counsel and vice president of the CMA, reportedly stated that "we are all but at agreement on this." Meanwhile the Carter administration was moving ahead with its own proposals. The basic goals of the administration bills were to establish liability, set up a fee system, and have the legal authority to begin dump-site cleanup before ultimate liability was resolved in court.

Good progress was being made when, according to personnel both in Congress and in the EPA, the industry withdrew from negotiations. They refused to participate in further discussions. In February 1979, a meeting was held between a CMA vice president and EPA representatives. At the meeting, according to two participants, the CMA executive stated that "We will beat you—there will be no compromise, no bill—society needs chemicals—society should pay for it."

Initial Congressional Hearings

Congressional hearings began in March 1979 before the House Subcommittee on Oversight and Investigations chaired by Bob Eckhardt (D, Texas) and before the Senate Subcommittees on Environmental Pollution and Resource Protection, chaired respectively by Edmund S. Muskie (D, Maine) and John C. Culver (D, Iowa).

Given the prominent media coverage of a chemical dump site called Love Canal, it made sense that Congressional hearings on hazardous waste disposal would begin by looking at that particular situation. The hearings produced several revelations that were quite damaging to Hooker Chemical Co., which dumped chemicals at the site, and to the entire chemical industry's credibility. Documents showed that Hooker had received complaints about the dump site as early as 1972; that Hooker did advise the city of Niagara Falls that hazardous wastes were disposed of in the site and warned the city against any construction activity of any kind on that site; and that exposed drums of chemicals in one lot posed a serious threat to children who played in that area.

During the time that these hearings were being held, Eckhardt announced that his subcommittee was conducting a survey of waste-disposal practices since 1950 of the fifty top chemical companies. The subcommittee's "objective is not to assess blame or give undue publicity regarding disposal practices of this industry or any component parts" but to locate abandoned waste sites before they became health problems.

The press was active and vocal on the issue. In April 1979 *Washington Post* editors addressed Hooker's claims in an editorial entitled "Who Pays for Poison?":

> The question left by this sad experience is how companies can be moved to take a larger view of their responsibilities and clean up their old toxic dumps before people are actually hurt. New laws, public pressure and the example of Love Canal have already raised the potential costs of doing nothing and changed corporate perspectives somewhat. Even so, it is still likely that many cleanup efforts will bog down in arguments over how the blame and the costs—which will be large—should be apportioned among the companies and the governments involved.

This editorial brought rapid response from the chemical industry. Robert Roland, president of the Chemical Manufacturers Association, responded in an editorial:

> One of the things that we must all realize in discussing the solid-waste disposal problem, including toxic or hazardous wastes, is that it is not just the problem of the chemical industry. It is a result of society's advanced technology and pursuit of an increasingly complex lifestyle. (April 2, 1979)

Thus, even before any legislation was introduced in Congress, the positions of the media, the industry, and the EPA were clearly sketched out.

Early Legislative Proposals

In the early summer, an important meeting was held at the White House. The issue was the superfund and who was going to pay for it. Representatives of the Department of Commerce, the Council of Economic Advisors, the Council on Wage and Price Stability, and the Office of Management and Budget argued for a fund totally generated from general government revenues. On the other side were representatives of the EPA; the Department of Health, Education and Welfare; the Occupational Safety and Health Administration; and the Council on Environmental Quality arguing for a shared funding approach between industry and the government. According to sources in attendance, President Carter himself decided on an 80 to 20 percent industry-government split.

In June, numerous bills to deal with hazardous wastes were introduced in the Congress. The administration bills (S 1341 and HR 4566) were introduced on June 14 and 21, respectively, and sought to create a $1.6-billion fund over four years, 80 percent of which would be raised through fees on oil and raw materials used to make hazardous chemicals. The rest would be supplied by the federal and state governments. Representatives Staggers and Florio introduced a bill (HR 4571) on June 21, 1979, which was essentially the same as the administration's bill. Representative John La Falce of Niagara Falls, New York, introduced a bill (HR 5290) in September, which had two significant differences from the previous proposals: first, it specified a smaller fund ($500 million) but did not require any industry contribution; second, it did provide for the payment of damages to individuals. Senator Moynihan introduced an identical bill in the Senate. Senators Culver and Muskie introduced another bill (S 1480) on July 11, 1979. It provided for a fund of $500 million totally collected from industry fees, and allowed injured individuals to collect damages. Their bill did not include oil spills.

The CMA's response to this flurry of activity was immediate and predictable. President Roland of the CMA argued that the bills unfairly singled out the chemical and related industries to bear a disproportionate burden of cleanup costs. In so doing, they failed to adequately reflect the society's responsibility for resolving a problem that everyone had helped create and for whose solution everyone should help pay.

Monsanto's response to a *Business Week* query on June 14, 1979, represented what was to become the industry's position.

> . . . based on a review of the Administration's fact sheet and the previous EPA proposal, we can state the following:
> 1. Abandoned sites are a separate and distinct problem from chemical spills and hazardous wastes and should be addressed as a separate issue.
> 2. The funding source for cleanup of abandoned sites where the liable party cannot be identified should be the Federal government because these sites represent a problem created by society, not just the chemical industry.
> 3. There are [sic] existing and/or proposed legislation and regulation that cover the problems of chemical spills, oil spills and hazardous waste management.

According to Marc Tipermas of the EPA, the "industry fought like tigers on the fees and economic impact" but were never able to show any real economic problems with the fees. Government officials believed that if the industry had been able to show economic damage, the bill would have died.

In July, an environmental affairs spokesperson for Union Carbide, Jackson Browning, represented the CMA before the Senate Subcommittee on Environmental Pollution and the Subcommittee on Resource Protection. He took the industry position one step further, suggesting that the proposed legislation was unconstitutional. Browning argued that public funding was appropriate for reasons of equity and sound public policy, and he claimed it was inequitable to place the burden on today's companies, stockholders, or customers for the practices, failures, or shortcomings of yesterday's industrial producers. Furthermore, he stated, many of the current problems were not known and were, in fact, unknowable at the time of the original disposal. Companies must not be assessed for disposal practices that were considered acceptable at the time, he argued.

Also testifying at this time were representatives of environmental organizations, who strongly argued that the industry's "ignorance is bliss" defense should not be accepted. The industry should not be rewarded for failing to identify risks associated with their practices until the government promulgates regulations. In September 1979, *Chemical and Engineering News* reported:

> CMA's criticisms of the superfund have drawn an unusually detailed and harsh response from the EPA. At his farewell press conference, EPA assistant administrator, Thomas C. Jorling, charged that the "superfund" proposal "has excited a frenetic and self-serving response from the chemical industry. The public deserves to know that much of the criticism raised against the proposal is incorrect and misleading."
> Noting the industry's contention that it is being unfairly penalized, Jorling responded that "the supposition of the Administration's proposal was that society should not bear the costs of protecting the public from hazards produced by those who have benefits from commerce relating to these substances. Many of those parties now wish to be insulated from any continuing responsibilities for the hazards to society which they created."

At the end of September, Representative Eckhardt's subcommittee released its report on hazardous wastes. It was critical of virtually every agency and congressional committee concerned with this issue and also questioned the integrity of the chemical industry. It called federal and state efforts to control disposal of hazardous wastes totally inadequate, said Congress may have been unrealistic in giving the EPA only eighteen months to develop national standards for the proper disposal of these wastes, and asserted that there was no excuse for the EPA's failure to promulgate regulations, enforce actions, or conduct a comprehensive search for hazardous waste sites. It also said that industry was sometimes lax to the point of criminal negligence in contaminating the land and adulterating the waters with its toxins.

On October 10 and 11, 1979, the last round of these initial congressional hearings began. These hearings were held before Representative Florio's House Subcommittee on Transportation and Commerce. Mr. Florio specifically challenged Robert Roland on CMA's withdrawal of its initial support for and commitment to hazardous waste cleanup efforts. He cited early statements by CMA spokespersons indicating that the industry should share social and financial responsibility, and asked, "What has taken place over the last couple of months that has changed your position?" Mr. Roland never clearly responded to this question and only noted that there were problems with the legalities of the superfund approach and that it was not equitable.

The various bills being introduced in the House and Senate at this time were causing some fragmentation in the industry positions as well. Industry trade associations held firm to the position that the fund should be financed through general revenues, but individual companies began investigating the Muskie-Culver industry fee plan. Some mining and petroleum companies preferred such a waste-based fee to the administration's scheme if it were based just on degree of hazard, not volume. Some chemical companies thought the Muskie-Culver approach would be cheaper and more equitable.

The industry, Congress, EPA, and the public were, at the end of 1979 entering what *Chemical Week* (October 3, 1979) termed "the eye of the superfund storm."

YEAR OF DECISION—PASSING THE SUPERFUND BILL

The year 1980 opened in an atmosphere of confusion and disarray on all sides. Multiple bills introduced by various representatives and committees in Congress complicated the voting process. Meanwhile, various industry representatives began to voice conflicting opinions, thus eroding the strength of the CMA's "united front." It would be a year of heated debate and political power struggles.

The opening of the CMA's attack on the superfund began in earnest in March 1980 with the release of an industry study on hazardous waste sites around the country. CMA president Roland claimed that the study "confirms our belief that the size of the superfund problem is not as great as the Environmental Protection Agency has estimated and that state agencies are acting in this area in a responsible manner to handle their own problems." The summary released by the CMA was attacked harshly by the EPA. Despite repeated calls for copies of the full study by the EPA, members of Congress, and congressional committees, no material was ever provided by the CMA.

In April, Representative Florio introduced his superfund bill, and it was referred to his own subcommittee for review. As the subcommittee was in the process of reviewing the bill a massive fire broke out at a chemical dump that had been used by the former Chemical Control Corporation in Elizabeth, New Jersey. Chemical wastes exploded, and a major catastrophe was avoided only because the winds blew the toxic clouds away from heavily populated areas. The cost of the cleanup was estimated at $10 million to $15 million. The catastrophe had an impact: one week after the incident, Florio's subcommittee approved the bill (HR 7020).

The erosion of the united CMA front against the superfund escalated at this point. While Florio's bill was in subcommittee, a difference of opinion over industry strategy unfolded. Union Carbide, Du Pont, Rohm & Haas, Olin, and Monsanto wanted to collaborate on the funding issue in exchange for other concessions. When the bill went to full committee, the compromise occurred. It involved the use of funds for cleaning up abandoned ("orphan") sites and for the removal of third-party liability. Florio was willing to compromise, and by midnight of May 14 the revised bill was adopted by the Commerce Committee.

The compromise did not meet with unanimous approval within the CMA. Though Rohm & Haas was strongly in favor, feeling that it secured "improved legislation . . . [it] could live with," Allied, Dow, and Du Pont were still arguing for an effort by CMA to kill all superfund legislation.

The chemical industry had other reasons for concern. In the Senate, the sudden departure of Senator Edmund S. Muskie to become Secretary of State was seen as damaging to the environmental goals, because he had been a leading advocate of environmental legislation. However, the chemical industry feared that the Senate might pass a very strong superfund bill as a final tribute to Muskie. In fact, the bills introduced in the Senate were more stringent on liability and they proposed higher funds for cleanup than those in the House.

Final Committee Hearings

The industry brought considerable pressure to bear on the House in order to have Florio's bill referred to the Ways and Means Committee. This was yet another shift in tactics. Industry representatives thought, because of the bill's revenue aspects, they could get a better deal this way. In previous Congresses, oil fund liability bills were not sent to Ways and Means. According to William Stover, CMA's vice president, it was thought that by going through Ways and Means the bill would be limited to "orphan sites . . . and hang the wrongdoer. If you can't find the wrongdoer, then use federal money."

The bill was referred to the Ways and Means Committee, but with a rule that allowed only thirty days to act. According to several observers, the CMA had strong bipartisan support for a $900 million superfund, but the CMA decided it could keep the figure at the original $600 million. Hearings were held, and in a surprise move the Committee voted to double the size of the bill—to $1.2 billion—and to increase the industry's contribution from 50 percent to 75 percent.

At the same time, superfund bills were moving through the Senate. In late June the Senate Environment and Public Works Committee approved a $4.1-billion fund to clean up sites and to compensate victims. The vote was 10 to 1 in favor.

As the pressure mounted for action on the superfund, the industry realized that it would have to pay something and that it may have lost the opportunity to determine how much. According to *Business Week*, the industry's best chance for stopping the superfund at this point appeared to be through delay.

Irving Shapiro, chairman of Du Pont, addressed the National Conference of Lieutenant Governors in August 1980 with a speech entitled "We Can Manage Hazardous Wastes." He argued strongly for a superfund bill, asserting that the chemical industry was willing to pay its fair share to make the environment safe from orphan dumps.

On September 23, the House of Representatives overwhelmingly adopted HR 7020—a $1.2-billion package, the industry paying 75 percent, government 25 percent. The legislation was sent to the Senate for its consideration. Roland noted that ". . . the bill, although not perfect, represents a conscientious bi-partisan effort to address the problems realistically and to establish adequate protection for the public and the environment."

Despite strong pressure for action from the media and the fact that the superfund legislation had become ". . . one of the best spectator sports now being played on Capitol Hill," the chance for passage was seen as only 50–50. The slowing of momentum was not lost on the White House. Although distracted by the Iranian hostage crisis, President Carter contacted legislators and asked what his administration could do to work to get legislation passed. This work, at the suggestion of several key Senators, took the form of meetings among the key actors. These meetings were helpful in moving the industry and Senate toward an agreement, but in early October, the industry, sensing that Ronald Reagan would win the presidential election, decided that they would not have to make any more concessions and could quite possibly succeed in stopping the superfund.

Enacting the Law

The presidential and congressional elections in November 1980 dramatically altered the power structure of superfund politics. The Republican party achieved a landslide victory in the presidential election and achieved substantial gains in the House. More importantly, they achieved control of the Senate where superfund legislation was being delayed. Further good news for the industry came when Senators Robert Byrd and Howard Baker (out-going and incoming majority leaders) announced that the Senate would not consider controversial bills in the lame-duck session between the election and the inauguration. At this point, the CMA was positive that the superfund was dead.

On November 14, 1980, a critical meeting took place between Mr. Roland and Representative Florio. Florio wanted the CMA to issue a statement clearly presenting its support of HR 7020. If the CMA would do this, Florio could guarantee the delivery of the Senate on HR 7020. Roland stated he could not issue a statement for the CMA but would need to get approval from the executive committee. He also noted that the CMA was opposed to the bill and would not provide such a statement of support, and he doubted that Florio could "deliver" the Senate. According to Florio, Roland also said that the industry could get a "better deal" from the incoming Republican administration. Florio left the meeting enraged and held a press conference to announce that Roland had reneged on his deal to support his $1.2-billion bill.

When asked later about these statements, Roland denied making them, but he went on to acknowledge that the new political climate could be more favorable to business and that the CMA did oppose the legislation passed in the House. Florio created sufficient publicity over the issue to tip the balance in favor of passage of a superfund bill.

All the publicity that was directed toward Republicans caused the incoming administration to request a position paper from the EPA addressing two key questions: (1) Why does the bill have to pass now?, and (2) How would the Reagan administration pass it? The EPA response highlighted four major points:

1. The passage of the bill next year would require a great deal of rebattling over the same issues and prevent the development and progress of the Reagan legislative program.

2. Any superfund bill would affect industry–government relationships. Passing superfund now would make it a Carter, not a Reagan, bill.

3. If passage was delayed, Reagan would have to use "chips" to get congressional support. (Chips are promises of support for individual representatives' legislation, appointments, or other political favors.)

4. The current superfund can be made acceptable to a broad spectrum of the industry.

Several major newspapers brought more pressure to bear on the Senate Finance Committee. The *Boston Globe,* the *Washington Post,* and the *New York Times* all ran articles in mid-November dealing with the chemical industry's political action committee's contributions to the Senate Finance Committee members in the 1980 elections. The same day in an unusual move, the Senate Finance Committee "washed its hands" of the controversy over the issue by offering a $4.2-billion bill that was certain to be either killed or significantly amended on the Senate floor.

Finance Committee Chairman Russell Long (D, Louisiana) brought the issue to a vote after only two hours of a scheduled three-day mark up in order, he said, to get action on the controversial subject before Congress adjourns. "This legislation should be decided by this Congress and this Senate, and we hope the Senate can act on it in these remaining days."

The industry stand against any superfund legislation cracked open on November 19, 1980. Irving Shapiro, Chairman of Du Pont, in an interview with the *New York Times,* stated that a fund for cleaning up toxic waste sites should be enacted in the current congressional session. "I want legislation in this session, rational legislation dictated by the facts," Mr. Shapiro said. He added that the compromise proposal for a $2.7-billion fund offered by Senator Stafford and Senator Randolph was unacceptable, but added that if the chief executives of the chemical industry got together with White House and Congressional representatives "we could have a sensible bill in two hours."

The industry association was surprised and its credibility damaged by Shapiro's break. It was surprised because Du Pont had been supportive of a hard-line approach by the CMA. The prestige and influence of both Du Pont and Shapiro opened the door for further fragmentation of the CMA position. The next day, both Rohm & Haas and Union Carbide announced support for "rational" legislation. This break in the industry ranks provided support that Republican leaders needed in order to press for a superfund bill.

On November 21, Senators Stafford and Randolph, sensing victory, further modified their compromise bill, reducing the funding size to $1.6 billion and requiring a contribution of 87.5 percent from industry and 12.5 percent from government. After intense negotiations, the compromise was agreed to, and passed by, the Senate on November 24, 1980.

The House considered identical legislation on December 3. President Carter, concerned about its prospects, telephoned sixty-five representatives in ninety minutes on the evening of December 2. After considerable debate, the House passed the bill by a vote of 274 to 94. The industry had lost its battle to stop the superfund from being born.

Chemical Week attempted to assess what went wrong with the industry's handling of the superfund:

> Caught unprepared by the wave of support for the compromise bill, CMA found itself alone in support of a $600 million Superfund bill approved months ago by the House Commerce Committee. "From my standpoint, CMA did not negotiate with us in any real sense," claimed an aide to Senator Stafford. The aide maintained that "CMA did not serve itself well." The CMA antagonized a number of congressmen by underestimating political realities and presenting no unified position on Superfund. An aide to a Republican congressman, sympathetic to industry, noted that the industry was "disorganized" when the House was considering Superfund. He recalls there were "too many people supposedly speaking for the industry, too many points of view, and too great a reluctance to make concessions." Another source says: "Had CMA been more constructive, this wouldn't have been so bitter at the end."

DISCUSSION QUESTIONS

1. What strategies and policies did the CMA and its members appear to have in managing their responses to the congressional action to create a "superfund" law? Specifically state the strategies at different points in time during the debate. (It may be helpful to draw a "timeline" identifying key dates and events.) Discuss how socially responsive these strategies were to the underlying public concerns.

2. Consider the public policy process (see Chapter 8) discussed in this case. Discuss the evolution of the superfund in terms of the public policy process model. What events corresponded to the various stages of the model?

3. Discuss the industry's argument that "society needs chemicals—society should have to pay for it." Contrast this with the EPA's argument that the cleanup funds should come from those segments of industry and consumers who are most responsible for imposing the risks on society. Which do you favor? Why? Analyze both arguments in terms of costs and benefits.

4. Why do you think Irving Shapiro and Du Pont changed positions in late 1980? Assess the importance of this action. If you worked for CMA, what would you say to Mr. Shapiro?

5. Evaluate the role of the chemical industry's trade association, the CMA. Did they do a good job of representing the industry? What factors might affect a trade association's position on such issues?

NESTLÉ AND THE INFANT FORMULA MARKETING CODE[1]

The Controversy

> Can a product which requires clean water, good sanitation, adequate family income and a literate parent to follow printed instructions be properly and safely used in areas where water is contaminated, sewage runs in the streets, poverty is severe and illiteracy is high?

With these words United States Senator Edward M. Kennedy, Chairman of the Senate Health and Scientific Research Subcommittee, opened the 1978 Senate Hearings on Infant Formula. These hearings were organized in response to outcries from health professionals and consumer groups who claimed that the increased use of infant formula was detrimental to infant health in developing nations. The purpose of the hearing was to hear testimony from individuals involved in the controversy, including industry representatives and their critics, and to develop a plan of action to protect infant lives.

The first official action to halt the trend away from breastfeeding had come six years earlier. The Protein-Calorie Advisory Group, an organ of the United Nations that coordinated other nutrition-related agencies, issued a statement in June 1972 suggesting that governments monitor the use of formula. The statement also urged formula companies to avoid aggressive marketing and to instruct consumers in the safe use of the product.

Critics of formula use in developing countries usually cite three principal causes of product misuse which lead to infant morbidity (illness) and mortality (death). The first is low family income. The purchase of infant formula in adequate quantities to feed a growing baby often represents a large portion of the family's income: the incentive is to overdilute it. The real cost of the formula is masked when the mother receives her first few cans of formula at no cost while she is in the hospital. In 1980, a week's supply of formula equaled about half of a laborer's weekly wage in Nigeria and other African nations. A study in Barbados found that about three-quarters of low-income

[1]This case was adapted from James E. Post, *First World Foods in Third World Markets: An Analysis of the Infant Formula Controversy*, Boston University, Public Affairs Research Program, 1987. Sources include James E. Post, "Assessing the Nestlé Boycott: Corporate Accountability and Human Rights," *California Management Review*, Winter 1985, pp. 113–131; Oliver Williams, "Who Cast the First Stone?" *Harvard Business Review*, September–October 1984, pp. 151–160; Nestlé, S.A. *The Dilemma of Third World Nutrition*, 1983; Nestlé, S.A., "Instructions to All Companies of the Nestlé Group and to Agents and Distributors Who Market Infant Formula under Trade Marks of the Nestlé Group," February 1982; press releases of the Nestlé Coordination Center on Nutrition (NCCN); quarterly reports of the Nestlé Infant Formula Audit Commission, 1982–1986; Michael deCourcy Hinds, "Nestlé's New Infant Formula Policy," *New York Times*, May 5, 1982, p. C-17; James P. Grant, "The State of the World's Children, 1982–83," United Nation's Children's Fund (UNICEF); and press releases of Infant Formula Action Coalition (INFACT), International Baby Food Action Network (IBFAN), and Interfaith Center on Corporate Responsibility; Herman Nickel, "The Corporation Haters," *Fortune*, June 18, 1980; and United States Senate, *Marketing and Promotion of Infant Formula in Developing Nations*, Hearings Before the Subcommittee on Health and Scientific Research of the Committee on Human Resources, 95th Congress, 2d Session, May 23, 1978 (Washington, DC: U.S. Government Printing Office, 1978).

families who relied on bottlefeeding were making a four-day supply of formula last between five days and three weeks. The result of overdilution is slow starvation and/or inadequate physical and mental development.

Secondly, critics allege that the huge majority of Third World residents do not have the sanitary systems necessary for safe formula use. Available water is often contaminated and homes lack facilities for sterilization and refrigeration. A sad reality of these poor hygienic conditions is that mothers, eager to protect their children from the "unsafe" environment, are more likely to be influenced by outside opinions on what is "best" for their babies. A marketer or health care worker can have tremendous influence on her. Infants fed formula under these poor hygienic conditions are more likely to contract debilitating bacterial diseases and diarrhea. As James P. Grant, Executive Director of UNICEF, said in a special report:

> [T]he low-income mother who is persuaded to abandon breastfeeding for bottle-feeding in the developing world is being persuaded to spend a significant proportion of her small income in order to expose her child to the risk of malnutrition, infection and an early grave.

The third major criticism of formula use in developing nations stems from the low literacy rate. Mothers who can barely read are at risk of not following the instructions correctly. These same women also are likely to be very vulnerable to pictorial representations of healthy and happy babies. The illiterate or semiliterate woman becomes an easy target for marketers.

A subtler aspect of the infant formula controversy was related to a common socioeconomic trend. In most developing countries, harsh economic conditions of the countryside were forcing many families to seek a better life in the city. There the low-income mother comes into more frequent contact with women from higher social classes. Many of these women have already abandoned breastfeeding in favor of the "more modern" method of infant feeding. Bottlefeeding became identified with the "better life" they had come to the city to find. The text on a can of Enfalac, sold in Peru, illustrates the themes of modernization and quality:

> "From Mead Johnson (owned by Bristol Myers) . . . the most modern infant formula . . . similar to mother's milk . . . the most modern and perfect maternalized infant formula, physiologically similar to mother's milk."

The label carried a picture of a white North American mother and baby.

Marketing in the Third World

As the birth rate in industrialized nations leveled off or declined in the early 1960s, formula companies began to look for new markets. They found them in developing nations where the birth rate was soaring and the media were reaching more and more people every day. The major formula companies (Nestlé, Bristol-Myers, American Home Products, and Abbott Labs) focused their attention on the foreign market.

Formula promotion in developing nations became very intense by the early 1970s. Whereas in their home countries food companies tended to advertise directly to consumers while pharmaceutical companies promoted mostly to health professionals, formula companies marketed to *both* consumers and health workers abroad. An expert familiar with the industry spoke of this marketing strategy during the 1978 congressional hearings:

> This promotion to both consumers and medical personnel has positioned the industry to take advantage of other development-related trends. Concentration of population in urban areas pays dividends for a radio advertising program; growth in medical services, hospitals, and live births in health clinics coincides with medical promotion and endorsement policies; and market presence in developing nations where births are rising is opportune when birth rates in industrialized nations are stable or falling. It is true, as the manufacturers assert, that many trends contribute to increases in women bottlefeeding their babies, but it is naive to believe that these firms have not deliberately positioned themselves to take advantage of such social change.

Marketing to the consumer meant changing knowledge and beliefs about infant feeding. All the media were used extensively—radio, television, billboards, and magazines. Labels on formula cans carried the message that formula use was ideal "for those who can't" breastfeed and for "when breastmilk isn't enough." Critics alleged that these phrases played upon unfounded fears of women that they would not be able successfully to breastfeed their children.

Formula cans also carried pictures of perfectly healthy babies, the race of the child dependent on where the product was to be sold. The implication clearly was that by drinking that formula, the newborn could be healthy and happy. Critics claimed that this was not only misleading, but it was also very dangerous. Formula use in economically depressed areas frequently took the child farther from good health rather than closer to it.

The formula industry also marketed through the various health care systems. Salespeople regularly visited physicians and hospital staffs, briefing them on new products and leaving generous amounts of samples. In many poverty-stricken areas, the formula companies donated supplies to the hospitals. Health care personnel would then, at their own discretion, pass the supplies to new mothers. During these crucial first few days while the mother was receiving free formula in the hospital, she would lose her ability to produce milk. The supply of free formula usually did not extend after the mother left the hospital, and the baby would then have to be fed on formula or some other breastmilk substitute.

Many formula companies also employed "milk (or mothercraft) nurses," women who were trained in nursing but whose primary responsibility was to promote formula use, both to mothers and to the professional community. They ran workshops and distributed educational material to health care workers, and they visited new mothers at home and in the hospital. Although called "nurses," these women were actually the mainstay of the infant formula salesforce.

Formula companies also supported hospitals and individual physicians with grants. Many maternity departments depended on these grants as part of the compensation package for their personnel.

The Boycott

By 1977 there was sufficient outrage over infant formula marketing to form a large coalition of consumer groups and international health agencies. Much of the protest focused on Nestlé, a company that controlled about half of the Third World (developing nations) infant formula market. A boycott of all Nestlé products was launched in June of that year. The next seven years were marked by court and media battles as Nestlé, the unwilling representative of the entire formula industry, fought the boycott and tried to minimize the damage being done to sales and its corporate image.

Nestlé's initial strategy to cope with the boycott was to try to discredit its leaders and to refute the allegations. At the Senate hearings, for example, Dr. Oswaldo Ballarin, president of Nestlé/Brazil, testified that "a worldwide church organization, with the stated purpose of undermining the free enterprise system" was heading the boycott. Under the direction of the world's largest public relations firm, Hill and Knowlton, Nestlé carried out a direct mail campaign where it mailed information packets to over 300,000 clergy and community leaders. Never recanting Ballarin's conspiracy allegations, Nestlé continued to challenge the factual bases for attacks on its marketing in the developing nations.

In October 1979, the World Health Organization (WHO) and UNICEF jointly sponsored a conference on infant feeding practices. Representatives from the formula industry, including Nestlé, and from different activist groups participated. Two major outcomes resulted from these meetings: the first was a preliminary set of guidelines for the marketing of breastmilk substitutes; the second was the recommendation that the Director General of the WHO should attempt to develop an international code of marketing behavior.

After the WHO/UNICEF meeting, Nestlé entered into its second phase of resisting the boycott. It contracted a different public relations firm, the Daniel Edelman Company, and adopted a new "low profile" strategy. Now the company steadfastly refused to acknowledge any wrongdoing in its marketing practices or to talk to boycott organizers. Instead of confronting its critics directly, Nestlé sent out hundreds of thousands of new press releases stating that its marketing practices were in accordance with recommended standards. It hoped to convey the message that the boycott was no longer necessary.

Leah Margulies from the Interfaith Center on Corporate Responsibility, a leading activist in the campaign to change industry practices, objected to Nestlé's claims that it was abiding by the new recommendations:

> The pattern that emerges is that even after ten years of debate, the infant formula industry continued aggressive promotion of infant formula that competes with breastmilk. While some of the most flagrant forms of promotion have been suspended (e.g., mass media advertising), overall promotional effort has, if any-

thing, intensified. The health institution and health care provider are now the central focus of an increasingly sophisticated campaign to promote artificial feeding in general and loyalty to a company's brand names in particular.

The third and final phase of Nestlé's resistance was characterized by its efforts to strengthen "the new right," a political coalition that strongly believes public welfare is advanced through private sector freedom. Nestlé supported organizations such as the Ethics and Public Policy Center (EPPC), headed by "the new right" philosopher Ernest Lefever. For its part, Lefever's organization publicized Nestlé's cause. In a mass mailing to potential donors, the EPPC included a reprint of an article entitled "Crusade against the Corporations" by Herman Nikel. In this article, the author called the churches' support for the boycott "Marxists marching under the banner of Christ." Four months later the *Washington Post* revealed that Nestlé had given $25,000 to the EPPC in 1980.

During this phase the company also funded "independent" research with the hope of improving its image and credibility. It formed a research foundation in Washington called the Nestlé Coordination Center for Nutrition, Inc. (NCCN). Raphael Pagan, Jr., formerly Vice President of Public Affairs at Castle and Cooke, Inc., was chosen to be its president. Favorable results from NCCN-sponsored studies were sent to the media, health professionals, and government agencies.

While the WHO Code was being drafted, Nestlé worked separately with an industry council to develop plans for self-regulation. To assist in this effort, they hired Dr. Stanislaus Flache to be the Secretary General of the International Council of Infant Food Industries (ICIFI). Dr. Flache had previously been Assistant Director General for the WHO.

Ratifying the Code

The WHO Code underwent several drafts and numerous revisions between 1979 and 1981. During that time all parties worked hard to advance their own positions. Activists recruited more churches, labor unions, and other organizations to publicly join the boycott. They stepped up their information dissemination and advertising in order to persuade more individual consumers to boycott Nestlé. They attended all WHO meetings where the new code was being discussed, and achieved official nongovernmental organization (NGO) status, a very important recognition in international affairs.

Nestlé, for its part, was also busy. It recognized that regardless of how strict the final WHO Code was, the company would actually have to abide by national laws, not international recommendations. It was therefore in the company's best interest to support national adoption of less stringent marketing codes. The International Baby Food Action Network (IBFAN)—the international activist organization—accused Nestlé of pressuring local governments to adopt the ICIFI codes rather than the emerging WHO Code. In Zimbabwe, Nestlé attorneys were able to cause a six-month delay in that country's Ministry of Health report on the dangers of bottlefeeding. When the report was finally published, Nestlé attacked it for being "erroneous" and "tendentious."

WHO is actually the staff organization for the World Health Assembly, which is composed of more than 100 member nations. It is the Assembly that actually votes to adopt actions such as the marketing code. The days immediately before the actual vote in the Assembly were marked with partisan efforts. Industry lobbyists and activists lobbied specific members to sway their opinions. The companies were also accused of playing "dirty tricks." For example, industry representatives circulated a letter among members of the Indian delegation that was supposedly from the "All India Medical Students Association." The letter suggested that Prime Minister Indira Gandhi did not completely support the code. The head of the Indian delegation countered with a communiqué suggesting that the first letter was not authentic. A similar example was a letter allegedly from the International Pediatrics Association withdrawing its support from the code. The president of the IPA publicly repudiated that claim.

Besides lobbying at the WHO Assembly, industry members voiced their opinions in the media. Among many statements released to the press, the following were representative:

> "We oppose the universal code and some believe it is a sign that the UN system is moving to control multinationals."—ICIFI Secretary General, Stanislaus Flache, *International Herald Tribune,* May 4, 1981.

> "The medical premise underlying the code is fundamentally faulty. . . . The WHO's proposed Code contains many unwarranted restrictions and prohibitions that are unconstitutional and represent a dangerous precedent. . . . We believe that the United States should vote 'no' on the proposed Code."—Bristol-Myers (Mead Johnson) Co., *Washington Post,* May 7, 1981.

The three United States infant formula manufacturers suggested that even if the WHO Code were passed in the World Health Assembly, they would not consider themselves bound by it. They argued that the decline in breastfeeding was due to changing life-styles, not to any sales efforts on the part of formula manufacturers.

Other food companies and organizations joined the formula companies in resisting the WHO Code, most notable among them were Heinz, Kraft, Gerber's, and the Grocery Manufacturers of America. Jointly, these companies lobbied officials in Washington to convince them that passage of the WHO Code would imply new laws, and these laws would violate both the First Amendment and U.S. antitrust laws.

Amidst all this battling, the WHO Code came up for vote in May 1981. Of the 118 member nations voting, 114 voted in favor of it, 3 abstained, and only 1 voted against it: the United States. Representatives from the Reagan administration said the Code violated the right of free speech and showed strains of being "totalitarian." The Secretary of Health and Human Services, Richard Schweiker, explained the U.S. position: "The administration honestly does not believe the WHO should be an international Federal Trade Commission. . . . The Code runs contrary to our constitution."

Reactions to the Vote in the WHO Assembly

Two pointed resignations quickly followed the United States' lone negative vote in the WHO. Dr. Stephen Joseph, a leading pediatrician, and Eugene Babb, a nutritionist, both resigned from their posts at the U.S. Agency for International Development in protest. Babb commented: "What we're saying (with this vote) to the world is that narrow commercial interests are more important to us than the health of infants in developing countries." Protests from the public were immediately seen in the media. *Newsweek* called the WHO Code vote the Reagan administration's first foreign policy disaster.

The WHO Code

The final version of the International Code of Marketing of Breastmilk Substitutes underlined the joint responsibility of all international, national, and private sector parties in the fight to promote infant health. The responsibility was shared, but actual implementation of the code had to be done on a local level; the WHO had no jurisdiction within national boundaries.

The code applied only to marketing of breastmilk substitutes. It put no restrictions on sales or distribution except where those tactics were used for promotional purposes.

Two major themes were bedrock for the rest of the code. The first was that all direct advertising and sampling to consumers be stopped. Billboards, point-of-sale advertising, all manner of outreach to new mothers was proscribed. Consistent with this idea was a set of guidelines for product labeling. Article 9 of the code specified that all packaging carry the message that "breastfeeding is best" for the baby and that formula should be used only on the advice of a health care worker. The label was not to carry any pictures or text that idealized formula, including pictures of infants.

The second central theme of the WHO Code dealt with the manner through which the formula companies could promote and distribute their products. Marketing could continue but only if it in no way undermined breastfeeding and if all efforts were filtered through health care personnel. Health authorities in member states were called upon to educate health workers on the benefits of breastfeeding.

The marketing practices that were allowed to continue were carefully spelled out in the code. Educational materials now had to include information on the benefits of breastfeeding and the potential dangers of bottlefeeding. Donations of informational and educational materials could be made only with written permission of the appropriate governmental agency. Donations or low-priced sales of supplies could be made to health care professionals but not as sales inducements. If the health care worker thought it was appropriate to pass the free product on to the mother, both the institution and the formula company had the responsibility to ensure a continued supply of that product as long as the baby needed it. All manner of support to individual professionals (fellowships, research grants, attendance at conferences) had to be disclosed to the institution with which that person was affiliated.

Other marketing practices were strictly prohibited. The health care facility could not be used for any sort of advertising or promotion, including displays, posters, or demonstration by industry personnel. "Milk nurses" were no longer permitted. Industry personnel could not be compensated on the basis of sales volume of formula. Sampling and gift giving to health care workers were curtailed.

The responsibility for monitoring compliance with the WHO Code and whatever local legislation resulted from it was left to individual governments. Nongovernmental groups were encouraged to call attention to the infractions they saw. The industry itself was called upon to "apprise each member of their marketing personnel of the Code and of their responsibilities under it."

Nestlé Agrees to Comply with the Code

The bitterness of the fight to pass the WHO Code in the World Health Assembly left industry executives, critics, and WHO officials disappointed and exhausted. There was no quick action to transform the code into national laws by the governments that had voted for it. For months, it seemed that the fight to pass the WHO Code had simply created a massive stalemate.

On March 16, 1982, ten months after the WHO Code was passed, Nestlé publicly announced that it would abide by the code. Telegrams poured into Nestlé's headquarters in Vevey, Switzerland, congratulating the company on its new direction. Raphael Pagan, head of the Nestlé Coordination Center for Nutrition, was quoted in *The Baltimore Sun* as saying:

> It's a quantum jump on the whole issue, the whole infant formula controversy. . . . I can assure you Nestlé is implementing a very stringent code of checks and balances to make sure it works.

Nestlé's critics were much less impressed with the "quantum jump." They wanted proof that the announcement would lead to real compliance in specific markets. The leaders of the Nestlé boycott vowed to continue action against the company until there was clear evidence of implementation of the code throughout the developing world. Douglas Johnson, an INFACT leader, said:

> Nestlé has now made a promise to all of us. We intend to see that they keep it. We will continue to monitor Nestlé's activity in the field, through our network of nearly 100 allied organizations in 65 countries. We will continue to report industry violations of the Code every month to the World Health Organization, UNICEF, national health ministries, our allied groups, and industry.

New Directives and INFACT'S Response

Nestlé issued a set of instructions to all its field personnel regarding the sale of infant formula one month before the company announced its intention to bring its marketing practices into line with the WHO Code. Although the new directives used the WHO Code as a starting point, they contained several major modifications. The result was a vague, and at times contradictory, set of instructions. To those eager to see operational compliance from the big formula company, it seemed that Nestlé's new strategy was to confuse the issue of infant formula marketing while creating an appearance of compliance.

INFACT renewed its efforts to influence Nestlé's marketing practices. It took exception to what it saw as the company's loose interpretation of the code. The critics did not trust Nestlé and were wary of any ambiguous language ("loopholes") in the company's instructions.

Nestlé's desire to end the boycott and INFACT's desire to see a major commitment to the WHO Code implemented by one of the infant formula manufacturers did help move the parties toward renewed negotiation. Although INFACT had a long list of criticisms of the Nestlé marketing instructions, four areas were singled out as pivotal for bringing the boycott to an end: the use of educational materials, the distribution of samples, the provision of formula supplies, and the giving of gifts to health workers. Each presented a difficult dilemma for the negotiators.

Educational Materials

The WHO Code specified that informational and educational materials of any type should provide positive information on the value of breastfeeding and information about the health hazards associated with bottlefeeding. Article 4.2 of the code is quite detailed about the content of these messages. Nestlé proposed a set of statements that it claimed struck a balance between factual information on formula feeding and appropriate warnings about the risks of bottlefeeding. INFACT argued for much stronger language to warn mothers about the risks of bottlefeeding. Whereas Nestlé sought to communicate the message that infant formula was a nutritionally satisfactory alternative to human milk, when used properly, INFACT sought a stronger message that effectively urged mothers to breastfeed because of the significant risks associated with bottlefeeding. Interpretation and implementation of this article of the WHO Code was the most difficult point in the Nestlé boycott negotiations of 1983–1984.

Samples

Article 5.2 of the WHO Code said:

> Manufacturers and distributors should not provide, directly or indirectly, to pregnant women, mothers or members of their families, samples of products within the scope of this Code.

Nestlé's directive stated:

> In accordance with existing instructions, samples (or free samples) may only be given to health workers . . . and not to mothers.

INFACT claimed that the company's instructions violated the code, because the giving of samples to health workers is simply an *indirect* way of ensuring that these product samples would be passed on to mothers. Thus, the end effect would be product promotion that the code sought to ban.

Supplies

The WHO Code defines supplies as "quantities of a product provided for use over an extended period, free or at a low price, for social purposes, including those provided to families in need." It was intended to allow supplies only for the purpose of social relief.

The use of supplies was among the most difficult facets of the code to implement. Many hospitals depended on donations of infant formula—both to help in their fight against malnutrition and to simplify the job of maternity ward nurses. The code implied that the formula companies themselves were to initiate changes in their lucrative relationships with hospital personnel by changing the nature and purpose of formula donations. If one supplier acted and others did not, however, a competitive disadvantage could result.

Nestlé's method to implement this new policy was to change the distribution process of its supplies. No longer would the company decide on the amount of formula to distribute. Henceforth, doctors would have to request supplies. Nestlé provided special request forms, hoping this new method would put the responsibility of formula use in the hospital upon medically trained personnel.

INFACT was critical of Nestlé's directives. It claimed that they did not explicitly make the distinction between supplies (given for the purpose of social relief) and samples (given as sales inducements). The recipient of the product was not likely to perceive the difference. Thus, a tighter control system was necessary.

Gifts

Gift giving to professionals took two forms prior to the WHO Code: giving "business" gifts to ensure a close working relationship, and giving supplies that doctors could use at home with their own babies. Both were discouraged by the code. The Nestlé directive stated that the former was allowed on special occasions, but they "must not be given or accepted as a condition or inducement for recommending the use of any Nestlé product."

Nestlé put the latter form of gift giving under the conceptual umbrella of sampling for the purpose of professional evaluation. "Recognizing that there is a legitimate interest on the part of doctors to familiarize themselves with the characteristics of a specific formula, samples of infant formula to be used for feeding a doctor's own baby may be given."

INFACT rebutted by saying that any gift, by its very nature, is an inducement for the use of a product. Thus, all personal gifts should be disallowed.

As negotiations between Nestlé and the boycott group continued, it was clear that compromise would be difficult to achieve. Yet without compromise, both sides would fail to achieve their respective goals.

DISCUSSION QUESTIONS

1. Evaluate the underlying problems of infant formula use in a risky environment. Then discuss and evaluate the basic strategies applied by Nestlé to deal with these problems and with WHO. Is it a company's responsibility to aggressively discourage its customers from misusing its product?

2. Who should resolve the different and conflicting interpretations of the code? Nestlé itself? The International Nestlé Boycott Committee? Another party?

3. What should Nestlé do regarding national governments? Should it abide by their individual codes, the WHO Code, or its own policies? Is consistency necessary?

4. How should the WHO Code be monitored and enforced? How can Nestlé's headquarters guarantee compliance by its field staff? How can it demonstrate its compliance to external critics and governments?

5. Are possibilities for industrial collaboration still alive? Is it appropriate for an industry organization to monitor compliance?

DOING BUSINESS IN SOUTH AFRICA

In the spring of 1987, institutional investors throughout the United States were forced to confront one of the most difficult, perplexing, and longstanding moral dilemmas: should they support shareholder resolutions asking American companies doing business in South Africa to withdraw and/or divest their holdings? Institutional investors, including churches, pension funds, "socially responsible" mutual funds, and, of course, universities, hold millions of shares of companies that have been doing business in South Africa. The investment managers of these funds are charged with producing financial returns, but they have increasingly been asked to do so within a framework of guidelines that the owners of the stock have developed. In universities, for example, it is often the vote of a committee that determines whether the university's shares will be voted "for," "against," or "abstain" on shareholder resolutions dealing with social issues and concerns. In 1987, as in previous years, these committees, fund managers, and institutional investors grappled with the issue of appropriate corporate involvement in South Africa.

BACKGROUND

One of the most controversial and important issues facing multinational business in the 1980s has been the question of social responsibility and corporate involvement in Third World nations. The focal point of this heated issue for most of the decade has been South Africa. The white South African government has enforced a policy of apartheid, forcing the segregation of the black and colored populations. This policy was challenged for decades by the South Africans living under restrictions, but it received little worldwide attention until 1960, when South African police officers armed with machine guns killed sixty-nine black protestors in Sharpeville. For two decades there have been periodic calls from around the world for political and economic sanctions against the South African government and for boycotts of products and exports, such as diamonds, gold, and other precious metals, from which the government derives a large part of its revenue. People inside and outside the country, including some of the businesses operating within its borders, began to insist that something had to break down the apartheid system.

Initially, in the United States, there were sporadic boycotts of companies doing business in South Africa, and a few random, scattered demonstrations. In 1971, a resolution was filed by the Episcopal Church at the annual shareholders meeting held by General Motors, which then operated a large large automobile manufacturing plant in South Africa. This triggered a response from other church groups, and similar shareholder resolutions were delivered to other corporations in the United States. These early resolutions were voted down overwhelmingly, South Africa maintained its segregationist policies, and American companies continued to operate there, taking advantage of low labor costs and accessibility to local resources and markets. But the moral issue had been raised.

It was not until the 1980s that the issue gained the full attention of both the U.S. government and all the corporations doing business in or with South Africa. Violence and unrest in that country began to escalate; protestors and innocent bystanders alike were being arrested, beaten, and even killed. Their funerals were often the scene of still more violence. By this time, the Free South Africa Movement had mobilized enough support to hold round-the-clock protests outside the South African Embassy in Washington, D.C. And activists unleashed a new weapon against companies doing business in South Africa: pressure from shareholder groups—most notably universities and pension funds—aimed at forcing their boards to divest all stock of companies doing business in that nation.

Not only had the problem become highly visible again, but new questions were raised about the economics of operating in such a turbulent and uncertain environment. Now, corporate boards and management were also saying, "Something must be done. The unanswered question is, what?" As time and circumstances in South Africa have changed, different answers have been offered, some in complete opposition to others, but almost all with valid arguments to support them. As the political situation continues to worsen, there is more pressure for companies to act. When boiled down to the most basic elements, the controversy seems to center around several major questions: Should U.S. corporations stay or leave? If they stay or leave, what kind of gain or loss will result? Who will be hurt and who will benefit?

A Force for Change

Initially, there was almost unanimous agreement among corporate managers that they could be a positive influence on the conditions in South Africa if they stayed. In 1984, almost every corporation, perhaps General Motors and IBM most adamantly, was vowing to stay on the grounds that it could be a force for "constructive change." In the first place, the corporations argued, their South African operations generally accounted for less than 2 percent of their total sales, and only a fraction of this percent was to state and local governments. Thus, they were not making any significant amount of money because of the apartheid system, nor were they supporting it. Secondly, the majority of these companies had signed the Sullivan Principles, created by Reverend Leon Sullivan in the 1970s, and in so doing pledged to maintain desegregated facilities, pay blacks the same wages as white workers and offer promotions to black and colored employees, and contribute to social development by subsidizing schools, housing, and medical facilities. United States corporations in South Africa became model employers and did, in fact, produce many of these positive changes in their areas of operation, even with opposition of the government. In the case of GM, the company's managing director advised the labor minister that he would be desegregating his facilities despite laws that prohibited such a policy. In the end, the labor minister was convinced to look the other way.

In addition to individual contributions benefitting local areas, South Africa as a whole has grown and developed far beyond where it would have been without the presence of multinationals. According to one expert, foreign companies operating in the Eastern Cape Province alone contributed 25 percent of the gross regional product in 1984 and provided 84 percent of the social welfare funds spent outside government budgets.[1]

The general feeling among corporate managements before 1985 was that if the companies pulled out, they would lose their influence and would not be able to make any positive changes. They would only harm those they had the ability to help if they stayed. United States businesses considered themselves both willing and able to challenge apartheid and to continue conducting a healthy business in South Africa. Taking the argument a step further, they considered the problem serious but resolvable and temporary. Thus, especially for companies like Goodyear and GM who had been in the country for 60 or 70 years, the idea of pulling out was not realistic. If they left, they would not be able to return when the situation improved, because European, Asian, or South African concerns by that time would have absorbed the market opportunities. And besides, if they left, activists across the United States might get the idea that they could force any company out of any country for any reason.

Pressure to Withdraw

By 1986, the attitudes of many managers had changed significantly, largely because the situation also had changed. Unrest was increasing, not only in South Africa, but in the United States. Though black activists in South Africa agreed that the multinationals were making valuable contributions, they were becoming increasingly convinced that the only way to pressure the government and the white society would be to cut the country off economically. Isolation would limit the availability of consumer goods to the white community, exposing those in power to the heat of the situation and forcing them to do something to resolve it. Any comforts and benefits the black people received from American companies—only 1 percent of blacks with jobs were employed by American companies, and social welfare funding went mostly to communities housing foreign operations—was only cooling the fire and slowing down the forces of change.

Meanwhile, opposition and activism was increasing in the United States. Sit-ins and mock shantytowns were cropping up on college campuses across the country as students and some professors tried to force their institutions to divest. Though these measures and various stockholder resolutions were now being taken more seriously, new weapons of protest were even more convincing. In the fall of 1986, California Governor George Deukmejian signed a sweeping divestment measure that mandated the sale of $9.5 billion

[1] Roger Thurow, "U.S. Exodus Touches Many South Africans," _Wall Street Journal,_ November 6, 1986, p. 36.

of securities from a total of $22 billion in state retirement funds.[2] Perhaps the most effective measure, however, has been the passage of so-called selective purchasing laws under which public contracts cannot be awarded to companies directly involved in South Africa. Thirty-one local governments and two states enacted such laws by the end of 1986, one of the most stringent of these laws being in Los Angeles. Within four months of its signing, at least six major municipal contracts, representing millions of dollars, had been blocked or held up because the winning bidders had business in South Africa.

At this point, the corporations began to realize that they could not bring about major positive changes in the system. Their efforts only provoked the government into more repressive action and prompted Andries Treurnicht, the leader of the right-wing Conservative Party, to assert that pressures for divestment were "blackmail" and that the ruling whites "will under no circumstances capitulate to a black government, GM or no GM."[3] Forced to realize that they could not "right the wrongs" in the African nation, and that they would lose money on the home front by trying, the corporations reached a new consensus: South Africa was a no-win situation. As one reporter put it, "Perhaps no other market has ever required so much anguish for so little reward as South Africa."[4]

So the exodus began—and then turned to a flood. Of the 325 U.S. companies with factories or offices in South Africa in 1984, 85 had disinvested in one way or another by the end of 1986, or they had announced plans to do so. These included GM, Ford, IBM, Coca-Cola, GTE, Honeywell, Xerox, Bell & Howell, and General Electric, which had started its relationship in 1894 by selling lighting fixtures in Johannesburg. The decision was not easy in any case, and it was usually based on a combination of factors, both moral and economic.

Bell & Howell, for example, had been operating an office equipment subsidiary in South Africa for over ten years when it decided to pull out. Company officials had been proud of the firm's presence; the company was a signatory to the Sullivan Principles, had helped build a local hospital, and had been energetically training and promoting black managers. But after ten years of thriving growth, the subsidiary lost $500,000 for two consecutive years, and in 1985 its sales plunged 27 percent, from $12.9 million to $9.5 million. Meanwhile, back at home, dealers from the company's textbook division began calling the Illinois headquarters in a panic, wondering how to handle the spread of selective purchasing laws. The textbook and information management divisions accounted for 50 percent of Bell & Howell's revenue, and were almost entirely dependent on sales to public schools. "We weren't going to endanger 11,000 employees (in the United States) for the sake of 150 in South Africa," said one company official. "We have a responsibility to our

[2]Michael Isikoff, "Threat to Profits Spurs U.S. Exodus from South Africa," *Washington Post*, November 17, 1986, pp. A-1, A-20.

[3]Roger Thurow, "South Africans Face Hard Time Living without U.S. Companies," *Wall Street Journal*, October 24, 1986, p. 2.

[4]Lee Smith, "South Africa: Time to Stay—Or Go?" *Fortune*, August 4, 1986, pp. 46–48.

shareholders to make money."[5] The company sold its assets for one-fifth their book value, and it withdrew in April 1986.

With companies pulling out one after another, the situation is changing yet again. As some had argued at the outset, the massive retreat did harm those it was designed to help. As the companies pack up and go home, so do the funds they spent on social welfare projects. And those who take over have no motivation or responsibility to continue supporting these projects. So, where children in schools have been receiving extra rations for lunch bought by funds from Ford, now they are back to one slice of bread. Though Ford negotiated "the most generous severance package in history" with its unions[6] and left behind funds for housing development and scholarships, these funds will dry up soon, and no more will be offered. As one former Ford employee put it, "the poverty and suffering in Port Elizabeth brought on by Ford's departure is so pervasive that a blind man can feel it with a stick."[7]

Some think the situation will only get worse. Though the number of jobs lost immediately has been minimal—only 600 out of roughly 8,600 held in the United States companies since 1984—this number is expected to rise dramatically as the general economic situation worsens. The South African economy has been suffering, the rand having devaluated to 30 percent of its 1981 value. Most companies were losing money before their American parents left, and one of the only ways their successors can turn a profit is by cutting jobs and/or wages. If the economy continues to fall, the workers will definitely suffer in the long run. Another former Ford employee was more graphic in his interpretation of the situation: "First comes unemployment. Unemployment leads to suffering. Suffering leads you to do anything, even steal and kill."[8]

As pressure builds in South Africa in response to the exodus, it is also building in the United States. Despite their absence from the immediate area, U.S. companies are not being let off the hook in terms of their effect on conditions in South Africa or their opportunism. Many of the companies that have left since 1985 have not only sold their facilities to their own local managers but have retained licensing and distribution contracts with these successor companies. Thus, in some instances the U.S. parent escapes anti-apartheid pressure at home, improves its image, maintains profitability by selling through low-overhead distribution agreements, and minimizes the risks of operating in an unstable economy. Meanwhile, the subsidiary is not a Sullivan Principles signatory, and it has neither the money nor the motivation to continue supporting social welfare programs. Critics claim, therefore, that the companies have pulled out all their support systems but still insist on turning a profit from a morally unjustifiable system. It is only a

---

[5]Isikoff, op. cit.

[6]Thurow, "U.S. Exodus Touches Many South Africans."

[7]Ibid.

[8]Ibid. See also, Ned Temko, "U.S. Divestment Misses the Mark in South Africa," *The Christian Science Monitor,* April 20, 1987, p. 1, 36.

matter of time, they say, before the new arsenal of weapons used to pressure these multinationals to unload their "direct investments" will be used to pressure them to sever their relations completely.

One company has already felt this pressure. Ashland Oil, which sold its South African Valvoline subsidiary to a European buyer in 1986, maintained a distribution agreement with this new owner through which it sold $300,000 worth of the product annually. In October of that year, the engineering firm of Daniel Mann Johnson & Mendenhall, an Ashland subsidiary in the United States, was to receive a $12-million sewage-treatment contract from the city of Los Angeles. Despite being the preferred bidder, the contract was not offered to DMJM, the mayor's office said, because that company's parents had business ties to South Africa. Less than a week after Ashland learned it was going to lose $12 million to save $300,000, officials from Ashland and DMJM presented the mayor with sworn statements pledging to terminate the South African distributorship within three months and refrain from any future sales to the country. The mayor accepted their promise.

THE 1987 RESOLUTIONS

Within this atmosphere of pressures and tensions, managers and corporations have continued to make decisions, trying to determine the optimal level and nature of their business relations with South Africa. In the spring of 1987, for example, two companies were facing shareholder resolutions on the issue of disinvestment. Caterpillar Inc. was being asked to withdraw from South Africa, and AT&T was being asked to use its "best efforts" to convince Olivetti, in which it is a minority stockholder, to "divest itself of its South African operations." The managements of both companies opposed the proposals.

Caterpillar Inc.

On April 8, 1987, the shareholders of Caterpillar Inc. voted on a resolution that asked that the company "implement a disinvestment program by withdrawal from South Africa and cessation of relationships with it" unless the system of apartheid was statutorily dismantled by the end of May 1987. The resolution was proposed by the New York State Common Retirement Fund, a pension fund for retired New York State employees, and was part of a campaign by the Retirement Fund to get all the companies in its common stock portfolio to withdraw from South Africa. The fund owned 586,000 shares of Caterpillar stock, with a market value in excess of $40 million in the spring of 1987. (See Figure 1.)

This was the first resolution on South Africa that Caterpillar had received and included in its proxy statement. The company had a good record of performance in South Africa and had been awarded a 1986 Sullivan rating of Category IIA ("Making Progress Based on Full Reporting").

Caterpillar's major line of business in South Africa consists of a parts

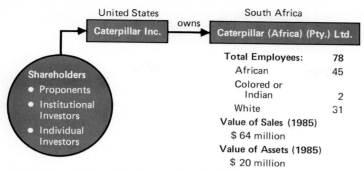

FIGURE 1   Caterpillar Inc. in South Africa.

warehousing operation that supplies replacement parts for Caterpillar construction, earthmoving, and mining machines to its independent dealers. Its
1985 sales in South Africa amounted to about $64 million compared to the
company's 1985 worldwide sales of $6.7 billion. Its South African assets
amount to approximately $20 million. Caterpillar products are primarily sold
through independent dealers in South Africa.

Caterpillar has developed a reputation as an activist company. It is a
member of the Sullivan Signatory Association, the American Chamber of
Commerce in South Africa (Amcham), and the East Rand Industrialists Network. The company's managing director, Ian Leach, is the chairman of Amcham's Social Justice Committee, and the company has supported social justice projects and lobbied the South African government both as an
independent company and as a member of these organizations. A 1987 report
to institutional investors portrayed the company as deeply and substantially
involved in community affairs projects in black communities, supportive of
legal assistance for blacks, and a leader in the development of joint actions
by companies to challenge South African racial policies.[9]

The text of the shareholder resolution and the statements of the proponents and Caterpillar's management are presented below.

EXCERPT FROM CATERPILLAR'S PROXY STATEMENT

Proposal 5—Stockholder Proposal

Mr. Edward V. Regan, the Comptroller of the State of New York, who advises
that he is the sole trustee of the Common Retirement Fund of the State of New
York, which includes 586,000 shares of the Company's common stock, has given
notice that he intends to present for consideration and action at the annual
meeting the following resolution:

---

[9]Investor Responsibility Research Center Inc., "Withdrawal of U.S. Companies from South Africa: Caterpillar Inc.," Proxy Issues Report, Analysis A, Supplement No. 6, Washington, DC:
IRRC, March 11, 1987.

Resolution Proposed by Stockholder

WHEREAS, the civil and human rights of the black population in South Africa continue to be denied under apartheid;

WHEREAS, numerous U.S. corporations subscribing to the Sullivan Principles provide excellent working environments for their employees and lobby the South African Government for the elimination of apartheid, nonetheless this abhorrent system persists as the major tenet of that Government;

WHEREAS, since January 1, 1984, at least 52 American companies have terminated operation in South Africa;

WHEREAS, both Reverend Sullivan and Bishop Tutu have called for the withdrawal of U.S. corporate investment if apartheid is not substantially eliminated during 1987;

WHEREAS, pension funds, endowment funds and other institutional investors are under legal and social pressure to divest their holdings in companies doing business in South Africa;

WHEREAS, the result will be financial harm to the beneficiaries of such funds;

WHEREAS, disinvestment—the withdrawal of corporations from South Africa—can result in real pressure for change.

NOW, THEREFORE, be it resolved that shareholders request the Board of Directors to establish the following policy:

The corporation shall implement a disinvestment program by withdrawal from South Africa and cessation of relationships with it unless by the end of May 1987 the system of apartheid is statutorily dismantled through

a. elimination of social segregation, including the Group Areas Act
b. establishment of equitable national education and health delivery systems
c. elimination of all elements of influx control
d. establishment of freehold rights for all South Africans regardless of race; elimination of residential segregation and removals
e. promotion of franchise rights for all South Africans in an equitable manner
f. elimination of the banning of people and organizations; strengthening the independence of the judicial system; and the unconditional release of political prisoners and detainees and those previously charged with treason

Statement of Proponent

United States corporations should not exist within the framework of apartheid which mandates the denial of basic human and civil rights to the Black majority. The use of violence to quell liberty rather than negotiating peaceful change is contrary to the fundamentals of our democratic society. Although significant strides have been made by U.S. companies toward eliminating apartheid within their South African operations, their efforts to lobby the Government of South Africa for statutory dismantling of apartheid have to date only had minimal effect.

As a pension fund, we do not believe selling shares as a statement of our abhorrence of apartheid will have any effect other than to harm present and future pensioners. On the other hand, most corporations have a very modest presence there and the weak economy and prognosis for future civic and social unrest suggest that disinvestment is a wise business policy.

It is time for shareholders to voice their opposition to the discriminatory practices of South Africa and for the corporation to make known through disinvestment that it cannot coexist with a system of slavery.

Accordingly, we seek the affirmative vote of all shareholders on this resolution.

Statement in Opposition to Proposal

The Board of Directors believes that the proposed disinvestment of Caterpillar's operations in South Africa and cessation of relationships with South Africa would not be a wise response to the challenge posed by the racial policies of the South African Government. We are fully aware of the perspective of the proponent that disinvestment and the cessation of relations is the only response remaining for those opposing the racial policies of the South African Government. We disagree with that conclusion. We do not believe that our presence in South Africa is of no value in the struggle to achieve a more just society there or that the interests of the Company and of those who depend on us should be ignored in weighing the issues.

Caterpillar products are sold throughout the world and we have operations and facilities in many countries. The Company strives to be a good corporate "citizen" of every country in which we do business. We believe that if we are able to operate ethically and honestly in accordance with our Code of Conduct in any country, we can legitimately claim the right to operate. We consider this position to be not only correct, but we believe that there is no other or better principle by which to guide our multinational operations.

Our operations in South Africa have been and are being conducted in full compliance with our Code of Conduct. In addition, we have over the course of many years participated fully in the extraordinary efforts that have been made by the American business community within South Africa to encourage the liberalization of the racial policies of the South African Government. We have taken many initiatives and have been involved in programs to improve the opportunities of South African Blacks. Our small South African work force is racially integrated. We have consistently followed the Sullivan Principles and have received good ratings from the Sullivan organization.

Caterpillar machines are sold in South Africa through an independent dealer which was appointed in 1927. Our in-country South African subsidiary, Caterpillar (Africa) (Proprietary) Limited, conducts a parts warehousing operation supplying replacement parts to the South African dealer and to dealers in several other countries in southern Africa. Caterpillar (Africa) currently employs 78 people. Caterpillar prime products and some componentry are imported directly by our South African dealer and one of its affiliates and are supplied from Caterpillar plants located principally in the United States. In a normal year 650 Caterpillar jobs and 1,300 supplier jobs in the United States are dependent upon exports to South Africa.

There is a large population of Caterpillar machines, built up over many years, operating in South Africa principally in construction, earthmoving and mining applications. We believe that the availability of these machines has been beneficial to all elements of the South African population. The function of our parts operation in South Africa is the support of this large machine population with replacement parts.

We believe we have obligations of both a moral and commercial nature not to abandon our employees in South Africa and the owners of our equipment, who have dealt with us in good faith upon the belief that we would keep faith with and honor our obligations to them. We also have an obligation to those of our employees in the United States and elsewhere whose livelihood depends upon our sales in and to South Africa. We do not believe that we can reasonably be asked to disregard our commercial interests, the interests of our employees in South Africa, the interests of our employees in the United States, and elsewhere, and the interests of those who have purchased our equipment in the belief that we would provide product support for it. We do not consider it to be our role or function as a commercial enterprise to make what is ultimately a political decision to terminate South African operations for reasons which do not pertain directly to our commercial activities.

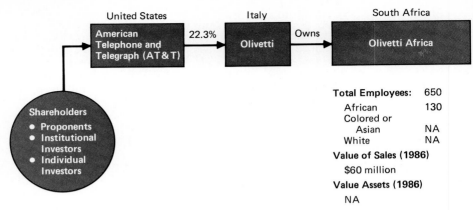

FIGURE 2   AT&T in South Africa.

We welcome the opportunity afforded by the current stockholder proposal to state to our stockholders our position on this difficult and important issue.

The Board of Directors recommends a vote AGAINST this proposal.

American Telephone & Telegraph Co.[10]

On April 15, 1987, shareholders of AT&T were asked to vote on a shareholder resolution sponsored by the Domestic and Foreign Missionary Society of the Episcopal Church, owners of 22,600 shares. The resolution commended AT&T management for its strong antiapartheid stand and requested the company "to use its best efforts, through its shareholdings and board memberships, to convince Olivetti, an Italian company, to divest itself of its South African operations." AT&T opposed the resolution. The company acknowledged that it owned 22.3 percent of Olivetti's outstanding shares, but it noted that this was a noncontrolling interest. While it has talked with Olivetti's management, AT&T argued that it would be inappropriate to intervene formally in Olivetti's South African operations.

AT&T has no direct operations in South Africa. (See Figure 2.) The company has neither a direct investment nor any employees or sales force operating in South Africa. However, in 1983 AT&T reached an agreement with Olivetti, Europe's leading office automation company, to acquire a noncontrolling interest of approximately 25 percent of Olivetti's common stock. This would make AT&T the largest shareholder in Olivetti, with the Olivetti family holding the next largest share of 21 percent. Six of the 21 directors on Olivetti's board are AT&T representatives. The two companies have agreed to distribute and possibly manufacture each other's products, with Olivetti handling AT&T products in several countries, including South Africa. In March 1985, AT&T launched its new line of personal computers and minicomputers in South Africa with Olivetti as the distributor.

[10]Investor Responsibility Research Center Inc., "Withdrawal of U.S. Companies from South Africa: American Telephone and Telegraph Co.," Proxy Issues Report, Analysis A, Supplement No. 14, Washington, DC: IRRC, March 20, 1987.

Olivetti Africa is located in Johannesburg and employs about 650 people, of whom more than 130 are blacks. According to AT&T, the Olivetti Africa operation consists of a small sales-and-service operation and a small assembly line of office products. Olivetti is not a signatory to the Sullivan Principles, although non-U.S. companies are welcome to become signatories. AT&T claimed that Olivetti conforms to the Sullivan Principles and adheres to the European Community code of conduct for companies operating in South Africa.

Olivetti Africa has been a very successful business according to South African business publications. The company had a 51 percent increase in unit sales in 1985 and projected a 30 percent increase for 1986. Olivetti's South African operations generated more than $60 million in annual revenues, out of a worldwide total of more than $4 billion for Olivetti. Olivetti's business strategy in South Africa is to emphasize "local assembly" of computers and to emphasize these local origins in selling to corporate business and government department customers. The company introduced two new products— an automatic teller machine and a consumer-activated terminal—to the South African market in 1986.

The text of the shareholder resolutions and the statements of the proponents and AT&T's management are presented below.

EXCERPT FROM AT&T'S PROXY STATEMENT

Shareholder Proposal 3:

The Domestic and Foreign Missionary Society of the Episcopal Church, 815 Second Avenue, New York, NY 10017, has submitted the following proposal:

"WHEREAS in response to a shareholder proposal submitted by some of its own employees, in April, 1986, AT&T adopted one of the strongest anti-apartheid stands of any major U.S. corporation; and

"WHEREAS although AT&T had not itself operated in South Africa, its new policy includes (i) a ban on sales of any of its products in South Africa; (ii) a pledge not to use any component, including platinum or palladium, imported from South Africa and (iii) a pledge not to provide improved telephone services within South Africa; and

"WHEREAS AT&T owns 22.3% of the stock of Olivetti, an Italian corporation, and has several representatives on Olivetti's Board of Directors, and

"WHEREAS Olivetti has a large presence in South Africa, including the assembling of computers there; and

"WHEREAS Olivetti is cooperating with the South African government's policy of building a fortress South Africa by increasing the 'local content' of its computers sold in South Africa; and

"WHEREAS a number of corporations, including IBM, General Motors, General Electric, Coca-Cola, American Express, Motorola, Martin Marietta, Phibro-Salomon, General Foods, Boeing, Atlantic Richfield, CBS, GTE, General Signal and Bell & Howell have divested themselves of their South African operations:

"THEREFORE, BE IT RESOLVED that the shareholders of AT&T commend its management for the strong anti-apartheid stand it has taken and in particular for the leadership AT&T has shown by the new policies announced in April, 1986; and be it further

"RESOLVED that the shareholders request AT&T to use its best efforts, thru its shareholdings and board memberships, to convince Olivetti to divest itself of its South African operations."

Statement of Support

"We believe that the actions of AT&T in pledging not to use any products (including platinum and palladium) or components imported from South Africa, together with its pledge not to sell any of its own products in South Africa or to assist in improving the South African telecommunications system, are indicative of a management which successfully integrates moral considerations into business decisions, thereby promoting the longer-term best interests of the corporation and of the United States. We therefore believe that management and the Board should be commended for their bold and creative leadership in fighting apartheid by instituting their own ban on imports from and exports to South Africa.

"Although AT&T has not itself operated in South Africa, AT&T does own 22.3% of the stock of Olivetti, an Italian corporation, and has several representatives on the Board of Olivetti. Olivetti has a major corporate presence in South Africa, including the production of computers there. Recently, Olivetti agreed to use more South African parts in the production of Olivetti's computers in South Africa, thereby assisting in developing an indigenous South African computer industry. We believe that Olivetti's presence in South Africa strengthens the apartheid system.

"We recognize that AT&T may be unable to convince Olivetti to leave South Africa. All we ask is that they use their best efforts, through their memberships on the Board of Olivetti and through their stockholdings, to *try* to convince Olivetti to leave South Africa."

Statement in Opposition

Your Directors recommend a vote AGAINST this proposal. Even though this proposal acknowledges AT&T's anti-apartheid stand, AT&T is being asked to use its influence on Olivetti, an Italian company, with regard to Olivetti Africa, a small wholly-owned Olivetti subsidiary located in South Africa, which accounts for approximately 3% of Olivetti's worldwide revenues.

AT&T owns 22.3% of Olivetti's outstanding shares, which is a noncontrolling interest. AT&T has no direct ownership interest in Olivetti Africa. AT&T has discussed its own anti-apartheid position with the management of Olivetti and has secured a commitment that Olivetti will not sell AT&T products in South Africa. Olivetti has informed AT&T that, although the Sullivan Principles are meant to apply only to U.S. companies, Olivetti, while not a signatory, voluntarily abides by them, and that Olivetti has long adhered to the Code of Conduct of European Community Companies doing business in South Africa.

AT&T's management will continue to discuss the situation in South Africa with Olivetti. However, in the opinion of the Directors, it would be inappropriate for AT&T to take formal action through its shareholdings or membership on the Olivetti board to attempt to intervene in the operations of Olivetti's subsidiary. Therefore, they recommend that shareholders vote AGAINST this proposal.

DISCUSSION QUESTIONS

1. Discuss whether U.S. companies have the ability to influence change in South Africa. If so, in what ways can they influence it? Do other foreign companies (for example, British, German, or Japanese companies) have such a power?

2. How is withdrawal of companies likely to affect prospects for political change in South Africa?

3. Some institutional investors have taken the position that because the disinvestment by such giants as IBM, GE, and Eastman Kodak did not lead to political change, the best available course is to strengthen support for activist companies such as Caterpillar. Evaluate this argument.

4. Is it appropriate for AT&T to use its influence to try to persuade Olivetti to withdraw from South Africa? Prepare arguments for and against such actions.

Epilogue

On June 3, 1987, the Reverend Leon Sullivan, the Philadelphia minister who created a code of conduct for U.S. companies doing business in South Africa, called on those companies to sell their investments there and end all commercial ties with that country. Reverend Sullivan called for complete withdrawal of U.S. companies within nine months.[11]

Leon Sullivan's campaign to break down apartheid through peaceful means and corporate influence appeared to have failed. The code of conduct that he created a decade earlier had drawn widespread support from the American business community operating in South Africa, in part because it had strong support from institutional investors in the United States. At his June 3 press conference, Reverend Sullivan said that of the 200 U.S. corporations operating in South Africa, 127 subscribed to the code. Despite their "notable record," however, their collective commitment had failed to undermine apartheid. Reverend Sullivan said: "Every American moral, economic and political force must be brought to bear to help influence the South African government to move toward dismantling the apartheid system while there is still time."[12] Despite the strides that companies had taken to expand equal opportunities, he continued, "The main pillars of apartheid still remain, and blacks are still denied basic human rights in their own country and are denied the right to vote."[13]

---

[11]Barnaby J. Feder, "Sullivan Asks End of Business Links with South Africa," *New York Times*, June 4, 1987, p. A–1.

[12]Ibid.

[13]Ibid.

In addition to withdrawal, Reverend Sullivan maintained that the most effective course for American companies was to reinvest in countries around South Africa while selling their South African operations only to buyers who would promote equal rights and black participation in ownership. Acknowledging that corporate power alone was insufficient leverage to move the South African government, Reverend Sullivan also called for a United States embargo on trade with South Africa and asked President Reagan to sever diplomatic relations.

Reactions

Reverend Sullivan's call for a corporate pullout drew a number of immediate reactions. A U.S. State Department spokesperson said that while the U.S. government has "enormous respect for Reverend Sullivan and the work he has done," the administration opposed the withdrawal option. "We deeply regret his announcement today. . . . Despite the difficulties on the ground in South Africa, we firmly believe that it is now more important than ever for U.S. firms to stay and work for an end to apartheid."[14]

The South African government's reaction was highly critical. The Foreign Minister said that Sullivan's decision was "neither in the interests of the workers nor of the United States itself. . . . The South African Government cannot allow itself to be threatened in this way. The Reverend Sullivan suffers from a persecution complex for which, apparently, nothing can be done."[15] A spokesperson for the reformist Progressive Federal Party called the Sullivan action "short-sighted" and "not calculated to encourage peaceful change."[16] A spokesperson for the African National Congress, the main guerrilla-backed nationalist movement, welcomed the Sullivan decision.

Activists applauded Reverend Sullivan's call for a pullout. Timothy Smith, director of the Interfaith Center on Corporate Responsibility, an organization sponsored by a broad coalition of American churches, said: "I think U.S. companies remaining in South Africa are really standing in a morally exposed position right now."[17]

The steering committee of the U.S. Corporate Council on South Africa, which consists of twelve chief executive officers of the largest multinational corporations based in the United States, issued a statement that expressed regret at Reverend Sullivan's decision: "The decisive arena of this historic struggle is inside South Africa itself, and U.S. corporate resources can be most effectively brought to bear there."[18] Allen Murray, Mobil's top executive said: "We owe a great debt to Leon Sullivan, but we will now have to carry out the Sullivan Principles without him."[19]

[14]Ibid., p. D-6.

[15]John D. Battersby, "South Africa Reacts Angrily to Sullivan Call," *New York Times,* June 4, 1987, p. D–6.

[16]Ibid.

[17]Feder, op. cit.

[18]Ibid.

[19]Ibid.

Asked if those principles could, in fact, go on without him, Reverend Sullivan replied "Well, they kept the Ten Commandments without Moses."[20]

QUESTIONS

1. Discuss the impact of Reverend Sullivan's new position on U.S. companies still operating in South Africa. Should they now withdraw from that country? If they decide to stay, should they continue to follow the Sullivan Principles, even if the South African government objects?

2. Discuss the strategic implications of Reverend Sullivan's decision. Does this action change the attractiveness of the South African business environment? Can the "business aspects" of operating in South Africa be separated from the ethical and political aspects?

3. Consider the position of an institutional investor—a pension fund or church endowment—that voted for Caterpillar's management in the main case. Now that Reverend Sullivan has altered his position, should the institutional investor support Caterpillar's continued activism in South Africa? What alternative actions can the investor take at this time?

[20]Ibid.

BHOPAL[1]

It began without warning at 12:56 A.M., December 3, 1984. As 900,000 people slept in and around the city and slums of Bhopal, India, a cloud of toxic gas consisting of methyl isocyanate (MIC) leaked from a storage tank at a Union Carbide pesticide plant. The evening's brisk winds pushed the cloud, within minutes, through the nearby dwellings, and within an hour agony had engulfed the lives of tens of thousands of Indians. Hundreds died in their beds, most of them children and the elderly weakened by hunger and frailty. Thousands more awoke to a nightmare of near suffocation, blindness, and chaos. They stumbled into the streets, choking, vomiting, sobbing, their eyes burning. Dogs, cows, and buffalos were stricken. Chaos filled the city, as death and panic spread.

By week's end more than 2,500 people were dead. Over 150,000 received medical care in the first week, and twice that many were treated by year's end. It was the world's worst industrial disaster. Two years later, lingering effects were still easily seen in Bhopal. Many residents suffered shortness of breath, eye irritation, and depression, and they continued to flock to hospitals, clinics, and rehabilitation centers. As many as 40,000 were estimated to be permanently injured from inhaling the poisonous fumes; many of these were so weakened as to be incapable of working or earning their livelihood.

Union Carbide Corporation

At the time of the accident, Union Carbide was the nation's third largest chemical producer, after Du Pont and Dow Chemical. The firm earned revenues of over $9 billion in 1982 and in 1983, though its net income fell from $310 million in 1982 to $79 million in 1983, which was its poorest performance in over a decade. In December 1983, Union Carbide had assets exceeding $10 billion, 99,506 employees worldwide, and a book value per share of $69.95.

In 1984 its strategic focus shifted away from the big cash generators of basic petrochemicals, which were swamped by global overcapacity, and metals and carbons products, which were hurt by poor conditions in the beleaguered steel industry. The firm announced in October 1984 an increased concentration of investment in three other lines of business—consumer products, industrial gases, and technology services and specialty products—all earmarked as growth areas. Just as this new corporate strategy was unfolding, the Bhopal disaster occurred.

Union Carbide's operations in India go back to the beginning of this century, when it began marketing its products there. In 1934, an assembly plant for batteries was opened in Calcutta. By 1983, Union Carbide had fourteen plants in India that manufactured chemicals, pesticides, batteries, and other products. The plant in Bhopal was built in 1969 to formulate a range

---

[1]This case was prepared by James Weber in collaboration with the book's authors. Information was drawn from the following sources: *Wall Street Journal, Business Week, Time, Newsweek, New York Times,* Union Carbide Corporation news releases and annual reports, and Paul Shrivastava, *Bhopal: Anatomy of a Crisis,* Cambridge, MA: Ballinger, 1987.

of pesticides and herbicides derived from a carbaryl base. In 1979, the company commissioned the Bhopal plant to manufacture MIC. At the time of its construction, the plant stood well away from most of Bhopal's population, but in intervening years many poor people had settled near the plant.

Union Carbide was one of a few firms in India in which the parent company was permitted to hold a majority interest. Normally investors are limited to minority ownership of equity in Indian companies, but the Indian government waived this requirement in the case of Union Carbide because of the sophistication of its technology and the company's potential for export. Union Carbide Corporation owned 50.9 percent of the Indian subsidiary, with the remaining 49.1 percent distributed among Indian shareholders. However, the involvement of the parent company in the Bhopal plant was limited, and the operations were supervised and staffed by Indian workers.

The Chemical Industry and Public Safety

Every day in the United States the chemical and petroleum industries produce about 275 million gallons of gasoline, 2.5 million pounds of pesticides and herbicides, and nearly 723,000 tons of dangerous wastes. Many of these hazardous materials, chiefly petrochemicals, are shipped across the country. Yet, in spite of the high potential for disastrous consequences, the safety record of these industries in the United States is exceptionally good. The chemical industry's safety record in 1983 showed 5.2 reported occupational injuries per 100 workers versus a 7.5 average for all manufacturing.

Although chemical companies insisted that they applied the same standard of safety and environmental protection in foreign facilities as at home, leading chemical industry executives were aware that, when operating in a Third World country, they faced many problems in attempting to reach the same standard of safety achieved in the United States. Most experts agreed that chemical companies building plants in the Third World rarely were seeking to dodge environmental rules at home. Nevertheless, weaker regulations and enforcement abroad, when combined with difficulties in maintaining quality control, posed worrisome possibilities for disaster.

Host government efforts to respond to the growing need for safety and environmental safeguards had been minimal. The number of environmental control agencies in developing countries had soared from 11 in 1972 to 110 in 1984. However, many of these were small, underfinanced, and only meagerly supported by their governments. In India, for example, the federal environmental department had a staff of about 150 persons, compared with the United States Environmental Protection Agency's headquarters staff of 4,400. A study by the International Labor Organization found that labor inspectors in developing countries had little status, poor pay, and huge territories to cover.

These conditions had contributed to disasters prior to the Bhopal tragedy. In Mexico City, November 1984, liquefied gas tanks exploded in a storage facility. The resulting fire took 452 lives and injured 4,248, and 1,000 people were reported missing. In Cubatao, Brazil, February 1984, gasoline from a leaky pipeline exploded into a giant fireball that killed at least 500 people. Near San Carlos de la Rapita, Spain, July 1978, an overloaded 38-ton tank truck carrying 1,518 cubic feet of combustible propylene gas skidded around a bend in the road and slammed into a wall. Flames shot 100 feet into the air, engulfed a tourists' campsite, and killed 215 people.

These and other incidents demonstrated the broad potential for danger since few of the developing nations had the elaborate system of safety regulations and inspections found in the United States. Yet workplaces in the Third World were fast acquiring many of the same kinds of complex industrial processes present in the United States. An environmentalist commented, "We're thrusting 20th-century technology into countries which aren't yet ready to deal with it. We've gotten away with it so far because there have been only minor tragedies. But the Union Carbide accident has really torn apart the whole cover on this, and things will never be the same again."[2]

Union Carbide's Assistance Program

As soon as the wire services carried news of the spreading tragedy in Bhopal, Union Carbide called an immediate halt to worldwide production and shipment of MIC. A company official explained that the firm took this precautionary step to determine if safety processes and devices were fully operational at their plants worldwide. To offset community fears near one of its MIC-producing plants in West Virginia, the company launched a public relations campaign that stressed the plant's excellent safety record and efficient safety equipment and procedures. On the day following the tragedy, Warren M. Anderson, Union Carbide's chairman, flew to India to provide relief and compensation to the victims. On December 6, Union Carbide employees around the world stopped work at noon to join in a moment of silence to show their grief and sorrow for those afflicted in the Bhopal disaster.

According to a Union Carbide fact sheet, the company responded to the Bhopal accident in three phases: immediate responses, intermediate responses, and long-term relief efforts.

Immediate relief efforts included Warren Anderson's trip to Bhopal on December 4; sending internationally recognized pulmonary and eye experts to treat survivors; dispatching a five-person medical relief and technical investigation team to Bhopal; offering a $1-million contribution to the Bhopal Relief Fund; contributing (through Union Carbide India) medicine, medical equipment, blankets, and clothing; and treating 6,000 persons at the plant's dispensary immediately after the incident.

Following these initial steps, the corporation focused on "intermediate" needs. These included collecting $120,000 through the firm's Employee Relief Fund; donating $5,000 toward a Bhopal eye center; sending additional donations of food, medicine, and clothing; and offering financial support for community rebuilding projects. However, the Indian subsidiary found its offers—of fully equipped medical care and research centers; facilities for re-

[2]*Wall Street Journal*, December 13, 1984, p. 1.

habilitation, vocational education, and job training; a mobile medical van; and educational scholarships—rejected or ignored by the state government of Madhya Pradesh where Bhopal was located. It was at this time that Union Carbide Chairman Anderson commented that the company was in a "negotiation mode."

According to Union Carbide, the company's long-term relief efforts were aimed at meeting health and welfare needs. United States Federal District Court Judge John Keenan, who held temporary legal authority over Bhopal matters, ordered the firm to disburse $5 million of Union Carbide's funds to assist survivors. Union Carbide began working with American investors to establish a prototype factory in Bhopal to manufacture low-cost prefabricated housing, but this project was later abandoned. Union Carbide India proposed to build dwellings for 500 residents, plus a job training center, a school, and a community center. In conjunction with Arizona State University, the United States firm developed a project to establish a Bhopal Technical and Vocational Training Center; this effort was not welcomed by the Madhya Pradesh state authorities who subsequently accused the project's management of fraudulent use of Union Carbide funds.

In addition, a pledge of $10 million was made by Union Carbide to establish a hospital in Bhopal, modeled on United States Veterans Administration hospitals that had been initially created to care for war-injured personnel. Some observers believed that this gesture was part of Union Carbide's efforts to establish a stronger negotiating position regarding legal settlements.

Explanations and Causes

The safety of the plant's design and operations was the subject of an internal report by Union Carbide (U.S.A.) in May 1982. Ten major deficiencies were reported. They included a potential for materials to leak from storage tanks, the possibility of dust explosions, problems with safety valves and instruments, and a high rate of personnel turnover at the Bhopal plant.

Union Carbide India responded to this report with an "action plan" to correct the deficiencies. Progress in upgrading the plant was described in three separate reports. The final report, dated June 1984, said that virtually all the problems at the plant had been corrected. The two remaining deficiencies, however, involved the operation of a safety valve used in the methyl isocyanate manufacturing process and the possibility that the tank storing MIC could be mistakenly overfilled. The report concluded that work on these two deficiencies was almost complete and depended on delivery of a control valve which was expected in July.

Human factors may have played a role. Employee morale was said to be low; some believed there were not enough staff, that training was inadequate, and that managerial experience was insufficient.

Various strategic factors and operating policies and procedures may have contributed to the accident and its aftermath. The Bhopal plant represented less than 3 percent of the firm's worldwide profits and thus was not critically important. Union Carbide's top management endorsed a plan in July 1984 to sell the plant because of the declining and increasingly competitive pesticides market. The facility had had eight plant managers in fifteen years, and it lacked contingency plans for dealing with major accidents. Indian insistence, like that in other developing nations, on placing operational control in the hands of host-country nationals may have worked perversely to reduce home-country headquarters control of the plant.

Finally, technological factors may have been involved. Various experts pointed to flaws in plant or equipment design, defective or malfunctioning equipment, the use of contaminated or substandard supplies and raw materials, and reliance on incorrect operating procedures. These failures might have been inadvertent or deliberate, or they might have been caused by negligence.[3]

Several investigations were conducted, and accusations surfaced regarding the cause of the accident.

On December 20, 1984, Union Carbide researchers arrived in Bhopal and conducted a three-month-long effort to reconstruct the sequence of events leading to the accident. They began by drilling into the remains of the MIC storage tank. Samples were sealed in twenty small glass vials and carried by courier to a West Virginia Union Carbide laboratory. The team's report was released in March 1985. It concluded that multiple systems failure and lapses, themselves linked to neglect of safety, maintenance, and operating procedures, appeared to have combined to cause the accident. The report stated that a safety valve opened as a result of a chemical reaction in the storage tank that contained 90,000 pounds of MIC. The valve remained open for nearly two hours before it reseated. During that period over 50,000 pounds of MIC in vapor and liquid form were discharged through the safety valve.

Other experts thought that the plant's scrubber system was not functioning or that the MIC gas leaked into the air through a loosened valve or ruptured tank without ever reaching the scrubber. The scrubber, a cylinder that washed the MIC with a caustic soda solution and converted it into safer substances, was the main safety device for preventing MIC gas from getting into the atmosphere.

In August 1985, Union Carbide suggested yet another possible cause of the disaster: sabotage. The company called attention to a wire service report that a group of Sikh extremists had claimed credit for the disaster. Sikh factions were pitted against the Gandhi government in a bitter political struggle that earlier had included armed repression of the Sikhs and the assassination by Sikhs of Prime Minister Indira Gandhi, mother of the present prime minister. The company said that it did not necessarily endorse the wire service report. A Union Carbide representative later said that the company believed that a large volume of water had been deliberately introduced into the storage tank, perhaps by a disgruntled employee rather than by a Sikh extremist. Previously the company had said the water could have been inadvertently allowed into the tank. In June 1987, Union Carbide claimed it

[3]For a discussion of these human, organizational, and technological possibilities, see Paul Shrivastava, *Bhopal: Anatomy of a Crisis*, Cambridge, MA: Ballinger, 1987, pp. 48–57.

had found evidence that several Bhopal plant employees had attempted to cover up their knowledge of the accident's start. This charge of sabotage and attempted cover-up was vehemently disputed by the former employees and by Indian government officials.[4]

The Role of the Indian Government

The Indian government, like Union Carbide, was active in responding to the anguish and devastation following the tragedy. In his first official pronouncement regarding the disaster, Prime Minister Rajiv Gandhi called the incident "horrifying" and established a $400,000 government emergency relief fund. A year later the Indian government had spent nearly $40 million on food and medical care for the 300,000 victims.[5]

Besides giving direct assistance the Indian government took an active legal role. Responding to the earliest reports of the tragedy, police arrested five plant officials on negligence charges and sealed off the factory. More arrests followed. On December 7, as Warren Anderson stepped out of the plane at the Bhopal airport, police arrested him on charges of death by negligence, criminal conspiracy, causing air pollution, and killing livestock. Two of the firm's top Indian executives were seized when they arrived at the airport intending to investigate the disaster. After Anderson posted $2,500 bail, he was ordered to leave the country.

On December 6, the Indian government, on behalf of the Indian people stricken by the tragedy, filed a criminal complaint against Union Carbide's Indian unit over the poisonous gas leak. Pursuant to the complaint, Indian police conducted an investigation to determine whether to prosecute. State authorities closed the plant in December 1984, declaring that it would never be allowed to reopen.

In March 1985, Union Carbide began talks with the Indian government in an attempt to resolve the growing number of liability claims against the firm which totalled over $15 billion in compensation and punitive damages. In an interview published in the *Financial Times of London,* Rajiv Gandhi said his government had rejected as inadequate a settlement offer by Union Carbide. The offer included an immediate payment of $60 million and an additional $180 million over the next thirty years. Three days later the Indian government filed suit against Union Carbide (U.S.A.).

Other negotiations also were under way between Union Carbide and lawyers for the Bhopal victims. On March 23, 1986, they agreed to settle the litigation claims, with Union Carbide to pay $350 million. When Indian government officials heard of this agreement, they proclaimed, "It has to be pointed out that there cannot be any settlement without agreement by India."[6] The Indian response further clarified that Union Carbide's proposed settlement was simply inadequate. There was pressure on the government

[4]*International Herald Tribune,* June 24, 1987, p. 2.

[5]*Business Week,* November 25, 1985, p. 96.

[6]*Business Week,* April 7, 1986, p. 39.

to push hard with its demands. A group of activists, the Poison Gas Episode Struggle Front, was calling for the nationalization of Union Carbide's Indian factories and for punitive damages equal to the total assets of the parent Union Carbide Corporation.

A critical legal question emerged shortly after the Bhopal tragedy. Should the claims be heard in American courts, since Union Carbide was the majority owner of the plant where the disaster occurred and a United States–based corporation? Or should the claims be settled in Indian courts, since the disaster occurred on India's territory?

The lawyers for the victims and the Indian government favored a trial in United States courts, presumably because these courts traditionally delivered larger awards to accident victims and delivered them faster than their Indian counterparts. Union Carbide understandably sought to have the claims tried in the Indian courts. The landmark decision handed down in May 1986 by United States Federal District Judge John F. Keenan, which had significant implications for all United States–based multinational corporations, ruled that the claims were to be decided in India, not in the United States.

Judge Keenan stated that to retain the litigation in the United States would be an example of imperialism, where an established sovereign inflicts its rules, its standards, and its values on a developing nation. The Indian courts, according to Keenan, have the proven capacity to mete out fair and equal justice.

After this court decision was handed down, the Indian government found itself in a weakened negotiating position. As settlement talks dragged on, the government took another bold step. On September 8, 1986, it sued Union Carbide in a Bhopal district court for an unspecified amount of damages arising from the poison gas leak. The suit said the firm failed to provide the required standard of safety at its Bhopal plant. It also blamed the company for highly dangerous and defective plant conditions. Two months later the Indian government disclosed that it would seek at least $3 billion from Union Carbide.

Wider Ramifications

Following the tragedy in Bhopal, fears spread through the community near Union Carbide's West Virginia plant, producer of MIC and other potentially hazardous chemicals. Three days after the Bhopal tragedy a gas bomb explosion rocked a Union Carbide plant in West Germany. The words "Poison Killer" and "Swine" were spray-painted on the plant's walls. A shipment of MIC, bound for France, was barred by the French Environment Ministry. Several European government agencies balked at continuing negotiations with Union Carbide over proposed plant construction plans.

Initially, the Union Carbide employees showed their sympathy and support for the tragedy's victims by contributing $150,000. Two years after the tragedy, a survey of Union Carbide employees in the United States discovered that many did not know how much was collected or what was done with the funds. Few knew, or seemed to care, about the progress of lawsuits or negotiations with the Indian government. They seemed to feel no personal responsibility for the tragedy and believed that the company was a victim of circumstances. "India forced the company not only to build a plant there but also to give control to its local subsidiary. We're bitter. A few incompetent, casual Indians put a black mark on my name," claimed one United States Union Carbide employee.[7]

The "black mark" also extended to the chemical industry and to United States–based multinationals operating in developing countries. "If I were a corporate manager, I would reexamine my profile of global activities, and in some cases I might pull out some products or processes where the risk is great and the profit marginal," said Ingo Walter, a professor at New York University's Graduate School of Business.[8]

These thoughts were echoed throughout the chemical industry. Ray R. Irani, president of Occidental Petroleum, said that the Bhopal incident meant that corporations must evaluate the reasons for establishing such operations in underdeveloped nations and managers must search their souls as to the benefits to the corporation and to the country. Both Du Pont and Dow Chemical noted difficulties in conducting hazardous operations abroad, and many chemical companies reviewed their safety operations and emergency response procedures, reduced the storage of some toxic chemicals, reevaluated the risks of operating in developing countries, and initiated programs for informing area residents about hazards. Union Carbide announced in March 1985 that it was tripling the number of safety inspections of all its plants.

These changes in corporate operations were a result of various external pressures. The insurance industry sharply reduced coverage for toxic waste sites while increasing premiums. This placed the chemical industry in a bind since the law required them to buy insurance, but the insurance companies either would not sell it or its cost was prohibitive.

Governments of several Third World countries imposed new curbs on chemical firms. For example, in Brazil, the world's fourth-largest user of agricultural chemicals, state authorities immediately restricted use of the deadly methyl isocyanate. The European Community's regulation, developed in response to a 1976 dioxin accident in Italy, required chemical plant operators to demonstrate that they had adequate safety measures and emergency plans and to inform residents in danger zones of the potential perils of accidents. In Germany new demands were made for stricter controls or even for plant closures.

Thousands of Americans living near chemical plants worried about their safety. The push for "right-to-know" laws increased. These laws require companies to list and label all toxic or potentially hazardous workplace chemicals, so that employees, transport companies, and public safety officials are informed about actual and potential risks. The city of Akron, Ohio, passed such a law just one week after the Bhopal disaster, and similar measures

---

[7]*Business Week,* November 25, 1985, p. 45.

[8]*Business Week,* December 24, 1984, p. 27.

were considered in hundreds of other communities and in nineteen state legislatures. Studies to develop federal legislation were begun shortly after the tragedy. "There's definitely heightened awareness," said Sandy Buchanan, director of the Toxic Action Project in Ohio. "Bhopal made it difficult for anyone to argue against people needing to know."[9]

The Long-Term Effects on Union Carbide

Bhopal weakened Union Carbide in a number of ways. In the week following the accident, the company's stock dropped to $35 per share from $49, wiping out 27 percent, or almost $1 billion, of its market value. Eighteen months later, Union Carbide announced a massive restructuring plan. The plan involved several plant closings and the dismissal of 4,000 employees, about 15 percent of the company's white-collar work force.

Analysts were divided on whether the restructuring was primarily due to the massive Bhopal lawsuit claims filed against the company or to an attempted takeover by GAF Corporation. Some observers thought Union Carbide's lowered stock value had increased its attractiveness as a takeover target. In August 1985, GAF increased its stake in Union Carbide to 7.1 percent, and rumors of a takeover circulated on Wall Street. In January 1986, GAF formally offered $5 billion for Union Carbide.

Union Carbide suppressed the hostile takeover with a defense that was upheld in the courts. The company's defense included putting on the selling block one of the firm's prime assets, the $2-billion Consumer Products Division, doubling Union Carbide's debt to $4.5 billion, and cutting the company's equity value to one-fourth of what it had been. Though Union Carbide claimed victory in this fight, the company emerged as a shadow of its former self.

Two-and-a-half years after the accident, negotiations to settle the potentially devastating lawsuits were stalled. The potential financial impact of a negotiated settlement or of court awards favorable to the claimants placed Union Carbide in a very precarious financial position. The possibility of being accused of "selling out" to a foreign multinational corporation made a negotiated out-of-court settlement politically risky for the Indian government. In an effort to restart the negotiations, Bhopal District Court Judge M. W. Deo called on both Union Carbide and the Indian government to make substantial payments to the victims of the disaster. Judge Deo said that his move reflected a fear that years of litigation would prevent aid from ever reaching the survivors.

DISCUSSION QUESTIONS

1. Assess Union Carbide's social strategy both before and after the Bhopal accident. Identify the company's strategic goals prior to the accident, and tell

[9]*Business Week,* February 18, 1985, p. 36.

how they were changed after the accident. Were these goals appropriate for the company and for its stakeholders?

2. Develop a stakeholder map for Union Carbide, based on the Bhopal incident. Include each stakeholder's major interest, and rank the stakeholders in terms of their relative power. How would such information help Union Carbide management in dealing with this crisis?

3. Of the various possible causes of the accident, which one do you believe to have been the most important? What could Union Carbide management have done to reduce or eliminate this causal factor? In your opinion, why did the company not take such action before the accident?

4. What are the main ethical issues of this case? Show how you would use utilitarian reasoning, rights reasoning, and justice reasoning to analyze these ethical issues.

GLOSSARY

Acid rain. Naturally occurring rain containing dilute solutions of nitric acid and sulfuric acid that are formed when nitrogen oxides and sulfur oxides combine with atmospheric water vapor.

Acquisition. (See **Merger.**)

Ad hoc coalition. Any informal and temporary group organized to lobby for or against a law or government regulation.

Administrative costs. The direct costs incurred in running government regulatory agencies, including salaries of employees, equipment, supplies, and other such items. (Compare with **Compliance costs.**)

Administrative learning. A stage in the development of social responsiveness within a company during which managers and supervisors learn the new practices necessary for coping with social problems and pressures.

Advocacy advertising. (See **Public issue advertising.**)

Affirmative action. A positive and sustained effort by an organization to identify, hire, train if necessary, and promote minorities, women, and members of other groups who are underrepresented in the organization's workforce.

Agrarian society. A society in which agricultural activities dominate work and employ the largest proportion of the labor force.

Ambient air quality standard. (See **Environmental-quality standard.**)

American dream. An ideal goal or vision of life in the United States, usually including material abundance and maximum freedom.

Annual meeting. A yearly meeting called by a corporation's board of directors for purposes of reporting to the company's stockholders on the current status and future prospects of the firm.

Biodegrade. A process of natural decomposition in which a substance is slowly absorbed back into the natural environment.

Biosphere. The land, air, water, and natural conditions on which life on earth depends.

Biotechnology. The use and combination of various sciences, including biochemistry, genetics, microbiology, ecology, recombinant DNA, and others, to invent and develop new and modified life forms for applications in medicine, industry, farming, and other areas of human life.

Blowing the whistle. (See **Whistle blowing.**)

Board of directors. A group of persons elected by shareholder votes to be responsible for directing the affairs of a corporation, establishing company objectives and policies, selecting top-level managers, and reviewing company performance.

Bottom line. Business profits or losses, usually reported in figures on the last or bottom line of a company's income statement.

Bribe. Something of value given to someone in power to materially influence a decision favorable to the briber.

Bubble concept. A pollution control plan that determines compliance by measuring combined total emissions from an industrial installation, rather than from each of the plant's individual pollution sources.

Business. The activity of organizing resources in order to produce and distribute goods and services for society.

Business and society. The study of the relationship of business with its entire social environment.

Business ethics. The application of general ethical principles to business behavior.

Business infrastructure. The basic underlying structure of facilities and services essential to the operation of a market-based business system, including a monetary system, standard weights and measures, transportation networks, a legal system to make and enforce laws, and similar components.

Cash cow. A company that generates large amounts of cash or liquid funds as a result of its normal operations.

Central state control. A socioeconomic system in which political, social, and economic power is concentrated in a central government that makes all fundamental policy decisions for the society.

Certificate of incorporation. A certificate, usually issued by a state government, authorizing a group of individuals to establish a business in the legal form of a corporation. (See **Federal chartering.**)

Charity principle. The idea that individuals and business firms should give voluntary aid and support to society's unfortunate or needy persons, as well as to other (nonprofit) organizations that provide community services.

Codetermination. A system of corporate governance providing for labor representation on a company's board of directors.

Collective bargaining. The legally protected right of employees to organize for purposes of bargaining with an employer concerning wages, working conditions, and benefits.

Command-and-control system. A pollution control system based on government regulations, environmental and emission standards, and legal penalties for noncompliance.

Commercial speech (in media presentations). The messages contained in paid commercial advertisements. Courts have ruled that commercial speech is not a form of free speech protected by the United States Constitution.

Community-employee-owned firm (CEF). A company owned wholly or in part by a combination of its employees and other persons and groups in the firm's local community.

Community relations. The involvement of business with the communities in which it conducts operations.

Competition. A struggle to survive and excel. In business, different firms compete with one another for the customer's dollars.

Compliance costs. The costs incurred by business and other organizations in complying with government regulations, such as the cost of pollution control machinery or disposing of toxic chemical wastes. (Compare with **Administrative costs.**)

Compound growth (economic; population). Growth (in production or population) that incorporates periodic increases into the (production or population) base, thereby compounding or multiplying the amount of growth experienced.

Concentration (corporate, economic, industrial, market). When relatively few companies are responsible for a large proportion of economic activity, production, or sales.

Concession bargaining. Bargaining between a labor union and an employer to reduce monetary benefits, change work rules, and/or modify fringe benefits in an existing labor contract in order to improve the competitive standing of the employing firm.

Consumer movement. (See **Consumerism.**)

Consumer responsibilities. The obligations of consumers to act fairly, intelligently, honestly, and helpfully toward sellers.

Consumer rights. The legitimate claims of consumers to safe products and services, adequate information, free choice, a fair hearing, and competitive prices.

Consumer sovereignty. The idea that consumers, through their purchases, decide what will be produced by business firms.

Consumerism. A social movement that seeks to augment the rights and powers of consumers.

Corporate culture. The traditions, customs, values, and approved ways of behaving that prevail in a corporation.

Corporate governance. Any structured system for allocating power in a corporation that determines how the company is to be governed.

Corporate legitimacy. Public acceptance of the corporation as an institution that contributes to society's well-being.

Corporate social involvement. The interaction of business corporations with society.

Corporate social policy. A policy or a group of policies in a corporation that define the company's purposes, goals, and programs regarding one or more social issues or problems.

Corporate social responsibility. A business obligation to seek socially beneficial results along with economically beneficial results in its actions.

Corporate social responsiveness. The ability of a corporation to relate its operations and policies to the social environment in ways that are mutually beneficial to the company and to society.

Corporate stakeholder. A person or group affected by a corporation's policies and actions.

Corporate strategic management. Planning, directing, and managing a corporation for the purpose of helping it achieve its basic purposes and long-run goals.

Corporate strategic planning. A process of formulating a corporation's basic purpose, long-run goals, and programs intended to achieve the company's purposes and goals.

Corporate takeover. The acquisition, usually by merger, of one corporation by another.

Corrective advertising. Advertising sometimes required by government that is intended to correct misleading claims made by the advertiser in earlier ads.

Cost-benefit analysis. A systematic method of calculating the costs and benefits of a project or activity that is intended to produce benefits.

Cost effective. Carrying out an activity by prudent and efficient use of resources.

Craft union. A union whose members possess a particular skill or craft, such as carpentry or plumbing.

Crisis management. The use of a special temporary team to help a company cope with an unusual emergency situation that may threaten the company in serious ways.

Crossownership (of media). The simultaneous ownership by one company of several different types of media, such as television stations, radio stations, newspapers, magazines, book publishing companies, and motion picture studios.

Cultural distance. The amount of difference in customs, attitudes, and values between two social systems.

Cultural shock. A person's disorientation and insecurity caused by the strangeness of a different culture. (Also known as _culture shock._)

Debt rescheduling. Rearranging the dates and periodic payments to be made on a debt owed to a creditor (which usually is a bank).

Deregulation. The removal or scaling down of regulatory authority and regulatory activities of government.

Discrimination (in jobs or employment). Unequal treatment of employees based on *non-job-related* factors such as race, sex, age, national origin, religion, color, and physical or mental handicap.

Disinvestment. Withdrawing a direct investment of funds and other resources that are used to operate a business or a portion of a business. A company that withdraws its operations from South Africa normally disinvests in this manner.

Divestment. Withdrawing and shifting to other uses the funds that a person or group has invested in the securities (stocks, bonds, notes, etc.) of a company. Institutional investors sometimes have divested the securities of companies doing business in South Africa.

Dividend. A return-on-investment payment made to the owners of shares of corporate stock at the discretion of the company's board of directors.

Ecological balance. A natural equilibrium maintained among any group of living things and the environment they occupy.

Ecology. The study of how living things—plants and animals—interact with one another and with their environment.

Ecosystem. The plants and animals in their natural environment, living together as an interdependent system.

Electoral politics. Political activities undertaken by business and other interest groups to influence the outcome of elections to public office.

Emission standard. A legally defined, specific amount of a pollutant permitted to be *discharged* from a polluting source in a given period of time. (Compare with **Environmental-quality standard.**)

Employment-at-will. The idea that an employee works at the "will" of an employer and can be discharged without legal recourse or appeal.

Employee stock ownership plan (ESOP). A company plan that encourages employees to invest money in that company's stock.

Enlightened self-interest model of social involvement. The view that social responsiveness and long-run economic return are compatible and are in the interest of business.

Environmental impact statement. A report on the expected environmental effects of a planned development; such reports are required when federal funding or federal jurisdiction is involved.

Environmental-quality standard. A legally defined, specific amount of a pollutant permitted to be *present* in an area, such as a plant where toxic substances are used or a region where auto traffic is heavy. (Compare with **Emission standard.**)

Environmental scanning. Examining an organization's environment to discover trends and forces that may have an impact on the organization.

Equal-access rule. A legal provision that requires television stations to allow all competing candidates for political office to broadcast their political messages if one of the candidates' views are broadcast.

Equal employment opportunity. The principle that all persons otherwise qualified should be treated equally with respect to job opportunities, workplace conditions, pay, fringe benefits, and retirement provisions.

Equal opportunity. The chance for all persons and groups in society to compete on the same basis for personal and social goals. Equal opportunity does not guarantee personal or social or economic equality because some persons are more talented or luckier than others.

Equal results. A goal to insure that all people in a social system actually have equal benefits such as education and income.

Ethics. The rules or principles that define right and wrong conduct.

Ethics audit. A systematic effort to discover actual or potential unethical behavior in an organization.

Ethics code. A written statement that describes the general value system and ethical rules of an organization.

Ethnocentric business. A company whose business standards are based on its home nation's customs, markets, and laws.

Expatriate. A citizen of one nation living and working in another nation.

Expediting payment. Gifts to lesser government and private employees, primarily to assure that they carry out promptly, cooperatively, and efficiently the duties for the gift giver that their job normally requires them to do.

Export of jobs. A loss of jobs in a business firm's home nation, and a creation of new jobs in a foreign nation, caused by relocating part or all of the business firm's operations (and jobs) to the foreign nation.

Expropriation. (See **Nationalization.**)

Fairness Doctrine. A requirement imposed on television broadcasting stations by the Federal Communications Commission to grant an opportunity for opposing viewpoints to be heard on major issues of public interest when one side of the issue is broadcast first.

Federal chartering. A proposed plan for giving the federal government power to issue certificates of incorporation for private business corporations.

Fiduciary responsibility or duty. A legal obligation to carry out a duty to some other person or group in order to protect their interest.

Flextime. A plan that allows employees limited control over scheduling their own hours of work, usually at the beginning and end of the work day.

Foreign Corrupt Practices Act of 1977. A federal law that regulates questionable payments of United States firms operating in other nations.

Freedom. An ability to make one's own decisions and take responsible actions without restrictions.

Free enterprise ideology. A set of beliefs about one way to organize economic life that includes individualism, freedom, private property, profit, equality of opportunity, competition, the work ethic, and a limited government.

Free enterprise system. A socioeconomic system based on private ownership, profit-seeking business firms, and the principle of free markets.

Free market. A model of an economic system based on voluntary and free exchange among buyers and sellers. Competition regulates prices in all free market exchanges.

Functional regulation. Regulations aimed at a particular function of business, such as competition or labor relations.

Future shock. A human reaction to rapid technological change whereby individuals experience difficulty in coping with the new conditions of life brought on by new technology.

Genetic engineering. (See **Biotechnology.**)

Geocentric business. A company whose business standards and policies are worldwide in outlook including multinational ownership, management, markets, and operations.

Golden parachute. A provision in a corporate executive's contract that guarantees all or some portion of the executive's salary and/or benefits if discharged as a result of a merger or corporate takeover.

Governmental politics. Political activities undertaken by business and other interest groups to influence government policies, forthcoming legislation, and the actions of regulatory agencies.

Government and business partnership. A subtype of socioeconomic system in which government and business work cooperatively to solve social problems. (Also known as *public-private partnership*.)

Hard-to-employ. Individuals who have never worked, who have been unemployed for long periods of time, who possess few job skills, or who otherwise have major disadvantages in seeking and holding jobs.

Hazardous waste. Waste materials from industrial, agricultural, and other activities capable of causing death or serious health problems for those persons exposed for prolonged periods. (Compare with **Toxic substance.**)

Home country. The country in which a multinational corporation has its headquarters.

Host country. A foreign country in which a multinational corporation conducts business.

Ideology. A set of basic beliefs that define an ideal way of living for an individual, an organization, or a society.

Individualism. A belief that each individual person has an inherent worth and dignity and possesses basic human rights that should be protected by society. Each person is presumed to be a free agent capable of knowing and promoting his or her own self-interest.

Industrial resource base. The minerals, energy sources, water supplies, skilled labor force, and human knowledge necessary for industrial production.

Industrial society. A society in which the building and mechanical processing of material goods dominates work and employs the largest proportion of the labor force.

Industrial union. A union whose members, regardless of their skills or craft, work in a particular industry, such as automobile manufacturing or the chemical industry.

Industry-specific regulation. Regulations aimed at specific industries, such as telephone service or railroad transportation, involving control of rates charged, customers served, and entry into the industry.

Inflation. Decline in the purchasing power of money.

Infrastructure. The internal social, educational, political, and economic conditions that affect a nation.

Institutional investor. A financial institution, insurance company, pension fund, endowment fund, or similar organization that invests its accumulated funds in the securities offered for sale on stock exchanges.

Institutionalized activity (ethics, social responsiveness, public affairs, etc.) An activity, operation, or procedure that is such an integral part of an organization that it is performed routinely by managers and employees.

Interactive model of business and society. The combined primary and secondary interactions that business has with society.

Interactive system. The closely intertwined relationships between business and society.

Interlocking directorate. A relationship between two corporations that is established when one person serves as a member of the board of directors of both corporations simultaneously.

International balance of payments. The net effect or balance of all payments made by a nation and all payments received by that nation in its trading and investment relationships with other nations. A favorable balance exists when net payments received are greater than net payments made; an unfavorable balance occurs when net payments made exceed net payments received.

"Invisible hand." A phrase derived from Adam Smith to describe market competition as the regulator of a free market economy.

Iron Law of Responsibility. The Iron Law of Responsibility states that in the long run those who do not use power in a way that society considers responsible will tend to lose it.

Issues management. Identifying, analyzing, developing recommendations, and implementing policies concerning issues that have special meaning and importance for a company.

Jeffersonian ideal. The preference, usually attributed to Thomas Jefferson, for a society composed of many small-scale producers, a representative political system, widespread dispersal of power, and individual freedom and responsibility for all citizens. (See **Populism.**)

Job redesign. Restructuring the work of employees to allow a more direct connection between an employee's personal effort and the tangible results of that work effort.

Job rotation. A plan that allows employees to move periodically from one job to another within an office or plant, as one way to reduce boredom and monotony and improve the quality of work life.

Junk mail. Unsolicited mail not wanted by the receiver.

Junk telephone call. An unsolicited telephone call not wanted by the receiver.

Justice. A concept used in ethical reasoning that refers to the fair distribution of benefits and burdens among the people in a society, according to some agreed-upon rule.

Knowledge society. A society in which the use and electronic manipulation of knowledge and information dominate work and employ the largest proportion of the labor force. (See **Postindustrial society.**)

Laissez faire. A French phrase meaning "to let alone," used to describe an economic system where government intervention is minimal.

Laws. A society's formally codified principles that help define right and wrong behavior.

Legitimacy of organizational influence. Acceptance by others of an organization's authority to require a specific standard of performance from them.

Lie detector. (See **Polygraph.**)

Loan guarantee. An agreement, usually by the federal government, to repay a bank loan if a borrower cannot repay it. The borrower pays a fee to the government for this guarantee.

Luddites. Groups of early-nineteenth-century English workers who, believing that machines took away jobs from workers, destroyed factory machinery.

Megacorporation. One of the very largest business corporations.

Merger. The joining together of two separate companies into a single company.

Microprocessor. A small silicon chip capable of a very large number of computational operations. (See **Semiconductor silicon chip.**)

Mitigation banking. A plan for acquiring, saving ("putting in the bank"), and later using credits to offset expected environmental damage, by taking actions to protect the environment before damage is done.

Mixed state-and-private enterprise. A socioeconomic system in which government owns some key industrial and financial enterprises but most businesses are owned and operated by private individuals and corporations.

Monopoly. An industry or market with one producer or seller.

Morality. A condition in which the most fundamental human values are preserved and allowed to shape human thought and action.

Multinational corporation. A company that conducts business in two or more nations, usually employing citizens of various nationalities.

Multiplier effect. A situation in which one event leads to more than one other related event.

Nationalization. Government taking ownership and control of private property with or without pay. (Also known as *expropriation*.)

Network television (or radio). A group of affiliated television or radio broadcasting stations that reach a certain percentage of the viewing or listening public. The affiliated stations agree to broadcast programs arranged by network officials.

New Deal. The popular name given to President Franklin D. Roosevelt's economic programs to combat the Great Depression of the 1930s.

Nomadic society. A society in which food gathering, hunting, and fishing dominate work and where human groups move as necessary to find such food.

Offset policy. A pollution control plan that permits excess pollution from one source if another polluting source reduces its emissions by an equal or greater amount.

Opportunity costs. The various opportunities that cannot be realized because money is spent for one purpose rather than for others.

Organizational commitment. A stage in the development of social responsiveness within a company when social responses have become a normal part of doing business. Therefore, the entire organization is committed to socially responsible actions and policies. (Compare with **Institutionalized activity.**)

Organizational society. A society, often technologically advanced, where most areas of life are organized and largely controlled by big organizations such as labor unions, corporations, government agencies, universities, military units, churches, and others.

Pandora's Box. In Greek mythology, a box that when opened let loose all kinds of misfortunes on society.

Philanthropy (corporate). Gifts and contributions made by corporations, usually from pretax profits, to benefit various types of nonprofit community organizations.

Pluralism. A society in which numerous economic, political, educational, social, cultural, and other groups are organized by people to promote their own interests.

Policy decision. A stage in the public policy process when government authorizes (or fails to authorize) a course of action, for example, by passing (or failing to pass) a law, issuing a court opinion, or adopting a new regulation.

Policy evaluation. The final stage in the public policy process when the results of a public policy are judged by those who have an interest in the outcome.

Policy formulation. A stage in the public policy process when interested groups take a position and try to persuade others to adopt that position.

Policy implementation. A stage in the public policy process when action is taken to enforce a public policy decision.

Political action committee. A committee organized according to election law by any group for the purpose of accepting voluntary contributions from individual donors and then making contributions in behalf of candidates for election to public office.

Pollution charge. A fee levied on a polluting source based on the amount of pollution released into the environment.

Pollution rights. A legal right to exceed established pollution limits; such rights may be bought, sold, or held for future use with approval of government regulators.

Pollution trade-offs. Accepting one form of pollution rather than another when it is not possible to eliminate both.

Polycentric business. A company whose business standards are based on the customs, markets, and laws of several different nations.

Polygraph. An operator-administered instrument used to judge the truth or falsity of a person's statements by measuring physiological changes that tend to be activated by a person's conscience when lying.

Populism. The preference for a democratic political system, family-operated farms, small-size business firms, and small-town life. (See **Jeffersonian ideal.**)

Postindustrial society. A society combining the features of a service society and a knowledge society. (See **Service society** and **Knowledge society.**)

Preferential hiring. An employment plan that gives preference to minorities, women, and other groups that may be underrepresented in an organization's workforce.

Primary interactions or involvement. The direct relationships a company has with those groups that enable it to produce goods and services.

Priority Rule. In ethical analysis, a procedure for ranking in terms of their importance the three ethical modes of reasoning—utilitarian, rights, and justice—before making a decision or taking action.

Privacy. (See **Right of privacy.**)

Private property. A group of rights giving control over physical and intangible assets to private owners. Private ownership is the basic institution of capitalism.

Privatization. The process of converting various economic functions, organizations, and programs from government ownership or government sponsorship to private operation.

Product liability. A legal responsibility of a person or firm for the harmful consequences to others stemming from use of a product manufactured, sold, managed, or employed by the person or firm.

Product recall. An effort by a business firm to remove a defective or sometimes dangerous product from consumer use and from all distribution channels.

Productivity. The relationship between total inputs and total outputs. Productivity increases when the outputs of an organization increase faster than the inputs necessary for production.

Profit maximization. An attempt by a business firm to achieve the highest possible rate of return from its operations.

Profit optimization. An attempt by a business firm to achieve an acceptable (rather than a maximum) rate of return from its operations.

Profits. The revenues of a person or company minus the costs incurred in producing the revenue.

Proxy. A legal instrument giving another person the right to vote the shares of stock of an absentee stockholder.

Proxy statement. A statement sent by a board of directors to a corporation's stockholders announcing the company's annual meeting, containing information about the business to be considered at the meeting, and enclosing a proxy form for stockholders not attending the meeting.

Public affairs function. An organization's activities intended to perceive, monitor, understand, communicate with, and influence the external environment, including local and national communities, government relations, and public opinion.

Public issue advertising. An advertisement appearing in the media that expresses the sponsor's viewpoint about a public issue. (Also known as _public policy advertising_ or _advocacy advertising._)

Public policy. A plan of action by government to achieve some broad purpose affecting a large segment of the public.

Public policy agenda. All public policy problems or issues that receive the active and serious attention of government officials.

Public policy process. All of the activities and stages involved in developing, carrying out, and evaluating public policies.

Public responsibility committee. A committee of a corporation's board of directors with the function of identifying social and political issues that may have an influence on the company and making recommendations to the directors about appropriate actions.

Public (or social) service leave. A type of corporate gift consisting of a leave of absence granted to an employee to engage in community service work, usually with full or partial pay provided by the employee's business firm.

Public trustee. A concept that a business owner or manager should base company decisions on the interests of a wide range of corporate stakeholders or members of the general public. In doing so, the business executive acts as a trustee of the public interest.

Publicly held corporation. A corporation whose stock is available for purchase by the general investing public.

Quality circle. A small group of supervisors and workers who meet to discuss ways to improve the overall quality of work done in their unit.

Quality of work life. The favorableness or unfavorableness of a job environment for an organization's employees.

Questionable payments. Something of value given to a person or firm, which raises significant ethical questions of right or wrong in the host nation or other nations.

Quotas (job, hiring, employment). An employment plan based on hiring a specific number or proportion of minorities, women, or other groups who may be underrepresented in an organization's workforce.

Right (human). A concept used in ethical reasoning that means that a person or group is entitled to something or is entitled to be treated in a certain way.

Right of privacy. A person's fundamental expectation of protection from organizational invasion of one's private life and unauthorized release of confidential information about the person.

Robot. Any automatic machine that performs work without the direct intervention of a human being.

Rule of Cost. The idea that all human actions generate costs.

Secondary interactions or involvement. The relationship a company has with those social and political groups that feel the impact of the company's main activities and take steps to do something about it. These relationships are derived from the firm's primary interactions.

Semiconductor silicon chip. A small computational device, made of silicon material, that is a key component of computers and other forms of electronic technology. (See **Microprocessor.**)

Service society. A society in which the provision of services, rather than the production of material goods, dominates work and employs the largest proportion of the labor force. (See **Postindustrial society.**)

Severance pay. A special payment made to an employee of a firm to compensate for an unexpected permanent layoff.

Shareholder. (See **Stockholder.**)

Shareholder proposal. A proposal made by a stockholder and included in a corporation's notice of its annual meeting that advocates some course of action to be taken by the company.

Shareholder suit (individual). A lawsuit initiated by one or more stockholders that attempts to recover damages *they* (as stockholders) *personally* suffered due to alleged actions of the company's management.

Shareholder's derivative suit. A lawsuit initiated by one or more stockholders that attempts to recover damages suffered *by the company* due to alleged actions of the company's management.

Social accountability. The condition of being held responsible to society or to some public or governmental group for one's actions, often requiring a specific accounting or reporting on these activities.

Social audit. A systematic study and evaluation of an organization's social performance. (See **Social performance evaluation.**)

Social forecasting. An attempt to estimate major social and political trends that may affect a company's operations and environment in the future.

Social involvement. (See **Corporate social involvement.**)

Social obligation. The posture of a company that takes only such social action as is minimally necessary and required by laws and regulations.

Social overhead costs. Public and private investments that are necessary to prepare the environment for effective operation of a new business or other major institutions.

Social partnership. A temporary or permanent coalition of interest groups who cooperate for the purpose of addressing or resolving some social problem.

Social performance evaluation. Information about an organization's social performance, often contained in a company's annual report to stockholders and sometimes prepared as a special report to management or the general public. (Compare with **Social audit.**)

Social regulation. Regulations intended to accomplish certain social improvements such as equal employment opportunity or on-the-job safety and health.

Social responsibility. (See **Corporate social responsibility.**)

Social responsiveness. (See **Corporate social responsiveness.**)

Society. The people, institutions, and technology that make up a recognizable human community.

Socioeconomic system. The combined and interrelated social, economic, and political institutions characteristic of a society.

Solid waste. Any solid waste materials resulting from human activities, such as municipal refuse and sewage, industrial wastes, and agricultural wastes.

Specialized learning. A stage in the development of social responsiveness within a company during which managers and supervisors, usually with the help of a specialist, learn the new practices necessary for coping with social problems and pressures.

Stakeholder. (See **Corporate stakeholder.**)

Stewardship principle. The idea that business managers should act in the interest of all members of society who are affected by their business decisions, thus behaving as stewards or trustees of the public welfare. (Compare with **Public trustee.**)

Stockholder. A person, group, or organization owning one or more shares of stock in a corporation.

"Survival of the fittest." A phrase derived from the ideas of Charles Darwin and Herbert Spencer meaning that only the strongest and most capable individuals are able to survive and excel in life's competitive struggles.

Technical elite. Highly trained and technically specialized members of an organization who may exercise great influence on policies and decisions from a purely technical point of view.

Technology. The tools, machines, skills, technical operations, and abstract symbols involved in human endeavor.

Technology assessment. An analytic attempt to understand, beforehand if possible, the economic and social effects of new technology, particularly the unintended, indirect, and possibly harmful impacts that may occur.

Technostructure. Members of an organization who possess and use specialized, technical knowledge in a group decision-making process.

Telecommuting. Performing knowledge work and transmitting the results of that work by means of computer terminal to an organization's central data bank and management center, while the employee works at home or at some other remote location.

Teleconference. A meeting of an organization's employees who are in widely separated locations that is made possible by two-way television transmissions.

Tender offer. An offer by an individual, group, or organization to buy outstanding shares of stock in a corporation, frequently in an effort to gain control or otherwise benefit themselves.

Third Wave. A period of widespread social change characteristic of high-technology, service-oriented, knowledge-based societies.

Third World nations. Developing nations as distinguished from more developed free world nations and communist nations.

Toxic substance. Any substance used in production or in consumer products that is poisonous or capable of causing serious health problems for those persons exposed. (Compare with **Hazardous waste.**)

Trade association. An organization that represents the business and professional interests of the firms or persons in a trade, industry, or profession; for example, medical doctors, chemical manufacturers, or used car dealers.

Trade-offs, economic and social. An attempt to balance and compare economic and social gains against economic and social costs when it is impossible to achieve all that is desired in both economic and social terms.

Trade secret. Private company information, not available to others, that is useful to the company business but could be financially harmful if known by others, especially competitors.

Unanimity Rule. In ethical analysis, a procedure for determining that all three modes of ethical reasoning—utilitarian, rights, and justice—provide consistent and uniform answers to an ethical problem or issue.

Utility (social). A concept used in ethical reasoning that refers to the net positive gain or benefit to society of some action or decision.

Values. Fundamental and enduring beliefs about the most desirable conditions and purposes of human life.

Videodisc. A disc on which television signals have been recorded for the purpose of storing digital data that may be played back.

Wall Street. A customary way of referring to the financial community of banks, investment institutions, and stock exchanges centered in the Wall Street area of New York City.

Wall Street Rule. A common practice among corporate stockholders of voting their shares of stock to support the company's management or selling the stock if they disagree seriously with management's policies.

Whistle blowing. An employee's disclosure to the public of alleged organizational misconduct.

Work ethic. The belief that human labor and work are inherently worthwhile, admirable, and both personally and socially valuable. The work ethic is sometimes called "the Protestant ethic" or "the Protestant work ethic" because of its origin among early Protestant theologians.

Zero discharge. An abstract, unattainable environmental goal that would involve the elimination or containment of all industrial and agricultural pollution.

PART I: THE CORPORATION IN SOCIETY

Corporate Social Responsibility

Bowen, Howard R.: *Social Responsibilities of the Businessman*, New York: Harper, 1953.

Bradshaw, Thornton, and David Vogel (eds.): *Corporations and Their Critics: Issues and Answers to the Problems of Corporate Social Responsibility*, New York: McGraw-Hill, 1981.

Chamberlain, Neil W.: *The Limits of Corporate Social Responsibility*, New York: Basic Books, 1973.

Committee for Economic Development: *Social Responsibilities of Business Corporations*, New York: Committee for Economic Development, 1971.

Dickie, Robert B., and Leroy S. Rouner (eds.): *Corporations and The Common Good*, South Bend, IN: University of Notre Dame Press, 1986.

Heald, Morrell: *The Social Responsibilities of Business: Company and Community, 1900–1960*, Cleveland: Case Western Reserve Press, 1970.

Worthy, James C.: *William C. Norris: Portrait of a Maverick*, Cambridge, MA: Ballinger, 1987.

Managing Social Responsiveness

Ackerman, Robert W.: *The Social Challenge to Business*, Cambridge, MA: Harvard University Press, 1975.

Blake, David H., William C. Frederick, and Mildred S. Myers: *Social Auditing: Evaluating the Impact of Corporate Programs*, New York: Praeger, 1976.

Chamberlain, Neil W.: *Social Strategy and Corporate Structure*, New York: Macmillan, 1982.

Fahey, Liam, and V. K. Narayanan: *Macroenvironmental Analysis for Strategic Management*, St. Paul, MN: West, 1986.

Freeman, R. Edward: *Strategic Management: A Stakeholder Approach*, Marshfield, MA: Pitman, 1984.

Heath, Robert L., and Richard Alan Nelson: *Issues Management: Corporate Public Policy-making in an Information Society,* Beverly Hills, CA: Sage, 1986.

Klein, Thomas A.: *Social Costs and Benefits of Business,* Englewood Cliffs, NJ: Prentice-Hall, 1977.

Lusterman, Seymour: *The Organization and Staffing of Corporate Public Affairs,* New York: Conference Board, 1987.

Miles, Robert H.: *Managing the Corporate Social Environment: A Grounded Theory,* Englewood Cliffs, NJ: Prentice-Hall, 1987.

Pinsdorf, Marion K.: *Communicating When Your Company Is Under Siege: Surviving Public Crisis,* Lexington, MA: Heath, 1987.

Post, James E.: *Corporate Behavior and Social Change,* Reston, VA: Reston, 1978.

Post, James E. (ed.): *Research in Corporate Social Performance and Policy: Center Themes in CSR Research,* volume 8, Greenwich, CT: JAI Press, 1986.

Preston, Lee E. (ed.): *Research in Corporate Social Performance and Policy,* volumes 1–7, Greenwich, CT: JAI Press, 1978–1985.

Preston, Lee E., and James E. Post: *Private Management and Public Policy,* Englewood Cliffs, NJ: Prentice-Hall, 1975.

Stone, Christopher E.: *Where the Law Ends: The Social Control of Corporate Behavior,* New York: Harper & Row, 1975.

Business Ethics and Values

Brodeur, Paul: *Outrageous Misconduct: The Asbestos Industry on Trial,* New York: Pantheon, 1985.

Cavanagh, Gerald F.: *American Business Values,* 2d ed., Englewood Cliffs, NJ: Prentice-Hall, 1984.

Chamberlain, Neil W.: *Remaking American Values: Challenge to a Business Society,* New York: Basic Books, 1977.

Clinard, Marshall B., and Peter C. Yeager: *Corporate Crime,* New York: Free Press, 1980.

Cochran, Thomas C.: *Challenges to American Values: Society, Business, and Religion,* New York: Oxford University Press, 1985.

DeGeorge, Richard T.: *Business Ethics,* New York: Macmillan, 1982.

Donaldson, Thomas: *Corporations and Morality.* Englewood Cliffs, NJ: Prentice-Hall, 1982.

England, George W.: *The Manager and His Values,* Cambridge, MA: Ballinger, 1975.

Frederick, William C. (ed.): *Research in Corporate Social Performance and Policy: Empirical Studies of Business Ethics and Values,* volume 9, Greenwich, CT.: JAI Press, 1987.

Marx, Thomas G.: *Business and Society: Economic, Moral, and Political Foundations,* Englewood Cliffs, NJ: Prentice-Hall, 1985.

McCoy, Charles S.: *Management of Values: The Ethical Difference in Corporate Policy and Performance,* Marshfield, MA: Pitman, 1985.

Mintz, Morton: *At Any Cost: Corporate Greed, Women, and the Dalkon Shield,* New York: Pantheon, 1985.

Schein, Edgar H.: *Organizational Culture and Leadership,* San Francisco: Jossey-Bass, 1985.

Schmidt, Warren H., and Barry Z. Posner, *Managerial Values and Expectations: The Silent Power in Personal and Organizational Life,* New York: American Management Associations, 1982.

Toffler, Barbara Ley: *Tough Choices: Managers Talk Ethics,* New York: Wiley, 1986.

Velasquez, Manuel G.: *Business Ethics: Concepts and Cases,* Englewood Cliffs, NJ: Prentice-Hall, 1982.

Walton, Clarence C. (ed.): *The Ethics of Corporate Conduct,* Englewood Cliffs, NJ: Prentice-Hall, 1977.

PART II: THE CORPORATION AND GOVERNMENT

Berry, Jeffrey M.: *The Interest Group Society*, Boston: Little, Brown, 1984.

Dolbeare, Kenneth M.: *Democracy at Risk: The Politics of Economic Renewal*, Chatham, NJ: Chatham House, 1986.

Epstein, Edwin M.: *The Corporation in American Politics*, Englewood Cliffs, NJ: Prentice-Hall, 1969.

Friedman, Milton, and Rose Friedman: *Free to Choose*, New York: Avon, 1981.

Garreau, Joel: *The Nine Nations of North America*, New York: Avon, 1981.

Gellhorn, Ernest: *Antitrust Law and Economics*, 3d ed., St. Paul, MN: West, 1986.

Lodge, George Cabot: *The New American Ideology*, New York: Knopf, 1976.

Marcus, Alfred A.: *The Adversary Economy: Business Responses to Changing Government Requirements*, Westport, CT: Quorum Books, 1984.

Navarro, Peter: *The Policy Game: How Special Interests and Ideologues Are Stealing America*, New York: Wiley, 1984.

Oxford Analytica: *America in Perspective: Major Trends in the United States through the 1990s*, Boston: Houghton Mifflin, 1986.

Peters, B. Guy: *American Public Policy: Promise and Performance*, 2d ed., Chatham, NJ: Chatham House, 1986.

Sealy, Albert H.: *Macro Blueprint: For Dialogue to Shape Tomorrow's Economy and Society with Enlightened Public Leadership and Corporate Governance*, New York: Interbook, 1986.

Sutton, Francis X., Seymour Harris, Carl Kaysen, and James Tobin: *The American Business Creed*, Cambridge, MA: Harvard University Press, 1956.

Wilson, Graham K.: *Business and Politics: A Comparative Introduction*, Chatham, NJ: Chatham House, 1985.

PART III: CORPORATE STAKEHOLDERS

Barcus, F. Earle: *Images of Life on Children's Television: Sex Roles, Minorities, and Families*, New York: Praeger, 1983.

Barnouw, Erik: *The Sponsor: Notes on a Modern Potentate*, New York: Oxford University Press, 1978.

Bloom, Paul, and Ruth Belk Smith (eds.): *The Future of Consumerism*, Lexington, MA: Lexington Books, 1986.

Bluestone, Barry, and Bennett Harrison: *The Deindustrialization of America: Plant Closings, Community Abandonment, and the Dismantling of Basic Industry*, New York: Basic Books, 1982.

Bradley, Keith, and Alan Gelb: *Worker Capitalism: The New Industrial Relations*, Cambridge, MA: MIT Press, 1983.

Corrado, Frank M.: *Media for Managers: Communications Strategy for the Eighties*, Englewood Cliffs, NJ: Prentice-Hall, 1984.

Davis, Keith, and John W. Newstrom, *Human Behavior at Work: Organizational Behavior*, 7th ed., New York: McGraw-Hill, 1985.

Gordus, Jeanne P., Paul Jarley, and Louis A. Ferman: *Plant Closings and Economic Dislocation*, Kalamazoo, MI: W. E. Upjohn Institute for Employment Research, 1981.

Herman, Edward S.: *Corporate Control, Corporate Power*, Cambridge: Cambridge University Press, 1981.

Kochan, Thomas A., Harry C. Katz, and Robert B. McKersie: *The Transformation of American Industrial Relations*, New York: Basic Books, 1986.

Kram, Kathy E.: *Mentoring at Work*, Glenview, IL: Scott Foresman, 1985.

Larsen, Otto N. (ed.): *Violence and the Mass Media*, New York: Harper & Row, 1968.

Liebert, Robert M., Joyce N. Sprafkin, and Emily S. Davidson: *The Early Window: Effects of Television on Children and Youth*, 2d ed., New York: Pergamon, 1982.

Mankiewicz, Frank, and Joel Swerdlow: _Remote Control: Television and the Manipulation of American Life_, New York: Times Books, 1978.

Michel, Allen, and Israel Shaked: _Takeover Madness: Corporate America Fights Back_, New York: Wiley, 1986.

Mitroff, Ian, and Ralph Kilmann: _Corporate Tragedies: Product Tampering, Sabotage, and Other Catastrophes_, New York: Praeger, 1984.

Rosen, Corey M., Katherine J. Klein, and Karen M. Young: _Employee Ownership in America: The Equity Solution_, Lexington, MA: Lexington, 1986.

Smith, James P., and Michael P. Ward: _Women's Wages and Work in the Twentieth Century_, Santa Monica, CA: Rand, 1984.

Theberge, Leonard J. (ed.): _Crooks, Conmen and Clowns: Businessmen in Television_, Washington, DC: Media Institute, 1981.

Vance, Stanley C.: _Corporate Leadership: Boards, Directors, and Strategy_, New York: McGraw-Hill, 1983.

Vogel, David: _Lobbying the Corporation: Citizen Challenges to Business Authority_, New York: Basic Books, 1978.

Werhane, Patricia H.: _Persons, Rights, and Corporations_, Englewood Cliffs, NJ: Prentice-Hall, 1985.

Westin, Alan F.: _Whistle-Blowing! Loyalty and Dissent in the Corporation_, New York: McGraw-Hill, 1981.

PART IV: MANAGING IN A TURBULENT WORLD

Blake, David H., and Robert S. Walters: _The Politics of Global Economic Relations_, Englewood Cliffs, NJ: Prentice-Hall, 1983.

Brooks, Harvey, Lance Liebman, and Corinne S. Schelling (eds.): _Public-Private Partnership: New Opportunities for Meeting Social Needs_, Cambridge, MA: Ballinger, 1984.

Brown, Lester R., et al.: _State of the World, 1987—A Worldwatch Institute Report on Progress toward a Sustainable Society_, New York: Norton, 1987.

Carson, Rachel: _Silent Spring_, Boston: Houghton Mifflin, 1962.

Epstein, Samuel, Lester O. Brown, and Carl Pope: _Hazardous Waste in America_, San Francisco: Sierra Club Books, 1982.

Frederick, Duke, William L. Howenstine, and June Sochen (eds.): _Destroy to Create: Interaction with the Natural Environment in the Building of America_, Hinsdale, IL: Dryden, 1972.

Gladwin, Thomas N., and Ingo Walter: _Multinationals under Fire—Lessons in the Management of Conflict_, New York: Wiley, 1980.

Kindleberger, Charles P., and David B. Audretsch (eds.): _The Multinational Corporation in the 1980s_, Cambridge, MA: MIT Press, 1983.

Kneese, Allen V., and Charles L. Schultze: _Pollution, Prices, and Public Policy_, Washington, DC: Brookings, 1975.

Lindblom, Charles E.: _Politics and Markets: The World's Political-Economic Systems_, New York: Basic Books, 1977.

McFarland, Dalton E.: _Management and Society: An Institutional Framework_, Englewood Cliffs, NJ: Prentice-Hall, 1982.

Naisbitt, John: _Megatrends: Ten New Directions Transforming Our Lives_, New York: Warner, 1981.

O'Toole, James: _Vanguard Management: Redesigning the Corporate Future_, New York: Doubleday, 1985.

Schlesinger, Arthur M., Jr.: _The Cycles of American History_, Boston, MA: Houghton Mifflin, 1986.

Sussman, Warren I.: _Culture As History: The Transformation of American Society in the Twentieth Century_, New York: Pantheon, 1984.

Toffler, Alvin: _The Third Wave_, New York: Bantam, 1981.

Tuleja, Tad: _Beyond the Bottom Line_, Washington, DC: Facts on File, 1985.

INDEXES

NAME INDEX

SUBJECT INDEX